MANDATE FOR CHANGE

The White House Years

MANDATE
FOR CHANGE

1953–1956

Dwight D. Eisenhower

HEINEMANN : LONDON

William Heinemann Ltd

LONDON MELBOURNE TORONTO

CAPE TOWN AUCKLAND

b 6401587

First published 1963

Excerpt from "Surprising Vote" from The New York Times *(Section 4), November 7, 1954. Copyright by* The New York Times. *Reprinted by permission.*

Excerpt from The Secret Diaries of Harold Ickes. *Copyright 1953, 1954 by Simon and Schuster, Inc. Reprinted by permission of the publishers.*

The letter from Robert E. Sherwood to Dwight D. Eisenhower is reprinted by permission of Mrs. Madeline H. Sherwood.

Printed in Great Britain
by Billing & Sons Limited, Guildford and London

To MAMIE

Some of the information included here is—or one day will be—available from other sources. But in the interest of making this already lengthy volume as useful as possible for most Americans; for the people of nations other than our own; and especially for students of history, I am including a number of quotations from documents, plus additional information which might help to clarify complex issues.

Contents

exchanged. Twenty-five thousand prisoners "escape." Walter
Robertson attains cooperation of Rhee as Communists continue attacks. Truce agreement signed.

parties for the staff, the vacation White Houses. Diplomatic
receptions and dinners. Military aides for the Commander-in-
Chief. The indispensable Secret Service. The end of 1953.

BOOK THREE

Farm surpluses. "Soil-bank" program. The agricultural dilemma. The ritual of adjournment.

Medical reports and speculations on a second term. Personal
and political considerations. Evening gathering for discussion.
Evaluation of the first three years. The final decision.

Illustrations

Maps

BY RAFAEL PALACIOS

BOOK ONE

As our heart summons our strength, our wisdom must direct it.

There is, in world affairs, a steady course to be followed between an assertion of strength that is truculent and a confession of helplessness that is cowardly.

There is, in our affairs at home, a middle way between untrammeled freedom of the individual and the demands for the welfare of the whole nation. This way must avoid government by bureaucracy as carefully as it avoids neglect of the helpless.

In every area of political action, free men must think before they can expect to win.

In this spirit must we live and labor: confident of our strength, compassionate in our heart, clear in our mind.

In this spirit, let us together turn to the great tasks before us.

—State of the Union message, February 2, 1953

CHAPTER I

Prelude to Politics

When a man assumes a public trust, he should consider himself as public property.

—*Thomas Jefferson*

O N January 20, 1953, I stood on a platform at the East Front of the Capitol in Washington to take the oath, administered by Chief Justice Fred M. Vinson, as the thirty-fourth President of the United States—an office I was to hold for eight years.

Those were to be momentous years and the problems challenging the new administration were complex and urgent. Two wars, with the United States deeply engaged in one, and vitally concerned in the other, were raging in Eastern Asia; Iran seemed to be almost ready to fall into Communist hands; the NATO Alliance had as yet found no positive way to mobilize into its defenses the latent strength of West Germany; Red China seemed increasingly bent on using force to advance its boundaries; Austria was still an occupied country, and Soviet intransigence was keeping it so. European economies were not yet recovered from the effects of World War II. Communism was striving to establish its first beachhead in the Americas by gaining control of Guatemala.

At home we faced large and continuing deficits, the value of our currency was eroding rapidly, industrial conflict had been prevalent, the economy was limping along under wage and price controls, and taxes were more than burdensome. Our confidence was eroding, too. Americans had become divided—over questions of loyalty, Communists in the government, and corruption of high public officials.

The story of our attack on such problems cannot be told in terms all black or all white. Those years brought to me—and often to the nation— satisfaction in many accomplishments, disappointments in certain failures.

They were prosperous years. In spite of one mild and one sharp recession the income and productivity of the nation advanced markedly;

steady progress toward fiscal responsibility was made; the divisions over internal security were ended; existing wars were stopped, threatening ones halted before they started. And although the aggressive purposes of Moscow and Peiping remained unchanged, the rolling advance of Communism came to a stop.

Great advances in science, contributing to both the values of peace and the weapons of war, brought revolutionary changes in our lives, but the advances in the first case were far from complete and the second had added, immeasurably, to our burdens.

For me those years were exciting—even if, at times, the ever-present routine became tiresome. They brought their joys and their sorrows— joys in old friendships and in new ones, sorrows when family members, good friends, and valued associates passed from among us. Above all they brought to me a constant stream of heart-warming messages (and visitors) from the cities, the farms, the villages—messages of encouragement and expressions of loyalty even when the authors found it necessary to criticize.

The American people gave me the priceless privilege of serving them in the Presidency. In this book I shall tell, as best I can, what I did and why.

*   *   *

So far as I can now recall, the earliest serious suggestion that I might become a presidential candidate one day was made by Virgil Pinkley in 1943. Pinkley, then a newspaper correspondent in the North African theater of World War II, came to see me shortly after the Allies in the Mediterranean had succeeded, at long last, in sweeping North Africa clean of Axis forces, overrunning Sicily, and landing in Italy. In the final stages of these operations all the Allied forces were under my over-all command, and as a result of their successes Mussolini had been ousted as the dictator of Fascist Italy.

Mr. Pinkley, remarking on the magnitude of these operations, observed that in view of a practice that had all but become an American tradition, I would, as the wartime commander of large and successful military groups, inevitably be considered as a strong presidential possibility.

Certainly much in American history supported Pinkley's contention that victorious command in the field often leads to later political consideration: George Washington, Andrew Jackson, William Henry Harrison, Zachary Taylor, and Ulysses S. Grant, largely but not solely because of their military achievements, had been voted into the office. George B. McClellan and Winfield Scott Hancock, probably the two most popular generals of the Army of the Potomac, were both nominated—but not elected—by the Democratic party. In more recent times this tendency had become less pronounced, though Leonard Wood and John J. Pershing had, after World War I, been accorded a great deal of support for political office.

Nevertheless, to say that I was astonished by Pinkley's suggestion is far from an exaggeration; my instant reaction was that he was something of a humorist.

"Virgil," I said, "you've been standing out in the sun too long."

In a difficult military campaign a commander cannot believe that anything else could be as important as winning the battle before him. He becomes so intent on tactical problems and strategical plans—indeed, his whole soul is so given over to achieving victory—that he cannot but react negatively to any suggestion that he should concern himself with extraneous possibilities. Certainly this was my feeling at that moment. I thought it completely absurd to mention my name in the same breath as the Presidency. Mr. Pinkley still chuckles as he reminds me of my rather violently phrased and somewhat embellished "No."

From that date onward similar suggestions[1] came to my attention periodically, but thereafter, on guard for the most part, I merely laughed them off, until the day when President Truman, riding with General Bradley and me in Berlin after the European armistice in 1945, abruptly said that he would help me get anything I might want, including the Presidency in 1948.[2] This put a more serious aspect on the matter but my prompt reply was that while I thanked him for his flattering thought I had no ambition whatsoever along political lines and would not consider the possibility of seeking a political position. I added that I would never in my lifetime experience a moment of more intense personal satisfaction than that which saw the surrender of Hitler's remaining forces at Reims, France, on May 7, 1945. I was very proud of the Allies and their performance, and of the great victory they had achieved

[1] Others during the war also foresaw the possibility: Senator Arthur Capper of Kansas, who favored my nomination in 1944 and later in 1948; the New York City American Legion Tank Corps Post in 1943; and George Allen, who in the same year wrote me, "How does it feel to be a presidential candidate?" and got the answer, "Baloney!"

[2] "I doubt that any soldier of our country was ever so suddenly struck in his emotional vitals by a President with such an apparently sincere and certainly astounding proposition as this. . . . To have the President suddenly throw this broadside into me left me no recourse except to treat it as a very splendid joke, which I hoped it was. I laughed heartily and said: 'Mr. President, I don't know who will be your opponent for the presidency, but it will not be I.' There was no doubt about *my* seriousness." *Crusade in Europe*, 1948, p. 444.

through the strategic and tactical plans that we had developed in the face of prolonged opposition from some quarters.

After that conversation I began to realize the necessity of expressing replies to queries about personal political possibilities in something more than jocular retort.

A few months afterward, late in 1945, I was ordered back to the United States and assigned as Chief of Staff of the United States Army. When I reported to the White House, the President was aware of my desire to retire, but I was naturally appreciative of the honor implied in his decision. Chief of Staff of the Army was a position that, prior to World War II, would probably have been, because of my age in grade and the vagaries of promotion and retirement laws, completely beyond my reach; though then it would have seemed challenging and interesting. But to me in 1945, returning to the United States only a few months after Hitler's destruction and having lived through years of war's excitement, drama, and never-ending anxieties, the prospect of directing the tedious job of Army demobilization—particularly in the light of my belief that unilateral disarmament on such a precipitate, almost helter-skelter basis was unwise—was frankly distasteful. But responding to the President's suggestion that I serve as Chief of Staff until General Omar Bradley could be released from his assignment in the Veterans Administration, I was ready to report for duty at any date he desired. The President thought that, on the basis, I would serve for about two years. My hope of retirement was, though not destroyed, for this period deferred. I took over General George C. Marshall's responsibilities in December 1945.[3]

Soon politics began to complicate my life in a really serious fashion. In Washington, I became more accessible than ever to an army of inquisitive reporters. Curiosity about my future plans, in spite of frequent denials of political ambition, heightened rather than abated. Since it is only human to value the good opinion of others, it would be foolish to say that this experience left me completely unmoved. Nevertheless I felt the questions to be irrelevant and the suggestions impractical, both because of my lack of ambition for a political career and of my isolation, from boyhood, from nearly all politics.

But with such questions becoming more and more frequent over many months, the matter became tiresome. I determined to stop it decisively. My sense of humor was beginning to show signs of wear and tear.

[3] Only President Truman, General Marshall, and I were supposed to know of this new assignment. Yet while visiting my Uncle Joel in Boone, Iowa, a few days before the President announced it, I heard a commentator disclose it on the radio. "What a place to keep a secret!" I said, referring to Washington.

Shortly before the scheduled date for the 1948 nominating primaries in New Hampshire, a newspaper publisher in that state, Leonard V. Finder, wrote me a long letter urging that I allow my name to be entered on the Republican slate there. Having thus been given a fine opportunity to clarify my position, I drafted a reply for public release. I hoped it would be responsive to every legitimate question concerning my personal intentions and would effectively answer those who asserted that I had an inescapable duty to the American people to make myself "available." In the letter I stressed that for me to assume that significant numbers of people desired me as a possible candidate would smack of effrontery; I explained the difficulty of phrasing a flat refusal without at the same time "appearing to violate that concept of duty to country which calls upon every good citizen to place no limitations upon his readiness to serve in any designated capacity." Then I reiterated my conviction that "the necessary and wise subordination of the military to civil power will be best sustained . . . when lifelong professional soldiers, in the absence of some obvious and overriding reasons, abstain from seeking high political office. . . ."

After expressing regret if I had previously, by a "too simple faith in the effectiveness of a plain denial," misled anyone to spend time and effort in my behalf, I concluded:

> In any event, my decision to remove myself completely from the political scene is definite and positive. I know you will not object to my making this letter public to inform all interested persons that I could not accept nomination even under the remote circumstances that it were tendered me.

The publication of this letter effectively stilled, for the time being, most of the political gossip and comment, and I congratulated myself on the wisdom of my action.

Several months earlier General Bradley had reported that he could soon leave the Veterans Administration, and in February 1948 I turned the office of Chief of Staff over to him. I promptly began terminal leave and in the spring of 1948 went to Columbia University as its president.

It was not long before many persons began to assume that my transfer from the military to the educational world made me a bona fide civilian and therefore that the reasons I had made public the previous January, in the letter to New Hampshire, were no longer valid.

Conveniently, they overlooked that by special law I was, with others, a General of the Army, theoretically on active duty for life. Although I was not filling a specific military post, this status accorded me the same pay and allowances and many of the same privileges as any other military officer of similar rank; it also imposed the same inhibitions, which precluded, to my mind at least, participation in partisan political activity. Furthermore, though I was now wearing civilian clothes and was engaged in civilian pursuits, these outward manifestations could not alter the fact that my entire adult life had, up to that moment, been devoted to the military service.

All this was ignored by many of the more persistent interrogators and self-appointed advisers. I continued to turn a deaf ear to those who refused to give up their attempts to make me a political figure.

This attitude did not mean that I was unconcerned about national affairs, including those with pronounced political overtones. Indeed, I was disturbed by what seemed to be a trend in thinking among our people, particularly the young, which held that problems—all problems—confronting us fell within the purview and responsibility of the federal government; that hard work on the part of the individual was no longer the key to his own social and financial betterment. I protested, in a casual although public talk, against a tendency to think that we, regardless of our earning capacity, should all eat caviar and drink champagne throughout our lives, where hot dogs and beer might be more appropriate. For this homely observation I was, much to my amusement, taken severely to task in an editorial in the Columbia College newspaper.

But the drift toward federal paternalism was not the only thing that disturbed me. The panic with which the public had demanded—and our political leaders had acceded to—rapid demobilization of America's armed forces after World War II presaged the possibility of a new wave of isolationism similar to that which followed World War I. Though we did not fully succumb to our traditional faith in isolation—largely because of the continuation of the Soviet conspiracy to achieve world domination —we were reducing our military forces drastically. There were too many who did not yet understand that without strength we could neither be isolated nor honorably involved in world councils. While we accepted such necessary measures as the Truman Doctrine and the Marshall Plan, and continued to support the United Nations, we had also allowed our military defenses to fall far below an adequate strength. Our severe reduction in military manpower after the war was one major reason for the administration's decision to pull United States occupation forces out of Korea.

My feeling about such issues had long since convinced me that it would be impossible for me ever to adopt a political philosophy so narrow as to merit the label "liberal," or "conservative," or anything of the sort. I came to believe, as I do to this day, that an individual can only examine and decide for himself each issue in a framework of philosophic conviction dedicated to responsible progress—always in the light of what he believes is good for America as a whole—and let the pundits hang the labels as they may.

Again I began receiving a volume of mail from people with politics on their minds—so voluminous that at times it overwhelmed the university's postal facilities. One incident threw my personal staff into an uproar. Not long after I arrived at the university, the radio commentator Walter Winchell asked that each of his listeners send a card or letter urging me to seek the presidential nomination. The mail quickly reached such proportions—approximately twenty thousand letters, cards, and wires in the first week—that there was no convenient place to store it at Columbia, pending its possible processing. To the chagrin of our overworked staff, I was not too distressed. Sure that the flow would stop as soon as the conventions had met and finished their work, I was amused but sympathetic with my assistants' problem. At the end of the first day I suggested that perhaps even my commodious office could be used for storage purposes until the sacks were sorted and the mail handled.

When I arrived at the office the following morning, the staff had a measure of revenge: there was barely room for me to sit at my desk. To work was impossible, and patently I could not receive visitors. I promptly announced a new plan; I was going off on a vacation until they could report that the place was cleared out. But for days there was insufficient space for incoming mail, and my assistants had trouble even counting the inflowing letters and cards. In the end the Columbia University Bureau of Applied Social Research, which was interested, among other things, in the study of the psychological reactions of people in the mass, came to the rescue and took over the task of analyzing this flash flood of correspondence. After help arrived, my assistants, greatly relieved, notified me that I could have my office back.

The 1948 Republican convention took place earlier than the Democratic. When the Republican delegates assembled in Philadelphia in late June, it became clear that Governor Dewey would probably be nominated. During the days immediately preceding the nomination, a number of Republicans, prominent in the convention, began trying to reach me by mail, telephone, and personally dispatched messages, to convince me that I should enter the political fight to prevent the nomination of a man who, they said, "could not be elected." Except for one devoted friend, William Robinson, who had been badgered to come as a messenger from the Philadelphia scene by those who did not think Dewey could be elected, I refused to see anyone, to answer any telephone call, or to reply to any telegram or letter coming from that city. I merely asserted that my New Hampshire letter of January 23 spoke for itself and still expressed my fixed decision.

Upon the nomination of Governor Dewey the bombardment took an unexpected turn. Many Democrats decided that my letter to Leonard Finder refusing to enter the political arena referred only to the Republican party; they apparently assumed that in their case my answer would be different. As the Democratic convention approached in mid-July, a renewed rush of messages, telephone calls, and visitors engulfed me. It became clear that another public statement was necessary. I sent for Robert Harron, the university's director of public relations, and gave him a message which he immediately distributed to the press. It reiterated my determination to remain as president of Columbia University, and concluded: "I . . . could not accept nomination for any public office or participate in a partisan political contest."

This solved the difficulty through the 1948 presidential election. Until November of that year my mind was free of the subject. But almost within hours after Truman's defeat of Dewey, the process began once again; now the pleas were that I should seek the Republican nomination in 1952.

Struggling anew with this problem, I received a message which definitely confirmed my continuing relationship to the military: the President and Secretary of Defense James Forrestal requested that I return to Washington intermittently to serve as an informal chairman of the Joint Chiefs of Staff. Such a post had not then been authorized by law, but the President's personal military assistant, Admiral William Leahy, had acted during the war and immediate postwar days in a similar capacity. Now, because of advancing years, the admiral was becoming less active, and for this reason the President asked me to chair the meetings of the Chiefs. He made this request, I believe, because of my known support of the concept of effective unification of the military services and of a strong Department of Defense—views which were far from unanimously held among those who wore uniforms. This additional assignment seemed to have a marked effect in diminishing political interest in my future intentions.

The two and a half years I spent as the active president of Columbia were satisfying occupationally and were personally most enjoyable. Certainly no university president could have enjoyed a more cordial association with his board of trustees than I did with the board at Columbia, which included my close friend Thomas J. Watson, who had been a key figure in persuading me to assume the presidency of the university. I became deeply interested not only in the educational, financial, and "public-relations" aspects of a university presidency, but also in helping establish certain new projects, including the American Assembly (a continuing program bringing together men of business, labor, the professions, political parties, and government for the study of major national problems), the program for the conservation of human resources, and a Chair of Peace. These ventures and normal duties kept me busy both in my office and in traveling around the United States. My wife and I were happy with the new career.

Part of my duties involved public appearances, and one statement I made in 1949 came to be of significance later. That year I accepted an invitation from the American Bar Association to deliver a Labor Day address at their convention in St. Louis. Thinking about what appeared to me to be trends of the time, I decided to speak about the "middle way," by which I meant "progress down the center, even though there the contest is hottest, the progress sometimes discouragingly slow." Naturally, there was a military metaphor or two in the talk. Its principles were basic to me:

> The frightened, the defeated, the coward, and the knave run to the flanks [I said], straggling out of the battle under the cover of slogans, false formulas, and appeals to passion—a welcome sight to an alert enemy. When the center weakens piecemeal, disintegration and annihilation are only steps away, in a battle of arms or of political philosophies. The clear-sighted and the courageous, fortunately, keep fighting in the middle of the war. They are determined that we shall not lose our freedoms, either to the unbearable selfishness of vested interest, or through the blindness of those who, protesting devotion to the public welfare, falsely declare that only government can bring us happiness, security, and opportunity.

Having broached the subject of government, I said that we expect in all cases government to be forehanded in establishing the rules that will preserve a practical equality in opportunity. We carefully watch the government,

> especially the ever-expanding federal government—to see that in performing the functions obviously falling within governmental responsibility, it does not interfere more than is necessary in our daily lives. We instinctively have greater faith in the counterbalancing effect of many social, philosophic, and economic forces than we do in arbitrary law. . . .

Extremists, I said, hope that we will lack the stubborn courage, the stamina, and the intelligent faith required to sustain this position. By appeals to immediate and selfish advantage, they would blind us to the enduring truth that no part of our society may prosper permanently except as the whole of America shall prosper. The intricate interdependencies of our highly industrialized economy, they think, would drive us to desert principles for expediencies. Above all, I said, we needed more economic understanding and working arrangements that will bind labor and management, in every productive enterprise, into a far tighter voluntary cooperative unit than we now have.

The purpose of this unity, I added, would be, without the subordination of one group to the other, to increase productivity and better the position of labor, of management, of all America.

World events determined that my career at Columbia University would be short. On the evening of December 18, 1950, while on a trip to Heidelberg College, my wife and I were sitting comfortably in a Pullman car on the sidetracks in Bucyrus, Ohio. There a railway employee reached us with a message that a telephone call would be coming through from the President of the United States. Since, to reach the station, I was compelled to wade several hundred yards in snow more than a foot deep, it took me a considerable time to reach the little freight office where the telephone was located, but the President's call came through almost instantly. After giving me a background of pertinent events in Europe, he said that he had just received, from the other nations of the North Atlantic Treaty Organization, notification of their unanimous preference for a military commander. They wanted me. He said that he agreed with the choice. Would I accept the appointment?

The request caused me an initial sense of disappointment. Such a change would inevitably mean a radical disruption in the life of which Mamie and I were becoming so fond, and I hated the idea of leaving. But I believed in the NATO concept; to my mind, the future of Western civilization was dependent on its success. Furthermore, I could understand why the nations of NATO would want to have as their commander an officer familiar with Europe and whose name, because of the Allied campaign in World War II, had become associated with victory. In any event, since I was still an officer in the Army, I replied that if the President, as Commander-in-Chief, felt that I could undertake the assignment with a better chance of success than any other soldier of his choice, my affirmative answer was inevitable.

It was merely a case of responding to military duty; though the orders came in the form of a request, no man in America's armed forces could possibly regard a request from his Commander-in-Chief as anything except a command.

In less than three weeks I made arrangements for a hurried trip to the capitals of the NATO countries to ascertain whether they were serious about raising and training troops, and whether they were ready to give ample and proper authority to the commander who would be responsible for their defensive organization and operations. On that quick trip I was assured. in conferences with all participating governments, of the sincerity of their resolve. I came back to the United States on January 27, 1951, and so reported to the President, then informally to a session of congressional members, held in the Library of Congress, and finally to the public.

Having decided to don a uniform once again and feeling the renewed pressures of many who wanted me in politics, I thought it advisable to draft a statement—with the purpose of making it public—of flat refusal to contemplate any political career at any time, including in my announcement a request that all Americans recognize its unequivocal character.

Before issuing it, however, I decided to find out whether both of our country's major political parties would support the concept of a collective defense of the Western world against possible Communist aggression. This question was controversial early in 1951. A deep difference existed between President Truman and a number of congressional leaders concerning the President's constitutional right, in peacetime, to deploy and dispose American forces according to his best judgment and without the specific approval of the Congress.[4] There was also under debate the number of American divisions that would go to Europe to participate in the collective defense.[5] In neither of these arguments was I a participant, even though I thought the President's rights were unchallengeable.

In the overriding question of the United States' commitment to share in the collective defense of the West, however, I was vitally interested. The success of NATO, I was convinced, would be doubtful unless this basic concept—and the decision to deploy American troops to Europe at least temporarily—received wholehearted support from all quarters of the American government. To satisfy myself on this score I sought out several political leaders, primarily Republicans, who seemed to question the soundness of the collective principle.

Several of these men I saw individually in strict confidence. One prominent leader, a senator, preferred to see me in the Pentagon, rather than in his own office. The senator arrived, was met at an inconspicuous spot by an aide, and was whisked up to a temporary office I was occupying. Only my staff knew of the meeting. The result of the conference was distressing.

I found my visitor concerned almost exclusively with the two specific questions of the number of American troops to be sent to Europe and the constitutional right of the President to send them. I told him that these

[4] Senators Robert A. Taft of Ohio and Kenneth Wherry of Nebraska headed the opposition to the President on this question.

[5] In April the Senate agreed to the dispatch of four additional American divisions to Europe in a resolution (S. Res. 99), but because the House failed to concur, this did not have the force of law. Four more divisions were actually sent during 1951.

points were outside my immediate concern and insisted on an answer regarding support of the collective principle. I failed to get assurance. From the senator I gained the impression—possibly a mistaken one—that he and some of his colleagues were interested, primarily, in cutting the President, or the Presidency, down to size. I obtained similar reactions from others with whom I conferred.

My disappointment was acute; I was resentful toward those who seemed to me to be playing politics in matters I thought vital to America and the Free World. In such a vast effort as this, the conviction of the United States—as determined by the entire government—ought to be understood at home and proclaimed to the world. In order to aid personally in achieving congressional support for the basic policy, I finally concluded that it might be more effective to keep some aura of mystery around my future personal plans. For the moment I decided to remain silent, not to declare myself out as a potential political factor, and went off to Europe.

The statement I had drafted was so unequivocal that if I had carried out my intention of publicizing it, my political life would have ended without ever starting. The paper was destroyed.

It is difficult to realize, now that NATO and the concept of collective defense are so well accepted in the United States and Europe, how much pessimism actually existed on both sides of the Atlantic regarding the undertaking. For one thing, the original plans were being made in an atmosphere of gloom caused by the situation in Korea, where the intervention of Chinese Communist troops in late November of 1950 had turned what appeared to be a victory into a crushing tactical defeat. At best the prospects in Korea appeared to be for an eventual stalemate; at worst they boded involvement with the Soviet Union and the beginning of World War III. In this latter contingency many felt that overwhelming Soviet ground forces would, despite our sole possession of the atomic bomb, overrun Western Europe in a matter of days, slicing through friendly territory upon which the United States would decline to inflict the terrors of Hiroshima.

There was also a strong suspicion that the nations of Western Europe, their economies depleted and populations weary, had little fight left in them. At a New York Christmas party given by W. Alton Jones before my departure (at which I was not present), nearly two hundred men of diverse careers and achievements gathered and—he reported to me—discussed almost nothing else but the problem confronting us all in Europe. A number expressed acute apprehension about the practicality of the NATO project. While realizing that my task would be difficult, I did not believe the Soviets would attack; moreover, I was confident of the support of the Executive branch of the government, of millions of citizens, and of my close friends.

During the months after arriving in Paris I was extremely busy with many problems (a few of which were still recurrent at the end of 1960). One of the time-consuming tasks was to obtain agreement among the NATO nations on a plan for bringing West German forces into our security organizations.

The plan I supported was known as the European Defense Community (EDC), originated by the French—a plan by which West Germany and five other European nations (France, Italy, Belgium, the Netherlands, and Luxembourg) would set up a supranational army with a common uniform and budget, to serve within NATO. Because of important differences among the European nations, particularly French fears of a rearmed Germany, it was difficult to achieve progress toward unanimity, despite the EDC's provision merging West German forces into the international European army. An integration of forces had to be attained. Germany as a full-fledged member was vital to NATO. Indeed, until we could find a satisfactory arrangement for bringing a strong German contingent into our forces, our defense arrangements could not be called effective. I met often and urgently with those governments that were reluctant to sign, trying to convince them that under EDC no one nation's forces would be self-sufficient, independent of the whole, not even those of the United States. To put it simply, we were all in this together—or should be.

Another problem always confronting the commander of a force comprising land, sea, and air elements is the intricate one of command relationships. This is particularly so when the force in question is multinational, with each nation holding different concepts of the way the theater should be organized. The United States Sixth Fleet, for example, operating in the Mediterranean, was assigned by the President to my command, as were the United States land and air forces. But others, the French in particular, were reluctant to approve the integration principle, especially in NATO; years later I was to find myself discussing the same question in strong terms with an old friend and comrade, General Charles de Gaulle, when he became President of France.

In addition to these politico-military matters, we had, of course, problems of a more strictly military complexion. Complete, integrated plans had to be drawn up for the defense of Western Europe against invasion from the east—as realistically as possible with the forces then existing. In February of 1951 only one American division (plus three armored cavalry regiments, computed as equivalent to a second) was stationed in Europe.

Plans had to be made for the staging, housing, and training of the

American reinforcements, a task of some magnitude, since most of the required assets in Germany, particularly housing facilities, had been returned to that government. In addition to working on administrative problems, we spent much time in preparing for extensive military-training exercises to be held in the fall of 1951, in the form of field maneuvers— the largest since the war's end. Following these we had planned a military-communications exercise of broad scope in early 1952, involving only the principal headquarters of SHAPE. It was known as Command Post Exercise Number One, and its successful completion would represent a great forward step in the setting up of inter-Allied staff procedures and in the theoretical implementation of defensive plans of the NATO force.

During all this time a stream of visitors from the United States was flowing into my headquarters with politics almost the single subject on their minds. Among them were important representatives of both political parties: senators, congressmen, governors, other political leaders, and personal friends. In my office appointment book for that autumn are some seventy-eight official sessions of this nature: many more visitors came to see me privately at my home in Marnes-la-Coquette. Invariably they wanted to talk about the political outlook.

Sometimes I would almost laugh aloud at their arguments, since all too often they would ascribe to me marvelous, almost unique, qualifications and traits. This became so much a feature of every conversation that I ceased making even pro forma denials; I found it easier just to answer their proposals and arguments with a simple, "I'm not interested." But this was no answer to be given to intimate friends: to them I merely elaborated—sometimes, I felt, ad nauseam—the points made in my letter to Mr. Finder of January 1948.

All this took valuable time. Fortunately my Allied staff had been built up into an efficient machine. It was headed by General Alfred M. Gruenther, whose brilliance and loyalty, added to his understanding of the international political problems of the military alliance, rendered him practically an indispensable individual. He was—and is—one of the ablest all-around officers, civilian or military, I have encountered in fifty years. As a consequence of his tireless work, I was sufficiently free of routine duty to receive, at least for a few minutes, almost every person who came to see me.

Senator Henry Cabot Lodge came on Tuesday, September 4, 1951, for a visit which turned out to be, for me, significant. While many had preceded him, he was different in that he said he was reflecting the known views of numerous large groups, many of whom now wanted to start organizing a nationwide movement to present my name before the 1952 Republican convention. Cabot, an associate and friend of mine from wartime days, presented his plea with the ardor of a crusader. Thinking to put him on the defensive at once, I asked, "You are well known in politics; why not run yourself?" Without pause his answer came back, "Because I cannot be elected," and he went on with his argument.

He started with a review of the political events in the last twenty years in the United States, particularly the five national elections of 1932 through 1948, all of which had resulted in defeats for the Republican party. Cabot asserted that unless this one-sided partisan dominance could be promptly reversed, the record presaged the virtual elimination of the two-party system, which we agreed was vital to the ultimate preservation of our national institutions.

But beyond this danger he went into the performance record of the recent succession of national administrations. This record he called one of gradual but steady accumulation of power in Washington, increased "paternalism" in government's relations with the citizens, constant deficit spending, and a steady erosion in the value of our currency. As a consequence he held, first, that these practices were becoming so alarming as to spell potential disaster for the country and, second, that corrective measures could not even be started unless we had a Republican victory in 1952.

On his opposition to centralization in the federal government and the cheapening of our currency, I was in substantial agreement. Indeed, I had while president of Columbia expressed myself on these issues in meetings, letters, and speeches. I believed that it was not merely enough to realize how freedom was won; it was essential to be awake to all threats to that freedom, including the danger that arises from too great a concentration of power of any kind in the hands of the few. In dwelling upon the dangers of centralization of government, I had said, in an address when inaugurated at Columbia, that the concentration of too much power in centralized government "need not be the result of violent revolution or great upheaval. A paternalistic government can gradually destroy by suffocation in the immediate advantage of subsidy, the will of a people to maintain a high degree of individual responsibility."

In voicing these and similar convictions through the next several years, I had always been careful to avoid sharply partisan implications, since my position as president of a great university, comprising both in faculty and student body people of every political persuasion, made no other attitude possible.

But now Cabot, sitting in my NATO office, turned to the subject of the Republican party itself and its problems in attempting to cope with the danger which faced our nation. He felt that the regular Republican leadership, cast in an opposition role for twenty long years, inescapably gave the country a negative impression. The principal figures of the party were, according to him, interpreted as saying that Americans faced the choice of doing the wrong thing under the Democrats or doing nothing at all under the Republicans. He said also that in 1951 the opposition of that part of the Republican leadership known loosely as the Old Guard to the sending of United States troops to Europe to serve in NATO had made the party appear unaware of the realities of the modern world.

Cabot believed that although the Republicans, during the past two decades, had nominated men with a variety of political opinions and beliefs such as Governor Alfred M. Landon and Mr. Wendell Willkie, none of their candidates had been able to generate an appeal strong enough to unify the party and at the same time attract the independent and Democratic support necessary for election. Moreover, the party was still blamed in many minds for the depression beginning in 1929. The Republican party, Cabot said, must now seek to nominate one who, supporting basic Republican convictions—which had come down to us from Lincoln and Theodore Roosevelt—could be elected and achieve at least a partial reversal of the trend toward centralization in government, irresponsible spending, and catering to pressure groups, and at the same time avoid the fatal errors of isolationism.

And then Cabot put forward the point of his presentation. "You," he said flatly, "are the only one who can be elected by the Republicans to the Presidency. You *must* permit the use of your name in the upcoming primaries."

To this I was not prepared to agree. But despite my protests he argued with the tenacity of a bulldog and pounded away on this theme until, as he left, I said I would "think the matter over."

At the moment this general remark seemed inconsequential; I had for a long time been compelled, consciously or unconsciously, to consider the possibility of entering politics. In my mind the words were routine. Certainly I did not feel that I had, in the slightest, changed my negative attitude toward personal involvement.

But as I look back on that incident, my promise, indefinite as it was, marked a turning point. For the first time I had allowed the smallest break in a regular practice of returning a flat refusal to any kind of proposal that I become an active participant. From that time onward, both alone and through correspondence, I began to look anew—perhaps subconsciously—at myself and politics.

In the ensuing months, although I could never dismiss the political dilemma completely from my mind, I was primarily concerned with my responsibilities in NATO.[6] Then came an entirely new kind of political

6 In November 1951, with Mrs. Eisenhower, I flew to the United States for discussions with President Truman and the military authorities. At a press conference upon

message and from an unexpected quarter. Under date of December 18, 1951, I received a letter from the President of the United States. It was written in longhand and is still in my possession. President Truman explained that while he would like to go back to Missouri in 1952, possibly to run for the Senate, he felt it his immediate duty to keep isolationists out of the White House. He requested that I inform him of my own intentions, implying that my answer would have a definite influence on his decision. He added that I should do what I thought best for the country.

Excerpts from my reply, which I wrote on New Year's Day, 1952, explain my sentiments of that moment:

> There has never been any change in my personal desires and aspirations, publicly and privately expressed, over the past six years or so. I'd like to live a semi-retired life with my family, given over mainly to the study of, and a bit of writing on, present day trends and problems. But just as you have decided that circumstances may not permit you to do exactly as you please, so I've found that fervent desire may sometimes have to give way to a conviction of duty. . . .
>
> I do not feel that I have any duty to seek a political nomination, in spite of the fact that many have urged to the contrary. Because of this belief I shall not do so . . . [and] because particularly of my determination to remain silent you know, far better than I, that the possibility that I will ever be drawn into political activity is so remote as to be negligible. . . .
>
> This answer is as full and frank as I am able to devise. But when one attempts to discuss such important abstractions as a sense of duty, applied to unforseen circumstances of the future, neither brevity nor arbitrary pronouncement seems wholly applicable.
>
> *Respectfully,*
> DWIGHT D. EISENHOWER.

The turn of the year brought about a second and important break in my hope of remaining forever outside the political world. The New Hampshire primary was scheduled for March 11, 1952, and a candidate's party affiliation had to be known by the authorities of that state before his name could be entered in the primary.

I had, up to this time, refused to make any public move that would even imply a personal choice between the two major political parties; but events now answered this question. Earlier, Senator Lodge had been in-

---

our arrival, the reporters outdid themselves trying to draw me into a discussion of politics, but I insisted on talking about defense. Finally, I told them:

"What I am trying to get at is that, as of this moment, I am trying to do a job, my staff is trying to do a job, and we think it's important, and we think that each of you would have a right to resent it if we would try to divert ourselves . . . from that job to talk partisan politics or to state a partisan preference."

formed on an authoritative basis, by General Lucius Clay, that I was a Republican and had consistently voted the Republican ticket since I had left active military service in 1948. With the pressure building up on Lodge and the others cooperating with him to enter my name in the primary, he finally, in early January, took it upon himself to say, on his own authority, that he could assure the New Hampshire officials that I was a Republican. He made the announcement without consulting me, probably to save me embarrassment. This done, the reporters in Paris clamored for corroboration, and I felt that, in the circumstances, I had to give it.

I was now publicly known as a Republican, but would say no more. This brought an immediate increase in the pressure, and from that moment on, the messages reached drumfire proportions.

Among my many visitors in the ensuing weeks were several who later became publicly active in the "Citizens for Eisenhower" groups, the at first informal organizations that never ceased their work until the climax later that year. Many were good friends; I could question neither their dedication nor their integrity. On February 10 Miss Jacqueline Cochran arrived on a special mission. Two days earlier there had been a mass meeting at midnight in New York's Madison Square Garden, arranged by supporters who were hoping by this means to add weight to their argument that I should become a candidate. The entire proceedings were put on film. As soon as the film was processed, Miss Cochran flew the Atlantic and brought it immediately to Paris. Her second task was to get me to sit still long enough to view it. By the time she reached our house, she had gone thirty-five hours without sleep.

As we conferred, Miss Cochran told me about the opposition of the so-called "pros" in politics, who, although part of the Eisenhower group, believed that no meeting of this kind, held after the completion of a Garden fight the same evening, could possibly draw a crowd at midnight. They felt that a poor turnout would slow up the "Eisenhower movement" which they thought was then gaining momentum. Miss Cochran asked that my wife be with me when we viewed the film. It was shown in our living room at Villa St. Pierre in Marnes-la-Coquette.

Fifteen thousand people had assembled in Madison Square Garden. It was a moving experience to witness the obvious unanimity of such a huge crowd—to realize that everyone present was enthusiastically supporting me for the highest office of the land. As the film went on, Mamie and I were profoundly affected. The incident impressed me more than had all the arguments presented by the individuals who had been plaguing me with political questions for many months. When our guests departed, I think we both suspected, although we did not say so, that our lives were to be once more uprooted.

After Jacqueline Cochran's visit I had a talk with General Lucius Clay on February 16, 1952. He flew to London, at the time of King George VI's death, and asked me to meet with him at the London home of Brigadier Sir James Gault—my British military assistant in World War II. George Allen and Sid Richardson, two friends from the States, were also there. At this meeting I tentatively agreed that I would return home to the United States as soon as I could complete my duties in Europe, and if nominated at the convention, would compaign for the Presidency. I was committed in my own mind to run if nominated, but not to seek the nomination.

I insisted that I would have to be the one to determine the date of my return. A letter written to Clay a few days later shows that I was not yet definitely decided about timing:

> As you can well see, my attitude has undergone a quite significant change since viewing the movie of the Madison Square Garden show and listening to your day long presentation of the activities now going forward in the United States. I assure you that I shall try to be co-operative and as understanding as I can. I ask only in return that you people regard my own position with some sympathy and remember that if I ever disagree it will only be in those cases where I feel I must, as a matter of conscience and conviction. . . .
>
> . . . Even though we agree with the old proverb, "The voice of the people is the voice of God," it is not always easy to determine just what that voice is saying. I continue to get letters from certain of my friends who are almost as violent in their urgent recommendations that I do not make an early visit home as those who believe that I should come.

Senator Hugh Butler of Nebraska gave me advice of a different kind; he told me that I had a "duty" to withdraw my name from any consideration by Republicans.

On Washington's Birthday nineteen congressmen[7] wrote me an impressive letter. These men, some of whom I knew well, a number of whom I knew not at all, urged me, on behalf of their respective constituents, to come home and seek the Republican presidential nomination. Incidentally, these congressmen later became so proud of their role in influencing me to be a candidate that they presented me with a silver blotter-holder for my desk, complete with their signatures, the presidential seal, and an emblem of Supreme Headquarters, Allied Powers in Europe. This memento still rests on my desk.

In March the New Hampshire primary was held on a day which, despite icy roads, a cold steady rain, and a bit of snow, saw a record

[7] Representatives Hope, Scott, Prouty, Bakewell, Javits, Sittler, Cole (Kan.), Case, Heselton, Denny, Cotton, Herter, Auchincloss, Morton, Ford, Tollefson, Riehlman, Cole (N.Y.), and Kean.

turnout. The considerable plurality[8] in that state seemed to be a clear demonstration that more people were interested in me as a political figure than I had believed.

This was followed by another persuasive event, the March 18 Minnesota primary. There, I was not listed as a candidate. Even so, citizens appeared who wrote my name on their ballots. The turnout was slightly overwhelming, the newspapers reported; some precincts ran out of printed ballots. Spellings of "Eisenhower" were various and imaginative. The effort to promote a write-in vote had, as with the Madison Square Garden meeting, been opposed by persons who, while participating in the effort to make me a candidate, believed that any write-in effort was doomed to miserable failure and would have a depressing effect. But the state chairman of the "Minnesotans for Eisenhower," Bradshaw Mintener, differed, and he and his organization, during the frenzied closing days of the state primary campaign, appealed to the voters of Minnesota for a "political miracle." It appeared to have happened: more than one hundred thousand people wrote in varying versions of my name.[9]

It was becoming clearer, every day, that I could not much longer remain actively in command of military forces with such constant political developments.[10]

But my personal situation remained complicated by my official situation, now not by the question of whether I should come home, but when. The key to the issue was my pledge to complete in Europe the task I was sent to do. Certainly there had never been any thought of my remaining indefinitely; indeed, my position of president of Columbia University was still being held for me. Rather I had felt that I could consider my task complete when the organizational phase was finished and the successful building of NATO was assured. I now felt that this was dependent on the signing of the EDC treaty by the French, which act, I judged, should be accomplished by June 1. Accordingly, I requested relief from my command as of that date, while doubling my efforts to expedite the French government's agreement to the treaty.

---

[8] Eisenhower: 46,661; Taft: 35,838.

[9] The day before the Minnesota primary a Navaho medicine man conferred an Indian blessing on Senator Taft. Unhappily, however, he left his turkey-feather wand at home and at the site of the ceremony had to improvise one of chicken feathers. When reporters asked the medicine man afterward how he estimated Taft's chances, he replied glumly, "Wand had chicken feathers instead of turkey feathers. Now Taft is finished."

[10] In a letter dated March 28, General Clay said that he was glad I was retaining a sense of humor. I had written to him and mentioned a "horse in the corral." As a boy I used to watch the horse being lassoed for the daily work. I rooted for him but observed that he was always caught. In 1952 I found myself in much the position of that horse.

In late March, I commented, in a letter to General Clay, on two memoranda which he had sent me on foreign affairs, written by John Foster Dulles. I first met Mr. Dulles in 1948. He had long been a prominent political figure and an avid student of foreign affairs. He had been interim senator from New York and had run in 1949 on the Republican ticket against Herbert Lehman for that office. As I read the Dulles memoranda my interest was excited by his theories, similar to those I had long been pondering, regarding the conservation of our national military power and influence through a policy which has commonly come to be called "massive retaliation." Yet while in substantial agreement, I felt he oversimplified certain parts of his argument. I said as much, questioning what we should do "if Soviet political aggression, as in Czechoslovakia, successively chips away exposed portions of the free world. Here is a case where the theory of retaliation falls down." And, I went on, "One of the great and immediate uses of the military forces we are developing is to convey a feeling of confidence to exposed populations, a confidence which will make them sturdier, politically, in their opposition to Communist inroads."

When I sent these same comments on to Foster himself a few days later, there began between us an active association and exchange of views which was to grow in intimacy and breadth through the next seven years.

On April 11, Command Post Exercise Number One—a significant staff training exercise, especially crucial in an Allied headquarters—was completed. And on that same day, April 11, the White House announced its approval of the letter in which I asked to be relieved of my NATO duties on June 1, and transferred to the retired list without pay.

While that announcement eliminated any further public question regarding the possibility of my indefinite continuance in active military service, it by no means spelled any personal relief from a life that had become little less than hectic. To the NATO training tasks that remained urgent—the effort to speed growth in combat forces and military facilities, and the vital functions of strengthening communication and command lines—was now added a program, self-imposed, of paying a final visit to NATO governments to make certain that I would not leave behind, unnecessarily, any loose threads and dangling questions.

On these journeys I omitted only Greece and Turkey, nations which I had recently visited. Each European Cabinet group with which I met expressed, confidentially, a hope that my replacement would be General Gruenther, not only because of his acknowledged ability, but because he had become well known, liked, and respected in European capitals as a soldier with a clear understanding of the special problems of Allied coordination.

These conclusions coincided with my own. I knew many of the leaders in our uniformed services and recognized their qualities. But the post of Supreme Commander of NATO, with the peculiar character and delicacy of its daily problems, puts a premium on specialized experience. All NATO countries wanted another American to succeed me, but of course the nomination of my replacement was the function of the President. He named General Matthew Ridgway, a man whom I had known before and during the war and who was an unusually competent combat commander. I thought the arrangement was satisfactory, particularly because I understood that General Gruenther would be continued in his post as NATO Chief of Staff.

There were many other future plans to discuss. By the time I had completed my final survey I definitely felt that policies governing initial organization, training, and national recruiting systems had been well established. It was particularly encouraging that in Paris on May 27 the Foreign Ministers of West Germany, France, Italy, Belgium, the Netherlands, and Luxembourg signed the treaty creating the European Defense Community. Though ratification by those governments was still to be achieved, the initialing seemed to indicate that the West had overcome a major obstacle to the incorporation of West German forces into its defenses.

While I was tidying up the final fragments of my activities at NATO, the announcement that I was soon to be retired from active service brought a fast increase in counsel and recommendations concerning my anticipated participation in 1952 politics. When military duties permitted, I tried to see each visitor and to answer all incoming communications. But, understandably, my personal schedule became more and more involved and difficult—so much so that, despite my regret in leaving SHAPE, I was relieved when the time came to say good-by.

For Mamie and me, as for most of us in the uniformed services, life had long been a constant series of partings from good friends and meetings with new people, as we confronted new duties. Yet this departure involved far more radical changes in outlook and activity than any formerly experienced.

In leaving SHAPE we were leaving a group of unusually interesting friends, intriguing duties, and pleasant home surroundings. Moreover, Mamie had fallen in love with Villa St. Pierre in Marnes-la-Coquette near our headquarters, undoubtedly the most unusual and comfortable home that we had ever occupied. It was acquired, rebuilt, and furnished by the French government, which had determined to establish, for the senior personnel at SHAPE, suitable quarters in the historic and beautiful surroundings near Versailles. Our neighbors were the soul of hospitality and friendliness.

Under Mayor Jean Minaud, Mrs. Eisenhower and I had been made honorary citizens of Marnes-la-Coquette, and he made certain that nothing occurred in the area to lessen our enjoyment of a beautiful villa and its spacious gardens. Indeed, when finally we had to bid farewell to a home that we had occupied for a few months only, the entire village turned out to bid us Godspeed. A touching feature of the parting was a serenade by the Petits Chanteurs à la Croix de Bois, a famous band of boy singers who later sang for us at the White House. It was a moving occasion.

Sometime later a letter written by George Washington on May 5, 1789, to Edward Rutledge,[11] was presented to me by Mr. St. John Terrell. On reading it I was struck by the solemn concern expressed by Washington as he proceeded "to embark again on the tempestuous and uncertain Ocean [sic] of public life.

"Though I flatter myself the world will do me the justice to believe that at my time of life and in my circumstances, nothing but a conviction of duty could have induced me to depart from my resolution of remaining in retirement; yet I greatly apprehend that my countrymen will expect too much from me. I fear if the issue of public measure should not correspond to their sanguine expectations, they will turn the extravagant (and I may say undue) praises that they are heaping upon me at this moment into equally extravagant (though I will finally hope unmerited) censures. So much is expected, so many untoward circumstances may intervene in such a new and critical situation, that I feel an insuperable diffidence in my own abilities."

It was with much the same feeling expressed by General Washington, but also with the expectation of new experiences and new opportunities for service, that my wife and I now turned toward the future that loomed before us.

---

[11] A member of the Continental Congress, a signer of the Declaration of Independence, and later a governor of South Carolina.

CHAPTER II

Candidate

Double, double, toil and trouble;
Fire burn and cauldron bubble.

—Shakespeare, Macbeth

IN Paris, through letters, cables, visitors, and newspaper accounts, I had come to know something of the growing numbers of people now joining those individuals who, for a long time, had personally urged me to go into politics. Nevertheless, I was astonished, upon reaching Washington on June 1, 1952, to learn of the scope and growth of the organizational and recruiting effort that had developed during the winter and spring.

Sometime in 1951 my friends General Lucius Clay, Governor Thomas E. Dewey and Republican National Committeeman J. Russel Sprague of New York, and Senator James Duff of Pennsylvania began working, with others, to arouse general interest in me for the Republican candidacy in 1952. Senator Frank Carlson and former Senator Harry Darby of Kansas soon teamed up with them, and at a meeting in Governor Dewey's suite at the Roosevelt Hotel on November 10, 1951, Cabot Lodge became campaign manager of this team of political pros, which also by that time included Herbert Brownell. Paul Hoffman joined in the spring of 1952.

This group set itself the immediate mission of generating delegate strength for the July convention to assure my nomination. Selecting for itself the colorless informal title of the "Initial Advisory Group," this small team worked so quietly that word of its existence rarely appeared in the press.

Another committee, highly important but also largely unknown to the public, included a small number of friends more or less revolving around Cliff Roberts. Aksel Nielsen, W. Alton Jones, William Robinson, Robert

Jones, Ellis Slater, Lucius Clay, and a few others[1] belonged to the group. As some of my most intimate civilian friends, they were a source of counsel and advice to me. They were not professional politicians and never acted as such.

In December of 1951, I later learned, this small group had a meeting in the Park Lane Hotel in New York City, where they decided to send Cliff Roberts and Bill Robinson to Paris to try to convince me that I should declare myself a Republican.[2]

In Washington a number of senators and congressmen (including Hugh Scott of Pennsylvania, former chairman of the Republican National Committee) had joined in the drive, as had many retired officers and enlisted men, old comrades of mine. And through most of the preceding year innumerable volunteers had begun work almost spontaneously across the country. Many designated themselves as "IKE clubs"; others adopted different names, all describing their purpose. I have never learned in what state or locality the first of these was founded.[3] But I did learn, on my return to this country in June, that beginning in the summer of 1951 two young men, Charles Willis and Stanley Rumbough, had worked in a loft in Hoboken, New Jersey, giving their entire time and energies almost twenty-four hours a day to the cause of nominating and electing me as President. These two were responsible for the formation of many IKE clubs, all over the country. Long before June 1952, such clubs abounded throughout the Union, even in the South. By February of that year, they numbered more than eight hundred.

This outburst of grass-roots volunteer action, I was told, was almost unique in American politics, at least in the magnitude and in the enthusiasm exhibited. The campaign seemed to have started small, here, there, then everywhere, and like a brush fire, spread in many directions. This phenomenon, representing strong sentiment on the part of substantial groups of citizens, provided one of the powerful arguments employed by friends in urging me to make myself available.

Practically all these groups, recognizing early the need for central direction and coordination, had associated themselves together on a national

[1] L. F. McCollum, L. B. Maytag, Albert Bradley, Burton F. Peck, Philip D. Reed, Douglas M. Black, Robert E. McConnell, Milton S. Eisenhower, and Philip Young.
[2] My good friend and outstanding supporter Roy Roberts, president of the *Kansas City Star,* had months earlier, after talking with me, described me as a "good Kansas Republican."
[3] I do know that out in Ponca City, Oklahoma, a druggist, Mr. T. J. Cuzalina, had for years been beating the drums and generating publicity to nominate me. By January 4, 1952, I was told that a group in Gettysburg, Pennsylvania, under the leadership of Raymond Pitcairn, of Philadelphia, was publicly petitioning me to run.

basis, forming an organization known as "Citizens for Eisenhower."[4] The co-chairmen eventually became Walter Williams of Seattle and Mrs. Oswald B. ("Mary") Lord of New York.

In spite of these developments, I had not acknowledged, even to myself, that I was an avowed candidate for the Republican nomination. I knew that once I should take the irrevocable step of declaring myself, I would be in a fight to the finish; a naturally combative disposition would never allow me to enter a contest except with the determination to exhaust every resource of energy and every honorable means to win it.

Soon I found that any personal decision as to my status was scarcely important. Having been persuaded that I should come back to the United States and make myself *available* for consideration by the public for political office, I now found that almost without exception everyone, both friend and political foe, interpreted my return as a pronouncement of positive intent to seek it. It was not long before it became far less wearing on my disposition to accept the situation rather than try constantly to convince others of the distinction I felt it proper to make between an availability and a candidacy.

Though in this I may have been less than astute, no voluntary or involuntary step I took toward the status of open candidacy was made carelessly or lightly. The matter was deadly serious, for I was not unaware of the grave tasks which fall to a head of government.

No individual can be completely or fully prepared for undertaking the responsibilities of the Presidency; possibly no one can even be fully aware of their weight and difficulty, except one who has borne them. It is generally assumed, I think, that any person seriously considered by the public as a possible nominee for the office will be the possessor of a satisfactory education and competence in rather traditional fields. Certainly his ability in handling and understanding people would be of interest to the average voter, as would his training and experience in making significant decisions. The basic features of his political philosophy should be fully exposed to the public and his lively interest in fundamental issues of his time should be obvious.

I was, of course, a political novice. Of certain characteristics and beliefs that would engage public interest about me as a possible candidate, little was known. Even though I had long been reading about national and world movements and trends, military life, while it had by no means precluded my concern with public matters, had assured that my opinions

[4] The New York City headquarters opened February 7, 1952. The organization was then headed by Arthur Vandenberg, Jr.

respecting them would be almost wholly personal and private. Only while I was at Columbia had I ventured to speak publicly about anything of a political nature.

But because of special experiences in my past life, I was probably more acutely aware than the average citizen of the complexities, anxieties, and burdens of the life led by a head of government.

In varying assignments, over a period of many years, I had had a chance to observe and work with, among others, Prime Minister Winston Churchill; President Franklin Delano Roosevelt; and the chief executives of the Philippines, an "emerging nation" (the term was not used then), and of France, an old nation.

My education, which gave me at least a fringe familiarity with decisions affecting high officials of the Executive branch, began relatively early in my military career. In 1929 I was assigned, as a major, to the Assistant Secretary of War (Patrick J. Hurley and, succeeding him, Frederick Payne) and later to the Chief of Staff of the Army, Douglas MacArthur. In Washington and elsewhere, as a personal assistant to these men, I had an opportunity to observe high-level activity in not only the Executive, but in the Legislative branch, particularly in matters pertaining to military budgets, public relations, and relations between the Executive branch and the Congress.

While it is never possible for a staff officer to feel the full weight of responsibility that rests on the shoulders of his chief, it is feasible for him to gain a degree of insight into the magnitude and intricacies of those of his chief's problems that come before him for study. He learns to live with the frustrating fact that many issues on which he is required to work have no immediate, and sometimes not even a satisfactory future, solution.

Following the completion of the military tour in Washington in 1935, I went to the Philippine Islands, which were to become, by law, a fully independent nation in 1946. My assignment was as senior assistant to General MacArthur, who had accepted the post of military adviser to the Commonwealth as it set about organizing a satisfactory defense establishment.

In this capacity I came into frequent and direct contact with President Manuel Quezon. He was an intelligent, energetic, and courageous man; to me he was an intensely interesting character. Here again my opportunities were unusually good to learn about the difficulties in the life of a chief executive.

I left the Philippines in December 1939, when all Western Europe was at war. After our own nation became engaged, I had a number of conversations with President Roosevelt, during which he sometimes detailed some of his problems, both current and future. These dealt primarily with military matters, but since his views were those of a head of state, they greatly intrigued me. The President had one quality that was particularly valuable in a wartime leader; he never, under any circumstances, entertained the slightest doubt that we could win.

Even as early as the Casablanca Conference, in January 1943, he referred, in a private conversation with me, to the future of the French colonies in North Africa. Tunisia was foremost in our minds not only because it was the scene of the current fighting, but also because of its strategic importance. Already he was casting his mind into postwar events. Our talk involved in addition to military operations, the local political scene, with which I was intimately familiar through my own experiences in the early phases of the campaign. We talked about De Gaulle, Admiral Darlan—only lately assassinated—and other French governmental leaders. I last saw the President early in 1944. The wear and tear on him was noticeable. I had no illusions about the burdensome character of his life.

With Mr. Churchill my association was far more intimate, because geographical proximity permitted us frequent opportunities for personal contact and because his position as Prime Minister did not place upon his movements the same restrictions as those surrounding the American President. He liked to visit field headquarters whenever possible.

From early 1942 until the end of 1945 my relations with Mr. Churchill were close and friendly. In addition, those years were particularly instructive because of his untiring attention to every problem of whatever kind affecting the British Empire—his memory respecting the deployment of specific military units, for example, was phenomenal.

He was quite personal in his relations with field commanders and never hesitated to suggest, from a location hundreds of miles from the scene of action, detailed plans of action; of course, he did not couch these messages in the form of orders, except when a major decision was required. He would send telegrams into the field, asking questions about the whereabouts and actions of particular regiments with which he was well acquainted. One evening I met him as he was drafting a message to a British mid-East commander. It dealt with specific items of a tactical plan; when he had finished he handed it to me for comment. After reading it I told him that I was not familiar with the details and even if I were I would not send such a message to a field commander. Why? he wanted to know. I replied that obviously the man in the field knew more about the detailed situation than anyone sitting in London. American practice was to give a commander a mission, and the means to carry it out, without interferences from superiors. Washington, of course, kept in touch with the situation, and sent such directions as were necessary concerning logistic support or changes in major programs. But so far as operations were concerned, our tendency was either to decorate a man or relieve him, depending upon success or failure. When he pressed me on the matter of his particular communication, I said, "If as an American commander I received such a message from the President of the United States, he would expect my resignation to be on his desk tomorrow morning—and I would make sure that it would be there." The incident was an illustration of the great differences between his and the American system of military command.

Despite occasional differences in viewpoint, conferences with the Prime Minister were always a pleasure. His sense of humor, conversational virtuosity, and habit of quoting from favorite authors made every meeting an adventure for me. He was farseeing in his attitudes toward the Soviets. I recall his repeated statement that he distrusted the Soviet leaders. Even though, when Hitler attacked the Soviets in 1941, he welcomed with open arms the help that Britain would now get from the Russian armies, he often reminded me that he was "suspicious of the Bear."

My later European experience at SHAPE, during 1951–52, compelled me to meet with the heads of the governments in NATO. There I had to urge a number of chief executives and their high-ranking associates to put more impetus behind efforts to provide for the common defense. The defense problem, of course, involved nearly every facet of government in each country, including the always difficult matter of budgets.

In addition, our headquarters was in France, where I had the chance to see what happens to a government of factions and fractions, and a parliament where there is virtually no penalty for failure. If the French political leaders made a mistake, the government "fell," which often meant that it simply re-formed, with various jobs juggled among the old job-holders.

All these experiences and responsibilities precluded any possibility that I might contemplate a campaign for the Presidency lightly.

In any event, while perforce recognizing the public impression that I was at last a declared candidate, there was one more condition to be satisfied before I could accept the Republican nomination, if offered: the convention would have to adopt a platform with which I could agree. I would not become the party's nominee, I told my intimates emphatically, unless I was prepared to carry out its basic campaign promises. In my view, the policies and programs of the party should be the vital factor in the decision of the American people.

Soon after I arrived in Washington on June 1, Secretary of Defense Lovett arranged a press conference for me in the Pentagon. Because I was still in uniform and speaking under military auspices, I told the reporters that I could comment only on military subjects. Before the meeting, I had mentioned this restriction to one of my old friends in the press corps. "This will be a mild cup of tea," he replied, "for a gang obviously expecting a cocktail of real authority." Of course the reporters there that day were far more interested in politics than in NATO; nevertheless they understood the limitation.

Thereafter, I took off for Abilene, the Kansas town in which I spent my boyhood, to lay the cornerstone for the Eisenhower Foundation, an institution initiated in 1945 by Kansans to honor the fighting men of World War II and to promote citizenship training in the United States.

Although I was in Abilene on a political errand, it would be callous to think that the nostalgic memories of childhood there did not cross my mind. The life we had together—my father, mother, brothers, and I[5] —had been complete, stimulating, and informative, with opportunity available to us for the asking. We had been poor, but one of the glories of America, at the time, was that we didn't know it. It was a good, secure small-town life, and that we wanted for luxuries didn't occur to any of us. As I walked the streets of Abilene that June 4 morning, the memory of that family life was much in my thoughts.

In the afternoon I was slated to deliver a televised outdoor speech, scheduled as the first of a series of personal appearances in which I was expected to outline to the public my basic positions on current American problems.

Rain began about noon. It was no Kansas spring shower; it was a drenching downpour, the kind we used to call, fifty years ago in that region, a "gully washer."

Friends' faces became longer as the rain persisted, but this was one condition that could not panic me. I had become hardened during the war to every kind of disappointment that weather could cause. During that conflict I had spent so many anxious and worrisome hours and days in frustrating inaction as we waited for weather to permit planned movements that at the war's end I vowed never again to allow myself to be upset by it. Rather, I would always, thereafter, gladly adjust my actions, and my disposition, to its vicissitudes.

So I was probably the least concerned of any of the principals participating in the event. Early in the afternoon, it became evident that few of the people crowding the town would be able to go to the park, and an aide ruefully remarked that the empty seats of the grandstand, pictured throughout the television network, could scarcely be taken as a good omen.

[5] My parents were David J. and Ida Elizabeth Eisenhower. My living brothers are Edgar, Earl, and Milton. Arthur died in 1958, Roy in 1942, Paul in infancy.

As the hour of my appearance approached, however, the deluge showed signs of ceasing, and we had at least a faint hope that the talk could be delivered as planned. The ride to the park, begun in slackening rain, took only a few minutes, and as we arrived the precipitation became scarcely more than a slow dripping and dropping, a sort of leaking from the overloaded clouds.

At five o'clock the time came for me to mount the rostrum. A raincoat was still a necessity, and to negotiate the mud and puddles of the open field between the car and the stand, I had to roll my trousers to the knees.

Probably no televised speech up to that moment was ever delivered under greater difficulties and more uncomfortable circumstances, or to a greater array of empty seats. Old friends and die-hard supporters were not, of course, deterred by the elements from coming; but in view of the condition of the field, it was fortunate that the thousands still in town did not try to crowd into the park.

Because the talk was the first of what was planned as a series between the time of my homecoming and the opening of the Republican National Convention, it was general in its tenor. I called attention again to the need for alertness and firmness in our attitude toward the ambitions of world Communism, and the utter futility of any policy of isolation. I deplored the secrecy of Yalta and the loss of China.

I spoke also of a series of internal dangers besetting us. The first of these I listed was the increasing trend toward unreasonable antagonisms among different economic groups in our country. Maximum productivity in our nation, I believed, demanded a favorable industrial climate provided by government; it also demanded intelligent cooperation among capital, management, and labor. I put myself on record as an enemy of inflation and expressed the conviction that excessive taxation could destroy the incentive to excel.

I spoke once more against the evil of centralization of government and against dishonesty or corruption in any of its levels. To summarize my belief concerning the basic needs of the United States in the area of defense and international responsibility, I said:

"Today, America must be spiritually, economically, and militarily strong, for her own sake and for humanity. She must guard her solvency as she does her physical frontiers. This means elimination of waste, luxury, and every needless expenditure from the national budget." I concluded by saying that military as well as other requirements must be approached with logic, not fear, and that as partners with others America must carry the burden of world leadership because of our strength.

That day was the first on which I was universally addressed and treated by everyone as a candidate. Conversations dealt exclusively with politics, especially the coming convention. A Mr. Arthur J. Weaver, already named as a delegate to the convention from Nebraska, called on me. He said he was to be a member of the convention's credentials committee and, after outlining some of the questions that he expected to meet, asked me for advice. I was quite well aware that there would be decisions involving the seating of rival delegations to the convention. In the hope of making clear that I had no personal ax to grind, I told him that he should examine the evidence in each case and vote nothing except his own conscience. He pursued the matter, adverting to a few of the specific charges and countercharges already made in the campaign, and sought my opinion about them. I reminded him that I was just home from Europe, that I was now becoming an interested party, and that it was not my business to talk about them. "These matters are your responsibility, not mine," I told him. "I have no counsel other than that I have just given you."

I can still recall that scene and that instant, in my corner room in the old Sunflower Hotel. Bill Robinson and my other advisers there looked at me in horror: they must have thought I was crazy! But from that first meeting, Mr. Weaver and I became stanch friends.

Throughout the rest of the day I was busy meeting delegates or people who expected to be delegates. I was invited by my old Abilene friend Charlie Case to come to his home for dinner. Once this became known, the people who wanted to see me put so much pressure on my host that I came not to dinner but to a political rally—incidentally, one of the few in eight years that was real fun!

Abilene was my boyhood town and many people still living had known me from boyhood. It was only natural that they should be biased. As a consequence, though the afternoon had been gloomy and soggy and the spirits of the managing group stood somewhere below zero, the crowds were happy, if not hilarious. In their minds' eye they unquestionably saw me already in the White House. Their attitude did not reflect the views of the outside world.

The next morning we confirmed, both from newspapers and telephone calls from friends, that the reactions to my afternoon performance were far from flattering. Criticisms were voiced about the weather, my appearance, my delivery and, finally, the substance of my speech. One rabid Taft supporter, Congressman B. Carroll Reece of Tennessee, said, "It looks like he's pretty much for home, mother and heaven."

I sympathized with the discouragement and low spirits of my friends but again refused to be disturbed. I did decide to use more impromptu talk thereafter and less calculated speech-writing—for although I had no burning ambition to win the nomination, I did want to make clear my ideas and attitudes. And on the credit side, the Abilene talk was useful later in the campaign as a reference for supporting speakers; for while it was general in nature, it came to be regarded as a good statement of sound progressive Republican doctrine.

That morning I was scheduled to meet with the press at the local theater, which in my youth we used to call the "Opry House." Late the prior afternoon there was bickering, renewed the next morning, between the representatives of the press and of television. The latter wanted to bring news cameras to the conference; most of the newspapermen were opposed. Hearing of this argument, I sided with the movie and television people, as did Bill Robinson, himself an important figure in the newspaper field. Why exclude them, I thought, as long as their presence did not interfere with the purpose of the conference? This decision made, we expected some expression of resentment, but most reporters seemed to be reconciled to the cameras.

In answer to an early question, I had an opportunity to outline what my policy would be both in the campaign and later, in dealing with queries about personalities. "In your speech yesterday," a reporter asked, "you said the loss of China was a type of tragedy that must not be repeated. On whom do you blame the loss of China?" My answer was unequivocal and prophetic: "I am not going . . . to indulge in personalities in anything I have to say. I believe in certain principles, certain procedures and methods that I will discuss with anybody at any time. I am not going to talk personalities."

The press conference covered almost every conceivable question, from the foreign policies of the Truman administration to my attitude toward wage and price controls, my connection with two Democratic administrations, conservation, farm price supports, and my estimate as to our probable delegate strength at the Republican National Convention. And of course there was the inevitable question: "Did you ever dream [that] someday when you left Abilene you would come back, running for the Presidency of the United States?" I told them that as a young boy I had great difficulty in determining whether I wanted to be a railroad conductor or another Hans Wagner. Later that day an Abilene friend called my attention to a youthful prophecy by a classmate writing in our high-school yearbook of 1909. I would grow up, he predicted, to be a professor of history at Yale; my older brother Edgar would be President of the United States.

Unlike the verdict on my first-day appearance in Abilene, friends and most of the press gave me a satisfactory grade on the morning's meeting. This was possibly because I have always enjoyed the give and take of the questions and answers of a press conference far more than I do the delivery of a set speech, even though it is easier in a prepared talk to present in more exact fashion a specific attitude on a difficult question than it is in an off-the-cuff answer.

My Abilene visit was, for me, the beginning of a new kind of life.

Though I had been, for years, thrown into frequent contact with political leaders and governmental officials of our own and other countries, I was not especially knowledgeable about the processes of nominating anyone for political office. Yet from then until July 12, in practically every meeting, every conversation, every verbal or written message, I found that this subject dominated.

The Initial Advisory Group had by this time concluded that the immediate requirement was to bring the Republican state delegations and me together, with the main effort to be directed at those delegations not rigidly committed to any candidate. Realizing that the time remaining before the beginning of the convention was exceedingly short, I approved the group's tentative plan which, in essence, was to invite these delegations to come to visit me, since in this way I could meet with several each day.

At Abilene I had seen a few people from six state delegations, but now I went back to New York City, returning to the house I had occupied as president of Columbia. I did, in fact, still hold this position, and if things had gone otherwise might indeed very well have returned to it. There my days were crowded with visits from delegations and with developing future plans. I was bombarded with questions, advice, and recommendations, all dealing exclusively with the nomination. Success in the convention balloting was the mission of Cabot Lodge and his group. They were, on that basis, engaged in planning the timing and character of my scheduled activities, while I was striving to give primary attention to explaining and supporting political convictions and beliefs. Though these differing objectives resulted in occasional mix-ups, some amusing, others irritating, they had no noticeable result except to promote a few unimportant arguments.

In meeting with visiting delegates a few advisers wanted me to stress things that they calculated would commend me to the delegation as a candidate, but I never asked anyone, anywhere, to support me as a person; only what I stood for. This distinction was, at the time, very real to me; in the long run I suppose it was inconsequential.

During the eight days I remained in New York, I talked with twenty delegations, largely from the Eastern seaboard. In the meantime we had developed our plans to the extent that we had decided upon the composition of a staff, headed by Arthur Vandenberg, Jr., to accompany me to the headquarters I had selected—Denver, Colorado.

On our arrival at Denver a crowd, estimated at a hundred thousand, turned out. That city was my wife's home, a sort of second home to me, and, because of its location, could be conveniently reached by delegations from the Central and Western states. We arranged a program that would permit me to meet the maximum number of political visitors. But there was no exclusiveness about these activities. From mid-June to early July, I talked not only to political delegations but to representatives of all kinds of professions, businesses, and occupations, outlining my position on issues, not all of which by any means were calculated to be popular with the specific audience with which I was faced. Indeed, I felt, and still do, that appeals to the special interests of selfish groups are both hypocritical and self-defeating.

Nevertheless, each group had, of course, its own interests to be dealt with. Thus I assured doctors I was against socialized medicine; I told residents of a Kansas area that I agreed their farms should not be inundated by a public-works project unless broad necessity for the construction could be proved; I told a delegation I was against sending an official ambassador to the Vatican if this was going to offend any considerable portion of our people, but told them, at the same time, that I admired and respected His Holiness and considered him a great champion in the fight against Communism; I told a Texas audience that I thought the state— like other Gulf states—should enjoy the right to the oil under the Gulf of Mexico, out of the state's historic boundary. I urged reducing the voting age to eighteen; I favored ending economic controls "as rapidly as possible." I told farmers that I thought the existing law affecting price supports should be allowed to operate until its then authorized terminal date, but that better methods should be devised to eliminate price-depressing surpluses; and all the time I urged increased attention to the world-wide Communist threat, the healthy growth of our economy, sound fiscal practices and integrity in government, and the avoidance of further deterioration in the value of our currency. "A bankrupt America," I said in a speech in Denver, "is a defenseless America."

Since my return to the United States I had heard arguments on both sides of a critical question: should I go to Chicago for the convention?

My answer was no. Every consideration of personal preference, health, and welfare, I believed, as well as of politics argued against the trip. In this view I was nearly alone; no one, except my wife, would agree with me. But one argument was effective in reversing my position. The shrewd people among the "Eisenhower group" seemed to understand that any man would be sensitive to the charge that he was "letting a friend down" or that he was remiss in his duty to others. All the work, the hopes, the sacrifices of hundreds of thousands, they argued, could go down the drain if I should fail to be on the spot when the decision was reached. It was "expected of me," they pleaded, by every club and everyone enlisted in the Eisenhower movement—and my failure to go would discourage, disappoint, and dishearten them all. So I went on my first political train ride.

A busy, hectic, and tiring ten days ensued.

During the journey I made nine speeches, visited Nebraska's capital, went to Iowa State College—and was nearly mobbed by a friendly crowd of between five and ten thousand people. My talks during the stops covered a variety of subjects, three of which I returned to time and again. The first of these was centralization of political authority and responsibility in Washington, which I opposed. I pointed out that the Democratic party had been in control of the federal government for twenty solid years and during those years our nation had experienced an uninterrupted drift toward more and more paternalism and control of the lives of its citizens.

Next, I urged the need for presenting Republicanism to young people in such fashion as to attract them to service under the Republican banner. I insisted that, without rejuvenating and strengthening the party by appealing to the vigor, vitality, and imagination of the young, we could not win the 1952 election. I asked for their help in sustaining individual liberty, competitive enterprise, and freedom of opportunity, as visualized by our Constitution.

The third subject on which I dwelt repeatedly had to do with charges of irregularity in the naming of certain state delegations. Following my return from Europe in June, I had for some time avoided any reference to these quarrels, primarily because of my lack of familiarity with the facts. As time passed, however, I found myself constantly seeking information, both as to practices and methods in these matters and to the specific charges and countercharges made about unfairness in Texas, Georgia, and Louisiana.

About Georgia and Louisiana, I said nothing because the cases seemed to me to be less clear and my information was less complete. The Texas affair, however, definitely involved principle. Under Texas law, each party's precinct conventions—open to any qualified voter—were to elect representatives to county conventions, who in turn would elect representatives to a state convention, who in turn would elect the delegates to the national convention. The law, however, raised a major question at the beginning: did a citizen have the right to cross the line and vote in the precinct convention of a party to which he did not belong?

The Republican National Committeeman Henry Zweifel, of Fort Worth, and his well-organized pro-Taft followers said no: by their order every voter at every precinct convention had to pledge in writing, "I am a Republican and desire to participate in Republican party activities in the year 1952."

This pledge did not deter the pro-Eisenhower Texans, headed by Jack Porter of Houston and Alvin H. Lane of Dallas.

"If asked to sign a declaration that you will support the Republican nominee," they broadcast all over Texas, "SIGN IT! The Supreme Court of Texas held that, in effect, you can vote Republican one day, Democratic the next, and vote in the general election the next day. . . ."

At the precinct conventions on May 3, usually held in private homes, unprecedented swarms of voters appeared. In precinct after precinct the Eisenhower followers outvoted the Taftites, who then walked out, convened their own rump conventions, and elected a rival slate of representatives to the county convention. At a precinct meeting in Zweifel's home a hundred Eisenhower supporters showed up and elected a slate; Zweifel bolted to his front yard, where he and his followers elected a rival delegation. All over Texas that day meetings broke up in fist fights.

At the succeeding May 6 conventions in most of the largest counties the same thing happened: the Taft forces, outvoted, walked out, then regrouped to vote again. Finally on May 27 a credentials committee for the Texas Republican state convention, controlled by the Zweifel group, gave a lopsided majority of the convention seats to representatives elected at the pro-Taft county meetings, charging that "Republicans for a day" had helped elect those pledged to me. "The Republican party," Zweifel declared, "has been saved from mob rule." The pro-Eisenhower representatives, locked out of one convention hall, crossed the street to another, packed it to the rafters, and elected their own slate of delegates to the national convention in Chicago.

On June 21 I had gone to Dallas, where I publicly expressed my attitude toward the Zweifel organization's arrogant overriding of the will of the majority, charging that in disenfranchising the delegates elected to support me, the "rustlers stole the Texas birthright instead of Texas steers." The credentials of both pro-Eisenhower and pro-Taft delegates had gone to the Republican National Committee, which was responsible for making up the temporary roll of delegates to open the convention. Because the committee had twice as many Texas delegates as seats, it declared these seats contested. Under the rules of the Republican National Convention of 1948, the members of the temporary roll—which necessarily included some of the contested delegates—had a right to take part in the final vote on the seating of all contested delegates except themselves.

I thought the national convention of 1952 should vote to change these rules. Believing that no man should be disenfranchised by the decision of a small committee, in which the prejudices of only one or two persons could be decisive, I had said in Dallas that I favored letting the national convention have the final say on contested seats. And I said further that I opposed letting any contested delegate have a vote on this question.

This suggestion foreshadowed the "Fair Play Amendment," a change in the convention rules submitted at the outset of the convention. The amendment provided that contested delegates who, in the selection of the temporary roll, did not receive an affirmative vote by two thirds of the members of the national committee could not vote to seat themselves or any other contested delegate. The immediate purpose was to assure that all the delegates from Georgia and Texas and thirteen of the fifteen delegates from Louisiana could not be seated until their qualifications had been approved by a majority of the rest of the delegates to the convention. The danger, of course, was that the thirty-eight Texas delegates for Taft—plus the thirteen from Louisiana and the seventeen from Georgia—could under the old rules, once temporarily seated by the national committee, vote each other into permanent seats.

This credentials quarrel practically monopolized the headlines for weeks prior to the opening of the convention, and I hammered away at it on the way to Chicago. The struggle was characterized by acrimonious public and private debate carried on between those in the Eisenhower camp on the one hand and, on the other, those supporting Senator Taft. My friends contended that complete control of the convention machinery had fallen into the hands of the other side and that justice in any important question involving the nomination could be obtained only by an appeal to the entire membership. These individuals pointed out, in support of their argument, that the keynote speaker (General MacArthur) as well as the temporary chairman (Walter Hallanan of West Virginia) and the permanent chairman (Joseph W. Martin of Massachusetts) owed their selection to the Taft forces. In turn, the Taft leaders charged that the Texas delegates for me had been elected by Democrats who wanted to force onto the November ballot a Republican who could be easily defeated.

The trip to Chicago took three days. At its completion everyone felt like a veteran of political campaigning.

When we arrived, on Saturday, July 5, and even before going to my hotel, I went to a reunion of the 82nd Airborne Division to speak at a luncheon commemorating the wartime exploits of that great organization. It was an exciting, even emotional, occasion—we were all old soldiers together—and the city's political atmosphere did nothing to dampen the enthusiasm or deportment of the diners.

When my party and I went on to our headquarters in the Blackstone Hotel, we quickly learned what it meant to be near the center of the political hurricane known as a national convention.

In spite of my efforts in New York and Denver to meet as many delegations as possible, I had been able to see only a fraction of those attending the convention. Senator Lodge and his associates now gave me a schedule for meeting most of the others, with no time whatsoever left free. Two living rooms were provided; while I was meeting with one delegation, another group would assemble in the second room. This went on every day, all day, with breaks coming only when it seemed desirable for me to dash off to meet a group that could not be accommodated in my suite. The evenings were normally reserved for special conferences.

At one such meeting we went over the important details of the platform. Foster Dulles had for six weeks been working on the foreign-policy plank, with Senator Taft's approval, despite the fact that Foster had declared his support for me; and Cabot Lodge had kept a sharp eye on the drafting of the entire document to make certain I could accept it. When I first saw the entire text, I was flabbergasted at its length. Who but a professional politician would read it all? I still believe that platforms would be more useful and more widely read if they were limited to a fraction of their current average length. Those portions of the 1952 platform devoted to indictment of the twenty-year record of Democratic stewardship were in some sections written in purple "prosecuting-attorney" style. I was not overly disturbed by this feature, since I understood that it was habitual in both parties. In any event, I was interested primarily in the platform's pledges, not its charges.

I concluded that its terms would not place me in a false position and I would therefore accept, if nominated.

On Sunday evening, July 6 (the eve of the convention), Governor Fine of Pennsylvania and Arthur Summerfield came in for a visit. These two leaders had long been wooed by Senator Lodge and the other men working on the floor at the convention. Responding to Mr. Brownell's urgent recommendation, I invited the two gentlemen to dinner. Brownell, who was present also, felt that if these two men, controlling as they did the pivotal Pennsylvania and Michigan delegations, would announce, early in the week, their support for my nomination, the effect would be to start a movement among the uncommitted delegates that would almost certainly assure a nomination on the first ballot. This, of course, was the great ambition of my advisers.

Our two guests did most of the talking. While each assured me that he personally was in favor of my nomination, the discussion revolved around the timing and techniques that would achieve in each of these state delegations the maximum number of Eisenhower votes.

The governor said that a public announcement of his decision within the next two days would serve this purpose better than further delay, which he thought would create uneasiness.

Mr. Summerfield had special reasons for avoiding an early revelation of his choice between the two candidates. He had for some time been the national committeeman from Michigan and, in addition, was the head of the state's delegation at the convention. In preparation for the convention activities many weeks earlier, he had assembled the delegation and urged each of its members to make his own choice among possible candidates, based on the best information and facts that could be assembled for study. In furtherance of this plan he had invited everyone who had been suggested as a candidate to come to the state to make a political address. He had personally contacted these potential candidates and assured each that when he and the members of his delegation finally made up their minds as to their choice, he would undertake promptly to inform all candidates as to the results. I was impressed by these steps to insure thoughtful, informed consideration of a delegate's responsibilities in a national convention. I think the nation's interest would be better served if such methods could be observed in all states.

Near the end of dinner in my suite, Summerfield said that he could not assemble and poll the delegation until all its members had been given adequate opportunity to make their own judgments. His word had been pledged to carry out these arrangements faithfully and he told me that while he was personally going to vote for me, he would not announce the position of his delegation until he had carried out all of his commitments. While he clearly understood the political value of making the Pennsylvania and Michigan announcements simultaneously, he said he was honor bound to wait. (On the first ballot the Michigan delegation cast thirty-five votes for me, eleven for Senator Taft.)

Obviously this discussion, which I later reported in detail to my associates, did not achieve a complete meeting of minds between the two men. At the end of the dinner Governor Fine stood up and said, "I will go along until Wednesday morning—but I'll then have to publicize my own decision regardless of the timing of the Michigan announcement."

Even after dinner my schedule for that Sunday evening was not complete. I met with the Minnesota delegation at 10 P.M. and later with Governor McKeldin and Mr. Brownell. This kind of thing went on incessantly until Thursday night and even on into Friday morning, when three separate delegations visited me, the last one leaving only an hour before the balloting for the nominations was scheduled to begin.

These talks were not academic. On that Sunday night I reportedly trailed Senator Taft by more than a hundred pledged delegates. After New Hampshire and Minnesota, the Senator had won primaries in Wisconsin, Nebraska, Illinois, Ohio, West Virginia, and South Dakota. (Slates pledged to me won in New Jersey and Oregon.) He had a total of 530— 458 uncontested and 72 contested and temporarily seated by the Republican National Committee. I had 427—406 uncontested plus 21 contested.

He needed fewer than a hundred more votes to go over the victory total of 604.

These figures indicate how critical was the issue of delegate seating.

Two days earlier the Republican National Committee had voted, as Taft suggested, to give him twenty-two of the Texas delegates, me sixteen. Cabot Lodge had in a bold move rejected this compromise. He was gambling on a change in the convention rules.

The next morning the convention assembled. For our side, Cabot and Sherman Adams directed the fight on the floor; behind the scenes Herbert Brownell mapped out strategy. Governor Arthur Langlie at once introduced the Fair Play Amendment. And after a heated argument the convention voted it into effect: the convention would vote on all the contests of Texas, Georgia, and Louisiana; and no contested delegate—unless put on the temporary roll by more than two thirds of the national committee—would have a right to vote on seating any other delegate.

A vote for the Fair Play Amendment was, as we saw it, a vote for honorable and orderly procedure, assuring that those on trial would not sit on the jury. But it also had a tendency to unite the delegates who supported my candidacy with the delegations from the so-called "favorite-son" states other than Ohio. Important states in this category were Maryland, whose favorite son was Governor McKeldin; Minnesota, whose favorite son was former Governor Stassen; and California, whose favorite son was Governor Warren. On a straight-out vote for the Republican nomination for President, if taken at the opening of the convention, the delegates from each favorite-son state would have voted for their own candidates, and the margin between the total vote for me and that for Senator Taft might have been extremely close. But all favorite-son states voted together in support of the Fair Play Amendment—for which there was a majority of more than a hundred votes. This gave our side a psychological boost at the very opening hour which, we began to hope, nothing could subsequently stop.

Even after the vote on the Fair Play Amendment, the credentials committee of the convention on July 8 upheld the national-committee decision by voting to seat the pro-Taft Georgia delegation, to give Eisenhower eleven Louisiana delegates, and to split the Texas delegation, twenty-two for Taft, sixteen for Eisenhower. But the next day the convention reversed the recommendations of the credentials committee and voted (607 to 531) to seat the pro-Eisenhower Georgia delegates; and voted by acclamation to seat all the Eisenhower delegates from Texas.

The end was in sight.

My brothers and several close friends gathered in my suite to watch the televised account of the final balloting for the nomination. But by that time I was tired, weary, and greatly worried about Mamie. She had contracted an infected tooth since coming to Chicago and proved allergic to the antibiotics prescribed. She had to stay in bed, undergoing such treatments as the doctors thought would relieve her excruciating pain. Consequently, I was not much concerned about the voting; half of the time I spent in her room, reporting to her briefly on the proceedings. (Fortunately, by Friday night she experienced a fine recovery, to my intense relief.)

I think it is common among political candidates to experience, at the time of balloting, a feeling of indifference, or perhaps numbness, toward the outcome. The fatigue and strain of a convention week are such that the candidate, having done his best, is looking forward principally to a short respite. Certainly this was true in my case. Although my friends and I were confident, I was sure at that moment that I would feel little disappointment if the balloting went against us. Consequently my main and immediate interest, except for Mamie's illness, was to visit and reminisce with my brothers about the past. As the voting went on we paid scant attention to the television set, which was filled with the dreary, time-consuming act called "polling the delegations." However, the principal events of the convention were so often reported and repeated over the television that, except by deliberately turning off the set, we could not have failed to keep abreast of the results.

At the end of the first ballot I had 595 votes—9 short of victory. Taft had 500, Warren 81. Suddenly the head of the Minnesota delegation, Senator Edward Thye, leaped to his feet, demanding the floor. He had earlier cast 19 votes for his state's favorite son, Harold Stassen. The chair recognized him.

"Minnesota," he said, "wishes to change its vote to Eisenhower."

It was all over.

Immediately after the balloting was finished, my first thought was to go to Mamie's room, down the corridor, to give her the news. It was, of course, a momentous thing, and both of us were somewhat overwhelmed by the future life our imaginations pictured for us. Curiously enough, neither of us expressed—and I am quite certain did not feel—any doubt, other than in fleeting moments, as to the November outcome.

After being assured that she was improving in strength, I decided to make a call without delay on Senator Taft, a man whom I respected and who had, up to this moment, I thought, every right to think of himself as the logical candidate of the Republican party. I walked into the room where my friends were still congregated and informed them of my intention. One or two remarked that this would violate precedent in such circumstances. I telephoned Senator Taft and asked for an opportunity to come across the street to call upon him. Although his voice indicated surprise, he agreed and I started on my way—a trip that proved to be far more difficult physically than I imagined. As I left my apartment, reporters, photographers, and crowds of the curious began to impede my progress, the press begging for a statement. Police officers detailed to me by the city of Chicago found it almost impossible to get me outside the hotel; but once in the street our real troubles began. I am quite sure that it took ten minutes to get across the street. Progress through the lobby and halls of Senator Taft's hotel was equally difficult, with the atmosphere of the crowds noticeably sorrowful and even resentful. I understood their attitude—I sympathized with it. All of them had worked for weeks and months with one purpose in view—to nominate Robert Taft. They wore great Taft buttons and ribbons. A not inconsiderable number of ladies were openly weeping.

Finally we reached the elevator and I was escorted to the senator's quarters.

The first thing the senator asked after I had reached his hotel room was whether his sons could be present. I agreed readily. In the course of the talk I said, "This is no time for conversation on matters of any substance; you're tired and so am I. I just want to say that I want to be your friend and hope you will be mine. I hope we can work together."

Senator Taft's reply was cordial and matter-of-fact. "My only problem for the moment," he said, "is that for the twenty minutes it took you to get over here I have been bombarded by requests from photographers for a picture. Would you be willing to have one taken?" We stepped into the hall to face the flash bulbs and our short chat was over.

I returned to my hotel under circumstances much easier than those of my former crossing.

When I entered my apartment I saw a marvel of communications that had never occurred to me. As I reached the door of my room my eye was attracted to the television screen in the far corner. On it, startled, I saw myself moving through my own door.[6]

The climax of the vote provided no opportunity for rest or relaxation. I was invited to come that evening to make my acceptance speech before the convention—and this meant hours of hectic preparatory work. We excluded everybody from my quarters except the workers. Aside from selected members of my staff, these included relays of secretaries who, already exhausted by weeks of never-ending writing, typing, revising, and retyping, were now called upon to work uninterruptedly and at top speed for a matter of seven hours.

My acceptance speech did not attempt to reach for eloquence or to become a vehicle for displaying any fancied oratorical ability. It was meant to be a serious, sober exposition of the problems before the

[6] This was the first national political convention to be broadcast on nationwide television.

Republican party and the purposes we hoped to achieve through a November victory at the polls.

I said that I accepted their summons to lead a crusade, a "crusade for freedom in America and freedom in the world. . . ."

Shortly after the presidential nomination was settled, a small committee came to ask about my choice for Vice President. This matter had often been the subject of discussion between me and my close associates. Many were considered highly qualified for selection, but of these a number, for varying reasons, were not available. For example, Cabot Lodge was running for the Senate, Dewey and Brownell disclaimed any interest in the post, Clay and others were deeply involved in business. Sometime before the convention I had made in longhand a short "eligible list" of those I thought both qualified and available. This list I carried in my billfold. As I recall, only one other, Herbert Brownell, knew the identities of the men named on it. When asked by the members of the committee for my preference, I read off my list, which was headed by Senator Richard Milhous Nixon of California. Since the committee enthusiastically approved my first choice, the names of the others were not published and I destroyed the slip.

The list, never before been made public, included (according to my memory, which is not necessarily infallible): Senator Nixon, Congressmen Charles Halleck and Walter Judd, Governors Dan Thornton and Arthur Langlie.

My reasons for placing Nixon's name on this list and at its head were my own. First, through reports of qualified observers I believed that his political philosophy generally coincided with my own. Next, I realized that before the election took place I would have attained the age of sixty-two. I thought we should take the opportunity to select a vice-presidential candidate who was young, vigorous, ready to learn, and of good reputation. Aside from this, the question of Communist infiltration and proper methods for defeating it in our country had become a burning and widespread issue. I had met Senator Nixon at my European headquarters a year earlier. Moreover, I had read about his record, as a congressman, in conducting a difficult investigation in the historic Alger Hiss case. In this instance Mr. Nixon had doggedly pursued a trail of evidence leading him to believe that Alger Hiss was in fact guilty of improper conduct in associations with Communists. The result, eventually, was the conviction of Mr. Hiss on charges of perjury. But the feature that especially appealed to me was the reputation that Congressman Nixon had achieved for fairness in the investigating process. Not once had he overstepped the limits prescribed by the American sense of fair play or American rules applying to such investigations. He did not persecute or defame. This I greatly admired.

There was one point in which my information about Mr. Nixon was not accurate. I had been told that he was forty-two years old. Actually, he was thirty-nine, but this correction, even though it was brought to my attention a few hours before I met with the Republican committee, did not seem to me too important.

That evening Mr. and Mrs. Nixon, Mamie, now feeling much better, and I went before the convention, and I delivered my acceptance speech. The events of seven and one-half months now seemed to completely contradict and belie everything I had been saying since leaving Europe in 1945. I learned again that the word "never" is rarely used correctly in expressing human intentions. My arguments, protestations, and sincere beliefs for years had now become as nothing.

The earliest national election that I can recall was that of 1896, in which William McKinley opposed William Jennings Bryan. As a little boy in Abilene, I had helped campaign that year by marching in a nighttime parade with a flaming torch made of a rag soaked in coal oil. Now, fifty-six years later, my own name was at the head of a Republican ticket.

CHAPTER III

Campaign—Trains and Planes

The foundation of all democracy is that the people have the right to vote. . . . At the bottom of all the tributes paid to democracy is the little man, walking into the little booth, with a little pencil, making a little cross on a little bit of paper. . . .

—Winston Churchill

THE Chicago week began and ended for my wife and me on a happy note. Upon reaching the city on Saturday we had arranged a trip for the following day to Fort Sheridan, just outside Chicago. Our three grandchildren, David, Anne, and Susan, were staying there temporarily with their maternal grandparents, Colonel and Mrs. Percy Thompson. The visit, of several hours, was almost the only pleasant personal interlude we were to have until the following Sunday, when John and his wife, coming from West Point, visited us at the Blackstone Hotel.

My son was then en route to Korea, where he had an assignment to an infantry unit. He and I had a long talk about the war and the living arrangements he had made for Barbara and the children during his absence.

I posed to him one disagreeable possibility—his capture by hostile forces. Certainly the risk of capture is one that faces every soldier going into combat, particularly with the infantry. "But in your case," I pointed out, "capture by the Communists would mean more than unusually harsh treatment and suffering for you, and anguish for your family. If I'm elected, the Communists will very likely consider that your capture gives them a powerful weapon for blackmail."

John was impressed, but far more because of the agony that such an event might bring his family and parents than because of what might happen to him. (Nevertheless, I had heartily concurred in his determination to go to a front-line battalion.) "You may be confident," John assured me quietly, "that I will never be captured."

Except for this one somber passage, we had a delightful reunion. We talked over the events of the week, the difficult schedules that Mamie and I would soon be pursuing, and the widely separated ways the members of the family would be treading. I invited our daughter-in-law to participate, just for the experience, in one trip on the campaign train, but Barbara's reply was a laughing "No thanks!" (Afterward, she did accompany us on one trip through Pennsylvania and the East.) Soon the clock warned us that the time had come to leave, and we faced a difficult farewell. In John's relatively short military career, this was the second time he was leaving for an active battle front.

With the tumultuous convention week behind, we went back to Denver. Strangely, I have never been able in recent years to recall a single incident of the return journey, not even the method of travel.[1] This failure of memory is interesting to me because I have often noticed in reading about investigations that the answer "I do not remember" seems frequently to draw from the questioner exclamations of incredulity and pseudo-amazement, as well as insinuations that the witness is not telling the truth. Since I am living testimony that the answer "I do not remember" is sometimes absolutely correct, even when referring to so important a detail as a journey of hundreds of miles during which there must have been important conferences, I have always felt a sympathy for any badgered, truthful individual forced to give such a reply.

By July 15 I was back in my Denver office, with the daily routine little different from that of preconvention days, except that now our attention was no longer centered on delegates—*all* the voters of the nation were the objects of our thinking and planning.

There were people to see and a heavy correspondence to read and answer. At the same time I had to devise a new headquarters organization, one section to take care of the chores devolving upon our base offices in Denver and New York and the other to accompany me throughout the campaign.

I was tired. Even before leaving Chicago I began to realize that weeks of uninterrupted political activity, following a heavy spring schedule in Europe, had put me in real need of a short vacation to store up strength for the physical demands I would soon face. Such a chance would be available only in these early weeks immediately following the convention; thereafter, the tempo of the election effort would rule out any further opportunity. On Thursday morning, July 17, with a few assistants, I went to a favorite vacation spot, a ranch near Fraser, Colorado,

[1] Research for this book tells me that it was an airplane flight, on the evening of July 14.

where I was the guest of my friend Aksel Nielsen. At an altitude of eighty-seven hundred feet, and with no adversary in the mountains other than a creek full of trout, I had a most enjoyable week. There was, inevitably, a constant procession of visitors, but almost without exception each was a friend and added to the pleasure of the vacation.

Of course, we could not wholly forget politics, including our opponents. One guest, George Allen, made it his business to keep in touch, by radio, with events at the Democratic convention. When he learned the hour at which its nominee, Adlai Stevenson, was scheduled to make his acceptance speech, all of us listened attentively. We were impressed by his speaking style and polish. But George, who had made politics his lifelong hobby, expressed his admiration for Governor Stevenson's effort in an odd way. He said, "He's too accomplished an orator; he will be easy to beat."

As always there was much use of the telephone—an instrument that has, from my boyhood, been a pet annoyance of mine. Still, one of the points I had to settle, by telephone, was the selection of my campaign manager. While Mr. Summerfield, the chairman of the Republican National Committee, could direct the Republican campaign in its entirety, in which the national ticket would play a vitally important part, he could not possibly serve simultaneously as my own representative in devising personal schedules and working out detailed plans. The man for this job would have to be at my side constantly until election day.

Brownell, who had become increasingly important in my advisory group, suggested Sherman Adams, governor of New Hampshire. Not only had Adams been the spark plug in the successful New Hampshire primary; he had been floor manager for our side in the convention struggle. After Chicago, the governor and his wife had gone on a fishing trip in Wyoming, leaving no address. He was difficult to locate. This was accomplished by July 22, and I told him on the telephone what I wanted. He promised to take the matter under advisement, but warned that he would have to consider a number of difficulties, not the least of which was that he was still governor of his state.

On the 26th Mr. Nixon reached Denver and the following morning came to Fraser. Though I had met him both in Europe and in Chicago, here in the quiet mountains it was easier to become better acquainted. I found him vigorous, alert, and intelligent. His visit provided a splendid opportunity for discussing plans, and we agreed to try to keep in contact sufficiently to assure effective coordination on major issues and appearances during the progress of our respective campaigns. Of course, we knew ourselves to be remarkably close together in political views generally.

On the following Monday I was again in my Denver office and met with Sherman Adams. He still had much to do in arranging his affairs if he were to undertake the assignment as my principal assistant in carrying on the campaign. But he was deeply interested in the prospect, and we held our discussions under the assumption that he would be able to settle his personal problems satisfactorily. Several days elapsed before he sent an affirmative answer and freed my mind on this score.

Our August sojourn in Denver was punctuated by hurried trips I felt it necessary to make. The first of these was to the Veterans of Foreign Wars convention at Los Angeles on August 5; another, five days later, to a large Indian convocation at Gallup, New Mexico; and a third one to Boise, Idaho, and Kansas City.

At Gallup ten thousand Indians from thirty-five tribes came riding covered wagons, limousines, jalopies, and horses to hear the speech. The talks at Los Angeles and Gallup were largely nonpolitical, but in Boise I tried to explain my convictions respecting America's domestic problems as well as the proper role of government in helping to overcome them.

There were two roads, I said, two extreme philosophies of government that were widely divergent—the Reactionary Right and the Radical Left. Both led to tyranny. The problem was to achieve a balance which would assure individual liberty in an orderly society.

The one thing absolutely necessary, it seemed to me, was that we achieve and maintain a climate in which the full potential of every individual could be realized. Also we had to recognize our responsibility to those in real need and alleviate their suffering by the aid of private and local institutions; if the job was too big for those institutions, then the government must help. Some of the goals our people had set for themselves were adequate security for old age; insurance for workers against unemployment, accident, and ill health; equal treatment and opportunity for all, regardless of race, color, or creed; improved educational opportunities; better housing; protection of the rights of working men and women; protection of the right to earn and save; stability for an expanding agriculture.

The Left proposed to tackle these problems, I went on, with one prescription—the centralization of power of all kinds in Washington. Those who advocated centralization believed they were infallible. They liked power, and they lacked faith in people. If America accepted that solution, we would not only fail in our goals—because history taught that such a course could lead only to ruin—we would also in the process lose our freedoms.

The only way we could achieve our unchanging goal, the full potential of each individual in an environment of freedom, was to pursue tirelessly the course our forefathers proposed—the middle way.

From Boise I went to Kansas City where, in a blinding rainstorm, the pilot brought our plane into a landing only by an admirable display of skill.

Early in August in Denver I had had an important visit with Arthur Summerfield and key staff members of the national committee. They outlined for us their proposed campaign plan, which was, so far as my own activities were projected, an ambitious one.

Mr. Summerfield's allover program had been carefully drawn up: a vast amount of campaign literature had to be prepared and distributed, television and radio programs had to be arranged, contracts made with transportation companies, programs laid out for supporting speakers and workers, and weak spots in organization detected and repaired. While we talked much of whistle-stopping and airfield meetings, motorcading was only briefly mentioned. However, later experience convinced me that motorcading is one of the most effective tools in campaigning, if the candidate has the physical endurance to continue it day after day, and the limitless capacity to respond enthusiastically and unfailingly to the cheerful greetings of the crowds along the way.

Yet as we viewed the plan, and approved of its basic methods, procedures, and purposes, I felt that it went into too much detail in attempting to prescribe my own movements and activities, even though we agreed on the need for unremitting work and incessant travel on my part. While the plan was broadly based and comprehensively conceived, it seemed to me to give too much weight to nationwide familiarity with my name, familiarity gained as a result of World War II. I was determined to emphasize principle and to voice my own convictions. To be sure, the executives of the national committee had a delicate task because they were supporting not only my campaign but also the simultaneous campaigns of the senatorial committee, the congressional committee, and the Vice President. But I told our visitors that of necessity I reserved to myself, assisted by Governor Adams, the authority to determine exactly what my activities would comprise; under any other system hopeless confusion would result. Mr. Summerfield and I agreed that our staffs would remain in frequent contact in the interests of over-all efficiency.

Later analysis of the November election results would appear to indicate that the coordination between the Republican National Committee and the senatorial and congressional committees was perhaps not as effective as that which existed between ourselves and Chairman Summerfield. For the difference in public support of the presidential and vice-presidential campaign and the congressional one, there were other important reasons, but even up to the time I left the government in 1961 the coordination between the national and the senatorial and congressional committees in the intervening elections left much to be desired.

In Denver, working day and night, we developed our plans with care, well knowing that once we began operating in the heat and smoke of politics we would be bombarded with recommendations to change important features. Long before, I had learned the lesson that whenever any program involving competition is developed under conditions favorable to exhaustive examination, cool calculation, and accurate planning, it is a bad mistake to abandon or to change it materially during the stresses and strains of the ensuing struggle. In such circumstances men, responding more to emotion than to logic and fact, are often led to argue heatedly and sometimes plausibly for a new strategy and new tactics; but to these entreaties the leader must normally turn a deaf ear. The Republican political campaign of 1952 was no exception. And later, as the struggle wore on, unusual incidents or developments brought forth a spate of recommendations and urgent pleas for violent changes in methods. We had every reason to be glad that our initial planning had been thorough. In fact, with few exceptions—such as a decision made by an assistant for me to go to Wisconsin after the state primary elections—we followed our original plans closely.

Moreover, because of the friendships and the mutual confidence that began to crystallize among the principal Republican figures in all phases of the effort, the cries of dissatisfaction and the arguments for major changes in the plot gradually slackened and almost ceased.

We talked, too, about the campaign plans for the "Citizens," drafted by Walter Williams and Mary Lord, co-chairmen of that organization. Their basic mission was to attract to our side independents and discontented Democrats, young and old. My own staff would, during the campaign, be looking to the Citizens for help, as we would to the national committee. Since we were the beneficiaries of two different organizations, we would inevitably be an additional connecting link between them.

One matter expected to cause trouble between the Citizens and the regular organization during the coming campaign was that of probable conflicts in fund-raising. The Republicans, both national and state, possessed lists of habitual donors, and the fear was expressed that the Citizens' solicitations would tend to dry up this source of support for the regular organization. While no foolproof scheme for avoiding conflict in this matter could be devised, Mr. Williams and Mrs. Lord were sure that they could minimize it.

To this particular kind of campaign preparation I was, of course, brand-new. In planning my own moves, however, I could draw to an extent on military experience. Staff organization was a far from new problem; extensive speaking engagements had been my constant chore for at least seven years, from the day in 1945 when I returned from Europe. What was new—and at times baffling—was the interrelationship between the presidential campaign and the various congressional, gubernatorial, and other campaigns. This network of purposes required visiting certain areas in which Republican candidates—particularly senatorial—were believed to be in trouble, areas which might profitably have been by-passed if I were the only candidate running. Furthermore, it was necessary for me to study local issues, to include local references—to public works, employment, attraction of private investment, a score of subjects, and above all, to the local Republican candidates. For the handshaking, motorcading, and innumerable short, impromptu talks on local affairs to small groups, my military training gave me little background to draw on; I had to find my way by deciding, from time to time, what seemed reasonably proper, necessary, and possible. In this planning phase in Denver I made two basic decisions which did much to establish the scope and nature of the campaign. One was to conduct an unceasing, whirlwind campaign— the other, to invade the so-called "Solid South."

The first of these was based on what I knew about human endurance. For weeks it had been dinned into my ears that one cause of the Republican defeat in 1948 was the entire party's overconfidence and lethargy. According to my informants, Governor Dewey had been advised that year to avoid "rocking the boat," to avoid antagonizing voters, making too many public appearances, speaking forthrightly on too many issues. He was, naturally, later made a scapegoat, probably by many whose advice he had heeded. I have come to believe that others, collectively, were far more responsible than he for the loss.

I was determined that should the fates again impose defeat on our party, no lack of personal effort on my part could be classed as a contributing cause. Once we began active campaigning, I decided, there would be no letup; the fight would be carried on to midnight of election eve at high intensity.

As an integral part of this decision I had to fix the date for beginning active operations. I alone had to be the judge of my reserve of physical energy, realizing that to start too soon could well result in exhaustion for the candidates and fatigue in the electorate, while to start too late would limit the scope of the effort and might raise again the charge of complacency. Indeed, soon after the adjournment of the Chicago convention in July, self-styled political experts as well as editorial writers began to express uneasiness and alarm about an alleged indifference to the importance of getting the campaign under way promptly.

The same sort of thing had happened to me more than once in wartime. Critics who had no comprehension of the infinite details of planning for systematic lifesaving and victorious effort but who loved to wear the convenient cloak of authorial omnipotence wrote voluminously about "obvious delay and timidity" in plunging into the fight—and more often than not would later, commenting in the pain and heat of battle, bitterly criticize the insensitiveness of the commander to the suffering of his soldiers.

In the impending campaign I believed that I could go at full speed for a matter of eight or nine weeks, assuming an average of seven hours sleep daily, with an occasional twenty-four hours reserved for complete rest and catching up with accumulated work at base headquarters. I fixed the 1st of September as the starting date of my active campaigning.

"Right after Labor Day, I'll really start swinging," I told a group of political and labor representatives who came to see me on August 28.

My second significant decision, to include the Southern states in nationwide campaigning, was flatly opposed by men far more politically experienced than I. They argued that to try to influence voters in the South was a waste of time, effort, and money, all of which could be used more profitably in areas where "there was some chance of winning." After all, since Reconstruction the Republicans had made no significant or permanent inroads into the South. Georgia, they told me, had never voted for a Republican presidential nominee. Arkansas, Alabama, and Mississippi last voted for one in 1872, South Carolina and Louisiana in 1876. Although Herbert Hoover carried seven Southern states—Virginia, North Carolina, Florida, Kentucky, Tennessee, Oklahoma and Texas— against Al Smith, they had gone Democratic or Dixiecrat ever since.

On this point I arbitrarily cut off argument. I was going South—even if I had to go alone. The pros accepted this decision, but their opinion of my political acumen was low, very low. Several asserted that no crowd a Republican could draw in the South would be larger than a "corporal's guard."

My reasons were simple but, I thought, logical. The first was purely personal. I had lived for years among the Southern people and liked them. I refused, as my party's nominee, to visit all other sections and ignore the South. Another reason stemmed from my concept of the Presidency. The man in the White House, I believe, should think of himself as President of all the people. Even though a party's nominee in a national election might lose every state in a major geographical region, he should not neglect the opportunity during the campaign to learn more about the problems and attitudes of that region and to make his own ideas and proposals affecting the nation known there.

So we thought and argued and agreed, and after the plans were set, I had homework to do. It was essential to focus my thinking on some of the more intricate and yet important domestic issues which were inextricably part of the campaign. On matters of principle my ideas were clear to me; on numerous matters of specific application they were not. For example, I had formed opinions on the Texas submerged-lands issue by virtue of exposure to it as president of Columbia University; on the other hand, the crucial question of revising the Taft-Hartley Act (a major piece of labor-management legislation) required study. When I set foot on shore from Europe in June, I could be excused—in fact, on occasion was complimented—for answering "I don't know" about certain domestic issues. Now, as the Republican nominee, I would be expected, and rightly so, to state concrete opinions on all relevant problems and to set forth what I planned to do about them if elected.

On August 24 I left Denver to go to New York City to address the annual convention of the American Legion. I had no intention of using such a platform for a purely political speech, but the meeting—at the very beginning of the campaign—with so many of my old comrades in arms had a sentimental appeal. With this move I shifted my headquarters to New York. In the coming weeks I was to be there only intermittently. The campaign trail ahead would extend more than fifty thousand miles by train and plane—a distance more than twice around the world, not counting thousands of miles of motorcading—with 232 stops in cities and towns in forty-five states. Each of those miles cost something in toil and sweat, and each day ended invariably in weariness, but they provided more than a balance in satisfaction and inspiration. Of course, the crowds I met were made up principally of political friends and supporters; consequently their enthusiasm was infectious and their desire to help obvious. They gave an uplift and encouragement particularly valuable to a rank amateur in political contests.

I soon found that my projected seven hours of daily sleep dwindled to more like five and my reserved twenty-four-hour rest days were scarcely less crowded than the others. But I did make it to the wire—barely!

Our first trip out of New York started on September 2—and we headed south, with Atlanta our destination. In the two days following we went in rapid succession to Jacksonville, Miami, Tampa, Birmingham, Little Rock, and back to New York. The crowds were large and enthusiastic, and at each stop I missed no opportunity to ask my lugubrious political friends to explain their idea of the size of a Southern corporal's guard.

The campaign was now in full swing. My continuing purpose was to explain to the maximum number of people my basic convictions as outlined in the Boise talk and their application to such subjects as the war in Korea, measures which might assure progress toward lasting peace, the need for honesty and integrity in government, and the evils of both inflation and political control over our economy. Moreover, I urged the creation of governmental attitudes favorable to economic stability and growth, and governmental encouragement of a spirit of cooperation and a feeling of confidence among *all* our people.

In region after region I spoke on subjects that commanded the interest of the people therein. For example, on September 6, I outlined my views on agriculture at the National Plowing Contest at Kasson, Minnesota; in the West I expounded the partnership principle in reclamation and water-power development. Everywhere I urged the need for uprooting Communism wherever it might be found in the United States—but accomplishing this by methods compatible with American tradition and ideals. "Freedom," I said in Milwaukee on October 3, "must defend itself with courage, with care, with force, and with fairness." I made hundreds of speeches during September and October, and the total audience was incalculable. The train, the automobile, and the podium served as in the past, but the plane and television extended the range as never before. Many were extemporaneous, made from the back platform of a railway train, on an improvised stand on an airfield, or in crowded auditoriums or stadiums, frequently with regional or nationwide television and radio coverage carrying the talk and with newspapers and magazines carrying the text to the country.

The composition, functions, and organization of a campaign staff operating under such conditions were intriguing. For any scheduled talk, first on the scene were the advance men; they went ahead of the train or plane to make certain that all arrangements including hotels, transportation, traffic, appointments, and publicity were interlocked so that not a moment would be wasted and no important chore overlooked.

The chief planner, supervisor, and coordinator was Governor Adams, who was not only tough-minded but quick and decisive in operation. He quickly won the respect and admiration of other members of the staff. Every man and woman accompanying us, whether assigned to general or special duties, would at times work personally with me but always with the knowledge of Governor Adams and with the responsibility of reporting to the governor the general results of our meeting.

Congressman Leonard Hall of New York provided most of our daily liaison with the Republican National Committee. Senator Fred Seaton of Nebraska participated in this work and served Sherman Adams as a deputy; he was also in effect the administrative manager of the entire group. James Hagerty was responsible for press and public relations. Thomas Stephens, whom I have always counted among the most politically astute of all my close associates, was assigned as appointments secretary. He made certain that I was started to the right places at the right time, and kept a complete list of everyone I saw and with whom I talked. His task was made more difficult because he had to distinguish between people who wanted to push their way forward only for their own purposes, and those who were genuinely trying to promote the success of the campaign.

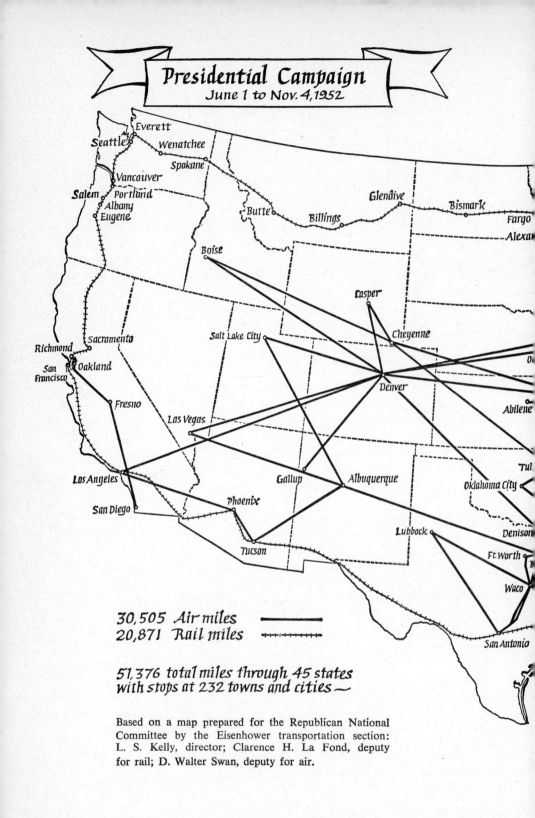

Presidential Campaign
June 1 to Nov. 4, 1952

Everett
Seattle
Wenatchee
Spokane
Vancouver
Salem   Portland
Albany
Eugene
Butte
Billings
Glendive
Bismark
Fargo
Alexan
Boise
Casper
Cheyenne
Salt Lake City
Richmond   Sacramento
San Francisco   Oakland
Denver
Fresno
Las Vegas
Abilene
Los Angeles
Gallup   Albuquerque
Tul
San Diego
Phoenix
Oklahoma City
Lubbock
Denison
Tucson
Ft. Worth
Waco
San Antonio

30,505 *Air miles* ———
20,871 *Rail miles* ‡‡‡‡‡‡‡

51,376 *total miles through 45 states*
with stops at 232 towns and cities —

Based on a map prepared for the Republican National
Committee by the Eisenhower transportation section:
L. S. Kelly, director; Clarence H. La Fond, deputy
for rail; D. Walter Swan, deputy for air.

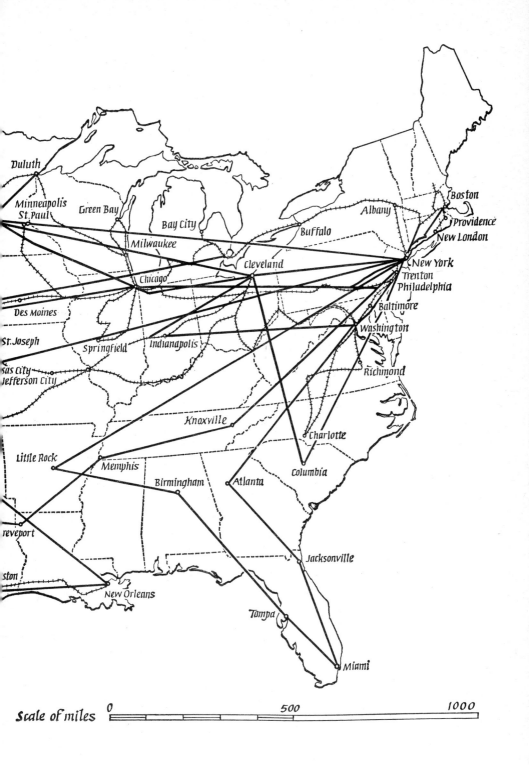

Scale of miles

0   500   1000

Others[2] were helpful in suggesting new ideas and thoughts, or emphasizing old ones, striving to see that at every stop I was sufficiently briefed, so as to meet individuals and crowds with appropriate information and tact—or a fair facsimile. Behind all these people was a devoted group of secretaries. Speeches had to be written and rewritten in racing trains and planes, in densely populated hotel rooms, while standing in halls, and even, at times, riding in automobiles. The work was made all the harder because I have never been able to accept a draft of a suggested talk from anyone else and deliver it intact as my own. Because drafts could be corrected only at odd moments, I never was able to get one completed to my satisfaction without repeated revisions. But the loyalty and efficiency —and patience—of the hard-working secretarial group never once let me down.

Morale was high, a fact all the more remarkable because of the kind of life we were leading. Early in the campaign the entire group seemed to have achieved, and constantly exuded, confidence in the final outcome. Long hours, broken sleep, and incessant work—much of it on an emergency basis—could get people tired and weary, but never downhearted. No man ever had a more intelligent, sensitive, and dedicated corps than I on that campaign train.

Only people who have lived and worked on a whistle-stopping train can fully grasp the urgent, whirling grind that is the daily and hourly portion of such a barnstorming organization. Though the airplane and television have worked to make this kind of campaign a thing of the past, the memories of my experiences in 1952, the last year in which whistle-stopping was the major mode of electioneering, still remain with me.

The train pulls into a station for a scheduled seven-minute stop, for example. The instant the wheels cease turning, the candidate, who lives in the rearmost section of the last car on the train, steps blithely out to face the crowd, doing his best to conceal with a big grin the ache in his bones, the exhaustion in his mind. Armed with a card on which he—or an assistant—has written three or four words to remind him of the par-

[2] I find it impossible now to assemble a complete list of my traveling companions. But they included, for varying lengths of time, Rachel Adams, Congressman Leslie Arends, Stephen Benedict, John Bird, Mary Burns, Mary Caffrey, Senator Frank Carlson, Robert Cutler, Senator James H. Duff, Milton S. Eisenhower, Ralph Fairley, Tom Golden, Edward Greene, Homer Gruenther, Gabriel Hauge, Stanley High, Katherine Howard, C. D. Jackson, L. S. Kelly, Senator William Knowland, Clarence La Fond, Robert Mathews, Mary Jane McCaffree, Kevin McCann, Arthur Minnich, E. Frederic Morrow, Edgar Nathan, Stanley Pratt, General Wilton B. Persons, Douglas Price, Stanley Rumbough, Congressman Hugh Scott, Bernard Shanley, Alice Smith, Dr. Howard Snyder, Harold Stassen, Walter Swan, Lou Swee, Anne Wheaton, Ann Whitman, and Charles Willis.

ticular subjects he must mention, and the local candidates for whom he wants to express support at this stop, he awaits cessation of the crowd's clamor—which he fervently prays will consume at least two minutes of his allotted seven. Then he launches into a talk that he is convinced, by his battered memory, must certainly fail because it has been delivered over and over again, never-ending and tiresome. But quickly he feels within himself a transformation. Although as he came out to the platform he was bored, resentful, or even sorry for himself, invariably the excitement generated by the crowd buoys him up—suddenly he is anxious to make his planned points; he strives for new thoughts; he speaks enthusiastically of Congressman Blank; he seeks for lucidity, conciseness, and logic in the exposition of his policies. He seems to feel that he owes it to these people to expose to them his beliefs, his convictions, his hopes and aspirations for our country. He almost wishes he could have those two minutes back, to share his wisdom more generously with his audience.

At the appointed time the train slowly moves out. Now, as he calls his good-bys, he feels a genuine regret that his stay has been so short. Then, out of sight once more, he stumbles back into the car, to an inviting couch where he tries, for a moment, to revitalize himself for the next chore.

During his seven-minute appearance a number of people have boarded the train. They will travel only as far as the next stop. These are political figures of the territory the train is now entering; they consider it important to their prestige in the upcoming town to be seen debarking from the same train that carries the candidate. Moreover, each needs a picture—which the local paper will print—of himself talking or shaking hands with the presidential candidate. The picture-taking goes on in the train's "conference car," the only one with sufficient space to accommodate group photography, and usually located about three cars ahead of the candidate's "office." After two or three minutes of rest the candidate starts forward to meet his political allies.

By this time the train is rushing ahead—indeed, at a maximum, jolting, and almost terrifying speed. To negotiate the three car lengths of narrow passageways, constantly guarding against injury from the lurching, jerking, unpredictable motion of the surging metal monster, is an ordeal. At its end, introductions are futilely made by the chairman of the visiting committee, whose voice, no matter what its carrying power, is drowned out by the clatter and din of speeding wheels and the groaning of the car's structure. As each visitor steps forward, the photographer obligingly flashes his light, and soon the deed is done. When the last visitor records his smile for posterity—and his constituency—the nominee, trying his best to look happy and hospitable, has now to repeat the ordeal of passage, this time to, rather than from, his car. (Even yet I try to figure out which was worse in politics—coming or going.)

Invariably, reaching the office car in the rear, the candidate is visited by two or three of the staff who have several services to perform on his behalf.

First and most important is a recitation of the subjects likely to excite the deepest interest of the people in the town next to be visited. Whether it is a bridge, a dam, agriculture, national defense, an anniversary, or a favorite son, it is the candidate's business, according to the pros, to demonstrate an awareness of each of their civic problems (and explain what he proposes to do about them) and share their civic pride.

On our 1952 campaign train one staff member would report what the papers were saying about matters of national import, being particularly careful to report on public and editorial reactions to my words and actions. If I should ever be reported as tired, vague, indifferent, rash, inaccurate, or wrong, I had to find a way to correct such mistakes.

This done, all assistants present normally participated in a discussion of the basic purpose of the next formal address to be prepared, especially if scheduled for broadcasting. Its delivery time might be a few days ahead —rarely more than two. In whatever time we had, five minutes or a half hour, we debated its theme and arguments.

(This discussion could go just so far in usefulness. Once the general subject, principal points, and length were agreed on, and possibly a rough draft thrown together, the rest was always up to me. No speech writer can make a talk sound exactly like the speaker's own or express with complete accuracy the speaker's convictions.)

Throughout the day, whenever there was a moment, I was always writing and correcting—at times missing a meal as a result. Only at the last possible minute was any speech ever finished, to be turned over to the typists and hurriedly mimeographed for the press.

The moment this happened, I normally began the process of preparing the next address. And about the time I could settle down to this, the whistle would blow for the next stop.

And every night there was a platform talk to be delivered, formal or informal.

Though the routine, repeated day after day, was grueling, there were too many unusual happenings along the way, serious or amusing, to class the experience as monotonous.

One time a teleprompter operator, failing to notice I was extemporizing, got so far ahead of me that I never could catch up. On another occasion a motorcycle policeman, eager to get me to my hotel, took me on a short cut—away from my own motorcade.

One thing that always sent a ripple of amusement through the staff was the failure of one or more of our group to catch the train as it left the station. Since little reliability could be placed on the announced duration of the stopping time, and everybody found it necessary to make an occasional purchase of stamps, toothbrushes, shaving soap, and the like, such accidents were bound to occur. The deserted staff member, if he failed to catch the train as it moved up the right-of-way, would have no recourse but to rush for a local airfield or taxi service in a desperate attempt to get back into politics. Sometimes these races covered many miles, much to the chagrin of the victim and the concealed sympathy and open delight of the others, almost all of whom had been victimized at least once.

Occasionally our train would be parked for brief periods in switching yards, and invariably this would become known to people in the neighborhood, who would promptly gather around the car where Mamie and I lived. When this happened at unseemly hours, my wife and I would find ourselves either asleep or otherwise unprepared for greeting well-wishers. More than once we had to appear on the back platform tousled, sleepy-eyed, and wearing old bathrobes, just to give a wave and a greeting. In Austin, Texas, we were serenaded at 2 A.M. by a crowd of students and we had to reach for our robes, hasten to the platform, and join in singing "The Eyes of Texas Are upon You." In Salisbury, North Carolina, the train stopped at about five-thirty in the morning. A crowd gathered around our car, and we had to respond to insistent cries to come to the platform to spend a minute or two with our laughing, yelling visitors. The men of the press, sleeping eight or ten cars ahead of ours, had always before been completely unaware of or had ignored these unscheduled stops and meetings. But in Salisbury a wakeful photographer had a feeling that something unusual was going on and came to the rear of the train. He took pictures of the scene. The photographs were most informal and unusual, but we had become so adjusted to the ever-ready, ever-present cameras that we thought no more of the incident until Jim Hagerty came to us a few hours later with a request from all the other photographers on the train—actually an earnest and prayerful petition—that we pose for pictures duplicating the one they missed early in the day. Otherwise, they said, their employers might accuse them of more than negligence.

Because of our friendship with the photographic group, we complied. At a convenient stopping place they herded back to the rear of the train while we solemnly donned bathrobes over our normal clothing and posed until they got the scene recorded on film. The gratitude of the group was satisfying; every man implied that he was going to vote Republican.

Intermittently our travels took us back through New York City. There we would usually stop twelve to twenty-four hours to catch up on any loose ends that seemed to be showing. On the morning of September 12, during one of these visits, Senator Taft, who since the convention had been vacationing in the northern woods of Canada, came to see me at Columbia. The meeting was highly publicized by the press, and many reporters tried to make the incident out as a vital turning point in the campaign, which, alarmists said, was "running like a dry creek." Actually, I had suggested in a wire to the senator on July 17 that we meet when he returned to this country, and he had agreed. In accordance with this months-old plan we got together to discuss the campaign; relaxed and refreshed, he was ready to do his part. After the bitterness of the pre-convention struggle, both of us agreed on the imperative necessity of healing the division within the party and getting all its members to pull together for a victory.

Accordingly, after we had talked for two hours at breakfast, Senator Taft went out to face reporters and cameramen and read a prepared text, which I had gone over. Then he said:

"I have tried to state here the basic principles in domestic policy which I think General Eisenhower and I agree on 100 per cent." He admitted that he did not accept all my views on foreign policy but emphasized that "our differences are differences of degree"—principally the degree of spending, he added, "although there is a fair agreement as to what we want to do now in total spending."

Long before this meeting each of us had, again and again, expressed a hope of reducing the federal budget. In our conversation we agreed that as soon as practicable it should be cut down to something like $60 billion, but we set no arbitrary dollar figure or time limit, and I insisted that any cuts not jeopardize the national defense.

In his text Senator Taft indicated our desire to reduce the federal budget to about $70 billion for fiscal year '54 and to reduce it further to $60 billion in fiscal year '55. (The government was then spending at an annual rate of $74 billion, and Congress had made appropriations for the year totaling more than $80 billion.) This goal seemed reasonable, although perhaps too ambitious in timing. I saw nothing startling in it.

Some journalists and the Democratic nominee, however, seemed to think that here was raw drama. The opposition saw in this meeting a great "surrender on Morningside Heights." The fact was that Senator Taft and I had agreed emphatically on the need for fiscal sanity in the government, as on most other issues, long before the breakfast talk. In the succeeding weeks he evidenced his enthusiasm for our common cause by a rugged round of campaigning which included more than thirty speeches in nineteen states.

Again, the staff and I boarded the train, and on this swing ran into the most troublesome problem of the entire campaign—the furor about the "Nixon fund."

On Thursday, September 18, a New York newspaper proclaimed: "Secret Rich Men's Trust Fund Keeps Nixon in Style Far Beyond His Salary." The story described what it called a "millionaires' club" which put money into a fund that benefited the senator personally as well as politically.

At first to many people this looked like just another sensationalized accusation of the type common in campaigns. As our train passed through Des Moines, Iowa, for example, a newsboy tossed a bundle of papers aboard containing only a short report on this charge. Later that evening, in Nebraska, more papers were brought in, with more on the story—back on page 57. Even the *New York Times* the following morning carried the story at the bottom of page one. But by that time aboard the train—with all its insulation from the outside world—we knew the Republican campaign faced trouble.

The storm of criticism that broke was of hurricane proportions. More and more Democrats, professing righteous indignation, gleefully jumped into the fray with the certainty that they had been given an unexpected opportunity to destroy the Republican ticket. This prospect was all the more welcome to them because of the emphasis we had been putting on the "mess in Washington." In the Department of Justice, in the Reconstruction Finance Corporation, and above all in the Bureau of Internal Revenue, so much evidence of woeful negligence and apparent crookedness had turned up, despite the administration's efforts to play it down, that I had again and again talked about the need for an administration that would renew Americans' faith in their government. In Duluth on October 4, for example, I cited the nine important tax collectors who had been fired or imprisoned for failing to do an honest job. Senator Nixon had been hammering away at the "scandal-a-day" national administration. Even Governor Stevenson found it necessary in the campaign to recognize the existence of this mess, pointing to his record as proof that he could clean up the tarnished face of government. Leaders of his party, writhing under the Republican attack, could make no plausible reply. But now, with the charges about the mysterious Nixon fund to fill the papers and divert attention, they saw their main chance.

Republicans were sharply divided. Many, leaping to a conclusion from the allegations in the papers, were genuinely shocked. Their reaction was "Nixon must be dumped." These people—who included several of my most trusted friends—bombarded me, through telephone calls, telegrams, and letters, with urgent pleas to remove Mr. Nixon from the ticket. A single moment's delay, I was told, would mean a Republican defeat; unless I acted with speed and decision I would make myself virtually a partner in Mr. Nixon's regrettable lapse.

From other Republicans I received exactly contrary advice. The whole affair, these people asserted, was manufactured. Should I hesitate for a second in condemning these trumped-up charges, they asserted, and thus showing my utter (and presumably blind) faith in my personally chosen campaign partner, our defeat was certain. One in this group was a brother of mine.

Only a few expressed confidence that I would or should decide what to do calmly. I disagreed with all who were insisting that I act instantly; to do so would cater to emotion, not to fact and justice.

Stories written with the purpose of damaging the reputation of a candidate have been a sleazy feature of many political campaigns. I resolved not to let such a story stampede me. Of course, I knew that within a reasonable time a decisive statement was required. But I also knew that should I decide without investigation and reflection, the American people would see me, justifiably, and on sober second thought, as one who was either desperately trying to court popularity through self-righteousness, or who would succumb to every pressure of noisy partisans. Quite apart from the fate of the ticket and the reaction to my conduct was the consideration that a young man's personal reputation and future were at stake.

Moreover, although I was comparatively new to political intricacies, I knew that in these circumstances either of two actions could prove fatal: the first, to try removing one vice-presidential nominee from the ticket and replacing him with another; the second, to exonerate a running mate through a shallow process which would leave about him at least some slight cloud of suspicion. Politically as well as morally there could be only one right course: a patient and judicial insistence on a disclosure of all the facts. And although I had never run for office before, this type of problem was not wholly strange. After all, in World War II, I had some difficult public-relations issues on my hands.

Accordingly, as my train went through Nebraska on September 19, I drafted a statement for Mr. Hagerty to issue to the press: "I have long admired and applauded Senator Nixon's American faith and the determination to drive Communist sympathizers from offices of public trust. There has recently been leveled against him a charge of unethical practices. I believe Dick Nixon to be an honest man. I am confident that he will place all the facts before the American people fairly and squarely. I intend to talk with him at the earliest time. . . ."

Our train rolled on to Kansas City, where I delivered a major speech that evening. The issue: corruption. I prefaced my remarks with a statement which we had received a few hours earlier from Senator Nixon: "I have asked the trustee of this fund," he said, ". . . to make a full report to the public."

"I have read this statement to you," I told my audience, "because I believe it is an honest statement. Knowing Dick Nixon as I do, I believe that when the facts are known to all of us, they will show that Dick Nixon would not compromise with what is right." The next day in an informal conference I told reporters the same thing, emphasizing that the drive to clean up corruption in Washington required that the Republican ticket leave no doubt among fair-minded people that it was as "clean as a hound's tooth."

By that time on Saturday, September 20, in Washington and Los Angeles lawyers and accountants from two distinguished firms, at our request, were examining the records of the fund. Dana Smith, a Pasadena attorney, had already reported its amount—$18,235 over the past two years; the names of its seventy-six contributors; and the disbursements, for political expenses, which he as trustee had made from the fund. The fund went out of existence when Senator Nixon became vice-presidential nominee. But the clamor for Nixon's withdrawal grew louder. On Sunday morning Harold Stassen wired him urging him to quit, as even the Republican *New York Herald Tribune* had done earlier.

That evening, from St. Louis, I telephoned Senator Nixon in Portland, Oregon. We agreed he should go on television, tell his full story to the country, and give the public time to respond—perhaps several days—before arriving at any decision. Though he offered to quit the ticket if I asked him to, I flatly refused.

The next day the lawyers' and accountants' report came in. From this source and others I learned that Mr. Nixon had allowed something to be done which was neither illegal nor uncommon among members of Congress; on this I had the testimony of a number of members themselves. It became clear that Mr. Smith personally made all payments out of the fund; that Mr. Nixon therefore never had access to it; that all payments went to cover political expenses only; that it had never been secret; that Senator Nixon had done no favors in return for anyone's contribution to it; and that the contribution limit was five hundred dollars. The fund was of the kind collected in every campaign to defray a candidate's expenditures; but this one was obviously intended to be used between, as well as actually during, active campaigns. In these respects it seemed that there was little difference between the fund and any other legitimate one intended to help in the election of a political candidate.

Richard Nixon, like many public figures, was not a wealthy man. The costs of running for public office can be staggering, and virtually all elected officials, including the wealthiest, are the beneficiaries, politically not personally, of campaign contributions. We had come a great distance indeed from the "secret millionaires' club" which was paying Mr. Nixon the alleged second salary out of which he was furnishing a fine house in northwest Washington. During these days of study and reflection and through the disclosure of the facts my deliberate decision to hold on to Nixon was formed; but the timing of my announcement was still to be determined.

On Tuesday, September 23, Mr. Nixon made his now-famous broadcast. In it he exposed his entire financial situation to the nation. It has been charged that he did this on an emotional basis and this is, of course, partly true. Tension had reached its highest pitch. His wires and mine were running three to one against him. And just before the broadcast Governor Dewey telephoned him from New York reporting the conviction of some of my supporters there that he should resign, which the young senator later said he had feared represented my views. To my mind, however, there was no question why emotion filled Dick's broadcast—or any doubt that it should have. Many people, because of a lack of information or for political advantage, were unjustifiably accusing him of fraud and crookedness. He had been attacked before; this was an attempt to kill him politically.

Sixty million people—a record number—reportedly watched the broadcast that night. With about thirty friends and associates I listened to it in the manager's office at the Cleveland Public Auditorium, where I was to speak later that night. None of us knew what he was going to say. But as soon as he had finished, I turned to Republican Chairman Arthur Summerfield, who was sitting nearby, and exclaimed: "Well, Arthur, you sure got your money's worth."

The timing of my public announcement became clear. First I threw away the prepared speech on inflation I had planned to give that evening. Taking a yellow pad, I sat down in a corner of the hotel room and wrote out a rough text of what I would say. I read it to Summerfield, General Persons, Bob Humphreys, and Congressman Les Arends, who were in the room.

There was one more thing to do. "Jim," I called to Hagerty, "grab some paper and send this wire to Dick Nixon."

"Your presentation was magnificent," I dictated. Though technically no decision rested with me, I went on, the "realities" required that I make a statement. "To complete the formulation of that personal decision, I feel the need for talking to you and would be most appreciative if you could fly to see me at once. Tomorrow evening I shall be at Wheeling, West Virginia. . . . Whatever personal admiration and affection I have for you, and they are very great, are undiminished."

I then left to deliver my speech. The crowd that evening stomped on the floor and roared with enthusiasm: "We want Dick! We want Dick!" The tide had turned.

"I like courage," I told them. "Tonight I saw an example of courage. . . . I have never seen any [one] come through in such fashion as Senator Nixon did tonight. . . . When I get in a fight, I would rather have a courageous and honest man by my side than a whole boxcar full of pussyfooters."

Mr. Nixon had asked his audience to write the Republican National Committee, and the wires and letters began pouring in, applauding him. The next night, September 24, after a mix-up due to the fact that my wire to him got lost, we appeared together on the platform in Wheeling before a large group. There I made clear in unmistakable terms that I trusted and believed in him, and that he would continue as the vice-presidential candidate during the campaign.

The underdog had come up off the floor to win a fight; his popularity was more firmly based than ever.

In his broadcast Mr. Nixon had referred to a charge then in the papers that Governor Stevenson had a fund, through which a group of business contributors had supplemented the salaries of officials in his state administration. Mr. Nixon challenged the governor to make public the secret lists of both donors and recipients; said that the Democratic vice-presidential nominee had his wife on his Senate payroll; and he called upon both Adlai Stevenson and vice-presidential nominee John Sparkman to bare their financial records in their entirety, as he had done. The result was that all four candidates on the two national tickets, including myself, laid open their private financial records to public inspection for the first time in American history.

Two days after the Wheeling appearance I again invaded the South, this time traveling through North Carolina and Virginia, the state of my mother's birth and girlhood. At Richmond the crowds were dense, with so many assigned to the temporary speakers' stand that it collapsed— fortunately without injury to anyone.

Next we made a long circuit through the Midwest and Far West. When we reached San Francisco I went immediately to the St. Francis Hotel, where our headquarters for that city was established. As usual, prominent local Republicans came in to talk about the outlook.

By this time I had grown accustomed to glowing predictions of victory, but the story this night was different. The burden of their message was that a third-party ticket, the existence of which had escaped my attention, was going to cut so deeply into California's Republican strength that the state would probably go Democratic and thus, several of my visitors believed, cost us the national election. Since my visitors were knowledgeable, this was a real blockbuster. They went on to say that it was still possible to have the third-party ticket taken off the ballot, provided its leaders so requested. Their contention was that I should use my influence to get this done. Though taken aback both by the report and the recommendation, I thought a moment and then remarked that the suggestion was in a sense rather laughable. "Would you suggest," I asked them, "that I also urge the Democratic candidate to take his party off the ballot?" The California group was not at all amused. But I took the stand that since I had heard nothing of this so-called danger in almost six weeks of campaigning, they were, in my opinion, allowing campaign jitters to overcome their own good judgment. The argument became a bit heated, and I think the suspicion was aroused that I was completely insensitive to public opinion and, more important, to the studied conclusions of men who knew far more about California politics than I.

Finally, before the matter got completely out of hand, Governor Earl Warren came in. I was delighted to see him. After a chat about personal matters I told him about the warning advice that I had just been receiving. He wasted no words. "General," he said, "you are going to carry California by at least half a million votes. Pay no attention to a third-party ticket, and don't take any action of any kind to urge its withdrawal from the ballot. I have been in politics in this state for a long time," he added, "and I think I know what I am talking about and can sense the temper of its people. Because of my confidence in the outcome of this campaign, I have made no more commitments for speeches in California; on the contrary, I'm going, on the request of the national committee, into a number of other states to do my bit in influencing the vote." His attitude was so firm that my visitors were silenced and I heard nothing more of the subject.

After the Western trip I once more moved into the South, this time stopping in Oklahoma, Louisiana, Texas, and Tennessee. On October 13, as we were leaving New Orleans, friends brought a huge cake to the train. The anniversary of my birth was celebrated the following day. The cake was the largest example of the confectioner's art that I had ever seen— almost large enough for us to eat it and have it, too—but the entire company of campaigners feasted on it (one of them, I believe, accidentally sat in part of it), and the cake disappeared.

That night we went on to Texas, a segment of our schedule that meant much to me sentimentally, because I was returning to that state exactly sixty-two years after I had been born there, in the town of Denison on the Red River. Moreover, I was happy that two of the supporters of the Republican national ticket were among the most prominent Democrats in that traditionally Democratic stronghold—Governor Allan Shivers and Price Daniel, who was a candidate for the United States Senate. (Elsewhere in the South I welcomed the support of Governor James Byrnes of South Carolina and the meaningful refusal of Senator Harry Byrd of Virginia to back the Democratic national ticket.)

The itinerary of the next two days is a flashing vignette in memory of the life we led throughout those two months.

We arrived in Houston, Texas, at 7:30 A.M. and left the train. After a motorcade and an early morning speech we left the city at 10:30 A.M. by plane. At noon we were in Waco for a half-hour meeting at the airfield. We flew to Lubbock in the Panhandle at two forty-five, and an hour later were again boarding the plane, this time for San Antonio, where thirty-seven years earlier I had met my future wife. That day I had two motorcades, delivered a speech, had a birthday party, and after yet another motorcade boarded the train at midnight. The following morning we reached Fort Worth early and a half-hour later went on to Dallas. We arrived there at nine-thirty, and at noon I made a speech at Shreveport, Louisiana. There, one hundred mayors were present, invited by the committee on arrangements, from cities all over southern Arkansas, eastern Texas, and Louisiana—the heart of traditional Southern sentiment and Democratic strength. We were in Shreveport only half an hour and arrived in Memphis about two-thirty. As usual, when our party entered a city, the occasion was featured by a motorcade and, of course, there were speeches.

At seven I was in Knoxville, and left there at seven-thirty. Later that evening we arrived at La Guardia Field, New York City, to end the day, many miles, many faces, and many talks from where we had started thirty-six hours earlier.

The next trip in mid-October was through Delaware and New Jersey, and the following one to New England, then at the height of its most beautiful and breathtaking season, with wooded areas clothed in a bewildering array of brilliant color.

By this time all of us felt that we were experienced campaigners, yet we ran into an affair at Harvard University that was nothing less than an adventure—one that carried with it a considerable risk of serious injury to numbers of people and all of it caused by youthful ardor and enthusiasm. The route of our motorcade took us to the university's limits. In that area a solid mass of humanity blocked the streets. For a few minutes, progress, while slow, was not completely blocked, but suddenly a spirit of hilarity seemed to seize the entire crowd. Each member apparently became bent upon securing a souvenir of the visit or, at the least, getting to a point in the crowd's center, which was, of course, my automobile. Under this kind of centripetal energy the policemen who had been attempting to plow a passageway through the human mass were driven to take refuge on top of the automobile. They and members of my staff took positions on the open car in such way as to protect me from clamorous youngsters who were intent on getting a button, a piece of clothing, or at times I thought even a part of my arm—all of them enjoying the whole affair immensely but each of them in imminent danger of being crushed against the car by the uncontrollable pressure of those in the rear. Fortunately, no one was seriously injured, but for minutes movement by car was impossible except with the certainty of serious bodily harm to those around us. Finally, members of the motorcade in the cars behind were able to secure the assistance of additional police and gradually we worked our way out into the open.

We had been delayed in our schedule by more than three quarters of an hour, but more than this, the souvenir hunters were so energetic and successful that we had to replace the chrome and other accessories taken from the car at an estimated cost of $750. I think that the astonishment of everyone in our party was all the greater because of our imbedded assumption that Harvard was America's outstanding example of conservative deportment, coupled with political liberalism. Two Harvard graduates among our entourage, Robert Cutler and Gabriel Hauge, seemed to be as amazed as all the rest of us.

In a Detroit speech on October 24 I announced my intention, if elected, to go to Korea before the following January and to determine for myself what the conditions were in that unhappy country. This idea had been bandied back and forth for days among a few of my associates and me, though we had not thought of making public such a purpose. A few days before the Detroit meeting, C. D. Jackson, a friend and adviser, came to me and said that he wanted to talk about an important possibility —so important and so delicate that he felt it unwise to impart it to any person other than me. The suggestion was that I should immediately announce an intention of going to Korea.[3]

I remember that I replied to him, grinning, "You're a great man, C. D., you agree with me." However, there was a difference: my feeling about

[3] The specific origin of such an idea is nearly impossible to establish. I was to learn later that in mid-August of 1952 Harry Kern, then foreign affairs editor of *Newsweek* magazine, had telephoned the suggestion for a Korean trip to the Republican National Committee, whose officials discussed it at length with members of my own staff. I was also told that in the following month Frank C. Hilton, of Reading, Pennsylvania, director of the veterans division of the national committee, came in with the same suggestion. Again the national-committee officials discussed it among themselves and with our group at the Commodore Hotel. Apparently Governor Stevenson's advisers also had thought of it at one point and rejected it. By late October, when I delivered the speech, it seems likely that this idea, possibly originating independently from several sources, had come into many minds.

the idea was the need for making the trip if elected; his was on the effect a public announcement of this intention would have on the election.

I made the announcement and the next morning's newspapers provided proof of Jackson's acumen. One reporter went so far as to say that the promise made the outcome of the election a certainty.

Political opponents challenged the seriousness of my statement and labeled it nothing but political claptrap. The fact was, as noted, that the matter had been weighing on my mind for some time, and my earnestness about it, quite apart from its political value, was obvious to my close friends, even if not to the opposition. Going to Korea was completely in keeping with my habits and convictions in visiting fighting units in World War II. In a book of war memoirs, *Crusade in Europe,* I had written in 1948:

> At times I received advice from friends, urging me to give up or curtail visits to troops. They correctly stated that, so far as the mass of men was concerned, I could never speak, personally, to more than a tiny percentage. They argued, therefore, that I was merely wearing myself out, without accomplishing anything significant, so far as the whole Army was concerned. With this I did not agree. . . . I felt that through constant talking to enlisted men I gained accurate impressions of their state of mind. . . .
>   . . . An army fearful of its officers is never as good as one that trusts and confides in its leaders.

On the final day of campaigning I returned to Boston where, in addition to a long motorcade through its narrow, crowded streets, a rally was held in the Boston Garden. Later, at 11 P.M., a nationwide television program was broadcast in which Dick and Pat Nixon participated with Mamie and me. The early part of this hour-long program involved answering live questions from citizens who had been encountered on the streets of many cities and encouraged to speak bluntly. It was an interesting performance, we were told, and those of our party certainly found it so, because it recalled the visits we had made only weeks earlier to the localities shown on the screen. The questions involved agriculture, education, the conduct of the campaign, taxes, and the inevitable predictions of the election's outcome. In the final minutes Dick and I urged all citizens to vote and conveyed our grateful thanks to all the people who had participated in this renewal of America's great quadrennial competition. On the stroke of midnight the campaigning was to end.

But there was one more wholly unscheduled, insignificant, but unforgettable incident to complete the day.

Hank Griffin, a photographer, had an idea that he thought would be interesting to his paper. He wanted to make a picture that would show the Republican nominees, with their wives, under a large clock, at the second midnight arrived.

To set up the photograph he had secured a large wall clock, but encountered great difficulty in finding a method of mounting it immediately over our heads for the desired composition. Finally he found a tall cloak stand and, using adhesive tape, fastened his clock to the upper hooks.

With everything ready, and the hour and second hands pointing to twelve, he asked, with a big smile, "Please look this way!" With this, bang! the clock fell, striking a sharp blow on my bald head and producing a cut from which the blood flowed for several seconds. Never have I seen anyone suffer more embarrassment and chagrin than Hank Griffin. Literally, he wept. He was inconsolable in spite of my assurance that I was not really hurt. Finally, to reassure him, I had the clock replaced in its precarious position (although with many additional yards of tape) and with Mamie, Pat, and Dick, sat underneath it until he got the picture he wanted. Even so he couldn't fully get his mind off an accident that caused him more pain than the victim.

There was little for us to do until the votes were counted and the election decided at some point during the following night. Taking the train for New York, Mamie and I, for the first time during all those weeks of travel, instead of going immediately to our beds after the day's work, went to the conference car to enjoy two or three hours of companionship with the staff. Fred Waring and his orchestra were with us that night and they entertained the entire company. Work was a thing of the past; everybody present was gay and thoroughly happy—even though sleepy.

We reached New York in the early morning and at six-thirty Mamie and I cast our votes, went to 60 Morningside Drive, and to bed. We slept or relaxed most of the day, and I was all in favor of staying in bed until around midnight, at which time custom demanded that I be present at headquarters to await the nation's verdict. But my associates persuaded us to come early, saying that there was to be a party at the Commodore Hotel throughout the evening, and the entire affair would be one of celebration from beginning to end because of confidence in the outcome. This attitude was so obvious that I could not help a secret shudder at the possibility that victory might disappear like snow under the summer sun if an adverse rush of votes fell upon us.

We went to the party, but in spite of all the excitement I could not quite summon the endurance to participate uninterruptedly in the gaiety. About ten-thirty Sherman Adams and my doctor induced me to go to bed in one of the suites and Sherman posted guards to see that I had a good rest until real significance was detected in the returns. I arose before midnight, after sleeping while the news came in. The verdict: we had taken about 55 per cent of the popular vote and 442 of the 531 electoral votes, winning by a landslide margin of more than six and a half million votes.

I was pleased and particularly delighted about the South, where Texas, Virginia, Tennessee, Florida, and Oklahoma gave majorities to the Republican national ticket. At around 1:30 A.M. Governor Stevenson conceded the election. Instantly the staff, the helpers, the workers, and every friend then in the hotel began to gather for a final jubilation. Standing on the balcony of the lobby, I took the microphone to thank them and to say again that I would do my best, in the office of the Presidency, to serve the people as a whole.

When Mamie and I left the hotel we were made sharply aware, through a very simple occurrence, of a complex change in our lives. As we walked out to Park Avenue and bent to get into our car, we found in the front seat, instead of our own driver, two complete strangers. There was a moment's pause—and then we knew. From that moment on we were to be transported, guarded, and protected by the United States Secret Service, a group which turned out to be one of the finest and most efficient organizations of men I have ever known.

The 1952 campaign was history.

CHAPTER IV

A Changed World,
Formation of a Cabinet,
a Mission to Korea

God give us men! A time like this demands
Strong minds, great hearts, true faith and ready hands. . . .

—*Josiah Gibert Holland*

A S we heralded political victory the night of November 4, 1952, it was a far different world from that of May 8, 1945, the day I had announced the military victory over the Nazis. In place of the exuberance we had felt then, there was now sober thoughtfulness, for the world was caught up in a grim long-range struggle between former associated powers—the Free World on the one hand and Soviet Russia, with the now communized China, on the other.

In spite of America's recognition of the U.S.S.R. in 1933, the Communist regime in the Kremlin had always been viewed suspiciously, with reason, by our people. Through the years the two nations had had few fruitful communications. But it was only natural that years of cooperation to defeat Hitler's legions, beginning in 1941, had raised in the United States, Britain, France, and other Western nations a bright hope that our wartime success might bring about a workable cooperation with the Soviets for the future. Instead, the main characteristic of the seven years between V-E Day and the day I was elected President had been a steady consolidation of two power blocs facing each other across the globe, the danger vastly multiplied by a growing arsenal of enormously destructive weapons on both sides.

In 1945, particularly between V-E Day in May and V-J Day in August, there had existed, on the surface at least, a spirit of mutual toleration between the governments of the Western Allies and the Soviet Union. On our side this atmosphere was engendered to a large extent by a widespread weariness of war and by a sincere hope that now, with the unconditional surrender of the Nazis, the world could live in peace and friendship. Our propaganda throughout the war had pictured the Russians, with some justification, as heroic colleagues in the common cause against Nazi brutality. Front-line American soldiers meeting with the soldiers of the Soviet Union on the banks of the Elbe and Mulde rivers in Germany had found them to be warm, generous, and as glad to see the end of war as we. Also encouraging for a time was the attitude of the Soviet leaders themselves, particularly in high-level conferences. Dedicated to the overthrow of Hitler, these men had been willing to adopt any façade of cooperation to achieve the aid so vital to their cause.

At these wartime conferences, among other things, the present occupation zones of Germany were determined. Prominent among the meetings was that held at Yalta in February 1945. I had advised my superiors before this conference that the Allied forces under my command would reach a line in Germany far in advance of that which was recommended by the European Advisory Commission[1] as the eastern boundary of the Allied occupation. However, with the Battle of the Bulge just completed in January of 1945, the political leaders of the West had probably felt at the time that they were achieving a fairly good bargain by agreeing to the recommended lines. But it meant that in the period immediately following the end of hostilities, American forces, in the center, had to retire some 130 miles from the forward position they had attained through force of arms.

Later in the year, at the Potsdam Conference, the Soviet leaders were informed that the United States had successfully developed a powerful new weapon and of our government's intention to employ it against the Japanese homeland. In addition, the request—completely unnecessary, many of my associates and I thought—was again made that the U.S.S.R. enter the war against the Japanese. Marshal Stalin repeated his intention, first set forth at Yalta, of entering the war three months from the date of V-E Day—which he did, much to the advantage of the U.S.S.R. They occupied vast territories with negligible losses.

From the end of the war we in Germany had local troubles with the Soviets even though the general atmosphere in Europe gave hope, during

[1] A commission located in London, established at the 1943 Moscow Conference of the Foreign Ministers of the United States, the United Kingdom, and the Soviet Union, to study "European questions arising as the war develops" and to make joint recommendations to the three governments.

the late summer and autumn of 1945, for some form of cooperation between our two nations.

One result of this hope was a frantic demobilization on the part of the West. The desire to bring our soldiers home, understandable in itself, had reached the proportions of hysteria. The nations of the West proceeded to take apart their mighty military machines in the swiftest manner possible.

At the end of the First World War, I had witnessed the same kind of reckless rush to civilian life. But now world conditions and my own had changed dramatically. The demobilization following the earlier conflict found me, a relatively junior officer, far removed from the levels of policy-making, with duties involving nothing more than supervising local staffs—which were totting up pay, bonuses, and allowances—and affixing my signature to the discharge slips of departing soldiers. But twenty-seven years later I was, as the government's chief Army adviser, involved in problems affecting the proper timing, methods, and extent of the United States' transformation from a war to a peacetime footing.

The differences in my own situations in those two demobilizations were nothing, however, compared to the nation's.

In 1919 America, behind her two ocean barriers, still felt secure from major and sudden attack. There was then some excuse, perhaps, for her impatience to resume her interrupted industrial, cultural, and social life. But the end of World War II provided no such excuse. Three atomic bombs had been exploded. Two fell upon enemy territory, each destroying the major part of a city, and it was clear that our nation could not for long hope to retain a monopoly in these destructive weapons. Bombers were increasing their range, speed, and carrying capacity—transoceanic plane trips had already become commonplace. Russia had become a strong military power, partially through the help we gave her during the war, while her suspicious and unfriendly attitude, clearly evident as early as the London meeting of the Foreign Ministers in the fall of 1945,[2] was emphasized in her attempt to keep her troops in Iran in the spring of 1946. She had no intention of abandoning the long-term Communist purpose: to rule the world by any means, if necessary by force.

My fellow officers and I in the military service, opposed to excessively rapid and extensive disarmament, argued that such measures could cost us heavily. In November 1945 I said in an address that:

[2] The purpose of the conference was to write peace treaties for Italy, Rumania, Bulgaria, and Hungary. The representatives failed to agree on Trieste, the disposal of Italy's colonies, the size of Italy's Army and Navy, Italian reparations, and the control of the Danube. The conference broke up over the technical question of the participation of China and France.

Based upon numberless contacts with many people of other nations, I hold the conviction that no other country fears a strong America; no decent preparations of our own will be regarded suspiciously by others, because we are trusted. Indeed I am convinced that others would interpret any return of ours to our former levels of unpreparedness as an intention to return to what we *thought* was isolation. They view with concern what they regard as our unseemly haste in disintegration of the mighty forces that did so much to bring Hitler and Mussolini to their knees. . . .

To be strong nationally is not a sin, it is a necessity! We must be strong first to defend ourselves, secondly, to give the necessary dignity and influence to the words of our leaders as they labor to perfect machinery by which the world may settle its difficulties legally and peaceably, rather than illegally and by force. A weakling, particularly a rich and opulent weakling, seeking peaceable solution of a difficulty, is likely to invite contempt; but the same plea from the strong is listened to most respectfully [see Appendix D].

Certain civilian officers supported my views, chief among them Secretary of the Navy Forrestal, who constantly voiced his suspicions of Soviet intent.

"There is strong pressure to bring Americans out of China, particularly the Marines," he wrote in his diary on November 20, 1945. "If we do, we invite a vacuum of anarchy in Manchuria, and it is obvious that into that vacuum ultimately either the Japanese or the Russians will flow. At the moment of course it will be the Russians."

His warning, along with that of the military leaders, was drowned out by the clamor of the troops to get home and of their families to hurry up the process. So, as always before at the end of America's wars, the uniformed services found themselves powerless to stem the impatience of a public and a government that assumed—because they wished it so— that wars were to be no more.

As the postwar years unfolded, there were other troublesome consequences. Western Europe, as a result of the war, found itself in a state of economic collapse. France, once proud, had been occupied by the German invader for a period of more than four years, and was set back proportionately, emotions tangled with serious fiscal and political problems. Britain had exhausted nearly every material resource; Germany, having likewise poured all of its assets into conflict, was now divided into four occupation zones and, having lost the war, was forced to pay heavy occupation costs, with its cities and industry in ruins and its people demoralized. Indeed, had certain officials in the Roosevelt administration had their way, Germany would have been far worse off, for there were those who advocated the flooding of the Ruhr mines, the wrecking of German factories, and the reducing of Germany from an industrial to an agricultural nation. Among others, Harry Dexter White, later named by Attorney General Brownell as one who had been heavily involved in a Soviet espionage ring operating within our government—and then an assistant to the Secretary of the Treasury—proposed exactly that.

In the Far East the defeat of the Japanese Empire left chaos in such areas as French Indochina, Indonesia, parts of Burma, and Malaya, with former colonial powers, nationalists, and Communists joining in a struggle for control. China itself was in a state of confusion and civil war, with both Chiang Kai-shek and the Chinese Communists claiming major roles in the defeat of Japan.

Thus the nations of the Free World were for only a short while a picture of joyous victory; too soon they reflected, in far too many cases, black disillusionment.

As time wore on, it became apparent that the Soviet Union had no intention of continuing its policy of friendship, even on the surface. By 1948 the mystery of Jan Masaryk's plunge to his death in Czechoslovakia (the Communists called it suicide) following the Communist coup, the Soviet use of the Red Army to support Communist regimes in Eastern Europe, Communist pressures on Italy and Finland, and the arrogant actions of some of the U.S.S.R.'s satellites, including the shooting down of two American transport planes over Yugoslavia,[3] made discernible to all the Soviet policy of holding occupied territory in bondage, while attempting to spread the growth of Communism through subversion, espionage, brutality, and fear.

Slowly the West began to react. Communist pressure, including subversion and support of dissident elements in the Balkans and Near East, had become so well established by March of 1947 the President declared what is now known as the "Truman Doctrine." Aid to Greece of $250 million and aid to Turkey of $150 million were requested of Congress and provided two months later, thus setting the stage for the consolidation of the southern flank of Europe.

That year the Marshall Plan, a farseeing program providing American assistance to rehabilitate the war-damaged economies of Europe, was proposed. Soon it was enacted into legislation and put in operation. (While at the time the administration estimated the project would take more than four years and cost some $17 billion, under the leadership of its statesmanlike Republican director, Paul Hoffman, the task was successfully completed, ahead of schedule, at a cost of $13.6 billion.)

One of the principal reasons for the success of the Marshall Plan was that the great expenditures of the United States went to rebuild and re-

---

[3] Five United States soldiers, occupants of the first plane, died in the crash; the Yugoslavs held in custody the occupants of the second plane. When the United States demanded their release, Tito freed them within forty-eight hours.

store countries sharing a common Western civilization, countries substantially similar to ours in traditions and practices. We were to learn later that in assisting the historically undeveloped or underdeveloped areas of the world, the United States would encounter a different problem—that of helping to create educational, social, and political administrative foundations for economic progress which had never before existed.

The year 1948 saw the institution of the West Berlin blockade on the part of the Soviets, which represented only the first crisis, although a crucial one indeed, of a continuing series over the fate of that unfortunate city. It was met by a response from the West that included a lifeline in the form of an airlift, directed by General Clay; the West will long owe him a large debt of gratitude for his resolution in this critical moment of history—a resolution which heroically reasserted the refusal of free men to quail before the threat of a tyrant. Further, in 1948 the world saw Hungary headed toward complete absorption by the Communists and Cardinal Mindszenty imprisoned and charged with crimes against the state.

A year of tragedy began in 1949. Most tragic was the defeat of Chiang Kai-shek at the hands of the Chinese Red Mao Tse-tung and Chiang's expulsion from the mainland of China. In 1945 General Marshall had been sent to China with explicit instructions to bring an end to the fighting, and to "broaden the base" of the country's representative government by getting Chiang Kai-shek and the Communists to sit down together to form a "strong, united, and democratic China." After 1945 many continued to believe or to hope that the Chinese Reds were merely "agrarian reformers" and not true Communists.[4] In 1949 the Department of State announced its opposition to a bill which would grant the Chinese Nationalist government $1.5 billion in economic and military aid, deploring Chiang's failure to make reforms, and resigning itself to a Communist victory.

When the mainland of China fell, one of America's stanchest personal allies was driven, with what forces he had left, across the Formosa Straits to that island which is now the remaining remnant of Free China.

[4] In 1946 when I was preparing for a trip to Nanking, President Truman told me that he was considering the appointment of a Secretary of State. The President was flattering enough to suggest that General Marshall and I were the two men most acceptable to him for the position, but before he went further, I hastened to say that I was going to China and would be happy to tell the general what the President had said about him.

General Marshall, while of course appreciative of the compliment, took the opportunity it offered to make a sardonic comment on the frustrations of his Chinese assignment. "Eisenhower," he said, "I would do almost anything to get out of this place. I'd even enlist in the Army!"

In the late summer of the same year the Soviets set off their first atomic explosion.

On the Western side, we signed the North Atlantic Treaty and formed NATO. Thus the year 1949 saw East and West consolidating their positions—face to face—along sectors of a line that stands substantially unchanged today.

Within the Free World itself many upheavals, also of vital significance, occurred. India and Pakistan had become independent members of the British Commonwealth in 1947. Though the Netherlands had brought Western civilization, economic progress, and orderly administration to the East Indies, the Indonesians—like nearly all colonial peoples—understandably insisted on their independence from the Dutch and won it in 1949. Jordan, Israel, and other nations were achieving independent status. The French, however, were still determined to retain their hold on Indochina and French Africa.

The turn of the decade, 1950, saw the outbreak of war in Korea. Coming back from a short trip into the Canadian woods in late June of 1950, I was saddened by the news that our country was again involved in hostilities. Accurate news of the affair was difficult to get, but I had the impression that the Defense Department, while already moving to the assistance of the Korean Republic, intended to intervene only with such air support as could be readily given from carriers and neighboring bases. This, if true, would be inadequate and therefore a mistake, I thought. Because of my long association with the individuals responsible for our defense establishment, I voluntarily went at once to Washington to visit with them, with no purpose except to ask for a briefing on the situation. General Bradley was ill, but I talked with friends in the Pentagon and later was given an opportunity to see the President. A detailed plan was not yet formulated and he asked for my views on the situation as it was outlined in the Pentagon.

I told the President that under the circumstances with which we were faced at the moment I thought the decision to intervene was wise and necessary. In this situation the United Nations would have a real test of its viability, I observed. As for the United States, the government now had to make certain of attaining its objective. (This was, according to my information, to assure the territorial integrity of South Korea.)

"Our nation has appealed to the use of force," I said. "We must make sure of success. We should move quickly to the necessary level of mobilization and begin at once to concentrate and use whatever forces may be required, including American ground troops. This act in itself," I said, "will remove any doubt of the seriousness of our intentions."

The President remarked that his thinking was along the same lines, though so far he had approved the use of American air and naval assistance only. In the meantime he was using his entire resources to get the United States rallied to the defense of South Korea, a purpose that I of course applauded.

United States forces were duly committed, and began to fight a heroic action in South Korea's defense. As of late 1952, fighting was still raging on a bloody front that had become fairly static.

Furthermore, the world situation had continued to degenerate. Premier Mossadegh had nationalized Iran's oil resources, and the country was drifting dangerously toward Communism. In Guatemala the Arbenz regime, since December 1950, had been attempting to establish a Communist state within the Western Hemisphere. In Indochina and Malaya there was fighting between the lawfully constituted governments and the Communists. Yugoslavia and Italy were still quarreling over their claimed rights in Trieste. Furthermore, although the United States had exploded its first H-bomb on November 1, three days before the election, it was probable that the Soviets would not be far behind.[5]

But the situation which faced our nation on that day can never be understood by looking at the externals alone. The attitudes of the government respecting domestic affairs, its people and policies, had increasingly disturbed me in the period leading up to my 1952 declaration that I was available for the office of the Presidency.

By 1952 numerous instances of malfeasance in office, disregard for fiscal responsibility, apparent governmental ignorance or apathy about the penetration of Communists in government,[6] and a willingness to divide industrial America against itself had reduced the prestige of the United States and caused disillusionment and cynicism among our people. These I felt must be erased if we were to remain a people of self-respect, capable of governing ourselves in a world of strife. This fact made it more essential than ever that we find candidates of the highest possible standing in character, integrity, and ability, to assist me in carrying on the proper functions of government.

* * *

On the day following the election, November 5, I went to Augusta, Georgia, for a degree of peace and quiet in which to make selections for

[5] The first Soviet thermonuclear test was detected the following August (1953). Benefiting from espionage and treason in the West, the Soviet Union probably began practical development of a thermonuclear bomb before the United States did.
[6] On August 5, 1948, President Truman, for example, charged that the Republican-controlled Eightieth Congress's investigation into alleged Russian spy rings within the government was a "red herring" designed to divert public attention from that Congress's failure to enact his programs.

future Cabinet positions and to devise plans for using to best advantage the time for preparation until Inauguration Day.

Another immediate task was to make arrangements with the outgoing administration for such liaison as would allow the incoming one to begin functioning efficiently.

Through an exchange of telegrams with President Truman, authority was granted for me to send appropriate representatives to key offices for briefing.

On November 5 President Truman wrote:

> Thank you for your prompt and courteous reply to my telegram. I know you will agree with me that there ought to be an orderly transfer of the business of the Executive branch of the government to the new administration, particularly in view of the international dangers and problems that confront this country and the whole Free World. I invite you therefore to meet with me here in the White House at your early convenience to discuss the problems of this transition period, so that it may be made clear to all the world that this nation is united in its struggle for freedom and peace.

The next day I replied:

> Thank you for your telegram. I am gratified by your suggestion that we have a personal meeting in the interests of orderly transition.
>
> Because I obviously require a reasonable time for conversations and conferences leading up to the designation of important assistants I respectfully suggest that we tentatively plan the proposed meeting for the early part of the week beginning November 17th. In the meantime with your permission I shall try to take immediate advantage of your suggestion concerning a budgetary representative and will additionally propose other individuals for indoctrination in several of the other departments in the federal government. In this way our own conference can achieve maximum results. I share your hope that we may present to the world an American unity in basic issues.

Under this authority I requested Joseph M. Dodge to cooperate with the Director of the Bureau of the Budget to the end that he could make recommendations to me for appropriate changes in the 1954 budget. I hoped that Mr. Dodge would later accept appointment as the new head of that bureau. At the same time I requested Cabot Lodge to represent me in liaison with other sections of the Executive branch.

I had known Joe Dodge from mid-1945 in Germany, where he had responsibility for fiscal affairs of the American occupation. Later he had gone to Japan in a similar capacity; and these experiences, together with his career as an American banker, eminently fitted him for the important post of Budget Director. More than this, he was a strong character, a believer in fiscal integrity, and completely selfless.

Cabot Lodge had unusual qualifications for service in government. Before the beginning of World War II he had been a member of the United States Senate and he had resigned that post early in the war to enter the Army.

These two appointments were merely initial moves in the process of preparing to take over the responsibility of government.

On November 18 I paid my formal visit to President Truman in the White House. He received me cordially; however, in such a short span of time the conversations, which included briefings by several outgoing Cabinet heads, were necessarily general and official in nature. So far as defense affairs were concerned, under the instructions of the President, I had been briefed periodically by General Walter Bedell Smith and his assistants in the Central Intelligence Agency on developments in the Korean War and on national security. This meeting therefore added little to my knowledge, nor did it affect my planning for the new administration, but I did thank the President sincerely for his cooperation.

Several of my close associates were already aware that I intended to ask them to accept important posts in the new administration.

Although no specific commitments had been made and indeed no decisive discussions among us had taken place, there had been no doubt in the minds of Foster Dulles, Sherman Adams, Herbert Brownell, Arthur Summerfield, Gabriel Hauge, Wilton B. Persons, James Hagerty, and others that I would want them with me if I should become President.

Promptly after the election results were known I asked Herbert Brownell and General Lucius Clay to become my principal assistants in searching out and screening the qualifications of persons we thought might be best suited for the numerous Executive positions to be filled. By that time I had reason to have developed confidence in the abilities and objectivity of Brownell, while General Clay was a lifelong friend who had been a brilliant career soldier, had held important assignments in civil posts, and had become head of a large industrial organization. In this screening work they were often assisted by Sherman Adams and, of course, called upon others for opinions and comment.

In the meantime it was necessary to plan the trip to Korea.

In his congratulatory message to me after the results of the election were known, the President had written that

The Independence [the presidential plane] will be at your disposal if you still desire to go to Korea.

In reply I had said:

I am most appreciative of your offer of the use of the Independence but assure you that any suitable transport plane that one of the services could make available will be satisfactory for my planned trip to Korea.

Before starting on such a trip I hoped to complete the slate of Cabinet designees and selections for other important posts. I told my staff to start planning for a departure date near the 1st of December.

By November 20 I had selected three prospective Cabinet officers— John Foster Dulles as Secretary of State, Charles E. Wilson as Secretary of Defense, and Douglas McKay as Secretary of the Interior. Governor Dewey, by his own declaration, had removed himself from consideration for any post, as had Paul Hoffman.

The selection of Mr. Dulles was an obvious one; the grandson of one Secretary of State and the nephew of another, he had carried on a lifelong study of American diplomacy. At the age of nineteen he was a secretary to the Chinese delegation at the 1907 peace conference at The Hague, and for nearly a half-century thereafter had worked in the field of foreign affairs both as a public servant and as a distinguished international lawyer. Before his appointment he and I had held a number of conversations on the international outlook and found ourselves in substantial agreement in our conclusions. He was a vigorous Republican who had represented bipartisanship in earlier years, a man of strong opinions and unimpeachable character.

Mr. Wilson was then head of the General Motors Corporation; I had met him several times since the war. He had a reputation as one of the ablest of our executives in big corporations. I sought an experienced man of this kind because of the huge procurement, storage, transportation, distribution, and other logistical functions of the Defense Department which, in my opinion, needed to be directed by experts. It seemed to me that a man of such qualifications could team up with professional soldiers to the great advantage of the nation. General Clay and others recommended him enthusiastically, and after a long conversation with me he agreed to undertake the duty.

The selection of Douglas McKay involved a number of factors, including geography. The great interest in conservation and water-power development of the trans-Mississippi states, especially those of the Mountain and Far West areas, practically monopolized the attention and activities of the Interior Department. Therefore, it seemed logical to appoint as its head a man familiar with the needs, history, and thinking of the West. The matter was made more complex by differences among several Western states over the amount of water each could take out of a river which flowed across state lines, such as the Colorado. The problem was to find a man of ability from that region who would be deemed by its people to be impartial in his administration of the affairs of the department and in helping to settle these differences. Any appointee from a state deeply involved in these conflicts—such as California or Arizona—would be suspect. Nebraska and Oregon, and possibly Washington and the Dakotas, seemed to be more nearly neutral than others and it was in them that we looked for a satisfactory individual.

Arthur Langlie of Washington, just re-elected governor of his state, was not available for consideration. But in Oregon, McKay was just ending a term as governor. Prior to that experience he had been a successful businessman, and our investigations indicated that his personal qualifications and his standing in the community were of a high order. After long consultations to determine the harmony of our views on the functions and problems of the Interior Department, I offered and he accepted the appointment.

The next day I announced George M. Humphrey as Secretary of the Treasury and Herbert Brownell as Attorney General. The appointment of the latter was practically a foregone conclusion in my mind, if he would agree to serve. He had become a close friend, and possessed an alert mind. Moreover, I so respected him as a man and lawyer that I did not seriously consider anyone else for the post.

George Humphrey was recommended to me by many advisers. His name was first suggested by Lucius Clay. The points that everyone emphasized were that he was impeccable in integrity and character, able as an administrator, and dedicated to sound fiscal and financial policies. He was reluctant to consider entering government and disclaimed particular qualifications for any post. From the beginning, however—I had never met him before—he and I seemed to get along together famously. After I told him why I wanted him and urged him to think of the country and ignore any other considerations, he agreed to accept, saying that he would do his best to discharge the vital responsibilities of that important post. For my part, my admiration, respect, and liking for him have never ceased to grow.

One of the positions I wanted to fill without delay was that of the head of the White House Staff. For years I had been in frequent contact with the Executive Office of the White House and I had certain ideas about the system, or lack of system, under which it operated. With my training in problems involving organization it was inconceivable to me that the work of the White House could not be better systemized than had been the case during the years I observed it.

Under the President there is a horde of activities that do not pertain, at least exclusively, to the established departments. For example, within the White House itself are the matters of public and press relations, liaison with both houses of Congress, scheduling visitors desiring to see the President, requests upon him for advice and speeches by educational, business, labor, and religious organizations, and the appointments of individuals to governmental positions other than those within the established departments.

Another duty is that of examining on behalf of the President actions that fall within approved policy but which do not normally demand his special action; meeting people who want to bring their problems directly to the White House but who do not need to see the President to obtain a satisfactory answer that is consistent with his convictions; procuring lists of individuals deemed suitable for governmental service in lower echelons; securing FBI reports upon prospective appointees; and minor transfers of appropriated moneys where the law requires presidential approval.

Still another group of duties has to do with coordinating, at levels below the top, the work involving two or more of the established departments and other parts of the Executive branch, such as the Council of Economic Advisers, the Bureau of the Budget, the General Services Administration, the Office of Defense Mobilization, the Civil Service Commission, and many others. When these problems of coordination assume sufficient importance to deserve the attention of the President, arrangements are made for necessary conferences with the heads of the agencies affected. But in countless cases, the appropriate staffs, operating on behalf of their respective chiefs, can settle differences efficiently. This is called "coordination at the staff level" and is most useful in civil government—as it is in the military services—particularly in saving the time of busy department heads and in prompt resolution of administrative details and difficulties.

The White House Staff, operating under approved policies, is responsible for these and other classes of duties. Obviously, to be successful the staff must be coordinated within itself by a responsible head.

In conformity with my conception of this staff and of its appropriate organization, I sought a competent administrator and a good friend to serve as its chief, who would be close to and trusted by me. The title I decided upon was "Assistant to the President." I believed, and still do, that the careful development by the President of a personal staff, able to assure the effective and unobtrusive performance of these several duties on his behalf, is one of the most important things he can do in the interests of efficient government.

Even before we had won the election, I began to ponder deeply and earnestly the identity of the man I needed. There were several military officers who, by reason of their abilities and broad experience, could have filled the post admirably—among them, Generals W. Bedell Smith, Lucius Clay, and Alfred M. Gruenther of the Army, General Lauris Norstad of the Air Force, and Captain George Anderson of the Navy. But having been a lifelong soldier myself, I felt it would create in many quarters a suspicion of excessive military influence to ask one of these to undertake this duty. Such an aide would have had, of course, the advantage of a thorough knowledge of staff functioning, which regrettably so many persons seem to misunderstand completely—sometimes, I think, deliberately. In any event, quickly discarding the idea of a military man, my mind turned to two others: Sherman Adams and Cabot Lodge. My list of prospects included also, for a time, the name of Herbert Brownell, but he, I had already decided, should be the Attorney General.

Either of the other two, I thought, could carry the responsibilities of the post satisfactorily, and each had special abilities. I wanted both in the government and had been considering each for a possible Cabinet post.

Circumstances helped me to make a selection. In November, Mr. Dulles suggested a change in the United States Representative to the United Nations because of the age of the incumbent. He strongly urged that I consider Cabot Lodge. I thought the idea admirable; Cabot's qualifications seemed almost unique. The post was one of vital importance— in fact, I later accorded its occupant Cabinet rank with a seniority just below that of the Secretary of State. Cabot, delighted with this opportunity for service, promptly accepted.

Sherman Adams therefore was, in my opinion, the logical individual to be the Assistant to the President. I explained to him the responsibilities of the post as I conceived them, and asked him to think it over. Initially he seemed reluctant to consider it at length, creating in me the feeling that he did not attach to the appointment the same importance I did. However, by November 24 he had reported that he would accept, and I informed him that as a matter of protocol he would have Cabinet rank.

Another designation I made that day was that of Ezra Taft Benson. When I told him that I was considering him as the future Secretary of Agriculture, he advanced a number of reasons why I should not select him.

"I am sure you know," he said first, "that I supported Senator Taft."

"Well, Mr. Benson," I retorted, "in view of your name, I am not surprised." That was no liability.

He went on to say that his responsibilities to his church—he was a member of the Council of Twelve, part of the governing body of the Mormon church—were not only sizable but provided the primary motivations of his life. To this I replied that I had met and liked David McKay, president of the Mormon church, and was sure that when he knew that

I wanted Mr. Benson for important service to the entire country, he would agree to the arrangement. I told Ezra of my hope that he could help solve the complex problems of agriculture, because I knew he agreed that political gimmicks and panaceas could not help farmers. Also I knew of his long years of experience in agriculture and had fine reports on him as a man of character and independent thinking. With his reservations resolved he accepted and his designation was announced.

The selection of a suitable Secretary of Labor was a delicate problem. I wanted no one who had evidenced extreme views in labor-management relations. Particularly I wanted no one whose pronouncements and actions labeled him, in my opinion, either as a supporter of socialism or as a "union buster." The man I picked would have to pass with flying colors— as indeed would every other individual I selected for service in the federal government—an exhaustive examination by the Federal Bureau of Investigation as to his past record, reputation, and standing in his community.

And here I digress long enough to say that there had come to my ears during this interregnum a story to the effect that J. Edgar Hoover, head of the FBI, had been out of favor in Washington. Such was my respect for him that I invited him to a meeting, my only purpose being to assure him that I wanted him in government as long as I might be there and that in the performance of his duties he would have the complete support of my office.

In seeking a Secretary who could represent in the government the viewpoint of labor as one of the vital elements of our economy, I hoped to find a satisfactory man from the ranks of labor itself. Long before, the old Department of Commerce and Labor had been divided, and Commerce was now traditionally headed by a businessman; I thought that as a counterbalance the Labor Department should be headed by one actually experienced in the labor movement.

To find a man meeting this list of qualifications was far from easy. The records of a number of men—not all of them actually a part of organized labor—were carefully examined and on one score or another rejected.

Finally Brownell reported on Martin Durkin of Chicago, head of the AFL plumbers' union and formerly head of the Illinois Labor Department. He was a Democrat and had been active in supporting my opponent in the campaign; but this did not disturb me provided he could measure up to the standards I had established.

In the meantime I had kept examinations into this matter secret, for I well knew that once my intention to select a man from one of the union organizations became known, violent criticism would make it almost impossible to get anyone to agree to serve in the post.

When the reports of necessary investigations came in, I invited Mr. Durkin to come to see me in New York.

I outlined for him my thoughts on the matter, taking special care to tell him that he would be expected to represent labor's viewpoint in the government but that he would no longer owe personal allegiance to labor, only to the nation. He would be expected to voice his own convictions honestly and forthrightly as a member of the government, but he would have to accept and abide by my decisions, once made. He seemed to have difficulty in making this distinction, which was to me quite simple. He likewise expressed concern for his future, if for any reason he might find it necessary to leave the government. I told him that if he served the nation impartially and intelligently, and as Secretary of Labor improved the attitudes between labor and management, he need have no fear about his future; such a success would make him so useful to both labor and management that his services would be in universal demand. After a period of consideration he accepted, informing me that his union was prepared to hold open his old position for a year, in the event that he might not want to continue in government. Both of us realized that the appointment was something of an experiment. For my part, I was committed to an attempt to minimize the mutual antagonisms which, in my view, were impeding progress in our economy. I was anxious to change this and to make a fresh start.

When the designation was announced, Senator Taft called it "incredible." Many others were no less critical. But I was determined to persist in the attempt. If it worked, the nation would be the gainer.

The case of Arthur Summerfield posed one problem that differed from any of the others. He had been chosen at the time of the Chicago convention as the chairman of the Republican National Committee. As such he had discharged his manifold responsibilities to my entire satisfaction, and had demonstrated a fine administrative ability. He was possessed of strong character and vast energy and he had become a friend. I wanted him in an important position.

In considering his future my first thought was to ask him to stay on as national chairman, in which position I thought he would be effective in consolidating and increasing the gains made by the party in the recent election. There were precedents for giving a Cabinet assignment to a national chairman of a successful campaign, while he continued on in the chairmanship. I thought this bad practice: it gave the appearance of using a Cabinet position and its facilities to promote the fortunes of a particular party. More than this, I thought that each of these positions should command the individual dedication and total abilities of its occupant. Dual assignments are not often satisfactory. ·

So I gave Arthur a choice, to take either the Postmaster Generalship or the chairmanship. His first reaction seemed to be that he would like both, but since I disapproved, he chose the Cabinet position and prepared to turn over the chairman's duties to a successor.

Very soon after the election the name of Mrs. Oveta Culp Hobby, a Texas newspaper publisher and Democrat-for-Eisenhower, was suggested to me as a possible appointee to the Cabinet. I had known her during the war when she was the head of the Women's Army Corps, in which work she had established a splendid reputation as an administrator and leader. I was hopeful of finding a woman of proven ability for a high post in government, and none seemed better fitted for such an appointment than she. She was told that I planned to propose to the Congress the consolidation of health, education, and welfare responsibilities into a single department, and to appoint her as its head. With this in mind I requested her to undertake, immediately upon my inauguration, the duties pertaining to the Federal Security Agency, telling her that pending the creation of the new department she would have Cabinet rank. After some urging she agreed to accept.

These designations left, in the Cabinet, only the Commerce Secretaryship to fill. A man who had been recommended to me highly, but whom I had never known before the beginning of the campaign just past, was Sinclair Weeks of Massachusetts. He was a former senator and former Republican National Finance Committee chairman. While I felt that he was well qualified for the Commerce post, I was at the same time still concerned about the vacancy in the national committee chairmanship, to be created by the resignation of Arthur Summerfield. I suggested this latter position to Mr. Weeks, believing that in this spot he might be able best to serve the party and the country, but I found that he strongly preferred the position in Commerce; he had no ambition whatsoever to fill the post of national chairman. I decided to nominate him as Secretary of Commerce.

The selection of my Cabinet was thus completed before December 1, 1952, a remarkably short time. This speed was necessitated to an extent by my forthcoming trip to Korea, which would occupy some two weeks, but it made it possible for several Cabinet-designees to accompany me on that trip and confer in a leisurely atmosphere on the problems which we all soon would be facing. Some designees, such as Secretary Benson, traveled the country at their own expense informing themselves during this valuable period. With this opportunity, including the pre-inauguration meeting we were to hold in January, I am certain that my Cabinet was as well-prepared for future governmental duties as any such team that ever assembled on Inauguration Day in Washington.

*   *   *

Although selected, one or two names of future Cabinet members were not announced to the public. This delay was planned deliberately in order to increase the credibility of a "cover story" devised by the Secret Service to keep a veil of secrecy around me in the days before my departure for Korea, now scheduled for November 29.

The cover story was a simple one: that I was remaining closely at my home at 60 Morningside Drive while working on the final Cabinet selections.

As a first step, all those detailed to accompany me were instructed to say nothing to anyone. They were to take special and separate routes to the airplane, which was scheduled to take off at an early hour, long before daylight. Staff members and other associates remaining in New York were given daylight schedules of visits to make to my home during my absence, carrying on the appearance of normal contact and activity. Another program controlled a series of announcements to be made from my home, including Cabinet designations. The plan was well conceived and successfully carried out until I had visited and departed from Korea, when the Secret Service decided that secrecy was no longer necessary.

My initial companions on the journey included General Bradley, Chairman of the Joint Chiefs of Staff; Cabinet-designees Wilson and Brownell; Press Secretary James Hagerty, and General Persons, an outstanding Army officer, long retired and one of my best and oldest friends. We were joined at Iwo Jima by Admiral Arthur W. Radford, Commander-in-Chief, Pacific.

We landed in Korea on December 2 and were met by General Mark W. Clark and General James A. Van Fleet. The war had been going on for more than two years.

The next day we were given a series of briefings by the senior commanders in Seoul and thereafter visited a number of combat headquarters, both air and ground. At one point I inspected a group comprising troops of fifteen different nations. On the 4th we had another round of inspections and briefings. The day's first visit was to the British Commonwealth Division, commanded by an old friend of World War II, Major General Sir Michael Montgomerie Alston-Roberts-West. My son, then on the Korean front, had recently been serving in the battalion of the 15th Infantry that I had proudly commanded as a Lieutenant Colonel at Fort Lewis, Washington, twelve years earlier. Aware of this former association, the division commander, Major General George Smythe, invited me to have an outdoor luncheon with a large group of the enlisted men belonging to my old command. It was an interesting meal even though the thermometer was registering subfreezing temperatures. The men freely told me about their daily lives in that mountainous and exposed terrain and described the discomfort they suffered because of the cold and the difficulty of maintaining underground shelters in decent condition.

One of my lunch companions was Corporal James A. Murray, who only weeks later was killed in action on patrol against the Chinese. War is the saddest of all human activities.

That day I witnessed a demonstration by the Capitol Division of the Republic of Korea. It involved a wide range of technical and tactical training, in which the men were obviously attaining an admirable proficiency. To this event I was accompanied by President Syngman Rhee who, in spite of the excessive cold and his advancing years, remained on the spot until the demonstration was completed.

On the 5th I had a number of conferences with military and civil personnel, mainly dealing with the military and economic future of the country, its crying need for schools, hospitals, roads, and a variety of equipment, and with programs for future military action in the event that the Red Chinese did not soon show a readiness to abandon aggressive purposes.

This was not my first trip to Korea. I had been there in the summer of 1946. On that trip, only a few months after the completion of World War II, the land was bleak, the climate hot, and the roads and fields dusty. This time we found contrasting conditions in temperature and climate. Military installations everywhere had turned the whole region into one gigantic battlefield.

The front ran roughly along the 38th Parallel, with the capital city, Seoul, included in the Allied lines. The forward elements of both armies were located in mountainous country, a fact that had added to the discomfort of our troops. From observation points we studied the hostile areas through field glasses and were told that the Chinese Reds in strengthening their positions had found an almost infallible way of protecting themselves while harassing our positions with artillery fire. They had gone to the trouble of boring tunnels through the mountaintops large enough to accommodate their artillery pieces. They would push their guns through the tunnels to fire once and withdraw immediately. Obviously they had undertaken a laborious task, but just as obviously they had plenty of manpower to use.

We used light airplanes to fly along the front and were impressed by the rapidity with which wounded were being brought back for treatment; evacuation was almost completely by helicopter since there were no landing fields for conventional planes in the mountains. Except for sporadic artillery fire and sniping there was little action at the moment, but in view of the strength of the positions the enemy had developed, it was obvious that any frontal attack would present great difficulties.

In the short time I was in Korea I was able to talk not only with President Rhee but with American and Allied personnel, from commanding generals to privates in the ranks. I was pleased by the obvious efficiency of the commanders. Many were friends. General Clark, commanding the Allied forces, and General Van Fleet, commanding the American Army, were both battle-tested, outstanding combat commanders. At corps, division, and regimental levels I was similarly impressed. The briefings given me at each level of command showed that our troops were alert, well-trained, and considering the circumstances of their existence, in remarkably good spirits. During my visit, however, I heard disturbing reports of a shortage of ammunition. I made a note to look into the matter promptly.

President Rhee, of course, was for all-out, full-scale attack to drive the invading forces up and off the peninsula. Such an attack would require an extension of the war across the Yalu River and attacks against the supporting bases of the invaders in China. At this time—December 1952— it had been tacitly accepted by both sides, including all of the Allied governments providing troops for the war, that we were fighting defensively and would take no risks of turning the conflict into a global war, which many feared would occur should we undertake offensive operations on a scale sufficient to win a decisive victory. We were also faced with the fact that negotiations between the two sides for an armistice had been going on for months. In our conversations, field commanders agreed that if these were not completed successfully within a reasonable time, our only recourse would eventually be to mount an all-out attack regardless of the risks. Under the circumstances of the moment, decisions of this kind could not even be made; but discussion was valuable. My conclusion as I left Korea was that we could not stand forever on a static front and continue to accept casualties without any visible results. Small attacks on small hills would not end this war.

All in all, the visit to Korea and to the rugged and barren terrain on which our lines were located left me with a renewed appreciation of the efficiency, durability, and fighting qualities of free men. While my principal attention was naturally given to American fighting forces, it was gratifying to see troops from such nations as Thailand, Ethiopia, the Philippines, and Colombia fighting as well and enduring hardships as uncomplainingly as were the fine men of Western Europe and North America. In particular I came away with an increased understanding of the advantages to be gained in training the Korean (ROK) soldier. I knew that I had not only achieved a better understanding of that battle-torn land, but had been inspired by the conduct of these fighters for freedom.

Late on the evening of the 5th I called on President Rhee and shortly thereafter went to the airport to start the return trip. There I said good-by to my son and to our military leaders and left for Guam, where I was scheduled to transfer to the cruiser *Helena*. At Guam, General Bradley and Admiral Radford left us, to proceed by airplane to Pearl Harbor. En route our ship passed Wake Island, where we were joined by Cabinet-designees Dulles, Humphrey, and McKay, and by General Clay and Mr. Dodge.

This rendezvous at Wake took place on December 7, and for the next several days on board the *Helena* we were busy. There was general agreement with my conclusion that we could not tolerate the indefinite continuance of the Korean conflict; the United States would have to prepare to break the stalemate.

On the voyage we also turned to making up slates of possible appointments for posts below Cabinet level, discussing practical means of reducing planned expenditures without reducing the nation's security or prospects for prosperity, and conferring on the basic features of my State of the Union speech, which I expected to deliver to the Congress in late January. While aboard the cruiser, I received word that the President, in a press conference, had attacked the trip to Korea as a "piece of demagoguery."

When I reached Pearl Harbor, we met with General Bradley and Admiral Radford again. I had earlier asked Mr. Wilson to talk with Radford, the Commander-in-Chief, Pacific, who had flown ahead to Honolulu, to form his own conclusions as to the suitability of this well-known naval officer for service on the Joint Chiefs of Staff. He was, of course, a qualified military man, but in my judgment, the Joint Chiefs should be acceptable to the civilian Defense Secretary. At one time Admiral Radford had been in the forefront of the service personnel who had bitterly opposed unification of the services. There is no doubt that in 1947 his efforts had been successful in preventing the level of unification that in my opinion was practical and desirable, but it was clearly brought out in the conversations between Mr. Wilson and the admiral that the latter's convictions on this point had undergone a radical change. He also knew the Far East. After Wilson's favorable report, I conferred with Radford myself and concluded that he could be extremely useful in Washington. He was, as it turned out, that rare combination—a man of tough conviction who would refuse to remain set in his ways. Faced with new facts, he would time and again modify his views to fit them.

Another man whom I had requested Mr. Wilson to see as soon as possible was Robert B. Anderson of Texas. I had met Anderson while I was at Columbia and had formed for him then a very high regard. He was intelligent, articulate, broadly experienced and educated, and, at forty-two, still a relatively young man. He had an extraordinarily good reputation in Texas. I asked Mr. Wilson to proceed to that state at once to look into the qualifications of Mr. Anderson, and to talk to him personally. In addition, I told Mr. Wilson that if, for any reason, he did not want Mr. Anderson in the Defense Department, I would myself have an equally important job for him in some other section in government. When again Mr. Wilson and I met in Washington, he was delightedly talking about his new "find," Robert Anderson, whom he planned to appoint Secretary of the Navy. I could not have been more pleased.

After two days in Hawaii we left for New York. I reached there early in the afternoon of the 14th. Meeting reporters, I made a statement that was brief but pointed: ". . . We face an enemy," I said, "whom we cannot hope to impress by words, however eloquent, but only by deeds —executed under circumstances of our own choosing."

When I reached the city I already knew that a visit from Prime Minister Churchill was imminent. I was happy with the chance to see once again one of the outstanding figures of our time. Our meeting took place at the home of our mutual friend Bernard Baruch, whose friendship with the Prime Minister dated from the days of World War I. Winston seemed in reasonably good health. However, at that time he was showing some effects of his seventy-eight years. I thought that he might be planning to retire in favor of some of the younger men in the party. He gave no hint of any such purpose; in fact, he talked of the future in terms of active participation on the many problems he saw looming ahead.

The Prime Minister voiced the hope that the United States and Britain would be able to build and sustain a special closeness in international relationships; in effect he hoped that we could so well coordinate our views and decisions that we could resume our wartime closeness and act jointly in the affairs of the family of nations.

I told him that the United States always put an unusual value on her relationship to Britain and that the history of World War II was in itself sufficient to assure particularly strong ties not only between us personally but between our two nations. On the other hand, I warned against the dangers of any concern in world opinion that we meant to form a two-power "coalition." To do so would create jealousies and suspicions that would be harmful in our work toward a world of justice.

We had long and earnest discussions about methods for combatting Communist encroachment. I told him I considered it our duty to make clear to the world the wickedness of Communist promises, and to convince dependent peoples that their only hope of maintaining independence, once achieved, was through cooperation with the Free World, which sought no domination of any kind over them. Not only did he agree, he

couched his concurrence in such eloquent and powerful language—
Churchillian phrases—as to make me wish now I could remember them
exactly and give them to the world.

During the next few days our headquarters in New York continued
with the same general plans and at the same pace. One new subject was
patronage. On Monday, January 5, I dictated this entry in my fragmentary
diary:

> The process of selecting a proper Governor for Hawaii has brought
> to me my first personal example of the traditional kind of political ap-
> pointment. . . . It has been my job to try to discover, in the United
> States, the individual that I consider best fitted for the discharge of a
> particular set of duties—after that my next chore was to make certain
> that I could get that individual for the job. (We have been remarkably
> successful in this regard. I had none of my choices even attempt to
> decline a Cabinet post; so far as I know, the Cabinet designees have
> had few declinations in their search for their principal assistants.)
> In the case of the Governor of Hawaii, there are two principal candi-
> dates who are themselves seeking the job. Each has developed a "pres-
> sure group" to support his claims. Such an approach to a public service
> position violates every instinct I have. To seek such a post is, to me,
> clear evidence of unsuitability. I feel that anyone who can, without
> great personal sacrifice, come to Washington to accept an important gov-
> ernmental post, is not fit to hold that post. This, of course, is not true in
> some of the more technical and professional positions, and it is unfair
> to assume that everyone should share my feelings in the matter when high
> positions are involved. But just the same, my respect and admiration
> for any individual who turns out to be a seeker after a political post
> diminishes almost to the vanishing point. . . .
> My experience in this case has generated in me the profound hope that
> I will be compelled to have little to do, during the next four years,
> with the distribution of Federal patronage. Having been fairly successful
> in late years in learning to keep a rigid check on my temper, I do not
> want to encounter complete defeat at this late date!

Appointments and patronage brought to mind a lesson taught me by
George Marshall in World War II. At one point he wrote saying that he
wanted to be sure that I understood that if I continued an officer in any
prominent position under my command, that meant I was happy with
him. He was not going to give me as an alibi for failure the fact that I had
ever used people of his appointment and not my own. Every man was
either to be my selection or have my approval. "Your success," he said,
"will be measured by their efforts." I applied this rule to my Cabinet-
designees and their choices.

An interesting early criticism came from a section of labor. Mr. Durkin had picked another AFL man as his principal assistant—the Under Secretary—in the Labor Department. The CIO disliked this action intensely.

At that time George Allen called my attention to a statement I had made in Paris exactly one year earlier: "I am a Republican."

"Now look what's happened to you," George said.

On January 11 I went to La Guardia Airport to meet my son, who had been ordered home from Korea for the inaugural ceremonies. Protesting, he made the trip.

The most important item on the remainder of my schedule before the inauguration was that of the meeting with the future Cabinet. The session convened at the Commodore Hotel in New York on the morning of January 12 and continued through the following day. We looked seriously upon the tasks we were assuming; our determination to go on preparing ourselves through study and frank discussion was evident in the agenda. It included a discussion of the roles of the Cabinet and the National Security Council. I wanted this fine group of men who had signaled their willingness to serve their country, and to help me, to understand the job as I saw it. A Cabinet member, they were to learn, was free to be concerned not only with the affairs of his own department but with virtually any question that concerned the government. No one was relieved of his responsibility or the opportunity to think broadly and to make suggestions. I read a draft of my Inaugural Address, and there was applause. That caused me to say that I had not read it for praise but for analysis and criticism. We then got down to a close scrutiny of the text.

The second day we talked organization and appointments. No individual claiming to be a relative or friend of mine was to receive, as long as I was in office, any special consideration or treatment. If anyone should ask a favor on the basis that he was my relative or friend, or because he had supported me politically, the request should be refused and the individual referred to my office for questioning or no longer be considered for any position. I was determined that none of us should be guilty of favoritism or nepotism.

Not everything was as serious. We had to make innumerable plans for the inauguration ceremony. I was determined that the parade should be as short as possible—having marched in too many of them myself. There was talk about headgear, and I suggested that we wear simple Homburg hats. It was said that tall silk hats were the tradition, and I answered that if we were worried about what had been done in years before, we could wear tricornered hats and knee breeches. Finally, Mrs. Eisenhower and I had received a handsome invitation to the inaugural ball, I remarked. We thought we might answer it by saying that we had another engagement.

*   *   *

My remaining days in New York were now largely taken up with preparation of an Inaugural Address. Shortly after election I had begun to ponder the character of the address I was to make. For help in the drafting, I turned first to C. D. Jackson. An assistant of his—both were from the *Time-Life* organization—Emmet J. Hughes, was a writer with a talent for phrase-making. Mr. Hughes became my assistant in working on the organization and wording of my talk; I determined its content in many discussions with him and with close advisers. It was largely completed by the time Mamie and I went from New York to Washington.

All four of my brothers and their wives came to the inauguration. In spite of my preoccupations, we were able to get together and reminisce. We stayed at the Statler Hotel, where Herbert Blunck, a friend and a very efficient hotel manager, had assigned an attractive suite to each brother and his family. For my part, a highlight was the dinner we all had together on my final evening as a private citizen.

The following morning was a busy one. After an early breakfast we attended the National Presbyterian Church, where the Reverend Edward L. R. Elson was pastor. Mamie had belonged to this denomination since girlhood, but until elected President, I had never had a formal connection with any specific church. In the military I had attended the post chapel and services conducted by ministers of various denominations. During the campaign many well-wishers urged me repeatedly to join a church, seeing a political advantage in such a move. I refused, however, until the election was over. Now, as a Presbyterian, I went with my family to a Communion service early on the morning of Inauguration Day.

Religion was one of the thoughts that I had been mulling over for several weeks. I did not want my Inaugural Address to be a sermon, by any means; I was not a man of the cloth. But there was embedded in me from boyhood, just as it was in my brothers, a deep faith in the beneficence of the Almighty. I wanted, then, to make this faith clear without creating the impression that I intended, as the political leader of the United States, to avoid my own responsibilities in an effort to pass them on to the Deity. I was seeking a way to point out that we were getting too secular.

Thinking on this as we came back from church, I decided to write a brief prayer to read before beginning my Inaugural Address. When I told Mamie of this idea she agreed enthusiastically, and within five or ten minutes I had written a text on a scratch pad and had it typed. I read it to my son and daughter-in-law and one or two close friends. They thought it was most fitting for the occasion, and it was with this hastily written prayer that I began my first Inaugural Address.[7] It was then time to go to the White House. When Mamie and I dismounted from our car, President and Mrs. Truman came to the front steps; we exchanged greetings and the President and I re-entered the first car, while Mamie and Mrs. Truman rode in the second.

To reach the Capitol, custom decreed that the outgoing and incoming Presidents ride down Pennsylvania Avenue together. The only comment of any consequence that I can recall during the short ride to the Capitol was asking the President the identity of the person who had ordered my son back from the combat area of Korea to be present at the inauguration. The President replied, "I did," and I thanked him sincerely for his thoughtfulness. My son had been upset when he first received the order because, not knowing the reason, he was fearful that he might lose his assignment in his combat division and be made some kind of aide or assistant of mine in the White House. When assured that he was coming to the United States merely for the inauguration and would immediately return to his post, he accepted the invitation gladly and I am quite sure had an enjoyable time in Washington as well as a pleasant reunion with his family.

The Inaugural Address was to the nation and to the world beyond. I said first that we sensed that the forces of good and evil were massed and opposed and that this fact defined the meaning of this day.

How far had we come in man's long pilgrimage from darkness toward the light? Our problems at home were dwarfed by this question, involving all mankind. The promise of our modern life—in which we turned rivers in their courses, used oceans and land and sky for our commerce, saw disease diminishing and life lengthening—was imperiled by the genius that had made it possible.

We had to proclaim our faith. It was our faith in the deathless dignity of man.

And the faith we held belongs, I said, "not to us alone but to the free

[7] "Almighty God, as we stand here at this moment my future associates in the Executive branch of government join me in beseeching that Thou will make full and complete our dedication to the service of the people in this throng, and their fellow citizens everywhere.

"Give us, we pray, the power to discern clearly right from wrong, and allow all our words and actions to be governed thereby, and by the laws of this land. Especially we pray that our concern shall be for all the people regardless of station, race or calling.

"May cooperation be permitted and be the mutual aim of those who, under the concepts of our Constitution, hold to differing political faiths; so that all may work for the good of our beloved country and Thy glory. Amen."

of all the world . . . the grower of rice in Burma and the planter of wheat in Iowa, the shepherd in southern Italy and the mountaineer in the Andes. It confers a common dignity upon the French soldier who dies in Indochina, the British soldier killed in Malaya, the American life given in Korea."

We were not the helpless prisoners of history; we had to be willing to accept whatever sacrifices might be required—for the people that values its privileges above its principles soon loses both.

"The peace we seek, then," I said at the close, is "more than the stilling of guns, easing the sorrow of war. More than escape from death, it is a way of life. More than a haven for the weary, it is a hope for the brave."

I had been given a rather rigid schedule for the day's activities, one item of which was a hasty lunch with the inaugural committee at the Capitol immediately after completion of the inauguration ceremonies. During the time allotted for the luncheon, the future officials of my administration, their families and wives, and the throng of visitors in the Capitol area would be proceeding to the grandstands along the route on which the parade was scheduled to move in the afternoon.

The parade that day was gay—and long. As the West Point cadets went by the reviewing stand, I recalled marching in the 1913 inaugural parade past President Woodrow Wilson.

Present were the traditional military contingents, a float for each state, innumerable bands, and an entry or two classified as high jinks. A California cowboy, riding a highly trained horse, got clearance from the Secret Service, stopped in front of me, and threw a lasso around my shoulders.

It had been a long time since the Republicans had had an opportunity to indulge in this kind of celebration. Consequently, the inaugural committee, headed by Senator Styles Bridges of New Hampshire, found it difficult to refuse any group that wanted to participate in the long and colorful review. The result was that I had to remain in the stand long after the hour set for the end of the parade; not until nearly seven o'clock did the last two elephants go by.[8] When late in the evening we entered the White House, the permanent household staff had made preparations for a gala reception.

The next problem was to get a bit of rest before going to the inaugural ball. The ball was actually two celebrations because the number of people

[8] I had arranged for not one but three Grand Marshals for the parade: General Leonard Gerow, General Carl ("Tooey") Spaatz, and Admiral Alan Kirk, all retired and all commanders of mine in the European theater of World War II.

accepting the committee's invitations for the evening's entertainment was so great that they could not be accommodated in any one structure in the city. But at last—sometime around one in the morning—the long day was over, and I went to bed as President of the United States.

BOOK TWO

... The United States pledges before you—and therefore before the world—its determination to help solve the fearful atomic dilemma—to devote its entire heart and mind to find the way by which the miraculous inventiveness of man shall not be dedicated to his death, but consecrated to his life.

—*"Atoms-for-Peace" speech, before the United Nations, December 8, 1953*

CHAPTER V

New Duties, New Faces

> . . . a wise and frugal government, which shall restrain men from
> injuring one another, which shall leave them otherwise free to
> regulate their own pursuits of industry and improvement, and shall
> not take from the mouth of labor the bread it has earned. This is
> the sum of good government. . . .
>
> —*Thomas Jefferson*
> *Inaugural Address, March 4, 1801*

O N January 21, 1953, shortly after 7:30 A.M., I entered the
oval room of the West Wing of the White House, des-
tined to be my office for the next eight years. The office of the President of
the United States, as compared to the sumptuous quarters of many business leaders and of most Cabinet officials, is a surprisingly plain room.
I had been in it many times before; its simplicity seemed to me most
appropriate for the American head of state.

There had been dramatic events in my life before—but none surpassed,
emotionally, crossing the threshold to an office of such awesome responsibility. Remembering my beginnings, I had to smile. If my chances of
walking into this room had been calculated when I was born in Denison,
Texas, in 1890, they would have been approximately zero. And yet the
homely old saw had proved to be true: in the United States, any boy
can grow up to be President.

I sat down at the massive desk. One drawer was locked. I rang for
William Simmons, the White House Office receptionist.

"Mr. Simmons," I asked, "is there a key to this desk? I can't get into
this drawer." He produced the key; there in the drawer lay a small pile
of confidential reports left by President Truman.

At two minutes after eight I had my first official conference as President, with Herbert Brownell, the Attorney General-designate. We discussed matters that had absorbed our attention for the weeks just past:

appointments, nominations to office, Senate confirmation of appointees, and conflict-of-interest laws.

As we talked, postal trucks were carting to the White House mail room, an office in the Executive Office Building across the street, the first sackfuls of letters and telegrams which I would receive as President—more than 6 million in eight years.

In the course of the day I asked Jim Hagerty to announce that I would continue the practice of holding regular news conferences, with the possibility that some of these might be televised. Twenty-nine members of the Palomino Mounted Police Patrol of Colorado, who had ridden in the inaugural parade, came in to shake hands, in their red jackets and white caps. Word arrived that the Chinese Communists had announced that their fighter planes had shot down a United States B-29 reconnaissance plane over Manchuria on the night of January 12. We knew it had been missing; now we knew that fourteen crew members had parachuted out: three had been killed and eleven taken prisoner. At luncheon former Governor Dan Thornton of Colorado and Governor Walter Kohler of Wisconsin wanted to discuss with me problems of mining, reclamation, and the conflict of federal and state taxes.

At three in the afternoon the members of the new White House Staff took their oaths of office. When this ceremony in my oval office ended, I expressed a hope which was much in my mind that day: "Gentlemen, I want the White House to be an example to the nation."

Then, in the East Room of the White House Mansion, the members of the Cabinet and Mrs. Oveta Culp Hobby, Director of the Federal Security Agency, were sworn in as officials of the government. From this group Charles E. Wilson was excluded because of the failure of the Senate to confirm his nomination. For the occasion I had brought up to the East Room the Cabinet table used by Abraham Lincoln, the first Republican President. Standing by it, the Honorable Fred M. Vinson, chief justice of the United States, administered the oaths.

*   *   *

The next day, January 22, activity speeded up markedly. My day started off with an 8:45 A.M. staff meeting. I worked on the State of the Union message and sent the names of twenty-three appointees to the Senate for confirmation.

By 6 P.M. I had met with nineteen men or groups, a wide-ranging calendar that included General J. Lawton Collins, Chief of Staff of the Army, Mr. Sam Stern of Fargo, North Dakota, Grand Exalted Ruler of the Elks, and Earl D. Johnson, Acting Secretary of Defense. Two of my brothers came to visit me—two who rarely agreed on anything—and amazed me by saying in unison that they thought the new office was satisfactory. My son and his wife, Barbara, came to bid me good-by, before he returned to his combat assignment in Korea and she went back to her home in New York State, where she and their children would live during his absence.

Washington was still crowded with inauguration visitors, who were full of congratulations and suggestions. I greeted as many of them as I could during those first few days. But I also turned at once to the unremitting tasks of the Presidency.

Serious problems were plaguing our nation in Korea and Vietnam. In the former, indecisive and costly fighting still dragged on. In Vietnam the French had not yet convinced the world that the struggle was between those who stood for freedom on one side and Communist rebels, supported by the power of Red China, on the other. Consequently a considerable portion of world opinion viewed the war there as merely a French effort to continue their prewar domination in the region. Until this point was clarified, it was difficult for any Western nation, including our own, to offer or provide any help to the French and loyal Vietnamese.

This was a matter that had troubled me greatly when I was serving as military commander of NATO in 1951–52. In that period the French government had found it necessary to deplete their NATO military contingent by a number of battalions so as to reinforce promptly French troops in Vietnam. In expressing my disappointment in that development I had strongly urged the government to interpret, publicly, their Far Eastern war effort in terms of freedom versus Communism. This could be done only through a French public commitment assuring to the Vietnamese, unequivocally, the right of determining their own political future. Such a pronouncement, I argued, would earn the approval of the Free World as well as its moral and greater material support.

During my service in NATO a considerable number of responsible officials in France had assured me of their complete agreement with this view. General de Lattre de Tassigny, who was then the commander of French forces in Vietnam, had come to the United States, at my urging, just a few months before his death and in a nationally televised speech in this country made just such a statement. But because his government did not follow with a public political pronouncement, the matter was still subject to misinterpretation and an American support for the French in that region could not achieve unanimous domestic approval. Nonetheless, recognizing the necessity of stopping Communist advances in that country, we started immediately after my inauguration to devise plans for strengthening the defenders politically and militarily within the proper limits.

In another conference that first day, with Budget Director Dodge, I discussed projected downward revisions in the budget recently sent to the Congress by the Truman administration. I was determined to put the federal government on a stronger financial footing as quickly as possible.

Another of the day's conferences, with the Attorney General, had to do with Defense Secretary-designate Wilson's difficulty with the Armed Services Committee of the Senate. The case had created a furor in the press. In the hope of having the Executive branch of government ready to operate by January 21, I had arranged to send to the Senate, some days before my inauguration, the names of all the individuals whom I planned to nominate for Cabinet and similar posts. Thus the appropriate committees would have an opportunity to conduct necessary investigations, and the entire Senate, I hoped, could confirm all nominations immediately after the inauguration.

But Charlie Wilson, being a blunt, outspoken man, with a wry sense of humor, was a natural for a clash with a congressional committee. The hearing on his nomination actually began on January 15, although the record was kept secret for nine days thereafter. The issue revolved around his ownership of thousands of shares of General Motors stock—he had been president of the company—worth several million dollars, plus a substantial bonus in cash and stock which he was to receive over the next four years. In addition, Mrs. Wilson also owned a block of General Motors stock.

The members of the Senate Armed Services Committee contended that the ownership of this much stock could conceivably create a conflict of interest in the case of a man who would, in his official position, influence governmental contracts for military equipment, many of them almost certain to be with the General Motors Corporation, a major supplier.

Wilson demurred. "I really feel you are giving me quite a pushing around. If I had come here to cheat," he told the senators who questioned him, "I wouldn't be here."

"I'm sorry you feel that way, Mr. Wilson," Chairman Richard Russell answered. "I am not trying to push you around, but I have my responsibilities too."

"I understand that," Wilson said. "But I am just human, and I am making a great sacrifice to come down here.

"If there was a nice clean way . . . to sell everything . . . and put it into government bonds," he went on, "I would do it. But the [tax] penalty is too great, gentlemen, and I do not know why you should ask me to do it."

"Would you make a decision adverse to General Motors?" This question prompted the most quoted—or misquoted—passage of the hearings. "For years," Mr. Wilson replied, "I thought what was good for the country was good for General Motors and vice versa." This was interpreted and broadcast—it still is—in the form of "What is good for General Motors is good for the country," and of course the breast-beaters had a field day.

One of the problems was in Mr. Wilson's style in testifying. Senators have never given especially warm receptions to those who appear to be lecturing them in their own forum. Nominees who do not are usually made somewhat more welcome. George Humphrey, for example, was also a man of considerable personal accomplishment and wealth, but he ran into no confirmation problems. In talking with Wilson, I gave him only one piece of advice. "Charlie," I said, "tell the whole works, so that there can be no question later." He probably did not need this reminder.

I must confess that this episode caused me considerable chagrin. On February 7, thinking about the general process of confirming men who have been nominated for high post, I wrote as follows in my spotty diary:

> While in every case the men I have named have been quite willing to comply with the provisions of the law (and I am referring to interpretations [of the law] given by some eminent men such as John W. Davis) I have found that some of our senatorial friends are so politically fearful that they carry the meaning and intent of the law far beyond anything that could be considered reasonable.
>
> The likely eventual result is that sooner or later [Presidents] will be unable to get anybody to take jobs in Washington except business failures, political hacks, and New Deal lawyers. All of these would jump at the chance to get a job that a successful business man has to sacrifice very materially in order to take. But it is the carrying of the practice to the extreme that will eventually damage us badly. . . .

The matter at issue is the extent to which a public servant's personal holdings will color his own decisions when the value of those holdings could be affected by his official actions. A man with no financial holdings whatever can be prejudiced, too. Other kinds of invisible prejudice are possible—the personal dislike of one person for another, to name a frequent one—and these can get in the way of judgment. The search must be for men who are, by the demonstrable evidence of their character and careers, as objective as possible in such matters.

The question arises most frequently when appointed officials of the government are involved; elected officials are apparently immune. Consequently there is no outcry in public when a member of Congress casts his vote on a bill that can conceivably affect the fate of his holdings.

Because the President and Vice President are elected officials, the so-called conflict-of-interest laws would not seem to apply to them. Nevertheless, in my own case I handled this matter in 1952 by making an irrevocable trust, to last during the period of my Presidency, in which I placed my moderate-sized investments. For eight years the trustee was not allowed to give me any information about investments or sales made on my behalf, nor was I allowed to know what securities were in the trust, or to give the trustee any instructions concerning them. The trustee's only obligation was to inform me annually of the amount of my taxable income derived from the investments made, so that I could make proper returns. Obviously, under this arrangement I could not know whether any decision of my own could affect the value of any part of the trust.

But a situation such as Secretary Wilson's could not be handled in this simple fashion. I agreed with his contention that men nominated to high office should be men of such integrity that the conflict-of-interest question becomes academic, and he was such a man. Yet the purpose of the existing laws seems to be that Caesar's wife (or a President's appointees) must be above even the suspicion of evil.

In my opinion "conflict of interest" is one of those matters that cannot be completely settled by law. It seems to me significant that our Founding Fathers, who wrote our Constitution and enacted the early laws to support its provisions, did not feel any necessity to raise the subject. I believe that any man who is elected President should have the right to select Executive-branch officials of his own choice. If any suspicion of malfeasance on the part of any of these individuals occurs, appropriate investigation can be made, and if improper conduct is demonstrated, the President himself should be responsible for the dereliction and for taking corrective action.

It soon became clear that Mr. Wilson would either have to sell his stock or ask me to withdraw his name—I had not yet sent up the formal nomination—from consideration for the vital post of Secretary of Defense. By the 22nd of January he had made his decision; he agreed to sell his stock, and I at once sent the nomination to Capitol Hill. That evening at seven twenty-one Jim Hagerty broke the news to the reporters. The next day the Senate Armed Services Committee approved his nomination and the Senate quickly confirmed him.

As I left my office late on the evening of January 22, I paused for a moment to write a note to myself:

My first full day at the President's Desk. Plenty of worries and difficult problems. . . . The result is that today just seems like a continuation of all I've been doing since July '41—even before that.

This attitude did not last long. One tiny incident that helped shatter it was nothing more than a telephone call from General Omar Bradley, then Chairman of the Joint Chiefs of Staff.

Hanging up the receiver, I turned to my secretary, Mrs. Ann C. Whitman.

"I've just learned a lesson from Omar Bradley," I said. "He addressed me over the phone as 'Mr. President.'"

These words may not have had at that moment any special significance for Mrs. Whitman, since she would have had at that time almost no way of knowing the closeness of my friendship with General Bradley. I had known him ever since we had entered West Point in 1911; we had played football together and belonged to the same company of the Corps of Cadets. Our association had been particularly close from the time he joined me in the African theater in early 1943 to the end of the European campaign. My telephone conversation was not with a stranger or short-time acquaintance—it came from a man who for forty years had called me "Ike," as I had called him "Brad." His salutation put me on notice: from then onward, for as long as I held the office, I would, except for my family, to a very definite degree be separated from all others, including my oldest and best friends. I would be far more alone now than when commanding the Allied forces in Europe in World War II.

*   *   *

On the morning of January 23 I got the chance to take care of a piece of personal business that had been much on my mind—a letter to my predecessor, former President Harry S Truman. It is true that one telling argument which led me to declare myself available for the Republican nomination in 1952 had been a conviction on my part that a long-term continuation of the domestic policies then supported by the Democratic administration would be ruinous to the nation. It is further true that the political campaign of that year had created some mutual antagonism, and I had resented President Truman's claim that my trip to Korea was nothing but a piece of demagoguery. But aside from this, I had been rather closely associated with the former President for nearly eight years—at least until he had learned of my Republican convictions—and in his last days in office he had shown a spirit of kindly cooperation in arranging governmental turnover and in ordering my son home for the inauguration. Therefore I wrote:

Dear Mr. President:

This note is to express my appreciation for the very many courtesies you extended to me and mine during the final stages of your Administration. The efforts you made to assure the orderly transfer of government, from your Administration to this one, are largely a matter of public knowledge but I am personally aware of the fact that you went to far greater trouble to accomplish this than almost anyone else could have known.

On the personal side, I especially want to thank you for your thoughtfulness in ordering my son home from Korea for the Inauguration; and even more especially for not allowing either him or me to know that you had done so.

I sincerely wish for you many years of happy and useful work; and of course, Mamie joins me in sending affectionate greetings to the ladies of your family.

With best wishes,

Sincerely,
DWIGHT D. EISENHOWER

His reply, dated January 28, was in warm and cordial terms, expressing his pleasure in helping in the orderly transfer, asking to be remembered to Mrs. Eisenhower, and wishing me the best. He would never have mentioned my son's return, he said, if I had not asked about it.

*   *   *

One of my first responsibilities was to organize the White House for efficiency.

There were many things that a good personal staff could and should do for a President—especially those things falling outside the responsibilities of major departments of the federal government. For such a group the name "White House Staff" seemed suitable; it could just as appropriately have been called "The President's Staff"; such a name, in fact, might have the additional advantage of setting this small group apart from the much larger "Executive Office of the President," which includes the staffs of the National Security Council, the Bureau of the Budget, the Council of Economic Advisers, and the Office of Defense Mobilization.

Organization cannot make a genius out of an incompetent; even less can it, of itself, make the decisions which are required to trigger necessary action. On the other hand, disorganization can scarcely fail to result in inefficiency and can easily lead to disaster. Organization makes more efficient the gathering and analysis of facts, and the arranging of the findings of experts in logical fashion. Therefore organization helps the responsible individual make the necessary decision, and helps assure that it is satisfactorily carried out.

I have been astonished to read some contentions which seem to suggest that smooth organization guarantees that nothing is happening, whereas ferment and disorder indicate progress.

There are men and women who seem to be born with a feeling for organization, just as others are born with a talent for art. But even the gifted natural artist needs training and experience, and so too anyone trying to find solutions to organizational problems must study them long and carefully. If he has not been so fortunate as to have personal experience, he must draw upon and trust the counsel of advisers who have.

I have often wondered, with occasional amusement, why so many who write on politics and public affairs apparently feel themselves experts on organization. Normally a writer is an individualistic rather than an organizational worker, and rarely has he gone deeply into the problems of organizing people into a great business or a large road gang, a vast military formation or a squad, a university or a governmental agency. Yet there are more than a few who seem to feel a compulsion, at times, to pontificate about organization.

I have read about "staff decisions" but I have never understood exactly what was meant by the expression, unless it is the assumption that decisions are sometimes made by group voting, as in a congressional committee, where a majority of votes controls the action. In my own experience—extending over half a century in various types of group mechanisms, large and small—I have never known any successful executive who has depended upon the taking of a vote in any gathering to make a decision for him. The habit of depending upon an "Aulic Council"—or for that matter, a Cabinet—to direct the affairs of a great nation, or of calling a "council of war" by generals to make decisions which were properly their own, went out of fashion long before most of us were born.

On a crucial question during the Civil War, Abraham Lincoln is said to have called for a vote around the Cabinet table. Every member voted no. "The ayes have it," Lincoln announced.

The Presidency still works the same way today.

Nonetheless, the President needs an efficient staff, and now more than ever before. In the early years of this century the White House had only one extension, the West Wing, built for the presidential offices in the administration of Theodore Roosevelt. One room in that wing was big enough for all who worked on correspondence, records, administrative services, and the delivery of messages. Across the street from it, an old ornate gray building housed three departments of government—State, War, and Navy. Executive-branch employees who were in a hurry to get downtown could take the shortest way, straight across the White House lawn. And even as late as the 1920s, at twelve noon, if they wanted they could stop by on nearly any day of the week, any week in the year, to shake hands with the President, who made a practice of setting aside this time for his constituents.

But during and after World War I, the New Deal, and World War II, employees in the old State, War and Navy Building spilled out into the Navy and Munitions buildings and then into the Pentagon, into a new State Department Building—now adjoining a still newer New State Building—and into an assortment of "temporary" office buildings and remodeled apartment houses scattered around the city.

In the great depression Harold L. Ickes presided over the construction of a new building for his Department of the Interior, covering not one city block like the old one, but two; and containing, incidentally, a set of secret elevators to permit private guests to come and go from his office without being seen by reporters. President Franklin D. Roosevelt added a second annex to the White House, the East Wing, and officials on the personal staff and in the Executive Office of the President overflowed into the erstwhile home of the Departments of State, of War, and of the Navy.

In 1933 the federal government employed 600,000 civilians; by 1952 that figure had nearly quadrupled. In 1933 it spent less than $5 billion; in 1953 it spent $74 billion, approximately fifteen times as much. In 1941, while the nation was involved in intensive preparations against the possibility of war, the United States government spent about $6 billion on major national security; when I entered the White House it was spending more than that to pay the interest on the national debt.

This expansion in the size of the government largely paralleled its growth in complexity and responsibility. The functions of government had multiplied enormously during the period, both those of the President and those of the Congress. This made more necessary than ever an efficient White House Staff in 1953.

In setting up this organization, one of the most important functions was that of maintaining liaison between the President and members of the Congress. To head a section for this purpose, I selected Major General Wilton B. ("Jerry") Persons. For many years, as an active officer in the War Department, he had operated in a similar capacity for the Army and was probably personally acquainted with more congressional members than any other individual in the city. After his second "retirement" he had served with me in NATO, and he long had been one of my admired and respected associates.

Named as General Persons' assistants were Gerald D. Morgan, an able lawyer closely associated with the drafting of the Taft-Hartley Act, and Bryce N. Harlow, formerly staff director of the House Armed Services Committee, an expert on military affairs, and a competent writer. After the death of Senator Taft, his administrative assistant, I. Jack Martin, joined the congressional liaison staff, which included also Homer H. Gruenther and Earle D. Chesney. All these men—except Jack Martin, who became a judge—remained with me, though some were in different posts, throughout my years in office.

Another important responsibility was the maintenance of orderly relations between the White House and the press corps. I selected James C. Hagerty as Press Secretary, the same post he had occupied on my personal staff during the political campaign. He was an experienced newspaperman and had occupied the post of press secretary to Governor

Dewey of New York. Possessed of an agile mind, a canny capacity for judging people, political shrewdness, and a healthy Irish temper, he had the respect of the White House correspondents as a "real pro."

"I have never lied to a reporter," he said; they knew they could count on his honesty.

To look after all communications of a top-secret character from or to the White House, I selected an outstanding young Army officer, Brigadier General Paul T. Carroll, who had served in World War II with distinction and been with me both in the Pentagon and in SHAPE Headquarters in Paris. If a document was incomplete, "Pete" Carroll would ask for additional facts to complete it. If coordination with other pertinent agencies was required, he would see to it that the matter was brought to their attention. His interests ranged far beyond defense and foreign policy. In his year and a half in the White House, before his tragic death at the age of forty-three of a heart attack, Pete selflessly campaigned for such causes as the World Day of Prayer and the metamorphosis of Washington, D.C., into the most beautiful city in the world, even while he handled, for me, communications of the utmost delicacy and importance.

His successor, in 1954, was another Army officer of exceptional capability, Colonel (later Brigadier General) Andrew J. Goodpaster.

There had to be a place to direct applications for governmental appointments. This section also had the responsibility for keeping lists of qualified individuals from among whom I would later select men and women for particular tasks as they should arise. Charles Willis was selected to handle this task, under Governor Adams' direction.

Many documents and proposals come to the President's office which require the immediate help of men with a professional knowledge of law and economics. While the nation's major legal affairs are handled by the Attorney General's office, and economic questions are primarily the business of the Council of Economic Advisers, innumerable day-to-day questions arise in which advice and counsel on these subjects is needed in short order. The Special Counsel is the President's lawyer, so to speak. He examines memoranda coming from the Attorney General's office, analyzes and often "translates" them before putting them on the President's desk. The Economic Assistant helps to assess the economic problems that are brought to the President from the Secretaries of the Treasury, Commerce, and Labor, and the Council of Economic Advisers. A third duty of importance is the responsibility for scheduling appointments, of sorting and sifting requests both from those whom the President wants and has to see and those who were seeking an opportunity to come to his office. This job requires tact, agility, and the ability to establish priorities.

In naming men to these three posts I decided to make a somewhat temporary arrangement. I had come to know and respect Thomas E.

Stephens, a New York lawyer who had been active during the political campaign. I had originally intended to appoint him Special Counsel, but because of his broad acquaintance with members of the government, particularly in the Republican party, I decided to give him the title of Special Counsel (the post he wanted at first) but to ask him to be responsible for appointments. In the meantime, I made another lawyer friend, Bernard M. Shanley of New Jersey, Acting Special Counsel. Dr. Gabriel Hauge, intelligent, widely informed, and of the highest integrity, became my personal economic adviser.

I created one position because of experiences in the preceding political campaign. As I toured the nation I had often been visited by representatives of what are called the minority groups. These groups had special, urgent problems which, it seemed to me, would require particular attention and study in the government. To meet the need of a specialist who could keep me advised of minority viewpoints, I found a buoyant young lawyer named Max Rabb, who had been administrative assistant to Cabot Lodge when Cabot was a senator. Because of Mr. Rabb's apparent enthusiasm and appetite for work, I later assigned him an additional duty, as Staff Secretary for the Cabinet.

One indispensable member of the White House Staff was the Executive Clerk, William J. Hopkins. A professional public servant—"as non-political as the Washington Monument," one reporter described him—he had served in the White House since the days of President Hoover. He knew more about—as he still does—procedure in all areas of government than anyone else with whom I have come in contact.

To assist me in preparing personal statements, certain correspondence, and drafts of speeches, I initially selected Emmet J. Hughes, followed several months later by an old friend who had been at Columbia and SHAPE with me, Dr. Kevin McCann, and by Bryce Harlow. During my entire eight years in the White House, Dr. McCann was president of Defiance College, in Ohio, but he was always ready and willing to come back to help me when I needed him—which was often.

At the top of the staff was, of course, Governor Sherman Adams. His task was to coordinate all of these sections and their operations, to make certain that every person in them understood the purport and the details of each directive issued, and to keep me informed of appropriate developments on a daily basis. He did not lay down rigid rules to restrict the staff members in their access to me; they worked flexibly, with a voluntary cooperation based on mutual friendship and respect.

Special groups and aides in the Executive Office of the President included the Council of Economic Advisers, first headed by Dr. Arthur F. Burns, a professor from Columbia University and one of the most brilliant economists in the United States; the Planning Board, which served the

National Security Council and was headed by General Robert Cutler, a Boston trust-company executive; and my adviser on psychological warfare problems, C. D. Jackson, now publisher of *Life,* a man who had had a considerable experience in this work during World War II. Then, of course, Joseph M. Dodge, as Director of the Bureau of the Budget, had by the nature of his duties the status of a direct personal adviser, counselor, and assistant to the President.

Alongside and supporting all these staffs was a selected group of first-class secretaries. My own confidential secretary, Mrs. Whitman, and each of those who was originally selected as the head of the secretarial group in each important section remained with me during the eight years of my two terms. They constituted a well-knit, knowledgeable, and efficient team, and all of them became my good friends.

Very quickly after my inauguration I learned another sad lesson about making appointments requiring Senate confirmation. I had planned to name Val Peterson, former governor of Nebraska, as ambassador to India, but in preliminary consultations with members of the Senate I encountered the vehement objections of Senators Hugh Butler and Dwight Griswold, both from Nebraska. They informed me that if I should send his name to the Senate they would find it necessary to state on the Senate floor that he was "personally objectionable"; the Senate has normally honored such an announcement by a senator from the same state by refusing to confirm the nomination. Their objections, they told me, did not involve his personal qualifications or character—which I knew to be beyond cavil—merely his political standing in their state. This seemed indefensible to me. I told both that I emphatically disapproved of their attitude but I was not going to embarrass Val Peterson and would appoint him to some responsible position where their attitude would be ineffective and his influence more pronounced. Through my eight years in office he served, in succession, as a member of the White House Staff, as federal Civil Defense Administrator, and—after his political enemies were gone—as ambassador to Denmark.

Like the appointment of Secretary Wilson, this case caused me to ponder the question of senatorial approval of nominations within the Executive branch. I believe that the custom of allowing one disgruntled senator to block an appointment by the phrase "personally objectionable" is unjustified and should be disavowed by the Senate. Indeed, I should like to see an amendment to the Constitution providing that any nomination within the Executive branch only—excluding judges, appointees to regulatory commissions, and the like—should be automatic unless, by a two-thirds majority, the Senate should reject it.

Of course, the matter of patronage is always present. I was scarcely nominated at Chicago when I was besieged by people seeking, condi-

tional upon my future election, promises for appointments for themselves
or for their friends. Arthur Krock, a veteran of the press corps whom I
admire, wrote a story in the first few days of my administration about
President Lincoln's troubles with patronage. Lincoln, thinking of the constant importunities for special favors with which he was constantly
bombarded while in the Presidency, once remarked, when told by the
doctors that he had a mild form of smallpox, "Now I have something I
can give everybody."

Faced with patronage problems, I recalled the pressures of the early
New Deal days. They had been so pervasive that they had reached me
when I was acting as an assistant to General MacArthur, who as Chief
of Staff had the job of organizing the Civilian Conservation Corps in
1933. While the work was going on, the War Department was charged
with a fault that seems ironic now: New Deal Democrats protested that all
the Reserve officers being called to duty were Republicans. The charge
was ridiculous; our records showed nothing about an officer's political
affiliation. But it did indicate how seriously these questions concern a
politician.

Well aware that there would be a bombardment of petitions for jobs
at the start of a new administration, I was determined to strengthen the
morale of the career Civil Service. Early in 1953 I appointed Philip
Young as chairman of the Civil Service Commission and as my own chief
adviser on personnel, and I backed him to the hilt. I rejected a suggestion
that every department should have the authority to discharge 10 per cent
of its people without regard to existing regulations. And I rejected repeated
demands from senators that I get rid of Young himself and throw open
the gates to political office seekers.

*   *   *

Many other matters, large and small, crowded the ensuing days, but
of all these the most urgent was that of preparing a suitable State of the
Union message, which, after arranging the date with congressional leaders,
I was to deliver on February 2.

With the chance for new policies and ideas to come into the federal
government after twenty years of another philosophy, I wanted to make
it clear that we would not be simply a continuation of the New Deal and
Fair Deal, either in purpose or execution.

"Our industrial plant is built," Franklin D. Roosevelt declared in a
famous speech in 1932, when the United States had a gross national
product of $58 billion—less than 30 per cent (in constant dollars) of what
it is today. And he went on, "The problem just now is whether under existing conditions it is not overbuilt. Our last frontier has long since been

reached. . . . Our task now is not discovery or exploitation of natural resources, or necessarily producing more goods. It is the soberer, less dramatic business of administering resources and plants already in hand . . . of distributing wealth and products more equitably. . . ."

I did not share the belief that the American economy was overbuilt; that parceling out scarcities was the way to economic justice; that the federal government had to establish a rigid economic order for the whole country; that only a Niagara of federal spending could power the country's economic progress; and that, all other things being equal, the federal government deserved first opportunity and had the right to solve any major problem that might arise in the nation.

In initiating a reversal of trends based on such beliefs—trends which by 1953 were twenty years old—we were setting in motion revolutionary activity. We suffered no delusion that such a revolution could become a reality through the frenzied drama of a first one hundred days, or that it could be the work of improvisation, however clever.

I therefore wanted to outline in the State of the Union message the philosophy of the new administration.

This message would be one of my most important pronouncements of policy; in every possible way I sought information, opinions, and advice on every subject that I thought might appropriately be included. During the twelve days between my inauguration and the delivery of the talk I made it the principal subject of two Cabinet and one National Security Council meetings. Among the many I saw was Senator Taft, with whom I had a long talk on reduction of federal expenditures and plans for the removal of governmental controls over the economy. As before, we were in substantial agreement as to principle.

In spite of study and research I was not certain that the message achieved exactly the tone I desired; possibly it contained too many details. I find in my files a note expressing my feelings, written on the morning of February 2:

> Today I give my first "State of the Union" talk before a Joint Session of the Congress. I feel it is a mistake for a new Administration to be talking so soon after inauguration; basic principle, expounded in an inaugural talk is one thing—but to begin talking concretely about a great array of specific problems is quite another. Time for study, exploration, and analysis is necessary. But—the Republicans have been so long out of power they want and probably need—a pronouncement from their President as a starting point. This I shall try to give. I hope— and pray—that it does not contain blunders that we will later regret.

At noon that day, having reached the Capitol and met an escorting committee of members from both houses, I proceeded with them to the entrance of the chamber of the House of Representatives and heard the doorkeeper, Tom Kennamer, call out, "Mr. Speaker, the President of the United States!" (It was the first time in our century—possibly in our history—when a President, preparing to deliver his first State of the Union message, could recall that this was the second time he had addressed a joint session of Congress. The first occasion was when I came back, temporarily, to the United States shortly after V-E Day in 1945.)

The principles of the message echoed those I had expounded during the political campaign just completed. They had as a backdrop the dark international reality outlined in the Inaugural Address—the recognition that the "forces of good and evil are massed and armed and opposed as rarely before in history," that "freedom is pitted against slavery, lightness against the dark."

Assuming these facts, I announced at the outset of the message these four aims:

> Application of America's influence in world affairs with such fortitude and such foresight that it will deter aggression and eventually secure peace;
> Establishment of a national administration of such integrity and such efficiency that its honor at home will ensure respect abroad;
> Encouragement of those incentives that inspire creative initiative in our economy, so that its productivity may fortify freedom everywhere; and
> Dedication to the well-being of all our citizens and to the attainment of equality of opportunity for all, so that our Nation will ever act with the strength of unity in every task to which it is called.

To others these may have been banal generalities. For me they were principles to which I intended to adhere.

In that first message to the Congress I announced that the government would seek to deter aggression and work for peace through a clear, consistent, and confident foreign policy. I pointed out that our foreign policy must be the product of genuine, continuous bipartisan cooperation exercised by both the Executive and the Legislative branches of the government. I hoped there would be no more disputes between Congress and President, such as those over our earlier policy in Europe, in China, and in Korea. It must be, I went on, a coherent global policy—one which did not put Asia first or Europe first or write off countries just because they were small or just because they were captive. As the Communist offense was one and global, the Free World's defense must be one and global. Under such a policy, I said, the United States would never acquiesce in the enslavement of any people in order to purchase fancied gain for ourselves.

In recent history it had been necessary for us to enter a war to prevent the overrunning of a small nation by a larger one. In the purpose of heading off such aggression, I said, mutual security would mean that "we shall give help to other nations in the measure that they strive earnestly to do their full share of the common task." No wealth of aid, I added, could compensate for poverty of spirit.

We would do all we could to get the countries of Western Europe to unite. And we would put our weight behind profitable and equitable world trade.

The biggest single headline of the message came in the announcement that I was issuing instructions that the Seventh Fleet, patrolling the waters between the island of Formosa and the Chinese mainland, no longer be employed to shield Communist China.

"In June 1950," I said, "following the aggressive attack on the Republic of Korea, the United States Seventh Fleet was instructed both to prevent attack upon Formosa and also to insure that Formosa should not be used as a base of operations against the Chinese Communist mainland." In the meantime the Chinese Communists had invaded Korea and attacked United Nations forces there. "Consequently," I added, "there is no longer any logic or sense in a condition that required the United States Navy to assume defensive responsibilities on behalf of the Chinese Communists." I assured the world that "this order implies no aggressive intent on our part," but I made it plain that "we certainly have no obligation to protect a nation fighting us in Korea."

It separated those who believed that the Chinese Communists were, if not agrarian reformers, at least agreeable men susceptible to reason, from those who realized that these Communists—like Communists everywhere—respect only force and hold fidelity to the pledged word in contempt.

The practical value of the announcement was simply this: like my visit to Korea, it put the Chinese Communists on notice that the days of stalemate were numbered; that the Korean War would either end or extend beyond Korea. It thus helped, I am convinced, to bring that war to a finish.

In that State of the Union message I announced policies which my associates and I were to pursue for the next eight years: to improve efficiency in defense; to reduce deficits, balance the budget, check inflation, and release the forces of private economic initiative; to cleanse the government of security risks and improve the efficiency and organization of the federal establishment.

Underlying these separate declarations was a realization of their connection—the connection between our ability to see international dangers and our ability to meet them with toughened military defenses; the connection between military strength, economic strength, and the health and education and welfare of our people; the connection between military strength, our productive power, the welfare of our people, and the honesty and integrity of men in public office.

All, in my view, went—and go—together.

"The hope of freedom itself depends, in real measure," I said, "upon our strength, our heart, and our wisdom."

I urged that we be strong in arms. This meant also that we had to be strong in the source of all our armaments—our productivity.

To stimulate that productivity I dwelt on the need for removing political controls over the American economy.

Our economic strength had developed, historically, freely and without artificial and arbitrary governmental controls. In times of national emergency, I said, controls had a role to play, but our whole system was based on the assumption that controls were not the answer. We were living in an international situation that was neither an emergency demanding full mobilization nor was it peace. We were going to be forced to learn many new things as we went along, clinging to what worked, discarding what did not. The weight of the evidence was against controls.

They had not prevented inflation; they had not kept down the cost of living. Ballooning costs and depreciating dollars were a characteristic of the time but we did not have to accept this passively. Accordingly, I said in the message, I did not intend to ask for a renewal of the present wage and price controls when the present legislation expired. We would take steps to eliminate controls in an orderly manner. Prices would change, some up, some down. But remove them we would.

"In facing all these problems—wages, prices, production, tax rates, fiscal policy, deficits—everywhere we remain constantly mindful that the time for sacrifice has not ended."

After delivering the State of the Union message I returned to the White House. Within hours I was presiding over a meeting on bringing wage and price controls to an end.

*   *   *

On the day I delivered the State of the Union message there were price ceilings on millions of products in American stores—tens of thousands of little white tags listing the lawful upper price limit on products, as set by the Office of Price Stabilization. The OPS, with its Washington headquarters in temporary buildings on the Mall, had a web of regional and district offices, and more than ten thousand employees scattered all over the country futilely trying to keep the lid on the cost of items from toasters, irons, and frying pans to textiles, clothes, and gasoline. On that afternoon also, millions of American men and women were working under wage ceilings set by the Wage Stabilization Board, a body

Madison Square Garden rally, February 8, 1952

"[Jacqueline] Cochran told me about the opposition of the so-called 'pros' in politics, who, although part of the Eisenhower group, believed that no meeting of this kind, held after the completion of a Garden fight the same evening, could possibly draw a crowd at midnight. They felt that a poor turnout would slow up the Eisenhower movement. . . .''

WE CAN WIN WITH IKE WE CAN WIN WITH IKE

Reunion in New York

"When I reached the city I already knew that a visit from Prime Minister Churchill was imminent. I was happy with the chance to see once again one of the outstanding figures of our time. Our meeting took place at the home of our mutual friend, Bernard Baruch, whose friendship with the Prime Minister dated from the days of World War I.... I warned against the dangers of any concern in world opinion that we meant to form a two-power 'coalition'."

En route to the inauguration

"To reach the Capitol, custom decreed that the outgoing and incoming Presidents ride down Pennsylvania Avenue together. The only comment of any consequence that I can recall during the short ride to the Capitol was asking the President the identity of the person who had ordered my son back from the combat area of Korea to be present at the inauguration. . . ."

Korea: The End of Bloodshed

"American casualties had reached a total of 21,000 killed, 91,000 wounded, and 13,000 missing. . . . I considered several possible lines of action. First of all would be to let the war drag on. . . . Continuing this way seemed to me intolerable."

In Korea as President-elect

Patrol duty at Kumgangsan

The day begins for the Chief Executive in the oval room of the West Wing

"The office of the President of the United States, as compared to the sumptuous quarters of many business leaders and of most Cabinet officials, is a surprisingly plain room."

Also shown: Executive Clerk William J. Hopkins

A handshake from grandson David at Augusta, Georgia

made up of four members from management, four from labor, and four from the "general public," with a stormy history of resignations, new appointments, and bad feelings.

The organizations, their bureaucratic methods, the ceiling prices, ceiling wages, price tags, compliance posters, and endless paper work had outlived their usefulness. We were determined to get rid of them.

There was no lack of dire predictions on what would happen if price controls were taken away. In May of 1952 President Truman had urged their continuation. At the height of the campaign that year a Democratic spokesman announced that 88 per cent of American housewives wanted controls kept on; he said they should be made even stronger. Accordingly, in the last days of the campaign, Governor Stevenson pledged "vigorous price controls" if the American people would elect him.

We rejected these views. But the question of how to remove controls remained. Should they meet quick and sudden death, as Secretary Humphrey and Secretary Wilson urged? Or should we extinguish them slowly, as Cabot Lodge and Harold Stassen recommended, to avoid skyrocketing prices? Arthur Flemming, Director of the Office of Defense Mobilization, took a middle position: we should lift controls gradually, category by category, but soon. Decontrols should begin that very week. Wages should be decontrolled in one action, and so at the same time should the prices of many consumer goods, including meats, furniture, and textiles. This was the plan I decided to use. Four days later I signed Executive Order 10432, and wage controls—along with some price controls—were history.

Six days later, on February 12, Dr. Flemming presented proposals for further decontrols. After a discussion in which Joseph Dodge warned that price rises would increase defense costs, and Foster Dulles reminded us that a worsening of the international situation might require the reimposition of controls, I remarked to the Cabinet that we could not live our lives under emergency measures and anticipated economic eruptions. Then I directed the decontrol of another group of items, including crude rubber, soap, poultry, lead, and glass. Controls on other items— among them tobacco, coal, and farm machinery—were to remain for a brief time, and controls on critical defense items for as long as necessary. We supported legislation to keep rent controls on until the state legislatures could deal with the problem.

The administration was not going to rigidly follow economic doctrine regardless of human hardship. I warned the congressional leaders at one meeting that we must always keep uppermost our concern for the individual, because "economic laws are sometimes slow to operate" and people can get hurt.

On the morning of March 5 I could tell the press that "I have been gratified to see that there has been little discernible evidence that anyone is trying to gouge, or take advantage of the situation." Prices were holding steady. They continued to hold remarkably steady through the administration's eight years. In 1951 Winston Churchill based his comeback campaign—victoriously—on the slogan "Set the People Free." In February 1953, with the sweeping away of economic controls, we had begun to do just that in the United States.

Now the administration (familiar with the history of the control system, which during its lifetime had seemed to be less a lid clamped on a boiling pot than an express elevator headed for the roof) deliberately took on the heavy responsibility of watching closely every economic indicator and of being ready to take any action necessary to strengthen the country's economic health. One of the most significant of these indicators is the consumer price index—which shows what consumers are paying for goods and services now by comparison with what they paid at a fixed date in the past.

Between 1945 and 1952 the consumer price index had gone up nearly 50 per cent; the value of the dollar went down more than 33 per cent. The price of children's shoes went up 73 per cent, of men's shoes 93 per cent. The price of white bread doubled; so did the price of a plow. The price of a semiprivate room in a hospital went up 170 per cent. Round-steak and veal-cutlet prices nearly tripled.

In nearly five of these eight years—from January, 1945 to June 30, 1947, and from September, 1950 to January, 1953—controls had been law. And the curious fact is that after a Republican Congress took the controls off—from 1948 to 1949—the consumer price index actually went down.[1]

Faced with these facts, one worker in a hundred protected his family with a clause in his contract—an escalator clause which would tie his wages to the tail of the price kite.[2] But the other workers whose wages were not hooked to prices had to run as fast as they could just to stay even. Moreover, some of those who were intent on stopping inflation felt that wage escalator clauses tied to the cost-of-living index were themselves inflationary.

*   *   *

Among many measures to restore stability to the dollar, one in particular commended itself: a rejection of a persistent policy of massive deficit

[1] The postwar figures (1957–59=100); 1945: 62.7; 1946: 68.0; 1947: 77.8; 1948: 83.8; 1949: 83.0; 1950: 83.8; 1951: 90.5; 1952: 92.5.
[2] By June of 1950 approximately 500,000 workers had such clauses; the civilian labor force then totaled approximately 63 million.

spending by the national government—of spending more than the government took in.

I had announced, in a 1952 campaign speech at Peoria, Illinois, that it would be a goal of the new administration to cut federal spending, to eliminate the budget deficit, and to reduce taxes. Throughout the campaign, to illustrate inflation I had used a length of board (sawed to the breaking point in two places) to represent the buying power of a 1945 dollar. To demonstrate the decline in the dollar between 1945 and 1952, I would break off the first third of the board. To illustrate the decline that was probable with eight more years of Fair Deal policies, I would break off another chunk of the board, ending up with a wooden equivalent of a thirty-three-cent dollar in terms of 1945 values. We expended a large pile of lumber in this lesson, but the point got across.

Whether used in a household, a business, or the federal government, the word "budget" conjures up visions of hard work, tough compromises, and regret—the last because of unnecessary expenditures of earlier years. The making of a federal budget imposes one of the most burdensome problems that confronts responsible officials. Seldom if ever will a government department recommend a reduction in current expenditures —the demand for more and more sums out of the federal Treasury is incessant and insatiable. Invariably the aggregate of these annual requests far exceeds the amounts projected in income.

Yet the objective of any conscientious budget maker is to balance the budget during the business cycle, and in recent times the federal budget makers have had to keep before their eyes, additionally, the depressing picture of a national debt of appalling size—a debt that they feel, or should feel, the necessity for reducing. Congress, of course, jealously holds on to the purse strings of government, and at first glance it would seem that it could limit spending through the simple expedient of specifying by law the maximum size of the debt. But though the Congress has time and time again enacted laws of this exact import, the effort has had limited effect. When the federal debt nears its legal limit, the Congress passes a new law setting the limit higher. The Congress, as a whole, has never been sufficiently committed to frugality and efficiency, in spite of the vast expenditures required for inescapable costs of government, to withstand pressures of special groups within the body politic and the determination of a few self-seeking political leaders to use the Treasury for furthering personal and party ambitions.

When my administration took over the reins of government in 1953, there was no one among my immediate associates not dedicated, in principle, to the proposition that both federal expenditures and the public debt must be reduced. We believed this to be vital to the expansion of our economy and the future prosperity of the nation.

We also knew that tax rates were so high, partly because of the requirements of World War II and the Korean conflict, that there was some likelihood of destroying the incentive—and the opportunity—of people to save and invest and create jobs. During the 1952 political campaign I had frequently voiced the hope that tax relief could be accorded within a reasonable time; otherwise, I thought serious results would be experienced.

As we began our studies, many people believed that federal expenditures and the national debt had become so great and accompanying tax rates so high that we faced the distinct possibility of living in a permanently controlled economy. If this situation were allowed to continue indefinitely, the country could not long pretend to be one of private, competitive enterprise; we would be accepting a controlled economy as a permanent feature of our society. The cloud of an unwanted socialism seemed to be, at least faintly, appearing on the economic horizon.

Convinced that only through a free and expanding economy could both our marvelous productivity and political liberty be assuredly sustained, we followed the move to eliminate controls with one that made stark necessity the single guide for budgeted expenditures. It was a backbreaking task.

Naturally, we all expected that the budget we inherited for fiscal year 1954 would once again be out of balance; and so it was, by nearly $10 billion. What we did not previously know was that our predecessors had piled on top of this mountainous debt additional C.O.D. purchases—largely in defense contracts—with no income whatsoever in sight to pay for them upon their arrival, over the next few years. These purchases totaled more than $80 billion—more than all the expenditures of the federal government put together from 1789 through World War I.

"The federal government," in Mr. Dodge's words, "resembled a family that had consistently lived well beyond its means; had undergone five years of severe adversity (related to World War II); had only three times in twenty years provided itself with more income than it had spent; had acquired a debt over four times its yearly income; owed more than a year's income on C.O.D.'s that would have to be paid for on delivery; normally had about one month's living expenses in the bank; had relatively little margin before reaching a fixed limit on its borrowing; faced an impending 10 per cent reduction in its income; and had no immediate plans for changing its habits."

The federal government, of course, could never default on paying its debts; but to meet its I.O.U.'s it would have to mire itself into deeper debt.

In addition to the sorry balance sheet we inherited, we had Republican promises to contend with—the promises of some lawmakers to balance the budget immediately and cut taxes no matter what the result. Representative Dan Reed of upstate New York, for example, filed a bill to reduce individual income taxes and announced his intention as chairman of the House Ways and Means Committee, which examined every piece of tax legislation, to let the excess-profits tax expire on June 30. His plan would cost the federal government $3.5 billion in revenue. Senator Taft, while agreeing to the extension of the excess-profits tax in 1953, was by no means disposed to go along the following year with a budget out of balance.

These facts put the administration in the middle. I, too, wanted reduced expenditures and balanced budgets, but I could never approve a plan to slash necessary defense spending just to contrast Republican economy with Democratic fiscal irresponsibility. Of course the day of deficits had to come to an end. As I told the Republican Legislative leaders later that year, if the Republicans had to continue deficit spending, "those others" might as well be in charge. But time was needed.

We all knew that given the prior administration's $78.6 billion budget for expenditures in the 1954 fiscal year (July 1, 1953 to July 1, 1954), there was not much elbow room to work in: $55.6 billion of that budget, or 70 per cent, went for the three major national-security items.[3] Another $14.4 billion went for relatively uncontrollable major programs under existing legislation, such as interest on the national debt, veterans' and agricultural programs, and grants to states for public assistance and unemployment compensation. Only $8.6 billion for other classes of spending was projected—not much in which to find savings sufficient to cancel out a deficit originally estimated at nearly $10 billion.

Recognizing the difficulty, on February 3 Budget Director Dodge, with my approval, sent to the head of every Executive-branch agency a memorandum outlining the policy for revising the budget. Every agency was to make a progressive reduction in the number of its employees, to proceed only with construction projects which were clearly essential, and in doing so, "to employ the strictest standards of economy" and to question the necessity for every program.

Persistently but selectively in those first months of 1953 we cut our inherited budget for fiscal year 1954; we scaled down the request for new obligational authority (new appropriations) from $72.9 billion to $63.2 billion and the estimated total expenditures from $78.6 billion to $72.1 billion.

On April 30 I met with the Legislative leaders. Describing our study of the problems and costs of national security, I told them it would be impossible for us to arrive at a balanced budget immediately; a too rapid reduction in the budget, I said, would have bad repercussions both

[3] Department of Defense (military functions); the Mutual Security Administration; and the Atomic Energy Commission.

at home and abroad. Roger Kyes, Deputy Secretary of Defense, pointed out that to get even this far we had had to make a cut in new appropriations in the military budget by $7 billion, justified only by the hopeful outlook for an early armistice in Korea. The upshot, I said, was a reduction of the deficit from the prior administration's $9.9 billion to less than $4 billion. (The actual deficit turned out to be $3.1 billion.)

The news astounded and upset Senator Taft. This administration, he argued heatedly, was spending almost as much as the preceding one, and the result would be either more debt or more taxes, and the certain defeat of Republican candidates in 1954. Two thirds of the Republican Congress, he predicted, would vote to cut the administration's revised budget, and the Republican party would be split then and there.

He recognized that the lion's share of the budget went into national security. But the trouble, he asserted, was with the people responsible for the military part of the budget. "I have no confidence whatsoever," he said, "in their judgment or their ability to break away from recommendations they have made in the past. There should be a complete resurvey of all military demands and a reduction all along the line." In an obviously emotional state, he went on to say he had opposed a tax cut this year, but could not do so again next year. "What has happened to the Republican hope," he wanted to know, "to get expenditures under the $70 billion mark at once?"

Foster Dulles, George Humphrey, and Joe Dodge, noting my reaction, jumped in, and each made a small speech. Finally, when they had diplomatically given me time to cool off before answering, I responded to Senator Taft's attack.

Of course, like all others present, I deeply respected Senator Taft's views and his dedication to the nation's welfare, but I could not agree that the country should have, or wanted, a tax cut ahead of a balanced budget or a balanced budget ahead of national security. In answer to Senator Taft I took time to review the international situation and this country's global strategy. I referred to the dangers in Iran and pointed out that Western Europe and the oil of the Middle East must in no circumstances fall to Communism. I reminded him of the alarming news of a new Communist invasion of Laos and the continuing wars in Korea and Vietnam. The important thing, I emphasized, was to take hold of the upward trend in appropriations and bend it down. I did not agree that the proposed budget would ruin Republicans in 1954, and in any event I did not believe that the administration could endanger the security of the United States by proposing an inadequate program. In this matter I felt competent to make a more accurate estimate than he could. "Regardless of consequences," I said, "the nation's military security will take first priority in my calculations."

Senator Taft soon calmed down and apologized; he was very much a man and had become my good friend. Though no one in the room knew the fact at that moment, he was even then living through the last painful months of his life.

The more we studied the financial statement we had inherited, the clearer it became that drastic action was indicated.

I wanted to see a tax reduction. But I wanted even more to stop the deterioration of the currency which had been going on for so many years under unsound fiscal and monetary policies. And, between the Scylla of a deep deficit and the Charybdis of an inadequate military budget, we had to make a start without encountering either.

Since 1930 there had been budget surpluses in only four years: 1930, 1947, 1948, and 1951. I had not promised, and I could not in good conscience produce, a balanced budget which would add fiscal year 1954 to that tiny group of years in the black. But I was determined, if humanly possible, to carry on the fight to conduct a revolution which would reverse the trend of the budgets of the past twenty years. It took us two years to do it, but we did achieve a balanced budget, while at the same time providing adequately for every essential function of government.

Moreover, it was part of our response to the global threat we faced. The Soviet leaders, I said in a nationwide address on May 19, "have plainly said that free people cannot preserve their way of life and at the same time provide enormous military establishments. Communist guns, in this sense, have been aiming at an economic target no less than a military target. . . .

"The course we must set for ourselves is a difficult one. It must avoid, on the one hand, the indefinite continuance of a needlessly high rate of federal spending in excess of federal income. It must avoid, on the other hand, any penny-wise, pound-foolish policy that could, through lack of needed strength, cripple the cause of freedom everywhere."

I knew that this approach did not scream shrilly of crisis and emergency, but it was realistic and at the same time quietly revolutionary. It called for some changes in our concept of the role of the National Security Council. On the last day of the preceding administration, top officials, in a report to the National Security Council, had recommended programs which—though never approved—would have run up an additional aggregate budget deficit over the next five years of $44 billion.

To help correct this kind of habit, on March 23 I announced that the Secretary of the Treasury, George Humphrey, would attend the meetings of the National Security Council. Thus the responsibilities of the NSC as an advisory body were broadened to recognize the relationship between military and economic strength.

On July 20 I approved the new plan requiring that every National Security Council policy paper include the estimated cost of the program it proposed. For example, it was unconscionable, I believed, that after months of work the Director of the Bureau of the Budget himself could never determine, within reasonable limits, the cost of the military operations in Korea.

It is easy to ignore the connection between national security and fiscal responsibility. To be sure, the Congress can appropriate bigger and bigger mountains of dollars—and cause deeper and deeper deficits—to pay for weapons which through this very process constantly increase in price. Unbalanced budgets and increasing costs have a reciprocal effect; as deficits deepen, prices tend to rise. But I am convinced it is far better to tailor defense to need, to scrutinize appropriations, to balance the budget over the business cycle, and thus help keep the price of weapons, like the price of everything else, from multiplying. In the five years between the end of World War II and the outbreak of the war in Korea, for example, the price of iron and steel in the United States nearly doubled. Such price increases, spiraling indefinitely upward out of anyone's control, I am convinced, can eventually wreck the nation's security. At home they provoke discontent among our people. Overseas they can lead to a decline in the reliability of the dollar in the international market—a decline which vitiates our friends' confidence in us and tempts our enemies to see us as weaker than we are.

Many military planners had a penchant for selecting a specific year in which they estimated an attack would come. We set another goal: to keep our defenses powerful not for one particular moment in time— an imaginary moment of greatest possible future danger—but day and night, every minute of every hour, for an indefinite period.

On April 30 I told the reporters at a weekly news conference, "This policy of ours . . . will not be tied to any magic, critical year [a year of estimated maximum national danger] which then has to be 'stretched out' because of economic or production problems, but will be based on the sounder theory that a very real danger not only exists this year, but may continue to exist for years to come; that our strength, which is already very real, must now be made stronger, not by inefficient and expensive starts and stops, but by steady continuous improvements. . . ."

Our earlier failure to keep a reasonable military posture, I said—a failure that required us to withdraw troops from Korea—may have been one of the important factors that helped trigger the Korean War.

I emphasized that I did not foresee a radically new kind of defense establishment, but that we did want to concentrate more on the latest weapons. In the build-up of this kind of strength we were determined to get "the latest and best to prevent the factor of obsolescence from over-taking us too quickly."

That remark of April 30 foreshadowed the later unveiling of a change in American defense: a greater reliance on deterrent nuclear weapons, which could be delivered by the Strategic Air Command and later by intermediate- and long-range ballistic missiles.

It was obvious that any change in military plans would mash the toes of special interest groups and inspire long and loud protests. Some of this was not too unpleasant to hear. The term "war babies," applied to some of our mushrooming munitions firms, was not one of endearment. But munitions firms were not the only objectors. Each service had its own association or league which, including in its membership some weapons producers, represented the interests of the particular service before the Congress and the public and, at the same time, served indirectly at least as a lobby for the affected manufacturers. "This administration," I had told the Legislative leaders that same morning, "will just have to go ahead, make responsible decisions, and then face the clamorings of the league for this and the league for that and other special interest groups."

But beyond this, I told the assembled reporters, "Security based upon heavy armaments is a way of life that has been forced upon us and on our allies. We don't like it; in fact, we hate it. But so long as such an unmistakable, self-confirmed threat to our freedom exists, we will carry these burdens with dedication and determination."

*   *   *

In the 1952 political campaign we had promised to overhaul the entire creaking federal establishment. On January 29 I signed my first Executive Order, establishing the President's Advisory Committee on Government Organization. Nelson Rockefeller was the chairman of this committee, and Dr. Arthur S. Flemming and my brother Dr. Milton S. Eisenhower were members. It based its initial recommendations on a report prepared by experts at Temple University, who in turn were studying the recommendations of the first Hoover Commission on Governmental Reorganization. Out of these studies plus recommendations of members of the Cabinet, came a number of organizational changes.

I had personally defined the duties of the White House Staff and approved the organization under which it was to work.

The Cabinet, from the beginning, met to consider together questions of general public concern and to give me recommendations on new government-wide policies and instructions. In the first six months, for example, the Cabinet discussed such dissimilar questions as Spanish air bases and postal rates. While the Secretary of State and the Postmaster General made the basic presentations, all present were invited to participate in any ensuing argument. I not only found a spirit of teamwork and friendship in the Cabinet, but I also found its deliberations and debates enlightening as I faced important decisions. To improve its usefulness I announced on June 5 a permanent secretariat for Cabinet meetings, a small group which would work up agendas for the discussions and see that all my decisions respecting them were properly reported and communicated to interested parties.

The history of past administrations had recorded much Cabinet bickering, personality conflicts, and end running, tale bearing, and throat cutting. Speaking of "just what use the Cabinet is under this Administration," Harold Ickes (Secretary of the Interior in the 1940s) had written in his diary, "the cold fact is that on important matters we are seldom called upon for advice. We never discuss exhaustively any policy of Government or question of political strategy. The President makes all of his own decisions and, so far at least as the Cabinet is concerned, without taking counsel with a group of advisers. On particular questions he will call into his office persons directly interested, but it is fair to say that the Cabinet is not a general council upon whose advice the President relies or the opinions of which, on important matters, he calls for. Our Cabinet meetings are pleasant affairs, but we only skim the surface of things on routine matters. As a matter of fact, I never think of bringing up even a serious departmental issue at Cabinet meeting, and apparently the other members follow the same policy, at least to a considerable extent."

Such instances do not seem to be among the most happy in American history. They make diverting reading but bad examples. I wanted my own administration free of them.

Constantly in those early months I searched for ways of improving the organization of the entire Executive branch.

Between March 12 and June 1 I sent to the Congress for approval, in accordance with the Reorganization Act of 1949, ten plans for changes in Executive-branch organization.

Reorganization Plan Number One, sent up March 12, established a new department of government, the Department of Health, Education and Welfare. Its principal functions were indicated by its title.

During the campaign, in speeches in Boise, Los Angeles, and other cities, I had hammered home the fact that the Republican party yielded to no one its concern for the human needs of human beings. To implement this promise, we hoped to extend social-security coverage to millions of additional workers.

The new Department of Health, Education and Welfare replaced the old Federal Security Agency, which by 1952 had become a conglomeration of bureaus employing more than thirty-six thousand people, getting its money through sixty-seven active appropriations, spending it at the rate of more than $4 billion a year, and lacking adequate administrative direction and control.[4]

When, on April 11, 1953, Mrs. Hobby, Federal Security Administrator, became Secretary Hobby, the Department of Health, Education and Welfare—the first new Cabinet department established in forty years— was on its way to becoming a far more disciplined and efficient servant of the ever-increasing number of American people.

My interest in organization in those early months of 1953 went to the limits of the federal establishment and beyond them. On March 30 I sent a special message to Congress urging that it set up a commission to study the division of responsibilities among federal, state, and local governments, to take a hard look at all programs of financial aid that reached down from Washington into the state and the individual community. This Commission on Intergovernmental Relations, which became a reality when I signed the legislation into law on July 10, had as its first chairman Clarence Manion, and as its second, an unusually astute man, Meyer Kestnbaum.

The same day I signed into law the bill establishing the second Hoover Commission—a commission to scrutinize specifically the functions and organization of the federal government.

Again and again I emphasized the need for efficient decentralization within each agency of the government. My principal assistants, I insisted, in the interests of sanity and efficiency, should save for themselves time for thinking and study. The only way they could get such time was to delegate as much as possible to their subordinates. "The marks of a good executive," I wrote to the heads of agencies on September 29, 1953, "are courage in delegating work to subordinates and his own skill in coordinating and directing their effort." And I should have added, as I so often did in wartime, to take personal responsibility for mistakes and give subordinates credit for success.

*   *   *

About three weeks after inauguration, we discovered that we had a situation wherein our government had promised to grant Brazil a loan to

[4] It included the Public Health Service, established in 1789; the Office of Education, established in 1867; the Social Security Administration, established in 1935. It had jurisdiction over the Food and Drug Administration, the Office of Vocational Rehabilitation, St. Elizabeth's Hospital for the mentally ill, the American Printing House for the Blind, the Columbia Institution for the Deaf, and Howard University, for Negro students.

help settle up its debts. Although George Humphrey and I believed that $100 million to $150 million was ample, the Brazilians wanted more like $300 million. There followed a two- or three-day round of intensive, heated discussion between the State Department (pro) and the Treasury Department (anti). Finally, State uncovered a note which showed that prior understandings made the government morally obligated to make the entire loan.

George came in on a Saturday morning. "Mr. President," he said, smiling through his tears, "we're hooked."

He showed me the pertinent papers and I signed.

As we got up to leave, he started out one door and I out the other. Then I stopped him. "George," I said, "do you realize that after kicking all this money around, and signing it away like that, I'll be out on a first tee in about thirty minutes at Burning Tree [golf course], fighting over handicap strokes on a one-dollar Nassau?"

In answer to a reporter's question one July morning, I said that we had not done all the things we wanted to do in six months, but "You cannot take a railroad and have a right-angle turn in it . . . ; you have to build a curve." In defense, in setting the economy free, in moving toward a balanced budget, in halting the ascent of prices, in reorganizing the government, we had not attempted to turn the train at a right angle.

But we had rounded a historic curve.

CHAPTER VI

Trouble in NATO,
Suez, Iran, Indochina

Suaviter in modo, fortiter in re.
—*Claudio Aquaviva*

O UR nation, born because of the dedication of its people to liberty and justice, has sought consciously to achieve a just and universal peace in freedom for all people. Hope ran high when, in 1945, many nations' representatives met in San Francisco to establish the United Nations Organization and a world in which law would supplant force as the arbiter in international disputes. That was hope's high point; from then onward every attempt to advance even a single step toward world peace encountered one unsurmountable obstacle—the implacable purpose of the men in the Kremlin to achieve Communist domination of the world.

Years of frustration in their attempts to reason with the increasingly powerful and ruthless Soviet government had led free nations to begin looking anxiously to their own capacity for self-defense. Obviously, free nations, particularly those directly exposed to Soviet threat, would each, standing alone, be in mortal danger. The United Nations of itself could exert no power other than moral, and the Soviets were scornfully contemptuous of any kind of power except materialistic. A degree of unity was essential among the nations so exposed.

Obviously, most of these nations, including even large ones remotely removed from the immediate danger, could not fail to recognize the eventual consequence of permitting the step-by-step domination of smaller countries by the Soviets, bringing the captured nations into the Communist orbit.

"From Stettin in the Baltic to Trieste in the Adriatic, an Iron Curtain has descended across the Continent." Between March of 1946, when at Fulton, Missouri, Winston Churchill spoke these somber words in warning, and January of 1953, when I entered the Presidency, the Communist curtain had also descended across Asia. Communist regimes, their realm now stretching eastward to the China Sea, ruled more than 800 million people.

The answer to Communist ambitions had to be in some form of collective defense. Formal and specific recognition of this need was given expression in the formation of the North Atlantic Treaty Organization, by which, in 1949, most of the nations of Western Europe had come together for security purposes with Canada and the United States.

Soviet propaganda against this organization began at once; it has never ceased. Well knowing that aggression by the whole Western coalition was a total impossibility, the Kremlin described the North Atlantic Treaty Organization as a wicked combination of greedy capitalists dedicated to the destruction of all "peace-loving democracies" and to domination of the uncommitted nations. Through constant repetition of this false charge, the Soviets have tried to create division and suspicion among the members of NATO.

This propaganda has not been a total failure. Though the NATO governments recognize the falsity and shallowness of the Communist cries, they cannot ignore the effect upon many of their less-informed citizens. The constant din of Soviet charges, threats, and lies finally begins to tell. Communist candidates have usually polled 20 per cent or more of the vote in both France and Italy—a tragic commentary on the twisted thinking fed by naïve trust in Communist promises.

The constant flow of this propaganda habitually reaches a peak when, for their own reasons, the Communist leaders want to create a special effect or are engaged in an unusual effort to discredit a NATO activity.

For example, when I set out on a tour of NATO capitals in January of 1951, the Kremlin directed the organization of great protest meetings in some of the cities I was scheduled to visit, with particular attention to Rome and Paris. There Communist strength was calculated to be sufficient to assure the effectiveness of the anti-NATO demonstrations. Intelligence officials had obtained copies of the instructions received by the local Communist organizations and were fully informed as to the scope and intensity of the planned disorders.

Since Rome was the first target city I was to visit, the Communists hoped that the demonstration there would be so impressive that the entire schedule would have to be abandoned. Threats were pasted on billboards, scrawled on convenient garden walls, and repeated in Communist periodicals. Because their propaganda is normally made personal whenever possible, most of the published attacks were directed more against me than against NATO. They charged that I was a cruel, military type, coming to Europe to start an aggressive war no matter what the cost in European lives.

In Rome the effort collapsed because of the efficiency of the local police forces. They watched closely every sensitive area. I left the city without even seeing, as far as I was aware, a single Communist. I saw instead large crowds of loyal Italians who, knowing the purpose of the Soviet propaganda, turned out to show me and the world that their sympathies were on freedom's side.

When we reached Paris, the Communist failure was even more complete, brought about by methods that included one peculiarly and delightfully French. Not only were the police, as usual, efficient, but the French developed a unique counterattack.

One of the ringleaders in the Communist effort was the party's newspaper, *L'Humanité*. Its assaults on me were bitter. But it happened that more than six years earlier I had become known as the "Liberator," a label which in the late summer of 1944 was used almost everywhere, even in laudatory headlines in *L'Humanité*. Now, in preparation for my 1951 visit, the French merely duplicated *L'Humanité*'s 1944 editorials, front pages, and headlines and posted them all over the city, side by side with current editorials from the same paper. Paris started laughing—and one thing the Communists cannot stand is ridicule.

The authorities informed me that all further scheduled anti-NATO demonstrations had been called off by orders of higher Communist authorities, who did not want to run the risk of similar failures in the capitals I was still to visit.

However, Soviet propaganda is relentless, and as President, in early 1953, I sensed that they were again making strenuous efforts to weaken NATO. Moreover, American embassies in Europe were reporting to Secretary Dulles an apprehension there, following my trip to Korea, that the new administration had slight interest in Europe and was fixing its attention instead on the Far East.

These reports dismayed me. From World War II, when I commanded the Allied forces in Europe, through the period when, as Supreme Allied Commander in Europe, my every effort was directed toward strengthening the collective security of the Western nations, to that very moment in early 1953, my conviction about that continent had remained fixed. On February 10 I wrote to General Gruenther, then Chief of Staff of the military forces of NATO:

If any one of my European friends has ever found—in anything I have ever said or done—any reason to believe that my interest in Europe was not continuous, intense and sympathetic and inspired by the realization that America's enlightened self-interest demands the closest cooperation in that region—then I should like to see such an individual point out to me the instance on which he bases his conclusion.

One of my first purposes therefore was to reassure the countries of Western Europe, whose military forces I had so recently commanded, that my interest in them was as strong as ever.

At the same time I had another concern. There were signs that not everyone in Western Europe realized the need for subordinating all lesser issues to that of achieving ever-growing practical cooperation and unity among NATO members. One immense need was ratification of the plan for a unified defense force, or the European Defense Community. Within my first few hours in office I had read messages from both Bonn and Paris describing meetings between Chancellor Adenauer of Germany and Foreign Minister Georges Bidault of France in which assurances were given of the support of both their governments for the principle of the European Defense Community. However, support of heads of government is one thing, support of parliaments is another. Reports in the press were rampant that the concept of a unified military force which would have to include both French and German units was far from accepted by the parliaments which would have to ratify it. For the moment the question was political, not military.

Accordingly, I decided to send Secretary Dulles promptly to several of the European capitals. Harold Stassen, as Director of the Mutual Security Agency, was to accompany him. He would be of assistance in obtaining the views of the European governments, and in analyzing their national needs. The mission was primarily one of observation and listening; Secretary Dulles and Governor Stassen were authorized to make no commitments beyond general reassurances to the Europeans.

As I wrote General Gruenther:

> I sent Secretary Dulles and Governor Stassen to Europe to further the same causes for which you and I have been struggling for the last couple of years. I wanted the European governments to be assured on an official basis that I had neither changed my personal views nor did I have any intention of denying the basic truth that only in collective security was there any real future in the free world. . . .
>
> All this I wanted done in the most courteous and sympathetic way possible—consequently I asked my two associates to go over there and do it personally. At the same time I thought this would dramatize the government's continuing interest in the region.

This was the first of Foster Dulles' overseas trips as Secretary of State, which were to take him, in the next six years, more than half a million miles.

The itinerary of my two emissaries included seven capitals: Rome, Paris, London, Bonn, The Hague, Brussels, and Luxembourg, over a period from the 30th of January to the 8th of February. Even before their departure there were renewed rumblings in the European press. On January 27 Foster Dulles had made a television speech to the nation in which he said:

> . . . It seems as though some of the French people and some of the German people want again to go on their separate ways. This is one of the reasons why President Eisenhower asked me and Mr. Stassen, who directs the Mutual Assistance Program, to go to Europe this week. We want to look the situation over at first hand and see whether this trend to unity is on the upgrade or is on the downgrade.

After assuring his audience that he and Mr. Stassen would be observers only, Mr. Dulles pointed out that the United States had made a big investment in Western Europe on the theory that there could be a greater degree of unity there. Of the $40 billion which we had sent abroad since the end of World War II, almost $30 billion had gone to Western Europe.[1] And he concluded, "If, however, there were no chance, and that I just refuse to believe, but if it appeared there were no chance of getting effective unity, and if in particular France, Germany and England should go their separate ways, then certainly it would be necessary to give a little rethinking to America's own foreign policy in relation to Western Europe."

This remark caused part of the press to describe the visit as a "shock treatment," and it caused anxiety in European capitals, an anxiety which Foster was able to dispel satisfactorily in conversations with Europe's leaders. From each capital he cabled the results.

On February 3, for example:

> Have had useful visit at Paris. Yesterday devoted wholly to talks with top French officials largely in relation to EDC. While political difficulties are great, Stassen and I feel that there is real determination on part of present government, particularly [French Premier] Mayer and [Defense Minister] Pleven, to push this to a successful conclusion. There is still a hard road ahead, but we feel that ultimate success is possible and even probable.

[1] By the end of 1952 United States' grants and credits to foreign countries totaled $40.7 billion. We had made economic and relief grants of $22.7 billion (which included the $13.6-billion Marshall Plan), military grants of $6 billion, and had issued credits (including those for the Export-Import Bank and the $3.7-billion British loan of the 1947 fiscal year) of $11.9 billion.

Your State of Union message was very well received and slight initial concern about Formosa was quickly dissipated, so that French press this morning takes sympathetic non-critical view.

Today we met at SHAPE with Ridgway, Gruenther and many of your former associates, and then with Ismay [Secretary General of NATO], NATO Council and OEEC [the Organization for European Economic Cooperation] and believe we contributed to their morale and to understanding of your administration's friendly policies.

Through more than six years Secretary Dulles made a constant practice, during his travels, of cabling me a summary of the day's events. At the end of his life, those cables, along with other memoranda which we had exchanged—sometimes almost hour by hour—made a stack more than four feet high.

In London, Secretary Dulles also had a highly satisfactory visit, holding discussions on Egypt, Iran, Formosa, and economic matters. Before I had left SHAPE in 1952 both Winston Churchill and Anthony Eden had told me of their great interest, if I should be elected, in the identity of the new American Secretary of State.

Anthony Eden had then expressed the hope that I might appoint someone other than Dulles. From anyone else I would have resented such a suggestion as an unwarranted intrusion in America's affairs. But my long association and friendship with him during war and peace, involving the frankest kind of exchanges between us, made such a remark understandable. So, at that moment, I made no reply except to say that I knew of no other American so well qualified as Foster to take over the duties of that particular office.

This trip provided the Prime Minister and Foreign Secretary with their first opportunity for an official discussion with the new Secretary. Naturally, I hoped that it would mark the beginning of a good relationship.

In Paris and London it was necessary for Foster to meet attacks from both governments on that portion of my State of the Union speech in which I had released the Seventh Fleet from the mission of protecting the China mainland. Concern was greatest in France and Britain, of course, since those nations had substantial interests in the Far East. On February 5 Anthony made a statement in Parliament that Her Majesty's government was convinced that our order to the Seventh Fleet implied no aggressive intent on our part. Concern was dissipated more easily in France than in England, but the British opposition was calmed by Eden's statement. This incident served to illustrate the sensitivity of friendly governments when they are afraid that one of their allies may take precipitous unilateral action.

Their mission completed, Dulles and Stassen returned early in February. David Bruce, formerly ambassador to France, agreed to proceed to Europe to follow up in the six EDC capitals the work which these two emissaries had so well begun.

*   *   *

Stalin was responsible for the anti-NATO propaganda just as he was responsible for the intransigent attitude that all Soviet ambassadors and representatives invariably displayed whenever conferring with free governments on the solution of an international problem. He was recognized both in Moscow and elsewhere in the world as an absolute dictator in the fullest sense of the word and his baneful influence was felt universally.

Before I assumed office Stalin had hinted in one of his rare interviews that he would like to meet with me. I had last met him on a trip to Moscow in August 1945. In long conversations he revealed himself to be what most people suspected: the iron-handed boss of the Soviet Union. He was also a man completely devoid of a sense of humor. For hours I had stood with him in a reviewing stand on top of Lenin's tomb watching Russian male and female athletes demonstrate their prowess in gymnastics.

"This develops the war spirit," Stalin said stolidly. "Your country ought to do more of this."

Even at a movie in the evening he was unable to unbend. We watched a Soviet picture on the capture of Berlin, featuring my old friend Marshal Zhukov with ranks of medals glittering on his best dress uniform. At the movie Stalin sat between Zhukov and me. At one point, I leaned over and said to our interpreter, who was seated directly behind Stalin, "Tell Marshal Zhukov that if he ever loses his job in the Soviet Union he can, on the evidence of this picture, surely get one in Hollywood."

Stalin listened to the translation in silence. "Marshal Zhukov," he informed me in a flat tone, "will never be without a job in the Soviet Union."

Now, more than seven years later, I doubted whether much that was productive could come out of meeting with such a man. Nonetheless, at a news conference on February 25, when a reporter asked if I would agree to leave the United States to meet with Stalin, I answered, "I would meet anybody, anywhere, where I thought there was the slightest chance of doing any good, as long as it was in keeping with what the American people expect of their Chief Executive."

The question became academic. Within ten days Stalin was dead.

Shortly after six o'clock on the morning of March 4, Allen Dulles, the director of the Central Intelligence Agency, telephoned me to say that Stalin had suffered a stroke and that he was believed to be dying.

Before eight o'clock I was in my office meeting with Foster Dulles, General Cutler, C. D. Jackson, and Jim Hagerty to go over the draft of a possible statement which they had already started work on. All that morning, there in my office and in a meeting of the National Security Council which followed, we discussed our possible moves. Although Foster Dulles had some reservations about making any statement at all in the circumstances—it would be a gamble, he thought, because it might be read as an appeal to the Soviet people in mourning to rise against their rulers—I believed the moment was propitious for the introduction of the right word directly into the Soviet Union.

By noon we agreed on this text:

At this moment in history when multitudes of Russians are anxiously concerned because of the illness of the Soviet ruler the thoughts of America go out to all the peoples of the U.S.S.R.—the men and women, the boys and girls—in the villages, cities, farms and factories of their homeland.

They are the children of the same God who is the Father of all peoples everywhere. And like all peoples, Russia's millions share our longing for a friendly and peaceful world.

Regardless of the identity of government personalities, the prayer of us Americans continues to be that the Almighty will watch over the people of that vast country and bring them, in His wisdom, opportunity to live their lives in a world where all men and women and children dwell in peace and comradeship.

The following evening, while I was at dinner with my wife, Jim Hagerty telephoned to report an announcement just made on Radio Moscow: "The heart of the comrade and inspired continuer of Lenin's will, the wise leader and teacher of the Communist party and the Soviet people— Joseph Vissarionovich Stalin—has stopped beating."

The next day the Soviet government announced the new leaders of the Soviet Union: Georgi Malenkov, Chairman of the Council of Ministers; Lavrenti Beria, First Deputy Chairman and Minister of Internal Affairs; V. M. Molotov, First Deputy Chairman and Foreign Minister; Nikolai Bulganin, First Deputy Chairman and Minister of War. All these became members of the Presidium (the inner ruling group) of the Central Committee of the Communist party, along with several others, including a little-known official named Nikita Khrushchev.

The new leadership in Russia, no matter how strong its links with the Stalin era, was not completely bound to blind obedience to the ways of a dead man. The future was theirs to make. Consequently, a major preoccupation of my mind through most of 1953 was the development of approaches to the Soviet leaders that might be at least a start toward the birth of mutual trust founded in cooperative effort—an essential relationship between the two great powers, if they and other nations were to find the way to universal peace.

Given any progress in the development of such trust, we could "proceed concurrently and constructively with the next great work—the reduction of the burden of armaments now weighing upon the world." The words are from a speech of mine before the American Society of Newspaper Editors on April 16, 1953.

This speech extended an offer and a promise to the new Russian hierarchy. But first I posed the alternative. In the eight years of fear and force engendered by the Soviets since 1945, I said, we had come down a dread road with no turning, where the worst threat was atomic war and the best hope was a life of perpetual terror and tension with the cost of arms draining the wealth and energies of all peoples. I counted that cost:

"Every gun that is made, every warship launched, every rocket fired signifies, in the final sense, a theft from those who hunger and are not fed, those who are cold and are not clothed.

"This world in arms is not spending money alone.

"It is spending the sweat of its laborers, the genius of its scientists, the hopes of its children.

"The cost of one modern heavy bomber is this: a modern brick school in more than thirty cities.

"It is two electric power plants, each serving a town of sixty thousand population.

"It is two fine, fully equipped hospitals.

"It is some fifty miles of concrete highway.

"We pay for a single fighter plane with a half-million bushels of wheat.

"We pay for a single destroyer with new homes that could have housed more than eight thousand people."

This was not a way of life at all, in any true sense, I said. Under a cloud of war, it was humanity hanging from a cross of iron. I argued that we had reached one of those times in the affairs of nations when the gravest choices had to be made, if there was to be a turning toward a just and lasting peace; therefore it was necessary for governments of the world to speak their intentions with simplicity and with honesty.

And I pointed out, "The world knows that an era ended with the death of Joseph Stalin. The extraordinary thirty-year span of his rule saw the Soviet Empire expand to reach from the Baltic Sea to the Sea of Japan. . . .

"The Soviet system shaped by Stalin and his predecessors was born of one world war. It survived with stubborn and often amazing courage a second world war. It has lived to threaten a third."

The new leaders in the Kremlin confronted a Free World aroused by the will to stay free. Our response in Korea and Southeast Asia, our formation of NATO and the European Defense Community demonstrated that the Free World demanded and expected the fullest respect of its rights and interests—and would accord the same respect to others.

"So the new Soviet leadership now has a precious opportunity to awaken, with the rest of the world, to the point of peril reached and to help turn the tide of history.

"Will it do this?

"We do not yet know. Recent statements and gestures of Soviet leaders give some evidence that they may recognize this critical moment.

"We welcome every honest act of peace.

"We care nothing for mere rhetoric.

"We are only for sincerity of peaceful purpose attested by deeds. The opportunities for such deeds are many. The performance of a great number of them waits upon no complex protocol but upon the simple will to do them. Even a few such clear and specific acts, such as the Soviet Union's signature upon an Austrian treaty or its release of thousands of prisoners still held from World War II, would be impressive signs of sincere intent. They would carry a power of persuasion not to be matched by any amount of oratory. . . .

"Again we say: the United States is ready to assume its just part.

"We have already done all within our power to speed conclusion of a treaty with Austria which will free that country from economic exploitation and from occupation by foreign troops."

Then I came to our specific offer. The subject was universal disarmament. I urged that with sincerity of purpose proved by appropriate deeds, "we could proceed concurrently with the next great work—the reduction of the burden of armaments now weighing upon the world. To this end we would welcome and enter into the most solemn agreements."

I suggested a number of channels by which such an objective might be approached, including limitation on numerical strength, on production of strategic materials, and on weapons of great destructiveness.

In addition, I proposed international control of atomic energy and universal prohibition of atomic weapons, with the establishment of adequate safeguards, including a practical system of inspection under the United Nations.

Details of disarmament programs were necessarily critical and complex, I argued, and no nation possessed a perfect, immutable formula. But the formula mattered less than the faith.

"The fruit of success . . . would present the world with the greatest task, and the greatest opportunity, of all . . . : the dedication of the energies, the resources, and the imaginations of all peaceful nations to a new kind of war. This would be a declared total war, not upon any human enemy, but upon the brute forces of poverty and need.

"The peace we seek, founded upon decent trust and cooperative effort among nations, can be fortified, not by weapons of war but by wheat and by cotton, by milk and by wool, by meat and by timber and by rice. These are words that translate into every language on earth. These are needs that challenge this world in arms. . . .

"This government is ready to ask its people to join with all nations in devoting a substantial percentage of the savings achieved by disarmament to a fund for world aid and reconstruction. . . .

"The monuments to this new kind of war would be these: roads and schools, hospitals and homes, food and health.

"We are ready, in short, to dedicate our strength to serving the *needs,* rather than the *fears,* of the world. . . .

"I know of only one question upon which progress waits. It is this: "What is the Soviet Union ready to do?"

Whatever the answer was, let it be plainly spoken, I said. The hunger for peace was too great, the hour in history too late, for any government to mock men's hopés with mere words and promises and gestures.

"If we strive but fail and the world remains armed against itself, it at least need be divided no longer in its clear knowledge of who has condemned humankind to this fate."

I delivered this talk under great difficulty, experiencing one of the most miserable periods, physically, of my life. For a few days I had been taking a brief vacation in Augusta, Georgia, and it was there that I put the finishing touches on the speech. The night before its scheduled delivery I endured an attack, one that several years later was diagnosed as the same kind that occasioned a serious operation for ileitis. I had by no means recovered the following morning, when I had to take the plane for Washington. The doctor provided medicines and sedatives, but when the time came for the luncheon at which my talk was to be made, the pain was such as to cause heavy perspiration on my face and head, and at the same time, chills of a very disturbing kind. The result was that I could concentrate on the text only by supreme effort; at times I became so dizzy that I feared I would faint. Immediately after lunch I had a short period for rest, but unfortunately the day's schedule called for two additional engagements. The first was the President's traditional presence in Washington at the opening game of the American League. Since my promise had been given weeks ahead, I felt it would be putting too important an interpretation on what I thought was a temporary illness if I should cancel the engagement. After leaving the ball game I had another appearance to make, this one in Salisbury, North Carolina, celebrating on that day the two-hundredth anniversary of Rowan County. I spoke for about ten minutes, and the press reported that I seemed to be enjoying myself. Finally, that evening in Augusta, I went to bed and with the continuous care of my very knowledgeable doctor, General Snyder, was able to get back on my feet within another thirty-six hours.

The proposals I set forth in my speech to the editors were deliberately specific. Though I had but little hope they could evoke any immediate favorable response in the Kremlin, I felt it wise to put the nation's deepest aspirations in the record, where they could be examined and studied by all the world, including the Russians. The men in the Kremlin were still in the turmoil of the succession period. For the moment, possibly, they were more anxious about individual survival and position than about Soviet long-term policy and foreign relations. On the assumption that the heads of the hostile system were temporarily torn by internal fear and feud, I believed that American leadership in the Free World might not only negate Soviet plots and plans, but also point out a path for the pursuit of peace that the whole world, including the Soviets, might follow.

Clearly, there are different methods that a man—or a nation—can use in attempting to influence others. I keep on my desk a piece of black wood given to me by Gabriel Hauge and inscribed with a Latin motto attributed to Claudio Aquaviva, a Jesuit general of the late sixteenth century: *Suaviter in modo, fortiter in re* (Gently in manner, strongly in deed). I have always deplored and deprecated table-pounding and name-calling; such methods, I have long believed, are normally self-defeating defense mechanisms. On the world scene, practiced by governments, such manners are tragically stupid and ultimately worthless.

To be effective in the nation's rightful role as a Free World leader, our people and their government should always, in my view, display a spirit of firmness without truculence, conciliation without appeasement, confidence without arrogance. I believe also that in an interdependent world, wracked by both communistic and nationalistic ambitions, only a leadership based on honesty of purpose, on calmness and inexhaustible patience in conference, and on a refusal to be diverted from basic principles could, in the long run, be influential in all its dealings with others—allies and potential enemies. Ultimate objectives must be paramount; immediate reactions are less important.

One great question was whether the new Russian regime was a one-man Malenkov dictatorship or a government by committee. The Intelligence experts inclined to the committee conclusion.

At first, they believed, Malenkov would play a cautious game and not break with the Stalinist past until he had all the power of the government securely in his own hands. Within a month, however, he began to make startling departures from the ways of his predecessor. Far earlier than anyone had expected, he launched a peace offensive, with three apparent purposes: to avoid a global war, to prevent the birth of a European Defense Community, and to slow up the rearmament of the United States and the West. These evidences gave us hope that perhaps the time had arrived when the Soviet leaders had decided, because of the discontent of their subjects, to turn their factories to producing more goods for civilian use and thus to raise the living standards of the Soviet population. By summer the Soviet Union under Malenkov was condemning the "cult of personality," which had flourished under Stalin, as "alien to the spirit of Marxism–Leninism." Day by day we scrutinized all such evidence to see whether, at long last, a satisfactory modus vivendi might become more than a hope.

Allen Dulles gave us evaluations—or impressions—of such individuals as Malenkov, Bulganin, Beria, Kozlov, Mikoyan, Khrushchev, and others. He and his associates made estimates of future developments and analyses of statements coming out of the Kremlin. He presented Intelligence estimates of Soviet military power, economic development, and possible intentions, particularly in Korea, Vietnam, and Germany. All of these things we studied constantly with experts in many fields.

While the Soviet problem loomed as the largest in global affairs and was never out of mind, only a fraction of our entire time could be given to it. A host of other problems, many of them offshoots of Communist operations beyond the Soviet borders, were constantly crossing and recrossing my desk.

For example, on April 12, 1953, four days before my speech to the American Society of Newspaper Editors, I addressed the Council of the Organization of American States—a talk which gave me a chance to affirm, in the midst of our critical concerns of those days, my determination to strengthen cooperation within the Western Hemisphere.

"The history of the Americas over the span of the sixty-three years since the founding of our regional organization [International Union of American Republics, founded April 14, 1890]," I said, "has not been spotlessly perfect. Like all peoples, our nations—every one of them, the United States included—have at times been guilty of selfish and thoughtless actions. In all dealings with our neighbors we have not always bravely resisted the temptations of expediency."

But I assured the assembled delegates that I was profoundly dedicated personally to doing all that I could to perfect the understanding and trust upon which the American community of nations must rest.

As our first step, I announced that day that I had asked my brother Dr. Milton S. Eisenhower, president of Pennsylvania State College, to visit Latin America in order to make specific recommendations for increasing friendship between us and our neighbors to the south.

*   *   *

On the day when the Soviet government announced Stalin's final illness, Anthony Eden, the British Foreign Secretary, and Foster Dulles came to the White House. The problem was the Suez Canal, and more specifically the right of the British to defend this narrow waterway through which tankers moved carrying oil—fuel for their factories and homes—from the fields of Saudi Arabia, Iran, Kuwait, and Iraq.[2] To defend that waterway, the British, in accordance with the Anglo-Egyptian treaty of 1936, had built a giant base along the banks of the canal—a base three miles wide and sixty-five miles long, with a billion and a half dollars' worth of workshops and supplies and eighty thousand troops. In July of 1952 General Mohammed Naguib had come to power and King Farouk had fled; the Egyptians in early 1953 announced their determination to throw out the "hated imperialists."

The British knew that they would probably have to make changes. But they did not want to leave unprotected their access to the oil of the Middle East.

Britain, despite its modern program of independence for countries once part of the Empire, continued in wide areas of the world to be damned as an exponent of colonialism. In Egypt, as in Iran, the attacks seemed to be rooted in a virulent nationalism and unreasoning prejudice, as well as in genuine misunderstandings. In both lands, however, the evidence of Communist meddling was evident. In the enlightened self-interest of the United States, I felt it advisable for us to do anything we could to promote mutual understanding, to help allay the anti-British sentiment, and to thwart the Communist campaign of violent hatred. Because of European dependence on the Suez Canal, the interests of the entire Free World were at stake in Egypt, and it was important that the bilateral quarrel then raging be settled promptly and amicably.

Anthony came to Washington to discuss a British plan. They would propose to the Egyptians a general settlement comprising the following five points:

1. Maintenance of the Canal Zone Base in time of peace with a view to its immediate reactivation in the event of war.
2. Arrangements for air defense in Egypt.

[2] British forces first entered Egypt on July 10, 1882. Under the Constantinople Convention of 1888—signed by Britain, Austria-Hungary, France, Germany, Holland, Italy, Russia, Spain, and Turkey—the canal was to remain open in time of both war and peace to every vessel of commerce or of war.

3. A phased withdrawal of British armed forces from Egyptian territory.

4. The participation of Egypt in a Middle East Defense Organization.

5. A program of military and economic assistance to Egypt.

Of these five points the knotty question would be that of the phased withdrawal of British armed forces from Egyptian territory. Here the British had in mind three alternatives. Certainly there was no basic disagreement between the British and the Egyptians on the removal of the bulk of the British troops stationed in the Suez Canal Base. These troops were expensive to maintain and were a constant source of irritation between the British and the host nation. The British always expected, under any agreement, to hand over the Canal Zone to Egypt, along with the Suez Canal Base area, during peacetime. However, within this base area, the British were anxious to keep certain existing depots and installations under British control. These depots and installations would serve as a working maintenance base for a portion of the Middle East land forces even during peacetime; this purpose would require the retention of some five thousand Army personnel and two thousand RAF personnel in installations within the Canal Zone Base area. In addition, this preferred British plan visualized an integrated Anglo-Egyptian air-defense organization, including headquarters and a few RAF squadrons, and an Allied-manned staging post. In our correspondence and conversations, this proposal came to be known, for short, as Case A.

In the event that the Egyptians would not accede to this arrangement, a second possibility was contemplated. The second plan would also allow the base to be placed under Egyptian control during peacetime, with the Egyptians taking over such depots and installations as the British thought should be continued there. The Egyptians would thereafter assume responsibility for keeping all communications in working order and for maintaining Allied war reserves and heavy workshops in a state to be reactivated on short notice. Some stores and equipment for use by Middle East land forces in peacetime also would be turned over. To assist the Egyptians in tasks for which they had little experience or training, a number of Allied supervisory and technical Army and Air Force personnel would be required, although far fewer than the seven thousand needed when these installations were actually run by the British. Integrated air-defense and the staging posts were visualized also under this plan, known as Case B.

In the event that none of these proved acceptable, the British as a last resort would propose Case C, a plan which would require them to evacuate almost completely, retaining only occasional inspection privileges. In all cases, A, B, and C, the Suez Canal Base would be available for Allied use, particularly British, in the event of war.

These three plans, with the flexibility regarding the phased withdrawal, seemed reasonable to me; and with minor changes in wording I agreed to support this position in any discussions the United States might have with the Egyptians.

However, the matter on which I saw difficulty was that of the tactics of presenting these to the Egyptians. Mr. Churchill would have vastly preferred a tripartite conference in which Britain and the United States would present these proposals as a solid position to the Egyptians. Unfortunately for this plan, General Naguib, three days after my inauguration, had asked the Egyptian people to pledge themselves to "get rid of the last traces of British imperialism"; I felt that if he were now to agree to such a conference, he obviously needed time and an excuse to withdraw from his extreme position. Still more unfortunately, news of the proposed conference reached General Naguib without warning or preparatory work.

On March 16 I wrote Anthony Eden, reminding him that I had previously expressed a reluctance to get too far involved until the United States could be assured of the desire of General Naguib, through an official invitation from him, for the United States to participate in the negotiations.

I had thought that we would be able to achieve an agreement for holding such a meeting, but we learned that Naguib declared such an idea unacceptable.

To Anthony, I expressed the conviction that while close British-American association meant much to the development of collective security and to the best interests of the whole Free World, we needed to avoid any charge of forming a bilateral combination in an attempt to dominate its international councils. I thought it was just as necessary to avoid this charge as it was to have a common understanding of our positions before going into international conferences. For example, I had more than once heard the French hint with considerable resentment that the United States and Britain were guilty of power politics at France's expense.

I was confident that we and the British would get much further along toward a satisfactory solution of our common problems if, while carefully coordinating basic objectives, we would each preserve an attitude of absolute equality with all other nations, in every kind of activity in which we might jointly participate.

I reaffirmed this government's approval of the proposed British plan and said I thought it would operate to the advantage of Egypt; it was in keeping with their just claims to sovereignty and equality. Likewise it would give the Free World assurance that the canal would remain available for use.

Within a few days of my letter to Anthony Eden, Mr. Churchill wrote to me to the effect that he regretted that the American government felt it could not do much about the Canal Zone. He expressed his pleasure that, broadly speaking, our two governments agreed upon the merits of the issue and that he could count on our good will. Even if we could not help him openly, he hoped we would not let it appear that we were helping Egypt. He said he felt like the American who prayed, "Oh Lord, if You cannot help me, please don't help that bear."

He had missed my point. So far as the plan was concerned, we supported him fully. Beyond this, by reason of personal and official friendships and our obvious community of interest, we were more than anxious to be helpful to Britain. I had merely expressed (in fact, repeated) the belief that it would be self-defeating for us to engage in international conferences with a joint position between us already publicly proclaimed.

In the dispute with Egypt the British government firmly believed it was discharging an international duty and was resolved not to be bullied any further by Naguib. Moreover, Mr. Churchill continued to believe that unless our two nations went into all conferences speaking with one voice, we seemed to be heading for a costly and indefinite stalemate, both in the Middle East and the Far East, instead of helping each other to reach conclusions furthering world peace.

In view of this, I replied to the Prime Minister:

> I am a bit puzzled as to the real meaning of your recent note to me. By no means have I, or my associates, indicated or implied that we are not in agreement with your Government in what you are trying to do in the Canal Zone. On the contrary, Anthony and I reached a clear understanding of the things we should strive to get under the various alternatives laid down by the staff, and both of us were very clear that the offer we would be making would be so fair to the Egyptians that we *hoped* it could not possibly be rejected.
>
> While he was here, I raised one question involving procedure. My question was: "How does the United States get into this consultation?"
>
> It was obvious that no one had thought very much on this point and it was recognized that a very awkward situation could result for our representative, and indeed, for the negotiations themselves, if an American should show up without some prior invitation and agreement between the principals, namely, your Government and the Egyptian Government.
>
> My point is this: If the United States walks into a conference with you, against the wishes of the Egyptian Government, then the only obvious interpretation would be that our two governments, together, are there to announce an ultimatum. An uninvited guest cannot possibly come into your house, be asked to leave, and then expect cordial and courteous treatment if he insists upon staying.
>
> So far as I know, this is the only point that has blocked the initiation of

the conference. But until it is ironed out, I do not see how we can possibly get into it.

I am sure that Anthony will confirm to you that I expressed exactly these sentiments to him when he was in my office.

Nevertheless, I was still more than ready to do my part to use United States' influence to bring about a settlement. I alerted General John E. Hull, a most able American Army officer, to be prepared to act as a special military adviser to Ambassador Jefferson Caffery (in Cairo) in the event that the invitation should be received from the Egyptians for our participation. I wrote to Naguib in the sincere hope that discussion between the Egyptian government and the United Kingdom on matters of great importance could now begin. I expressed the interest of the United States government in the results and our understanding of the natural aspirations of Egypt for full sovereignty over her territory. Furthermore, I told him of my conviction that it was the genuine intention of the British government to meet Egypt's basic requirements, consistent with the requirements of the area's defense. I pointed out the British were justified in fearing the consequences of a military vacuum in the area, and in asking that the immensely costly base facilities could be readily used by the Free World in any time of crisis.

In my letter I told Naguib that the United States shared with Britain the desire that the discussion of the canal would include the broader problem of the defense of the entire Middle East. I congratulated him on the pact which Egypt and the British had signed conferring independence within three years on the Anglo-Egyptian Sudan, and assured him of America's willingness to assist Egypt materially in fulfilling its new role as a sovereign nation.

At about this point when prospects took a slightly favorable turn, Anthony Eden wrote me (on the 1st of April) explaining that the British planned to stand by their five-point proposal and that no agreement would be signed on any single point alone. It appeared to both of us that the five points which we had discussed early in March would seem reasonable under almost any conditions. Eden strongly argued, however, that the Egyptians would be quick to take advantage of any rifts between us, and would, if possible, try to get the United States to pressure Great Britain into making further concessions.

On this point we had reassured our friends again and again. But we also had to express again and again our recognition of the fact that since public opinion in Egypt was so strongly anti-British, it was necessary that Naguib, in order to stay in power, be treated as a complete equal in the world's councils. For one thing, a meeting on his territory could be arranged only by his invitation, as I, at least, thought was now obvious.

It soon appeared that our three-cornered correspondence was getting nowhere. So I recommended that the British begin negotiations with the Egyptians, being reasonably certain that when the discussions reached the point where Egypt's need of military assistance came to the fore, the United States might then be invited to join the group. General Hull would, at that time, be ready to depart for Egypt. On April 28 the British and Egyptians did open a series of talks, which broke down on May 5.

Naguib's reply to my letter was disappointing. It was cordial, and it expressed great admiration for the American tradition of freedom, but it also showed a suspicion and a resentment of the British which was something to reckon with:

> The road to an understanding would be clearer were it not for the moral and physical barriers and obstacles besetting it, most conspicuous and most serious of which is the destructively persistent stationing of British armed forces on Egyptian territory.

General Naguib denied that withdrawal of United Kingdom armed forces from Egypt would create a military vacuum. Egypt, he said, was fully aware of its responsibilities in defense of world peace and in providing its own security against aggression, in accordance with the letter and spirit of the Charter of the United Nations.

Soon thereafter, Secretary Dulles and Harold Stassen began another trip, this time to twelve Middle Eastern countries. The first stop would be Cairo. On May 8 I wrote a letter of introduction for the two to General Naguib. I told him that my two emissaries would wish to establish personal bonds of friendship, which could contribute much to understanding between us. The next day Foster Dulles and Harold Stassen left.

Here an incident occurred which, while amusing in a way, indicates the sensitivity of national governments to the smallest and most trivial event, if an unexpected interpretation can be read into it. While Foster and Harold Stassen were preparing for their trip, a question came up regarding a modest gift which I might present to General Naguib. The thought occurred to me that since I had several Colt revolvers, one of these might make a fine gift, particularly in view of the distinctive American flavor of this weapon, which would be as exotic and interesting to the general as an old Egyptian sword would have been to me. By the time Foster reached Egypt with this gift, however, the talks between the British and Egyptians had broken down temporarily, and the news of my sending a firearm to Naguib was received with much consternation and resentment in Britain. The act was considered symbolic of our desire to arm the Egyptians regardless of any arrangements they came to with Britain. As a result, I had to ask our ambassador in London some time later to assure Mr. Churchill that presenting one Colt .38 to General Naguib did not presage a flow of planes, tanks, and guns to arm that nation. Winston himself appeared quite relieved.

In Cairo, Foster found the situation even more serious than we had imagined. The temporary suspension of the negotiations was due to a difference over a detail: whether British Suez Base personnel should receive instructions directly from London or whether these should be communicated through Egyptian authorities. In essence, the British were sticking to the provision which we had called Case A in our discussions in early March, which involved the stationing of some seven thousand British military personnel to maintain the Suez Canal Base. Foster realized that there was no easy way to break the deadlock without loss of face to one side or another. Tension mounted daily.

The Secretary of State spent five hours with Naguib on May 11, and the latter apparently appreciated the letter and gift. But it soon became apparent that the personal relationship with Naguib, agreeable though it was, could not correct the deep Egyptian distrust of the British, a distrust which seemed to override any fear they might have of the Soviets. When Foster reached Baghdad a few days later, he found further evidence of this distrust prevalent throughout the Middle East. Meanwhile the danger of hostilities in the Canal Zone grew, although Naguib and his Council of the Revolution did agree that they would attempt to avoid this type of action until Foster's return to the United States, when we could have a further exchange with the British.

Home once more, the Secretary of State delivered, on June 1, a report over radio and television in which he described the purpose of his trip and his visit with Naguib. He emphasized again that the presence of large numbers of British troops was no issue at all, since both sides had already agreed that such should be withdrawn. Subsequent authority, after withdrawal of troops, over the gigantic base, airstrip, depots, and supplies was the matter at issue. The Secretary said that there was nothing irreconcilable between the rights of the nations signatory to the 1888 treaty and the requirements of Egyptian sovereignty, which statement struck a responsive chord with Mr. Churchill.

Meanwhile, I continued an active correspondence with the Prime Minister, in the hope that an agreement could be concluded which would provide for the retention of a minimum number of British soldiers and airmen in the Suez Canal Base. But Winston still seemed to cling to the belief that something resembling Case A would be accepted by the Egyptians. Cases B and C were apparently forgotten and with them any purpose of compromise or conciliation. Our information pointed to the conclusion that public opinion in Egypt was so strongly negative that such an agreement was virtually impossible. In the meantime we wondered why the Egyptians were presently stalling negotiations. In the British view the

Egyptians were weakening. In our opinion they were merely waiting to see what would happen next.

On the 10th of June, I wrote to the Prime Minister, saying that the question of maintenance and availability of the base in time of war was the salient issue. I solicited his views on a thought that Britain might make the base available to all the Arab states with which they were allied—primarily Jordan and Iraq, and secondarily Saudi Arabia. If satisfactory arrangements could be made with Egypt and these other nations, Naguib might then invite the United States and the British to discussions on over-all security in the Middle East. Meanwhile, the United States would continue to defer arms aid to Egypt pending a final settlement between Naguib and the British.

This idea was not acceptable to Mr. Churchill. He said that we were leaning far too much toward the Egyptian viewpoint, that in our discussions in early March the British had made far-reaching concessions and should not be asked to make more.

Winston went on to say that the Egyptian dictatorship had washed its hands of discussions with the British, timing this move with Foster Dulles' visit. The British were quite ready to resume the talks and had no objection to our trying to persuade the Egyptians to do so. But they were not ready, he insisted, to make any change in principle in the terms on which the British and the Americans had in the main agreed. After all, he said, there were other bases in other countries not even established by formal treaty—for example, the American bases in the United Kingdom.

If the United States should depart from the agreement it had reached with the British in March, he added, the British would feel they were not being treated fairly by their great ally. And if as a result of American encouragement Naguib decided to turn his threats into action, bloodshed might well result, bloodshed for which the British would disclaim all responsibility.

In view of this attitude we ceased to urge the Egyptians to negotiate further at this time. If the British negotiators were required to insist upon the maintenance of substantial numbers of British troops in the Suez Base, there would be little basis for fruitful negotiations between the countries. Case B, which visualized the provision of British technical supervisors under Egyptian command, seemed to us to be far more realistic. Of course, Mr. Churchill knew of our preference for Case A and of Foster's statement in Cairo that the Egyptians would not be able to get arms from us until they and the British agreed. That statement, I told Winston, should allay any feeling he might have of our deserting an agreed position or exhibiting a weakness.

This assurance seemed to put my old friend's mind at ease; but unfortunately he was soon taken ill. This resulted in a temporary postponement of the conference that the French, British, and American governments had been planning for Bermuda. We had hoped to discuss the Suez Base with the British at that time.

In the meantime, at the Prime Minister's behest, Lord Salisbury came to the United States for conversations. In these, as well as in subsequent correspondence, I continued to reiterate my belief that it would be a grave error to ignore the intensity of Egyptian feeling and its impact on the actions of Naguib.

At this point things reached more or less of an impasse. About the middle of July, Naguib wrote a letter which, while again cordial in tone, said bluntly that Egyptian willingness to conclude an agreement concerning the Suez Canal Base was conditional upon immediate evacuation of all British personnel in the Canal Zone with the exception of a minimum required number of technicians. He would make no commitment regarding wartime availability of the base unless he could show, in return, something more than vague assurances. In this last he was referring to his desire for a supply of arms by the United States to Egypt. What disturbed me most about this letter was its atmosphere of gloom and distrust; moreover, he raised a new obstacle by saying that any agreement he signed would be effective for only three years.

This letter obviously required an answer, and I sent one promptly, protesting in particular the three-year limitation. But now the United States recommended resumption of contact between the Egyptian government and the British representatives in Egypt, stating our willingness to assist Egypt in its plans for economic development and the strengthening of its armed forces. I assured the Egyptians that the United Kingdom would be willing to do the same.

On July 30, 1953, a series of informal meetings in Cairo began again between representatives of the United Kingdom and Egypt, with Case B at the heart of the discussion. The two main subjects still in disagreement were (1) the number of technicians who might be allowed to remain under a modified Case B and (2) the details of the rights of re-entry in the event of war. There were many complicating questions, even extending to such details as the wearing of military uniforms by the British technicians in the Canal Zone Base, and whether they should be privileged to carry arms. The British wanted to retain broad rights of re-entry, in the event, for example, that the United Nations should recommend sanctions against an aggressor or that there should be an attack on a non-Arab Middle Eastern country, specifically Turkey or Iran. The Egyptians objected.

"Don't press the British on specifics," I instructed Foster Dulles as these talks went on. "Leave them responsible for working out a peaceful solution."

Sporadically, during this time, between spring and November of 1953, Egyptian terrorists killed, wounded, or kidnapped British soldiers stationed in the Canal Zone.

And in Britain itself, as late as December of 1953, some Conservative members of Parliament, led by Captain Charles Waterhouse, opposed the idea of any troop withdrawal from Suez—an item which had been agreed on in principle from the start. Thus Prime Minister Churchill had to contend not only with emotional Egyptians but also with aroused fellow members of his own Conservative party.

Finally, by January of 1954, Egypt agreed that the British could re-enter the Canal Zone if an aggressor should attack a member of the Arab League or Turkey—though not Iran. But the two could agree on no more. As the year ended, the problem was far from settled.

*   *   *

Another troubled area that compelled our concern during 1953 was Iran—a country of 19 million people which shares a border with the Soviet Union and which holds beneath its soil a large percentage of the world's reserves of oil.[3]

In 1909 the Anglo-Persian Oil Company was formed, to take over the operation of a sixty-year concession under which it had exclusive rights to explore and exploit the oil of southern Iran. The British government controlled 52 per cent of the stock in the company. In 1949 the company negotiated an agreement with the Iranian government under which it would pay the government 25 to 30 per cent of its net profits. Under the powerful pressure of members of the Moslem clergy, and members of the Tudeh (Communist) party—outlawed because of an attempt to kill the Shah in 1949—the Iranian government failed to ratify this agreement and on May 2, 1951, put the entire oil industry of the country under national ownership.

The leader of this drive was Iran's Premier, Dr. Mohammed Mossadegh, a semi-invalid who, often clad in pajamas in public, carried on a fanatical campaign, with tears and fainting fits and street mobs of followers, to throw the British out of Iran, come what might. "It is better to be independent and produce only one ton of oil a year," he said, "than to produce 32 million tons and be a slave to Britain."

In October of 1951 the British shut down Abadan, the world's largest refinery, on the Persian Gulf, and the last British employees and their families sailed for home. The British government, supported by other gov-

[3] In 1947, for example, half the entire crude oil and natural gas produced in the Middle East came from Iran.

ernments of the West, clamped a boycott on all Iranian oil. For two years the British and Iranians stayed at loggerheads. No oil flowed through the southern Iranian pipelines to the Abadan refinery and to the waiting tankers which would carry it to the homes and factories of the West. No oil royalties flowed in the opposite direction into the treasury of the government of Iran, which from this great natural resource had previously received as much as 30 per cent of its national income and 60 per cent of its foreign exchange. To most Iranians outside Teheran, living at a subsistence level off the land as in the days of Cyrus, this deadlock probably meant little. And to many Englishmen, it meant only that the oil came from Kuwait or Saudi Arabia—alternative sources under British control —rather than from Iran.[4] But the disagreement was dangerous; it could not go on forever.

The Iranian problem had come to my personal attention even before I was inaugurated. While president of Columbia University, I met the young Shah of Iran, Mohammed Reza Shah Pahlavi. At that time I developed —on short acquaintance—some confidence that he would prove an effective leader of his people. Then, early in January of 1953, while I was still living on the Columbia University campus, I received a cable from Premier Mossadegh, who by that time was ruling the country by decree. In his cable, three pages long, he congratulated me on the election results, and then plunged into an extended dissertation on the problems of Iran, which he feared had already been presented to me by those who did not see eye to eye with him on his country's future:

> I dislike taking up with you the problems of my country even before you assume office. I do so partly because of their urgency and partly because I have reason to believe that they have already been presented to you by those who may not share my concern for the future of Iran and its people.
>
> It is my hope that the new administration which you will head will obtain at the outset a true understanding of the significance of the vital struggle in which the Iranian people have been engaging and assist in removing the obstacles which are preventing them from realizing their aspirations for the attainment of . . . life as a politically and economically independent nation. For almost two years the Iranian people have suffered acute distress and much misery merely because a company inspired by covetousness and a desire for profit supported by the British government has been endeavoring to prevent them from obtaining their natural and elementary rights.

I immediately assured Dr. Mossadegh in an answering cable that I had in no way compromised a position of impartiality and that no one had

---

[4] Iranian production fell from 424,000 barrels a day in 1947 to 59,000 in 1954; in the same years daily production in Saudi Arabia rose from 246,000 barrels to 953,000, in Kuwait from 45,000 barrels to 952,000.

attempted to prejudice me in the matter. I expressed the hope that our own future relationships would be completely free of any suspicion, and said I would be delighted to receive either personally and directly, or through established diplomatic channels, any communication of his views on any subject in which we might have a common interest.

In January of 1953 the Iranian parliament extended Mossadegh's dictatorial powers for another year. The following month, Mossadegh, pushing his strength, denounced the Shah, the constitutional monarch, for intrigues with "foreign interests." Pressed by Mossadegh, the Shah on February 28 announced he would abdicate "for reasons of health." This brought on serious riots; the Shah's supporters, along with rival supporters of Mossadegh, choked the streets. As a result, in a direct challenge to Mossadegh, the Shah within hours canceled his plan of abdication.

Meanwhile, the United States ambassador in Iran, Loy Henderson, presented proposals to Mossadegh in an effort to get him and the British to cooperate in some solution to the oil problem. Under one of these proposals, a consortium of oil companies would replace the Anglo-Iranian Oil Company and buy oil from Iran's nationalized industry. Mossadegh contemptuously turned this suggestion down as a "form of plunder." On May 28 Premier Mossadegh once again wrote me a long personal message, referring back to his earlier communication:

> During the few months that have elapsed since the date of that message the Iranian people have been suffering financial hardships and struggling with political intrigues carried on by the former oil company and the British government. For instance, the purchasers of Iranian oil have been dragged from one court to another, and all means of propaganda and diplomacy have been employed in order to place illegal obstacles in the way of the sale of Iranian oil. Although the Italian and Japanese courts have declared Iranian oil to be free and unencumbered, the British have not as yet abandoned their unjust and unprincipled activities.
>
> Although it was hoped that during Your Excellency's administration attention of a more sympathetic character would be devoted to the Iranian situation, unfortunately no change seems thus far to have taken place in the position of the American government. . . .
>
> As a result of action taken by the former company and the British government, the Iranian nation is now facing great economic and political difficulties. There can be serious consequences, from an international viewpoint as well, if this situation is permitted to continue. If prompt and effective aid is not given this country now, any steps that might be taken tomorrow to compensate for the negligence of today might well be too late. . . .

Then he made a direct appeal:

The Iranian nation hopes that with the help and assistance of the American government the obstacles placed in the way of sale of Iranian oil can be removed, and that if the American government is not able to effect a removal of such obstacles, it can render effective economic assistance to enable Iran to utilize her other resources. This country has natural resources other than oil. The exploitation of these resources would solve the present difficulties of the country. This, however, is impossible without economic aid.

In conclusion, I invite Your Excellency's sympathetic and responsive attention to the present dangerous situation of Iran, and I trust that you will ascribe to all the points contained in this message the importance due them. . . .

I refused, however, to pour more American money into a country in turmoil in order to bail Mossadegh out of troubles rooted in his refusal to work out an agreement with the British. Accordingly, on June 29, I replied:

The failure of Iran and of the United Kingdom to reach an agreement with regard to compensation has handicapped the government of the United States in its efforts to help Iran. There is a strong feeling in the United States, even among American citizens most sympathetic to Iran and friendly to the Iranian people, that it would not be fair to the American taxpayers for the United States government to extend any considerable amount of economic aid to Iran so long as Iran could have access to funds derived from the sale of its oil and oil products if a reasonable agreement were reached with regard to compensation whereby the large-scale marketing of Iranian oil would be resumed. Similarly, many American citizens would be deeply opposed to the purchase by the United States government of Iranian oil in the absence of an oil settlement. . . .

I fully understand that the government of Iran must determine for itself which foreign and domestic policies are likely to be most advantageous to Iran and to the Iranian people. In what I have written, I am not trying to advise the Iranian government on its best interests. I am merely trying to explain why, in the circumstances, the government of the United States is not presently in a position to extend more aid to Iran or to purchase Iranian oil.

In case Iran should so desire, the United States government hopes to be able to continue to extend technical assistance and military aid on a basis comparable to that given during the past year. . . .

A crisis was approaching. Three months earlier Mossadegh had tried to get the parliament to pass legislation making him Commander-in-Chief of the Iranian Army, replacing the Shah in this position. The parliament refused. On July 19, therefore, Mossadegh called for the dissolution of the Majlis, the second house of the Iranian parliament, and for a plebiscite to be held August 2. Less than a week after this announcement, reports were coming in that Mossadegh was moving closer and closer to the Communists. More and more, he was refusing to crack down on violent Tudeh-party demonstrations in the streets. And, one report said, he was looking forward to receiving $20 million from the Soviet Union, which would keep his treasury afloat for the next two or three months. By the end of July the Tudeh party came out openly for Mossadegh, the Soviet Union sent a new and hopeful ambassador to Teheran,[5] and the Shah, his life in danger, was forced to take refuge.

In the plebiscite three days later Mossadegh got 99.4 per cent of the votes. Iran's downhill course toward Communist-supported dictatorship was picking up momentum.

For the Shah, the time had come to check that course. As he later told an observer, Mossadegh had become "absolutely mad and insanely jealous, like a tiger who springs upon any living thing that it sees moving about him." Mossadegh, the Shah thought, believed that he could form an alliance with the Tudeh party and then outwit it; but in doing so, the Shah recognized, Dr. Mossadegh would become to Iran what the ill-fated Dr. Beneš had been in Czechoslovakia—a leader whom the Communists, having gained power, would eventually destroy.

The Shah, however, decided not to conduct a military coup; instead he resolved to do what the Constitution permitted him to do—appoint Mossadegh's successor. He decided on a general named Fazlollah Zahedi.

This critical decision made, the Shah left Teheran for his palace on the Caspian Sea. From there on August 13 he sent his letter appointing Zahedi, giving it to a trusted Army colonel, who was to deliver it to Zahedi. Zahedi, in turn, sent the colonel to break the news to Mossadegh. A day went by. Nothing happened: the colonel got to Teheran too late to make the delivery. The second day was a holiday; again, nothing happened. By the third day Mossadegh's spies had brought him the secret, and when the colonel showed up at his house to deliver the sad word, Mossadegh had him arrested.

The three days of delay had been disastrous. Mossadegh began arresting everybody he could get his hands on. For forty-eight hours his mobs ran through the streets rioting, smashing statues of the Shah and his father, and screaming, "Death to the Shah!" On the morning of August 16 the Shah left his Caspian Sea palace in a Beechcraft with one pilot, one palace official, and his Queen. At ten-fifteen he landed in Bagh-

[5] "Negotiations initiated by the Soviet Union are now being conducted [with Iran]," Malenkov said in a speech to the Supreme Soviet on August 8, "for the settlement of certain border problems and also mutual financial claims. We anticipate that the negotiations will be successfully concluded. Recently [June 12] a mutually advantageous agreement was reached on increasing trade between both countries."

dad. On that day he obviously believed he would probably never return to his homeland.

But we did not stop trying to retrieve the situation. I conferred daily with officials of the State and Defense departments and the Central Intelligence Agency and saw reports from our representatives on the spot who were working actively with the Shah's supporters.

Then, suddenly and dramatically, the opposition to Mossadegh and the Communists—by those loyal to the Shah—began to work. The Iranian Army turned against officers whom Mossadegh had installed. The Army drove all pro-Mossadegh demonstrators off the streets, leaving them open to anti-Mossadegh rioters who swarmed through government buildings, and looted and burned Mossadegh's residence. General Zahedi rumbled through the avenues of Teheran in a tank and led in the capture of the main Iranian radio station. Rumors spread that the Shah, by then in Italy, was coming back.

The next day Mossadegh, in pajamas, surrendered. He was placed under arrest. Zahedi's forces rounded up and jailed the Tudeh leaders. It was all over.

Throughout this crisis the United States government had done everything it possibly could to back up the Shah. Indeed, some reports from observers on the spot in Teheran during the critical days sounded more like a dime novel than historical fact. On the Shah's triumphant return, I cabled him. as well as General Zahedi, my congratulations.

Further encouraging news reached me at the beginning of September in Colorado. There I received from Bedell Smith, Under Secretary of State, a memorandum prepared by an American in Iran, unidentified to me, who had seen General Zahedi, the new Premier, and the Shah a few days earlier.

According to the American, the Premier was particularly appreciative of the message I had sent. He believed that prompt and substantial assistance from the United States—assistance which would produce immediate and visible results—was essential to Iran.

General Zahedi, our informant wrote, had no love for the British. But he recognized the importance of establishing good relations with them and repeated over and over again his strong desire for the resumption of diplomatic contact and for an oil settlement as soon as possible.

This was good news, but what followed in the memorandum, concerning the Shah personally, was even more heartening. I reproduce this verbatim as I read it in the Colorado mountains because it represents the kind of clear and succinct reporting by an observer that enables a recipient to evaluate a distant situation, particularly when he has some personal knowledge of the principal character himself.

The Shah is a new man. For the first time, he believes in himself because he feels that he is King of his people's choice and not by arbitrary decision of a foreign power. The Shah is not bitter about the past, but does feel that both Britain and America—but especially Britain—have made mistakes and have interfered unwisely in Iran in the past. He also feels that promises have been made to him by the United States which were not honored. He recognizes now his debt to us and hopes, as he puts it, that we have a realistic understanding of the importance of Iran to us.

Like General Zahedi he stressed the urgent need for prompt and substantial economic aid. He also spoke to me of military aid, a subject on which he has become more realistic in recent years. He no longer talks of jet planes and hundreds of tanks, but does talk of the equipment and training assistance needed to produce crack mountain troops. He is fully aware of the importance of the army to the security of his country and is also convinced—as are many members of our military mission—that with the proper help Iran can become a significant link in the Free World's defense.

The Shah was obviously determined to provide the leadership his country needed and was counting on us to give him the necessary help. He sent a message to me expressing a hope that between us we could change the whole strategic picture in the Middle East by taking advantage of the Iranian renaissance.

The same American also reported that on his way home he had discussed Iran with Winston Churchill. The Prime Minister, he said, understood the necessity for prompt economic aid to Iran without waiting for either the restoration of diplomatic relations with Britain or an oil settlement. In fact, Winston said emphatically that if it were necessary, he himself would provide economic aid to Iran before the restoration of diplomatic relations, although he did not explain how this might be accomplished. We had a wonderful and unexpected opportunity in Iran which might change the whole picture in the Middle East, he continued, and he concluded by asking our correspondent to tell me that he was feeling much better and could "hang on as long as may be necessary."

On the 4th of September, Ambassador Loy Henderson and Premier Zahedi exchanged letters to the effect that the United States could now continue its planned technical-aid program of $23.4 million for the current fiscal year. Largely as a result of a letter which I had received from Premier Zahedi on August 25, outlining the country's difficulties and need for aid and desire to align itself with the freedom-loving countries of the world, I decided that under the circumstances the technical-aid program as planned was insufficient. I announced on September 5 an additional $45 million for emergency economic assistance. In all, American aid to Iran that fiscal year came to nearly $85 million.

On October 8 I wrote in my diary:

Now if the British will be conciliatory . . . ; if the Shah and his new premier, General Zahedi, will be only a little bit flexible, and the United States will stand by to help both financially and with wise counsel, we may really give a serious defeat to Russian intentions and plans in that area.

Of course, it will not be so easy for the Iranian economy to be restored, even if her refineries again begin to operate. This is due to the fact that during the long period of shutdown of her oil fields, world buyers have gone to other sources of supply. These have been expanded to meet the need and now, literally, Iran really has no ready market for her vast oil production. However, this is a problem that we should be able to help solve.

On December 21, 1953, an Iranian court sentenced Mossadegh to three years in solitary confinement. In 1954 the country held new elections. And in August of that year the Iranian government reached an agreement with an international consortium to buy Iran's oil.[6]

Under a special ruling by the Department of Justice, based on the national-security needs of the United States, American oil companies participated in this consortium without fear of prosecution under antitrust laws.

For the first time in three years Iran was quiet—and still free.

*   *   *

Through 1953 we scrutinized another region where Communist aggression might damage us seriously—Southeast Asia.

In Indochina local fighting had broken out almost immediately after the Japanese surrender which ended the hostilities of World War II. Originally the fighting was popularly supposed to be between French occupation forces and so-called "patriots," who were trying to destroy French domination in the region. But from the beginning the French insisted that the rebellion was Communist in origin. In its early stages the struggle attracted little world attention because it appeared to be not only local in scope but relatively unimportant in global significance. However, the French themselves were unable, in the early postwar period, to provide the forces that could have quickly re-established order and brought about political reorganization. While the dissident forces were then neither numerous nor well equipped, they were never completely brought under control.

With the Communist victory on the Chinese mainland in 1949, the situation changed rapidly. Red China began providing support for the

[6] In the work leading to the consortium agreement, Herbert Hoover, Jr., later Under Secretary of State, performed one of his most outstanding public services.

rebelling elements in Vietnam. The French were compelled, in spite of their unsatisfactory economic and military situation at home, to send additional troops into the region. The struggle became more intense and began gradually, with Chinese intervention, to assume its true complexion of a struggle between Communism and non-Communist forces rather than one between a colonial power and colonists who were intent on attaining independence. Unfortunately, as I have noted, successive French governments were slow in making a convincing world pronouncement placing themselves unequivocally in the role of defending the people of Indochina against Communist domination and assuring the region the right of self-determination. However, a NATO resolution adopted unanimously on the 17th of December, 1952, recognized that the French resistance to the Chinese-supported rebels was essential to the defense of liberty, acknowledged that the resistance was in harmony with the aims and ideals of NATO, and therefore agreed "that the campaign waged by the French Union forces in Indochina deserves continued support from the NATO governments."

The following day the Mutual Security Administration, with President Truman's approval, announced a $30.5-million defense-support program for the three Associated States which make up Indochina—Laos, Vietnam, and Cambodia. About the same amount was earmarked, simultaneously, for economic aid and resettlement of refugees from the war in Vietnam. The United States government on December 21 endorsed Vietnam, Cambodia, and Laos for membership in the United Nations.

The picture at the time of my inauguration indicated the growing size and importance of the war. The French had deployed, at that time, forces numbering over half a million men under arms. During the seven prior years of fighting, casualties had totaled 132,000 wounded and 48,000 killed. In 1952 the French lost more officers than were graduated that year from its military college, Saint Cyr, and in prosecuting the war, the French had spent more than $3.5 billion out of their war-damaged economy. But the French had still not unequivocally promised to the Associated States the right of self-determination.

In the meantime, with the Korean War still going on, I had pointed out in my State of the Union message of February 1953 that there was a definite relationship between the fighting in Indochina and that in Korea. In late March, French Premier Mayer, with Foreign Minister Bidault, came to Washington for a conference. For part of our consultations the ambassadors of Cambodia and Vietnam were present.

With Foster Dulles and several of our chief assistants we entertained our guests on the presidential yacht, *Williamsburg,* going down the Potomac as far as Mount Vernon. I recalled Bidault's courage as a fighter of the resistance in World War II, and I hoped that in this meeting the

United States might get some agreement from France on both the European Defense Community and the war in Indochina. On EDC, however, Bidault continued to talk on both sides of the question. And on Indochina he evaded, refusing to commit himself to an out-and-out renunciation of any French colonial purpose.

The final communiqué of the conference included an expression of concern that a cease fire in Korea would free the Chinese Communists to reinforce their support of the rebels in the Indochina area.

The developing scene had ominous aspects. The Chinese Communists were constantly threatening aggressive action against Formosa and the government of Chiang Kai-shek. Ever since World War II, the United States had recognized the strategic necessity of maintaining the integrity of the Western Pacific island chain, including Formosa as one of its principal links. Our readiness to go to the defense of that island, if it were attacked, had been announced as a governmental policy before I was inaugurated, and I had personally emphasized the importance of this island's safety to our nation's security.

In the Philippines the Huk (Communist) activities had long created serious problems for that government. Any weakening of our determination to maintain the defense of Formosa or to support any other threatened area could easily have had a most serious effect in that archipelago.

Manifestly the loss of Indochina would have been equally disastrous. Unless checked decisively and promptly, the situation could become really alarming. We as a nation could not stand aloof—unless we were ready to allow free nations to crumble, one by one, under Communist pressure.

At this time, the spring of 1953, our main task was to convince the world that the Southeast Asian war was an aggressive move by the Communists to subjugate that entire area. To make this clear was a real necessity: our own people as well as the citizens of the three Associated States of Indochina had to be assured of the true meaning of the war. In a midyear report I received from the State Department appeared the following description of the situation:

> Failure of important elements of the local population to give a full measure of support to the war effort remained one of the chief negative factors. Notwithstanding France's action of 1949 in granting "independence within the French Union" to the three States of Laos, Cambodia, and Viet Nam, certain symbols of the former colonial era remained, and French authority remained paramount over foreign and military affairs, foreign trade and exchange, and internal security. France continued to maintain a near monopoly in the economic life of the Associated States. However justified this situation may be by the paramount French role in financing and defending the area, it was disliked by large elements of the native population. This discontent impeded the development of fighting

spirit among the growing indigenous armed forces, particularly among the irregulars and in the Royal Khmer Army. The rate of formation of the Vietnamese Army was adversely affected to an indeterminate extent.

A point of crisis in the relations between the Associated States and France was produced in June in the disaffection of the King of Cambodia, who presented the French a demand for full and real independence within the French Union, similar to Dominion status within the British Commonwealth, with a threat to fight for it if denied.

As the period under review closed, the newly formed Cabinet in France was preparing a new basis for political relations with the three States in the form of a declaration of France's readiness to enter into negotiations for completing their sovereignty and independence. It remained to be seen whether this would produce the necessary response among the native peoples and provide the stimulus for a new turn in the war.

But, though the French were slow to awaken to the seriousness of the problem of making their intentions plain, I felt that aid should not be delayed. Those of us most concerned went to work. I sent a message to the Congress on the 5th of May in which I pointed out the need, in our own interests, to make available greater resources to the French and Associated States against the Communist invasion.

A few days later the Under Secretary of State, General Smith, pointed out that the Indochina affair had become a global problem and that real help to the French had become a necessity for our nation.

In order to increase the efficiency of the military effort by our friends, in June I sent one of our outstanding combat soldiers, Lieutenant General John W. ("Iron Mike") O'Daniel, to Saigon to confer with the French Army.

By September, the necessary legislative processes having been completed in Washington, we were able to announce a commitment of $385 million up to the end of 1954, in addition to other aid funds already earmarked for the prosecution of the war. On the 17th of that month Secretary Dulles said in a speech before the United Nations General Assembly:

> . . . The French Government by its declaration of July 3, 1953, has announced its intention of completing the process of transferring to the Governments of the three Associated States all remaining powers as are needed to perfect their independence to their own satisfaction.
>
> The Communist-dominated armies in Indo-China have no shadow of a claim to be regarded as the champions of an independence movement.

This unequivocal statement would, I hoped, demonstrate once and for all that the fighting in that unhappy region was not for the purpose of reimposing French domination. Unfortunately the official character of governmental declarations does not necessarily assure their penetrating to all the people to whom they mean most. In this instance the hope for improvement of morale in Vietnam would be realized only if every man and woman in the country could be convinced that, in fighting alongside the French, they were now fighting for their own independence and freedom.

With the establishment of military liaison between the United States Defense Department and the forces fighting for freedom in Vietnam, and the provision of substantial American financial support for carrying on the war, one immediate crisis was passed. But the passing of 1953 did not eliminate our troubles in Vietnam; far more serious ones were still to come.

CHAPTER VII

Korea: The End of Bloodshed

Never take counsel of your fears.

—A motto of General George S. Patton, Jr.

Older men declare war. But it is youth that must fight and die. And it is youth who must inherit the tribulation, the sorrow, and the triumphs that are the aftermath of war.

—Herbert Hoover
Republican National Convention, 1944

O F the manifold problems confronting me early in 1953 none required more urgent attention than the war in Korea. By election time in 1952 American casualties had reached a total of 21,000 killed, 91,000 wounded, and 13,000 missing, making this the fourth most costly conflict in United States history, ranking only behind the Civil War and the two world wars.

Like every other American, I deeply resented the unprovoked and cold-blooded attack against South Korea on that June day in 1950, and believed that we could not afford to yield an inch to the Communist aggression there. My trip to Korea as President-elect gave me some personal knowledge of the situation, including the terrain, the combat conditions, and the prominent leaders involved.

In 1953 the first thing to do in developing new plans or policies respecting the war was to review the history of the entire conflict. Nearly all of the mobile military action took place while I was at Columbia University and, later, at SHAPE. Nevertheless, the nature of the war itself had to be clearly understood if we were to attack intelligently the problem of bringing it to an honorable end.

* * *

The entire world was startled when, at four o'clock in the morning of June 25, 1950, approximately seven assault infantry divisions and one tank brigade of the "North Korean People's Army" jumped off from positions along the 38th Parallel against the weaker army of the Republic of Korea (ROK). Forces facing the North Koreans were the 1st ROK Division along the Kaesong Peninsula, the 7th ROK Division guarding the approaches from Chorwon, and units of the 8th ROK Division along the east coast. Relatively undermanned and poorly armed, these ROK forces were rapidly driven southward, and by the evening of the 28th of June, Seoul had fallen to the North Koreans and the battle line was to the south of the Han River.

Jarred by this unwarranted aggression, the United Nations reacted immediately. On June 25, the day the attack began, the UN Security Council adopted a resolution calling for cessation of hostilities and the withdrawal of North Korean troops to north of the 38th Parallel, and calling upon UN members to assist the UN in the execution of this resolution. The next day President Truman pledged United States assistance. On June 27 President Truman, noting North Korea's flouting of the first resolution, and responding to a second resolution recommending that UN members furnish the Republic of Korea the assistance necessary to repel the attack and restore peace, announced that he had ordered United States air and sea forces to give cover and support to ROK troops. He also ordered the United States Seventh Fleet to prevent any attack on Formosa and to make certain the forces of Chiang Kai-shek did not attack the mainland. The UN Security Council had adopted its two resolutions in the absence of the Soviet member, Jacob Malik, who, by walking out some time before—fortunately for the Free World—deprived his government of the opportunity to veto the action.

The United States entered the Korean War to carry out a "police action," with no objective more ambitious than the expulsion of Communist forces from the Republic of Korea. It is quite probable that the Communists expected, when they made their attack, a cheap and easy victory, believing that neither the United States nor any other Western power would assume the risk of general war in order to defend that newly independent country. Unquestionably, the Communists were encouraged in such beliefs by the diminution of our military strength in the area because of excessive postwar disarmament, and by the gratuitous announcement of the Secretary of State in a speech at the National Press Club on January 12, 1950, that our "defensive perimeter runs along the Aleutians to Japan and then goes to the Ryukyus . . . [and] from the Ryukyus

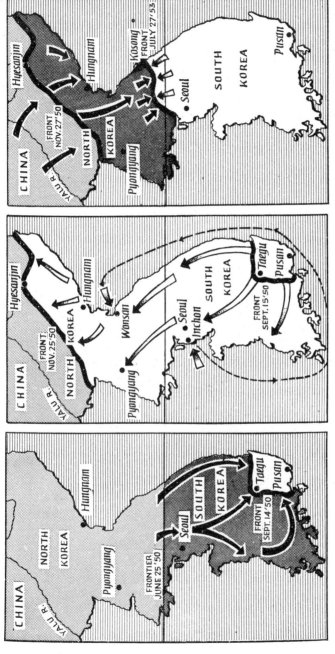

June to September 1950
Opening situation—North Korean
penetration to the Pusan Perimeter

September to November 1950
United Nations counterattack

November 1950 to July 1953
Toward the cease-fire line

THE KOREAN WAR: THREE PHASES

to the Philippine Islands"—an announcement which set Korea outside our defense perimeter. Since the beginning of the war, no statement of American or UN military objectives went further than to express the determination to re-establish the northern frontier of the Republic.

On the fifth day after the first attack it was obvious that the ROK Army, with United States air and sea support alone, could not drive back the invaders. That day President Truman announced that he had instituted an embargo on all United States exports to North Korea, a naval blockade of the entire Korean coast, Air Force bombing missions against North Korean military targets, and the use of "certain supporting ground units." At the same time Ambassador Warren Austin in the UN Security Council said that the *United States government's action was solely for the purpose of restoring the Republic of Korea to its status prior to the invasion.*

But the fact that the United States Army had been ordered into action had a vast significance. It meant, in effect, that the United States was in earnest when it committed its soldiers to ground combat in defense of South Korea.

Had it not been for the valiant conduct of the ROK Army and United States troops whose advance elements finally made contact with the North Koreans near Suwon, the tale of the initial days of the war would have been one of complete disaster. Vastly outnumbered, the ROK and American units (the latter initially consisting of only two understrength rifle companies from the 24th U. S. Infantry Division) were compelled to trade space for time while other units could be brought to the theater. As the ROK forces and the Americans fell back, suffering heavy losses in one delaying action after another, the remainder of the 24th and later, on July 18, 1950, the 25th Infantry Division and the 1st Cavalry Division began moving in from Japan. Even under favorable conditions, it takes a long time to build up a respectable fighting force in a remote area.

The 29th Regimental Combat Team followed, and, on July 31, the 5th Regimental Combat Team. Also on that day, over a month following the beginning of hostilities, a regiment of the 2nd Infantry Division, the first ground unit from the United States, arrived. This was followed on August 2 by the arrival of the 1st Provisional Marine Brigade.

On July 8 General Douglas MacArthur was named by the United Nations as their commander. Since, as commander of the United States armed forces in the Far East and of the occupational forces in Japan, he kept his headquarters in Tokyo, a field command had to be established for the day-to-day conduct of the battle. It was particularly fortunate for the United Nations, I thought, when on July 14 my old friend General Walton Walker, who had commanded XX Corps in Europe during World War II, was named commanding general of the United States Eighth Army, which was to direct ground operations in Korea.

The task of the United Nations forces at that moment was still to gain time, pending arrival of reinforcements, and to retain the southeastern corner of the Korean Peninsula, where the important port of Pusan was located. Thus, defending behind the Naktong River, in a small area about the size of the state of Massachusetts, the United Nations troops could hope to hold off enemy attacks by dint of shorter supply lines, effective interdiction on the part of our Air Force, and the rugged nature of the terrain. Even in this restricted area United States and ROK units were spread thinly. More than one division had to occupy a frontage of nearly forty miles. The battle for the "Pusan Perimeter" raged for weeks.

By September 15 the American and ROK build-up had reached sufficient strength to justify a counteroffensive. On that date the United States X Corps, which had been a separate force consisting primarily of the 7th Infantry and the 1st Marine Divisions,[1] landed at Inchon on Korea's western coast and moved inland to capture the city of Seoul. The Eighth Army, then made up of the 1st, 3rd, 6th, 8th, and Capitol ROK Divisions, the 1st U. S. Cavalry Division, and the 2nd, 24th, and 25th U. S. Infantry Divisions, launched an attack to fight its way back along the routes over which it had made its heartbreaking retreat only two months earlier. The North Koreans had suffered heavy losses; now, with virtually no air support, with long supply lines badly hampered by our Air Force, and unable to move in the daytime, they crumbled. The swift and decisive pursuit reduced the North Korean Army to practical impotency—at least temporarily.

General MacArthur elected, rightly in my opinion, to fight a military campaign north of the 38th Parallel to complete the destruction of the North Korean force. On October 7 the United Nations General Assembly adopted a resolution recommending all appropriate steps to insure a condition of stability throughout Korea; all "constituent acts" to establish "a unified, independent, and democratic Government in a sovereign state of Korea." It contemplated the cooperation of both North and South Korea in this process and asserted that UN forces should not remain in any part of Korea except as necessary to achieve the country's unity and independence.

Two days after the Security Council voted this resolution, UN forces crossed the 38th Parallel in strength. During the month of October the X Corps embarked from Inchon to land at Wonsan, on the east coast, and from there continued to advance toward the Yalu River, moving on the right flank of the Eighth Army, while the Eighth Army itself drove up the

[1] The X Corps did not come under command of the Eighth Army until after its evacuation from Hungnam following the general counterattack over two months later. At this time General Edward Almond took his orders straight from General MacArthur's headquarters in Tokyo.

center of Korea. By October 20 the North Korean capital of Pyongyang had fallen to the 1st U. S. Cavalry Division and six days later the 6th ROK Division was given the distinction of being the first United Nations force to reach the Manchurian border.

Jubilation was high. The North Korean Army had been beaten and was fleeing northward; victory seemed complete. But then, on the horizon, loomed a new menace: the Red Chinese.

In an effort to limit the war to the borders of Korea, the United Nations forces were prohibited by political directive from firing across the Yalu River—a prohibition which made a sanctuary of Manchurian territory. Our troops along that river were not allowed to interfere with any enemy concentrating on the north bank. In late October, Chinese Communist prisoners were identified among those taken by the Eighth Army in North Korea. These identifications were reported in the press, but largely discounted because they were few in number and the captured soldiers were classed before the UN Security Council by the Communist Chinese as "volunteers"—not members of organized units. Other events, however, tended to increase the ominous significance of the prisoners' identification. On November 2 the 8th U. S. Cavalry Regiment was virtually decimated at Unsan, indicating the presence of strong reinforcements, and temporarily halting the Eighth Army's advance in the West.

Consequently, during November 1950 a general situation existed in North Korea that was difficult to evaluate. If the Chinese Communists were present in large numbers, they represented a definite threat to the United Nations forces, which were then badly extended both in depth and frontage as their forward units pursued the beaten enemy. Immediate concentration for battle would become vitally necessary. But if the reports were untrue, then the opportunity still remained to destroy the last vestiges of the enemy's strength by vigorously continuing the attack in both corners of North Korea. The latter course was chosen by the high command. Enthusiasm remained high, and on November 24 the "end-of-the-war offensive" was launched by the Eighth Army and the X Corps. Three days later the full grim truth came out: Chinese Red troops were moving down from the Yalu in great force, and promptly had initiated a major offensive against the Eighth Army's right flank at Tokchon. The next day General MacArthur reported that the United Nations forces were now in "an undeclared war with Communist China"; he estimated that over 200,000 Chinese Communists were deployed in North Korea. Before long, a general withdrawal on the part of the X Corps was begun toward Hungnam. The eastern port of Wonsan was abandoned; units of the 1st Marine Division at the Changjin Reservoir and the Army's 7th Infantry Division on the Yalu found it necessary to attack backward through Chinese Communist forces to reach the Hungnam area. There, after a grueling withdrawal in sub-zero temperatures, these elements of the X Corps were evacuated by sea under protection provided by the 3rd U. S. Infantry Division, now undertaking its first action in Korea. These three divisions were redeployed to the south and then integrated into the Eighth Army. All the Allied forces in the peninsula were now operating under single tactical command.

On December 23, at Columbia University, I received sad news. Walton Walker had been killed in a jeep accident, ending the career of a gallant fighting soldier.[2] Walker was replaced by General Matthew Ridgway, who flew out from Washington to take command. By this time the entire front had been forced to fall back south, with Seoul once more evacuated.

General Ridgway promptly initiated and implemented a policy which was invaluable to the morale of the UN troops. It was known, bluntly enough, as "Operation Killer"—the idea being that UN troops were there not to occupy real estate but to destroy Communists.

Now the Korean campaign turned into a series of large-scale seesaw

[2] Walton's death was not only a shock; it carried me back through almost forty years to the days when we had been second lieutenants together in the 19th Infantry in Texas. When I joined the regiment in 1915, we were a closely knit group of youngsters, and I was the junior of the lot. The regiment, known from Civil War days as the Rock of Chickamauga, was proud of its history and its reputation as a good, rough, tough—and some said hard-drinking—outfit.

In those days there were very few general officers in the Army, none higher than major general. Of these I can remember seeing only four before our entry into World War I, and I had never spoken to any one of them. Second lieutenants were so respectful of high rank that we made a deliberate effort to keep out of the way of such exalted personages. None of these general officers had come from the 19th Infantry, a fact that we second lieutenants, for some reason, took pride in proclaiming to other units stationed at Fort Sam Houston.

Following America's entry into World War I, the members of the regiment were scattered. We never again met as a body. But a quarter of a century later, when World War II broke out, this group of lieutenants produced, in the ground forces, Generals Leonard T. Gerow, Walton Walker, Wade Haislip, J. L. Bradley, and me. Davenport Johnson and Michael Scanlan became major generals in the Air Force. This accounted for more than two thirds of all the second lieutenants in the regiment of that period. The ironic fact was that no one of rank higher than second lieutenant in the regiment of that time ever rose above the rank of colonel.

During the hard European fighting in the fall of 1944, Gerow, Haislip, and Walker commanded Army corps. Each established a fine reputation as a battle leader. Because of their good performances I recommended them for promotion, and all three attained the grade of lieutenant general almost simultaneously. Visiting the front one day I stopped at Walker's XX Corps headquarters and casually remarked to him that I was glad that he had received this deserved promotion. He looked at me rather oddly and said, "Yes. And I see that Gerow and Haislip were also promoted. If anyone ever finds out that we were all 19th Infantry second lieutenants together, I am very much afraid that you are going to be accused of rank favoritism." Later, these three became four-star generals.

attacks. On January 25 the UN forces attacked to the north, and by April 27 were in possession of Seoul and, along the entire front, had reached a line near the 38th Parallel. At this time the Chinese Communists, in their turn, launched a counteroffensive which drove UN forces once more to the south of Suwon, and Seoul fell into Communist hands for the third time.

Ten 'days earlier, General Ridgway had departed from Korea to assume the position of UN commander in Japan, because of General MacArthur's relief by President Truman. Named to succeed Ridgway was another soldier with no superior as a stout fighting man, General James A. Van Fleet, a West Point classmate of mine.

Following the Communist offensive, the last attack of which was made on May 16, General Van Fleet launched a final assault, recaptured Seoul, and established a line extending along the Han and Imjin rivers north of Seoul on the west, to Kosong on the east coast. Then on June 23, 1951, the Soviet representative, again active in the UN Security Council, put out peace feelers. Soon truce talks at Kaesong began.

Eventually the lines crystallized where General Van Fleet's offensive had halted, mostly north of the 38th Parallel. Later in the summer, sharp, violent clashes occurred over key terrain features, as each side fought to improve and protect its main positions. From that time on fighting was of a localized, even though bloody, nature, rarely over a battalion in strength. Under these circumstances the Korean War stalemated; there were no major military movements, but for many months more the war was to grind out painful lists of casualties without significant changes in situation or disposition.

In these circumstances the Department of State said repeatedly that the attainment of a unified, independent, and democratic Korea—as described in the UN resolution on the eve of General MacArthur's invasion of North Korea—was the UN's political goal. Its military goal, the Secretary insisted in testimony on Capitol Hill, had remained unchanged from the beginning: to repel the attack and restore the peace. "Neither the United Nations nor the United States," he said, "has ever undertaken the obligation to unify Korea by force."

This was the situation I saw when visiting the Korean front in December 1952.

*   *   *

But now, in the spring of 1953, I was President and I considered several possible lines of action. First of all would be to let the war drag on, without a change in policy. If a satisfactory armistice could not be quickly achieved, continuing this way seemed to me intolerable. We were sustaining heavy casualties for little, if any, gain.

Another plan might be to attack to the north to gain an all-out military victory by conventional means. This was the least attractive of all plans. The Chinese and North Korean Communists had sat on the same defensive line for a solid year and a half. Being diligent workers, they had done a remarkable job of digging interlaced and underground entrenchments across the entire peninsula, with positions organized in depth. They had partially overcome former logistical deficiencies by bringing in large quantities of artillery and stores of ammunition during quiet periods, and had a force in Korea superior in numbers to that of the ROK and United Nations forces combined.

These facts would not in themselves necessarily preclude an attack. The UN enjoyed air superiority, and, with the superior weapons and equipment and highly developed logistical system of the UN forces, an attack might well have been successful, particularly if accompanied by an amphibious landing in the enemy's rear. Nevertheless, any such attack would be costly, whether the objective was local or unlimited. The big tactical problem would be the breakthrough of the defense positions. Moreover, if the purpose were to occupy the major part of the peninsula of Korea, success would put us in an extremely awkward position, with a substantial occupation of territory but no ability to use our weapons to complete the victory—that is, unless the "sanctuary" concept were discarded and attack on airfields and targets in Manchuria were allowed. Such a change would increase the danger of spreading the war.

An attack launched merely to move the line of contact to the narrow waist of the peninsula between Sinanju and Hungnam would not in itself prove decisive and would never merit the cost in lives.

Clearly, then, a course of action other than a conventional ground attack in Korea was necessary.

In the light of my unwillingness to accept the status quo, several other moves were considered in the event that the Chinese Communists refused to accede to an armistice in a reasonable time. These possibilities differed in detail, but in order to back up any of them, we had to face several facts.

First, it was obvious that if we were to go over to a major offensive, the war would have to be expanded outside of Korea—with strikes against the supporting Chinese airfields in Manchuria, a blockade of the Chinese coast, and similar measures. Second, a build-up of both United States and ROK forces would be necessary. I had already authorized the raising of military aid to the ROK Army to permit an increase from 460,000 to 525,000 troops and the organization of two new divisions. This would bring the ROK Army up to fourteen divisions, as a step toward a total of twenty. In addition, there were more United States units available. In Japan, for example, the 24th Infantry Division and the 1st Cavalry Division[3] were made up largely of personnel experienced in Korean fighting. A second Marine division was available from the United States. Build-up of Korean ammunition stocks would also be required, which would cut, undesirably but not fatally, into ammunition already committed to NATO.

Finally, to keep the attack from becoming overly costly, it was clear that we would have to use atomic weapons.

This necessity was suggested to me by General MacArthur while I, as President-elect, was still living in New York. The Joint Chiefs of Staff were pessimistic about the feasibility of using tactical atomic weapons on front-line positions, in view of the extensive underground fortifications which the Chinese Communists had been able to construct; but such weapons would obviously be effective for strategic targets in North Korea, Manchuria, and on the Chinese coast.

If we decided upon a major, new type of offensive, the present policies would have to be changed and the new ones agreed to by our allies. Foremost would be the proposed use of atomic weapons. In this respect American views have always differed somewhat from those of some of our allies. For the British, for example, the use of atomic weapons in war at that time would have been a decision of the gravest kind. My feeling was then, and still remains, that it would be impossible for the United States to maintain the military commitments which it now sustains around the world (without turning into a garrison state) did we not possess atomic weapons and the will to use them when necessary. But an American decision to use them at that time would have created strong disrupting feelings between ourselves and our allies. However, if an all-out offensive should be highly successful, I felt that the rifts so caused could, in time, be repaired.

Of course, there were other problems, not the least of which would be the possibility of the Soviet Union entering the war. In nuclear warfare the Chinese Communists would have been able to do little. But we knew that the Soviets had atomic weapons in quantity and estimated that they would soon explode a hydrogen device. Of all the Asian targets which might be subjected to Soviet bombing, I was most concerned about the unprotected cities of Japan.

---

[3] These two units had been returned to Japan from Korea after long continuous combat duty. They had been replaced by two U. S. National Guard divisions, the 40th and 45th.

Meanwhile, General Mark Clark (who had succeeded Ridgway as United Nations commander) began to suspect that the Communists were building up forces in the Kaesong "sanctuary" area. He requested permission to launch an attack in the event he became convinced that a Communist attack there was pending. This authority I thought unwise to delegate at that time. But the question of the privileged ground which we had accorded the Communists for the negotiations was ripe for reexamination. Therefore, on the recommendation of the Joint Chiefs of Staff, I asked the Secretary of State to look into the possibility of ending these privileges in case the armistice negotiations were unjustifiably prolonged.

The lack of progress in the long-stalemated talks—they were then recessed—and the nearly stalemated war both demanded, in my opinion, definite measures on our part to put an end to these intolerable conditions. One possibility was to let the Communist authorities understand that, in the absence of satisfactory progress, we intended to move decisively without inhibition in our use of weapons, and would no longer be responsible for confining hostilities to the Korean Peninsula. We would not be limited by any world-wide gentleman's agreement. In India and in the Formosa Straits area, and at the truce negotiations at Panmunjom, we dropped the word, discreetly, of our intention. We felt quite sure it would reach Soviet and Chinese Communist ears.

Soon the prospects for armistice negotiations seemed to improve. On the 22nd of February, General Clark wrote a routine letter to the Communist high command to ask whether they would be willing to repatriate seriously sick and wounded prisoners of war in accordance with the Geneva Convention. The sending of this kind of letter was almost a common practice, but this time the Communists expressed willingness to repatriate and to resume truce negotiations. This exchange of letters resulted in a dramatic operation called "Little Switch," in which all sick and wounded prisoners (684 United Nations personnel and 6670 Communists) were returned from the hands of their captors to their own lines.

On April 9 Korean President Syngman Rhee wrote me a frank letter of protest criticizing the Communists' recent offer for resumption of peace negotiations. If a peace agreement should be arranged that would allow the Chinese to remain in Korea, Rhee wrote, South Korea would feel justified in asking all her allies to get out of the country except those who would be willing to join in a drive northward to the Yalu. The United States forces, if they remained, he said, might then follow the fighters on the front lines, giving them support and coverage with planes, long-range artillery, and naval guns on both sides of the peninsula; but, he added, if the United States wanted to take its forces out of Korea, it could do so.[4]

The Rhee letter was drastic in tone and extreme in its terms. I answered promptly, in an effort to restrain and reassure him.

I expressed sympathy with his aspirations and those of the Korean people to bring an end to the artificial and unnatural division of their country, and with their desire to expel the Chinese invader. But I emphasized these points:

> First, the action taken by the United Nations in Korea was to assist your valiant country in repelling the armed attack directed against it initially by the North Korean regime and subsequently by the Chinese Communists. This has successfully been accomplished.
>
> Second, the task of repelling the armed attack having been accomplished, it would not be defensible to refuse to stop the fighting on an honorable basis as a prerequisite to working out the remaining issues by peaceful means.
>
> Third, the United States and the United Nations have consistently supported the unification of Korea under conditions which would assure its freedom and independence. Neither the United States nor the United Nations has ever committed itself to resort to war to achieve this objective. To do so would be a complete negation of the basic tenets of this country and the United Nations.
>
> Fourth, any agreement to stop the fighting on an honorable basis presupposes a willingness on the part of both sides to discuss the remaining issues and to make every reasonable effort to reach agreement thereon. As I said in my address of April 16 an honorable armistice "means the immediate cessation of hostilities and the prompt initiation of political discussions leading to the holding of free elections in a United Korea."

In addition, I said we would seek a settlement of the problems confronting Korea but that such an effort would be nullified if the Rhee government should take actions which could not be supported by the United States and others of the United Nations in Korea's defense.

Three days later, armistice negotiations were resumed. One of the issues was our insistence on settling the prisoners-of-war question before proceeding with the rest of the truce negotiations. This issue, of repatriation, we believed should serve as a test of the good faith of the Chinese Communists. All the time, however, there was the danger that the resumed truce negotiations would serve simply as a platform for further propaganda. In one White House meeting early in May there was considerable discussion about the current Red Chinese propaganda in favor of substituting a political conference—which, because of its extended nature, would probably hold us indefinitely to the status quo—for the armi-

---

[4] On the 15th of April, I also received a forthright letter from Generalissimo Chiang Kai-skek recommending a time limit on the truce talks at Panmunjom.

stice conference on the prisoners-of-war issue. All present at the meeting concurred in my conclusion that this was another stalling action and should be flatly rejected.

On May 30 President Rhee sent me a letter stating that the acceptance of any armistice arrangements which would allow the Chinese Communists to remain in Korea would mean "a death sentence for Korea without protest." As an alternative, he suggested a simultaneous withdrawal of both the Communist and United Nations forces in Korea on the condition that a mutual defense pact between the Republic of Korea and the United States could first be accomplished. President Rhee pointed out that North Korea had a military pact with Red China, while the latter had another with the Soviet Union. He requested an increase in ROK armed forces, and provision of adequate supplies of arms, ammunition, and general logistical materials. He requested, further, that United States air and naval forces remain in place so as to deter the enemy from another aggression. If this proposal were unacceptable, he begged us to allow the Koreans to continue the fighting, for this "is the universal preference of the Korean people to any divisive armistice or peace."

In reply I assured Dr. Rhee that (1) the United States would not renounce its efforts by all peaceful means to effect unification of Korea, (2) that I was prepared promptly, at the conclusion of an acceptable armistice, to negotiate with him a mutual defense treaty along the lines of the treaties heretofore made between the United States and the Republic of the Philippines, the United States and the Commonwealth of Australia, and the United States and the Dominion of New Zealand, (3) that the United States government, subject to requisite congressional appropriations, would continue economic aid to the Republic of Korea to permit restoration of its devastated land.

On the 4th of June the Communists submitted a prisoners-of-war proposal which seemed highly favorable. My old friend Robert Murphy was temporarily serving, at the completion of his tour as ambassador to Japan, as political adviser to General Clark. When the Communist offer was received, Mr. Murphy informed me through the State Department that its terms accorded substantially with ours of May 25. The Communists were willing to go further than we could have expected on the question of release to civilian status of prisoners electing not to be returned to their homelands. We knew that many soldiers captured by United Nations forces would want to stay in South Korea. It now appeared to Mr. Murphy that the prisoners-of-war issue had been solved and there should be little hindrance to our reaching a full agreement. He pointed out, however, that it would be difficult to agree on a truce line, in the light of the ebb and flow of battle, which had been severe during recent weeks, in which period the Communists had made numerous gains against ROK units.

Mr. Murphy's analysis proved accurate. On June 8 the Communists agreed to voluntary repatriation of prisoners of war, for months the biggest thorn in the side of negotiators. The next day the negotiators at Panmunjom began dealing with the question of a final cease-fire line.

World reaction to progress in the armistice negotiations was universally favorable. The day after the agreement to voluntary repatriation Prime Minister Nehru, for one, cabled the Secretary of State:

> . . . I should like to offer my respectful congratulations to President Eisenhower for his leadership at this critical moment. I earnestly trust that this agreement will be for peace not repeat not only in the Far East but elsewhere. [Signed] Jawaharlal Nehru

At this time it seemed desirable to ask President Rhee to visit the United States, for a confidential exchange of views. Ambassador Briggs reported that the President had expressed great pleasure on the receipt of this invitation from the United States and had re-emphasized the necessity for the United States and the Republic of Korea to maintain their friendship despite "divergence on individual issues." But at that moment, demonstrations against the truce occurred in Seoul. President Rhee felt it necessary to urge Secretary Dulles that these demonstrations not be misinterpreted. He repeated that the United States was entitled to go its own way in foreign policy; but he promised that, should he find it necessary to take action on his own with the forces of the Republic of Korea, he would inform General Clark in advance.

Because of the unsettled situation, President Rhee declined to come to the United States at that time. He thanked Foster Dulles for his invitation but said conditions in Korea were such that he could not leave the country even for a short while. He countered by asking the Secretary of State to make a trip to Korea. This idea, while attractive on the surface, had its disadvantages. Foster felt it was important to get Rhee to accept an armistice quickly and at the same time to provide him with a way of saving face, following his much publicized opposition to any peace settlement short of his own ideas. If Foster went to Korea and gave specific assurances on a security pact, and on coordinated action in political conferences to follow, we might possibly obtain concurrence without loss of prestige for Rhee. But we thought also that until President Rhee had at least taken a favorable position toward an armistice, it would be best for a representative other than the Secretary of State to go. Foster recommended Walter Robertson, Assistant Secretary of State for Far Eastern Affairs, or Douglas MacArthur II, the department's counselor.

On the 17th of June, Rhee sent me a letter in which he reiterated his old argument on the fatal nature of the truce about to be signed. He expressed his gratitude for the help that the United States had given to Korea, and his letter was cordial, but there was no doubt that he was highly emotional. His attitude caused us much uneasiness.

The ink was scarcely dry on all this correspondence when a bombshell exploded. Twenty-five thousand North Korean non-Communist prisoners had somehow escaped from the stockades in which they were being held.

Shortly thereafter, Rhee's government admitted complicity in the incident.

These twenty-five thousand prisoners of themselves did not constitute the real issue. Since the prisoners were largely non-Communists, they were probably little threat to the supply lines or to the security of the rear area. However, what Syngman Rhee had done was to sabotage the very basis of the arguments that we had been presenting to the Chinese and North Koreans for all these many months. In agreeing that prisoners should not be repatriated against their will, the Communists had made a major concession. The processing of the prisoners was observed by representatives of both sides. This condition was negated in a stroke by Rhee's release of the North Koreans. The Communists asked at this juncture—and, I must confess, with some right—whether the United States was able to live up to any agreement to which the South Koreans might be a party.

This situation required immediate action. That day I dispatched through the State Department the following message to President Rhee:

I have learned with grave concern that you have ordered the release of North Korean prisoners held by the United Nations Command in camps which are under the authority of the UN Command. Responsibility for the safeguarding of these prisoners was in part entrusted by the UN Command to the military forces of the Republic of Korea. Your order has been carried out by the use of open violence by South Korean elements against the authority of the UN Command.

On July 15, 1950, you formally advised the Commander-in-Chief of the United Nations Command that in view of the joint military effort of the UN on behalf of the Republic of Korea you assigned to him and to such military commanders as may exercise UN Command authority within Korea or in adjacent seas "authority over all land, sea and air forces of the Republic of Korea during the period of the present state of hostilities." I am informed by General Clark and by General Taylor that within recent days you have given them unqualified assurance that you would take no unilateral action at variance with the foregoing without prior consultation with them.

Your present order and the action thereunder constitutes a clear violation of this assurance and creates an impossible situation for the UN Command. If continued, such a course of action can only result in the needless sacrifice of all that has been won for Korea by the blood and bravery of its magnificent fighting forces.

Persistence in your present course of action will make impractical for the UN Command to continue to operate jointly with you under the conditions which would result therefrom. Unless you are prepared immediately and unequivocally to accept the authority of the UN Command to conduct the present hostilities and to bring them to a close, it will be necessary to effect another arrangement. Accordingly, the UN Commander-in-Chief has now been authorized to take such steps as may become necessary in the light of your determination.

As your personal friend I hope you will find an immediate way to correct this situation. Accordingly, I am not now making this message public. I am confining myself to a brief statement deploring your action which I feel compelled to do to keep faith with my own people and our allies.

The next day the matter was discussed at great length at the White House. Fundamental, and obvious to us all, was the fact that Rhee's action had put us in an extremely embarrassing position. We were now in a place where we could really not vouch that we could keep our end of any bargain we might make with our opponents. Another matter we had to explore was a follow-up message to President Rhee which could be made public. While it was necessary to convince him that any action of this type, if repeated, would sabotage our efforts to aid him in his struggle against Communism, it was vital that we not give the Communists the impression that the United States contemplated a withdrawal from Korea itself. Such a result would be a surrender to the Chinese, handing them on a silver platter everything for which they had been fighting for three years. Several of my associates even thought that we should make certain of United States forces' ability to extricate themselves— without disastrous losses from harassment by former friends—in the event that the United States should decide to withdraw from the Korean Peninsula. I discounted this apprehension.[5]

I came to the conclusion that the situation could be salvaged. Foster Dulles expressed the opinion vigorously that if the Communists desired a truce as much as he thought they did, they would overlook Rhee's impetuosity and would be content to sign an agreement, provided they were

---

[5] A long time afterward, I was amused to find that my confidence was shared by my politically unconcerned son, then a major in the 3rd Division in Korea. On June 20, 1953, he had written his grandmother:

"Dear Nana: Just a note to let you know all is going along well. The weather is pretty nice and life, all in all, is not too bad.

"I guess Syngman Rhee pretty well scuttled the truce. Exactly what will come of all this, of course, nobody can tell. I sure am glad, though, that the U.S. has enough force here to take care of itself no matter what happens.

"The war has been pretty active lately. . . . Johnnie."

given proper assurances. Three days later the Secretary sent a sharp letter to Rhee taking him to task for his action and informing him that Assistant Secretary Walter Robertson would come in person, for the hour was too grave to risk the lack of understanding which could come from cabled messages. He assured Rhee that Walter Robertson had the complete confidence of us both.

Meanwhile, as might be expected, the feeling on the home front was one of bewilderment. There seemed to be some confusion in the minds of many people as to the identity of the real enemy, and I found it necessary in a news conference on July 1 to remind a questioner, "The enemy is still in North Korea." I said we were witnessing an acute example of the difficulties that arise when allies, dedicated to the same principles and the same basic ideas, draw apart on the means of attaining their objectives. This was the history of coalitions, I said, and we should not be too discouraged about it. In this case the differences were very real. Moreover, when people were emotionally upset—as President Rhee was—they were apt to overstate their cases and become extraordinarily difficult when others were trying for calm solutions.

Robertson flew to Seoul and began talks with Rhee. They required the utmost tact, diplomacy, fortitude, and patience. Day after day he argued with this fiercely patriotic but recalcitrant old man on the futility of trying to go it alone. He gave assurance of United States support if Rhee would be reasonable. Finally, on July 8 General Clark was able to assure the Communists that the South Korean Army would observe the armistice. On the 12th of July, Rhee publicly promised to cooperate.

Mr. Robertson's conduct in the course of these negotiations was exemplary. Syngman Rhee himself took the time out to send me a letter expressing great pleasure with Mr. Robertson's performance and with the fine spirit of consideration and understanding which he had shown. Dr. Rhee assured me that he would not obstruct in any way the implementation of the terms of the armistice. He did, of course, express his usual misgivings about the long-term results.

In the meantime the fighting had gone on, with the Communists resuming large-scale attacks on our lines. Some time earlier, they had attacked Allied salients in North Korea and had advanced five miles. Now they resumed this aggressive activity on a much larger scale, and in an unexpected quarter.

The Korean Peninsula is shaped like a somewhat flattened S. On the western side of this peninsula the terrain is rolling, hilly rather than mountainous. On the eastern side, however, the terrain is rugged; indeed, the continental divide of the Korean Peninsula lies only a few miles from the east coast.

The key avenue of approach between North and South Korea lies ap-

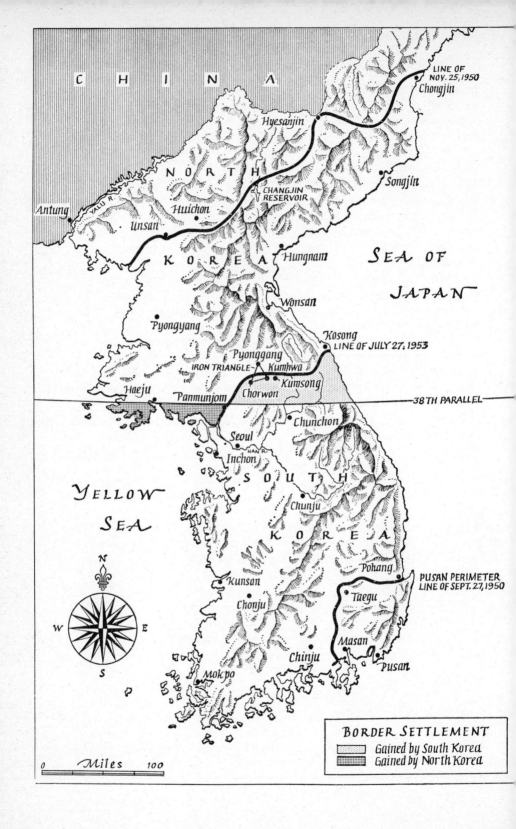

CHINA

LINE OF
NOV. 25, 1950

Chongjin

Hyesanjin

NORTH

Songjin

CHANGJIN
RESERVOIR

Antung

YALU R.

Huichon

KOREA

Hungnam

SEA OF

Unsan

JAPAN

Wonsan

Pyongyang

Kosong
LINE OF JULY 27, 1953

Pyonggang

IRON TRIANGLE

Kumhwa

Kumsong

Haeju

Panmunjom

Chorwon

38TH PARALLEL

Chunchon

Seoul

HAN R.

Inchon

SOUTH

YELLOW

Chunju

SEA

KOREA

Pohang

PUSAN PERIMETER
LINE OF SEPT. 27, 1950

Kunsan

Taegu

Chonju

Masan

Chinju

Pusan

Mokpo

N

W   E

S

BORDER SETTLEMENT
Gained by South Korea
Gained by North Korea

0   Miles   100

proximately in the center of the *S,* running north and south. This is the Chorwon Valley, which runs from Seoul on the south to a plain on the northeast coast on which are located Hamhung, Hungnam, and Wonsan. At the line of contact between the UN and the Communist forces in this Chorwon Valley is an area which came at the time to be known as the "Iron Triangle." This was the scene of intense fighting through much of the war, but the attack made at this time, surprisingly enough, was in the nearly impassable country east of the Iron Triangle in the vicinity of the site where a town named Kumsong once stood. On the night of July 13–14 several Chinese armies, each the size of a Western corps, attacked on a front held by the Capitol ROK Division, the unit which I had visited as President-elect in December of 1952. In a vicious assault the Communists succeeded in overrunning the entire infantry elements of the division and virtually destroying a supporting United States field-artillery battalion.

On the 14th, the 3rd U. S. Division some miles to the west, which had been relieved the night before by the 2nd U. S. Division, was ordered, after six continuous months on the line, to move into this hazardous gap. The movement was unusually swift, since the 3rd Division had been supplied with additional trucks, those that had brought the relieving troops. The 3rd Division moved into the attack area, and during the night of July 14–15, the 15th and 65th Infantry Regiments of the division struggled up the steep slopes in the driving rain, trying to make contact with each other, and hoping that the next voices they heard would not be those of the Communists.

For some unknown reason, the Chinese never followed up their successful attack.

Undoubtedly, however, they had been able to identify the 3rd Division as a United States unit on the day of the 14th, and it is probable they wanted to avoid a general engagement with our troops.

Many believed that the policy of the Chinese Communists was to split the allies by attacking ROK units only and ignoring those of the United States. This assumption seemed further substantiated by the fact that the next day large-scale attacks were launched still farther to the east in the vicinity of the ROK II Corps. Here several divisions were hit badly and gains up to several miles on the part of the Chinese Communists were realized. The mountainous masses in this area afforded little opportunity for exploitation; therefore the attacks, costly as they were to the Communists, were of little consequence. One possibly useful result was to remind President Rhee of the vulnerability of his forces if deprived of United Nations support.

The whole military operation gave me a renewed touch of pride in my old unit, the 3rd Division. I did not then realize that July 15–27, 1953, would be the last period of fighting action of United States troops under my direction, either in uniform or as Commander-in-Chief of American armed forces.

By this time, mid-July, it became apparent that a truce would probably be signed in the near future. In a White House meeting on July 23 our discussion hinged around the possible desirability of reinforcing UN units in South Korea, since a truce would mean that no more troops could be brought in on either side. Knowing this, I promptly authorized the movement to Korea of some United States units, including the 24th Infantry Division and the 1st Cavalry Division then in Japan, plus the 3rd Marine Division, located in the United States. I felt that no publicity was necessary, since there was no intent or possibility of concealing the move from the Chinese Communists.

In spite of seemingly favorable progress toward an armistice, I soon found myself writing a memorandum in near exasperation about our uncertain situation with respect to the South Korean government and the effects of this lack of close coordination on the struggle against the Communists. Our nation and the United Nations went into Korea for one reason only, to repel aggression and restore the borders of the Republic of Korea—not to reunite Korea by force. An armistice therefore would presumably mark the beginning of political discussions which would hope to reunite Korea and accomplish evacuation of the country by all troops —Chinese and United Nations'. But I had to add, "There has been so much backing and filling, indecision, doubt and frustration engendered by both Rhee and the Communists that I am doubtful that an armistice even if achieved will have any great meaning."

Fortunately I was wrong. The truce was signed three days later, on July 27, 1953.

It represented, for us, an acceptable solution to a problem that almost defied, in view of world sentiment and the political situation, any solution at all. The day before, I had prepared a statement which, while never issued in this form because its ideas were included in an address I made to the nation that evening, still expressed my feelings completely in welcoming the armistice:

> All of us share certain thoughts at this moment.
> We think—first of all—of our brave sons who gave their lives to bring this armistice with honor. Their sacrifice has proved again the valor of free men.
> We think of other sons wearied by months of imprisonment behind enemy lines. The swift return of all of them will bring joy to many homes. It will also be welcome evidence of the good faith of those with whom we have signed this armistice.

We think, too, of the enemy prisoners in our hands. We have steadfastly sustained their right to choose their own future, to live in freedom if they wish.

In the statement, I said that we thought, too, of our allies, the men of twenty-one nations who went with us through the long, battle-scarred months, and in particular the valorous armies of the Republic of Korea. Though he put patience to the test, I could not but express admiration for Syngman Rhee, who inspired the armies with his fighting spirit. They had done more than prove their title to freedom; they had given peoples everywhere an example of courage and patriotism, and an example of the fact that men of the East and men of the West could unite and fight side by side for their freedom.

But [I continued], one thought above all, at this moment, must discipline our emotions and steady our resolve. It is this: we have won an armistice on a single battlefield—not peace in the world.

This means that for the coming months, during the period of prisoner screening and exchange—which we hope will be brief—and during the possibly longer period of the political conference which looks toward the unification of Korea, we and our United Nations allies must stand guard. . . .

We shall take every precaution to see that the United Nations and American military position in Korea is not impaired during the armistice period. For we know that manifest strength alone can guard the just and lasting peace we seek.

As Foster Dulles and I sat and talked it over, we viewed the outcome with a measure of satisfaction. Yet this was tempered by the haunting doubt that any peaceful negotiation could reunite Korea until the basic conflict between the Free World and Communism would one day be resolved. Soon Foster would travel to South Korea to talk with Dr. Rhee and to make preliminary arrangements to help in rehabilitating that unhappy country. Our tasks would be tedious and difficult, but they would stand in heartening contrast to what had gone before. Three years of heroism, frustration, and bloodshed were over.

CHAPTER VIII

The Platform: Promises to Keep

One must have a good memory to be able to keep the promises one makes.

—Friedrich Wilhelm Nietzsche

IN the congressional session of 1953 we were obligated to redeem promises made in the Republican platform of 1952, to keep pledges I had made in the campaign, and to follow through on the recommendations submitted in my State of the Union message on the 2nd of February.

Stern facts influenced our approach to these tasks.

One fact was the slimness of the Republican majority in Congress. When the Eighty-third Congress assembled on January 3, 1953, for its first session, the Republicans had a majority of only eleven votes in the House (221 Republicans, 210 Democrats, one independent; three of the 435 seats were vacant). A shift of six Republican votes on an issue could cause the Democrats, if they held solid, to prevail. In the Senate the Republican margin consisted of just one man: forty-eight Republicans assembled on one side of the aisle, forty-seven Democrats on the other; one independent, former Republican and future Democrat Wayne Morse of Oregon, would vote with the Republicans on few issues.

Another relevant fact was the unfamiliarity of Republicans with either the techniques or the need of cooperating with the Executive. Not since 1931—nearly a quarter of a century before—had a Republican President had a Republican majority in both houses of the Congress. Not a single Republican senator arriving in Washington in January of 1953 had ever served with a President of his own party. Of the 221 Republicans in the House, only fifteen had served with a Republican President.

Moreover, Republicans who came to Washington that January to take their seats in the two wings of the Capitol displayed a wide variety of political and philosophic views. Among them were internationalists and isolationists, public servants of splendid integrity and headline seekers, men dedicated to promoting the national welfare and others concerned solely with their own areas.

On their side of the Senate aisle, the Democrats were likewise divided. Among them were men—like Senator Byrd of Virginia and Senator George of Georgia—on whom I could count in many critical votes. Among them also were Senators Estes Kefauver of Tennessee, Paul Douglas of Illinois, and Hubert Humphrey of Minnesota, who if they were ever to vote on our side—particularly on domestic issues—would do so only coincidentally.

With such a line-up on Capitol Hill, I knew from the beginning that noisy, strong-armed tactics would accomplish nothing, even if I were so inclined. A friend, William Phillips, wrote to me that he had become "deeply troubled" by the widespread impression, after the congressional session was under way, that certain senators of my own party were outspokenly differing with my policies and thus impairing my leadership. He was referring, plainly, to Senators Henry Dworshak and Herman Welker of Idaho, Hugh Butler of Nebraska, George W. Malone of Nevada, William Jenner of Indiana, and Joseph R. McCarthy, among others. In my reply I described to him some of my thoughts on leadership in general:

> Clearly, there are different ways to try to be a leader. In my view, a fair, decent, and reasonable dealing with men, a reasonable recognition that views may diverge, a constant seeking for a high and strong ground on which to work together, is the best way to lead our country in the difficult times ahead of us. A living democracy needs diversity to keep it strong. For survival, it also needs to have the diversities brought together in a common purpose, so fair, so reasonable, and so appealing that all can rally to it. . . .
>
> Speaking from a more distinctly personal point of view, the present situation is, I think, without recent precedent in that the particular legislators who are most often opposing Administration views are of the *majority* party. People like to think of Mr. Roosevelt as a leader; in the situation where his own party was delighted to hear a daily excoriation of the opposite political party, his methods were adequate to his time and to the situation. As of today, every measure that we deem essential to the progress and welfare of America normally requires Democratic support in varying degrees. I think it is fair to say that, in this situation, only a leadership that is based on honesty of purpose, calmness and inexhaustible patience in conference and persuasion, and refusal to be diverted from basic principles can, in the long run, win out. I further believe that we must never lose sight of the ultimate objectives we are trying to attain. . . .

In these circumstances I thought it necessary to establish several lines of communication between the Executive and Legislative branches.

I urged each Cabinet member to become acquainted and develop friendly contacts with the members of every committee with which he had special dealings. (The Secretary of State, for example, himself a former senator, was mainly concerned with the Foreign Relations Committee of the Senate, the Foreign Affairs Committee of the House, and the appropriations committees of both houses.) I encouraged department heads to meet committee members collectively and individually, both officially and socially.

In addition, in each department special representatives kept abreast of all legislative proposals under consideration in their respective committees, so as to be fully prepared to provide information and advice as desired by legislators.

For my part, I early embarked on a program of discussing issues, in a social atmosphere, with groups of congressmen and senators of both parties, in the hope that personal acquaintance would help smooth out difficulties inherent in partisanship.

As I have already noted, I set up a staff section in the White House with the mission of maintaining effective liaison between the Congress and me, with General Persons at its head.

But of all the mechanisms for developing coordination between the White House and the Congress—particularly with the Republican members—by far the most effective was the weekly meeting I held with the Legislative leaders.

On the morning of Monday, January 26, less than a week after the inauguration, I entered the Cabinet Room of the White House for the first such meeting with the Republican leaders of the Senate and the House. Around the long table sat, from the Senate, Vice President Nixon; the majority leader, Senator Robert Taft; the president pro tempore, and chairman of the Committee on Appropriations, Senator Styles Bridges; the chairman of the Republican Policy Committee, Senator William Knowland; the chairman of the Finance Committee, Senator Eugene Millikin; and the majority whip, Senator Leverett Saltonstall. From the House there was Speaker Joseph W. Martin; Majority Leader Charles Halleck; Majority Whip Leslie Arends; and, from my staff, Governor Adams, General Persons, and General Persons' assistants.

I knew all of these men. Among the senators I knew Bob Taft best. Styles Bridges had been in the Senate since 1937, longer than any other of the group. Knowland, who had been with me during the campaign, was the youngest. Millikin I probably knew the least. On the House side, I knew Charlie Halleck best.

In this first meeting I said first that it was my intention to redeem the pledges of the platform and the campaign. To my astonishment, I discovered that some of the men in the room could not seem to understand the seriousness with which I regarded our platform's provisions, and were amazed by my uncompromising assertion that I was going to do my best to fulfill every promise to which I had been a party. (More than once I was to hear this view derided by "practical politicians" who laughed off platforms as traps to catch voters. But whenever they expressed these cynical conclusions to me, they invariably encountered a rebuff that left them a bit embarrassed.)

I had hoped that the first Republican national victory in twenty years would provide a strong, unifying influence within the party and among its representatives in the Senate and the House. But my hope for unanimity was quickly shattered.

It was clear that habitual, almost instinctive opposition to the Chief Executive, as well as differences in political convictions, would create difficulties in Executive-Legislative relations.

Some Republican senators, for example, had long been opponents of the mutual-security program, in which I believed implicitly. Others opposed my insistence that postal rates be increased, in the fear that the reaction of voters would be unfavorable. Some wanted to reduce income taxes at once, regardless of Korean War costs and current deficits. Others were unhappy with the Trade Agreements Act, and a few even hoped we could restore the Smoot-Hawley Tariff Act, a move which I knew would be ruinous. A considerable number was against fulfilling the platform pledge of statehood for Hawaii, and others wanted to raise the level of farm price supports despite all our pledges of economy.

Though we eventually succeeded, it took sustained hard work in early 1953 to build effective cooperation between the Legislative and Executive branches, partly because of the traditional jealousy between them, dating from Washington's time (some senators were seemingly proud of this), and partly, too, because of genuine philosophic differences.

Senator Taft, however, was a shining exception. I quickly learned I could count on his stanch support. "Senator Taft has been the model of cheerful and effective cooperation," I wrote in my diary on February 7. I soon learned also that within the leadership group I could normally count on Senators Saltonstall and Dirksen, and Congressmen Joe Martin, Charlie Halleck, and John Taber.

At the end of another meeting, on February 9, Senator Taft and Speaker Martin met with reporters in the West Wing of the White House and gave them the first of several lists of legislation which the administration wanted passed that session. The list—far from complete—included legislation to bring Hawaii into the Union as a state; to amend the Labor-Management Relations Act of 1947 (the Taft-Hartley Act); to give the states clear rights to the submerged lands within their historic boundaries; to expand international trade by extending the President's power to reduce United States tariffs reciprocally; to simplify customs procedures; and to add two members to the board of commissioners of the District of Columbia.

This list, like the sweeping away of wage and price controls, conformed to principal administration themes—encourage free men to trade competitively; confirm the rights and responsibilities of the states; give labor and management a square deal, with no coddling, no favoritism, no coercion.

I especially wanted prompt action in revising the Taft-Hartley Act and eliminating the annual and growing deficit in the Post Office Department.

For a long time I had felt—and so expressed myself before the AFL in New York City during the campaign—that in some ways the Taft-Hartley Act could be repressive to labor. Certain aspects of the law could be used to get rid of a union, as, for example, the provision that employees who struck for economic reasons, rather than because of unfair practices, lost their right to vote for collective-bargaining agents. These defects I felt should be corrected. In addition, it seemed to me unfair that union leaders should be required to take an oath that they were not members of the Communist party, whereas management representatives with whom they dealt were not required to do so.

On the other hand, it was essential that the rights of management and the general public be observed. Hence, I set up a committee to study the law and submit recommended amendments to me for transmission to the Congress. The hope was that we could develop amendments which would be considered by the majority of the Congress and the people to be fair to management, labor, and the general public. The committee consisted of Secretary of Labor Durkin, Secretary of Commerce Weeks, Mr. Shanley of my office, Senator H. Alexander Smith, of New Jersey, Senator Taft, and Representative Samuel K. McConnell, Jr., of Pennsylvania.

In a Legislative-leaders meeting on May 25 I was informed of difficulties among the members of this committee. Secretary Weeks and Secretary Durkin were "poles apart" in their recommendations for the amendments.

Martin Durkin, a devout and honorable man, had little experience in public affairs. It was difficult for him to understand the function I wanted him to perform as Secretary of Labor.

Before his appointment I had held a long conversation with him on this subject in the Commodore Hotel in New York. I explained that there were a number of ways in which he could, as a union member, be most effective. His presence in the Cabinet, I believed, would serve notice on the unions and the public that governmental deliberations at the highest levels were open and aboveboard and precluded the possibility of any cabals developing counter to the interests of labor. Next he would, as a lifelong union member, reflect a labor viewpoint in all our counsels and should therefore be able to help round out any debate or discussion that had to do with subjects of interest to labor specifically or with our economy as a whole. But I cautioned him that he was not to consider himself as only a direct representative of unions; rather he was, with a labor background, to help develop policies and programs that would have as their sole aim the welfare of the entire nation. Just as every laboring man is first of all an American, I wanted him to use his office to serve America—with a special interest, to be sure, in all workers, organized and unorganized.

In purpose, he tried to be completely cooperative; he had a pleasing personality and was liked by his associates. But he had real difficulty in functioning as an impartial adviser; he seemed to carry a bit of a chip on his shoulder. Whenever a matter came up of special interest to labor, he unfailingly said that his duty was to participate in "collective bargaining" on the issue. He told me that, in dealing with other members of the administration, he was at a disadvantage in collective bargaining because in every conference he was but one man representing labor, while everyone else present was either a capitalist or a member of the professions.

One morning, in a conversation between the two of us, I reminded him that though I had never held a union card, I was of the opinion that almost nobody of his acquaintance had ever worked longer and harder than I had in my pre-West Point days. To suggest that I had any prejudice against labor, either as work or a political and social force, was perfectly ridiculous and, from my viewpoint, unthinkable.

By the 1st of July the initial talks on revising Taft-Hartley seemed to have stalled. But a month later, on August 3, the *Wall Street Journal* published the full text of what it described as a proposed presidential message to the Congress comprising nineteen amendments to the Taft-Hartley Act, most of them favorable to labor. One amendment, for example, would have repealed Section 14 (b) of the act—the section which permits the individual states to decide whether or not to authorize compulsory union membership. When the leak appeared, the White House emphasized that the text was not definite, that work on a draft had not yet approached even the "semi-final stage."

On August 19 I made a trip to New York from the Summer White House in Denver for the purpose of attending a ceremony honoring Bernard Baruch. On this trip Secretary Durkin met me for luncheon at the Waldorf.

I wanted to talk with him because of my increasing concern that he regarded himself in the Cabinet as a special pleader for labor rather than as my principal labor adviser. It seemed to me that he kept thinking of himself as an employee of a labor union, serving in the Cabinet merely on an interim basis while on vacation from his true work.

As we talked that day, he told me that unless he could be assured of the administration's support on a number of the nineteen points he considered vital, such as the repeal of 14 (b), he would be disowned by his union and no job would exist for him when the time came for him to end his governmental tour of service.

"Martin," I said, "if you will work along with the rest of us in a common effort to develop fair amendments to the law, your success will assure you a good position in the future—without question."

He appeared deeply touched by this statement of purpose and indicated his readiness and ability to function in the manner I described. The staff group in Washington, he said, had been making great progress toward recommendations for amendments to the law.

Neither accepting nor rejecting his own specific recommendations, I told him that if all my advisers on that body could, despite their diverse views, come to a unanimous agreement, I should of course give great weight to their conclusions.

Within two weeks Secretary Durkin sent me his letter of resignation. He had found it necessary, he said, to return to his position as head of his union. He gave no other reason for resigning.

Through Governor Adams, I sent Mr. Durkin a message that I planned to accept his resignation under the terms he specified, which were that he remain as Secretary until September 9, and that no announcement be made before that date. On September 10 I made a one-day trip to Washington to attend the funeral of Chief Justice Vinson, who had died suddenly. That morning Secretary Durkin visited me.

I discovered that he felt that the two White House representatives on the committee, Mr. Shanley and Mr. Morgan, had, as he expressed it, broken faith in their "collective bargaining." It was very clear to me that he did not understand the function that the White House representatives were performing—trying, without expressing personal opinions themselves, to find recommendations which the members of the committee would all agree to.

He said also that my opposition to points to which he thought I had previously agreed was wrecking the progress of the "collective bargaining" between us. As long as the subject was still under examination, I replied, and I had not reached and announced a final decision, there was nothing inconsistent in our talking it out further, even if I had inadvertently misled him in some particulars. Moreover, I added, his repeated use of the expression "collective bargaining" startled me. I explained to him very earnestly that he was not a "bargainer" in my Cabinet, he was my principal adviser on labor; that the discussions of the committee were not like contract negotiations; and that he was perfectly free to make to me such recommendations and offer such advice as his own convictions and wisdom dictated. But he merely kept repeating, "I think you should accept my resignation." I told him that of course I would.

Secretary Durkin's was the only case in my eight years in the White House in which a resignation was tendered because of failure to achieve a meeting of minds between me and any principal subordinate. Personally I liked and respected him. During his term as Secretary of Labor no one knew that he was suffering from the first effects of an illness which was to cause his untimely death in November of 1955.

On September 23, 1953, I sent a message to the convention of the American Federation of Labor outlining my efforts to arrive at a set of recommended amendments which would be fair to all, explaining the delay in receiving the committee report, and promising to submit my own recommendations to the Congress in January. Immediately the new Secretary of Labor, James P. Mitchell, began working on a new set of suggested amendments to the Taft-Hartley Act, which he reported at the Legislative conference on December 17. They were approved and thus we were prepared to make our recommendations at the opening of Congress in 1954.

In the meantime, the administration was waging tough campaigns on the fiscal front. We wanted to increase postal rates, decrease expenditures across the board while making adequate provision for the nation's security, and postpone tax reduction until the budget was in balance. One major fight the administration lost; another it won.

To make the Post Office Department a self-supporting enterprise was an objective we pursued incessantly from 1953 onward.

Large postal deficits began to occur shortly after World War II. Their history, by 1952, had been one of growth, almost uncontrollable growth. Relatively few citizens failed to see the logic of requiring the costs of mail delivery to be borne by those who used the mails; certainly I rarely received a message opposing the increase of postal rates needed to eliminate postal deficits. But the Congress had long refused to attack the problem, and continued to do so. For reasons not clear to me, congressmen often seem to feel that they will put their political lives in jeopardy if they vote to put the Post Office Department on a pay-as-you-go basis; instead, they prefer to vote for frequent and sometimes unjustified pay raises for postal employees on the assumption that they will thus help assure their own re-election. The officials of the postal workers' unions and associations of course tried to stimulate this attitude. In this matter too many legislators, of both houses, have habitually exhibited a lack of courage that to me is deplorable. Part of this attitude is engendered by some influential periodicals with nationwide circulations. In 1953 the Post Office Department calculated that it incurred large losses in delivering second- and third-class mail, and contended that these losses were completely unjustified; but the influence of publishers, paper manufacturers, and direct-mail advertisers constituted one of the causes for congressional failure to make rate increases.

An additional cause of increased deficits was the popular and understandable desire for constantly increased efficiency in postal deliveries. The department could have cut costs markedly by providing fewer and slower deliveries, and otherwise reducing the quality of service. But lower quality of service could be harmful to every individual, company, and institution in the nation; so the obvious cure was to increase both service and charges therefor.

On the firing line during every congressional session in the long, bitter, and largely losing struggle to balance the postal budget was Arthur Summerfield, Postmaster General for the eight years of my Presidency. Tirelessly he sought support for our program of improving service and cutting down the deficit, which in 1953 would amount to more than a half billion dollars. He visited and argued with members of the Congress, with publishers of nationally-circulated periodicals, and with audiences in nearly every state. He was earnest, indefatigable, and inspired.

At the Legislative-leaders meeting on July 14, for example, I emphasized that postal-rate increases should take priority over such projects as the St. Lawrence Seaway, vital as they were. When one senator volunteered that there was but dim hope that the Congress would enact the increase that summer, I said that perhaps the congressmen should give up their vacation, stay in Washington, and get the job done. Several faces around the table turned ashen.

We lost the fight. We could not overcome congressional timidity and the lobbies.

In the ensuing eight years we never stopped striving to get Congress to put the Post Office Department on a pay-as-you-go basis. Only once, in 1958, did the Congress authorize rate changes; these increased postal revenues about $550 million—but Congress also voted simultaneous increases in the pay of postal workers, which cost $265 million. This resulted only in slowing the rising deficit line and left the problem to the next administration.[1]

[1] Unfortunately, the succeeding administration, as this is written, has been no more successful in overcoming the postal deficit than we were, and this in spite of the fact that my successor enjoyed a large majority in both houses of the Congress, whereas for six years I had had to deal with a Congress controlled by the political opposition. In his second effort on this problem, my successor got through an increase of about

I believe strongly that every American citizen, regardless of party, should rise in his wrath either to obtain prompt action in eliminating mail deficits or to defeat members of Congress who so fearfully cater to the demands of selfish lobbies. Otherwise, the deficit will soon climb to more than $1 billion a year.

In contrast to our defeat on the postal problem was our success in a closely related fight in which Congressman Dan Reed of New York and his followers were determined to cut federal taxes, regardless of consequences.

Reducing taxes was one of my major goals, but timing was of paramount importance. At Columbia, South Carolina, in the 1952 campaign (May 19), I had made a speech on National Tax Freedom Day—the day each year when the average American citizen has earned enough money to pay his annual tax bill, and can start earning money to keep for himself and his family. On another occasion I cited the 151 taxes on a loaf of bread, the 192 taxes on a gallon of gasoline, the 206 taxes on an automobile. And at Peoria, Illinois, I had emphasized, "My goal, assuming that the cold war gets no worse, is to cut federal spending to something like $60 billion within four years. Such a cut would eliminate the deficit in the budget, and would make way for a substantial tax reduction."

Yet I could not accept the argument that early 1953 was the time to begin reducing taxes. Our effort to balance the budget without damaging the nation's security demanded that the existing level of revenue for the year be maintained. My promise to cut taxes had been predicated on a simultaneous balancing of the budget.

Congressman Daniel A. Reed of New York, Republican chairman of the influential House Ways and Means Committee, took a different view. As soon as Congress came into session he introduced a bill (H. R. 1) to advance from January 1 of 1954 to July 1 of 1953 a scheduled elimination of the 11 per cent increase in personal income taxes adopted in 1951 because of the Korean War. He had also announced his intention to let the wartime excess-profits tax expire as scheduled on June 30, 1953. These two measures would cost the government more than $2 billion in revenue.

I was emphatic in my opposition. On May 20 I recommended an extension of the excess-profits tax for six months, to New Year's Day, 1954, and asked for a repeal of the 5 per cent reduction on corporate income taxes, scheduled for April 1, 1954. I recommended a postponement of the cut in excise taxes, scheduled for the same date, and

---

$600 million a year, offset by postal pay raises totaling $363 million a year. (The same piece of legislation gave other federal employees an increase in pay costing $686 million a year; the annual pay increases therefore totaled more than a billion dollars.)

asked that the 11 per cent increase in personal income taxes not expire until the date originally scheduled, December 31, 1953, not six months earlier, as Chairman Reed wanted.

Mr. Reed was adamant. He believed that by lowering some and eliminating other taxes, government revenues would rise because of the stimulating effect of tax relief on business. The administration, always sharing his desire to lower taxes, insisted that the favorable effect on business would not produce sufficient increase in revenues to enable us to balance the budget the following year.

A prolonged debate ensued. I used every possible reason, argument, and device, and every kind of personal and indirect contact to bring Chairman Reed to my way of thinking, for his congressional position was a powerful one in tax affairs, and I wanted his support. When I could not make him see reason I informed him that we would fight the matter to the end.

Speaker Martin and Majority Leader Halleck led the administration forces in the House of Representatives. Backed by other Republicans, they succeeded in bottling up Chairman Reed's tax-cutting H. R. 1 in the House Rules Committee. We had more trouble, however, pushing through our extension of the excess-profits tax. Twice, on June 20 and June 23, I talked with Chairman Reed, urging him to call for a vote on this legislation in his committee. He refused, earning for himself from one commentator the label, in those days of Korean troubles, "the Syngman Rhee of Capitol Hill." On June 25, however, the House Rules Committee, with adroit and persistent prodding from Martin, Halleck, and others, voted to bring the excess-profits tax-extension bill to the floor without the approval of Reed's Ways and Means Committee. When Reed heard of this, his resistance melted. His committee voted to report the bill out. Two days later it passed the House, a week later the Senate. On July 16 I signed it into law.

On July 31 I made an entry in my diary after a visit of Ben Fairless, one of the country's chief industrialists, who had talked about the extension of the excess-profits tax:

> Ben Fairless came in several weeks ago. The call was merely a personal one, but as President of United States Steel, he mentioned the question of the excess profits tax, which I was then attempting to have extended by the Congress. He said: "The extension of the tax will cost our company 80 million dollars. We think you ought to insist upon extension. You cannot possibly favor one group in the country at the expense of another—and we are willing to bear our share until you find a more equitable way of dealing with the matter the excess profits tax was supposed to cover. Everybody agrees that it is a vicious and stupid form of

taxation, but in the light of the circumstances, you should continue it until next January."

The point of registering his statement—in almost his exact words—is that he is a representative of the class that the so-called liberal is always calling "thief," "robber," "economic tory," and all of the other names that imply venality and utter selfishness.

Of course, all of us are selfish. The instinct of self-preservation leads us into short-sightedness, and self-centered actions, often at the expense of our fellows. But the very least that we should attempt to do, it seems to me, is to think of our long term good as well as of our immediate gain. One thing that the long term good of each of us demands is the fiscal, economic, industrial and agricultural soundness of America. There is no future prosperity for any except as the whole shall prosper.

So what I am probably trying to say concerning my reactions to the above incident, is that at least Ben Fairless exhibited a more intelligent kind of selfishness than did the politicians seeking special favors for an individual or an industry demanding a completely privileged position for itself.

END OF TIRADE!

This tax fight, I am glad to say, did not cost the administration the friendship of Congressman Reed. In all our discussions he had been perfectly honest in his own convictions and kind enough to say he respected mine. Though the fight was tough, happily it never descended to personalities, even though it revealed a division within Republican ranks which time and work would have to heal.

In May 1953 the administration fought and won on a second important issue and made good a campaign pledge to shore up the rights of the states against the implacable expansionism of the federal government.

In 1894, off the coast of California near Santa Barbara, geologists struck oil for the first time in massive and unmeasured deposits beneath the floor of the Pacific Ocean. In 1938, off Louisiana, the Superior Oil Company and the Pure Oil Company together built a drilling platform in fourteen feet of water, drilled, struck oil a mile down, and, on March 11, brought in the first well in the open waters of the Gulf of Mexico.

In the years following World War II, these events led to a wrangle over one question: who owned the oil?

The stakes were immense. More than 15 billion barrels in potential reserves, the geologists estimated, lay beneath the sea off the coasts of Texas, Louisiana, and California—an amount equal to more than a third of the total proved petroleum reserves in the United States. Those 15 billion barrels of oil were worth about $40 billion.

The issue was generally identified as the tidelands controversy. Actually, none of the oil in dispute lay under the tidelands, that is, lands between the high and low tide marks, which everyone agreed belonged to the states. It lay under the continental shelf—submerged land extending seaward from the low tide mark out to an irregular line marking the place where the ocean depth dropped off to more than six hundred feet. In places in the Gulf of Mexico that line marking the end of the shelf extends out two hundred miles.

How far out did the rights of the states go: to the low tide mark? To the traditional three-mile limit recognized in international law as the outermost limit of a nation's right to ownership? To a "historic boundary" more than three miles out? Or to the edge of the shelf?

The answer was not one of mere academic interest. Texas, for example, claimed a historic boundary three marine leagues (about ten and a half miles) out to sea. Within this boundary it had an estimated 1.2 billion barrels of oil. But within a three-mile boundary, it would have had only 400 million barrels, a third as much.

For more than a hundred years these questions had been answered in one way, the way the Supreme Court answered it in 1845: "The shores of navigable water, and the soils under them, were not granted by the Constitution to the United States, but were reserved to the States respectively." As late as 1933 even Secretary of the Interior Harold Ickes refused to grant a federal oil lease in the lands off the coast of California, saying that those lands properly belonged to the state.

In September 1945, however, President Truman issued two Proclamations and two Executive Orders asserting federal jurisdiction over all natural resources of the entire continental shelf. The next year the Congress answered him by passing a joint resolution relinquishing any federal title to the submerged lands. President Truman vetoed the resolution and the Congress failed to override.

Then came a turning point. On June 23, 1947, the Supreme Court reversed itself. In a historic decision in the case of the *United States v. California,* the Court declared that California "is not the owner of the three-mile belt along its coast, and that the Federal Government rather than the State has paramount rights in and power over that belt, incident to which is full dominion over the resources of the soil under that water area, including oil." The Court had therefore denied ownership of the three-mile marginal belt to California. But it had specifically refused to confer outright ownership of the belt on the United States. The result was confusion—confusion which made compelling the need for congressional action to settle the dispute.

In May 1952 the Congress passed an act which would give the states ownership of the submerged lands. Again President Truman vetoed the bill, and once again the Congress failed to override. As the convention and campaign of 1952 approached, a hard line was therefore drawn between those who claimed states' rights and those who charged "giveaway."

Long before I had given permission in 1952 to enter my name in the nominating contest of the Republican party, I had learned of the coastal states' deep interest in this kind of legislation. On a visit to Texas in 1947 I was presented copies of historical documents on which that state based its claim to these lands up to the limit of three leagues from the coast. These papers included copies of documents pertaining to the Texan effort to achieve annexation to the United States. From these it seemed clear to me that in achieving the status of an independent nation, Texas had acquired the same claim to offshore lands as was possessed by Mexico, which had, in turn, derived its claim from Spanish law. Under the old Mexican law, territorial waters extended to three leagues offshore.

In its later annexation negotiations with the United States, the Texas government, wanting the United States government to take over its national debt—then calculated at no more than $10 million—offered the federal government all its public lands plus $350,000 in exchange.

The United States government rejected this proposal as a bad investment. The joint resolution of Congress annexing Texas in 1845 specified that Texas would retain both its debts and its lands. Consequently, according to Texas interpretation, that state was still entitled to ownership of its coastal areas—ownership which extended to three leagues from the shore—the distance established by the statutes of Texas during its years as an independent republic and ratified by the United States when Texas came into the Union.

I accepted this conclusion, on the historical evidence.

Other Gulf states, however, had similar claims. The two most interested were Louisiana and Florida, which also at one time had been Spanish colonies, and so had followed the Spanish custom of setting a boundary three leagues out to sea.

Louisiana claimed that the act of Congress admitting Louisiana into the Union in 1812 fixed a three-league seaward boundary for the state; "all islands within three leagues of the Coast," the act read, lay within the confines of Louisiana. Florida claimed that in 1868, when the Congress approved the state's constitution upon its return to the Union, the Congress ratified a boundary three marine leagues out into the Gulf.

Should these two states have the same rights as those claimed by Texas? If so, should all coastal states be equal in this respect, or should the others have rights only out to the traditional three-mile limit? The final decision on setting these boundaries would rest with the Congress and the courts.

In 1952 the Republican platform pledged "restoration to the States of their rights to all lands and resources beneath navigable inland and off-shore waters within their historic boundaries."

In a campaign speech at New Orleans on October 13 I amplified this commitment:

> The attack on tidelands is only a part of the effort of the administration to amass more power and money. So let me be clear in my position on the tidelands and on submerged lands and resources beneath inland and off-shore states which lie within historic state boundaries. As I said before, my views are in line with my party's platform. I favor the recognition of clear legal title to these lands in each of the forty-eight states. This has been my position since 1948, long before I was persuaded to go into politics. State titles in these so-called tideland areas stand clouded today. The Supreme Court has declared in very recent years that there are certain paramount federal rights in these areas, but the Court expressly recognized the right of Congress to deal with those matters of ownership and title. Twice, by substantial majorities, both houses of Congress have voted to recognize the traditional concept of state ownership of these submerged areas. Twice, these acts of Congress have been vetoed by the President. I would approve such acts of Congress.

The next day I said the same thing at Houston. My convictions thus known, President Truman, on January 16, 1953, just four days before leaving office, issued an Executive Order setting aside all the submerged lands of the continental shelf as a naval petroleum reserve. But by that time, Senator Spessard Holland of Florida and thirty-nine others of both parties introduced Senate Joint Resolution 13—the misnamed "Tidelands Bill"—which would restore these lands to the states.

On February 9 I repeated to the Legislative leaders my campaign pledge: if this legislation passed, I would sign it.

On March 2 Attorney General Brownell, in testimony before the Senate Committee on Interior and Insular Affairs, urged that the federal government not relinquish title in favor of the states but rather confer on them the right to administer the development and removal of natural resources landward to their historic boundaries. Moreover, to preclude long litigation, he urged the Congress to draw a line setting those boundaries.

State Department witnesses echoed the Attorney General's concern, particularly over giving the states outright ownership of land beyond the three-mile limit. Recognizing a boundary farther out, the department said, could conflict with international law.

I respected the right of both departments, in their testimony favoring submerged-lands legislation, to express their independent opinion on the technical distinction between outright ownership and mineral rights. I had made clear my own determination to try to restore ownership to the states, and my belief that by reason of history the limit of that ownership and the three-mile limit set by international law was one to be resolved by either the Congress or the courts. Accordingly, on April 24 I wrote Senator Clinton Anderson urging "prompt passage" of the submerged-lands resolution.

The argument became particularly warm in the Senate (the bill passed the House by a vote of 258 to 108 on April 1). Opponents charged "give-away," asserting that the federal government was conferring on a few states "resources which belong to all the people." States not on the sea-board fought the resolution because they wanted a share of the oil royal-ties. The other side pointed out that these interior states had never offered to split up profits from their mines.

After a long debate, in which Senator Wayne Morse set a filibuster record of twenty-two hours and twenty-six minutes, the Congress made its decision—it passed Senate Joint Resolution 13, conferring ownership on the states. I signed the bill into law on May 22.

The Congress had rejected Attorney General Brownell's request that it draw the boundary lines. Instead, their resolution set the seaward bound-ary for each coastal state at three miles from the coastline and declared that no boundary could extend beyond that distance in either the At-lantic or the Pacific. But the resolution went on to say that it in no way prejudiced any state's claim to a boundary beyond the three-mile limit in the Gulf of Mexico "if it were so provided prior to or at the time such State entered the Union or if it was heretofore or hereafter approved by the Congress." That refusal to draw a line threw the decision into the Supreme Court. In May of 1960 the Court granted a three-league limit in the Gulf to Texas and Florida and set a three-mile limit for the rest of the Gulf states. The Court rejected Louisiana's argument. The state had sought to prove that the Congress, admitting it to the Union in 1812, had in fact approved a boundary three leagues out. That decision of the Court settled the question.

There is a sequel to this history. The Submerged Lands Act gave the states ownership of the continental shelf out to their historic boundaries. But another piece of legislation, sponsored by the administration and passed later in 1953, established the federal government's mineral rights on the rest of the shelf, an area which by far outstrips in scope and wealth that of the section of the shelf ceded to the states. Whereas Louisiana, for example, had 250 million barrels of oil within its boundary, the fed-eral government, on its section of the continental shelf off the Louisiana coast, retained 3.75 billion barrels of oil. Whereas Texas, within its three-league limit, has 1.2 billion barrels, the United States government, in its section of the shelf off the Texas coast, retained 7.8 billion. By the end of 1962 bonuses, rentals, and royalties on the outer continental shelf land had brought in federal revenues of nearly $800 million. Thus the rights of all—both states and federal government—were respected.

A legislative matter of utmost importance to our economy and to the conduct of our foreign relations was the extension of the Trade Agreements Act.

Between 1949 and 1952 the United States exported more than one fourth of all its tobacco, grain sorghums, wheat and flour, cotton, and rice. In 1950 it exported more than 10 per cent of all its motor trucks, agricultural machinery, diesel engines, oil-field machinery, printing machinery, tractors, machine tools, and textile machines. The conclusion was clear: if foreign countries were to continue to buy from the United States on such a scale, and pay in the medium of international exchange, the American dollar, they somehow had to continue to get a reserve of American dollars. They could get dollars in just two ways: through foreign aid or through foreign trade—sales of their own products in the markets of the United States. The administration thought we should keep those markets open under programs that would prove beneficial to both sides.

On September 5, 1901, at the Buffalo Exposition, in what was to be his last speech before his assassination, President William McKinley (never known as a rabid internationalist) made an eloquent plea for the expansion of international trade. The half-century intervening had, in my view, only intensified the validity of his argument. In October 1952 Joseph Stalin, in his last public political pronouncement, asserted that so much of the world had become alienated from the West that Britain, France, and the United States could make no place in international markets for the products of Germany and Japan. Stalin concluded that inevitably Britain and France would "break from the embrace of the United States," and that West Germany and Japan would "try to smash United States domination." At a crucial instant in this desperate battle for markets, Stalin predicted, would arrive the Soviet Union's "moment for the decisive blow."

Despite overwhelming evidence, however, many members of the Congress continued to stand firm for high tariff rates to protect United States industry, regardless of the effect of such action on our foreign markets.

The immediate question in early 1953 was what to do about the Trade Agreements Act, due to expire on June 12 of that year. In essence this act authorized the President to enter into reciprocal agreements with other nations to raise or lower duties within 50 per cent of the 1945 rates. The first such legislation was passed in 1934 and similar laws had been passed periodically since then. The act at the time I was inaugurated had been extended in 1951 for two years. In the two decades between the first legislation in 1934 and the 1953 inauguration, average United States tariff rates had been cut in half under its provisions through thirty-eight agreements with fifty countries.

The administration, to be sure, never proposed to blow a Joshua's trumpet which would bring all tariff walls crashing down. We recognized that this course could visit hardship on many workers and their families. We recognized, too, that the Soviet threat and the demands of free countries' national security impaired the free working of pure economic law by requiring individual countries to be at least partly self-sufficient, able to produce goods for their armies and navies which other countries, if war should end forever, might better produce for them. To go full out in the direction of free trade, I insisted, the world would need permanent peace.

In the circumstances, the 1951 Trade Agreements Act then on the books seemed to me adequate, although I recognized that certain features might be modified. On April 7 I therefore sent a special message to the Congress recommending the renewal of the act in its present form for one year. That year would give the administration time to undertake a broad study of American foreign-trade policy in its entirety—a study to be conducted by a joint Executive-Legislative commission on foreign economic policy, which I also asked the Congress to establish by legislation.

The friends of freer trade—for example, the League of Women Voters, the Committee for Economic Development—backed the administration on this request.

The foes of freer trade backed another bill, introduced by Congressman Richard Simpson of Pennsylvania, which would have raised tariffs, set new import quotas, expanded the Tariff Commission from six to seven members to "rescue it from the blight of domination by executive powers," and required the President to follow the commission's recommendations in specific instances. It thus would have made him a messenger boy, and hamstrung him in his negotiation of reciprocal trade agreements with other countries. The effect of such legislation, if enacted, would have been to restrict seriously the President's capacity to deal intelligently with some of our foreign-relations problems.

Through more than two thousand pages of testimony before the House Ways and Means Committee that spring, the protectionist supporters of this bill made known their arguments for higher and thicker tariff walls. The almond growers of California, the manufacturers of band instruments from coast to coast, the members of the Bicycle Institute, the members of the Maraschino Cherry and Glacé Fruit Association, fish canners, wool-hat manufacturers, straw-hat manufacturers, wool growers, cigarette-lighter manufacturers, walnut growers—all these and hundreds of others added their voices to the powerful pleas of the producers of lead and zinc and of oil and of coal, who were to get specific protection through import quotas written into the legislation introduced by the Pennsylvania congressman. A representative of the Pin, Clip, and Fastener Association demanded from the House committee "an absolute import quota" with respect to safety pins. Altogether, these protectionists claimed they represented more than 5 million people.

Their arguments were not a trifle. For example, the Trade Agreements Act included a provision called the "escape clause," under which the Tariff Commission could recommend an increase in United States tariffs, to go into effect immediately upon the approval of the President. Early in 1953 I had been asked to approve a Tariff Commission recommendation for an increase in the tariff on briar pipes—plain, smoking pipes, produced in quantity in Italy, France, Britain, and Austria. Such an item would have been inconsequential insofar as the total volume of imports was concerned and in view of the small numbers engaged in making pipes here in the United States. However, it was considered an important case from the standpoint of establishing the administration's attitude and future policy; Secretary Weeks informed me that the whole world as well as Congress would be watching the result.

Certainly, from a legal point of view only, the conditions for the application of the escape clause to raise tariffs were clear-cut. On the other hand, raising a number of such tariffs might constitute a severe blow to the economies of some of our allies. Therefore, while members of the administration would probably, to a man, favor retaining the rates then in effect, the problem was that certain congressmen, of both major political parties, had no love for the principle of reciprocal trade agreements in the first place, and a presidential veto on the pipe recommendation of the Tariff Commission might very well provoke the Congress and result in a failure to re-enact the Trade Agreements Act itself.

Thus was the matter dramatized. In effect we had an issue where the good of the United States as a whole was pitted against the power of influential lobbies in Congress, with briar pipes in the middle.

On February 19 I announced my refusal—at least temporarily—to follow the commission's recommendation and raise the tariff. As we foresaw, Europeans read in the decision a declaration of the administration's intent, a hopeful omen for the future [see Appendix G].

Against the background of such executive decisions, the arguments in Congress roared on. The coal, lead and zinc, and other forces continued to push for the Simpson bill. In the heat of the fight Congressman Halleck facetiously reported a rumor on Capitol Hill that Foster Dulles had said the United States would make no more trade agreements. "If that's so," I retorted just as facetiously, "we'll get a new Secretary of State!"

Finally we won out. The Simpson bill came up for debate in the House on July 23. The representatives voted to send it back to committee. Then the administration bill went sailing through. On August 7 I signed it into law; we now had the Trade Agreements Act extended for a year and a commission established to start an intensive study of our foreign economic policy. This commission was composed of seventeen members. I was fortunate in obtaining as its chairman an outstanding American, Mr. Clarence B. Randall, chairman of Inland Steel Corporation.

In late February, I learned from the Secretary of State that a number of senators were determined to block my nomination of Charles E. Bohlen as American ambassador to Moscow.

When the new administration came in, "Chip" Bohlen was serving as the State Department's counselor. Since 1929 he had had a distinguished career in the United States Foreign Service and had become the State Department's foremost specialist on the Soviet Union.

But his experience was not his crime. His crime, in the eyes of men who opposed him, was that he was a high-up holdover from the "Acheson days" and, moreover, a holdover who had sat next to President Roosevelt at the 1945 conference at Yalta.

"The Government of the United States, under Republican leadership," the 1952 platform had declared, "will repudiate all commitments contained in secret understandings such as those of Yalta which aid Communist enslavements." Carrying out this pledge, I announced in my first State of the Union message that I would ask the Congress to join in a resolution making clear that the United States government recognized no commitment "contained in secret understandings of the past with foreign governments" which permit enslavement.

I submitted such a resolution to the Congress, writing in most of the "whereases" myself. I wanted such a resolution enacted, one which would declare to the world that the United States had never acquiesced in the subjugation of free peoples. But I refused to do what extremists asked: repudiate in their entirety the Yalta agreements and thus endanger United States rights in Vienna and Berlin, affirmed at Yalta, and raking over the ashes of the dead past. And I refused to shut my eyes and reject an expert and loyal man on the single ground that he had served President Roosevelt at Yalta as a Russian-language interpreter.

On Capitol Hill a storm blew up over the wording of the resolution. Then on March 5 Stalin died. His death silenced the wrangling of the congressmen. And it heightened the justification for filling the ambassadorial post in Moscow (it had been vacant since 1952, when the U.S.S.R. declared George Kennan *persona non grata*), for sending an experienced

American to the Soviet capital to watch and report through those un-certain days.

The name of Charles E. Bohlen had come up early in my conversations with Secretary Dulles as we sought out the right men to represent us abroad. I knew Bohlen and had learned to respect and like him. So when Foster stated that Bohlen's known qualifications would be especially valu-able at this time, I gladly approved the Secretary's recommendation. How-ever, he went on to say that a number of senators would oppose con-firmation on the ground that Bohlen had been at Yalta.

This seemed to me a flimsy argument. Knowing that Mr. Bohlen was a Foreign Service officer, I understood full well that he had been duty bound to act in accordance with the instructions of the President. Clearly he could not be thought personally culpable unless he had been present in an important advisory capacity to the President and then only if it could be shown that his advice was of a kind as to cast suspicion on his loyalty or judgment.

In 1951 when I was the Allied commander in NATO and Bohlen was the United States representative at the "Rose Palace" in Paris, where sub-ordinate officials from the United States, the United Kingdom, France, and the Soviets were trying to develop an agenda for a future Foreign Ministers conference, I had many conversations with him concerning our difficulties with the Soviets. So fully did I believe in his tough, firm but fair attitude in the wearying negotiations in which he participated and which lasted for months that I came to look upon him as one of the ablest Foreign Service officers I had ever met.

Therefore, when Foster warned me, I persisted in making the appoint-ment. Once I had an opportunity to explain to opposing senators my reasons for the action and to express my personal confidence in Bohlen, their objections would disappear.

Not so; too many of them had already expressed their opposition.

There was nothing to do but fight it out. I submitted the nomination, and Senator Taft promised to lead our forces in the Senate.

The Senate Foreign Relations Committee questioned Bohlen intensively on what he did at Yalta. When the sessions ended, the committee unani-mously approved his nomination, and those voting included Republicans Hickenlooper, Taft, Langer, Ferguson, and Knowland.

The nomination would now go to the Senate for a vote.

At a news conference on March 19 I was asked to comment on the statement the day before by Senator McCarthy that it was a serious mis-take for me not to withdraw the Bohlen nomination. I replied that I had a full report (as well as an enthusiastic recommendation) from the Secre-tary of State, and that Bohlen seemed to me a fine appointment.

The next day, when the Senate began its debate, McCarthy, McCarran, and Malone led the drive to get Bohlen's scalp. "We find," Senator McCarthy alleged on March 25, "that his entire history is one of complete, wholehearted, 100 per cent cooperation with the Acheson-Hiss-Truman regime." "Don't send Bohlen to Moscow," Senator Herman Welker of Idaho urged; "send General Van Fleet instead." Senator McCarran charged on the Senate floor that Scott McLeod (the State Department's head of the Bureau of Security and Consular Affairs) had refused to clear Bohlen because of derogatory information in his FBI file, and that Secretary Dulles had overruled this decision.

The suggestion that Bohlen was unacceptable to the FBI led to senators' demands to see the security file. On the morning of March 23 I therefore telephoned Attorney General Brownell about a proposal of Senators Wiley (Republican of Wisconsin) and Smith (Republican of New Jersey) that a committee of two senators, one from each party—Senators Taft of Ohio and Sparkman of Alabama—take a look at the file. The Attorney General feared that giving such permission would "open Pandora's box." I felt, however, that agreeing would not set a precedent. I gave the order that the two senators should be permitted to see the FBI summary—a paper purged of raw information and names of informants. Taft and Sparkman read the file and reported that it contained nothing which should stand in the way of Bohlen's confirmation.

On March 27 the Senate approved the nomination by an overwhelming vote, seventy-four to thirteen. But it was disquieting that those thirteen included only two Democrats, McCarran of Nevada and Johnson of Colorado, while the other eleven were Republicans—Bricker, Bridges, Dirksen, Dworshak, Goldwater, Hickenlooper, Malone, McCarthy, Mundt, Schoeppel, and Welker.

Bohlen went on to serve with distinction, first in Moscow, then in Manila, and finally in Washington as a special assistant to the Secretary of State.

Despite difficulties, by April 1 I was looking ahead with optimism. "Senator Taft and I are becoming right good friends," I wrote in my diary. "The relations between the Executive Branch and Republican leaders in Congress are getting better and better." "Only yesterday," I wrote, "someone came to me with the argument that I should set quietly about the formation of a new party. The method would be to make a personal appeal to every member of the House and Senate; to every Governor; and to every National Committeeman whose general political philosophy and purpose" square with " 'the middle way.' " Though such a course, I wrote, might become necessary, to build solidarity among the Republicans would be "much the better way."

My hope at that moment was that we might eventually be able to split off a number of senators from the "McCarthy-Malone axis" and thus reduce the remaining splinter group to practical impotence. If we could do so, I believed, we might go ahead toward building a splendid progressive and responsible record despite the Republicans' narrow margin in the Congress, and the persistent opposition of many Democrats.

But given these difficulties the work was hard and long that year. On May 28, for example, the Senate Appropriations Committee reported out a bill with a rider barring any American contribution to the United Nations in the next fiscal year if Communist China were admitted to membership. The chairman, Styles Bridges of New Hampshire, told reporters that only three of the twenty-three committee members had voted against that rider.

That day at a news conference I told reporters I opposed both Red China's admission and this provision. To express my opposition further, I called a special conference with the Legislative leaders to bring the question at once to a showdown.

At eleven fifty-five on the morning of Tuesday, June 2, I walked from my office to the Cabinet Room to meet with Senators Knowland, Millikin, Bridges, and Saltonstall; and Representatives Martin, Halleck, Arends, and Taber.

I came right to the point.

"I am distressed," I said, "that this rider might become law. I oppose it because I believe that the United States cannot properly serve notice on the United Nations in such a manner, and more fundamentally, that the United States cannot live alone."

I was not attempting to tell the members of Congress what they should think or what they should say, I continued, but I assured them that I was convinced that the rider, if enacted into law, could seriously hamper me in the conduct of foreign affairs.

"The United Nations," I said, "is essential because global war is now unthinkable as a result of the development of new and devastating weapons. Communist China is not yet in the United Nations. But it is not wise to tie our own hands irrevocably about affairs in advance. For example," I went on, "just think back to 1945, when Germany was our deadly enemy; who could then have foreseen that in only a few years it would become a friendly associate?" Finally, I emphasized to the congressmen the damage we would do ourselves in the eyes of the world by taking a penny-pinching monetary approach in order to prove our opposition to Red China's entry into the United Nations.

As soon as I had finished, Senator Bridges began. He and Senator Saltonstall and Senator Knowland, he explained, had voted for the rider because they thought their action would strengthen the hand of the President by laying down the rules of the game before a crisis appeared. Although they would not want to embarrass the President, they believed they were making a legitimate attempt to let the world know what the Congress thought.

"The admission of Red China," Senator Knowland said, "would violate every one of my basic beliefs. Already rumors are rampant that the British will start pushing for the admission of Red China soon after the negotiation of the cease fire in Korea. Under ordinary procedures the United States could not possibly come out on top in this issue if it came to a United Nations vote; therefore, we have to take an active and aggressive stand now."

I disagreed. The rider, I said, was the wrong instrument. If we were to have a workable world organization, every nation must expect to undergo defeats in the UN from time to time. The destruction of the UN would lead to the destruction of NATO, and where would we be then, how could we then maintain our own security?

Senator Knowland began to talk toward a compromise. Perhaps, he said, the senators should seek another way of showing congressional disapproval, such as a resolution which would have no legal effect on the President and cut off no funds.

With this proposal I quickly agreed. If the resolution did not lay the ax to appropriations, I could go to the heads of foreign governments, let them know the attitude of the Congress and its leaders, and warn them that if they forced the issue, I could not answer for the response of the United States.

Accordingly, Bridges announced that he and his associates would scrap their rider.

That skirmish was over. But striving to preserve the Executive branch from congressional encroachment was in no sense ended. Slightly more than a month later, on July 9, 1953, I picked up the telephone and called Congressman Walter Judd of Minnesota. The Congress, I told him, was getting ready to adopt an amendment which would prevent my obligating any mutual-security funds until the European governments ratified the treaty which would set up a European Defense Community, including West Germany. Among other things, it was an insult, I went on, for a Republican President to face such a restrictive policy when the Congress had not forced it on his Democratic predecessor. Though Congressman Judd defended his original support of the amendment, he agreed to work for a compromise.

This exchange was just one round in the first of eight battles which I fought with the Congress over the annual appropriation for the mutual-security program. In his last Budget message, President Truman had recommended new mutual-security appropriations of $7.6 billion. I had scaled this request down to $5.1 billion. But there was a host on Capitol Hill determined to chop the figure further. The Congress, one member declared, should "bring to an abrupt end this utterly useless and ineffective attempt to buy support and friendship from other nations." At the head of the ever-popular attack on mutual-security programs stood Congressman Otto Passman of Louisiana, who had made—and still is making —a career out of irresponsibly cutting back mutual-security money each year. Yet every two years his constituents return him to Congress, where, under the present system of organization, his views and actions fall with an unfortunately heavy impact upon this crucial national program.

By July 18 the House Appropriations Committee had cut my $5.1-billion request down to $4.4 billion. Four days later the House rejected two proposals by Republican Congressman Jacob Javits of New York to restore part of the money—money which would help our European allies. Only forty-one congressmen voted for the first Javits proposal, thirty-six for the second.

The next day the Senate Appropriations Committee added $100 million, and there the figure stood—$4.5 billion—at the end. The administration had lost more than a half-billion dollars of its request, with only a few Republicans supporting the amount I requested. Everett Dirksen was first among them.

In another international-affairs contest—for emergency immigration legislation—the administration once again had to take on Senator Pat McCarran, Democrat of Nevada.

On April 22 I asked the Congress to enact legislation admitting to the United States 120,000 Europeans each year for the next two years. During World War II, migration from one country to another had virtually ceased. After the war, millions became refugees, fleeing from Communist Eastern Europe. Other millions had become expellees—Germans thrown out of Eastern Europe by the Communist rulers. In 1952 the Congress—over President Truman's veto—had enacted the McCarran-Walter Immigration and Naturalization Act, a restrictive measure which retained national-origins quotas based on the United States population of 1924. This needed revision.

The administration's Emergency Migration Act of 1953 (its original title)—though it left the 1952 McCarran-Walter Act for the moment untouched—provided for the admission of 110,000 East German escapees and expellees now in the Federal Republic of Germany, in West Berlin, and in Austria; 15,000 escapees from Communism presently in NATO countries and in Trieste; 75,000 Italians (to ease the burden of Italy's colossal overpopulation and acute unemployment and thus help Premier Alcide De Gasperi, a stanch ally); and 20,000 immigrants from Greece and the Netherlands, both badly devastated by the war.

Administration witnesses argued for the bill on humanitarian grounds.

They testified to the contribution these new European immigrants could make to America, including a start on our farm-labor problem. They assured the Senate Judiciary Committee that these new citizens would not fall with heavy impact on the American labor market.

A representative of the DAR was sure that these foreigners, if admitted, would take away Americans' jobs. Congressman Walter of Pennsylvania feared spies would be planted among them. All true anti-Communists, other House members argued, should stay where they belonged, in Europe, right up against the Iron Curtain, ready to leap to the bugle call for a war of liberation. Above all, Senator McCarran and his supporters opposed the admission of people who were not refugees. "We must be careful," he said, "not to pass a surplus-population bill in the guise of a refugee measure, or permit classification of refugees in such a way as to open the door to Communist penetration."

On the morning of July 14 Senator Arthur Watkins, Republican chairman of the Senate Judiciary Committee, telephoned me to say that the administration was in trouble with the bill. Senators Butler (Republican of Maryland) and Jenner (Republican of Indiana), he went on, wanted Senator Watkins and Senator McCarran to come to see me about it, particularly about the Italian quota. Butler and Jenner, Senator Watkins said, did not want the total figure to exceed 175,000, a figure which Senator Watkins and I agreed was not enough. I looked at my calendar and told him I could meet with him and McCarran at twelve-thirty.

As soon as the conversation ended, I picked up the telephone again and asked for Secretary Dulles.

"I've just learned," I told him, "that McCarran wants to cut the total figure to 175,000, eliminating the quota for Italian nationals on the assumption that they are not refugees. How many Italians," I asked, "are also displaced persons?"

A few minutes later Secretary Dulles phoned back the answer. "There are nearly a half-million Italian displaced persons from North Africa and Trieste," he said. "They could fill to overflowing our suggested quota of 75,000."

Senator McCarran finally arrived. With these facts I tried to persuade him to go along. I made about as much impression on him as beating on an anvil with a sponge.

Three days later, on July 23, however, the Senate Judiciary Committee reported out a bill which would admit 215,000 immigrants over the next three years. The bill, by committee amendment, was now an all-refugee measure except for a provision for 4000 visas to "eligible orphans." Senators McCarran, Eastland, Jenner, Welker, McClellan, and Olin Johnston still opposed the bill as it stood. But at nine o'clock that morning

Senator McCarran again came to see me. This time he had a compromise: 190,000 adults and 4000 children. If I accepted it, he said, he would neither fight the bill nor vote for it.

I refused. And when the fight had ended, the administration had authority to admit the number recommended by the Senate committee, 215,000 over three years. McCarran himself went along. On August 7 I signed into law the bill named the "Refugee Relief Act of 1953."

Despite the difficulties, the Eighty-third Congress, under Republican leadership, had by adjournment day built a record that gave us hope for the future. To be sure, the administration's plea for two more commissioners for the District of Columbia had died in committee. So—after it passed the House—had the administration's plea for legislation to make Hawaii a state. But the Congress had, among other things, passed the tax extensions, the Trade Agreements Act extension, the Refugee Relief Act, the Submerged Lands Act, a bill providing federal aid for school districts overloaded by nearby federal installations, and one sending emergency wheat to drought-stricken Pakistan.

Moreover, in eighty-three test votes on "Eisenhower issues" that year, seventy-four had turned out to be victories. And in these eighty-three test votes, the nonpartisan *Congressional Quarterly* reported, a majority of the Republicans had voted with me 80 per cent of the time, a majority of the Democrats 55 per cent of the time. Ten Republican congressmen supported the administration on 97 per cent of the votes, and one—Wigglesworth of Massachusetts—turned in a performance of 100 per cent.

On the Senate side, even Malone, Williams, and Welker voted with the administration on nearly 60 per cent of the test issues; and Saltonstall, Ives, Flanders, Payne, Bush, and Duff supported us 90 per cent or more of the time (Duff registered 100 per cent).

Despite the headlines on Republican discord, the Republicans in the Congress were falling into line behind the administration. Perseverance was producing results.

But in the midst of all these gains that year, the administration, and I personally, suffered an inexpressibly sad loss in the death on July 31 of Senator Robert A. Taft.

In the short time that Senator Taft lived after my inauguration, we worked together to rebuild unity in the Republican party and to put through legislation we both felt necessary to the welfare of the country.

As far back as the preinaugural days, I had sent word to him from the Commodore Hotel in New York that I should be highly pleased if he would serve as the Republican leader in the Senate. I had already learned that he would like to continue in the office. I was delighted when he agreed, and even to this day I believe that if fate had permitted him to continue in his post, the Republican party would have developed into a much stronger and better-unified political organization.

During the weeks we worked together a sound friendship developed between Senator Taft and me. It was not a Damon-Pythias affair, nor was there any unfailing compatibility of political viewpoint. On the one or two occasions when he voiced his differences impatiently and in vehement fashion—as in the April 30 Cabinet meeting—his behavior seemed at the time inexplicable; his illness then was unsuspected.

At any rate, Senator Taft and I early reached an amicable and definite understanding as to methods of handling our common problems and, indeed, he never once failed to carry forward vigorously any mission that I asked him to undertake in the Senate.

In some things I found him unexpectedly "liberal," specifically in his attitudes on old-age pensions, school aid, and public housing—attitudes, incidentally, which were miles away from those of some self-described "Taft stalwarts." One day after a Legislative-leaders meeting, he walked into my office to continue the discussion.

"You know, I hate federal bureaucracy," he said. "The best way I can think of to combat its growth and at the same time help people would be to have the federal government pay a flat fee to the states for every child in school, and automatically to send out a monthly pension check, also of a fixed amount, to every man and woman who reached the age of sixty-five."

When I heard these things, I had to chuckle. "Why, Bob, with those views you're twice as liberal as I am. How did you ever come to be called a conservative?"

"Oh, you know how it is," he replied. "A label like that gets applied to you, and afterwards you just have to live with it."

In almost all domestic matters, however, he and I stood firmly together. In these fields the main point of difference between us lay in our views on how quickly we could implement those things on which we agreed in principle, especially the reduction of federal expenditures.

In the foreign field Senator Taft and I never disagreed when we discussed questions academically or theoretically. He supported—somewhat reluctantly, it is true—the theory of cooperative security and mutual aid. But when the matter became specific in terms of actual loans or grants, he found it difficult to agree.

Nevertheless, Senator Taft, throughout the period of his active service after my inauguration, cooperated so well with the Executive branch as to excite my admiration and certainly to exceed by far any expectations that I held in December of 1952. In particular, whenever we could foresee a definite fight in the Senate—as in the matter of the Bohlen appointment—he, on my request, would invariably take the part of a loyal and effective lieutenant and exert the finest kind of leadership.

Senator Taft's death came so quickly after we really appreciated the seriousness of his illness that even those of us who had some little warning were dismayed, and deeply grieved.

In April he had come to the Augusta National Golf Club, in Georgia, at my invitation, and on the following day we played a game of golf. It was a cold, raw, damp day, and when he remarked to me that his hip hurt him and that he had noticed some pain in that region for several days, I thought little of it. After all, neither of us was any longer young and we were naturally subject to aches and pains after exercise. However, I did suggest that upon his return to Washington he should see the doctors at Walter Reed Hospital. He thought he would probably do so, remarking that he planned to consult his own doctor later in Cincinnati, but a preliminary examination at Walter Reed might indicate no necessity for hurry.

A few days later in Washington the senator told me that he was not feeling well, and that the pain in his hip was more severe. In spite of my insistence that he go to the hospital, he still did not do so—I was told— until May 20. A week later my doctor, General Snyder, told me confidentially that there was a strong suspicion of the presence of cancer, although the examination in Walter Reed was thus far only of a preliminary nature. This possibility was kept secret, first because it was the kind of thing that could not be determined accurately at that moment, and second, it would have been unfortunate for any news to leak out, true or untrue.

Soon after leaving Walter Reed, he went on to Ohio, where he entered another hospital. I was then given to understand that there was a serious question as to the exact nature of his trouble. For a while the doctors held out the hope that he might have only a kind of glandular disorder and might be able to resume his normal duties, but by June 1 I had hints that he might be seriously incapacitated.

Senator Taft's condition remained very much of a question mark for the next week or so. However, while I was in Minnesota to address the Junior Chamber of Commerce convention on June 10, I was shocked to receive a message that he had decided to give up his leadership duties in the Senate. Even this did not mean that he was necessarily fatally ill, but he was suffering considerable discomfort and felt that he could no longer carry on the duties of Senate leader. He was still hopeful that he could retain an active part in the Senate's deliberations.

A short time later Senator Taft came to the White House to attend a conference. This was the first time I saw him using crutches, and while he told me that they were helpful in relieving the pain in his hip, I thought that he was beginning to have the appearance of a very sick man. Nevertheless, he kept hard at work. On June 24 he came to the White House for breakfast with other Legislative leaders and on the following day he came to a luncheon of the same kind.

Four days later he attended a Legislative-leaders meeting in the Cabinet Room. After the close of the meeting he came to my office for an informal conversation. On this day, by contrast with his appearance of ten days earlier, he looked fine, had a good color, and was jovial. He was particularly delighted with his physical improvement and told me that although he had lost twenty-five pounds since he first became ill, he had in the preceding week gained four of them back. Bob Taft was quite sure that he was on the road to recovery. My elation was shattered, however, when, only hours later, I was informed by the doctors that his temporary improvement was the result of a particular type of treatment, affording no real promise that his health would be permanently improved.

Finally, in early July, Senator Taft went to New York, and on July 8 an exploratory operation was performed. General Snyder had told me that the senator was due for such an operation earlier but had postponed it because of his confidence in his marked improvement.

I was anxious to avoid bothering him, but I kept in contact through messages carried by the doctors, and on July 21, with their permission, I called him on the phone. He was feeling well and he announced that within a week he was going to leave the hospital and come back to Washington. We discussed a number of specific matters, one of which was the appointment of an Assistant Secretary of Labor, of whom Senator Taft heartily approved. A statement he made during that conversation will remain vividly in my memory always. "I have just one ambition— to come back and help you make this administration completely successful."

He made the same statement to others several times. On July 31 he died, never having left the hospital.

Whenever the life of a distinguished man comes to an end before his work is done, one cannot but wonder what might have been if he had continued. Thus, with the news of Senator Taft's passing, I paused and reflected on this—and, more generally, on the impact of personality on the current of human affairs. What would have been the outcome of the Battle of Gettysburg had Stonewall Jackson been spared to act once more as "Lee's right arm" in that engagement? What would have come from the Congress of Vienna without the personality and influence of Metternich? How brilliant would have been the victories of Revolutionary France had its armies been commanded by Joseph Hooker rather than by Napoleon Bonaparte? Without Grant how long would the War between the States have endured? How much bitterness might the nation have been spared had Lincoln lived into the days of Reconstruction?

These questions, of course, must be dismissed finally as idle though absorbing conjectures. But I could not help feeling that with the loss of Senator Taft—with his dedication to the principles of the Republican party, his determination that the Republicans would act virtually as a unit under the leadership of the President, his towering stature in the Senate—the party and, more importantly, the nation had suffered a blow which would be felt for a long time, a loss which possibly could never be made good.

CHAPTER IX

Some Early Decisions

. . . a Government of laws, and not of men.

—The report of a Constitution or
Form of Government for the
Commonwealth of Massachusetts (1779)

O N my desk, when I took office, lay a document which was to lead to much controversy throughout the spring of 1953. Submitted to the Department of Justice but not acted upon in the final weeks of the Truman administration, it was an appeal for executive clemency in the case of Julius and Ethel Rosenberg who, convicted of espionage against the United States, were under sentence of death.

More than a decade earlier, Mr. and Mrs. Rosenberg had become members of the Communist party in New York City. At the height of World War II, in the summer of 1944, Mrs. Rosenberg's brother, David Greenglass, began work as a machinist at the atomic weapons center in Los Alamos, New Mexico. In January 1945, six months before Potsdam, eight months before Hiroshima, he gave the Rosenbergs his first sketches—rough drawings of a high-explosive lens used to detonate the bomb. Later the Rosenbergs sent a courier, Harry Gold, who identified himself by showing Greenglass a torn piece of a paper box which matched the other half sent to Greenglass by the Rosenbergs; Gold carried away from this rendezvous more sketches of the lens. In September, Greenglass passed another crude drawing to the Rosenbergs, this time of the atomic bomb itself, with a set of explanatory notes.

No one will probably ever know exactly how much these grubby scraps of paper, passed in secrecy from hand to hand, changed the course of history and the safety of the United States.

Four years passed. Then a sequence of events occurred, each caused by an earlier one, like a row of dominoes going down. In England, Klaus Fuchs confessed to espionage for the Soviet Union. He implicated Gold, who in turn named Greenglass. In June 1950 Greenglass confessed, naming the Rosenbergs, and in January 1951 they were indicted.

For cooperating with the prosecution, Greenglass' sentence was for fifteen years of imprisonment, Gold's for thirty. In England, Fuchs drew only fourteen. But the Rosenbergs pleaded not guilty. The jury returned its verdict in March 1951; Mr. and Mrs. Rosenberg became the first Americans in peacetime to be sentenced to death on a charge of espionage.

The United States Court of Appeals upheld the conviction in February 1952. In October the Supreme Court granted a stay of execution during action on a petition for reconsideration of its earlier refusal to review the case. The next month the Supreme Court denied reconsideration. After denying judicial clemency, the original sentencing judge stayed the executions to allow the Rosenbergs to apply for executive clemency. There the question hung in January of 1953.

The Communist press screamed that the United States government had hypocritically convicted the Rosenbergs of espionage, framing them because they were Jewish. With them joined, at least in sympathy, other Americans who, not denying the Rosenbergs' indisputable guilt, questioned the severity of their sentence. After all, they argued, Gold, Greenglass, and Fuchs got off with their lives and even without life imprisonment. Why, for the first time, give the death sentence in this case? Because the Rosenbergs, others answered, refused to confess. Execution would make them martyrs, the pleaders for clemency contended. But softening their sentence, the answer went, would keep other spies from confessing in the future. (Gold and Greenglass, who had confessed, escaped the death penalty.)

Despite these rebuttals, many people sincerely believed that life imprisonment might be a better judgment, particularly because the Rosenbergs were the parents of two small sons and because one of the condemned was a woman.

On February 11, 1953, I made public my decision.

The nature of the crime for which they [the Rosenbergs] have been found guilty and sentenced [I wrote] far exceeds that of the taking of the life of another citizen; it involves the deliberate betrayal of the entire nation and could very well result in the death of many, many thousands of innocent citizens. . . .

The courts have provided every opportunity for the submission of evidence bearing on this case. . . . All rights of appeal were exercised and the conviction of the trial court was upheld after full judicial review. . . .

I have made a careful examination into this case and am satisfied that the two individuals have been accorded their full measure of justice. . . .

During the spring the Communist press and its cohorts, and others, including those opposed to capital punishment, protested the sentence.

Through mass meetings and picketings, the Communists went all out to twist public sympathy in their direction. On May 25, however, the Supreme Court delivered its decision: it again refused to hear the appeal. On June 15 it denied a plea to stay the execution.

The next day, because this problem was very much on my mind, I wrote to my son, John, then serving in Korea, about one aspect of the case:

> To address myself more specifically to the Rosenberg case for a minute, I must say that it goes against the grain to avoid interfering in the case where a woman is to receive capital punishment. Over against this, however, must be placed one or two facts that have great significance. The first of these is that in this instance it is the woman who is the strong and recalcitrant character, the man is the weak one. She has obviously been the leader in everything they did in the spy ring. The second thing is that if there would be any commuting of the woman's sentence without the man's then from here on the Soviets would simply recruit their spies from among women.[1]

In the letter to John, I had explained that the incidence of threatening letters was such that, as a precautionary measure, I had to double the security guard around his children.

On June 19 the Supreme Court vacated a stay of execution which had been granted two days earlier on a point of law by Mr. Justice Douglas (whether the federal district judge had the right to impose the death penalty when the jury had not recommended it). And that night, with Communist and anti-Communist demonstrations up and down Pennsylvania Avenue in front of the White House, the sentence of the courts was duly executed.

---

[1] In a letter addressed to a friend who was opposed to the execution of the Rosenberg sentence, I included the following:

"As to any intervention based on consideration of America's reputation or standing in the world, you have given the case for one side. What you did not suggest was the need for considering this kind of argument over and against the known convictions of Communist leaders that free governments—and especially the American government—are notoriously weak and fearful and that consequently subversive and other kinds of activity can be conducted against them with no real fear of dire punishment on the part of the perpetrator. It is, of course, important to the Communists to have this contention sustained and justified. In the present case they have even stooped to dragging in young and innocent children in order to serve their own purpose.

"The action of these people has exposed to greater danger of death literally millions of our citizens. The very real question becomes 'how far can this be permitted by a government that, regardless of every consideration of mercy and compassion, is also required to be a *just* government in serving the interests of all its citizens?' That their crime is a very real one and that its potential results are as definite as I have just stated, are facts that seem to me to be above contention."

*   *   *

Not all of the tasks that fell to me as President in the first few months of office were onerous or unpleasant. There were many occasions on which the privileges and honors of the office of the Presidency made themselves apparent. One such occasion came on March 3, 1953, when Foster Dulles sent me a memorandum stating that he had now completed, on my behalf, the composition of a delegation to the coronation of Queen Elizabeth II. Proposed was the name of General George C. Marshall to serve as my special representative, and Governor Earl Warren and Fleur Cowles to serve as assistant representatives. General Omar N. Bradley, chairman of the Joint Chiefs of Staff, was to represent the three United States services. These invitations were quickly issued and accepted.

*   *   *

On the morning of September 8, at the Summer White House in Denver, I received the tragic news that the chief justice of the United States, Fred Vinson, had died in the night of a heart attack. He had long been a good friend, but entirely aside from the personal distress that his death brought to me, it was obvious I had to begin a search for the man best fitted for the post.

I became hopeful of making an appointment before the beginning of the fall session of the Court. Among the factors that guided me in the search, partisan politics had no place. At the time of the chief justice's death, out of the nine members of the Court eight had been classed as Democrats before joining the Court and only one—Associate Justice Harold Burton—as a Republican. Naturally, for the good of the country, I hoped eventually to achieve a better balance in this regard. As I said in a speech some years later, I did not want the Court to be "a repository of unbalanced partisan attitudes." But I had no intention of selecting a chief justice merely on such a basis. My goal was a United States Supreme Court worthy of the high esteem of the American people.

At the beginning of my administration I had informed the Attorney General that in submitting to me recommendations for vacancies in the federal Judiciary, character and ability would be the first qualifications to seek.

I told him also that I would appoint no one who did not have the approval of the American Bar Association and the respect of the community in which he lived. I further directed Brownell to use the FBI in making a thorough investigation of a prospective appointee's reputation and of every pertinent detail of his life, a practice that I followed respecting major appointments from the very beginning. Another qualification I thought important was that of age. I finally fixed sixty-two as the upper age limit for initial appointment to the federal courts, although I said also that I would be ready to waive this requirement, allowing a margin of a year or so if other qualifications were unusually impressive. The general health of the person proposed would also be an important factor. Finally, I told Brownell that I placed great value on solid common sense—a quality hard to define but well understood by most—and that we would exclude from any list of prospects candidates known to hold extreme legal or philosophic views. I wanted federal judges who commanded the respect, confidence, and pride of the population.

For the office of chief justice, additional factors had to be considered, over and above these instructions which applied to all appointments to the federal Judiciary.

A chief justice, I felt, should in addition to meeting all the criteria I had established for the selection of other judges, be a man of national stature, who had such recognized administrative ability as to promise an efficient conduct of the affairs of the Court and who could be expected to provide a leadership that would be favorably received by all the courts of the land. In finding the man who met these criteria, I was determined, as I told one friend who telephoned with a name to suggest, "not to make any mistakes in a hurry."

A number of candidates immediately came to my mind, or were suggested by the Attorney General and others. Among these were Judge John J. Parker of North Carolina, of the Fourth United States Circuit Court of Appeals; Arthur T. Vanderbilt, chief justice of the Supreme Court of New Jersey; Judge Orie Phillips of the Tenth United States Circuit Court of Appeals in Denver; John W. Davis, a highly respected and esteemed lawyer and a former presidential nominee of the Democratic party; and Governor Warren of California. In addition, I gave serious thought to the possibility of appointing John Foster Dulles.

Most of these prospects were automatically eliminated either because of advanced age or a record of unsound health. Although Foster Dulles exceeded the age limit by three years, at that time he seemed so vital and vigorous that I determined to take up with him, but with no commitment, the possibility of his selection, because of my belief that he was one of the few men who could fill the post with distinction.

He eliminated himself instantly and unequivocally. He said, in effect, "I have been interested from boyhood in the diplomatic and foreign affairs of our nation. I'm highly complimented by the implication that I might be suited to the position of chief justice, but I assure you that my interests lie with the duties of my present post. As long as you are happy with my performance there, I have no interest in any other."

Disabling factors among other prospects—and Foster's decision—began to narrow further consideration to members of the Supreme Court and to Governor Warren. I had been informed that two or three of the members of the Court were failing in health, and another was well over the established age limit. Two others represented what I thought were extreme views in matters that could be expected to come before the Court for decision.

Governor Warren was a man whom I had long respected, although my personal contacts with him had been few. But because of his qualifications for public service, I had made, even before the election, a number of inquiries about his career and his standing both in his own state and throughout the nation. I learned that he had served for a number of years as the attorney general for the state of California. As its governor he was frequently mentioned as a presidential candidate. His personal reputation was impeccable, and while here and there some people voiced questions involving his political philosophy, these questions were generally casual or without significant substance.

A few months prior to the death of Chief Justice Vinson, I had talked to Warren about his basic philosophy and been quite pleased that his views seemed to reflect high ideals and a great deal of common sense. During this conversation I told the governor that I was considering the possibility of appointing him to the Supreme Court and that I was definitely inclined to do so if, in the future, a vacancy should occur. However, neither he nor I was thinking of the special post of chief justice, nor was I definitely committed to any appointment. Now in the fall of 1953, my attention became more and more centered on him. However, realizing that my own sketchy contacts with Earl Warren did not form a sufficient basis for final decision in this vital matter, I told the Attorney General that I wanted to gain a more definite opinion on the governor's record of attainments as a lawyer, as district attorney, and as attorney general of California, and that I needed the conclusions of a qualified lawyer on the matter. Brownell, who was well acquainted with him, flew to California to talk with him. To avoid speculation by others, I had told the Attorney General that I would not attempt to meet with the governor personally. He was to keep his meeting secret.

Long before the conference between Governor Warren and Brownell, however, gossip concerning the possibility of his appointment had developed and I received a number of letters, some of which vehemently opposed any thought of putting Governor Warren on the Supreme Court bench. Several writers argued that appointment of the governor would be merely the payment of a personal political debt, supposedly incurred at the time of my nomination.

The truth was that I owed Governor Warren nothing. The ridiculous character of this accusation was amply proved, I thought, by the history of the 1952 convention. Governor Warren would not take any action to throw his seventy California votes to me and thus assure my nomination even after he realized that on the first ballot my nomination could be assured by a change of only nine votes. Minnesota supplied those votes, and even then Governor Warren's delegation refused to switch until after the motion was made to make the selection unanimous.

The Attorney General, on his return, gave me a helpful report, and I decided to name Governor Warren chief justice. Because the Congress had adjourned, I made a recess appointment, and he took his oath of office on October 5. The following January, I sent the nomination to the Senate. After Senator William Langer, chairman of the Committee on the Judiciary, bottled the nomination up for nearly two months, the Senate approved it in eight minutes, on March 1, 1954.

At the time of Governor Warren's appointment to the Court there was pending the question of racial segregation in our schools. The issue had been argued before the justices in December of 1952 and it would be reargued in December of 1953. With the publication of its historic decision on May 17, 1954, declaring school segregation unconstitutional, much criticism and, indeed, consternation arose in some quarters, even though the decision was unanimous and despite the fact that on the Court were three men of Southern birth and upbringing (Associate Justices Hugo L. Black of Alabama, Stanley F. Reed of Kentucky, and Tom Clark of Texas). Some of those who disliked the decision directed their criticism against the chief justice on the theory that because of his position it was obvious that he was responsible for the Court's decision, which reversed an earlier one of 1896.

This criticism, too, I have always discounted; the chief justice had been on the Court such a short time—he was its newest recruit—that I do not believe he could possibly have exercised the amount of influence ascribed to him over this group of men, who are notable for the independence and variety of their views. I have questioned many eminent lawyers on the soundness of this decision, and without exception they have expressed the opinion that it conformed to the Constitution of the United States.

This issue was to become increasingly critical among the many federal concerns of this decade and the one that followed. In the absence of federal law on the subject, the Supreme Court found it necessary to issue instructions to lower courts on school desegregation rulings for the enforcement of the decision reached in May 1954. This later move placed upon each locality the responsibility to plan for bringing about what the

Court called desegregation with "all deliberate speed." These plans had to be approved by the appropriate local federal district judge.

Although, as President, I never expressed either approbation or disapproval of a Court decision, in this instance there can be no question that the judgment of the Court was right.

During eight years in the Presidency I was called upon to make five selections for the Supreme Court. They were, in addition to Governor Warren, Charles Evans Whittaker of Missouri, John M. Harlan of New York, Potter Stewart of Ohio, and William J. Brennan of New Jersey. In each case I went to great lengths to satisfy myself that the appointments were given to the best-qualified men on the basis of the criteria laid down early in 1953. Justice Brennan, for instance, a Democrat, was suggested by New Jersey Chief Justice Vanderbilt, a Republican, one of the most highly respected and best-known figures in American jurisprudence. Judge Vanderbilt said that, in his opinion, Brennan possessed the finest "judicial mind" that he had known in a long experience, and was of the highest character.

Early in my administration I added another item to the criteria I had initially established for the appointment of men to our higher courts, particularly to the Supreme Court. I told the Attorney General that I would not thereafter appoint anyone who had not served on a lower federal court or on a state supreme court. My thought was that this criterion would insure that there would then be available to us a record of the decisions for which the prospective appointee had been responsible. These would provide an inkling of his philosophy.

*   *   *

I was determined to do my best to unite, strengthen, and invigorate the Republican party. To make this clear, and to stimulate the participation of younger people, I journeyed in June 1953 to the Mount Rushmore National Monument in South Dakota and addressed the National Young Republican organization.

". . . One of the many responsibilities I acquired last year," I said, "was that of becoming leader of the Republican party. I am very proud —and I may say I am kept intensely aware—of this special responsibility."

Most Americans, I suggested to the young people, would agree with me that it would be inappropriate for the President of the United States to indulge incessantly in partisan activities. Many of the critical problems before the country were in no sense party issues. But from John Adams onward, we had held the conviction that representative government required a healthy two-party system and that the vigor of the party in power required leadership by the President.

The audience seemed to be full of the vitality we needed in the Republican party. "Having been all my life a member of a militant organization, it would be strange indeed," I remarked, "if I should lack satisfaction in a meeting with militant Republicans." And the young Republicans had certainly earned the adjective "militant." Their zeal, their courage, their energy excited my admiration and commanded my respect. I could only hope that we would have the sense to encourage them further, not to discourage them with the prospect of bucking an old-line party organization or the feeling that new faces were not really welcome until they became old faces. I wanted to increase our gains in the South, to strengthen our appeal to sensible Democrats and independents, to get away from constricting—and largely meaningless—labels like "liberal" and "conservative," and to destroy the concept that the Republican party belonged to a minority which, though the party might be a wreck, was determined to "own the wreckage." The Citizens groups who had helped us win were perfectly willing to vote Republican just as long as we could command their respect and interest. They were just as willing to forget any party affiliation if the hierarchy of the party ignored or resented them. I was anxious to keep the Citizens on a permanent basis, but there were those who thought of them as anathema. In speaking to the young I knew that I was appealing to a group which had the courage to label their convictions at an early age. We needed them—and I liked them.

For that reason it was important to point out that, even though head of the party, I was President first and could not go around cracking heads together, and that responsible groups within the party would have to help it build on the momentum created by our election in 1952. Here assembled was a part of the Republican future. I thought it would be well to warn them of what was ahead.

Members of the opposition would, of course, "view with alarm" everything we did. But I urged my audience to be philosophic and patient, noting that this kind of sound and fury is another characteristic inherent in our two-party system. Consequently, I urged them always to keep their sense of humor, pointing out that since time immemorial man has heard no cry more agonized than that of the deposed bureaucrat or the demoted politician.

In Hershey, Pennsylvania, at a great political rally on October 13, 1953, a group of friends gave me a birthday party and possibly the most splendid birthday present I have ever received. I liked the evening's entertainment—the music was by Fred Waring and his orchestra—and, except for the fact that I had to make a speech, I enjoyed the occasion. But the real significance of the evening was the announcement of the Eisenhower Exchange Fellowships. They were established to finance extended visits to and from the United States, not by students or by men and women exclusively from the academic world, but rather by outstanding people in mid-career from a variety of fields—education, journalism, government, business, and the professions. This nonpartisan program of broad scope[2] is one of the few two-way international exchange programs not financed by the government.

I was grateful to my friends for conceiving such an idea. To keep in touch with the progress of these grants, I have talked with the Fellows, both American and foreign, who have received them.

By June of 1963 the grants had brought to the United States 160 Fellows from fifty foreign countries and had sent abroad 22 from the United States. It was fine to feel on that birthday evening that so many were expressing in such a practical way their faith in the promotion of understanding among peoples everywhere, of whatever station, as one basis for achieving mankind's greatest goal, peace with justice.

One early decision of a relatively personal and yet official nature involved my conduct of periodic press conferences. These devices for informing the public had been handled differently by each President since the practice began. I determined to hold them weekly, depending on the amount of news, my location, and my involvement with other official matters. Furthermore, we decided on an innovation: to allow verbatim transcription—and, later, television and radio tapes—of my statements and responses. This decision made a number of people nervous. Some, not including my astute and dedicated Press Secretary, Jim Hagerty, were concerned that an inadvertent misstatement in public would be a calamity. A word-for-word transcription, of course, seldom reads like a polished text. One of my brothers, moderately noted for the fluency and logic of his speech, once told me he was dumfounded whenever he received a stenotypist's record of what he had said; the experience, he indicated, always injured his pride. Nonetheless, I soon learned that ungrammatical sentences in the transcripts caused many to believe that I was incapable of using good English; indeed, several people who have examined my private papers, many in my handwriting, have expressed outright astonishment that in my writings syntax and grammatical structure were at least adequate. By consistently focusing on ideas rather than on phrasing,

---

[2] The board of trustees includes representatives of both major political parties, educators, businessmen, and members of the professions. Its chairman since its first year has been Thomas B. McCabe and its executive director J. Hampton Barnes of Philadelphia.

I was able to avoid causing the nation a serious setback through anything I said in many hours, over eight years, of intensive questioning.

One problem that confronts every chief executive and affects his meetings with the press is security. The more a President knows, the less likely he is to remember at any given moment what is in the public domain. It is far better to stumble or speak guardedly than to move ahead smoothly and risk imperiling the country.

Not only closely held secrets may be involved, but individual reputations also. Running the risk of sounding bad seems slight when compared to the danger of embarrassing subordinates. Admitting that one does not know all the details of everything going on in all departments of the government seemed preferable to pretending to an intimate knowledge no one man can have.

The number of press conferences held during my administration—by department heads and myself—suggests the strength of our conviction that informing the public was essential.

At one point I allowed an impression about my own feelings toward newspapers to gain currency—and it was, as it happened, both false and taken at face value. Asked once whether I had read a certain critical article, I brushed the question off by saying that I did not read newspapers. This seemed to please those who welcomed the idea that I never read anything other than short memos and Westerns. Actually, I was up early every morning, and when my aide, Colonel Robert L. Schulz, would come to start the day, he usually found me sitting beneath a sun lamp, with the better part of at least two newspapers read. I say the better part because I did not believe that slavish cover-to-cover reading was warranted, and certainly not the guesswork and personal interpretations of many columnists. There were journalists whose work I read regularly— Arthur Krock, Roscoe Drummond, Larry Burd, Robert Donovan, David Lawrence, and two or three, such as Kenneth Crawford, Walter Lippman and Marquis Childs, who consistently opposed me. But when I found that the writings of any newsman or columnist consistently strayed too far from the facts, I thereafter ignored his column.

Not all of the misstatements and misinterpretations of federal activity I found in the press were due to reporters. A newspaper, magazine, or television editor may delete portions, add material, assign positions, dictate headlines, or, as they say in the parlance of the business, decide how to "play" the story. More than once, what was played up missed the true importance in a policy, or a statement, or an action. Generally, however, information reaching the public from my press conferences was accurate and well "played."

I rarely found press conferences boring. One aspect that intrigued me was the psychological revelations apparent in the actions of the reporters themselves. To the amusement of their colleagues, a few members of the Washington press corps took themselves most seriously. These reporters insisted upon being heard at every conference—usually posing ponderous, academic, or minutely local questions. But most newsmen take such conferences in stride; their questions are normally worthy of careful answers, and a few of the best almost never ask any questions at all.

As a general in war, as Chief of Staff in Washington, as a university president, as a peacetime Allied commander in Europe, and as the nominee of my party, I had been meeting with the press since 1942. The sessions with war correspondents had been the most useful and informative, by and large; those at the White House, except when they were littered with an overabundance of questions involving personalities or partisanship, ranked in my estimation immediately after the wartime conferences. A goodly portion of the Washington press corps is of a stature to command respect; several became my friends, not mere faces in a crowd.

*   *   *

A matter which needed Executive impetus in the early months of 1953 was civil rights. My philosophy on this subject had often been stated. I believe that political or economic power to enforce segregation based on race, color, or creed is morally wrong and should by all practicable and reasonable means be abolished as soon as possible. My feelings could well be summed up by one sentence: There must be no second-class citizens in this country.

The two previous administrations had made much of their concern for the plight of minority groups, particularly the Negroes, in America. Certainly some progress had been made during these two administrations: during President Truman's time, for example, the integration of the armed forces had begun. However, these administrations had exerted the bulk of their effort on securing civil-rights legislation—antilynching, anti-poll tax, and FEPC measures, for example—which habitually met defeat from opposition led by members of the Democratic party itself.

It seemed to me that much could be done by Executive power alone. Integration in the District of Columbia, which should be the showpiece of our nation, was not a fact on the date of my inauguration. Elsewhere—in installations of the armed forces and in veterans hospitals, for example, particularly in the South and in the border states—segregation was still practiced. The very least the Executive could do would be to see first that the federal house itself was in order and that segregation in all installations where federal money was spent should become a thing of the past.

To point up this philosophy, I had included passages in my State of the Union speech in February 1953 which indicated that the new administration was committed to the principle that our civil rights formed a central part of the heritage we were striving to defend on all fronts with all our strength:

> I believe with all my heart that our vigilant guarding of these rights is a sacred obligation binding upon every citizen. To be true to one's own freedom is, in essence, to honor and respect the freedom of all others.

A cardinal ideal in this heritage, I said, is the equality before the law of all citizens.

> We know that discrimination against minorities persists despite our allegiance to this ideal. Such discrimination—confined to no one section of the nation—is but the outward testimony to the persistence of distrust and of fear in the hearts of men.
> This fact makes all the more vital the fighting of these wrongs by each individual, in every station of life, in his every deed.
> Much of the answer lies in the power of fact, fully publicized; of persuasion, honestly pressed; and of conscience, justly aroused. These are methods familiar to our way of life, tested and proven wise.
> I propose to use whatever authority exists in the office of the President to end segregation in the District of Columbia, including the federal government, and any segregation in the armed forces.

It came to my attention, however, that my desires in this regard were not being pushed as I wanted. After a reporter had asked at a news conference about the charge that at posts in some Southern states the Army had segregated schools, I checked and received the assurance that such segregation was to be ended by the fall term. But several months later I learned from my Associate Counsel, Max Rabb, that some government agencies were neglecting their duty.

Accordingly, I charged Max, who also served as Special Assistant in charge of minority affairs, with the task of seeing that all that could be done in the federal government was actually accomplished. To start with, Max went to see Robert B. Anderson, Secretary of the Navy, about segregation in naval installations at Norfolk and in South Carolina. Secretary Anderson was a Texan, who at the beginning of the administration was registered as a Texas Democrat. His response was so immediate and so decisive as to excite my intense admiration, a feeling for him which has grown ever since. With no fanfare—in fact, with much care to avoid making an open issue of things—segregation was soon completely and almost painlessly eliminated at all naval installations.

Thereupon, at my personal request, Max Rabb set about to track down any inconsistencies of this sort in the rest of the departments and agencies of the government. New orders, issued quietly, immediately took effect. For example, children on Army posts going to schools administered by the Department of Health, Education and Welfare were no longer to attend segregated classes. The forty-seven veterans hospitals which had been practicing segregation were no longer to separate the races. By the end of the year segregation in the Navy and Air Force was a thing of the past, and the Army was getting ready to eliminate its last all-Negro unit.

More difficult, however, was the problem of desegregation in the District of Columbia, for there many of the offending institutions were privately-owned and not subject to direct governmental control. I saw the owners of the movie theaters in Washington and persuaded them of the rightness of this effort. On June 8 the Supreme Court in a unanimous decision ruled that restaurants in the District could not refuse to serve Negroes; the Attorney General, appearing personally before the Court, had appealed for such a decision. And the Committee on Government Contracts, revitalized with the Vice President at its head, and with such persons as George Meany, John Roosevelt, and Helen Rogers Reid among its members, performed an invaluable service in persuading such facilities as the Capitol Transit Company to end bans against Negro employees.

Especially satisfying was a development which occurred some years later as a result of such efforts. Dr. Ralph Bunche, Under Secretary of the United Nations, called on me on October 24, 1956. He said that in 1949 he had been offered the position of Assistant Secretary of State but had felt it necessary to refuse because he could not raise his son in a self-respecting manner within the District of Columbia. Now he would not again feel it necessary to decline on that basis.

After I left the White House, one man's act reminded me that not all a President's results or rewards are statistically measurable. In October of 1962 I was informed that Dr. William Hinton, the first Negro professor at Harvard University, had provided in his will that his life's savings, amounting to some $75,000, should be used to establish a Dwight D. Eisenhower Scholarship Fund for graduate students at Harvard. Dr. Hinton's will—he died in 1959—provided that this should be done in recognition of steps toward the acceptance of equal opportunities during my administration. When notified by Dr. Nathan M. Pusey, president of Harvard, of the professor's sentiments, I told Dr. Pusey that I could not recall having been given a personal distinction that had touched me more deeply.

CHAPTER X

With Churchill and Laniel
in Bermuda—Atoms for Peace

Since no future peace can be maintained if land, sea, or air armaments continue to be employed by nations which threaten, or may threaten, aggression outside their frontiers, [we] believe, pending the establishment of a wider and permanent system of general security, that the disarmament of such nations is essential.

—*The Atlantic Charter, 1941*

ON September 28, 1953, Mrs. Eisenhower and I welcomed to Washington President and Señora Remón Cantera of Panama. This official visit was the first of thirty-seven made to the White House by heads of state, and the first of 210 meetings which I was to have with heads of state and heads of government, in and outside the United States during my Presidency.

The President and his wife, a charming couple, endeared themselves to Mamie and me by their kindnesses toward our grandchildren, to whom they brought colorful native costumes.

Señora Remón was deeply involved in social work in Panama; she headed the Panamanian Red Cross. During her stay in Washington she visited its American headquarters and talked extensively with officials of the new Department of Health, Education and Welfare.

President Remón spoke about dissatisfactions in his country concerning the operations of the Panama Canal—dissatisfactions, for example, over different pay scales in the Canal Zone for American and Panamanian workers and over our failure to return to Panama lands once granted to the United States for the effective operation of the canal, but no longer needed. None of the complaints was of earth-shaking proportions in itself, but the number of them was such that earlier in the month the two governments had begun discussions. In my conversations with President Remón I recalled that two decades earlier, as a major working in the office of an Assistant Secretary of War, I had been involved in similar problems in Panamanian-American relations. Since that time, under the Treaty of Friendship and Cooperation of 1936, the United States had renounced its obligation to guarantee Panama's independence—though if Panama were threatened by attack the two countries would consult on mutual defense—and had relinquished its right to continue to expropriate Panamanian lands outside the Canal Zone. Nonetheless, with an American facility so stupendous as the canal operating in Panama, the greatest single employer of labor in the nation and a major source of revenue for the local government, it was inevitable that there should constantly arise frictions and difficulties between the two countries.

I was glad that at the close of President Remón's stay in Washington, we could announce the resolution of some differences over lands and pay scales and the making of arrangements to attempt solution of others.

*   *   *

Less than a month later I made my first presidential good-will trip out of the country. On October 19 I met with President Adolfo Ruiz Cortines of Mexico at Falcon Dam on the Rio Grande, on the common border of our two countries.

From the beginning of my administration I had been seeking opportunities for early meetings with the heads of this nation's nearest neighbors, Canada and Mexico. I wanted to make a personal and specific effort to assure these nations of the new administration's desire to cooperate in mutual respect and friendliness.

In spite of all the difficulties that have beset these relationships—beginning even before our Revolutionary War—the necessity for firm friendships among the three of us has long been obvious.

On the northern border our major difficulties disappeared earlier than on the southern. But even as late as the 1840s a successful presidential campaign, James K. Polk's, was waged on a slogan of "fifty-four forty or fight": the assertion of a claim to all the land on our northwestern frontier lying south of that degree of latitude. After the compromises with the British in that decade resulted in common recognition of our present boundaries, relations had steadily improved. Today the Canadian-American border, bare of military installations, is one of the strongest international boundaries in the world, for it is defended only by friendship.

But on the southern border—more than two thousand miles in length—difficulties between our two nations persisted well into this century. Spanish discovery and colonization in the southwest had been far ahead of our own exploratory activities. As American frontiersmen pushed into those regions, trouble developed, intensified by differences in languages, customs, and cultures. The conflict was persistent and often violent, breaking out into two wars—between Texas and Mexico in 1836 and between the United States and Mexico in 1846, almost immediately after our annexation of Texas. The continuing internal conflict in Mexico following upon the overthrow in 1911 of the modern dictator, President Porfirio Díaz, had kept the entire territory in turmoil on both sides of the border. As a young lieutenant stationed in Texas, I became well acquainted with these antagonisms: to the Mexicans, for example, we were the hated "gringos." In 1916 we had even mobilized a great portion of our National Guard to reinforce the Regular Army, most of which was then stationed along our southern land border, to prevent irregular incursions into our territory, primarily by the bandit leader Pancho Villa.

After World War I conditions gradually improved, although even in President Franklin Roosevelt's time many in this country called for war when Mexico decided to nationalize its oil industry, in which some of our citizens had invested heavily.

By no means are our common problems yet completely solved, but in the past two decades each side has increasingly emphasized the need of settling these by peaceful negotiation.

Holding to the wisdom of this purpose, I hoped to establish personal contacts that would prove useful in its attainment. In December 1952 the Vice President-elect had gone to Mexico for the inauguration of its new President, Ruiz Cortines. On his return to the United States he added his urging to my own desire for an early meeting. I accepted the invitation to participate in the joint dedication of the Falcon Dam.

This five-mile-long dam, spanning the Rio Grande and forming a reservoir more than fifty miles long, was, even before the dedication ceremony, helping to prevent the wasting of more than 3 million acre-feet of water a year; giving protection against floods (the dam got its name from an old Texas town which a flood had washed away); and storing water to irrigate farms on both sides of the border.

By prearrangement I crossed the international border to call upon the Mexican President in the municipal building at Nuevo Guerrero, where he received me in appropriate ceremonies which included a Mexican fiesta. After the visit I returned to American territory, where in the administration building of the Falcon Dam I received President Ruiz Cortines, who came to return my call. There were interesting variations in our customs and rules: I needed no permission to leave the United States, but Ruiz Cortines had to obtain special clearance from the Mexican national legislature to step across the border and spend part of the afternoon.

I tendered his party a luncheon, after which we went to the dam itself for the dedication. Under a ninety-degree sun I made a speech in which I tried to reach not only the people of Mexico but all those in Latin America.

In speaking of friendship I assured our neighbors to the south that I was "by no means talking of that pale sentiment by which we often describe a chance meeting with an acquaintance on the street, nor do I mean for it to be used as a mere salute or as used, sometimes, in formal diplomatic language." I meant "the kind of friendship that seeks—seeks earnestly and persistently—to understand the viewpoint of the other, and then labors with sympathy and with all that is in the heart to meet the viewpoint of his friend."

In the Falcon Dam I saw living testimony to the understanding and the cooperation binding our peoples. "More than any volume of words, the sound of its rushing waters and spinning generators speaks of this understanding. And more meaningful and powerful than all the energy it shall generate is the force for common good which we can found in this cooperation."

The lands to our south, I said, needed capital to provide vital stimulus to industry and agriculture—to all production. They needed technical assistance, and an opportunity to sell their products in United States markets. "We know these matters," I therefore said, "to be the common concern of all other nations and peoples—for whatever touches one of us touches all of us.

"And above all we know this: the conquest of these problems is within the power of our united energy, skill, and determination. . . .

"Ours is the imperishable spirit of free men, unswayed by the cheap promises of totalitarianism, undismayed by its blustering threats.

"Our common purpose is the pursuit of a peace that is productive and lasting."

Out of that meeting grew a friendship between the Mexican President and me that was not only personally gratifying but provided an easy and effective line of communication as our two governments approached the problems involved in the rights of United States citizens to fish in offshore waters over which Mexico claimed sovereignty, the disposal of United States surplus cotton, the illegal entry of thousands of Mexican migrant laborers into the United States (called "wetbacks" because many swam the Rio Grande) for seasonal work on American farms, and United States tariffs on incoming lead and zinc, which Mexico produced in quantity.

On the 18th of November, I received a report from my brother Milton, who as my personal representative had returned from South America after analyzing the economic and social problems of the Latin American republics, and now recommended ways to strengthen trade and economic cooperation between them and us. Between June 23 and July 29 he, and the delegation he headed, had visited the ten republics of South America. He had traveled many thousands of miles and talked with a great number of people—not only heads of government, but also leaders in agriculture, industry, finance, labor, and education. Throughout my Presidency, I was to lean heavily upon his counsel and upon his detailed and sympathetic knowledge of the problems of the other nations of this hemisphere.

*   *   *

Also in November, I had an opportunity to visit our neighbor on the north. The Governor General of Canada, representing the British sovereign, was Vincent Massey. Our ambassador was Douglas Stuart, a most able public servant and my good friend. Louis St. Laurent, whom I had known from NATO days, was Canada's Prime Minister.

My wife—who celebrated her birthday while there—and I thoroughly enjoyed our three-day visit to Ottawa. Addressing the Parliament, I assured this nation, too, of my government's intention to approach all our common problems in a spirit of friendly understanding.

Problems did in fact exist. The Canadian government, for example, was becoming impatient about United States slowness in agreeing to the joint building of the St. Lawrence Seaway. I was fully committed to this effort but was hamstrung until I could obtain necessary legislation from the Congress. Beyond that immediate problem stood a continuing concern of both governments—how best to warn and defend the people of North America against nuclear attack. We were concerned as well about how best to encourage the flow of goods in both directions across our border without damaging producers on either side. (The Canadians were then vigorously objecting to any increase in United States restrictions against imports of lead, zinc, oats, and fish.)

These and other problems I discussed with leaders of the Canadian government. But specifics were not so much on my mind at the time as was my desire to create an atmosphere in which difficulties could be discussed and composed.

In the Parliament, I began by attempting in my execrable French a few words of salutation to its French-speaking members. ("I shall now do something very brave," I remember Winston Churchill once told a similar audience. "I shall say a few words in French.") Then I went on to discuss the common defense of the northern half of the hemisphere.

"Canada and the United States are equal partners," I said, "and neither dares to waste time. . . . These days demand ceaseless vigilance. We must be ready and prepared. The threat is present. The measures of defense have been thoroughly studied by official bodies of both countries. The Permanent Joint Board on Defense has worked assiduously and effectively on mutual problems. Now is the time for action on all agreed measures. . . ."

I knew that, because of the comparative size of our two nations, our Canadian friends sometimes suspected us of arrogance. As I told my audience, our country made no claims to a monopoly on wisdom. I said we were not only willing but anxious to discuss with them and with any others all possible paths to cooperation and peace. I promised to use every means, from the normal diplomatic exchange to the forum of the United Nations, to further that search.

"Beyond the shadow of the atomic cloud," I concluded, "the horizon is bright with promise. No shadow can halt our advance together. For we, Canada and the United States, shall use carefully and wisely the God-given graces of faith and reason as we march toward it—toward the horizon of a world where each man, each family, each nation lives at peace in a climate of freedom."

*   *   *

But my concern in strengthening personal ties extended far beyond our immediate neighbors.

For special purposes, I strongly believe that in the conduct of foreign relations, personal discussions between heads of government can be helpful, even imperative. This is one reason for the many invitations to visit Washington that we sent to heads of state during my years in office, and for my own numerous journeys to other capitals.

Upon entering office I was personally acquainted with the heads of state and of government of many nations, including every one in Western Europe except those in Spain, Yugoslavia, and Sweden. I had known these officials—noble and commoner, civilian and soldier—both in war and in peace, and it seemed only natural that a resumption of our earlier association would be helpful. Early in my first administration, I told Foster that I should like to meet soon with Prime Minister Churchill and felt that we should try to arrange such a conference with France's representative present. The Secretary quietly made necessary inquiries and after a number of difficulties had been overcome, the three governments agreed to meet in Bermuda in June 1953.

On May 21, however, the French government of Premier René Mayer fell. For five weeks, in the eighteenth Cabinet crisis since the liberation, France had no leader. By the time Joseph Laniel came to power, on June 26, both Winston and Anthony Eden had become ill. After these delays, and the usual administrative difficulties surrounding a planned visit by governmental heads to foreign soil, the conference was finally set for December 4–8, 1953, in the British possession of Bermuda.

This meeting with the Prime Minister of Great Britain and the Premier of France had no purpose that could be translated into terms of hoped-for agreements among the three participating nations. At least twice, prior to the meeting, I announced in press conferences that its sole objective was to provide friends in responsible positions an opportunity to meet and talk more intimately about world problems than could be done through letters, telegrams, and special messengers. Winston shared this idea.

We knew that the presence of only three friendly governments at a conference could create misunderstanding on the part of other powers and the world press. I warned correspondents, in advance, that there would be no agenda; soon I began to regret that I did not also say "no communiqué."

The Bermuda Conference convinced me that issuing a final communiqué tends to destroy the intimacy and value of informal talks. In Bermuda the presence of a very large press representation constantly put conferees under pressure to give out "news." Even more important, it made it necessary at times for some of the participants to engage in talk which was primarily for the benefit of their constituents back home. The most potent argument for communiqués is that without them visiting journalists may manufacture stories out of whole cloth. Such stories can sometimes distort and sometimes completely reverse the facts.

Another factor that helps to defeat the purpose of a purely friendly exchange of views is the presence at meetings of an excessive number of experts, technicians, and assistants. The heads of some governments at that time—for example, the French—did not have the same clear right and opportunity enjoyed by a President of the United States to make their own selections of principal subordinates. As a result, a number of those accompanying Premier Laniel to the Bermuda Conference were not only of different political belief, but were opponents of his on many important questions. M. Bidault, his Foreign Minister, had been a candidate for election as Premier, and had lost out by only one vote in the French National Assembly. (A few weeks after the conference they would be rival candidates again.)

Because the conference was intended to be and was, in fact, informal, its significance was not so great as to deserve here any extended account of the proceedings. However, because it was the first "heads-of-government" conference in which I participated for discussion of problems of global significance, I believe it is worth while to try to give something of its atmosphere and an abbreviated record of our conversation.

While each principal had nine or ten members in his party, we had more enlightening conversations when, for the discussion of special subjects, we reduced the size of each delegation to no more than three. At high political levels, as in businesses and in families, three persons can often accomplish more than thirty.

Subjects discussed at the conference included: prospects for approval of a European Defense Community in the North Atlantic Treaty Organization; Indochina; Egypt and the Suez Canal; Korea; and an answer from our three nations to a Soviet note concerning a possible meeting of the Foreign Ministers of the four powers.

The discussion of the European Defense Community and the North Atlantic Treaty Organization was mainly a monologue by Foreign Minister Bidault. Since the tentative approval of EDC by the French government before my departure from NATO, little had been accomplished toward ratification. The purpose of Bidault's remarks was to set forth in detail the difficulties his government was encountering in its effort to obtain parliamentary approval of the EDC treaty. More particularly, Bidault emphasized that certain conditions would have to be met before the treaty stood any possible chance of approval.

"This," he emphasized to Mr. Churchill and me, "you should clearly understand."

First, he said, there would have to be a settlement satisfactory to the French of the Saar question. After World War II the nine hundred square miles of the rich industrial Saar territory—with its population of nearly a million persons, most of them German—had been detached from Germany and set up as an autonomous state under the control of France. As a precondition of Germany's becoming once again a sovereign armed state, France insisted that the Saar territory remain autonomous; Germany, however, insisted that historically, as part of Germany, the Saar could have its ultimate status set only by a peace treaty for all of Germany. Dwelling at length on the history and significance of the Saar, Bidault asserted that unless Germany (apparently to be influenced by the United States and the United Kingdom) should make the concessions that the French thought necessary, there would be no hope of obtaining parliamentary approval of EDC.

He then took up the question of American and British ground strength in Europe. He insisted upon a twenty-year guarantee that these forces would remain in Europe in substantially their present strength. To this, neither Winston nor I would agree, but Bidault asserted that without such assurances the treaty was doomed in the French parliament.

He repeatedly asserted that France, alone among the great Western powers, was making the humiliating sacrifice of "integrating its forces with those of another nation which had long been its enemy." Because of this "sacrifice," he said, the United States and Great Britain would not only have to be very understanding, but would have to be ready to make greater contributions in other fields in order to obtain French approval.

I liked Bidault and knew him for a courageous man; his argument, however, made little sense to me.

"Just what nation does France now regard as a potential enemy," I asked him, "Germany or Russia?"

The answer was obvious, but the long-standing distrust of Germany was, at that moment, still so prevalent that many French political figures feared to espouse EDC and its great potential for assuring European security against Communist aggression.

After the first meeting I had a long private talk with Bidault. He said in effect that what he was compelled to say about EDC in the conference did not, of course, represent his deepest views and convictions. He assured me that he believed, as I did, that EDC was a necessity; but he was compelled to do his duty in representing his chief, M. Laniel. He then said that if he was not in the new government, to be formed after the election of a new Premier later that month, he would go throughout France, even to its music halls and cinemas, to proclaim the truth about the matter.

In the second meeting, which M. Laniel missed because of illness, Winston's reaction was emphatic. He was polite enough to make several cordial references to Bidault's personal courage in World War II and his statesmanlike actions since that time. But he also said that implicit in everything Bidault said was France's fear that Germany would become predominant and controlling in a European Defense Community, with France relegated to a secondary position. For this reason Mr. Churchill felt that the French government was demanding, in advance, a settlement of the Saar issue and the indefinite presence of British and American troops. EDC would protect France, he said; moreover, it was a concept which had been brought out three years earlier by the French government itself. At that time, he went on, he had opposed the plan; he did not see how it would work.

But two things had become clear to all of us, he said with characteristic force and clarity. Western Europe could not be defended without German troops, German productivity, and the German geographic position to give depth to the whole theater, and it was clear that France would not, by any manner or means, agree to the rearming of Germany on an independent basis. EDC was therefore the only practicable solution. He could not understand M. Bidault's statement because in the proposed

EDC organization, Germany could not have any complete military force of its own.

Winston remarked that he was chagrined and astounded that Bidault had spoken of EDC in such defeatist terms. He emphasized that EDC must be accepted. If it were not, he for one was going to urge the unilateral rearmament of Germany. He was convinced that a rearmed Western Germany was absolutely indispensable to the safety of the Western world.

After he had finished his statement (during which I recalled that two years earlier I had used every resource at my command, including argument, cajolery, and sheer prayer, to get Winston to say a single kind word about EDC) I intervened in the hope of straightening out misunderstandings that had arisen between the two.

As chairman of the conference, I said that I had invited Bidault to present all of his problems and list the ways in which we could be of help in obtaining early French approval of EDC. I suggested that Winston not criticize Bidault personally for his full presentation; but I decidedly stood with Winston in refusing to consider EDC a failure. I told Bidault that EDC would function effectively as a part of NATO; without EDC the whole NATO concept would have to be overhauled.

We could not shake Bidault from his position, largely, I think, because of the fact that he was talking not only for another, but in the presence of too many people. Two or three weeks earlier he had made a bold speech in the French parliament in favor of EDC, including, however, the promise that at Bermuda the French government would seek to get the United States and Britain to keep troops on the Continent in order to guarantee it.

He did say that support of EDC was the continuing policy of the French government. This was about as strong a statement as he felt able to make.

Indochina was also a subject on which Bidault expounded at length. Nothing particularly new developed from his discussion, but the French considered that the situation there was better than it had been for a long time. While he did not mean that they were really hopeful of securing an early and decisive military victory, he did mean that for the first time they were thinking of winning eventually.

The United States had been supplying equipment for that operation at a generous rate, and there was evidence that the French had more equipment than they could use effectively. In addition, we were at that time in the process of turning over to the French a second aircraft carrier, about twenty-five C-47 transports, and helicopters. All of these actions were intended to give the French better air support and greater flexibility in the use of their paratroop battalions and, above all, to insure higher morale.

I was surprised to find the touchy Egyptian question proposed by the British. At first I questioned the propriety of discussing at a tripartite meeting the question of the Suez Base, which did not seem to involve the French directly, but I approved it for the agenda, on being informed that Winston had insisted upon its inclusion. When we finally got to this subject, it developed that Winston had made a mistake. He wanted to talk *to the Americans only* about Egypt. The Prime Minister asked that we skip the item in the plenary meeting, saying that he would talk to us individually about it. French suspicions were instantly alerted, and they insisted upon being a party to the talks on Egypt.

At that point Winston was caught in an embarrassing situation, but he masterfully retrieved his error by discussing—fluently as always—a problem about the Suez Canal of little significance, and so succeeded in occupying time in the tripartite meeting. Later he told us, in a short letter, what he really wanted to say: he wanted more positive United States support in resolving the two remaining points in the argument he was having with the Egyptians over the Suez Base. Britain wanted to keep in uniform all its technicians who remained in Egypt; moreover, it wanted the UN to have the responsibility of deciding when the peace of that area was threatened and of authorizing British troops to come back into Egypt to use the base for defense purposes.

As to the second of these points, I was disposed to support the Prime Minister very strongly; as to the first, I felt there was little substance to his argument.

At one point in the proceedings Winston spoke on imperialism. After delivering himself of an impassioned talk about the absurdity of trying to set up independent nations composed of people unready for self-government, he predicted history would record that Britain's desertion of her duty in India was a serious blunder. Although he might personally not live to see all of the unfortunate results that would flow from that tragedy, he went on, he felt certain that there were people around the conference table who would eventually see this act bring grief and sorrow to the entire Western world.

Philosophically, much could be said for his view that many of the countries attempting to assume the rights of independence were unaware of the inescapable responsibilities and burdens of self-government, despite such training in public administration as the British, for example, had given them. Great difficulties were certain to arise. But the truth that Winston chose to ignore was that any attempt by European powers to sustain by force their dominant positions in these territories would have long since resulted in furious resentment, unrest, and conflict. The hard fact was that the spirit of nationalism had become rampant and often uncontrollable in the world.

When I indicated some disagreement with Winston on phases of his argument on this subject, he countered, in good humor, "You're just like the young Turks in my government."

We talked, also, of Korea. Lucidly, Foster Dulles described the position in Korea, the personality and attitude of President Rhee, the measures we had taken to prevent the resumption of hostilities provoked by Rhee acting alone, and the plans that we were making for a better redeployment of all our troops on the theory that the present armistice would last for a long time. He gave, in addition, a brief outline of our plans for operations in the event that the truce was broken by a deliberate Communist offensive.

The only part of the discussion that led to definite opposition from Winston was our announcement that in the event of renewed attack, we would feel free to use the atomic bomb against military targets, whenever military advantage dictated such use. This awakened in Winston many fears. Britain, he argued, was a small crowded island; one good nuclear bombing could destroy it, and recklessness might provoke such a catastrophe. I earnestly assured Winston that I had no intention of acting rashly, saying that I merely wanted our friends to know that past limitations on our actions, in the event of a heavy attack on us, would not necessarily be observed.

Our three governments decided to answer the Soviet note of November 26 requesting a four-power conference. We directed our Foreign Ministers to be prepared to meet the Russians in West Berlin and take up with them certain distinct European problems, notably those of Germany and Austria. We agreed among ourselves that our representatives would remain in the meeting long enough to determine whether or not the Russians were acting in good faith, but that if after two or three weeks we concluded that they were simply using the meeting for propaganda purposes, we would find a way to terminate it. On the other hand, if there were any promising developments, we would stay in the negotiations as long as there was a slight hope for progress.

The Soviets had been beating the drums for a five-power meeting consisting of the United States, the United Kingdom, France, the U.S.S.R., and Communist China. The American delegation declined to discuss such a proposal but did say that if either of the other two wanted to give its view on this, it could do so. Neither felt any need to do so. Though the British had recognized Communist China early in 1950, I explained that I would ignore the claim of Communist China that it should be received into the United Nations or at a conference table, until it had established its right to be treated as a respectable member of the family of nations. Among the requirements were withdrawal from Korea, cessation of support for the Communist faction in Indochina, adoption of decent deportment in its contacts with the Western world, and a commitment to abandon its military threat against Formosa.

The final afternoon and evening of the conference were given almost wholly to an attempt to agree upon a communiqué. This was boring to me, because of my opposition to the issuance of any joint statement. I knew, of course, I would have to bow to custom, but on the subject of support for EDC the communiqué was probably the least emphatic of any signed by the three Western nations during the preceding several years.

The conference was for me a sort of home-coming, a renewal of an old and close relationship. Once again, Winston Churchill and I were working together, each of us with heavy responsibilities and both engaged in a common effort to resolve momentous problems. Although the years had aged the Prime Minister, adding in the process a new weapon to his defensive armament—a partial deafness which he seemed able at times to turn on and off to suit his purposes—time had not dulled his mind or tongue.

On several occasions we seized the opportunity to talk privately. Immediately after our arrival, we settled ourselves comfortably in my sitting room and discussed a number of subjects, one of which was recognition of Red China. He remarked that although he had originally opposed British recognition of that government, the existing relationship between Britain and Red China had become a sort of habit, and he had no intention of breaking it. But he assured me he would certainly always vote with the United States to bar Red China's admission to the United Nations. "After all," he said dryly, "we do prefer the United States over Red China as an ally."

Later, I went alone to the Prime Minister's suite for a luncheon. Again, he had much to say about the need for Washington and London to coordinate and crystallize their views whenever they had mutual interests in any spot on the globe—for example, India, Egypt, Iran—and then to publicly present a solid front to the third party in the dispute.

I gave my approval to part of his argument—to confer confidentially in searching for joint solutions that would be approved by world opinion as just, equitable, and considerate. But I expressed the thought that if any other party in the dispute had the slightest semblance of justice on its side, it now could appeal to the United Nations. Unless we recognized the equality of member nations of that body, we could, in many cases, be made to look like arbitrary imperialists if we tried to "gang up" publicly in supporting the principles in which we both believed.

He made one point in our luncheon talk that he did not document and it is possible that I misunderstood him. I gathered that he thought it impossible at times for subordinates in the British Foreign Office to talk freely with our staffs concerning important problems because of the American tendency in discussion to get annoyed, if not angry. I suggested that he and I take an opportunity to tell our staffs jointly that we expected between them the freest and fullest kind of discussion and argument, even in those cases where they thought it impossible to reach an agreement.

I am not sure just what he had in mind, but during the luncheon he expressed his admiration of the way Bedell Smith, my brilliant Chief of Staff in World War II, and I used to work together. He said that he had been in my headquarters on a day when Bedell was carrying on a heated argument with me. I not only allowed him to argue; I urged him to continue. The Prime Minister thought the incident a quite notable clash of views and men. But then, he said, I made a decision which settled the proposition and, to his amazement, Bedell's instant reaction was exactly as if he had got his own way—which he had not. I assured Winston that this was the accepted American practice in this kind of work, and I hoped our joint staffs could operate similarly.

In other private chats with the Prime Minister the conversations were mainly on atomic matters—the earmarking of a certain number of atomic bombs which could be stored in England in our custody for use by British bombers in the event of war; and a proposal that I was planning to make to the United Nations immediately after we left Bermuda.

Even as in World War II, Winston was still a man of rocklike convictions which he expressed in masterly fashion. He believed that the best hope for strengthening Free World security and progress was in public pronouncement of British-American decisions on each significant problem. He pointed out that nationalism was on the march, and that world Communism was taking advantage of it to cause dissension everywhere. Moscow was leading misguided people to believe they could count on Communist help to achieve and sustain their nationalistic aims. Actually, the Communists hoped to take advantage of the confusion resulting from destruction of existing relationships and so further the aims of world revolution and the Kremlin's domination of all peoples.

In these circumstances I felt that the last thing the two strongest Western powers should do was to appear before the world as a combination of forces to compel adherence to their announced views, especially when these views concerned existing or former relationships between a mother country and a colony. The Free World's hope of defeating Communism was not based on always blocking national aspirations or supporting the status quo. That hope could be realized only by convincing newly independent peoples that their sole assurance of maintaining independence, once attained, would be through cooperation with the Free World.

The Prime Minister did not by any means propose to disregard the legitimate aspirations of weaker peoples. But he did take a somewhat paternalistic approach. He said that we, with our experience and power, would be required to support and carry the heavy burdens of realistic international plans as well as to aid infant nations toward self-dependence. Therefore, he said, other nations should recognize the wisdom of our suggestions—and follow them. That might be true, in the abstract, I agreed, but in real life, long and patient negotiations, understanding, and equality of treatment were essential.

In any case, Mr. Churchill's presence in Bermuda made my participation in the conference much easier and more pleasant. My affection and respect for him have never been dimmed either by years or heated debate. I wrote him as our visit ended:

> As I depart from this lovely spot, I leave this note behind to thank you once again for acting as our host for a very interesting and, I hope, profitable conference. While my disposition has not always been equal to the pressures of some of the lectures (especially those requiring translation) I think that I came through my first international conference—in a political role—in fairly good shape.

*   *   *

At four the same afternoon, having flown directly from Bermuda, I delivered my second major speech in the field of foreign relations, this time before the General Assembly of the United Nations, in New York. I had taken the draft of the talk with me to Bermuda. My primary purpose was to continue working to make it a precise statement of my views. At the same time I wanted to talk to Winston about it in detail, and to M. Laniel in general. I wanted to ensure that these gentlemen understood what I was getting at, so that no chance phraseology—should some creep in—would wound our allies. Mr. Churchill and his advisers, Anthony Eden and Lord Cherwell, thought there were two such phrases in the draft, and that their inclusion would tend to weaken its peaceful or constructive purposes—and tend also to emphasize American belligerence and toughness. Foster and I talked the matter over, decided there was merit in their suggested changes, and made two modifications.

C. D. Jackson, who was on the airplane carrying us back to New York, collaborated, throughout the journey, with Foster Dulles, Lewis Strauss, then the Chairman of the Atomic Energy Commission, and me in final revisions and editing. We worked so late that to give Mrs. Ann Whitman time to finish typing, I had to ask Colonel Draper to circle New York for half an hour before landing. Foster, Lewis, and C. D. pitched in then, too. It was amusing to see the Secretary of State, the Chairman of the

Atomic Energy Commission, and my principal adviser on "propaganda" help run the mimeograph machine and do the stapling.

In time, this talk followed the April speech before the American Society of Newspaper Editors by more than seven months. In logic, it should have come first, for my purpose was to promote development of mutual trust, a trust that was essential before we could hope for success in the specific disarmament proposals made before the editors.

Earlier in 1953 I had asked C. D. Jackson to work with me on a speech to awaken the American people and the world to the incredible destructive power of the United States stockpile of nuclear weapons. He and his aides produced draft after draft. But when they had finished, Jackson and I agreed that the exposition left the listener with only a new terror, not a new hope.

Therefore, as I wrote to a friend, "I began to search around for any kind of an idea that could bring the world to look at the atomic problem in a broad and intelligent way and still escape the impasse to action created by Russian intransigence in the matter of mutual or neutral inspection of resources. I wanted, additionally, to give our people and the world some faint idea of the distance already travelled by this new science —but to do it in such a way as not to create new alarm."

One day I hit upon the idea of actual physical donations of isotopes from our then unequaled nuclear stockpile, to a common fund for peaceful purposes. This would have to mean donations by both Russia and the United States—with Britain also in the picture in at least a minor way. I wanted to develop this thought in such a way as to provide at the very least a calm and reasonable atmosphere in which the whole matter could be considered.

Accordingly, in September, I told my Special Assistant for National Security Affairs, General Cutler, of my thought. Within minutes after he left my office he was writing to Lewis Strauss. "The President suggested that you might consider the following proposal which he did not think anyone had yet thought of. . . . Suppose the United States and the Soviets were to turn over to the United Nations, for peaceful uses X kilograms of fissionable matter. . . ."

In the weeks following, Strauss, Cutler, Jackson, and their aides worked intensively on the implications of this idea. Out of their deliberations came Admiral Strauss's suggestion for storing the uranium diluted and in solution to prevent theft, and a proposal for setting up a new International Atomic Energy Agency. To work on the draft of the speech on this subject, Strauss and Jackson met again and again at the Metropolitan Club in Washington for breakfast; appropriately, the project took on the code name "Wheaties."

Rosenberg-case demonstrators

"With . . . demonstrations up and down Pennsylvania Avenue in front of the White House, the sentence of the courts was duly executed."

Senate investigating subcommittee in action

"Cameras and klieg lights were installed in the Senate committee room where [Senator McCarthy] held hearings ... which helped still more to sustain public interest in his appearances and incited him to become even more extreme in his accusations."

The President greets Mrs. Eisenhower after White House lawn ceremonies

"I have heard people who in the past had been familiar with the White House characterize it as a cold, unlivable 'institution'. My family and I felt none of this."

Press conference at the Executive Offices Building, January 13, 1954

"I rarely found press conferences boring. One aspect that intrigued me was . . . the actions of the reporters themselves."

Finally, only minutes before delivery of the speech, the work was done. The text, which I had revised again and again, lay open before me, re-typed for the last time, as I began speaking to the delegates to the United Nations General Assembly on December 8. The core of the speech, after a recital of the calamitous horror all the world faced in a nuclear war, came in these paragraphs:

> To hasten the day when fear of the atom will begin to disappear from the minds of people . . . there are certain steps that can be taken now.
> I therefore make the following proposals:
> The governments principally involved, to the extent permitted by elementary prudence, to begin now and continue to make joint contributions from their stockpiles of normal uranium and fissionable materials to an International Atomic Energy Agency. We would expect that such an agency would be set up under the aegis of the United Nations. . . .
> Undoubtedly initial and early contributions to this plan would be small in quantity. However, the proposal has great virtue that it can be undertaken without the irritations and mutual suspicions incident to any attempt to set up a completely acceptable system of world-wide inspection and control.
> The [World] Atomic Energy Agency could be made responsible for the impounding, storage, and protection of the contributed fissionable and other materials. The ingenuity of our scientists will provide special safe conditions under which such a bank of fissionable material can be made essentially immune to surprise seizure.
> The more important responsibility of this Atomic Energy Agency would be to devise methods whereby this fissionable material would be allocated to serve the peaceful pursuits of mankind. Experts would be mobilized to apply atomic energy to the needs of agriculture, medicine, and other peaceful activities. A special purpose would be to provide abundant electrical energy in the power-starved areas of the world. Thus the contributing powers would be dedicating some of their strength to serve the needs rather than the fears of mankind. . . .

Then, announcing that the United States was ready to participate with others—including the Soviet Union—in developing plans for expediting the peaceful uses of atomic energy, I added:

> The coming months will be fraught with fateful decisions. In this Assembly; in the capitals and military headquarters of the world; in the hearts of men everywhere, be they governors or governed, may they be the decisions which will lead this world out of fear and into peace.
> To the making of these fateful decisions, the United States pledges before you—and therefore before the world—its determination to help solve the fearful atomic dilemma—to devote its entire heart and mind to find the way by which the miraculous inventiveness of man shall not be dedicated to his death, but consecrated to his life.

My objectives in this talk were several. The principal one was exactly as stated—to make a clear effort to get the Soviet Union working with us in a noncontroversial phase of the atomic field and thus begin to divert nuclear science from destructive to peaceful purposes.

The second was that if we were successful in making even a start, it was possible that gradually negotiation and cooperation might expand into something broader; there was hope that Russia's own self-interest might lead her to participate in joint humanitarian efforts.

A third objective was to call the attention of smaller nations to the fact that they too had an interest in the uses to which the world put its limited supply of raw fissionable material. Too many small nations had looked upon nuclear science as a matter of concern only to the U.S.S.R. and the United States—except, of course, for the fear that their own countries might be targets in the event of atomic war.

My hope was to awaken in these nations an understanding that new and promising opportunities were steadily opening up for using these materials and skills for their benefit. Thus world opinion might build for turning efforts toward these constructive purposes.

Some feared that my proposal for the Soviets and ourselves to contribute fissionable material—at an agreed ratio—to a UN stockpile would cause an unjustified drain-off from our stores of fissionable materials. Our technical experts assured me that even if Russia agreed to cooperate in such a plan solely for propaganda purposes, the United States could afford to reduce its atomic stockpile by two or three times the amount the Russians might contribute, and still improve our relative position.

A further reason for the address was to give the American people the reassurance—the certain knowledge—that they had not poured their substance into nuclear development with the sole purpose of using it for world destruction.

Finally, it provided the opportunity to tell America and the world about the size and strength of our atomic capabilities—and yet to do it in such a way as to make the presentation an argument for peaceful negotiation rather than a story told in an atmosphere of truculence, defiance, and threat.

Underlying all this, of course, was the clear conviction that as of that moment, the world, as it still is, was courting disaster in the armaments race, that something must be done to put a brake on this momentum. Certainly there were few so foolish as to think that the brake could be composed only of words and protestations, however eloquent or sincere. But ideas expressed in words must certainly have an effect in getting people to think of specific ways by which future disaster can be avoided.

In the circumstances of that time the proposals were revolutionary. A few nights before my delivery of the speech, both Winston Churchill and

Anthony Eden told Foster Dulles at Bermuda that American thinking was evidently years ahead of that of the British in atomic matters.

At home and overseas, editorial and public reaction to the speech was good. Though the Soviet Union did not immediately give the world its final answer, I had achieved most of my short-term purposes. The United States had set the stage for a practical approach to the development of confidence among the great powers of the world—if the Kremlin so desired.

The press spontaneously gave the proposal a fitting title, "Atoms for Peace."

CHAPTER XI

Life in the White House—
Tricycles in the Corridor

I Pray Heaven to Bestow
The Best of Blessings on
THIS HOUSE
and on All that shall hereafter
Inhabit it. May none but Honest
and Wise Men ever rule under This Roof!

—*President John Adams*

THE White House is not only the seat of authority in the nation, it is the home of the President and his family. It is the place where he greets and entertains a constant stream of guests, foreign and domestic, most of whom bring him a variety and richness of knowledge and understanding that can scarcely be obtained in any other post in the world. Among the great free nations of the North Atlantic we, except for modern France, are the only one with a form of government which makes its head of government also the chief of state. While this fact increases the volume of duties devolving upon the man occupying the Presidency, it does provide opportunity for exercising an influence in a way that is almost uniquely personal and powerful.

The English sovereign "reigns but does not rule." The King or Queen is the center of many occasions of solemn pageantry and ceremony, and is the symbol of Britain's traditions, history, and might. But the sovereign interferes in no way with the workings of the government itself, headed by the Prime Minister. I once read an account of the development of government among the English-speaking peoples in which a statement appeared—I cannot vouch for its accuracy—that the sovereign is required to sign any governmental decree placed before him by the British government, even his own death warrant.

Whether or not this is literally true, it does illustrate the complete separation of the duties and responsibilities between the chief of state and the head of government under the British parliamentary system.

The American system places all this responsibility and authority in the hands of the President, and the White House has for us the significance of Buckingham Palace and 10 Downing Street combined. Consequently we accord to the words "White House" a respect that amounts almost to veneration. Architecturally, such structures as Buckingham Palace and Windsor Castle in England, the Elysée Palace in Paris, Rome's Quirinal Palace, and the Rashtrapati Bhavan in New Delhi make the White House appear, by comparison, a simple and modest cottage. But I am quite sure that no American would like to see the White House revised materially in its general lines and appearance, or replaced by the most magnificent structure ever devised by the hand of man.

The north side of the White House, facing upon Pennsylvania Avenue and looking across Lafayette Square with its equestrian statue of Andrew Jackson, has three stories. The south side, looking over the broad White House lawn, across the Mall and, through a cut in the trees, to the distant memorial to Jefferson, has four stories. The principal feature of the lowest of these, commonly called the ground floor, is known as the Diplomatic Reception Room. In quieter days of the past it was quite convenient for the President to arrange periods during the week when he could, in appropriate formal clothes, and with reasonable pomp and circumstance, receive the credentials of the personal emissaries of other chiefs of state. I am not certain when the President abandoned the custom of receiving ceremoniously those ambassadors from nations with which we have diplomatic ties, but it happened before my time. Except for a few special occasions, I received diplomats in my office, in simple, informal meetings. Nevertheless, the oval room on the ground floor was still known, to the staff and to older Washingtonians, by its original name.

On the ground floor in the main building were located, also, during my administration, the kitchen, the theater, the library, and the Gold and China rooms. In the Gold Room is stored an impressive gold service bequeathed to the White House by Mrs. Anthony Biddle during my first term. In the China Room were displayed samples of the china used by each President. (Washington never lived in the White House, but pieces of the tableware he used are included in the collection.)

Still other rooms, on the same floor, were given over to the White House physician, the housekeeper, and facilities for presidential broadcasts.

The next floor above, reached by an elevator and by a broad stairway, was the one most commonly and publicly used. It was normally entered through the north or Pennsylvania Avenue side, which brought a visitor immediately into a spacious lobby. To the far left was the East Room or Ballroom, the largest in the house. From east to west beyond the lobby were the Green, Blue, and Red rooms—they have, I believe, since been renamed—all used for entertaining. The center one is oval, standing immediately above the Diplomatic Reception Room. At the west end is the State Dining Room which, with crowding, can accommodate a hundred guests.

Next to it is a room, then used as a private dining room, that was, during my tenure, listed in the book titled *The 100 Most Beautiful Rooms of America.*

The traditional living quarters of the First Family have been at the west end of the second floor. In the center of this floor, facing south and adjoined by an outside balcony, is still another oval room, then known as the President's Study. I used it for receiving visitors informally in the evening, whenever a somewhat homier atmosphere than could be obtained in my office was desirable. It was decorated largely with personal mementos of a fairly long life, from a number of regions and nations throughout the world; most were from my military career but some were gifts brought to the American people by heads of government and state. They were kept there for a temporary period only, and later were transferred to a suitable museum—the Smithsonian, the Library of Congress, or the museum which bears my name in Abilene, Kansas.

The east end of the second floor comprised what, in our time, was called by the staff "The Royal Suite." Until Blair House, the presidential guest house across the street, had undergone complete renovation and decoration during my first administration, I used these rooms for putting up any chief of state visiting the United States. A formal dinner would be held on the first evening of his arrival, and the visitor and his family would spend that night in the White House. On the following day they would go to their respective embassies, and on the second night following, my wife and I would be entertained by the visiting King, Queen, or President at his embassy.

The Royal Suite is divided by a hall that runs the full length of the second floor. On the south side was the Lincoln Room, so named because in it were furnishings used by President Lincoln; and there he signed the Emancipation Proclamation. Immediately across was the Queen's Room, although how the name originated I do not know. I do know that whenever Sir Winston Churchill was entertained in the White House, he always occupied the Queen's Room. It was there, in fact, that he and I had our first meeting. Early in World War II, President Roosevelt suggested that General Mark Wayne Clark and I come to the White House to meet the visiting Prime Minister. Entering the room, we found Winston installed in a big bed, working at a sheaf of papers. I learned later it was his custom to do a morning stint before leaving his sleeping quarters. I liked him from that moment on.

The third floor has a number of guest rooms, opening on another long hall running the length of the main structure. A distinguishing feature, on the south side, was a solarium, sunny and light, and much used by our grandchildren when we were so fortunate as to have them with us. On the same floor were also rooms for household servants and storage space.

In 1902 the increasing size of the government forced President Theodore Roosevelt to make an addition to the White House, which up to that time had been not only the home of the President and his family, but his working offices as well. The new addition was called the West Wing and its principal interior feature was another oval room—the President's Office—built as a near replica of the President's Study on the second floor of the main structure. The new West Wing also provided space for the Cabinet Room, personal assistants to the Presidents, press representatives, and waiting rooms for visitors.

In 1942–43 in the administration of President Franklin Roosevelt, increased crowding caused another addition to be erected, this one called the East Wing. We used it strictly for offices.

As might be expected, during my time in the White House, the need for additional space again became plainly evident. I appointed a group of distinguished citizens to study the needs of the Executive Offices, approved their recommendations, and passed them on to the Congress in July 1957 with a request for appropriate action. The Mansion and the two wings would not be affected. The Congress, in a mood of unjustifiable penny-pinching, failed to act. That body had rarely stinted itself when providing additional attractive working space for its own members and their growing staffs, but seemed curiously blind to the needs of the Executive.

In a minor way I was relieved that nothing was done during my administration to improve the Executive quarters because, had the Congress acted favorably, we would have had to live through the confusion and inconvenience of the construction period. But I did think that in view of the fact that the time element alone would prevent me from ever occupying the proposed new quarters, I would be doing a useful service for my successors.

I have heard people who in the past had been familiar with the White House characterize it as a cold, unlivable "institution." My family and I felt none of this. On the contrary, we liked the place and all it stood for. First occupied by John Adams—whose prayer of dedication is carved in the mantelpiece in the State Dining Room—it conveyed to us much of the dignity, the simple greatness of America. Because of this feeling, we never felt that we had any right to make major changes in the structure itself or in its principal furnishings.

The White House had been occupied fourteen years when it was burned by the British in 1814. By 1817 it was rebuilt. Then, in the early twentieth century it was enlarged. And it was completely rebuilt, save for the outside walls, in 1949–50. Growing and developing with the decades, the Mansion itself has always remained largely the same. In the rebuilding of 1949, architects took careful notes to ensure that the new structure within the old walls would be a faithful reproduction of the old.

My conviction is that the White House has been and should always remain a place to be venerated by its occupants as well as by all Americans. I believe that because of the White House's meaning for America—and assuming its stability in structure and surroundings—a visitor of the generation of 2050 or 3050 should be able to gain from it the same sense of humility, pride, reverence, and history that my wife and I felt every day of the years we were privileged to live in it. For the White House is not just a well-run home for the Chief Executive; it is a living story of past pioneering, struggles, wars, innovations, and a growing America. I like to think of it as a symbol of freedom and of the hopes and future accomplishments of her people.

The White House is also a place of work. Within it, many specialists helped to make it for us a pleasant dwelling and a useful, efficient place in which the nation's business could be conducted. The household staff was an experienced group. The head usher, Howell G. Crim, his successor, J. Bernard West, and their assistants[1] were cheerfully helpful. The entire household functioned so well under the direction of the usher's office that I cannot recall a single unpleasant incident involving the staff during our years there. From some of them we still receive cards and greetings on days of special significance.

One of my wife's interests was, of course, in the housekeeper's domain and in the cuisine. With the usher, the social secretary, the florist, and the headwaiter she planned meals and the details of social functions and housing of guests. The social secretary, Mary Jane McCaffree, occupied an important and respected position. She sent out invitations as directed, and supervised entertainments. When these involved foreign visitors, she had to coordinate the guest list with that of the chief of protocol of the State Department, initially John Simmons, later Wiley Buchanan. Mrs. McCaffree was remarkably efficient and at the same time had a warm

[1] Messrs. Thomas B. Carter, Charles K. Claunch, Ray M. Hare, Jr., Rex W. Scouten, and Wilson Searles.

and engaging personality. She got along well with the distinguished guests entertained at the White House—not a few of them of quite uncertain temperament.

There were, in addition, plumbers, carpenters, engineers, and painters, all highly skilled craftsmen whose real pride in the White House was evident in their work.

One characteristic that endeared the entire household staff to us was their fondness for our grandchildren. Like other grandparents we looked forward eagerly to their every visit, and since the two of us would often be busy with our respective engagements for hours on end, only the staff would be present to watch over the smaller ones and keep track of the older ones.

On the third floor of the Mansion the hall, the playroom, and solarium provided space for television, electric trains, and all the other equipment now vital to children from the ages of three to twelve. The swimming pool, between the Mansion and the West Wing, was a favorite spot. The movie theater on the ground floor, between the Mansion and the East Wing, was patronized assiduously. Roads through the South Grounds became proving grounds for bicycles and the electric carts given to the children by friends. The ground floor of the Mansion itself was far from immune to use by the grandchildren as a race track. Tricycles left standing in the corridors were a familiar sight to visitors entering the Mansion through the Diplomatic Reception Room, and to the members of the White House Staff in transit between the East and West wings.

These visits from David, Barbara Anne, Susan Elaine, and Mary Jean were highlights of our domestic life. David, the eldest, was not quite five years old when I was inaugurated. Mary Jean, the youngest, was born in 1955 and was christened in the Blue Room, where President Cleveland had been married. During the years, we gave one birthday party for each grandchild in the ground-floor library. The guest of honor was privileged to make up the guest list, which invariably included the school friends of the honoree, and the only formality observed was the "receiving line," established at the moment when my wife and I appeared at the party. Each youngster was gravely presented to us by the guest of honor, who then took the entire crowd to a movie, followed by the inevitable mountain of ice cream and cake.

The cowboy actor-singer Roy Rogers and his wife, Dale, fine people with a deep love of children and a gift for entertaining them, came to the first party and volunteered to sing a few songs for the children. Though for years the two of them have enjoyed a solid popularity, I am sure that they have never had a noisier or more enthusiastic audience. At later parties different forms of entertainment were provided—all to the delight of the small fry.

The whole household always entered into the bubbling spirit of such occasions. Everyone had such a fine time that the only persistent social problem was to induce enthusiastic guests to go home at the time they were expected by their parents.

*   *   *

Because the life of a President involves a considerable number of more formal occasions, a group required in his role as Commander-in-Chief consists of his three military aides, each representing one of the three main branches of the armed services. Attached to or under the supervision of this group were special military sections, including an Army signal detachment, Army chauffeurs, and a combined Marine and Army helicopter detachment. One special facility was an Army medical detachment, directed by my doctor, General Howard Snyder, and his assistants, Colonel Walter R. Tkach and Nurse Genevieve Herrell.

Each aide had important duties in addition to his responsibility of accompanying me at ceremonies and acting as a liaison officer with his service. Colonel Robert Schulz, my Army aide-de-camp, was responsible for taking care of my personal affairs, including bank accounts, insurance, and expenses.

Captain Edward Beach (succeeded by Captain E. P. Aurand) was my naval aide. He was in charge of emergency evacuation plans for our family and my immediate staff. He also supervised, on my behalf, the presidential retreat, known as Camp David, useful not only as a recreational spot on weekends, but as an admirable place for holding large, confidential conferences, both domestic and international. The Marine and Army helicopter detachments were established in 1957—the first year helicopters were considered safe enough by the Secret Service for a President's use. They were under the command of Colonel Victor Armstrong and Colonel William Howell respectively, and since they were at first primarily for emergency transportation, they also came under the supervision of Captain Aurand.

The Air Force aide, Colonel William Draper, who had been my personal pilot ever since I first went to NATO, was in charge of the two presidential airplanes. Because of the nature of his duties I saw less of him, except on trips, than of the other aides, but he was no less valuable. I trusted implicitly in his skill and judgment.

Colonel Schulz and Captain Aurand established a helpful method for keeping me informed on military affairs falling within their respective areas of interest. Almost daily new developments arose in the organization, matériel, and techniques in the Army and Navy which though not worth formal reports were nevertheless interesting to me both as President and as an old soldier.

These aides kept abreast of these developments and told me about them, using for the purpose the walking time between my room in the Mansion and the office in the West Wing. Colonel Schulz would arrive every morning at seven-thirty to accompany me to the office, an hour that cannot have been particularly convenient, since his home was some fifteen miles away in Virginia.

"Pete" Aurand would come to my office about lunch time, waiting there to walk with me back to the Mansion. This practice, voluntarily established by the two, was, from my viewpoint, not only useful but enjoyable.

Colonel Draper would take advantage of our frequent airplane trips to keep me similarly informed on Air Force details.

Still another military group of the utmost usefulness was known as "White House aides." They came from all four services and were invariably present to assist in formal functions in the Mansion or on the grounds, at receptions, dinners, luncheons, and formal teas. In uniforms suited to the occasion, their duties were to be helpful to guests in every possible way. Their presence was always noted with approval by visitors, especially those from other countries. In the later years of my administration I added to the White House aides, with the enthusiastic concurrence of their superintendents, one cadet from each of the service academies. West Point, Annapolis, Air Force, and Coast Guard cadets so detailed always appeared in full dress, and served for a single evening ceremony only. (It was surprising to me, because of my own instinctive aversion to the many ceremonial events of my cadet days, that the cadets themselves warmly approved the practice.)

*   *   *

A state, or formal, evening during my years in the White House followed a fairly fixed pattern. Dress for men was white tie, and guests assembled in the East Room before my wife and I appeared. During the time that guests were being introduced to each other by the aides and arranged in order of official precedence in the receiving line, Mrs. Eisenhower and I would be visiting with the guests of honor in the living quarters on the second floor.

Just before the hour for meeting the entire company, we and our honored guests posed for a photograph, then proceeded to the first floor. Arriving there, we would all stand at attention while the President's march, "Hail to the Chief," and other honors were rendered by the

Orchestra of the Marine Band, after which we could proceed, surrounded by aides, to the entrance of the East Room. After we arrived, the company moved past us in single file for introductions.

Then I would claim the wife of our guest of honor as my dinner partner, while Mrs. Eisenhower would take the arm of the visiting head of state and proceed the length of the lobby to the State Dining Room.

The tables were arranged in the form of an *E,* with the four of us seated in the middle of the *E*'s vertical column, looking over the three branches of the table. Mr. Robert M. Redmond, the White House florist, always did his work well; on the tables and in the room flowers would be grouped in profusion. Mamie loved carnations in particular, and they were always a part of the décor, massed in attractive arrangements.

Dinner served and completed, the company next proceeded to the Red and Green rooms for coffee, the ladies to the first, the men gathering in the latter. After some twenty minutes ladies and gentlemen would meet in the Blue Room, with each man claiming his dinner partner once more as all the guests went to the East Room for the evening's entertainment. This was varied, conforming as far as we could arrange, with the reported tastes of our foreign visitors. One potentate loved and composed jazz; we provided it, but it was not my favorite. At other times we had such artists as Risë Stevens, Gregor Piatigorsky, and Artur Rubinstein, Marian Anderson, Patrice Munsel, Gladys Swarthout, the Mormon Tabernacle Choir, and the Westminster Choir. Fred Waring and his orchestra appeared several times in response to numerous requests from former guests who were themselves repeaters at such affairs. Music from the several military services always seemed to please our guests. Aside from the Marine Orchestra, which was always present, there were on different occasions the Army Chorus, the "Singing Sergeants" from the Air Force, and a group from the Navy who presented sea chanties.

Entertainment normally lasted for half an hour and with its end the evening was completed. During our first several years in the White House my wife and I would withdraw with the guests of honor to the second floor for more coffee and conversation, but after the renovation of Blair House, which again provided a convenient and handsome guest house for foreign visitors of the highest station, we would, at the evening's close, escort them to the front portico. Other guests then left, except that, on occasion, when old friends were present, I might ask the aides to seek them out and bring them to our quarters for a short after-dinner chat.

Shortly after I entered the White House, I instituted a different and personal type of social event in the form of all-male or "stag" dinners. These were usually small, rarely involving more than sixteen guests. Dress was either a business suit or dinner jacket. I sent each guest a note rather than a formal invitation. Each, as he arrived, was brought to the President's Study on the second floor. My guests were drawn from government, business, publishing, the professions, agriculture, the arts, labor, and education. Normally the guests were a mixture of all these. The after-dinner period was devoted to extended informal conversation, with the group seated in a circle in the Red Room. This conversation was not purely social. I used these dinners to try to draw from leaders in various sections of American life their views on many domestic and international questions. Thus the stag dinners were, for me, a means of gaining information and intelligent opinion as well as of enjoying good company. When the evening ended, I escorted my guests to the door to bid each good night. It was a particular pleasure for me to have a moment alone with each man.

I remember one evening when, after walking a friend to the door, I looked at him and saw that tears were running down his face. He was a strong man, a hardheaded businessman, and I exclaimed, "What's the matter?"

"Mr. President," he said, "I just wanted to tell you what it has meant to me, a farm boy from the Midwest, to spend an evening and dine in the White House. . . ."

He did not have to explain any further. The White House seen quickly in a photograph or in passing, is one thing; but if a man pauses long enough to contemplate what it has meant to so many Americans, it is something else again. The castles of Europe are splendid, but they were built by monarchs and rulers of all sorts, including despots; they have meant pomp and splendor. This house, from the beginning, has meant freedom.

*   *   *

Two men on the household staff who had been immensely valuable to me for many years were Sergeant Leonard Dry and Sergeant John Moaney. The former had been my chauffeur and the latter my orderly, both joining me during the early months of the war in Europe. When we came to the White House, Sergeant Dry was assigned to drive the car used by my wife, since the handling of my own transportation had now become a responsibility of the Secret Service. Mrs. Eisenhower had complete confidence in his skill, judgment, and reliability, and he never disappointed her. Another helper, beloved by everyone, was my wife's companion and personal maid, Rose Woods. For fifteen years she has been a most important member of our ménage.

During the years, Sergeant Moaney had made himself valuable, almost indispensable, to me. But when I decided to resign my Army commission upon nomination for the Presidency in 1952, I had to tell him that due to my new civilian capacity, he and I would of necessity be separated. I would no longer be entitled to his services.

He quietly replied that if I left the Army, he was going to do the same. He did not hesitate a second in casting his lot with me in my new undertaking.

I warned him that if I were elected President, he would be reinstated in the Army, at his old grade, of course, but should I fail to win the election, both of us would be without jobs or pay. I shall never forget his smiling answer:

"Don't worry, General," he said, "I think you and I can always make a living."

Such loyalty touched me so deeply that I remember going back to the room in the Blackstone Hotel in Chicago, where Mamie was ill in bed, to say to her, "Isn't it fortunate for all of us that there are so many things that money cannot possibly buy?"

The presence of Sergeants Dry and Moaney during the years in the White House meant just as much to me as it did during earlier years. More than this, fortunately for us, Sergeant Moaney's wife, Delores, has likewise been a member of our household for many years—a most happy arrangement in our family.

Sergeant Moaney's first duty in the morning was to awaken me, but habit formed during years in the Army took care of this matter automatically. Only on rare occasions was I not reading at 7 A.M., Moaney's regular time of arrival. Because members of my personal staff insisted on arriving at the office earlier than I did, I usually remained in the Mansion until at least seven forty-five. Even so, in view of the distances many had to travel in reaching the office, I think some of the staff were inclined to agree with a reporter who once, having to catch a very early plane to accompany me on a trip, remarked sleepily and disgustedly, "What this country needs is a President who knows how to sleep in the mornings."

*   *   *

The dateline "White House" carries a meaning far broader than a mere structure or location; the White House, in newspaper stories, always means the President's headquarters, all the time, even when dispatches identify it as the "Summer" or the "Vacation" White House. But the atmosphere and the sense of history surrounding 1600 Pennsylvania Avenue itself, the feeling of being at the center of the world, and the excitement of directing or supervising, day by day, programs of the utmost importance to the nation and its relations with others were exhilarating. Also the proximity of the departments of government and the Congress and the excellent communication facilities to and from the White House made it desirable for me to stay in Washington most of the time.

Quite early, however, I found it advisable, and at times essential, to seek periods of relaxation and recreation away from Washington. Such so-called vacations could not materially reduce the need for incessant study and conferences, but they did have some effect in slowing the pace of personal activity. This came about largely because absence from Washington made me less accessible to those in and out of government who were seeking appointments for reasons of secondary import, as well as to those who merely wanted to "drop in." This relief was provided by the comparative isolation of such spots as Denver, Colorado; Augusta, Georgia; and Newport, Rhode Island. Moreover, wherever I was, I always had the valuable assistance not only of my staff but also of military personnel and communications, furnished by the Air Force at Lowry Field in Denver, the Army at Fort Gordon, near Augusta, and the Navy's installation at Newport.

But a President is President no matter what his location. For example, during eight weeks in Denver in 1954 my staff and I worked every day other than Sundays, including six that I spent in the mountains at Fraser, Colorado, with Aksel Nielsen. During those weeks I saw 225 visitors, not including my own immediate staff, made four official trips out of Denver, delivered six speeches, made three television appearances, attended five official luncheons or dinners, considered 513 bills from Congress, signing 488 into law and vetoing 25. Finally, I signed 420 other official papers or documents—all of this business of direct concern to the running of the Executive branch. While this schedule might sound like a strangely hectic vacation, it was largely free from purely ceremonial activities and, as I have said, from welcome but time-consuming visitors.

My two favorite fishing places were at Aksel Nielsen's place, the Norgren-Nielsen ranch near Fraser, and Bal Swan's ranch on a branch of the Platte River. At both spots my hosts made our party most welcome— they were thoughtful of my need for some privacy and generous in their provision of every convenience.

Once when visiting briefly in Denver, Aksel and I took a drive through the foothills, pausing for a short visit with Bal at his ranch. Bal urgently invited me to do a little fishing but I explained that, because I knew I would have to be on my way quickly, I had not bothered to obtain a license. But Bal sensed that I was fairly itching to put a line in that stream. He asked me to wait for a moment, disappeared, then came back and kept me engaged in conversation about ranch affairs for some minutes. But realizing that I should be going to keep an engagement, I was just interrupting to tell him so when a great smile broke out on his face. A man came up and handed him an envelope. Taking it, Bal shoved a rod in my hand, saying, "Here's your license and here's your equipment—now do a little fishing!"

To get the license he had rushed a helper, at breakneck speed, down to a close-by village. I promptly found that there were important reasons for postponing my previously made engagement. Fortunately, my luck was in—I caught several beauties in about half an hour and then left. I think I've never seen anyone as pleased as Bal at the complete success of a surprise stratagem. So was I.

In the Fraser area, which I started to visit just after World War II, Aksel and I liked to stay for several days at a time. The gatherings were always a small group of men, and I—with my faithful Moaney—always the cook. In simpler, pre-presidential years, this meant cooking, at the most, for three or four. But once I started traveling with Secret Service men, signal detachments, and staff assistants, our simple fishing expeditions became as elaborate as troop movements. While these men worked in shifts, the distance from the town, where they lived, was sufficient to make it more practical for Moaney and me to feed some of them rather than to send them into Fraser. This was especially true at breakfast. We were early risers—at least I was, and the others felt that they had to conform. At that altitude, with the early morning temperatures in August around freezing, appetites seemed to go up. I lost a bit of my enthusiasm for cooking when, after preparing breakfast one morning, a friend reported to me in the kitchen, that a policeman cooperating with the Secret Service had consumed, in addition to liberal portions of sausage and bacon, seventeen of my corncakes, swimming in butter and syrup.

At least Moaney and I felt complimented by his demonstrated approval of our culinary skill.

The White House detail of the United States Secret Service is an indispensable group in the life of a modern President, in Washington or out of it. The Secret Service, originally organized to combat counterfeiting, is, by law, charged with the responsibility for assuring the safety of the person of the President and the members of his family.

In my administration the detail was headed by James J. Rowley, who has since, to my delight, been promoted to the post of chief of the entire Secret Service. Jim was capable, decisive, and easy to work with, heading an organization that was painstakingly thorough. Furthermore, to add an important fact, his birthday was October 14, the same as mine.

The responsibilities of the detail are to be in instant readiness, prepared for any kind of move by the President and, where necessary and possible, to arrange in advance for cooperation with the local police. When crowds are expected, the detail reconnoiters the route first, going over it with care, checking on the adequacy of the arrangements of the city police. Before the President goes on a deliberately planned journey Secret Service men are part of the advance party that goes ahead, days before the President arrives. They "sweep" every room in which he is to appear, pronouncing judgment on which rooms are "safe" and "clean," i.e., without hidden microphones. They investigate any known or potentially unfriendly members of groups that will come into proximity.

Their duty is to protect the President from embarrassment, as well as from physical harm. In a motorcade they follow the President in an open car, in all kinds of weather, jumping out of their car to provide a protective cordon when he stops, surrounding his car when it is proceeding slowly. There are Secret Service men in the crowd wherever the presidential car is expected to stop. On the golf course there are agents in the woods.

At the same time the Secret Service takes pride in imposing minimum restrictions on the President. Their philosophy is that if he wants to try a new golf course or visit a strange factory, he has a right to do so. They do not object when their work takes them away from home at Christmas time.

My driver, Deeter B. Flohr, was assigned as a personal bodyguard whenever I was outside the White House grounds. On all journeys away from Washington he was constantly at my side, and even in Washington, except for his normal days off, he was rarely more than a few feet away.

While the men of the detail took their responsibilities most seriously and were alert to see that no threat of violence approached, I tended for my part to discount the need for such careful surveillance and, at times, apparently worried these protectors by my unthinking disregard of their advice. But I did respect and admire them deeply—and was always grateful for the skillful way in which, without hurting the feelings of spectators, they protected me from discomfort and inconvenience, which arose at times out of the friendly and enthusiastic exuberance of crowds.

One of the necessary facilities that the detail invariably provided was almost instantaneous communication between me—no matter where I might be—and the White House. Automobiles were equipped with radiotelephones, and even on the golf course there were communication facilities, carried, in this instance, in golf bags by agents somewhat thinly disguised as players.

After my 1955 heart attack the Secret Service carried along a supply of oxygen and special medicines. At one point, after I had climbed a long, ancient staircase in Afghanistan, General Snyder recommended that I take a whiff of oxygen, which was duly reported as evidence of an illness, when it was nothing but a simple precaution on his part. All in all, in view of the many kinds of help provided so cheerfully and efficiently by the Secret Service, I shall always be personally indebted to them.

*   *   *

Life in Washington was not all problems and decisions and precautions. There were many lighter moments—I prized them highly.

One consistently enjoyable time during life in the White House was the occasional weekend bridge session that I was able to arrange with close friends who like the game. Among these were General Gruenther, George Allen, and James Lemon, all men who lived at least part of the time in Washington. Others on whom I could call to help make up a game included W. Alton ("Pete") Jones, Sig Larmon, Barry Leithead, Ambassador John H. Whitney, Clifford Roberts, William Robinson, Ellis Slater, Charles S. Jones, and Clarence Schoo. I had known all these men for years and always sought one or another of them out as companions for any planned recreation. Two of them, Bill Robinson and Pete Jones, responding to a call I sent out once when leaving Paris, caught a midnight plane out of New York and flew the Atlantic for two days of golf and bridge with Jock Whitney and me in Scotland.

Another favorite form of relaxation was informal visits with friends late in the day. Habitually starting the day's work at seven or even earlier, I was always ready to stop at six and look about for some friendly soul who could come in for a chat. For such meetings I made no specific prior arrangements; at the last minute I would ask Mrs. Whitman to try to find some friends who might be free around 6 P.M. to spend an hour with me.

Al Gruenther, who returned from his post at SHAPE in Paris in 1956, and George Allen, because they lived in Washington, were more readily available than other old friends. After Gruenther's assumption of the presidency of the American Red Cross his office was only a few blocks from the White House. Thus we were able to continue in person the close communication we had maintained by correspondence ever since my return from Europe four years earlier. In the White House a talk with him after a hard day's work never failed to give me a lift. He was perceptive and interested in public affairs, with a quick, incisive mind and an outgoing personality.

George Allen, a businessman, always brought something highly interesting and entertaining to a conversation. He was a master storyteller, and at the same time a shrewd and highly intelligent observer. His reputation as a wit overshadowed the fact that politics was his avocation. I have never known a more capable judge of national political trends. Once a Democrat, he never spoke against his old friends. In spite of a self-advertised aversion to physical activity, he had wide interests and traveled throughout the United States so incessantly that he was never without a new idea, item of information, or opinion on American sentiment and reaction to current events. At the same time, he also had the gift of appropriate silence. I first met George in London in the early days of World War II, and ever since had been trying to get him to watch his calories. Though my accomplishments along this line were purely negative, he was a congenial, stanch, and thoughtful friend.

General Robert Cutler, twice assigned as my Special Assistant for National Security Affairs, was one whose company I always enjoyed and who became a very close friend. Cabinet officers and members of my staff would have been involved more often in the before-dinner talk but 6 P.M. seemed, for them, one of the busiest hours of the day and they could only occasionally drop in for these informal gatherings.

At times an out-of-town friend, having business that brought him to Washington, was able to join in these conversations. In this group were my bridge-playing companions as well as old friends from the armed services and Columbia University and, more recently, politics. Aksel Nielsen came to the city periodically. Bob Woodruff of Atlanta never failed to report to my office on his Washington visits and whenever possible responded promptly to my invitation to come to the second floor of the Mansion.

The desirable qualities in a President's friends are, in large part, the same as for friendship everywhere—compatibility, with each person having similar if not precisely matching tastes in people, recreation, humor; the ability to talk easily, bringing unsought reward to each other for time spent together; the naturalness that comes from backgrounds or careers which have elements in common—especially from years of work or experiences together, at times under strain, which puts acquaintanceship to the test and creates out of it genuine friendship. In addition, the President must have loyal men around him, men he can trust. Not one of the friends I have mentioned—and some whose names I have surely and inadvertently left out—has ever, to my knowledge, written a sentence or uttered a word that could have been embarrassing to me. Every one of them made it a matter of personal honor to avoid any attempt to influence a governmental policy or official by reason of close association with me. These were men of discretion, men who, already successful, made no attempt to profit by our association. It is almost impossible for me to describe how valuable their friendship was to me. Any person enjoys his or her friends; a President needs them, perhaps more intensely at times than anything else.

*   *   *

The year 1953 wound up for us pleasantly. Highlights in our household, as elsewhere, were the celebrations of Thanksgiving and Christmas. We went to Augusta to celebrate both these holidays, because our son was then stationed at Fort Benning, with his family nearby, and the only way we could get together was to bring them to Augusta from that nearby station. Thus the Tuesday before Thanksgiving we stopped at Fort Benning, picked up John and his family, and proceeded to Augusta for a family visit. David made a small sensation (at five years of age) when he arrived wearing a large Pilgrim hat nearly as tall as he was. He had just learned of the Pilgrim fathers and their dress, and so he made out of cardboard a hat in the Pilgrim style and painted it black to be in fashion. In the circle in which he moved that Thanksgiving—the warm circle of our family—he could not have been more fashionable.

The weather was perfect, our stay far too short. John had to get back to his duties and we returned to Washington on Sunday.

Just before Christmas, back at the White House, we arranged for a reception for all the staff, for everyone: doormen and gardeners, special assistants, secretaries and military aides, telephone operators, painters, plumbers, carpenters, and policemen. We gave a great deal of thought to a little memento that we could give to each one. It was difficult to think of anything that could stand as a token of our appreciation of their dedicated service through the year, which would be personal and yet suitable for each person. Finally someone had the idea that we should reproduce one of my amateurish efforts at painting, an idea that was startling, if not dismaying to me. However, when no one produced a better idea, I went along.

My painting was an attempted likeness of President Lincoln, on which I had worked from a book of photographs. The reproduction looked far better than my painting, which was fortunate.

Our reception was held at about noon, to give the maximum number of people a chance to be present. The East Room was decorated with traditional Christmas-tree ornaments, and a nativity scene was the center of attention.

This ceremony was repeated annually, providing my wife and me with an opportunity each year to meet all the employees, rather than only those whose household duties as cooks, waiters, and doormen, for example, brought us together. The attendance varied somewhat from year to year after 1953; I think the average was on the order of eight hundred.

On Christmas morning, 1953, we again left for Augusta by way of Fort Benning. We picked up John, Barbara, and the children, and finished out the eventful year as a happy and thankful family.

BOOK THREE

Don't join the book burners. Don't think you are going to conceal faults by concealing evidence that they ever existed. Don't be afraid to go in your library and read every book, as long as that document does not offend our own ideas of decency. That should be the only censorship.

How will we defeat Communism unless we know what it is, and what it teaches, and why does it have such an appeal for men, why are so many people swearing allegiance to it? It is almost a religion, albeit one of the nether regions.

And we have got to fight it with something better, not try to conceal the thinking of our own people. They are part of America. And even if they think ideas that are contrary to ours, their right to say them, their right to record them, and their right to have them at places where they are accessible to others is unquestioned, or it isn't America.

—Remarks at Dartmouth College, June 14, 1953

CHAPTER XII

The Executive and the Congress

The President shall be Commander-in-Chief of the Army and Navy of the United States, and of the militia of the several States when called into the actual service of the United States. . . .

He shall from time to time give to the Congress information of the state of the Union, and recommend to their consideration such measures as he shall judge necessary and expedient. . . .

—The Constitution of the United States

THE history of 1954 is the history of the resolution of a host of problems, many of them old ones. The year began with a deep division over the Bricker amendment; it ended with that issue laid to rest. It began with serious concern about security risks in government; it ended with that concern largely allayed. It began with Senator McCarthy riding high and ended with his being practically a political cipher. It began with a recession and ended with the American economy climbing toward new heights of prosperity. It began with a pro-Communist regime in Guatemala and Italian-Yugoslav contention over Trieste; when it ended, these troubles had been ended as well. During the year the fighting in Indochina came to a halt, and members of the North Atlantic Treaty Organization cleared the way for the effective build-up of European military forces, including units from the Federal Republic of Germany.

The year opened when the administration announced a list of legislation of wide scope which it wanted the Congress to pass. But before starting in earnest on the long, hard work to turn these requests into reality, the Congress focused its attention on a piece of unfinished business—an amendment to the United States Constitution (Senate Joint Resolution 1), introduced on the first day of the first session of Congress the year before by Senator John Bricker of Ohio.

*   *   *

Senator Bricker was a respected member of the Senate, a lawyer who had been governor of his state. He, along with some other members of the legal profession, had for some time been deeply concerned over a tendency in certain governmental circles to consider treaty-making as a way to effectuate domestic reforms—reforms in areas usually regarded as properly within the jurisdiction of the states. He warned, for example, against imposing on the United States "socialism by treaty." He and those who shared his viewpoint believed that sub-agencies of the United Nations —such as the Human Rights Commission—were actively influencing our State Department to favor using treaties as a device to circumvent provisions of the Constitution, including the Bill of Rights. Under fire especially was a proposed "Covenant on Human Rights." His suggested solution was to amend the United States Constitution to set forth explicit limitations on the power of the President and the Senate to enter into treaties [see Appendix E].

This amendment was co-sponsored by sixty-two other senators, from both major parties, when it was first introduced. It set the stage for a full-scale review of the decision made by the Constitutional Convention which drew up our original Constitution that the treaty-making power of the federal government should be broad in scope and binding upon the several states.

The controversial treaty provision in the Constitution, Article VI, states that "This Constitution, and the laws of the United States which shall be made in pursuance thereof; and all treaties made . . . under the authority of the United States, shall be the supreme law of the land . . . anything in the constitution or laws of any State to the contrary notwithstanding."

The Supreme Court in 1920, in a case relied upon by the proponents of the Bricker amendment, decided that a treaty with Canada regulating the hunting seasons for migratory birds was properly within the treaty-making powers of the President and the Senate. The Court rejected the argument that the treaty on this subject was prohibited by Article X of the Constitution—the Article which reserves to the states the powers not delegated to the federal government.

Some lawyers believed that the language of Mr. Justice Holmes in this Supreme Court decision was so broad in scope that any future and unscrupulous President, if supported by a two-thirds majority of unscrupulous senators, might make a treaty which would take away basic rights now protected by the Constitution and jeopardize our entire American system of government. These lawyers had support among many thoughtful persons and, in addition, others guided primarily by emotion. The latter knew little of law and nothing of Supreme Court decisions, but they distrusted the pacts and Executive agreements (which were not treaties) of World War II, particularly those made by President Roosevelt at Teheran and Yalta, which they feared had sacrificed vital United States interests to the Soviet Union.

Together, therefore, a number of organizations[1] of varying kinds and strengths, believing that both treaties and Executive agreements could imperil our system, decided that the Constitution required amendment.

For the adoption of such an amendment, which for enactment would require approval of two thirds of the Senate and House and three fourths of the state legislatures, Senator Bricker led the fight with his Joint Resolution 1.

The first skirmish in the Senate involved three months of hearings in the Senate Committee on the Judiciary during the spring of 1953. During that period the committee wrote into Senator Bricker's resolution two provisions: One gave the Congress "power to regulate all Executive and other agreements"; this clause, limiting the President's constitutional power to conduct foreign policy, would, its sponsors hoped, prevent any future "Yaltas." A second provision, labeled the "which clause," read, "A treaty shall become effective as internal law in the United States only through legislation which would be valid in the absence of a treaty." This clause would, its sponsors hoped, limit the power of the President and Senate to make treaties only on "international" as opposed to "internal" or "domestic" subjects. The impreciseness of the amended Bricker resolution, and the conflict among experts over the meaning of the language, caused many hours of debate on and off the Senate floor, and in the end contributed mightily to the fate of the proposal.

On the Senate floor Senator Bricker rose on March 13, 1953, to speak in defense of his amendment. To buttress his argument, he quoted several sentences from a talk which Foster Dulles had made before a regional meeting of the American Bar Association in Louisville, Kentucky, in April of 1952. There, Mr. Dulles had discussed the status of treaties in international law and under the Constitution. He pointed out that the Constitution specifically says that approved treaties "become the supreme law of the land." He added that "they are indeed more supreme than ordinary laws, for congressional laws are invalid if they do not conform to the Constitution, whereas treaty law can override the Constitution. Treaties, for example, can take powers away from the Congress and give

[1] Including the American Bar Association, the Daughters of the American Revolution, the United States Chamber of Commerce, the Veterans of Foreign Wars, and the American Legion. Opponents included the American Association of University Women, the CIO and AFL, and the Association of the Bar of the City of New York.

them to the President; they can take powers from the state and give them
to the federal government or to some international body, and they can
cut across the rights given the people by the constitutional Bill of Rights.
. . . This extraordinary power seems to have been deliberately intended
by our founders in order to give the federal government untrammeled
authority to deal with international problems."

To Senator Bricker these quotations showed that Secretary Dulles acknowledged that there was a need for the Bricker amendment. But in the
hearings of the Judiciary Committee, Secretary Dulles testified that the
one clause in his speech, "treaty law can override the Constitution," did
not accurately reflect his views. He said that he recognized that any governmental power, including the treaty-making power, was subject to abuse.
The treaty powers of the Constitution, however, had not in fact been
abused in the 165 years since the Constitution was adopted. He also
pointed out that the Supreme Court had stated several times that a treaty
which conflicted with the Constitution would be invalid. He said the
proper way to prevent misuse of the treaty power was to rely on education
and public debate. He said further that the language of the proposed
constitutional amendment, even if it succeeded in curing potential abuse
of the treaty power, was so broad and inflexible that it created a risk of
drastically limiting the traditional power of the President to conduct
foreign affairs—a far worse danger to our Republic.

Later, in a letter to me, the Secretary amplified his views at considerable length and stated the case for the opposition to the Bricker amendment clearly:

> In the West Pacific and Asia, the vital security interests of the United
> States are involved in steadily evolving relations with the free nations
> of that area.
> It would be difficult to deal with these matters in a way which will serve
> the United States and the cause of peace if the Senate, by a two-thirds vote
> proclaims to the world that the United States plans permanently to dis-
> enable itself from making treaties and conducting foreign relations in the
> historic manner to which the United States and the world are accustomed
> and which, for 165 years, has served us well.
> I realize that action by the Senate is but the first of many steps in the
> process of constitutional amendment. I would myself be confident that
> on reflection the further steps would not be taken because sober thought
> would convince the nation of the danger of a program which would, in
> large measure, reproduce the international impotence which marked the
> Confederation during the period preceding the adoption of our Constitution.
> Nevertheless if the Senate with its great influence and prestige should by a
> two-thirds vote adopt the proposed amendment, this would be taken by our
> friends and by our enemies as foreshadowing a revolutionary change in
> the position of the United States.

In my own intensive study of the question I had as counselors distinguished lawyers in government, beginning with Herbert Brownell and Foster Dulles, who was an international lawyer of high repute. Early in 1953 I sent a memorandum to every Cabinet officer asking him to study the implications of the amendment. I also had advice from many outstanding members of the Judiciary and private members of the bar. Among these, several whom I deeply respected were John W. Davis, Judge John Parker, Judge Orie Phillips, and Professor Edward S. Corwin.

As President, I had no prescribed function in the process of amending the Constitution. But as the head of government, a government that in important aspects would be seriously handicapped if this amendment were adopted, and as the head of a political party, it was my duty, in a matter of such moment to the nation's future, to participate according to my own convictions and conscience.

My position of opposition, while buttressed by expert advisers, had been developed partly from my knowledge of the difficulties involved in the enforcement of the Treaty of 1783 between the United States and Great Britain. The treaty provided for the satisfaction of certain debts owed to British merchants by former colonists, for the restitution to British Loyalists of confiscated property, and for Britain's evacuation of forts lying on our northern frontier. Many states refused to comply with the provisions on debts and on the return of the Loyalists' estates. The central government had no power to compel compliance with the treaty. And Great Britain used this failure to comply as a reason for refusing to abandon the forts.

Such a glaring weakness in the Articles of Confederation was clearly one of the reasons for the development of the American Constitution. It is inconceivable that our founders did not study thoroughly the language by which they conferred on the President the authority to conduct the nation's foreign relations and by which they described the place and standing of a properly made and approved treaty.

The Bricker amendment would have denigrated the status of a legitimate treaty. Every treaty of the future and possibly of the past would be subjected to ceaseless challenge by any of the states, under Article X. Lawsuits, controversy, and confusion would replace the simple and efficacious processes visualized by the Founding Fathers, and, I believed, chaos in international affairs would result.

As the months wore on, I was visited by many individuals and groups whose purpose was to urge my support for, or my opposition to, the amendment—mostly the former.

From these meetings I soon learned that there was a great gulf of misunderstanding between the experts who clearly realized what the effect of an amendment would be, and those who, in the stress of fear that the Constitution would be betrayed and destroyed without the amendment, made great personal sacrifice of time and travel money to acquaint me with their concern.

For a time there was a tremendous emotional surge in the country, and this was in itself a matter of grave concern to me. I constantly urged my visitors to remember that I was sworn to uphold the Constitution, and therefore their determination to make certain that nothing should be done to destroy it could be no greater than my own. I began a practice of assuring visitors that I would support an amendment which would say only, but in unequivocal language, that any treaty or Executive agreement violating the Constitution would have no force and effect. Many who came to see me on the issue were satisfied by this answer, but the more knowledgeable of the opponents quickly protested that even such a simple amendment might give to the courts opportunity to make some unpredictable interpretation.

But the popular fear that our entire Constitution could be overridden by a treaty grew so widespread that I realized such apprehensions had to be quieted by an action such as I had said I would support. Of course, I knew that the lawyers favoring the Bricker amendment could never accept this simple statement as fulfilling their objective, since they would clearly see that it was innocuous and represented no departure from the Constitution. They would also realize that such a widely publicized statement by the head of the government would do much to take the emotion out of the public's view of the issue, and greatly weaken the fight for the full Bricker amendment.

On July 22, 1953, Senator Knowland submitted an amendment eliminating the "which clause." It stipulated that any provision of any treaty which conflicted with the Constitution of the United States should be of no force or effect; that Senate ratification of any treaty would require a yea-and-nay vote; and that when the Senate so provided, a treaty would become effective as internal law in the United States only through the enactment of appropriate legislation [see Appendix F].

The difference between the Knowland and Bricker amendments on this last point was that under Knowland's the Senate, if it desired to require legislation to make a treaty effective as internal law, would have to take action while considering ratification of the treaty, whereas under Bricker's, after the treaty was ratified, both houses of Congress would always be required to act to make the treaty effective as "domestic" law. If they did not so act, the states would not be bound by the treaty as to "domestic" matters. Senator Knowland's amendment seemed acceptable to me because it was based on the principles of sustaining the power of the President and the Senate in treaty-making and of the President's authority in conducting our foreign relations.

For months members of my administration, including the Vice President, Secretary Dulles, Secretary Humphrey, Attorney General Brownell, and Secretary Weeks, had met with Senator Bricker, trying to get him to modify his proposal to something similar to the simple language I had proposed. I had conferred with him myself on June 16, and we seemed close to agreement. A week later, however, he sent word that he would not give up any part of the "which clause."

This made it clear to the country, as it had long been to the administration, that his "which clause" was the vital concern of the revisionists. The lines of difference were now sharply defined. It was no longer possible for the supporters of the Bricker amendment to say that their purpose was merely to clarify the meaning of the Constitution. Their aim was to change it radically.

There was nothing else to do but get ready for a fight to the end.

As the battle opened in the 1954 session of the Eighty-third Congress, senators supporting the amendment, recalling the approval they had obtained from the Senate Judiciary Committee in 1953, felt that their chances of victory were bright. On the other hand, the public had been hearing powerful voices in opposition.

Late in 1953, for example, I received from John W. Davis a pamphlet published by the Committee for the Defense of the Constitution—with himself, Professor Edward S. Corwin, General Lucius Clay, and others as co-signers:

> We are opposed to amending the Constitution by the so-called Bricker Amendment. . . . the proposed Amendment would cut down the treaty-making power of the Federal Government and alter the existing division and balance of powers between the legislative and executive branches.
>
> In so doing it would write into the Constitution three new and dangerous provisions. First: The proposed Amendment would require that a treaty become effective as internal law "only through legislation."

After a treaty had been negotiated and signed, the pamphlet said, it would have to be approved by the Senate, as before, and then turned into an internal law requiring a majority vote in each house and final approval of the President. This provision, they pointed out, would make "our procedure for carrying out our treaty obligations the most cumbersome in the world, impose needless delay and seriously weaken our bargaining position."

> Second: The proposed Amendment would limit implementing legislation to that "which would be valid in the absence of treaty"—the so-called "which clause." This is an attack upon the union itself. It would confine the Federal Government's power to make an effective treaty (as well as to implementing treaties) to those subjects on which Congress may legislate

under the powers otherwise delegated to it by the Constitution. . . . The Bricker Amendment would thus make acquiescence of the legislatures of the forty-eight states necessary to the effectuation in the United States of such vital international agreements as the traditional treaties of friendship, commerce, and navigation, narcotics control convention and possible arrangement for international control of atomic energy.

Third: The proposed Amendment would give Congress the "power to regulate" executive and other international agreements. It would go beyond the extensive powers which Congress already has and exercises in this field. . . . It would let Congress destroy the President's power to make necessary international arrangements to meet emergencies, like the Berlin blockade, as they occur.

Each of these three changes was objectionable, their analysis showed, and all were both unnecessary and harmful.

Many senators tried to devise language that would meet the objections of the Committee for the Defense of the Constitution but which would also assure the public of the sanctity of our Constitution. Senator Bricker's supporters refused to consider anything that omitted the "which clause," and this was completely unacceptable to me and to my administration. We refused to take anything that in reality would change the substance of the Constitution as it stood.

Volumes of words were written, far more were heatedly spoken, in and outside the halls of Congress. One angry wag charged that the Constitution was being taken apart "brick by brick by Bricker." I spent hours on the telephone conferring with Republicans in the Senate, with Secretary Dulles and Attorney General Brownell. Test votes in the Senate— the legislation never reached the House—were exceedingly close. On February 17, 1954, the Senate rejected the "which clause" forty-four to forty-three. On February 25 it rejected Senator Bricker's last try by a vote of forty-two to fifty. But in the crucial final vote on February 26, a compromise amendment sponsored by Senator Walter George, which was also unacceptable to the administration, received sixty "aye" votes. Just one more would have given the amendment a two-thirds majority of the ninety-one senators present and voting.

With that vote the weeks of controversy ended, for all practical purposes. The powers of future Presidents to conduct our foreign relations were preserved, as since 1789, unimpaired.

I have heard it said that the struggle over the Bricker amendment was in reality a contest between "liberals" and "conservatives" or between "isolationists" and "internationalists." Yet George Humphrey, to name just one, who had always classed himself as a conservative, was flatly opposed to the amendment. And certain senators, usually known as liberals, on both sides of the aisle, voted for the George amendment. They included Senators Margaret Chase Smith, Clinton Anderson, Mike Mansfield, and Lyndon Johnson. My brother Edgar, a lawyer who always liked to refer to himself as a "constitutional conservative," argued hotly—so far as an argument by letter can be so characterized—that the amendment was absolutely necessary to save the United States from coming disaster. My own opinion was that the contrary was true. Being a lawyer, he felt somewhat frustrated that I could not agree with him on a legal matter, but my best retort was that the subject was far above legalistic interpretation in importance. Both of us felt so strongly about the amendment that by common consent it was finally dropped as a subject of correspondence between us.

Initially, presentations made to me in favor of the amendment were studded with the names of organizations recorded as in support. The list was impressive in length, but as time went on, it became clear that many prominent members and sections of these organizations were in conflict with the committees or spokesmen who had expressed the supporting view. The breakup of this solid phalanx was one of the developments that finally brought about the defeat of the amendment, which I still think would have spelled tragedy for the future of America. In any event, the matter, after its defeat in the 1954 session, never again became a subject of formal congressional debate during my time in the White House.

On March 1, 1954, I told the Republican Legislative leaders that, with the debate over the Bricker amendment now a thing of the past, I hoped everybody could turn to the work of moving forward the administration's legislative program.

*   *   *

In developing a program we had definitely been making a new beginning. When my administration began, in January 1953, it perforce undertook the work of modifying and revising the documents and programs earlier sent to the Congress by the Truman administration. The budget for the period from July 1, 1953, to June 30, 1954, had been prepared by the previous administration in detail, and our own opportunities at that time for making the necessary studies and analyses for extensive revision were limited.

But at the close of 1953 the story was far different. We now had had the time to scrutinize every area of government in detail. With the advent of the 1954 calendar year my administration had the entire responsibility for the content of the State of the Union message, the Budget message, and the Economic Report, the three major messages sent annually by law to the United States Congress. Beginning with these messages, we intended to ask the Congress to pass a variety of new laws which would set forth for the first time definitively the administration's thinking on many major public policies.

At a three-day conference of the Republican Legislative leaders, beginning December 17, 1953, I presented this legislative program for 1954. I asked those attending this special meeting to comment on it and on the priority in which it could be pushed through the Congress. By holding such a meeting I hoped to further the consolidation of the Republican party and its support of the recommendations that I intended to send to the Congress.

"In 1954," I told the Legislative leaders, "the party should deliver on commitments made in the platform of 1952. There are minimum limits of achievement below which we must not fall."

When the conference ended, I wrote to one of its participants, House Majority Leader Charlie Halleck:

> The three day conference has come and gone. Unquestionably the over-all result was good, although naturally I had disappointments— particularly when I found that some of our people still seem to believe in caution rather than courage, and in evading rather than meeting issues.
>
> Happily, this attitude is far from universal and I want to tell you again how gratified I am by your readiness, always, to take the thorniest problems in your hands—whenever the problem is one calling for political solution —and staying with it until the job is done.
>
> Unquestionably, we should arrange for the earliest possible bipartisan meeting to go over such matters as foreign policy and national security. Because of the thin Republican margins in both Houses, both you and Knowland obviously require Democratic support in almost every tough vote. This being so, we must by all means quickly show our readiness to cooperate in every decent way, and particularly in those areas where bipartisan action is vital to the national interest.

On January 7, 1954, I delivered my annual State of the Union message. Three days earlier I disapproved a suggestion that I deliver this message, for the first time in history, at night on television: such an innovation, I felt, would reflect badly on the Congress. The message listed and described specific legislative measures. It set out dates for subsequent special messages to the Congress, which would expand on particular subjects—for example, agriculture, labor, and social security. This commitment to deliver specific messages on specific days kept my staff, at times, working around the clock, but every message arrived at Capitol Hill on time. Some of the requests for legislation came out of the 1952 platform. Others arose from our studies in 1953. As a whole, these requests constituted the most massive and comprehensive set of recommendations of my entire eight years. The prestige of the administration was riding on their enactment into law.

Following up on the overhauling of the security regulations of the year before, and keeping to our pledge to do everything possible to clean the country of subversives, I asked the Congress to enact legislation providing that an American citizen convicted of conspiring to advocate the overthrow of our government by force or by violence be treated as one who had renounced his allegiance to the United States and had forfeited his citizenship.

I also requested "immunity-bath" legislation which would permit the Attorney General to grant immunity from prosecution to witnesses testifying before a grand jury or a congressional committee, where such witness would otherwise invoke the Fifth Amendment privilege to protect fellow conspirators. While I knew that some so-called liberals would object strenuously to this proposal, I believed that our nation had a fundamental obligation to protect itself against palpable disloyalty. Incidentally, I pointed out that both Canada and Britain, resolute in defense of civil rights, had laws similar to the one I wanted.

One set of proposals was designed to fortify the American economy and thus to add to the United States' prosperity and security. A second set was framed to further the health and welfare of the individual.

A giant item in the first group was one which for nearly a half-century, since the days of Theodore Roosevelt, had been considered an impossible dream, a law which would permit the United States to cooperate with Canada to deepen the St. Lawrence River. Such an accomplishment would permit seagoing ships to sail from the Atlantic more than two thousand miles through the Great Lakes to the heart of the Middle West.

I had long favored the construction of the St. Lawrence Seaway. As Chief of Staff of the Army from late 1945 to early 1948, I expressed the conviction that this waterway would strengthen the security of both countries. Now as President I had become convinced that the seaway would be, in addition, an economic asset to both nations. While certain interests, primarily Eastern seaports and the railways of that region, might suffer some disadvantages, I was persuaded that the over-all benefit to the nation would more than counterbalance any harm suffered. I insisted, however, that the law provide that the seaway, through tolls, eventually pay for itself.

In another major economic request, four days after my State of the Union message, I sent the Congress a special message outlining a break with the present agricultural law, inherited from the preceding administration.

During the 1952 campaign, at Kasson, Minnesota, I had pledged to uphold the price-support law then existing, until it expired on December 31,

1954. I was keeping that pledge. But with the expiration of the old law, the time would have arrived for a new and better one.

The old law set a "parity price" for farm products—a price calculated to give the farmer a fair return in comparison with his costs. It compelled the federal government to support six products—wheat, corn, cotton, tobacco, peanuts, and rice—at 90 per cent of this parity price. At harvest time, if the market price had fallen below the support price, a farmer who had planted only on a number of acres fixed by the government, could get a loan from the government, with his crops as collateral, for the full support price. If the market price then rose above the support price, the farmer paid the government back; if not, he kept the loan, and the government took his crop.

This law, enacted to encourage all-out food production during World War II and the Korean War, had failed. In 1952 farm prices fell; they continued to do so in 1953. And all the while, farm costs rose. The farmer was in a tighter and tighter squeeze despite the fact that crop and livestock yields had gone up, and new machines had helped the individual farmer produce more than ever before.

In 1947, for example, a farmer could buy a pickup truck with what he made from selling nine bales of cotton. By the end of 1952 the same truck cost not nine bales, but fourteen. In 1947 a farmer could buy a tractor with 800 bushels of corn. By the end of 1952 that tractor cost more than 1300 bushels—two thirds more. In 1947 a farmer could buy a combine with 930 bushels of wheat; by the end of 1952 that same combine cost 1600 bushels.

The chief beneficiaries of the system of high, rigid price supports were the 2 million larger, more mechanized farms, which turned out about 85 per cent of America's agricultural output. There were 3.5 million smaller farms producing only 15 per cent.

Moreover, under this system, the government was doing no better than the farmers. It was becoming the proprietor of a heightening mountain of wheat and corn, tobacco and cotton, piling up in the warehouses of the federal Commodity Credit Corporation. By 1954 the government had enough wheat and cotton under padlock to supply all the needs of the market for an entire year. These products plus all the others owned by the government were worth $2.5 billion. On top of them the government had under loan another $2.5 billion worth. To store these foods and fibers, American taxpayers were paying a bill of a half-million dollars a day.

In these circumstances I pointed out that we had two choices: first, we could tell farmers to cut down still further on the number of acres they planted with basic crops, and at the same time clamp rigid federal controls on these additional acres taken out of basic crop production. Such a decision would move us toward regimenting the production of every basic crop and putting every producer of those crops under the domination and control of the federal government. This plan, I argued, would be expensive; it would go against fundamental interests both of the farmer and of the nation as a whole; it would not reduce surpluses. It was no solution whatsoever.

The other choice was to allow a free market for these agricultural products a chance to achieve gradually a greater influence on production-planning by farmers. Accordingly, I proposed that the federal government support the prices of the basic crops not at the compulsory fixed 90 per cent of parity, but at varying levels between 75 and 90, in accordance with the relationship of the total supply to a supply considered normal.

Moreover, I proposed a new definition of "parity." The old parity formula was based on the ratio between prices and costs in 1910–14, when the two were closely balanced. The administration proposed to substitute for this outdated formula another one taking account of the higher costs of many tools and pieces of equipment and technological benefits which did not exist in 1914, a formula based on the cost-price ratio of the past ten years. This modernized parity formula would go gradually into effect over the next two years.

To make the plan effective, I asked the Congress to pass legislation that would block existing surpluses from the normal channels of trade. In computing the support price the government could then ignore this $2.5 billion worth of stored products. Instead, I proposed, these should go into special noncommercial programs. These would include lunches for school children, disaster relief, emergency assistance to foreign populations stricken by famine or other catastrophes, and stockpiles against a national emergency.

These improvements, I insisted, including modernized parity and flexible price supports, would have to be made gradually: in no case should we permit an abrupt drop in the dollar or percentage level of price supports.

We had drawn up these recommendations with extreme care:

> . . . This administration [I said] resolved to get the benefit of the best thinking of the nation's farmers, as well as that of its farm experts. Over sixty different survey groups, and more than five hundred of the most eminent farm leaders in the country, have participated in these studies. Agricultural colleges and research institutions contributed their work and thought. Scores of producer, processor, and trade groups, as well as national farm organizations, gave their findings and proposals. Mail from thousands

of individual farmers, and opinion polls among farmers, have been analyzed and weighed. The bipartisan, broadly representative national Agricultural Advisory Commission has steadily worked and consulted on the problem for the past twelve months. Numerous commodity organizations have been consulted. Many members of the Congress have shared their own rich experience in this effort.

None of us was blind to the fact that in attempting to liberate agriculture from the artificial system of marketing in vogue since World War II, we were undertaking an effort that would call forth angry protests from vote-seeking politicians and from certain sectors of the agricultural community. However, we had some ardent supporters on our side. As soon as my message reached Capitol Hill, newspaper reporters were kept busy jotting down instantaneous reactions to it: "Excellent," said Republican Senator Aiken of Vermont, chairman of the Senate Agriculture and Forestry Committee, "it will be enacted." "Sound and effective," pronounced Charlie Halleck. "I don't think," Sam Rayburn countered, "the Congress will give up the 90 per cent parity for basic farm products." "The program means less protection and less money for the farmer," Lyndon Johnson declared. From Senator McCarthy came the conclusion that support prices "should not go as low as 75 per cent and ought to go perhaps even above 100"! And from Senator Hubert Humphrey came an excited mixed metaphor: "The same old disastrous slide-scale idea dressed up with a temporary sedative." The American Farm Bureau Federation, largest of the farm associations, approved the administration program. The National Farmers Union completely opposed it, advocating "100 per cent of parity price supports on all family farm production."

The fight to free the farmers and make the agricultural industry more responsive to a competitive market was destined to continue throughout all the years of my Presidency. It circulated, partly at least, around the personality and convictions of Ezra Taft Benson.

A firm believer in private enterprise, his conclusions once formed were earnestly held and argued, though not always with the maximum of tact. But he and I agreed that high, rigid governmental price supports could never solve the farm problem, and so I supported his every effort—and they were honest efforts because he was and is a man of unimpeachable integrity—to make American agriculture more responsive to a free market.

In my 1954 Agricultural message I said that "special attention" would be given to "the problems peculiar to small farmers"—the million and a half with incomes of less than $1000 a year. There followed a year-long, nationwide study, with the result that in April of the next year the administration launched its Rural Development Program.

On the same day, January 11, 1954, I sent the Congress a message suggesting amendments to the Taft-Hartley Act. In the weeks before, I had received quantities of advice on these amendments, some favoring labor, some favoring management. The new Secretary of Labor, James P. Mitchell, a former Assistant Secretary of the Army recommended by Charlie Wilson, began working out a set of amendments which would be fair to both labor and management. Mitchell had entered office the preceding October and I soon recognized from his performance that as long as he wanted the job and I was President there would be no need to appoint a successor to him. At the Legislative-leaders meeting in December he presented the administration's suggested proposals, which quickly won the general acceptance of everybody around the table.

The Taft-Hartley Act (the Labor-Management Act of 1947) outlawed the secondary boycott. A secondary boycott occurs when unions, with a grievance against a (primary) employer, seek to intensify pressure on him by taking economic action—striking, picketing, refusing to handle goods—against another employer (secondary) with whom the first has business relations, even though the unions have no grievance against the secondary employer. In my message I proposed cutting back on the definition of the secondary boycott. My amendment would permit a boycott against an employer doing "farmed-out work" for another employer whose employees were on strike, because such a secondary employer could not call himself "an innocent third party" outside the dispute. My proposal would also permit a boycott against an employer on a construction project who, along with a primary employer, was doing work at a project site. A picket line at a construction site against one employer, of course, tended to put pressure on all employers; but outlawing such a picket line, we believed, would take from the union its right to strike against its primary employer. So I favored rewriting this part of the law. And whereas the Taft-Hartley Act required the general counsel of the National Labor Relations Board to ask the courts for an injunction against any secondary boycott, I favored amending the law to let the general counsel do so at his own discretion.

Following through on my 1952 commitment against "union-busting," I urged a change in the part of the law which prohibited employees who struck for economic reasons from voting in elections to choose their collective-bargaining representatives. Under this provision of the Taft-Hartley Act an employer could conceivably provoke a strike and replace the strikers with new permanent employees, who could then hold an election in which the strikers could not vote.

In another proposal I insisted that the Communist-disclaimer oath either be required equally of employers and employees or be dropped from the law.

Most labor leaders liked these changes, though the National Association of Manufacturers did not. But my message included provisions which provoked just the reverse response. Under the interpretation of Taft-Hartley, for example, employers had claimed that no limitation existed on the claims a union might make during a representation election, whereas management had to exercise great care over what it said to avoid the charge of interference. I proposed that the right of free speech should apply equally to labor and management.

I reaffirmed the right of the states to take action in emergencies which endangered the health or the safety of their citizens, despite "any conflict with federal laws."

Further, my message recommended guaranteeing the right of the employee, when called on to strike, to vote by secret ballot under federal auspices for or against continuing the strike. It seemed to me that the government had been so preoccupied with authorizing, supporting, and protecting union organizations that it had ignored the need of assuring the individual union member a full and untrammeled right to a voice, by secret ballot, in any decision on a strike, which was, in effect, a decision on his own weekly paycheck.

I declined to ask the Congress to repeal Section 14 (b), which permits the states to make their own decisions respecting "right-to-work laws," which ban compulsory union membership.

Reading these changes, labor leaders objected to the provision asserting the right of the states to act in any emergency endangering health or safety, arguing that state laws, including the right-to-work laws of thirteen states, were more repressive to labor than federal laws. Walter Reuther, head of the CIO, cried that the amendments would make the Taft-Hartley Act worse than it already was; the secret-strike-vote provision, he alleged, reflected a deep-seated antilabor prejudice. Why a secret vote in a democratic institution implied a prejudice against labor, he did not attempt to explain. Miners' union leader John L. Lewis thought these amendments could not make "a slave law palatable to free born citizens. . . . It should," he thundered, "be repealed in toto."

My own concern, in the midst of this controversy, was above all with the worker, not with his union leaders. In any event, it was clear that this message would provoke a prolonged fight in the Congress.

Late in February the Randall Commission on Foreign Economic Policy, established the preceding August, reported its conclusions. And on March 30, based on them, I sent a special message to the Congress. This called for legislation to extend for three years the Trade Agreements Act, with amendments to authorize tariff cuts on specific items up to 15 per cent over the three-year period, to simplify our customs procedures, and to increase American businesses' investments abroad by setting corporate income taxes on income from foreign subsidiaries at a rate 14 per cent lower than the regular corporate rate in the United States.

My proposals would not make a sweeping across-the-board reduction in tariffs. The law would retain its historic peril-point and escape-clause provisions to protect American businesses against serious injury[2] from foreign competition. And the American economy would therefore suffer no sudden sharp decline. The report went on to show the advantages to the United States of increasing two-way trade instead of cutting back on our exports or forever providing aid in order to eliminate the "dollar gap"—the lack of dollars abroad due to the fact that we had been exporting far more than we had been importing. Each year since World War II the deficit had averaged about $4 billion.

I outlined the purpose of these and other recommendations at the end of the message: "Conceived as a whole, this program consists of four major parts: Aid—which we wish to curtail; Investment—which we wish to encourage; Convertibility[3]—which we wish to facilitate; and Trade—which we wish to expand."

On March 29, the day before this message went to the Hill, I discussed it with the Republican congressional leaders. As members of the Randall Commission itself, Senator Millikin and Congressmen Reed and Simpson had refused to sign the conclusions of the majority. At the March 29 meeting, comments from Senator Knowland, Speaker Martin, Congressman Reed, and Senator Millikin indicated clearly that they doubted the wisdom of any further effort to liberalize our foreign-trade laws. Clarence Randall answered all their questions clearly and patiently.

"The United States," he assured them, "isn't trying to give away something for nothing."

Congressman Halleck stood squarely with the administration, recognizing the need for the United States to expand international trade, cut production costs, and boost its exports. "I'm not supporting this bill be-

[2] The peril-point provision requires the Tariff Commission to report to the President, before he can enter into any tariff negotiations, on (a) the limit to which a tariff can be lowered without causing serious injury to a domestic industry or (b) the level to which a tariff should be raised to prevent such injury.

The escape clause forbids the continuation of any tariff reduction on a product which is being imported into the United States "in such increased quantities . . . as to cause or threaten serious injury to the domestic industry producing like or directly competitive products."

[3] The free exchangeability of currencies, possible when trade between any two countries flows in roughly equal amounts both ways.

cause I don't care what happens to the American purchaser," he said. "Frankly, I'm supporting it because I think it will be good for the country."[4]

Another message, delivered to the Congress on February 17, called for authority to exchange with our allies "such tactical information as is essential to the development of defense plans and to the training of personnel for atomic warfare"; and provided for the protection of information about atomic energy. But it did much more. Looking beyond the horizon of national danger, it set out for the first time in history a program for harnessing atomic energy for the commercial production of electricity. For that program I asked the Congress for legislation to permit the private manufacture, ownership, and operation of atomic reactors under licensing systems administered by the Atomic Energy Commission. I asked also for authority to allow the commission to supply these private manufacturers, at cost, materials and services to launch this new industry.

These recommendations rejected the fearful warning that the government should retain its federal monopoly over the development of atomic power, to prevent the growth of an insidious "private monopoly." They followed my "Atoms-for-Peace" address at the United Nations in December, 1953. And they foreshadowed the ground-breaking for the United States' first civilian atomic power plant at Shippingport, Pennsylvania, on Labor Day of 1954.

With these proposals, and the Budget message, which sought seriously to restore fiscal responsibility, the Congress and the country had before them the administration's economic objectives for 1954: build the seaway, unshackle agriculture, correct faults in labor-management legislation, lower tariff walls, lay the foundation for a new industry to produce light and power.

---

[4] After Clarence Randall had presented the report to the commission, I asked him to stay in the government to help carry its recommendations into effect. To that end I appointed what was known informally as the trade committee, consisting of the appropriate Assistant Secretaries from each Cabinet department, with Mr. Randall himself as chairman. At the same time I asked Joseph Dodge, who by then had left as Budget Director, to study the whole subject of coordination from the White House. Mr. Dodge recommended that foreign economic policy be thereafter coordinated continuously by a group to consist of selected Cabinet officers and the heads of other appropriate agencies. Adopting this recommendation, I established the Council on Foreign Economic Policy, with Mr. Dodge as the first chairman. He and Mr. Randall then worked in parallel for a time. Not long after, however, Mr. Dodge had to return to private affairs, the trade committee was disbanded, and I named Mr. Randall chairman of the Council on Foreign Economic Policy. He continued to serve in that capacity throughout my two terms, during which the council proved its value time and again.

In a second set of proposals that year, the Congress and the country could read a large measure of concern for the individual—for his rights as a citizen and for his welfare. As in the campaign of 1952 and the legislative program of 1953, I recommended legislation to confer statehood on Hawaii, to permit the residents of the District of Columbia to vote, and to give the same right to every man and woman who reaches the age of eighteen. This last reflected my opinion, formed during World War II, that a man old enough to take up arms for his country was old enough to cast a ballot intelligently.

In a special message I renewed the recommendations I had made in 1953 that the Congress broaden social-security coverage to include ten million additional people—self-employed farmers, doctors, dentists, lawyers, and others. I also recommended an increase in social-security benefits and a new provision to protect the benefit rights of disabled persons. This program would gradually decrease the need for public assistance payments shared by federal, state, and local governments to the destitute.

I sent the Congress a short special message on the health needs of the American people. It called for a limited federal reinsurance service to encourage private and nonprofit health-insurance programs. We asked for a greater federal program to rehabilitate the disabled through vocational training. And we recommended an increase in the federal investment in hospitals and other facilities for medical care.

Another special message asked for broadening of the Housing Act of 1949 to authorize loans and grants to communities for slum clearance. For low-income families, I proposed the construction of 140,000 homes in a four-year period. The purpose was, thereafter, to displace governmentally financed housing projects with a program to insure long-term loans to those who might otherwise not be able to obtain essential funds from private lenders.

I was especially anxious to clean up slums and rebuild blighted areas. Any such undertaking needed "a jaundiced eye and a good microscope," but I insisted that this housing program, within limits, not be blocked by budgetary considerations. I was delighted—and surprised—to discover that my enthusiasm was shared by the most economy-conscious man in the administration, George Humphrey.

"The State of the Union message," I reminded the Cabinet on November 12, 1953, "will emphasize the administration's determination to provide for the needs of all Americans, particularly the 'little fellow.' The budget is going to contain specific items to demonstrate that our good intentions are not just good words." Specifically, I was thinking of our health, social-security, and housing recommendations. We planned to double expenditures for urban redevelopment, and recommended new starts on six irrigation, eight flood-prevention, and eight navigation projects.

Initiation of these humanitarian programs did not deter us from our determination to reduce the federal budget. I told the Legislative leaders that balancing the budget was a cold phrase for an imperative necessity. And again and again I emphasized that our concern for fiscal responsibility was in the end a concern for people.

I argued that the balancing of the budget was not merely some abstract, statistical feat to be performed by government accountants but was to give each family the kind of dollar with which it could begin balancing its own budget. I believed that without a sound dollar, every American family would face a renewal of inflation, an ever-increasing cost of living, the withering away of savings and life-insurance policies. Bigger and continuing deficits, I said, would in turn inflate the dollar still more and would cheat every family in America. It would strike most cruelly at the poor among us.

The Budget message for fiscal year 1955 brought to the Congress estimated Treasury receipts and contemplated expenditures. After many months of study, analysis, and debate concerning world and domestic conditions, it reflected the administration's determination both to meet national needs and to achieve, as soon as feasible, a balance between income and expenditure.

"Meeting these twin objectives," Joseph Dodge, the Budget Director, said in a masterpiece of understatement, "will be a real headache."

During the period of budget construction, at the close of 1953, Director Dodge and I worked together almost daily. In early November he wrote me a memorandum which succinctly set forth our mutual understanding; it was to serve as a weapon in his economizing efforts with federal agencies:

(1) . . . Both appropriations and the level of expenditures for fiscal year 1955 must be reduced substantially below those for the 1954 fiscal year.

(2) To achieve this objective every possible reduction will have to be made and every item included in the Budget must meet the test of necessity rather than of desirability. This policy of reduction must be applied with relative uniformity, though equitably, to all agencies.

(3) Pressures to protect favored expenditures or programs must give way, except in the most unusual cases, to the greater pressure to reduce overall Government expenditures.

(4) It will be necessary to anticipate results from improved management in the agencies by making reasonable reductions for improved efficiency in operations. Such reductions either take account of efforts already under

way or will stimulate efforts to accomplish them in the twelve months beginning July 1, 1954.

This approach leads inevitably to differences concerning the amounts between the Bureau of the Budget and the agency. Unless all concerned clearly understand that it has the full support of the President, agencies can be expected to appeal to the President directly and in many cases on what will appear as relatively unimportant decisions. Therefore I should like to have your approval or modification of the approach outlined so that I may be guided accordingly in subsequent recommendations.

My approval was promptly given, and the Budget Director used the memorandum with good results.

Finally, the budget was ready for the Congress. In the Budget message I pointed out that our current review of the 1954 budget—the one under which we were then operating—showed that requests for new obligational authority (new appropriations) were reduced more than $11 billion and expenditures were reduced $7 billion below the totals estimated for that year by the preceding administration. And I added that similar reductions were planned in the new budget which I was recommending for the next fiscal year.

These reductions would permit us to do one of two things: cut taxes or turn in a 1955 budget surplus. So that most of the new savings could be passed along to taxpayers, with beneficial effects on our entire economy, I believed it appropriate to adopt a course leading toward both lower taxes and a balanced budget.

The reductions in the 1954 budget expenditures had been devoted to reducing the large deficit forecast in it. The anticipated savings in 1955 budget expenditures justified our reducing taxes.

As early as September 1953, I had decided that because the danger of immediate inflation had given way to the possibility of recession, the administration would not oppose the tax reductions already scheduled to take effect on the next New Year's Day. So, with the administration's approval, the Korean War emergency increase in individual income taxes and the wartime excess-profits tax expired in January 1954.

But my Budget message went much further than this in tax reduction. Under the changes we proposed: Parents would be able to claim as dependents children earning more than six hundred dollars per year; widows and widowers with dependent children would be permitted to file the equivalent of a joint return and thus pay at a lower rate, as married couples were permitted to do; foster children could be claimed as dependents; working mothers could take a tax deduction for the cost of child care. Further, taxpayers would be able to claim an allowance for medical expenses in excess of 3 per cent of their income, compared with the 5 per cent then in effect; double taxation—the taxation of the same earnings both as income to the corporation and as income to the individual stockholder who receives a dividend—would end, and depreciation allowances would be liberalized.

At the same time, the administration opposed any reduction in the total revenue brought in by excise taxes, or in the general corporate income tax.

Although these changes meant we might have a budgetary deficit of slightly less than $3 billion in fiscal year 1955, I insisted that by continuing to search for every possible economy, we could reduce the projected deficit as the year went on. And I was confident that in the succeeding period—July 1, 1955, to June 30, 1956—we could achieve a surplus.

During 1954 I made 232 specific requests for legislation to the Congress. I knew that the struggle for passage of a program of this magnitude would be continuous and arduous, for Republicans had in the Senate an even more precarious majority than in the previous year. After the death of Senator Taft, the Democratic governor of Ohio, Frank Lausche, appointed Thomas A. Burke to fill the vacancy. That appointment left in the Senate a line-up of forty-seven Republicans, forty-eight Democrats, and independent Wayne Morse, who early in 1955 would cross to the Democratic side. With the Vice President presiding and casting the deciding ballot, and Morse siding with the Republicans, a straight party vote in the Senate would give the administration a majority of exactly one.

The death of Senator Taft had left also the large problem of selecting a new majority leader. During his months of service as majority leader, Senator Taft had used Senator Knowland, a young, vigorous, and forthright man, as his principal assistant, and upon relinquishing the duties of that office, he suggested that Knowland take his place.

Several of my associates urged me to favor a man of their choice, using patronage as a coercive method of getting my way. Under other circumstances this might have been the thing to do. But what my friends did not appreciate was that the parties were so evenly balanced that we needed the vote of every one of our Republican senators to put through the legislation in which we believed. Senator Taft had bent over backward to work for party unity. To ignore his suggestion and sponsor some other individual as majority leader—even if I had been so inclined—would certainly alienate senators whom Senator Taft had been able to hold in line. To obtain desirable legislation not only required us to keep the backing of most Republicans, but also often to win Democratic votes; so we had ceaselessly to explain, persuade, cultivate the understanding and confidence that go with personal friendship, and even cajole senators and representatives. Later, when the Republicans were a definite minority in the Senate, similar and sometimes intensified measures had to be used to achieve the support I wanted, and they were, more often than not, successful.

Accordingly, Senator Knowland became Senator Taft's successor.

Frequently I discussed with the Cabinet the many ways we might use to induce the Congress to support the administration's program, including the continuing cultivation of personal friendships. My conclusion was that we would have to employ *every* honorable and effective means at our command.

Through the succeeding months the administration fought for its beliefs. At one meeting of the Legislative leaders both Senator Knowland and Congressman Halleck urged me to accept a compromise in the new farm legislation, setting dairy price supports at 85 rather than 75 per cent of parity. I rejected this and continued, with final success, to fight for the 75 per cent floor. Congressman Halleck foresaw a major fight over an increase in personal income-tax exemptions which was suggested and supported by the Democrats; Senator Millikin believed it would be impossible to prevent an increase of one hundred dollars in exemptions. Hence on March 15, I took our case to the people in a radio and television address. Reviewing the administration's proposals for overhauling the tax laws, I came out flatly against the proposed exemption increase, pointing out that a raise of one hundred dollars would cost the government $2.5 billion in revenues and that a raise of four hundred dollars would cost the government $8 billion and excuse one taxpayer in three from paying any tax whatsoever. Again, we succeeded.

The March 29 meeting with the Legislative leaders focused largely on the administration's foreign economic policy. One senator said he believed my request for authority to lower tariffs reciprocally would cause more trouble within the party and the country than any other recommendation I had yet put forward. At the end of the discussion I remarked that though I did not consider my views sacrosanct, I did believe that the party had to redeem its platform pledge and that on such an issue we all had to pull together. I was constantly being urged to make speeches, I went on, and I felt that any public talks I made must be focused on the record being made by the Republican Congress. We needed speedy action so that I could have a solid basis for talking about the efficient, business-like methods of this party, whose leaders were working together for their country.

Of course, the Presidency assured me of a sizable audience in any public appearance, but to those audiences I wanted to convey information not only of purpose but of deed. I wanted to talk constructively on behalf of the party, without becoming arrogantly partisan, about strengthening the country, building the structure of peace, and lessening fears among the people. I was ready to do my part, I told the leaders; they also had to do theirs. We should decide at once exactly what Republicans wanted to do, and then do it, despite all opposition. "This program," I said, "is better than anything the Democrats have ever offered. The Republican party can win solid support from the country if we all get to work and put the program through."

My exhortation had noticeable effect in the meeting; most of those present responded warmly. But later experience demonstrated more than once that good resolutions by a politician cannot always stand up against pressures that involve possible votes for him in the next election.

These Legislative meetings were sometimes tiresome. Indeed, after a long and wearying discussion with the Legislative leaders one day, I remarked it was about time all of us did something about strengthening whatever sense of humor we might possess. Considering the frustrations in dealing with 531 separate political opinions on Capitol Hill, I knew that a sense of humor, though not a guarantee of success, was at least indispensable to sanity.

But it was not always easy to laugh. One day I presented to the leaders my ideas on agricultural problems and repeated that I could not possibly approve any legislation which continued the present program into the following year. Extension of the present program for another year, even though approval were given for a subsequent initiation of a new program, would mean that the administration was left exactly where it began, I said, "and next year we'll just have to start the fight all over again."

One legislator mentioned that consumers in the industrial areas would support the administration in any knockdown fight with the farm bloc, to get rid of high price supports.

"That's not the point," I told him. "I don't want to play one section of the country off against another. In the long run the consumer could not benefit from a depressed agriculture. What I want is a good bill which, by its reasonableness and demonstrable practicability, will strengthen a delicate economic situation."

Once we had a lengthy discussion of postal legislation. A question arose: would Congress sustain a veto, if the legislation were such that I felt I had to veto it?

I said that failure to sustain a veto would serve to release me immediately from the plans that were being built up around my personal participation in the 1954 campaign. I would not go to the country and work for people who would not support me in a pinch. "The administration and its Republican friends in the Congress," I said, "have to stand and fight."

When Senator Knowland suggested at one meeting that his task in getting needed legislation would be much easier if Republicans had a majority like that of the Democrats in 1933, I responded at once to clear up any doubts he and his associates might have. Not for one moment, I said, should anyone think that I was complaining against the leadership. I just wanted all Republicans to keep working for every single item we, as a party, had promised to the nation.

In May the administration's determination began to pay off: the Congress passed the St. Lawrence Seaway bill—a historic victory.

Twenty years earlier, a treaty authorizing American participation in building the seaway fell short in the United States Senate by just twelve votes. In 1948 and 1952 other seaway bills had ended up caught in committee. But early in 1953 both supporters and opponents of the bill had to face a hard new fact: that if the United States refused to join in the work, Canada would, by herself, build the seaway on her side of the border, and leave the United States without a clear right to a voice in the seaway's construction, control, operation, and tolls, in time of either peace or national emergency.

On January 23, 1953, Senator Alexander Wiley (Republican of Wisconsin) introduced a new bill. By eliminating a provision for federal construction of associated hydroelectric facilities on the St. Lawrence River,[5] and by eliminating for the present a plan to deepen the waterway all the way to Duluth, Senator Wiley's bill cut the United States' costs from $566 million to less than $100 million. This provision won over many who favored the seaway but regretted its high cost. The bill picked up additional support as more legislators came to realize that our principal source of high-grade iron ore, in the Mesabi Range in Minnesota, was starting to run out, and that the United States needed a sure way, in time of any emergency, to ship supplementary high-grade ore up the St. Lawrence from Labrador.

To me, this fact was central and overriding. Moreover, in time the St. Lawrence Seaway would become an economic necessity. The United States should move now, I was convinced, before a national crisis forced it into a crash program at a much greater cost. Administration witnesses supported the Wiley bill, and on June 16 the Senate Foreign Relations Committee favorably reported on it.

Upon the opening of the 1954 session of Congress, Senator Wiley reminded his fellow senators: "Canada is unwilling to delay longer. This is our last chance to insure that our interests will be protected by joint

[5] In January 1953 the New York State Power Authority asked for designation by the Federal Power Commission as the United States agent to cooperate in the construction of these power dams in the International Rapids section of the St. Lawrence. Canada was ready to proceed to build the seaway as soon as the commission issued this license.

cooperation." A week later the Senate passed the Wiley bill. Twenty-five Republicans and twenty-five Democrats favored it; fifteen Republicans and eighteen Democrats opposed it. The fight then shifted to the House of Representatives.

Appeals rained down on congressmen from powerful lobbies—the Association of American Railroads, John L. Lewis' United Mine Workers, coal operators of Pennsylvania and West Virginia, and the Port Authorities of New York, Boston, Baltimore, Newark, New Orleans, Houston, Savannah, Philadelphia, Wilmington, and Norfolk. Nevertheless, in February the House Committee on Public Works reported favorably on the bill. A minority group on the committee opposed it, charging that the seaway would be frozen and unusable for four or five months every year, and alleging that the cost of attempting to defend the seaway would greatly exceed any possible wartime value it might have. The majority report, however, hammered away at one key question: "Should these works be on the American side with joint American and Canadian control of the entire waterway, or should they be on the Canadian side with the entire waterway under Canada's exclusive control?"

Week by week, Speaker Martin and Majority Leader Halleck shepherded the progress of this legislation. Finally, during the first week in May it came up for debate. A Maryland congressman charged that it would tend to destroy the railroads because it would create a competitor at government expense. A congressman from Virginia alleged that it would hurt the great ports of New York, Philadelphia, Boston, Baltimore, and others, and destroy a great part of the economy of this country along the Atlantic seaboard. A congressman from West Virginia asserted that the administration had engaged in boondoggling, logrolling, and lobbying to get the seaway bill through. Congressman Brownson of Indiana proposed an amendment: the United States, he said, should finance the seaway through the public sale of non-government-supported corporation bonds. Congressman George Dondero of Michigan, fighting for the bill, said that the purpose of this amendment was to kill the bill. Congressman Halleck reported that I opposed the amendment, and the House then voted it down.

The next day the bill passed. One hundred and forty-four Republicans and ninety-six Democrats voted for it; sixty-four Republicans and ninety-four Democrats voted against it. On May 13 I signed it into law.

I observed that it marked the legislative culmination of an effort that had taken thirty years to reach this point. With this bill[6] the administration won a major victory.

[6] The legislation established a St. Lawrence Seaway Development Corporation, authorizing it to sell up to $105 million worth of interest-bearing revenue bonds to the United States Treasury, to be repaid within fifty years out of the corporation's

THE EXECUTIVE AND THE CONGRESS 303

In the summer months that followed, however, the administration did not find itself on an easy downhill course. The Army-McCarthy fight was in full swing, filling the headlines and the hours of millions of people who watched television in the afternoon. The legislative wheels in Congress ground to a virtual stop.

With the exception of the seaway bill and the Federal Aid Highway Act of 1954, which I had signed on May 6, and which provided the largest two-year sum—nearly $2 billion—ever invested up to that time to modernize the United States' highways, this congressional session had produced little by the middle of July. Then came the deluge.

On August 2 I approved the administration's housing bill. The next day I signed the bill increasing federal payments to the states to help rehabilitate the disabled, and a week later a bill to modernize the tanker fleet. On August 16 came the administration's tax-revision bill—the last in a series of measures which gave the American people a tax cut in 1954 of $7.4 billion, a reduction unmatched in any previous year in our history.

The next day I approved a bill to amend the Water Facilities Act, one of three administration measures that year to help farmers and ranchers do a better job of conserving water in the upper sections of this country's watersheds. The theme was "nailing the raindrop where it falls."

A week later, on August 24, I signed the Communist Control Act, with the immunity-bath provision. Four days later I approved the administration's agriculture bill, with provision for modernized parity and flexible price supports. Two days later came the administration's Atomic Energy Act of 1954, and on September 1 a bill extending unemployment insurance and another providing for an increase in social-security benefits and an extension of social-security coverage to approximately 10 million additional people.

In the 1954 session, as these pieces of legislation and many other minor ones became law, I also vetoed forty-two bills; not once did the Congress override. Though the Congress had rejected health reinsurance, Taft-Hartley revision, Hawaiian statehood, increased postal rates, and voting rights for eighteen-year-olds, and had extended the Trade Agreements Act for only one year, it had approved thirteen of my nineteen major proposals. And of the entire 232 which I had requested, the Congress had approved 150, giving the administration an extraordinarily favorable

---

revenues. The bill authorized the corporation to construct and operate, in cooperation with Canada, canals and locks in the International Rapids section of the St. Lawrence and to dredge the Thousand Islands section. Before the seaway was created by deepening, the volume of cargo through it every year averaged about 13 million tons; in 1959, the year the improved seaway opened, the volume climbed to nearly 21 million tons.

record for that session. We had made this progress despite the fact that these changes caused major difficulties with individual congressmen, despite the distractions of Senator McCarthy—and despite a recession.

* * *

For more than twenty years economic depression had been the skeleton in the Republican closet, locked in by demogogues. In many minds the suspicion lurked that this problem might once again prove to be the party's undoing. To dispel this fear, in 1954 the Republican administration, with Republican supporters in the Congress, had to pass through a trial of fire.

That trial had begun late in 1953. On September 25 Dr. Arthur Burns, chairman of the Council of Economic Advisers, reported to the Cabinet on what he had told me earlier. His economic indicators showed the need for further precautionary planning against a downturn which seemed already to have begun. At that meeting I recalled the Republican party's commitment to use the full resources of the federal government to prevent "another 1929."

In the second quarter of 1953 the gross national product of the United States had reached a yearly rate of $370 billion. But in the third quarter the rate fell to $367 billion and in the last quarter of the year dipped to $361 billion. By January of 1954 unemployment had reached 3 million—4.9 per cent of the civilian labor force.

The basic causes of the 1953–54 contraction were an imbalance between production and sales, an increase in inventories, and reductions in defense spending following the end of the Korean War. A contributory cause may have been the government's effort in the spring of 1953 to tighten up the money supply to prevent inflation; in January of 1953 the Federal Reserve Board had raised the discount rate (from 1.75 per cent to 2 per cent), and in April the Treasury Department put out a thirty-year bond issue which competed for cash that otherwise might have gone into corporate bonds and mortgages.

Faced with evidences of a possible decline, politicians, economic writers, and labor leaders called for drastic action at once. In November, Colin Clark, a British economist writing in the *Manchester Guardian,* made a prediction. It created a stir here. Clark foresaw a deep American depression, with 6 or 7 million unemployed, unless the federal government cut back taxes on a massive scale. A cut of $20 billion in "excise and other consumptive taxes"—with no reduction in federal spending— beginning July 1, 1954, would do the job, he believed, as would less severe measures taken earlier. In January, as unemployment reached 3 million,

Walter Reuther urged me to call a national conference on unemployment. I declined.

On January 15 I met with the Cabinet to discuss the Economic Report, soon to go to the Congress. I wanted to avoid false expressions of confidence, and yet to refrain from suggesting that the federal government was powerless to act to strengthen the economy.

The report set forth our determination to move swiftly with preventive action to arrest the downturn before it might become severe; to avoid a doctrinaire position; to do everything possible to stimulate consumers to spend more money and businessmen to create more jobs; to use, wisely and if necessary, any and all weapons in the federal arsenal, including changes in monetary and credit policy, modification of the tax structure, and a speed-up in the construction of useful and previously surveyed public works, to deal with particular instances of economic hardships as they might arise; and to maintain a steady, unshakable public confidence in the capacity of the American economy for continued growth. Confidence, we believed, was as real as a gang plow or a blast furnace.

Many items in our 1954 legislative program, valuable in themselves, would, when enacted into law, also fortify the economy: the bills, for example, on taxes, housing, social security, highway construction, and agriculture. The announcement in January of these legislative proposals, nearly all of which were subsequently enacted by the Congress, in itself contributed to the public's confidence that, under Republican management, the economy would revive and prosper.

In February unemployment went up again, to 3.6 million. In these circumstances it might have been easy—particularly for Republicans, haunted by the memory of 1932—to fly into a frenzy, to push the button for a crash program of government activity. The administration, however, remained watchful but refused to panic. I refused to urge a massive program of federal intervention in the economy before we had compelling evidence that it would do more good than harm. And I opposed an increase, proposed in the Congress, in individual income-tax exemptions.

But the government had to stand *ready* to act. At the Cabinet meeting of March 12 I instructed Dr. Burns to report (at every subsequent meeting) on the state of the economy and governmental actions needed. A week later, on March 19, he gave us the heartening news of a lengthening workweek and signs that the unemployment increase was coming to a stop.

We did not know then, however, that the economic slowdown was nearing an end. Accordingly, at the next Cabinet meeting I asked Dr. Burns to make a list of the administration's legislative proposals which, if enacted, would most help the economy. At the Legislative-leaders meeting three days later, Congressman Halleck assured us that the House would move quickly on those items. On March 31 I signed into law a bill which, while extending some excise-tax rates, previously scheduled for re- duction on April 1, cut other excise taxes and reduced federal revenues by nearly a billion dollars. Although I had asked for no decreases in the total excise-tax revenues, I expressed the hope, as I signed the bill, that the cut would help the economy and that the revenue loss would not be damaging.

On April 2 Dr. Burns listed additional measures which the govern- ment could take to invigorate the economy. For example, the Federal Reserve Board, he said, might make credit both more abundant and cheaper; the Internal Revenue Service might start sending out checks immediately on taxpayers' claims of overassessment; Executive-branch agencies might consult with the states on the acceleration of public works. I ordered these things done except for the first: the Executive branch did not control the independent Federal Reserve Board.

Though conclusive figures were not yet in, the signs of an early eco- nomic recovery were multiplying. Nonetheless, in April 1954, in the face of evidence of a probable upturn, David McDonald, head of the United Steel Workers, was still arguing for a massive governmental program, in- cluding a $5-billion public works outlay, a $5-billion housing and slum- clearance effort, a $3-billion increase in unemployment compensation and pensions, and a $4-billion cut in income taxes—a proposal that in one swoop would have offset, with interest, the great sums we had cut out of the budgets.

My own belief was that such a full-out response to the evidence we then had was not only unjustified, in the long run it would be harmful. Public-works projects, for example, usually take a year or two to get into motion. If we had followed the prophets of gloom in March and April of 1954, the effects of their advice would have been felt not that year but in 1955 and 1956, when the economy soared to a new high, and federal spending on this scale might have brought on severe inflation.

But when the administration held back on committing itself to a crash public-works program, Walter Reuther convened his own national full- employment conference, and Mr. Truman charged my administration with "creeping McKinleyism." This gave a bit of comic relief in a worrisome situation.

Through April and May, Dr. Burns reported with increasing optimism. In June he could see clear evidence that recovery was under way, and on July 23 he reported the decline definitely at an end.

The year 1954 went on to become one of the most prosperous peace- time years to date in our history. President McKinley would have been pleased.

The experience through which the nation had passed provided new, or reaffirmed old, lessons. The outstanding feature of the 1953–54 recession was the transition from federal to private spending, from armaments to consumer goods.

In this transition we saw demonstrated the fact that if the government acts wisely and early, and resists panic, it can do much to stave off serious difficulties later. Economic contraction can be slowed up even when governmental expenditures and budget deficits are declining, if effective means are taken to build confidence. Further, we demonstrated that the monetary policy of the government can be a powerful instrument of economic recovery, as long as the confidence of consumers and businessmen in the future remains high. We learned other things, too: that economic stabilizers, such as unemployment insurance and a judicious tax system, automatically help check a recession; that a minor contraction in this country need not produce a severe depression abroad, and that the expansion of the economy of the world can help buttress the economy of the United States in a time of temporary trouble. These lessons would serve us well in the years ahead.

Most important, however, we had our faith renewed in a cardinal Republican concept: that while the groundwork for economic recovery must be laid by the government, *recovery itself is the work of the American people*. This surely proved to be true in 1954. Though the government reduced taxes, most of the administration's major legislative proposals did not become law until the recession had evaporated. The big public-works program, ready if necessary to help bail the country out of a crash, never came off the shelf. It is likely that the public's knowledge of this governmental attitude and readiness to act went far to instill a mood of confidence. But it was the mood and not governmental measures —the people and not a spending program—that wrought the change.

Without a depression, the United States moved in 1954 from a wartime to a peacetime economy. And the Republican party exorcised a specter.

CHAPTER XIII

Problems of Internal Security

> . . . a reverence for the characteristic rights of free men, and a regard for the public harmony.
>
> —*George Washington*
> *First Inaugural Address*

IN the early postwar years Americans had gradually become aware of the danger to their freedom posed by international Communism. Even more slowly, perhaps because we did not like to admit it to ourselves, we came to realize that not all danger came from without—that there were dangers from within as well. By the time of the 1952 election, sufficient evidence had piled up (the Rosenberg case was only one example) to induce the public to express its insistence that the government effectively tighten its regulations and rid the federal establishment of employees who, for whatever reason, were potential sources of danger to the national security.

Frequently during the political campaign, I had pledged to do just this, having been openly critical of the government's attitude. President Truman had approved a program of two parts. The first, which extended throughout the government, was designed to test only a federal employee's actual loyalty to the United States; the second, limited to sensitive departments, extended the criteria to include other personal traits which might make an employee, even though loyal, a security liability in the job he held. Because loyalty comprises only one aspect of security, I felt this double-standard program to be inadequate; it had appeared to me to reflect either a complacency or skepticism toward security risks in government.

Immediately after inauguration I set to work to close this gap in our defenses. In the first Cabinet meeting on January 23, 1953, I set three standards which were to be observed in tightening security regulations.

First of all, the legitimate rights of employees must be protected. Second, procedures for implementing all regulations had to be simplified for clarity and more uniform standards applied throughout the government. Third, security rather than loyalty must be the test. In regard to the third standard it is important to realize that many loyal Americans, by reason of instability, alcoholism, homosexuality, or previous tendencies to associate with Communist-front groups, are unintentional security risks. In some instances, because of moral lapses, they become subjected to the threat of blackmail by enemy agents. I emphasized that working for the government must be regarded as a privilege and not a constitutional right.

Immediately we set about to ensure that all presidential appointees were given extensive background investigations by the Federal Bureau of Investigation. This had not been uniformly done before. Interestingly, Mrs. Hobby reported that in her agency, half of the security officers themselves had never had such a background investigation.

On the morning of April 27 the Attorney General presented to the Republican Legislative leaders the text of Executive Order 10450, which I had approved, establishing the new employee security program.

The new order eliminated the double standard of testing some as loyal citizens and others as security risks. No person could hold a job thereafter in the federal government if his employment was not clearly consistent with the interests of national security.

The new program included new procedures. Under the former program, only new applicants underwent investigation by the Civil Service Commission; only those whose files contained information indicating disloyalty and those who worked in sensitive jobs underwent full field investigation by the FBI. Under the new system, all employees *not previously checked* had to undergo investigation by the Civil Service Commission.

Under the old program each department head had the responsibility for making sure his agency harbored no disloyal employees. To this end, he had the duty of appointing loyalty boards composed of at least three officers of his department. Any departmental employee suspected of disloyalty had a hearing before such a board. If the board recommended his removal, he could appeal to the Loyalty Review Board of the Civil Service Commission, which heard the case and made an advisory recommendation to the department head, who made the final judgment.

We eliminated both the departmental boards and the Civil Service Loyalty Review Board. Now the file of an employee suspected of being a security risk went to the head of his department, who had three choices: he could decide the evidence was too flimsy to warrant investigation; transfer the employee to a nonsensitive job while adjudication continued; or discharge him. If the department head took either the second or third course, the employee had a right to a hearing before a three-man board drawn not, as before, from his own department and thus possibly from among his own friends or enemies, but from a selected list of officials of other federal agencies. This board, appointed by the employee's department head, had the power to study and recommend; but the power to decide resided with the head of the department, unencumbered by the further hearings and recommendations of the old Loyalty Review Board with its many regional panels.

While we applied the same standards for all departments, our attention focused on the "sensitive" agencies, especially the State and Defense Departments, the Central Intelligence Agency, the Atomic Energy Commission, and others where the nation's security might be most affected.

The Executive Order was effective. By October 23 of that year we announced that during the first four months of its operations more than fourteen hundred employees had been dropped from the federal payroll, including more than eight hundred who had been dismissed. The others had resigned when notified of the unfavorable reports in their files.

This program drew criticism from some, a few of whom were personally involved. But never has any thinking person won me away from the basic principles I had outlined: that working for the government is a privilege and not a right, and that the United States, while always displaying fairness and rationality in its methods, cannot afford to relax for one moment its vigilance in protecting the internal security of our government.

*　　*　　*

One case that attracted a great deal of public attention involved a brilliant scientist who had been a central figure in the development of the atomic bomb—Dr. J. Robert Oppenheimer.

On December 2, 1953, I had a long telephone conversation with Secretary of Defense Wilson. The Secretary told me of a report which he and Lewis Strauss (Chairman of the Atomic Energy Commission) had received directly from FBI Director J. Edgar Hoover. The report contained allegations against Dr. Oppenheimer, some of which were new.

This report jolted me. Dr. Oppenheimer had been the chairman of the General Advisory Committee of the Atomic Energy Commission. He was an important figure in the whole history of nuclear development. His service had been continued as a contract consultant, and he was well acquainted with many of the nation's most important secrets. Indeed, he had helped to create several of them. To increase the seriousness of the matter, the new charges were brought not by an unknown citizen, but by William Borden, a lawyer who had been executive director of the staff of the congressional Joint Committee on Atomic Energy under the preceding Democratic administration, and who obviously was aware of the gravity of his charges.

Among other concerns, Secretary Wilson had been informed that Senator McCarthy was aware of this report, and he feared the consequences to all, including Dr. Oppenheimer, if this information should be handled in an irresponsible manner.

The McCarthy aspect I dismissed, at least as it touched on the relations between him and my administration. I wanted to make sure, however, that Attorney General Brownell knew about this report, if (as seemed unlikely) he had not already learned of it. I warned that we were not going to be in a position of making accusations against anyone without solid evidence.

The next morning, after further consultations, I notified the Secretary of State, the Secretary of Defense, the Director of the Office of Defense Mobilization (Dr. Arthur S. Flemming), the Chairman of the Atomic Energy Commission, and the director of the CIA that pending a full examination, they were to put a "blank wall" between Dr. Oppenheimer and any information of a sensitive or classified character. Then, I noted in my diary:

> I directed a memorandum to the Attorney General instructing him to procure from the Director of the FBI an entire file in the case of Dr. Oppenheimer and to make of it a thorough study. I assured them that I did want a thorough and prompt recommendation from him as to what further action should be taken. . . .
>
> It is reported to me that this same [security] information, or at least the vast bulk of it, has been constantly reviewed and re-examined over a number of years, and that the over-all conclusion has always been that there is no evidence that implies disloyalty on the part of Dr. Oppenheimer. However, this does not mean that he might not be a security risk. . . .

At the moment Dr. Oppenheimer was in Europe. Because of his official connection with the Atomic Energy Commission, it was Admiral Strauss who informed him of the allegations on his return. Dr. Oppenheimer said that he knew that his file contained information which would necessitate a review, and, in accordance with the security regulations of the AEC, he elected to have a hearing. He was told that as a necessary step his security clearance was suspended pending the completion of the examination.

The investigation (which produced three thousand pages of testimony) consisted of a thorough examination of all available records and a confidential hearing before a review panel before which forty witnesses appeared. To conduct the hearing, a three-man board was appointed, with my approval, consisting of outstanding citizens, headed by Gordon Gray,[1] who had been Secretary of the Army under President Truman and had occupied other posts of trust and responsibility in government. He was a man of the highest character, integrity, and fairness.

The examination ran several weeks, and the committee finally found, by a vote of two to one, that Dr. Oppenheimer was indeed a security risk, though a loyal citizen. On May 27 the Gray board submitted this finding to the AEC, whose five commissioners approved it a month later by a vote of four to one.

Dr. Oppenheimer's friends charged that the finding was based almost exclusively on the circumstance that Oppenheimer had opposed the development of the hydrogen bomb. Certainly I, and I am sure the members of the investigating committee of the AEC, gave no weight to this fact.

Professor Oppenheimer's opposition to the hydrogen-bomb project could well have been a matter of conscience; it could have been his belief that, as a practical matter, the world would be better off if this development was stifled before birth.

Years earlier an experience of my own had given me a striking example of the truth that conflicting judgments about the nation's security could be forcefully expressed without carrying the implication that either side deserved the charge of "security risk."

The incident took place in 1945 when Secretary of War Stimson, visiting my headquarters in Germany, informed me that our government was preparing to drop an atomic bomb on Japan. I was one of those who felt that there were a number of cogent reasons to question the wisdom of such an act. I was not, of course, called upon, officially, for any advice or counsel concerning the matter, because the European theater, of which I was the commanding general, was not involved, the forces of Hitler having already been defeated. But the Secretary, upon giving me the news of the successful bomb test in New Mexico, and of the plan for using it, asked for my reaction, apparently expecting a vigorous assent.

During his recitation of the relevant facts, I had been conscious of a feeling of depression and so I voiced to him my grave misgivings, first

[1] The Honorable Gordon Gray was president of the University of North Carolina. The other two members were Mr. Thomas A. Morgan, former president of the Sperry Corporation, and Dr. Ward V. Evans, professor of chemistry, Loyola University, Chicago. Since the AEC went by special security legislation, these men came from outside government. However, the hearings were conducted under the procedures of Executive Order 10450.

on the basis of my belief that Japan was already defeated and that dropping the bomb was completely unnecessary, and secondly because I thought that our country should avoid shocking world opinion by the use of a weapon whose employment was, I thought, no longer mandatory as a measure to save American lives. It was my belief that Japan was, at that very moment, seeking some way to surrender with a minimum loss of "face." The Secretary was deeply perturbed by my attitude, almost angrily refuting the reasons I gave for my quick conclusions.

But in spite of his instant rejection of my opinion, it never occurred to Secretary Stimson to question my loyalty to America, or for me to think that anyone else would or could do so. In the same way I refused to accept any implication that Dr. Oppenheimer was disloyal to America or was a security risk merely because he had opposed the development of a weapon many hundreds of times more terrifying than anything we had then produced.

It was entirely on other evidence, including Dr. Oppenheimer's own testimony, that I concurred in the recommendations of the investigation committee and approved the vote of the Atomic Energy Commission, the majority of whom cited "fundamental defects in his character," instanced by his repeated falsehoods to security officers about Communists whom he knew. Professor Oppenheimer's clearance was not reinstated.

The publicity in such unhappy situations always brings forth a spate of criticism and comment, pro and con. It was said that the rigidity of the security system, exemplified in the Oppenheimer case, would make it impossible to induce scientists to work for the government. Since that time, of course, many dedicated scientists have gladly devoted their talents to government service. Others said that the entire investigation was organized by anti-Semitic groups, and other accusations of even less validity were hurled.

One man singled out as the particular villain by these critics was the Chairman of the Atomic Energy Commission, Lewis Strauss, alleging that he had engineered the verdict against Oppenheimer motivated by personal revenge rooted in their disagreement over whether the United States should proceed to develop the hydrogen bomb.

I had appointed Admiral Lewis Strauss Chairman of the commission in June of 1953. Since the administration of President Woodrow Wilson, he had served in public posts of national importance, always with the highest distinction, integrity, and selflessness. The Oppenheimer case marked the beginning of a persistent drive by enemies of his in politics and the press to discredit him and destroy his usefulness as one of this country's outstanding public servants—a drive that extended through the turmoil of the Dixon and Yates case in 1954–55 and ended with the inexcusable refusal of the Senate to confirm his nomination as Secretary of Commerce in 1959.

Not all the mail, however, was abusive. I received a letter dated April 13, 1954, from Mr. Robert E. Sherwood, for instance, one of the nation's most respected dramatists and the author of *Roosevelt and Hopkins,* which read:

> The announcement of the manner[2] in which you are handling the case of Dr. Oppenheimer came like a breath of clear, fresh air on the front pages this morning.
>
> I do not know Dr. Oppenheimer, but I do know Dr. Conant and Dr. Vannevar Bush, and it was dreadful to contemplate that the enormous contribution of these distinguished American scientists should provide a series of field days for the McCarthy carnival merely because, apparently, Dr. Oppenheimer had been guilty of political naivete in some phase of his career.
>
> The way you are directing this matter is precisely the way it should be done: with dignity, with fairness, with respect for the rights of the individual and with the great authority which is constitutionally yours.
>
> Also—and I must confess that this gives me and many others particular satisfaction—you have taken an entirely proper and wise action which will deprive McCarthy of a great deal of the headline thunder to which I am sure he was looking forward eagerly.

*   *   *

An episode of another kind, when press reaction reflected the tension of the time, involved Harry Dexter White, an Assistant Secretary of the Treasury in the last administration. President Truman, on January 23, 1946, had appointed him director of the United States Mission to the International Monetary Fund. White had resigned from the government in April of 1947, and in August of 1948, while being accused of an association with a Russian spy ring in the government, had died of a heart attack.

On November 6, 1953, the Attorney General, in an effort to call attention to the real dangers of Communist penetration, told members of the Executives Club of Chicago, with the data of the Federal Bureau of Investigation to support his statement: ". . . Harry Dexter White was a

---

2 Dr. Oppenheimer, like others whose records were under review, had the right to challenge the appointees of the panel, to produce witnesses on his own behalf, to be represented by counsel, and to have his counsel cross-examine adverse witnesses. He also had the right to appeal the findings of the panel and did so. At the close of the procedures, his counsel volunteered that the hearings had been conducted fairly.

Russian spy. He smuggled secret documents to Russian agents for transmission to Moscow. Harry Dexter White was known to be a Communist spy by the very people who appointed him to the most sensitive and important position he ever held in Government service. . . . I can now announce officially . . . that the records in my department show that White's spying activities . . . were reported in detail by the FBI. . . ."

The day before his statement, Attorney General Brownell had told me in a telephone conversation that he planned to reveal the record. I said that, as a responsible official of the government, he had to make that decision. If he felt that it was his duty to review this case in public, he should do so on a purely factual basis. If there were repercussions, I would support him.

A rash of criticism broke out. The reports of the FBI showed that White had concealed his involvement in a Russian espionage ring while holding a responsible office in government. The central point in the case was this shocking FBI evidence, but a host of partisan critics chose to ignore this and to attack the Attorney General for "trying to make political capital" out of incontrovertible evidence.

The Attorney General made these facts known to awaken the public, as well as many uninformed people in government, to the existence of the Communist threat from within and to show that any individual, even though high in government, if found to be a security risk, should be promptly and without apology dismissed. J. Edgar Hoover supported the Attorney General by testifying that at no time did the FBI approve the previous administration's promotion of White for the avowed purpose of making it easier to keep him under FBI surveillance. But the long, heated argument left many scars.

*   *   *

During the course of 1953–54, 8008 cases of security risks were identified by properly appointed boards. As a result, 3002 were dismissed as security risks, and 5006 resigned before their cases were acted upon. At the same time, there were tens of thousands of records examined, and many employees were transferred without prejudice from sensitive to nonsensitive positions. The percentage of all government employees found untrustworthy was small indeed, and many publicized and debated cases resulted in exoneration. Despite the critics, the United States still had a government of laws. We constantly reviewed our security program, trying to improve it, remembering always the welfare of the country and the rights of the individual.

*   *   *

The problem of security in government was troublesome and was exaggerated by the extravagant and often baseless charges made against many individuals and groups by Senator McCarthy, chairman of the Permanent Investigations Subcommittee of the Senate Committee on Governmental Operations. Other members of the committee were Republicans Mundt, Dirksen, and Potter, and Democrats McClellan, Jackson, and Symington.

His methods were frequently such as to arouse the resentment and the opposition of informed Americans. He had achieved nationwide notoriety before the beginning of my administration. Americans, of course, would never disagree with or criticize anyone who was honestly and properly dedicated to identifying Communists holding positions of trust in the United States and exposing them and their activities. But Senator McCarthy's general and specific accusations were, from the start, so extreme, often involving unsupported and unjustified allegations of the gravest kind, that his attacks, which at times degenerated to persecution, became known as "McCarthyism." Protected as he was by congressional immunity, anyone could be irresponsibly attacked. Strong resentment against McCarthyism developed among the educators, the press, and the clergy—indeed, among all informed groups. The question was often—and justifiably—asked, "Who is safe?"

Because of the passions Senator McCarthy stirred up, the frequency with which his name appeared in the headlines of the nation's press, the bitterness with which his opponents condemned him, and the fervor with which his partisans applauded him, the story of his rise and fall cannot be told in a paragraph.

Senator McCarthy had been a little-known junior senator from Wisconsin until a day in early February 1950, when he made the traditional Lincoln's Birthday speech before a Republican gathering in Wheeling, West Virginia. In this talk he claimed that he had in his possession a list of 205 card-carrying Communists employed in the State Department. McCarthy did not later reaffirm this figure; indeed, he reduced it drastically in subsequent talks. Ironically, as has been suggested, it might well have been forgotten if the Truman administration had not challenged it, demanding that he produce his source of information or quit talking. Being independent of Executive control, Senator McCarthy did neither—but he was now in the headlines. He had found a horse to ride, and ride it he did.

Because of my absence from the United States during 1951 and the first half of 1952, relatively little of this had come to my attention until my nomination for the Presidency. Soon thereafter I was told that many observers believed that McCarthyism would be a national issue in the 1952 political campaign. I took the personal position that as a consistent and established opponent of Communism and all it stood for, I would, if elected, initiate measures to make certain that no Communist or fellow traveler would remain in government. At the same time I pledged that, in the attempt to discover and uproot Communists, I would countenance only methods that were completely consonant with American juridical practices and that respected the individual rights of those accused. This placed the matter on a positive basis and I declined to be drawn into arguments with, or accusations against, Senator McCarthy himself.

Although he was a Republican senator and I, as the presidential nominee, would be expected in the campaign of 1952 to support all Republican candidates for office, I was determined to give no appearance of aligning my views with his. Consequently, I told my staff to make no plans for my visiting Wisconsin. Later, while I was preoccupied with the daily demands of strenuous political campaigning, itineraries for my travels were fixed before I became aware that they provided for a tour through Wisconsin, with a number of whistle stops and one formal speaking engagement.

This occasioned the sharpest flareup I can recall between my staff and I during the entire campaign. My irritation did not reflect any personal embarrassment about going into the state, where McCarthy had in the meantime become the party's nominee. Obviously it would be a simple matter to make my own attitude perfectly clear. But for two reasons the blunder rankled. The first was that either attitude I might take—refusal on the one hand to brawl publicly with McCarthy in his own state or, on the other, refusal to imply personal acquiescence in his methods—could create unfortunate political division in Wisconsin and lend further currency and power to his charges. The second reason was nothing more than frustration that my specific instructions had been overlooked and a speaking program so definitely arranged that it was now impossible for me to repudiate it. I was caught in a position that allowed me no alternative.

In these circumstances I decided that my first talk in Wisconsin would demonstrate clearly that I would have no part in indicting people except under methods that were accepted as in harmony with American ideals and practices. Several of my advisers seemed to think that this, too, would cause an explosive and divisive effect in that area.

I replied that I would do it my way or I would cancel that part of the itinerary.

The night before I was scheduled to go into Wisconsin, Governor Kohler, of that state, came to see me in Peoria, Illinois. His purpose was to pour oil on troubled political waters and to try to make sure that we would not have an unfortunate incident among Wisconsin Republicans that in the general election might put his state—and conceivably the entire election—in the Democratic column. I told him about my own decision, and he agreed with it. However, he noted that I had personally written a short paragraph in the speech I was to deliver in Wisconsin expressing my admiration and respect for General Marshall, who had, I was informed, been criticized by Senator McCarthy as a dupe of the Communists. This paragraph had become the subject of staff concern because I had thrown it in the talk with little supporting context, and including it was obviously, as the governor and my advisers asserted, "dragging it in by the scruff of the neck." They pointed out, moreover, that only a short time earlier I had, in a Denver news conference, made a strong statement emphasizing my deep feeling concerning General Marshall's outstanding character and achievements[3]; the intended repetition could be interpreted only as a "chip-on-the-shoulder" attitude. By thus arousing new public clamor, I could be inadvertently embarrassing General Marshall.

After listening to them I agreed to the deletion. When this became known, it gave the opposition and some segments of the press an opportunity to charge that I had "capitulated" to the McCarthyites. This was, of course, completely untrue. Indeed, if I could have foreseen this distortion of the facts, a distortion that even led some to question my loyalty to General Marshall, I would never have acceded to the staff's arguments, logical as they sounded at the time.

The next day Senator McCarthy got on the campaign train. His purpose was to ask me about the attitude I planned to take toward him and his investigations. In a somewhat strained interview I told him that I was going to make clear, when I spoke in his state, my opposition to un-American methods in combatting Communism. He said, "If you say that, they [the audience] will boo you." To this, I replied with some heat that I had no concern whatsoever about booing, that I had often been criticized for my actions, and would gladly be booed for standing for my

[3] "George Marshall is one of the patriots of this country, and anyone who has lived with him, has worked with him as I have, knows that he is a man of real selflessness —a man who has suffered with ill health. Maybe he has made mistakes. I do not know about that, but from the time I met him on December 14, 1942, until the war was over, if he was not a perfect example of patriotism and a loyal servant of the United States, I never saw one. If I could say any more, I would say it, but I have no patience with anyone who can find in his record of service for this country anything to criticize. . . ."

own conceptions of justice. I made no change in my planned talk as a result of my meeting with the senator.

My train that morning stopped at Green Bay, where I had to make one of the customary "back-platform" talks. In order to emphasize at once my position, I included in my remarks the statement that like all other loyal Americans, I was very concerned about Communism, pledging that we would take every appropriate action to uproot it wherever it might exist. But I said that we could not, by any manner of means, use methods that were un-American, and in particular I could not approve of making baseless accusations against people who had not been proved guilty of wrongdoing. I went on to say that I would fight against such practices if I were elected.

I was anxious to get this matter of un-American methods into the clear light of day. If there was to be any booing, I wanted to hear it right away. But there were no boos, only hearty applause from the considerable crowd that gathered at the railway station that fall morning.

Some members of my staff were worried. They thought that if the national election should prove to be close, and my failure to support McCarthy enthusiastically should lose the state to the Democrats, it would be charged that my stubbornness had denied to us a Republican victory. I replied that if this were the case, Republicans would deserve to lose. It was gratifying, later, to learn that in Wisconsin the national ticket ran ahead of McCarthy by more than a hundred thousand votes.

From that time on, however, it could not be expected that my relations with Senator McCarthy would be cordial. As time went on, he began to include my associates and me in his innuendoes and sometimes in his all-out attacks.

Some of my good friends and most trusted advisers would, periodically, become infuriated at his irresponsible actions and urge me to censure him publicly in the strongest possible language in the hope of destroying his political position and his capacity to distort the American ideal before the world. I even had letters from Americans arguing that, as President, I should "fire McCarthy"—a circumstance that made me wonder wryly, at times, how much the average citizen really knows about the institutions and composition of his government.

Senator McCarthy seemed quite aware that his publicity value depended upon consistent attack. On the floor of the Senate he opposed the nomination of Mr. Bohlen as ambassador to Russia; in a letter to me he made wild charges against James Bryant Conant, president of Harvard University, when I nominated that distinguished educator as United States High Commissioner to the Federal Republic of Germany. Again and again the truth defeated him, but he continued to revel in the publicity he so much coveted. In working sessions of the Legislative leaders he was remarkably quiet.[4]

It seemed that almost every day I had to point out that if I were to attack Senator McCarthy, even though every personal instinct so prompted me, I would greatly enhance his publicity value without achieving any constructive purpose. I was convinced that his influence, such as it was, would be gone completely if he lost his headline value. Indeed, the newspapers which most violently condemned him were simultaneously giving his baseless charges greater and greater coverage. Television and radio increased his audiences. Cameras and klieg lights were installed in the Senate committee room where he held hearings, a circumstance which helped still more to sustain public interest in his appearances and incited him to become even more extreme in his accusations. Ultimately, and ironically, television helped to bring about his downfall.

Convinced that the only person who could destroy McCarthy as a political figure was he himself, and finding evidence piling up that he was gradually doing exactly that, I continued in my determination to ignore him. But at the same time I declared—almost every week it seemed— that I opposed, to the limit of my official power and personal influence, all unfair, unjust, and un-American practices in trials, investigations, and inquiries. The opportunities for opposition were certain to come.

The senator was undeterred. On one occasion he sent two of his assistants, Roy Cohn and G. David Schine, to investigate American overseas libraries to determine the numbers of books there that followed the Communist line. He then proceeded to investigate a governmental official who had criticized the antics of the two investigators. In another incident I felt impelled to condemn publicly an article written by the executive director of the McCarthy subcommittee staff, entitled "Reds and Our Churches." The author of the article resigned from the subcommittee.

At one point, Senator McCarthy insisted that the government get rid of all the books in our overseas libraries that he decided were subversive and un-American. Informed of this while on a visit to Dartmouth College, I seized the opportunity in an impromptu talk to deplore the ignorance and stupidity of "book burners." I told the audience that there was no hope of eliminating evils—such as Communism—until we were able to learn exactly what Communism was. To hide our heads in the ashes of ignorance, I asserted, would, far from defeating Communism, merely contribute to our own confusion and defenselessness.

[4] Despite their later charges of the administration's "softness" on subversives in government, it should be noted that in early 1953 both Senator McCarthy and Congressman Velde were present at the Legislative-leaders meeting at which the Attorney General unveiled the new security regulations. Neither registered an objection to the new Executive Order.

McCarthyism was a much larger issue than McCarthy. This was the truth that I constantly held before me as I listened to the many exhortations that I should "demolish" the senator himself. Although he was striving to make himself the embodiment of the anti-Communist, antisubversive movement in the United States, he too often forgot the complex and precious American issues of personal liberties and constitutional process; and he all too frequently ignored the incalculably important doctrine of the relationship between the Legislative and Executive branches. His avowed purpose became hopelessly entangled with, and frustrated by, his methods. It was his methods that were labeled as McCarthyism.

Of one thing I was certain: McCarthyism antedated the appearance of Joseph McCarthy of Wisconsin and would last longer than the man's power or publicity.

Lashing back at one man, which is easy enough for a President, was not as important to me as the long-term value of restraint, the due process of law, and the basic rights of free men.

That is why I condemned book-burning, rather than bandying about the names of the men of the moment who would burn the books.

At the height of all the furor, on May 31, 1954, I went to New York on the occasion of the two-hundredth anniversary of Columbia University and delivered an address aimed at curbing tendencies which seemed to be alive in the land.

> Amid . . . alarms and uncertainties [I said], doubters begin to lose faith in themselves, in their country, in their convictions. They begin to fear other people's ideas—every new idea. They begin to talk about censoring the sources and the communications of ideas. . . . We know that when censorship goes beyond the observance of common decency, . . . it quickly becomes, for us, a deadly danger. . . .
>
> Without exhaustive debate—even heated debate—of ideas and programs, free government would weaken and wither. But if we allow ourselves to be persuaded that every individual, or party, that takes issue with our own convictions is necessarily wicked or treasonous—then we are approaching the end of freedom's road. . . .
>
> Effective support of principles, like success in battle, requires calm and clear judgment, courage, faith, fortitude. Our dedication to truth and freedom . . . does not require—and cannot tolerate—fear, threat, hysteria, and intimidation.
>
> As we preach freedom to others, so we should practice it among ourselves. . . .

As the months went by, my advisers gradually became practically unanimous in agreeing with my methods for defeating McCarthyism. Indeed, by this time I was getting reports from all sides that the strain on the senator was beginning to show.

Senator McCarthy's last and most ambitious attack was on the Army. The first charge involved an alleged espionage plot in the Army Signal Corps Radar Center at Fort Monmouth, New Jersey. On December 10, 1953, after a long, drawn-out, and dreary investigation, the charge collapsed completely.

Senator McCarthy, however, pressed on. In the following month, January of 1954, he made a new discovery, this time in the person of one Dr. Irving Peress, an Army dentist stationed at Camp Kilmer, who had been inducted in October 1952, and in accordance with the doctors' draft law had been given a commission in the Medical Corps. Subsequently issued a loyalty questionnaire, he had refused to answer all the questions. During a loyalty investigation which followed, Captain Peress had been promoted to the grade of major. This was in line with the policy of adjusting the rank of doctors to conform, insofar as possible, with their professional qualifications. The investigation completed, the Army decided to discharge Peress at his own pleasure within ninety days after January 18. Meanwhile, Senator McCarthy, having got wind of the case, called Peress for questioning in New York. After having pleaded the Fifth Amendment to some of the senator's questions, Major Peress immediately applied for his honorable discharge and received it on the 2nd of February.

The discharge of Peress infuriated Senator McCarthy. He demanded a court-martial for him and punitive action for all those involved in the handling of his case, on the grounds of conspiracy. This demand, insofar as it applied to Peress, was impossible; he had been discharged, could not be recalled, and, transcending these facts, there were no grounds for court-martial against him.

Secretary Stevens came to see me on the 10th of February. He gave me the facts as he knew them and asked for my advice. I told him that I thought his course of action was clear. He should, I said:

First, admit at once whatever error, if any, had been committed.

Second, give to the investigating subcommittee, upon request, every pertinent fact, leaving nothing more to be uncovered.

Third, point out how the mistake occurred, explaining the means he was applying to make certain of no repetition.

Fourth—since he had already informed me that he was taking full responsibility—instruct all his officers acquainted with the facts to testify openly and without fear as to these facts.

Fifth, having done all this, he should renew his expression of confidence in the efficiency and loyalty of the Army and stand on that.

He was *not* to placate or appease anyone or to demean himself in any way. He was to remember that he was the civilian Secretary of a proud and honorable organization, which boasted an unimpeachable record of patriotic service to the nation. Having made his position clear, he should demand the courteous treatment that was his due as a citizen and public servant. If any "browbeating" were attempted, he should leave the hearing and inform the chairman that he would return only when he could be assured of courteous treatment. I further advised him to instruct any of his juniors in the Army, who might be called before the subcommittee, to follow the same line of conduct. If they were personally badgered, I wanted a report.

The investigation continued. On February 18 a hearing was held in New York. Besides Peress himself, the witnesses were the commanding general of Camp Kilmer, Brigadier General Ralph W. Zwicker, and three other officers. Peress refused to answer a total of thirty-three questions.

Senator McCarthy's conduct at this time proved, partially at least, his later undoing. He ordered Mr. John Adams (the Army's counsel, representing Secretary Stevens) from the room and demanded within twenty-four hours the names of all persons involved. Enraged by General Zwicker's refusal to produce the names, Senator McCarthy accused the general of shielding Communist conspirators, and reportedly said the general was "not fit to wear the uniform." He threatened to put the general on public display the following Tuesday, February 23.

Upon learning of the episode Secretary Stevens immediately instructed General Zwicker and the others that they were not to appear before the McCarthy subcommittee. Stevens announced that he himself would testify.

Before the hearings resumed, other members of the McCarthy subcommittee made an effort to patch things up. They induced Senator McCarthy to postpone the hearings until Thursday and arranged a "secret" luncheon to be held at Senator Dirksen's office in the Senate Office Building for Wednesday, February 24. Republican members—but not Democrats—of the McCarthy subcommittee were invited. Secretary Stevens agreed and, true to the understanding, informed nobody in advance of the event.

The result of this apparently harmless meeting was embarrassing indeed. What actually occurred was that, in return for assurance that witnesses would no longer be abused and would be treated with respect, Secretary Stevens agreed to rescind his orders to his subordinates not to appear before the subcommittee and would provide McCarthy with the information requested. But, when the "secret" meeting adjourned, he found the press assembled outside the door. A memorandum of the conversation was released with the terms of the agreement favorable to Senator McCarthy's side included but the assurances regarding the treatment of witnesses left out.

The newspapers, with only the memorandum available, painted the meeting in the blackest terms, using words such as "surrender," "capitulate," and "retreat." Senator McCarthy made the most of the situation.

Secretary Stevens was understandably furious. My own reaction upon reading the newspapers the next morning was not pleasant. I immediately called for the facts. It soon became obvious that Secretary Stevens had definitely received the proper assurances and had simply said that "under *these* conditions my boys will come down to Congress and testify like anybody else." An honorable gentleman, both in character and deportment, who throughout this entire difficult episode conducted himself with courage, dignity, and poise, it did not occur to him to demand a written statement to ensure compliance by both sides with the agreement. So I was more than a little annoyed to learn that the impression was rife that I had instructed Stevens to go down and settle with McCarthy at practically any price, my advice having been exactly the opposite.

The day after the luncheon Secretary Stevens, Governor Adams, the Vice President, General Persons, and I worked on a memorandum designed to set the record straight. Afterward the Secretary proceeded to Jim Hagerty's office where, at 6 P.M., he issued his statement from the White House. It confirmed (1) that he had not retreated from any of the principles on which he had stood and that (2) he would not stand for Army personnel being browbeaten and humiliated. He made clear that he had received assurances from members of the committee that they would not permit such conditions to develop.

The next day both Senators Potter and Mundt, who had been present at the meeting, confirmed the truth of Secretary Stevens' statement.

At the Legislative-leaders meeting on Monday, March 1, I admonished my colleagues from the Capitol that we had better get to work on our legislative program despite the noise of the opposition. It was essential that our program and our legislative accomplishments be something on which the party could run in November. But everyone's mind was on the McCarthy situation. When the discussion reached that subject, I made my position plain. I would not, I said, ever challenge the right of Congress to make legitimate investigations of the Executive department, for that right is inherent in the division of powers under the Constitution and necessary to the process of legislation. I stressed, however, that we could not fight Communism by destroying the basic concepts of our form of government.

I gave the conference all the facts respecting the luncheon meeting, including one they had not before known. Secretary Stevens had gone to the meeting under a pledge of secrecy—he had not even told me his intention to attend. The consensus seemed to be that Stevens had been "double-crossed."

Two days later, at a press conference, I took the occasion to restate my position:

The Department of the Army made serious errors in handling the Peress case and the Secretary of the Army so stated publicly, almost a month ago.[5] The Army is correcting its procedures to avoid such mistakes in the future. I am completely confident that Secretary Stevens will be successful in this effort.

I went on to say that I had spent many years in the Army, during the course of which I had sometimes appeared before congressional committees. I had never seen the Army fail to render due and complete respect to every member of the Congress, and in all that time I had never seen any members of the Congress guilty of disrespect for the public servants appearing before them. My intention was to see to it that the Executive branch observed and applied this tradition as long as I might hold my official position. I expressed my confidence—and America's pride—in our military services and their leaders, and specified that in my tribute to the services I meant to include General Zwicker, who had been decorated for gallantry in the field.

I added:

> . . . Except where the interests of the nation demand otherwise, every governmental employee in the Executive branch, whether civilian or in the armed forces, is expected to respond cheerfully and completely to the requests of the Congress and its several committees. In doing so it is, of course, assumed that they will be accorded the same respect and courtesy that I require that they show to the members of the Legislative body. Officials in the Executive branch of the government will have my unqualified support in insisting that employees in the Executive branch who appear before any type of Executive or congressional investigating body be treated fairly.

In early March I invited Senator Dirksen to breakfast. He had already shown the potential of a strong Republican leader, and I wanted to enlist his help. At the breakfast he promised to try to influence Republican members on the McCarthy subcommittee to promote the observance of proper procedures.

Elsewhere, Senator McCarthy's immunity was wearing thin. Defense Secretary Charlie Wilson, in one of his less quoted but more significant statements, said that the idea that the Army was coddling Communists was "just damn tommyrot."

[5] On February 18, 1954, the Army made public a letter from Secretary Stevens to Senator McCarthy which said in part: "The developments of this case have made it obvious to me and to the Army staff that there were defects in the Army procedures for handling men called to duty under the provisions of the Doctor's Draft Act. . . . As a result of these disclosures I have already issued instructions for corrective changes in current practices. . . . We do not defend this shortcoming and intend that such cases shall not recur."

Senator Flanders of Vermont, a courageous Republican, got up on the floor of the Senate and denounced McCarthy for trying to shatter the party.[6]

This effort of Senator Flanders' was the beginning of a movement in the Senate to "do something" about the antics of their colleague, which were scarcely in keeping with what members liked to call the "dignity of the Senate."

Our majority leader, Senator Knowland, however, seemed less concerned with Senator McCarthy's methods than with the prospect that such a move toward censuring the senator might create difficulties between the Executive branch and the Senate. Sensing my sympathy with Senator Flanders' action, he cited President Franklin Roosevelt's efforts to "purge" senators he did not like. I told him that I would not be trapped into any purging action; the matter belonged in the Senate and, so far as I was concerned, there it would stay.

Then the Army moved over to the attack. Fed up with the continual harassment from the McCarthy subcommittee, Secretary Stevens, encouraged by Senator Potter and others, determined to make public a memorandum of facts, which, at Governor Adams' direction, had been in preparation for two months. The paper recorded, among other things, details in the military career of G. David Schine.

In November of 1953 Schine had been drafted and had been assigned to Fort Dix for basic training. Almost immediately upon his arrival, the Army had been bombarded by demands from Schine's former associate Roy Cohn to give the new soldier special privileges. Cohn was still the McCarthy subcommittee's counsel. The demands were varied in character. Unless they were met, Cohn threatened, he would proceed to "wreck the Army." Schine himself, while apparently a less talkative individual than Cohn, made his own contribution to the comedy by asserting at Fort Dix that he had been drafted to "modernize the Army."

When the memorandum was complete, the Army put it to use. On March 11 a copy of the report was issued to each Republican member of the McCarthy subcommittee, extra copies were given to the press, and a few reached the hands of other senators. This attack put McCarthy on the defensive for the first time. He knew that he had been hurt. At a press conference on the 12th of March he called the report "blackmail," and counterattacked with an accusation that Secretary Stevens was trying to divert the investigation to the Air Force and Navy. In spite of the senator's efforts, however, the majority of his committee now demanded that

[6] "He [McCarthy] dons his war paint. He goes into his war dance. He emits his war whoops. He goes forth to battle and proudly returns with the scalp of a pink Army dentist. We may assume that this represents the depth of the seriousness of Communist penetration at this time."

Cohn be questioned. The next day McCarthy said he would testify under oath in the case, with another senator presiding. The Army-McCarthy hearings were launched.

My main concern in the matter was that it be done with minimum publicity and maximum dispatch. From my own viewpoint I could see much potential harm and no gain for the Republican party in an emotional spectacle in which most of the principals were Republicans —and, more important, I could see more harm to the United States.

The Senate has often been called the "world's most exclusive club," and its members tend to defend each other under the most extraordinary circumstances, particularly when there is any hint that any senator, no matter how wayward, is under attack, especially from the Executive. Nevertheless, the hearings began on April 22, and as a result of the rules on cross-examination and the fact that the proceedings were televised, the public was subjected to more of an extravaganza than a dignified committee hearing. Actually at issue were two rather simple questions; first, had Senator McCarthy and his staff exercised improper pressures in behalf of their former colleague, Private G. David Schine; and, on the other side, had Secretary Stevens attempted to "appease" McCarthy or attempted improperly to divert McCarthy's attention to the other services with promises to aid any such maneuver?

But the questions themselves were soon lost in a welter of personalities and emotion. In the whole sorry mess of thirty-six sessions, stretching over some fifty-seven days, the television audience was absorbed in such details as innumerable points of order, cropped photographs, wrangles over procedures, the duties Private Schine performed or did not perform, the authenticity of letters produced as evidence, the admissibility of monitored telephone calls, and finally a near fist fight between Roy Cohn and the counsel for Democratic members of the subcommittee.

On one issue only was the White House brought directly into the fracas. Early in May, Senator McCarthy produced a letter, supposedly written to the Army by the chief of the Federal Bureau of Investigation, J. Edgar Hoover, which the senator claimed he had received from an Army Intelligence officer acting outside orders of his legal superiors. On May 11 J. Edgar Hoover denied the authenticity of the letter, but said it contained several paragraphs of a secret memorandum that he had sent to the Army.[7] Brazen as this was, the acting chairman of the investigating subcommittee defended the practice of seeking classified information from the Executive branch through pressuring subordinates. On

[7] The "letter," of a little over two pages (alleging espionage at Fort Monmouth) contained seven paragraphs of a report Hoover had sent to Major General A. R. Bolling, chief of Army Intelligence, on January 26, 1951.

the same day he made a request for the names of all military personnel who had any connection with the case.

Almost immediately Secretary Wilson called for guidance on Chairman Mundt's request. I could see little connection between the Peress case and the current discussions in the subcommittee, but as a general principle I advised that the Army should provide the subcommittee with any information that security and efficient administration would permit. Military officials in particular, I felt, should not appear to be covering up.

However, with this general rule there was one condition to be imposed. On the matter of discussions within the Executive branch there was the principle of respecting vital confidences. This principle is of consummate importance, for if a staff officer cannot give advice to his chief without fear of exposure, he will find it difficult to continue to give that advice freely. Eventually it would become impossible for the Executive branch to function. Therefore, two days later I wrote a letter to Secretary Wilson, made public on May 17, specifying that matters that belonged to the Executive department exclusively should not be disclosed at the present hearing [see Appendix H].

This letter caused a certain amount of furor and the term "blackout" was applied in some quarters. However, distasteful as such action was, I deemed it essential and I made it stick.[8]

By the second week in June it was obvious that the hearings were finally coming to an end. The Army had now been able to present its case; and it was apparent that McCarthy's influence was slipping badly.[9]

June 17 was the last day. Chairman Mundt announced that the essential facts had been produced and that the hearings were adjourned. The confused and largely petty issues had finally boiled down to the main one, which now overshadowed all the others—that of Legislative versus Executive authority. On this matter, the age-old one of "Executive privilege," the bulk of the senators, both Republican and Democratic, supported my position. But while the end result was great damage to Senator McCarthy, there was also damage to the Republican party. In only one respect could the party conceivably have gained: with McCarthy neutral-

[8] The next week Senator McCarthy stated that the 2 million federal employees had a duty to give him any information which they had, regardless of any presidential secrecy directive. In answer to this I issued a statement, "The Executive branch has the sole responsibility for the enforcement of our laws and the responsibility cannot be usurped by an individual who may seek to set himself above the laws."
[9] The American Institute of Public Opinion found that in January, 50 per cent of the American population was favorable to McCarthy and only 29 per cent unfavorable. By May the samplings indicated the favorable disposition to McCarthy had been reduced to 35 per cent, and those unfavorable had risen to 49 per cent. These trends were most pronounced in the Midwestern states.

ized as a major force in the 1954 political campaign, the focus could now be put on the administration's legislative program. For by the time the hearings were over, Republican leaders were becoming wary of McCarthy's participation in the campaign.

But the senator's troubles were not to end there. On July 30 Senator Ralph Flanders (Republican, of Vermont) introduced Senate Resolution 301: "Resolved, that the conduct of the Senator from Wisconsin, Mr. McCarthy, is unbecoming a Member of the United States Senate, is contrary to Senatorial traditions, and tends to bring the Senate into disrepute, and such conduct is hereby condemned." During the first week of August, by a bipartisan vote of the Senate, a special six-man Select Committee, appointed by Vice President Nixon, was established to examine the whole McCarthy question and report back to the Senate before adjournment. This committee consisted of six respected members of the Senate, under the chairmanship of Republican Senator Arthur Watkins of Utah, a former judge.[10]

When the Watkins committee hearings began, Senator McCarthy tried his old tactic of grabbing the initiative and confusing the issue. He was, however, up against a group far different from those he had contended with before. The hearings were not televised. And whenever McCarthy's conduct was out of order, he was informed of this fact in no uncertain terms.

On September 27 the results of the Watkins committee hearings came out. While bending over backward and giving Senator McCarthy the benefit of the doubt on some points, the committee recommended censure on two charges: contempt of the Senate, and the senator's treatment of General Zwicker. In view of the senatorial restraint toward colleagues, this was a victory indeed for the anti-McCarthy forces. There the matter sat until after the congressional elections.

Elections over, the Senate reconvened in November for the purpose of addressing the McCarthy issue. The debate was scheduled to begin on the 10th of November, a Wednesday, but Senator McCarthy issued a statement the previous day (which he merely inserted in the record as his opening speech) that did much to damage his position. The statement said, "I would have the American people recognize the fact that the Communist party has now extended its tentacles to the United States Senate. It has made a committee of the Senate its unwitting handmaiden."

The ensuing debate was characterized by parliamentary maneuvering and much argument. For a while it appeared that the vote would never come about, since McCarthy was hospitalized for days with a sore el-

[10] The others were Carlson (Republican of Kan.), Case (Republican, S.D.), Johnson (Democrat, Colo.), Stennis (Democrat, Miss.), and Ervin (Democrat, N.C.).

bow. There was a danger that a filibuster might carry the proceedings to an inconclusive end.

However, on the 2nd of December the matter was brought to a final vote. On an amended resolution which mentioned neither the word "censure" nor the name of General Zwicker, sixty-seven out of eighty-nine Senators voted to condemn McCarthy for conduct "contrary to senatorial traditions." [See Appendix I.]

It is doubtful that this result would have ever come about had I adopted a habit of referring to McCarthy by name in press conferences, thus making the issue one of Executive versus congressional prestige. I felt impelled, however, to express my appreciation to the man who was the hero of the episode, Senator Arthur Watkins. Accordingly I invited him to come to my office on Saturday morning, December 4, so that we might have a few words in private. He came "off the record," arriving at the East Wing and walking across through the basement of the Mansion to avoid notice, and the two of us had a pleasant conversation. Senator Watkins said his only regret was that the censure motion on McCarthy's treatment of Zwicker could not go through as originally worded.

Across the hall, outside Jim Hagerty's office, a larger crowd of newspapermen than usual had assembled. Word of Senator Watkins' visit had got out. Just as the senator was ready to leave, Jim walked in.

"The reporters would like to interview the senator on his way out," he said. "Is it O.K.?"

The senator was willing and I at once gave my approval. "Tell them," I said to Jim, "that I asked Senator Watkins to come down here so that I could tell him how much we appreciate his superb handling of a most difficult job."

Upon learning of this meeting, Senator McCarthy finally made what has been termed his "break" with me—why it was called such at that late date I could not fathom. He claimed that the administration was soft on Communism and apologized for having supported me in 1952.

But one thing was apparent. By a combination of the Senate's vote and the loss of his committee chairmanship, the senator's power was ended. Senator McCarthy died an untimely and sad—even pathetic—death in 1957, but as a political force he was finished at the end of 1954.

On the whole sorry experience I had no public comment to make but I did have an urge to go back into my memory to review the developments and to contemplate their meaning.

McCarthyism took its toll on many individuals and on the nation. No one was safe from charges recklessly made from inside the walls of congressional immunity. Teachers, government employees, and even ministers became vulnerable. Innocent people accused of Communist associations or party membership have not to this day been able to clear their names fully. For a few, of course, the cost was little—where the accused was a figure who stood high in public trust and respect, personal damage, if any, could be ignored or laughed away. But where, without proof of guilt, or because of some accidental or early-in-life association with suspected persons, a man or woman had lost a job or the confidence and trust of superiors and associates, the cost was often tragic, both emotionally and occupationally.

Not all these accusations were made by Senator McCarthy himself; but he and his cult were never known for any sense of discrimination either in their choice of targets or in determining who held the gun. The attack on General Zwicker made me furious; the innuendoes about some others, whom I knew intimately, I found ridiculous.

Measured against all the mental anguish unfairly inflicted upon people and all the bitterness occasioned by baseless charges against them, the benefits flowing from the McCarthy "investigations" do not loom large. I was told by members of the Executive departments, including the Federal Bureau of Investigation, that those discovered by the subcommittee to be, on reliable information, disloyal or unreliable were few in number. Moreover, in most of the cases, where damaging evidence was made public by them, I was informed that the truth of the matter usually had been uncovered by appropriate officials, without committee intervention.

Supporters of McCarthyism represented it as simply a dramatic effort to awaken the public to the existence of some Communist penetration into all facets of our national life and to warn everyone of the need for universal alertness. Perhaps at its beginning the movement may have had some such usefulness. But almost immediately its methods defeated its purported objectives. Un-American activity cannot be prevented or routed out by employing un-American methods; to preserve freedom we must use the tools that freedom provides.

CHAPTER XIV

Chaos in Indochina

Enemy advances, we retreat; enemy halts, we harass; enemy tires, we attack; enemy retreats, we pursue.

—*Mao Tse-tung*

IN 1954 the seven-and-a-half-year-old war in Indochina came to an end. It was a war which at its beginning in 1946 seemed to be only a "local disturbance." But several small countries and finally many nations were to some extent caught up in it. Merely listing the highlights of the communications, conferences, negotiations, and military tactics of those many months would be a long process. Yet such a list could give only a faint idea of the anxious hours and days when the leaders of the Free World tried to find among themselves at least a temporary, workable unity—when diverse intentions, plans, and purposes caused chaos, misunderstanding, and tragedy in that unfortunate land.

*   *   *

The strategic importance of Indochina, made up of the three Associated States—Vietnam, Laos, and Cambodia—is obvious. Before World War II it had long been under French rule. The land, about the size of Texas, is shaped roughly like a bent dumbbell, with a population in 1954 of nearly 28 million people living largely along the coast and in two river deltas. The rich Red River Delta lies in the north, and through it the Red River empties into the South China Sea. (The Red River Delta is referred to, in most official documents, as the Tonkin Delta, a name derived from the province through which the river flows.)

The Mekong River Delta is to the south. To the west of Indochina is Thailand; on the east and south is the South China Sea; on the north lies Red China. This area, particularly the elongated land of Vietnam along the east coast, became the scene of a bitter war between opposing groups within it. One group, the Vietminh, was inspired and led by Communist elements, and this fact made the conflict important to the major powers.

The loss of all Vietnam, together with Laos on the west and Cambodia in the southwest, would have meant the surrender to Communist enslavement of millions. On the material side, it would have spelled the loss of valuable deposits of tin and prodigious supplies of rubber and rice. It would have meant that Thailand, enjoying buffer territory between itself and Red China, would be exposed on its entire eastern border to infiltration or attack.

And if Indochina fell, not only Thailand but Burma and Malaya would be threatened, with added risks to East Pakistan and South Asia as well as to all Indonesia.

Unfortunately, from a military point of view, the Red River Delta in the north of Vietnam, where the city of Hanoi and its port, Haiphong, are located, was directly exposed to Chinese-supported Communist attack. Easy access routes run along the Red River and parallel valleys from northwest to southeast, starting in the Chinese province of Yunnan, and no natural barriers protect the northern border of Vietnam. Moreover, the rough terrain and almost incredibly dense jungle lend themselves ideally to guerrilla operations, at which the Communists are expert. This vulnerable area was also the richest part of Indochina.

During the first forty years of the twentieth century the region was relatively quiescent, its economy based largely on its tin ore and natural rubber. Then, when the Japanese entered World War II, their armies moved into the region and rapidly took over complete control, a condition which persisted until the final Japanese defeat in August 1945.

This was the signal for the French to come in again to reassert control. Shortly thereafter, trouble developed between the French and the natives, many of whom were tired of overlordships of all kinds and wanted independence. This unrest mushroomed into fighting that gradually grew more widespread in scope and intense in character. By 1950 France had strong Regular Army units deployed in the area and was doing its best to raise, equip, and train loyal native troops to assist in quelling the rebellion. The disaffected forces were led by a man, Ho Chi Minh, who had once, in 1946, been Premier of all Indochina, with the blessing of the French.

Ho Chi Minh was, of course, a hard-core Communist, while the Vietminh, the forces under his command, were supported by the Chinese Communists in the north. Although guerrilla fighting was sporadic, the French controlled the deltas and the cities and an area along the waist of Vietnam, whereas the back country, including most of the province of Tonkin and a sizable area in central Annam, was controlled mainly by the Vietminh.

C H I N A

MEKONG R.

RED R.

TONKIN

Dien Bien Phu

Hanoi

Haiphong

HAINAN I.

Vinh

SOUTH

CHINA

SEA

Hué

THAILAND

MEKONG R.

Binh Dinh

N

W   E

S

Angkor Vat

C A M B O D I A

Saigon

INDOCHINA
JULY 1953
Communist China
Communist Penetration
Free Territory
Neutral Countries

0   Miles   200

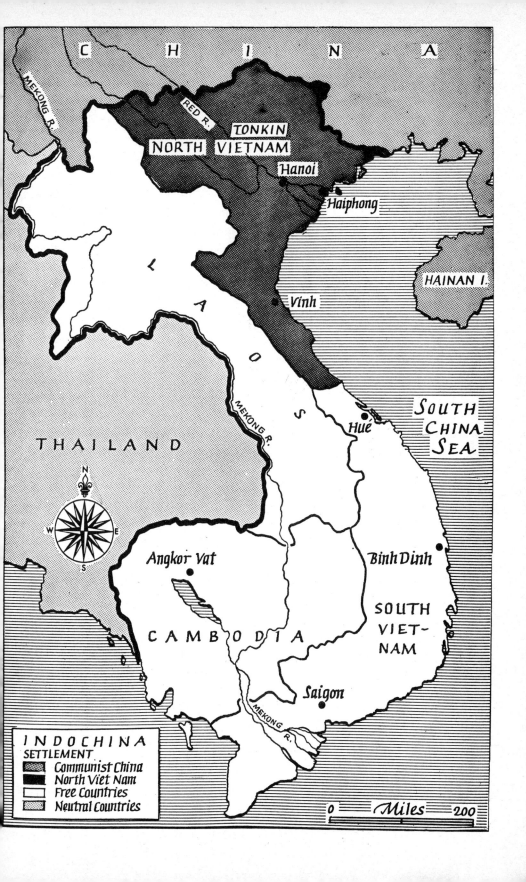

C H I N A

MEKONG R.

RED R.

TONKIN

NORTH VIETNAM

Hanoi

Haiphong

L

A

O

S

Vinh

HAINAN I.

THAILAND

MEKONG R.

Hué

SOUTH
CHINA
SEA

N

W   E

S

Angkor Vat

Binh Dinh

C A M B O D I A

SOUTH
VIET-
NAM

MEKONG R.

Saigon

INDOCHINA
SETTLEMENT
Communist China
North Viet Nam
Free Countries
Neutral Countries

0   Miles   200

In early 1951 the Indochina affair had come emphatically to my attention when I was Allied commander of the NATO troops with headquarters in Paris. The NATO defense needed greater French participation, but this was largely denied because of France's losses and costs in the Indochina war, as mentioned earlier.

These losses and costs to the French might be lessened, I believed, if allies could be brought in to carry part of the load in defending Indochina. Such a development would depend, of course, upon a clear appreciation throughout the Free World that the war was in no sense an effort on the part of the French to sustain their former domination over the area, but was in fact a clear case of freedom defending itself from Communist aggression. To bring about such an appreciation, there would have to be a definite and public pledge on the part of the French to accord independence and the right of self-determination upon the Associated States as soon as military victory should be attained.

I repeatedly urged upon successive French governments the wisdom of publishing to the Free World such an unequivocal commitment. But the French government did not make its position unmistakably clear, especially to the people most concerned, the Vietnamese. Had it done so, the effect would soon have been—we in NATO believed—to make the war the concern of all nations outside the Iron Curtain, and could have assured France of material help, as well as the support of world opinion. Furthermore, it would have immeasurably raised the fighting morale of the loyal Vietnamese.

At that time the French government apparently saw no need to publicize any such sincere, simple, and selfless pronouncement. As far as I could tell, this reluctance seemed to have its source in the French conviction that making an all-out statement would weaken their leadership in the war and might have serious effects in other portions of the French Empire, including Algeria; moreover, the civil officials with whom I often talked invariably agreed that while in this one special situation their difficulties could be greatly diminished by making clear their intention to offer freedom to Indochina, they felt also that an announcement of voluntary withdrawal from the area during hostilities would be a tremendous blow to French prestige and influence in the world.

In the absence of such a statement, the war was naturally looked upon in most cases as a domestic difficulty between France and one part of her empire. This attitude precluded the possibility that other free nations could help in what the French themselves considered so much a family quarrel that it could not even be submitted to the United Nations for adjudication.

Both Europe and the United States understood the great political and strategic significance of the Southwest Pacific and Southeast Asia. But so important did the French consider their exclusive responsibility to resolve the conflict favorably that, even after the United States began to provide money and material to assist them, they would accept such aid only on the basis of using it according to their fixed political and military policies. Even when they later asked us for active military intervention, they did not base the request on the defense of freedom and international peace; they simply requested American help, to be used under French commanders solely as they saw fit.

The French, in more than seven years of fighting to subdue the rebels, were to suffer some 150,000 casualties, one third of them dead or missing. The cost to France amounted to about $5 billion.

By the time I entered the Presidency the French nation had become weary of the war, and their government—at least in official circles, if not publicly—was promising eventual self-rule and even independence to Indochina. Undoubtedly the conflict was coming to be recognized as having global significance, but what the French political leaders said semipublicly about fighting against Communism and what the Army and the population in Vietnam believed about the character of the war were quite different.

The forces of the French Union fighting in Vietnam comprised approximately 200,000 French and 200,000 natives from the Associated States of Indochina. Patriotic Frenchmen fighting there naturally expected to see their sacrifices accrue to the good of France. But Frenchmen, initially told that they were fighting in Indochina for France and the preservation of her empire, might react adversely to an announcement and a series of actions that would inevitably lead to a breakaway of the Associated States from France.

This was a time in history when France, along with other old colonial powers, did not necessarily want to continue maintaining—expensively in more than a few cases—its colonies. Initially their troops had been sent to preserve the status quo, but the cause, not the meaning of the war, was changing.

This put the French on the horns of a dilemma. Delay or equivocation in implementing complete independence could only serve to bolster the Communist claim that this was in reality a war to preserve colonialism. To American ears the first French pronouncements, soon made to the world, were a distinct step forward, but it was almost impossible to make the average Vietnamese peasant realize that the French, under whose rule his people had lived for some eighty years, were really fighting in the cause of freedom, while the Vietminh, people of their own ethnic origins, were fighting on the side of slavery. It was generally conceded that had an election been held, Ho Chi Minh would have been elected Premier. Unhappily, the situation was exacerbated by the almost total lack of leadership displayed by the Vietnamese Chief of State, Bao Dai, who, while nominally the head of that nation, chose to spend the bulk of his time in the spas of Europe rather than in his own land leading his armies against those of Communism.

Toward the end of 1953, the effect of the termination of hostilities in Korea began to be felt in Indochina. Overt Red Chinese aggression was not anticipated—that government had been adequately warned by the United States—but the Chinese Communists now were able to spare greatly increased quantities of matériel in the form of guns and ammunition (largely supplied by the Soviets) for use on the Indochinese battle front. More advisers were being sent in and the Chinese were making available to the Vietminh logistical experience they had gained in the Korean War.

To combat this, General Navarre, who had succeeded to the French military command in Indochina, proposed in 1953 an over-all scheme under which, hopefully, he would end the war successfully. Under the Navarre Plan the French were to send nine more battalions of troops and supporting units to Indochina, increasing the size of the French Expeditionary Forces in that region to 250,000. In addition, the French would train enough native troops to raise the strength of the Vietnamese Army to 300,000 during the following year. Thus, the planned strength of the French Union should be 550,000 troops by the end of 1954. Since the estimated strength of the Vietminh was not more than 400,000, it appeared that if the French Union could then lure them into open battle, they might be able to knock out the regular Vietminh forces by the end of the 1955 fighting season, reducing the fighting in Indochina to mop-up operations which could be conducted for the most part by native troops. In order to make this plan possible, the United States agreed on September 30, 1953, to grant France, in addition to the aid already earmarked, another $385 million to be available by the end of that calendar year; these funds were to supply and equip additional French and native forces during the build-up phase.

In this light the military situation was not alarming, but it was, at times, confusing. In October the French Union forces launched a fairly successful offensive against the Communist forces in central Vietnam, and on November 7 the French command reported a victorious conclusion of the battle. On November 20, French Union forces moved west from the Red River Delta in Tonkin and occupied an area ten miles from the border of Laos. This place was later to become a household word throughout the Free World: Dien Bien Phu.

It was difficult then—as it is now with the advantage of hindsight—to understand exactly why (a year in advance of the build-up contemplated in the Navarre Plan) the French decided to send ten thousand crack troops into this position, strong as it was, whose only means of resupply was by air.

One reason they offered was that they wanted to occupy the plain on which Dien Bien Phu was located so as to prevent the organizing and mounting in this region of the guerrilla strikes which were continually harassing the Red River Delta. Another reason was to cut the road which led from the heart of Vietminh territory to the border of Laos, a state also being invaded by the Vietminh. It was argued that during the rainy season the enemy would be roadbound, and the Dien Bien Phu position would therefore prove a real cork in the bottle. To remove it the Communists would attempt to reduce Dien Bien Phu, which would enable the French to induce the main Vietminh forces into a pitched battle on ground where the French could concentrate their supposedly superior forces. A third bit of reasoning was the conviction that the Chinese Communists would not supply the Vietminh with artillery, and that even if they did, it could not be brought to the high ground surrounding Dien Bien Phu where it could fire effectively. They were wrong.

Whatever the reasons, the occupation of Dien Bien Phu caused little notice at the time, except to soldiers who were well acquainted with the almost invariable fate of troops invested in an isolated fortress. I instructed both the State and Defense Departments to communicate to their French counterparts my concern as to the move.

Bastogne, the critical road junction denied to the Germans during the Battle of the Bulge in World War II, was a far different story. There, beleaguered troops had to be resupplied by air. But Bastogne was an episode in a large campaign; it was far from being a deliberately contrived and semi-isolated maneuver.

Soon there were ominous portents. On December 30, 1953, Allen Dulles, director of the CIA, reported a recent attack by the Vietminh in the strength of eight battalions. Some estimates indicated that as many as ten thousand Vietminh troops were involved. The French were gathering forces in the south, and it appeared that a battle there might be imminent. But the real danger spot, Mr. Dulles concluded at the time, was in the north, where Vietminh forces were apparently trying to encircle Dien Bien Phu.

About a week later, reports came in that the French garrison at that important outpost was surrounded by approximately three Vietminh divisions—outnumbering the besieged forces by three to one. The garrison was not considered in immediate danger and it was not clear whether the Vietminh would launch a frontal attack on the French position or try to contain it while moving other troops southward into Laos toward the Thai frontier. General Navarre told Admiral Radford that the position might be taken if the Vietminh were willing to pay the price, but Radford believed, correctly, that for the moment the enemy would not be able to conduct both operations simultaneously.

In our discussions in Washington we recognized that while the location of Dien Bien Phu was of minor military significance, the far-reaching psychological effects which the loss of this garrison of fine troops might have on the French would be serious.

The situation confronting the United States in our hope of finding ways to help the French effectively was complicated. The most obvious and least risky method was to provide material aid, and we were already giving this, through our commitments and actions in support of the Navarre Plan. In our judgment this kind of aid was being sent in as rapidly as French capacity to absorb it permitted. Without United States technical personnel to train the French and Vietnamese in the maintenance and operation of advanced equipment, much more would be superfluous.

As I viewed the prospects of military intervention in the relative calm of early 1954, it seemed clear that if three basic requirements were fulfilled, the United States could properly and effectively render real help in winning the war. The first requirement was a legal right under international law; second, was a favorable climate of Free World opinion; and third, favorable action by the Congress.

Regarding the legal right, the course was clear. Any intervention on the part of the United States would scarcely be possible save on the urgent request of the French government, which request would have to reflect, without question, the desire of the local governments.

World opinion represented a different question. We carefully examined methods and procedures calculated to win the approbation of most of the Free World. One method would have been for the three Associated States of the French Union to go to the United Nations and request help of that body. Another would be to confine United States intervention to participation in a coalition, including Britain, the ANZUS[1] powers, and some of the Southeast Asian nations. While we recognized that the burden of the operation would fall on the United States, the token forces supplied by these other nations, as in Korea, would lend real moral standing to a venture that otherwise could be made to appear as a brutal example of imperialism. This need was particularly acute because there was no incontrovertible evidence of overt Red Chinese participation in the Indochina conflict.

[1] A security treaty (September 1, 1951) signed by Australia, New Zealand, and the United States.

Another consideration in any conceivable intervention was the type of forces which might be employed. There seemed to be no dearth of defensive ground strength in Indochina. I told my associates in January of 1954 that I could not at that moment see the value of putting United States ground forces in Southeast Asia.

One possibility was to support the French with air strikes, possibly from carriers, on Communist installations around Dien Bien Phu. There were grave doubts in my mind about the effectiveness of such air strikes on deployed troops where good cover was plentiful. Employment of air strikes alone to support French forces in the jungle would create a double jeopardy; it would comprise an act of war and would also entail the risk of having intervened and lost. Air power might be temporarily beneficial to French morale, but I had no intention of using United States forces in any limited action when the force employed would probably not be decisively effective.

As a result we concentrated our efforts on attempting to convince the French and the British of the necessity for achieving a coalition which would give moral meaning to intervention, on taking further measures to convince the Vietnamese and the world of the sincerity of France's intention to grant complete independence in the shortest possible time to the Associated States, and to stepping up our material aid in every practical way.

This last was far from simple. Providing material and technicians was not difficult and we sent certain numbers of B-26s by the middle of February 1954. However, we were not legally allowed to send Air Force personnel on a permanent basis. After consultation with the leaders of both houses of Congress, we sent two hundred technicians to Vietnam in February, to remain only until the middle of June.

To study further feasible steps for supporting the Navarre Plan, I directed the formation of an ad hoc committee consisting of Under Secretary of State Bedell Smith, Deputy Secretary of Defense Roger Kyes, the Joint Chiefs of Staff, and Allen Dulles. Because we needed military information and judgment from sources in which we had the utmost confidence, I ordered that Lieutenant General John W. O'Daniel, then in Indochina on a temporary basis, be designated as chief of the United States Military Advisory and Assistance Group with the Vietnamese.

Indochina at this time was what Bedell Smith aptly called a "real-estate war." Both sides pursued each other, occupied territory, and indulged in minor combat only. Dien Bien Phu represented the principal exception. Allen Dulles reported on January 14 that the French garrison, now consisting of fifteen battalions, totaling about eleven thousand French troops, was down to six days' supply of rations. But timely airlift, it was believed, could avoid any real supply difficulty. Against these eleven thousand troops, however, it was estimated that the Vietminh numbered some twenty-four thousand. In view of the alleged strength of the position, the garrison seemed in no immediate danger. Meanwhile, the French began fighting effectively in the south and eliminated a penetration the Vietminh had made all the way across Laos.

The war seesawed. On January 30 a Communist Vietminh force invaded northern Laos and drove down toward the capital city of Luang Prabang. Although, because of supply difficulties and French Union resistance, the invading troops never reached the capital, they did reach a point thirty or forty miles away. This advance drained off some enemy forces confronting Dien Bien Phu and lessened the threat of a frontal attack on that position. In the meantime, the supply situation at Dien Bien Phu was reported improved.

But French Union efforts to mop up Vietminh centers in southern Vietnam were only partly successful—the advance warnings passed on to the Vietminh by the civilian populace were a disturbing and critical fact.

This was the situation that existed when representatives of the United States, France, Great Britain, and the U.S.S.R. met at Berlin for a conference in 1954.

The Berlin Conference of Foreign Ministers[2] convened on January 25, without agenda. Its purpose was to discuss such world problems as Austria, Germany, and the Far East.

Before departure for Berlin, Foster Dulles said that this meeting might represent the last major Soviet effort to disrupt the Western Alliance. If they were successful, we would have to reassess our views on at least two features of that alliance, EDC and NATO. If they failed, we could count it an achievement. There was a possibility of obtaining a peace treaty for Austria; none of us held a shred of hope on the reunification of Germany at this conference.

Mr. Molotov, the Soviet Foreign Minister, lost no time in bringing up his pet proposal for a "Big Five" conference—to include Communist China. In a Soviet note the previous November, a five-power conference had been proposed as a condition precedent to any discussion of the German and Austrian problems. Now Molotov tapered down his demands to make the five-power meeting solely on the problems of Asia. This was still unacceptable to us.

Unfortunately, Molotov was fully aware of the political pressures on French Foreign Minister Bidault to achieve a settlement in Indochina.

[2] This was the conference that the French, British, and ourselves agreed to at Bermuda the month previously.

Bidault, in fact, felt that if the Laniel government was to survive, he had to bring back at least a tentative pledge to discuss Indochina at a meeting scheduled later for Geneva.

The life of the Laniel government was important to United States policies. We were convinced that no succeeding government would take a stronger position than his on the defense of Indochina, or in support of the European Defense Community. We had to be sympathetic to the French desire. But there was danger in the attitude developing among the Western allies which, to us, seemed to put too much faith in the validity of negotiations with the Soviets and Chinese Communists. Secretary Dulles attempted to discourage Bidault from overanxiety to negotiate, pointing out that this could lead to further deterioration of morale in Indochina and France itself.

Bidault persisted. On February 9 Foster notified me from Berlin that French pressure for a conference on Indochina at Geneva was mounting. He held little hope of being able to withstand it, and said that if the United States was held responsible for blocking such a conference, the moral obligation to carry on the war in Indochina might be shifted from French shoulders to ours. Finally, Foster himself found it necessary to propose a restricted four-power conference on the Far East.

There were good reasons for Foster's action in addition to the desperate straits of our French friends. Since the British and French both were seeking Far East talks, it would be less of a sign of disunity if the United States proposed it formally, and carefully restricted it to that area. In addition, if discussion was inevitable, it was desirable to initiate it prior to any unfavorable developments in the Indochina fighting. In adopting this course of action Foster warned Bidault that prospects of this later conference would increase Communist efforts toward a military knockout this season and those efforts would have to be met with corresponding determination.

At the same time, the Secretary found it necessary to assure the French that our agreements to continue material aid in Vietnam would be carried out. Some of our congressmen, Senator Stennis and Senator Richard Russell, for example, were uneasy about any American participation whatsoever.

On the 10th of February, I cabled Foster in Berlin:

> . . . It is true that certain legislators have expressed uneasiness concerning any use of American maintenance personnel in Indochina. They fear that this may be opening the door to increased and unwise introduction of American troops into that area. Administration has given assurances to guard against such developments. . . .
> There is no ground whatsoever for assuming we intend to reverse or ignore U. S. commitments made to French. Those commitments were

based upon assumptions that French would act comprehensively and vigorously in prosecuting war; and their commitment in this regard is as binding as is ours in providing additional money and equipment. The so-called Navarre Plan visualized substantial victory by summer of 1955.

General O'Daniel's most recent report is more encouraging than given to you through French sources. I still believe that the two things most needed for success are French will to win and complete acceptance by Vietnamese of French promise of independence as soon as victory is achieved. To summarize, administration has no intention of evading its pledges in the area providing the French performance measures up to the promises made by them as basis for requesting our increased help.

In the meantime, Bidault's problems became more severe and finally, as the result of the clamor of the French government and the skillful manipulations on the part of Mr. Molotov, Bidault found himself in the position of practically pleading with Molotov for the inclusion of Indochina on the Geneva agenda. Thus on February 18, 1954, the Berlin Conference came to an end after four weeks of polemics and argument with nothing more constructive than agreement to meet at Geneva on April 26 to discuss problems of Korea and Indochina.

On March 13, only twenty-three days after the conclusion of the conference, a blow fell. The Vietminh units investing Dien Bien Phu had been heavily reinforced and on that date made their first large-scale assault against that stronghold. Two days later, French airstrips at Dien Bien Phu were put out of action, at least temporarily, by Vietminh artillery fire. Within five days, Allen Dulles said that the Vietminh had already lost the equivalent of five battalions in their assault and the French had lost two battalions, which had been replaced by airdrop. Although it was impossible to predict the eventual result of these assaults, our Intelligence people estimated that the French had only about a fifty-fifty chance of holding out. The French government was not hopeful.

This news was serious. It was difficult to understand, in the light of General Navarre's earlier statements that he hoped to be attacked by the enemy at Dien Bien Phu, why the French had suddenly become so very pessimistic. It seemed to me that odds of two to one favoring an attacker against a position well dug in and determinedly defended should not be regarded with alarm.

During the ensuing week Dien Bien Phu was fairly quiet, possibly because the Vietminh were short of ammunition and supplies. The French improved their position but did not bring in additional replacements.

It was perplexing, too, that the French had not been able to prevent a Vietminh division, which had made a new incursion into northern Laos, from returning to Dien Bien Phu. If there was only one road, as reported,

I could not see why the French could not at least interdict this route. General Ridgway, Army Chief of Staff, advised me that apparently the French were encountering so much guerrilla resistance that they were unable to carry on such operations in the hinterlands as would prevent the division from returning.

The Vietminh were able to replenish their supplies in the course of about a week, and on the 30th of March launched another large-scale attack at Dien Bien Phu.

A new issue now arose. What would be the United States reaction in the event that the Chinese Communists themselves attacked French positions in Vietnam with their MIG aircraft? General Paul Ely (French Chief of Staff), General Valluy (French representative on the military group of NATO), and Admiral Radford had discussed this question with Secretary Dulles, who sent me a memorandum in which the following appeared:

> I said that I would not, of course, attempt to answer that question. I did, however, think it appropriate to remind our French friends that if the United States sent its flag and its own military establishment—land, sea or air—into the Indo-China war, then the prestige of the United States would be engaged to a point where we would want to have a success. We could not afford thus to engage the prestige of the United States and suffer a defeat which would have world-wide repercussions.

He said also, that if the French wanted our open participation, this would call for a greater degree of philosophical and practical partnership than had prevailed to that time, notably in relation to proclaiming plainly their intentions regarding independence for the Associated States and in working cooperatively to expand training programs for indigenous forces.

The ever-present, persistent, gnawing possibility was that of employing our ground forces in Indochina. The war had been going on for a long time and unless the French were successful a great many people could be swept under Communist rule. We had helped the French in the ways open to us, and they were losing ground; still, they were convinced that only they could devise successful military operations there. Nevertheless, I let it be known that I would never agree to send our ground troops as mere reinforcements for French units, to be used only as they saw fit. Part of my fundamental concept of the Presidency is that we have a constitutional government and only when there is a sudden, unforeseen emergency should the President put us into war without congressional action.

Some of my advisers felt that the French had actually reached the point where they would rather abandon Indochina, or lose it as a result of a military defeat, than save it through international intervention. As an example of governmental despondency in France, Bedell Smith informed me on March 12 that the Defense Minister of the French government had told five American correspondents that the Indochina problem could be resolved only by Communist China, that Communist China would want recognition and an easing of the Free World nations' trade embargo against her, imposed during the Korean War, *and that the key nation in making these concessions must be the United States.* Bedell added a pointed comment: "It seems to me that [the Defense Minister] has been extremely free with our negotiating position."

On the 4th of April I made an effort to have the British join with us in organizing a regional grouping of the United States, France, and the Southeast Asian nations. I wrote to Winston Churchill:

> I am sure . . . you are following with the deepest interest and anxiety the daily reports of the gallant fight being put up by the French at Dien Bien Phu. Today, the situation there does not seem hopeless.
>
> But regardless of the outcome of this particular battle, I fear that the French cannot alone see the thing through, this despite the very substantial assistance in money and matériel that we are giving them. It is no solution simply to urge the French to intensify their efforts. And if they do not see it through and Indochina passes into the hands of the Communists the ultimate effect on our and your global strategic position with the consequent shift in the power ratios throughout Asia and the Pacific could be disastrous and, I know, unacceptable to you and me. . . . This has led us to the hard conclusion that the situation in Southeast Asia requires us urgently to take serious and far-reaching decisions.
>
> Geneva is less than four weeks away. There the possibility of the Communists driving a wedge between us will, given the state of mind in France, be infinitely greater than at Berlin. I can understand the very natural desire of the French to seek an end to this war which has been bleeding them for eight years. But our painstaking search for a way out of the impasse has reluctantly forced us to the conclusion that there is no negotiated solution of the Indochina problem which in its essence would not be either a face-saving device to cover a French surrender or a face-saving device to cover a Communist retirement. The first alternative is too serious in its broad strategic implications for us and for you to be acceptable. . . .
>
> Somehow we must contrive to bring about the second alternative. The preliminary lines of our thinking were sketched out by Foster in his speech last Monday night when he said that under the conditions of today the imposition on Southeast Asia of the political system of Communist Russia and its Chinese Communist ally, by whatever means, would be a grave threat to the whole free community, and that in our view this possibility should now be met by united action and not passively accepted. . . .
>
> I believe that the best way to put teeth in this concept and to bring greater moral and material resources to the support of the French effort is through

the establishment of a new, ad hoc grouping or coalition composed of nations which have a vital concern in the checking of Communist expansion in the area. I have in mind in addition to our two countries, France, the Associated States, Australia, New Zealand, Thailand and the Philippines. The United States government would expect to play its full part in such a coalition. . . .

The important thing is that the coalition must be strong and it must be willing to join the fight if necessary. I do not envisage the need of any appreciable ground forces on your or our part. . . .

If I may refer again to history; we failed to halt Hirohito, Mussolini and Hitler by not acting in unity and in time. That marked the beginning of many years of stark tragedy and desperate peril. May it not be that our nations have learned something from that lesson? . . .

With warm regard,

IKE

Three days later I received a message from Winston to the effect that his government would talk over the matter with Foster in London on April 12.

His brief answer showed that the British had little enthusiasm for joining us in taking a firm position and it seemed clear that the Congress would not act favorably unless I could give assurances that the British would be by our side. Indeed, Foster Dulles had previously held a meeting with Deputy Secretary of Defense Roger Kyes, Admiral Radford, and eight congressional leaders, as a result of which he concluded that it would be impossible to get congressional authorization for the United States to act alone. Congressional support would be contingent upon meeting three conditions:

(1) United States intervention must be part of a coalition to include the other free nations of Southeast Asia, the Philippines, and the British Commonwealth.

(2) The French must agree to accelerate their independence program for the Associated States so there could be no interpretation that United States assistance meant support of French colonialism.

(3) The French must agree not to pull their forces out of the war if we put our forces in.

There was nothing in these preconditions or in this congressional viewpoint with which I could disagree; my judgment entirely coincided with theirs. The meeting did, however, give Secretary Dulles sufficient assurance of congressional support if these conditions were met to feel perfectly able to talk to other nations and tell them that if they would go along with our proposal we would be ready to participate in a regional grouping. Thus we could get to work.

As a next step I decided to attempt the organization of a regional grouping before the opening of the Geneva Conference and arranged for Foster Dulles to go to Paris and London for that purpose.

Shortly after reaching England, Foster reported back with some optimism, expressing the belief that he had accomplished much toward dispelling the British reluctance to say or do anything before Geneva. He noted that the communiqué issued that day indicated a large measure of acceptance of our view of the danger and necessity for united action. Differences remained, however. The British, fearful of becoming involved with ground forces in Indochina, took a more optimistic view of the results in the event that the French lost northern Vietnam than did the military in our country.

"Press generally friendly," Foster cabled in winding up his report, "and Daily Worker paid compliment of saying am most *un*welcome guest since 1066."

In Paris, Mr. Dulles received assurances from M. Laniel and M. Reynaud that the French had promised total independence to the Associated States and that France would keep its word. A treaty had recently been signed with Laos giving the Laotians full satisfaction. The Vietnamese wanted two treaties, one granting their total independence and a second governing the continuing relations between France and Vietnam. The idea was to form a "fraternal association" of free and equal states which, under the name of the French Union, would work together for the development of their civilizations, the advancement of the well-being of their people, and the assurance of the security of each of them. The concessions on the part of the French were such that Reynaud hoped that now, finally, the French would never again be regarded as colonialists. The Vietnamese had been satisfied.

The French government's statement issued at this time, so long and so tragically delayed, should have, by its wording, assured the world that the French were fighting for freedom and against Communist penetration. But the problem of achieving understanding and belief among the populations most affected was never completely solved.

In spite of Secretary Dulles' apparent progress in Paris and London, the attitude of the British was still disturbing, in that they seemed to put such heavy reliance on the value of negotiations with the Communists. The British stand at the time was that the war in Indochina could not be won by the French and that the best they could do would be to secure a cease fire by negotiation on some—nearly any—sort of terms. Any preparations made in advance of the Geneva Conference for united action, the British felt, would be unacceptable, apparently for fear of irritating the Communists.

We, in Washington, found it difficult to understand such a position, but finally concluded that the British conviction stemmed from several factors: British diplomacy had kept that small island a world power for a long time and, as they were always acutely aware that today's enemy may be tomorrow's friend, this awareness had caused them to put much faith in the process of negotiation. With this I had no quarrel in principle, but in its application to dealings with the Communists, I considered it unrealistic. To my knowledge the fact that Communists were to participate in any international conference never implied that they would either make concessions or keep promises.

For whatever reasons, the British were hesitant, and even before Foster left for Paris and Geneva, they had, possibly through misunderstanding, repudiated what he had thought was a firm agreement for the ambassadors of nine countries to meet in Washington to discuss unified action. On April 19 Foster gave me his guess that the British insistence on calling off this meeting was possibly due to pressure from Nehru, who had very little sympathy with any efforts to assist the French.

In any event, the West started off for Geneva under a pall: the situation at Dien Bien Phu had degenerated rapidly during the month of April.

When Foster Dulles arrived in Paris to meet with Bidault prior to the opening of the conference, Bidault expressed the opinion, which Ely confirmed, that the situation in Dien Bien Phu had become virtually hopeless. Breakout was no solution, since it involved abandonment of wounded and equipment. As they had so often before, Bidault and Ely suggested that nothing could save the situation except, possibly, massive air intervention, which the United States would have to supply. Foster said that he understood that there were already more planes in Indochina than could be handled by crews and technicians. Ely denied that the situation regarding utilization of equipment was as bad as Foster seemed to think, while Bidault suggested an emergency consultation between Navarre and General O'Daniel on the spot. The emphasis he gave to the suggestion was clear indication that Navarre's reported aloofness in dealing with General O'Daniel was deliberate. Bidault implied that while he had in the past opposed internationalizing the war, he would now favor it if United States action would save Dien Bien Phu. He wrote off the matter of British participation, saying that their contribution would not amount to much anyway.

The next day the French command reported that Vietminh forces had driven a dangerous wedge into French defensive positions at Dien Bien Phu. Upon receiving Foster's message I could feel the distress under which he must have been operating because of the defeatist attitude of one of our best friends, the one that had the most to lose. Accordingly, I wrote him on the 23rd of April:

My first reaction upon reading your report on your initial conversation with Bidault is to assure you of my full understanding of the feeling of frustration that must consume you. I refer particularly to our earlier efforts to get French to ask for internationalization of the war, and to get the British to appreciate the seriousness of the situation at Dien Bien Phu and the probable result on the entire war of defeat at that place. There is little I can say now to help you . . . , but I am so confident of the unity of conviction you and I hold on these and related matters, that I do not even feel the need of assuring you again of my complete support. . . .

D.D.E.

The days before the opening of the Geneva Conference on April 26 were tense. On Friday afternoon, April 23, I had two messages from Foster. At 8 P.M.:

Please inform President and Radford urgently that Bidault received in the middle of afternoon council session copy of message from Navarre to Laniel which he gave me to read. He will talk to me further on subject at dinner tonight but, in brief, situation at Dien Bien Phu is desperate. Attempt to regain Huguette has claimed last reserves. Only alternatives Navarre sees are (1) operation Voutour which would be massive B-29 bombing (which I understand would be U. S. operation from U. S. bases outside Indochina) or (2) request for cease fire (which I assume would be at Dien Bien Phu and not throughout all Indochina).

I told Bidault B-29 intervention as proposed seemed to me out of question under existing circumstances but that I would report all this urgently to the President and that I would discuss it with Admiral Radford immediately upon latter's arrival in Paris tomorrow evening.

Bidault gives the impression of a man close to the breaking point. His mental condition at this morning's session was greatly improved over yesterday, but it has been painful to watch him presiding over the council at this afternoon's long session. He is obviously exhausted and is confused and rambling in his talk. Dulles

Another was timed 10 P.M.:

Please pass following message to the President; I am deeply touched by, and grateful for, your message. The situation here is tragic. . . . There is, of course, no military or logical reason why loss of Dien Bien Phu should lead to collapse of French will, in relation both to Indochina and EDC. It seems to me that Dien Bien Phu has become a symbol out of all proportion to its military importance. . . . Dulles

The fears I had expressed long ago concerning the wisdom of the French taking up a fortress position at Dien Bien Phu were turning out to be grimly accurate. When a French diplomat had told me of their plans at the time, I said, "You *cannot* do this!"

"This will bring the enemy into the open," he said. "We cannot find them in the jungle, and this will draw them out where we can then win."

"The French know military history," I said. "They are smart enough to know the outcome of becoming firmly emplaced and then beseiged in an exposed position with poor means of supply and reinforcements."

Never before had I been so sad to be so right.

That evening I telephoned Bedell Smith about the French request for direct intervention, and agreed that Foster's position should stand unchanged. There would be no intervention without allies.

In Paris, Foster decided to bring the British position into the clear. In a conference with Anthony Eden, Foster told him, unequivocally, that major combat action by United States forces in Indochina would need the consent of Congress, but that Congress would be more amenable if assured that Britain agreed to participate in unified action. Admiral Radford had convinced Eden in another meeting that day that the United States military chiefs took a gloomier view of the situation than the French had given the British most recently. That evening Eden flew back to London, for a Cabinet meeting on Sunday, April 25. The Churchill government decided, once and for all, that unified action must wait until all possibility of settlement by negotiation had been tried and failed. This ended for the time being our efforts to find any satisfactory method of Allied intervention. I was disappointed but such was my confidence in Prime Minister Churchill and the British government that I accepted their decision in the confidence that it was honestly made, and reflected their best judgment of what was best for Britain and, from their viewpoint, for the Free World.

Meanwhile, from the other side of the world, messages continued. General de Castries, the gallant commander of the garrison at Dien Bien Phu, had asked urgently for more reinforcements, but the over-all commander, General Navarre, refused to drop reinforcements on the basis that he would then have spent his entire reserve. There were other possibilities, yet the French did not seize them.[3]

Thus the Geneva Conference could not have begun or been conducted under worse conditions. On April 27 I wrote a memorandum for the files:

[3] General O'Daniel had outlined a plan for the relief of Dien Bien Phu involving forces available, which would make use of a parachute drop of three battalions, plus an attack from Hanoi to Dien Bien Phu by armored groups and mechanized infantry elements. Despite O'Daniel's confidence in his plan, he felt reluctant about submitting it directly to General Navarre in view of Navarre's sensitivities and O'Daniel's limited terms of reference as chief of the United States Military Advisory and Assistance Group (MAAG). Therefore he passed it on to our chargé d'affaires, Mr. McClintock, who spoke to the French Commissioner General, M. Maurice de Jean. The plan was considered but never attempted by the French high command.

Latest reports from Foster Dulles indicate that the British have taken a definite stand against any collective conversations looking toward the development of an anti-Communist coalition in Southeast Asia. Moreover, Eden has apparently gone into the Geneva Conference under strict instructions to press earnestly for a "cease fire" in Indochina.

I was informally told, at the time, that both Australia and New Zealand were ready to listen to any proposals the United States government might make to them for collective action for entering the Indochina war. This would have been a very difficult situation for us, for even though I believed the British government was not fully aware of the risks we and the Commonwealth were recognizing in that region, I would have been most unhappy to urge collective action with other members of the Commonwealth without sturdy Britain as a participant.

As a curtain began to come down on Dien Bien Phu and another was raised at Geneva, I wrote to General Gruenther at NATO, who had sent word of French gloom and shakiness:

Dear Al:

I am most appreciative of your letter.

As you know, you and I started more than three years ago trying to convince the French that they could *not* win the Indo-China war and particularly could not get real American support in that region unless they would unequivocally pledge independence to the Associated States upon the achievement of military victory. Along with this—indeed as a corollary to it—this Administration has been arguing that no Western power can go to Asia militarily, except as one of a concert of powers, which concert must include local Asiatic peoples.

To contemplate anything else is to lay ourselves open to the charge of imperialism and colonialism or—at the very least—of objectionable paternalism. Even, therefore, if we could by some sudden stroke assure the saving of Dien Bien Phu garrison, I think that under the conditions proposed by the French the free world would lose more than it would gain. . . . Consequently, we have had to stand by while the tactical situation has grown worse and worse. Now, unless there should be a sudden development of discouragement on the part of the enemy, it looks as if Dien Bien Phu could scarcely survive. . . .

In any event, I do believe as follows:

(a). That the loss of Dien Bien Phu does not necessarily mean the loss of the Indo-China war.

(b). The heroic exploits of the French garrison (which are all the more wonderful in view of the weak support they have had from Paris) should be glorified and extolled as indicative of the French character and determination.

(c). We should all (United States, France, Thailand, United Kingdom, Australia, New Zealand, et al) begin conferring at once on means of successfully stopping the Communist advances in Southeast Asia.

(d). The plan should include the use of the bulk of the French Army in Indo-China.

(e). The plan should assure freedom of political action to Indo-China promptly upon attainment of victory.

(f). Additional ground forces should come from Asiatic and European troops already in the region.

(g). The general security and peaceful purposes and aims of such a concert of nations should be announced publicly—as in NATO. Then we possibly wouldn't *have* to fight. . . .

DE

The Geneva Conference convened on April 26, but the first few days were devoted to a repetition at a higher level of the fruitless talks which had been going on at Panmunjom about a political settlement for Korea. More meaningful events occurred outside the conference room—in private meetings between diplomats at Geneva, in Washington and Paris, and in Indochina itself.

Indochina remained very much in the public mind in our country. In Washington at a news conference on April 29 I was asked what we would accept by way of a peace in Indochina. I pointed out that, under the conditions then existing, we would probably get not what we would like by way of settlement at Geneva but rather a modus vivendi, a pragmatic and workable rather than a desirable arrangement. There was no plausible reason for the United States to intervene; we could not even be sure that the Vietnamese population wanted us to do so. In response to another question, I said that the aid we had been giving the French was authorized by the terms of the mutual assistance pact.

Vice President Nixon had made a speech on April 16 which suggested the qualified possibility that we might one day have to send troops.[4] Naturally this was always a possibility; the question was under constant study. At my news conference the question was posed respecting a rider introduced in the House on an appropriations bill the day before, seeking to limit the President's authority to dispatch troops anywhere in the world without the consent of Congress. I replied that an appropriations bill was not the place to legislate Executive responsibility, and far beyond this in importance was that such an artificial restriction would damage the flexibility of the President in moving to sustain the interests of the United States wherever necessary. I would have vetoed the bill if presented and made this known. The rider failed of passage.

[4] In a talk before the American Society of Newspaper Editors, he said in a speech "not for attribution" and thereafter widely attributed, that ". . . if to avoid further Communist expansion in Asia and Indochina, we must take the risk now by putting our boys in, I think the Executive has to take the politically unpopular decision and do it."

That afternoon Acting Secretary of State Bedell Smith reported on be-hind-the-scenes movements in Paris and Geneva. Eden's position was that the British would support any peace agreement the French would make and would be willing to guarantee it; i.e., to put their weight behind its enforcement. They were not willing to enter into any regional defense agreement with non-Communist countries to safeguard Southeast Asia un-til *after* the Geneva Conference.

Bedell's report included the statement that Australia and New Zea-land had withdrawn from their original position favorable to united ac-tion. More encouraging was the news that the French had signed a new, preliminary agreement with the Associated States the day before in Paris, and that nearby Thailand was showing that they recognized the Com-munist danger to themselves by asking us to increase the level of our military assistance.

The French kept alive the possibility that we could solve some of our "constitutional problems" and launch a unilateral air strike—on their terms. They were said to be trying to prevent the fall of Dien Bien Phu for three weeks in this hope.

The situation at Dien Bien Phu, however, had now become impossible. The French defense area had shrunk to a perimeter fifteen hundred yards in diameter, making it extremely difficult to drop supplies to the garrison. The French force was down to 8500 effective infantrymen and 1200 ar-tillerymen—against a Vietminh force of 40,000. One relief column of 3000 native troops had made a feeble effort to rescue Dien Bien Phu, but obviously could not affect the battle.

We discussed once more the possibility of United States intervention by an air strike in Indochina. Although the three service chiefs—Army, Navy, Air Force—had recommended against this course, there was some merit in the argument that the psychological effect of an air strike would raise French and Vietnamese morale and improve, at least temporarily, the entire situation.

During the course of this meeting I remarked that if the United States were, unilaterally, to permit its forces to be drawn into conflict in Indo-china and in a succession of Asian wars, the end result would be to drain off our resources and to weaken our over-all defensive position. If we, without allies, should ever find ourselves fighting at various places all over the region, and if Red Chinese aggressive participation were clearly iden-tified, then we could scarcely avoid, I said, considering the necessity of striking directly at the head instead of the tail of the snake, Red China itself.

But in the meantime, the problem was to solve the current dilemma. Even without a mechanism for united action, we could still go on giving the French considerable material aid. Moreover, Bedell Smith at my direction was to go to Geneva the next afternoon and invite the ANZUS deputies to meet with him that evening. Bedell was not at all sure that merely because the British had turned down our invitation to join a regional grouping we should abandon the whole effort.

On the next day, April 30, Foster Dulles reported to me on a frank discussion with Anthony Eden. Foster had said bluntly that we were disappointed when, in the first week of the Geneva Conference, the Communists poured invective on the United States' "imperialistic actions," and the British delegation stood silently by. Then he said that he had come back to Washington from London with an understanding that both countries were agreed that he should start to set up conferences in Washington to discuss an alliance with the nations involved, and the British government had seen fit to repudiate this understanding without offering an alternative.

Foster went on to assure Eden, he reported, that no matter what the British might have inferred from strong statements by any of our officials (Admiral Radford had apparently alarmed the British and encouraged the French), the United States was not seeking large-scale intervention in Indochina or war with China.[5] We were earnestly trying to avoid any such developments—but they could best be avoided by a show of Western firmness. The conversation did much to clarify to the British government our concern about our common problems in the Far East.

Dien Bien Phu was now near the end. On May 1 the Vietminh launched their third major assault on the dwindling French Union forces, and by the next day they had captured three of the French strong points in fierce fighting. Two weeks earlier, I had sent the following message:

> In common with millions of my countrymen, I salute the gallantry and stamina of the commander and soldiers who are defending Dien Bien Phu. We have the most profound admiration for the brave and resourceful fight being waged there by troops from France, Vietnam, and other parts of the French Union. Those soldiers, true to their own great traditions, are defending the cause of human freedom and are demonstrating in the truest fashion qualities on which the survival of the Free World depends. I would be grateful if you would convey to the commander of the gallant garrison of Dien Bien Phu this expression of my admiration and best wishes.

Now, on May 6, under dramatic circumstances General de Castries, heroic to the end, replied:

[5] Statements by members of the State Department which seem to be at variance with statements by members of Defense can best be explained, perhaps, by their differing emphases. The United States policy is that we are for peace but that we are ready to fight for our rights and our liberty, if necessary. State voices this with an emphasis on "We are for peace" while Defense underscores "We are ready to fight."

I have been deeply moved by the expression of admiration of gratitude and of confidence that President Eisenhower was kind enough to send me on behalf of the American people. The Free World may be assured that the defenders of Dien Bien Phu, whatever their origin, conscious of the importance of the fight they are waging, are determined to do everything in their power to continue to deserve this confidence and to fulfill right to the end the mission which has been entrusted to them.

That day it was reported that two additional positions had been lost since the last report. A river which ran through the French position was flooding, cutting the position in half. Four thousand effective troops were left and only 450 additional men had been dropped in since April 25. On May 7 the fortress fell, the final position having been reduced to a size no larger than a baseball field.

Though we could see the end coming, the final capitulation of the garrison of Dien Bien Phu was saddening.

Military history has many examples of small, fiercely courageous bands holding out against overwhelming odds. The exploits of the defenders of the pass at Thermopylae, the garrison of the Alamo, the Light Brigade, the Filipinos and Americans on Bataan, and the outposts of Korea are all actions in which soldierly performance has commanded the veneration of both soldiers and civilians. The conduct of the defenders of Dien Bien Phu ranked with the best of them.

Yet as men die, the world is often unaware of their sacrifice. The claims for our attention are many. Other struggles are lost or won at the same time. On the day of the fall of Dien Bien Phu, the front page of one metropolitan paper did not mention it.[6] A column on that page covers the maneuverings at Geneva—maneuverings which were to be sharply altered or rendered meaningless by the news of the surrender. Another story reports that the Democrats, led by former President Truman and Senator Lyndon B. Johnson, had launched an attack on our foreign policy. They put the administration on notice, the story said, that the bipartisanship of the last sixteen months was breaking up. Other articles on that day reported that United States participation in the St. Lawrence Seaway was approved by the House (241 to 158), and that the four-minute mile was run for the first time by Roger Bannister in England.

But the lead article—the banner headline—pertains to none of these, not the fall of a French fortress or the Geneva Conference, not the Democrats on foreign policy or the St. Lawrence Seaway. Instead it covers Senator McCarthy's demand for a test of the Executive's right to bar secret data to congressional investigators.

[6] The final word of its surrender had not arrived in time for print.

It is instructive now, when emotions are quiet and time has passed, to ask how much lasting significance each of these events has had. The battle in Indochina still goes on, though with a difference. The St. Lawrence Seaway, now completed, provides an invaluable service to the entire North American continent and world shippers from all points. The right of the Executive to decide to withhold information in the interest of national security has been challenged but is still upheld and practiced. The four-minute mile has been broken many times, and Senator McCarthy ceased to command public attention shortly after that day in history.

On the 8th of May the French government submitted to the Geneva Conference a proposal for ending the hostilities in Indochina. Essentially, these proposals treated the problem in two parts: (1) that of Laos and Cambodia, where the Vietminh had committed aggression from without, and (2) that of Vietnam, where the situation was officially recognized as being primarily internal.

For Cambodia the proposal was simple. There should be evacuation of all regular and irregular forces of the aggressor Vietminh and disarmament of related military elements not belonging to the Army or law-enforcement agencies.

In Vietnam, on the other hand, the French proposed military groupings in delimited zones—which means that all Red formations would move north of one established line, all those loyal to the French Union would pull south of that parallel. All combatants except the police forces were to be disarmed, prisoners of war were to be freed and, as in the Cambodian proposal, control was to be vested in an international commission.

To me these French proposals presented two major difficulties. First, the grouping of the regular military units of both parties in delimited zones implied nothing else but partition. We knew, from experience in Korea, that this would probably lead to Communist enslavement of millions in the northern partitioned area. In addition, the proposals for a cessation of hostilities immediately upon signing of an armistice failed to specify whether the control measures for enforcement were to be made effective *before* the cease fire. I had long ago learned that no agreement with Communists is worth the paper it is written on unless it contains its own self-enforcing procedures.

Our direct interest in these negotiations arose out of the assumption that the United States would be expected to act as one of the guarantors of whatever agreement should be achieved.

I approved instructions to the United States delegation that the United States would not associate itself with any proposal from any source for a cease fire which would take effect *in advance of an acceptable armistice agreement,* including international mechanisms for enforcement.[7] We would, however, "concur in initiation of negotiations" for the armistice itself. In the meantime, we would encourage the French Union forces to continue the fight in Indochina while the conference progressed, would provide more aid, and would go on with our efforts "to organize and promptly activate a Southeast Asia regional grouping. . . ." The negotiations were long and tedious, and every day the military situation worsened in Vietnam. Indeed, the Communists now began to prolong and stall the conference, obviously taking advantage of the overwhelming military initiative they enjoyed in the Red River Delta. The longer they could stall, the more nervous the French would become—and Indochina, particularly the delta, would go farther down the drain. No longer was anyone complacently decrying the capabilities of the Vietminh to redeploy and to move supplies. We knew that the Red River Delta was in immediate danger, even though at that moment the French Union forces there were estimated to number 192,000 against 76,000 regular Vietminh. With five hundred additional trucks, Allen Dulles estimated that the Vietminh would be able to effect an operation against the delta in two or three weeks. The French forces were of necessity enclosed in fixed strong points with little mobility, affording the more mobile rebels the ability to concentrate overwhelming force at almost any point they chose. Again, the problem involved local public opinion. The enemy had much popular sympathy, and many civilians aided them by providing both shelter and information. The French still had sufficient forces to win if they could induce the regular Vietnamese soldiers to fight vigorously with them and the populace to support them. But guerrilla warfare cannot work two ways; normally only one side can enjoy reliable citizen help.

Now we were feeling the full impact of the earlier refusal to undertake any united action until after the Geneva Conference. The Communists realized that if they could draw out the conference, they need fear little by way of any intervention by outside powers.

Even if others were reluctant to act, we could not afford to sit on the side lines and do nothing. I felt that a prompt French decision to abandon their claim to exclusive direction of the fighting against Communism in the area should come soon, and that they should seek instead a coalition of power to carry the burden. However, Foster and I thought it best to defer pressuring the Laniel government into immediate decision, primarily because we believed that the impact of Dien Bien Phu had not had time to register fully on the French mind. When the French came to realize the

---

[7] The Vietminh actually did submit a proposal which appeared conciliatory at first glance, but which specified that the conciliatory measures were to take place only after an uncontrolled cease fire. This proposal was lost in a new outburst of vituperation.

alternatives they faced—either internationalization of the conflict or virtually abject surrender—a satisfactory outcome could be expected. But to urge this immediately might cause the Laniel government to reject it outright, thereby leaving only the second alternative. Therefore, we decided to inform Ambassador Dillon in Paris of the preconditions under which I *might* ask Congress for authority to use armed forces of the United States. This would give Dillon the chance to discuss them with Laniel informally, with Dillon to tell us if he thought the time was not right.

Although the French government was aware of the bulk of these conditions, we felt it necessary to spell them out again: that the United States military participation be formally requested by France and the three Associated States, that the ANZUS powers be invited to help also.[8] We insisted that the United Nations be brought in to form a peace-observation commission; that France guarantee complete independence to the Associated States, including an "unqualified option to withdraw from the French Union at any time"; that France keep its forces in action, with the United States assistance—"principally air and sea"—as supplements, not substitutes; and that agreement be reached on our participation in training native troops and working out a command structure for united action. Further, we would require that all these decisions not only be accepted by the French Cabinet (in view of its shaky nature), but also be authorized or endorsed by the French National Assembly.

As Foster and I talked these conditions over, we were concerned by two possibilities. One was our Intelligence community's estimates that intervention by the United States would have a fifty-fifty chance of bringing on the Chinese Communists in force. This, of course, is the type of danger that sometimes must be faced, and we were prepared, if necessary, to meet it. The other was the implication of going into Indochina without British cooperation, even though New Zealand and Australia might participate. Such action would inevitably tend to weaken our normally close and highly valued relationship with the British.

In accordance with his instructions, Dillon went to see Laniel. Maurice Schumann, the Foreign Minister, was also present. Most of the points we had made they understood completely. The matter that gave them the most concern seemed strange in the light of the promises of independence made in the past. Laniel and Schumann apparently could not tolerate the idea that the French should accord to the Associated States the right of withdrawal from the French Union. Naturally, both France and the individual states wanted to retain a loose association in a French Union.

[8] With the understanding that Thailand and the Philippines would accept at once, Australia and New Zealand would probably accept following the Australian elections, and the United Kingdom would "either participate or be acquiescent."

Not all the important ties between nations show on a map; their economies are based on a single currency, convenient trading possibilities are
open, the smaller countries can more easily seek foreign aid from the old
"mother" country. But the French could not see how a statement giving
the Associated States the *right* to withdraw from the Union if they should
later decide to do so was an important right—in fact, one which would
make the promise of independence genuine.

In the course of the discussion Dillon concluded that the French were
not looking forward to substantial involvement of United States ground
troops in Indochina, but would like a token force of perhaps one Marine
division so that our participation would not be limited to strictly naval
and air forces.

Several days later Schumann notified Dillon that the French had found
another concern in our desire that the French keep their forces completely intact for the entire period of united action. He pointed out that
such action might last a number of years, and the Navarre Plan had always contemplated reduction of French forces on a gradual basis. He
said that approval of the European Defense Community, another major
matter then being considered, could not be secured if the French would
have to keep full forces indefinitely in Indochina. The viewpoint of gradual reduction of French forces was reasonable. But I was never happy
at subtle references tying the fate of EDC to our willingness to do things
in Indochina as the French government desired.

On the matter of the United States assuming the burden of training
the Vietnamese forces in Indochina we had little difficulty. "Iron Mike"
O'Daniel, despite his nickname and his tough exterior, was a man of
great ability and tact. His discussions with General Navarre on the subject went well.[9]

In one conversation Bidault said to Bedell Smith, possibly with justification, that Navarre should be replaced; in view of the French superiority
in men and weapons something was obviously wrong when the French
suffered defeat after defeat. Bedell gave a straightforward answer: he
told Bidault that any second-rate general should be able to win in Indochina if there were a proper political atmosphere.

There were a few encouraging signs. The French Cabinet decided on
May 29 to request the National Assembly's approval to send conscripts
to Indochina, a decision long overdue. Encouraging, too, was the fact that
the rainy season, which would hamper operations, was due soon.

[9] One of the seemingly slight but actually significant steps agreed upon among the
military staffs at the time was that Vietnamese units would be organized on a
divisional basis, thus giving them equal status with foreign units, rather than being
restricted to *groupes* or battalions as had been their lot in the past.

On the command condition, French Chief of Staff Ely, after surveying the situation in Indochina, briefed Major General Thomas B. Trapnell[10] in Paris. Five Vietminh divisions released from Dien Bien Phu were on the move in the Red River Delta. Ely was adamant on command responsibilities—with justification under the circumstances—because at the moment there could be no question of the United States sharing responsibilities for operational planning. On the other hand, if a satisfactory arrangement was made for United States intervention, General Ely agreed that our officers might be integrated into French planning staffs. Ely may have felt that one or two divisions of United States ground troops would be sufficient to prove good faith but not large enough to create any threat to the French right of over-all command.

On May 28 Secretary Dulles, Deputy Secretary of Defense Anderson, Admiral Radford, and General Cutler came to my office. One of the renewed questions was that of United States response to overt military aggression by Communist China or forces directed by them. The Joint Chiefs of Staff agreed that we should not in such a circumstance rely upon a static type of defense as in Korea, but rather upon an offensive against Communist China—not, however, necessarily going to the industrial sources of Chinese power or destroying cities, but striking areas and facilities supporting a Chinese offensive, airfields, communications lines, and bases. Another feasible project might be to mount an amphibious attack against an island position on the Chinese coast, such as Hainan. This would serve to divert Chinese attention and hit them where it would hurt by threatening Chinese lines of communication and by creating another Formosa-like position opposite the South China mainland. I approved of this kind of contingency planning, although I did not believe overt Chinese Communist aggression was likely.

The French continued to regard overt aggression with Communist MIG airplanes as a contingency completely separate from any other in which the United States might be asked to intervene. In fact, General Ely told General Trapnell that Admiral Radford had previously assured the French that United States aircraft would intervene in this eventuality. Ely later admitted this was an understanding between Chiefs of Staff only, and that he knew it was subject to veto at political echelons. Ely, however, was pressing for a positive answer on automatic United States response so that he could plan on this support.

The French were obviously contemplating a possible withdrawal from the Red River Delta under fire, in which they feared they could be virtually massacred by Chinese air attacks. One of their estimates was

[10] Major General Thomas B. Trapnell had been sent to Paris to confer with Ely. He had considerable prior experience in Vietnam.

that a massive Chinese attack by 120 planes could knock out French air capabilities in the delta and so seriously damage Haiphong that it would be impossible for the French to withdraw. They expressed once again the old threat that if the French Expeditionary Force were to be seriously defeated because the United States had not come to their rescue, then a movement would be strong in France in favor of making peace at any price with the Communists rather than continuing to count on United States support through NATO.

While there was misunderstanding between us and the French, I determined to make certain that none should exist among members of the administration. Therefore, I took the opportunity at a meeting on June 3 to clarify my attitude. If the United States should, by itself, and without the clear invitation of the Vietnamese people and satisfactory arrangements with the French, undertake to counter Chinese Communist aggression, I said, this would, of course, mark the collapse of the American policy of united action. Moreover, if the nations of the Southeast Asian area showed a complete indifference to the fate of Indochina, it would be the signal for us to undertake a reappraisal of basic United States security policy. I was convinced that it was in our interest to commit United States armed forces in the event of overt Chinese aggression, but I was determined that Southeast Asian nations could not disclaim responsibility for their own safety, expecting the United States alone to carry all the burdens of Free World security. If I should find it necessary to go to the Congress for authority to intervene in Indochina, I wanted to say that we had allies such as Thailand, Australia, New Zealand, the Philippines, and above all, the bulk of the Vietnamese people, ready to join with us in resisting such aggression.

In spite of the warnings our government had issued to the Chinese Communists and which Secretary Dulles had given to Molotov privately, I could not see why we would be compelled to tell the French or any other ally, in advance, in what manner we would respond to Chinese Communist intervention, unless these same allies were prepared to join and cooperate with us effectively on a partnership basis, should this contingency arise.

Misunderstandings of the problem were evident everywhere. People seemed to assume that the United States was carrying primary responsibility for defense of Indochina, as we had in Korea. Secretary Dulles was asked in a news conference in early June how long the United States and other free nations could continue to sit at Geneva in a sincere effort to negotiate while the Communists dragged their feet and intensified the war in Indochina. Foster pointed out once more that primary responsibility lay with the countries carrying the principal burden of the fighting, namely France and the Associated States, and that we recognized their primacy in the matter. The length of the Western powers' stay at Geneva would be decided by the French.

In the meantime, evidence piled up that the French government grew, daily, more discouraged.

On June 8 I received a letter from General Gruenther in which he described a meeting he had just had with René Pleven, the French Minister of Defense. Pleven, one of France's finest statesmen, a fighter of Communism and a friend of the United States, was like many of his countrymen an excitable person. It was in such an emotional state that General Gruenther had found him.

> . . . Yesterday Pleven asked me to come and see him to discuss certain matters in connection with the 3 new divisions the French are about to activate to send to Indo-China—(Maybe!). We handled our business satisfactorily which dealt with the kind of letter he should send me telling about the stripping which would take place in the French NATO divisions. . . .
>
> . . . He is very very much discouraged—and he sees no hope except some kind of cease fire solution—very vague in nature.
>
> At one stage he said: "If we should lose the delta area it would be a catastrophe for France and a great set back for the whole Free World. It would start a wave of anti-allied outbursts in France with great bitterness because the Allies let us down. The British would bear the brunt of this attack because the French people feel that the British are blocking united action. But it would be more than anti-British. It would really develop into an anti-NATO campaign with a strong 'let's go it alone' type of hysteria. . . . The American Government must realize how serious it would be if we suffered a serious defeat in the Delta. Everything the U. S. stands for in Europe would be endangered."

My reply to Gruenther contained these pertinent paragraphs:

> I was struck by a sentence in your letter in which you quote Pleven as saying, "It (the loss of the Delta) would start a wave of anti-allied outbursts in France with great bitterness because the Allies let us down."
>
> Pleven knows as well as you and I do that, beginning in early 1951, every kind of presentation has been made to the French Government to induce that government to put the Indo-China war on an international footing. . . . We urged further that France not only declare her intention of making Indo-China independent and that she was fighting for the right of Indo-China to be independent—but that she should take steps to place the issue before the U. N. At the very least, this latter action would have had the effect of legitimizing any kind of coalition that might then have been formed to fight the war.
>
> As the conflict has dragged on, the United States has more than once

offered help of a kind that would tend to keep our participation in the background, but could nevertheless be very effective. I refer to our efforts to get a good guerrilla organization started in the region, our offer to take over a great part of the burden of training native troops, and numerous offers of help in the logistic field.

Most of these have been rebuffed. . . .

In recent months, the French government has begun to speak out of the other side of its mouth, and has been demanding help of various kinds. But it is noteworthy that all these requests for help have been for help on France's own terms—her government has consistently insisted upon promises from us of certain kinds of technical help which we would presumably turn over to them without question to be used by them as they saw fit.

Yet at the same time, they have made no single effort to meet the conditions that we have insisted upon for three years as constituting the only sound basis on which any European government could be fighting in South East Asia. . . .

. . . Take, for example, the fact that while the United States was sending conscripted soldiers to Korea to fight a war in which we as a nation never had any of our political or economic interests involved, the French refused to send conscripts to Indo-China, which had been for years merely one of their colonies. . . .

During this period I often expressed a thought in conversation with Secretary Dulles. "France ought to recall General de Gaulle," I said.

On May 5 we had received a message from Bedell Smith at Geneva outlining a proposal by Anthony Eden that the United Kingdom take part at once with the United States, France, Australia, and New Zealand, in an examination of the Indochina-Southeast Asia situation by a "Five Power Staff Agency," located in Singapore. This represented a considerable advance in the British position: it visualized including Indochina in British planning and for the first time showed their willingness to try to do something before the end of the Geneva Conference. The proposal had the drawback that it was confined to "white" nations. Accordingly, I said that any reply to Eden (along with my acceptance of his proposal) should make clear that a Five Power Staff Agency along with other nations was not to the United States a fully satisfactory substitute for a broad political coalition of Southeast Asian countries in a cooperative defense effort. It would, of course, take time to develop such a comprehensive international organization.

Obviously a change was taking place. A meeting of the same five powers was set up to convene in Washington in early June. This, and discussions by the military representatives in Washington, helped to make the world aware that the Geneva Conference could not be used as a vehicle for handcuffing the Western world into inaction in Indochina.

On June 3 the French government assigned General Ely to the dual post of French Commissioner General in Indochina and **Commander-in-Chief** of French Union forces in that area. He was a man in whom the French government had great trust and who was known by all of us to be in favor of a strong stand in defense of the Red River Delta. He was taking over a disintegrating situation. On the day of Ely's appointment General Valluy, French representative on the five-power military talks in Washington, said that the French expected an all-out Vietminh attack on the Red River Delta within the next ten days. Valluy was not optimistic about withstanding such an attack, since morale was low and the French Expeditionary Force was tired. Despite the fact that French Union forces included seventy-nine battalions and eleven *groupes mobiles* available for defense of the delta, which should be highly useful in this open terrain, General Valluy was convinced that the Vietminh would try to capture Hanoi, by negotiation or by force.

In early June the Vietminh made major attacks on the Hanoi-Haiphong rail line. The victorious troops from Dien Bien Phu were now fairly well redeployed, and while they were not yet prepared to make massive attacks on the delta, our attaché expected such attacks soon.

As the days wore on, with Communist stalling at Geneva, and more intense fighting in Indochina, certain issues began to be clarified. By this time it was generally accepted that partition would occur in Vietnam and possibly even in the other Associated States.

At the maximum the French hoped to retain a permanent enclave in the Red River Delta consisting of both Haiphong and Hanoi; as a minimum they had to retain the port of Haiphong for a period of time in order to evacuate the French Expeditionary Force and such civilians as had sided openly with the French.

In a June 9 talk with Anthony Eden, General Smith became convinced that the British were running out of patience with the negotiations and might now be prepared to resume talks on unified action, deferred since April. However, the French had still taken no position on our preconditions for intervention.

In these circumstances Eden proposed to see Molotov once more and then break from the conference, meanwhile recommending that Laos and Cambodia put their case before the United Nations. These tactics recommended themselves strongly to us.

The next day I sent Bedell a message which said that if France should insist on continuing negotiations in spite of their obvious futility, our best move would be to reduce our delegation in stature rather than completely withdraw it. Bedell Smith would return to Washington, leaving a diplomat of lesser rank in charge and suggesting the United Kingdom do the same.

But now events overtook us. There had been hope that Molotov in a speech he was scheduled to make on June 8 would modify his earlier use of nothing but invective and vituperation. Instead, he launched into a renewed tirade against the United States. That evening Bidault dejectedly left for Paris.

On the 12th of June the Laniel government failed to gain a vote of confidence in the French Assembly by a vote of 306 to 293. France was without a leader and without a government.

We decided that it was best for the United States to break off major participation in the Geneva Conference. The days of keeping the Western powers bound to inaction by creating divisions of policy among them in a dragged-out conference were coming to an end.

On the 18th of June, Pierre Mendès-France took office as Premier of France on the strength of the pledge that he would secure a peace in Indochina by July 20. M. Mendès-France, a member of the Radical-Socialist party, came in riding a vote of confidence of 419 to 47. He assumed the position of Foreign Minister as well as of Premier.

The next day Bedell flew to Paris for a meeting with Mendès-France. The new Premier said it was now essential to make every effort to end the war promptly. This, he hoped, would revive the ancient spirit of France and put an end to the differences that divided the French people. At the same time, Mendès-France asserted that he would not accept a peace in Indochina that was a surrender to the Vietminh, even a disguised one. He informed Bedell of his plans, which included the possibility of meeting with Chou En-lai, even though this might have an unfavorable impact on American public opinion.

Mendès-France had only one request: that we use our influence with the Vietnamese Premier, Ngo Dinh Diem—newly appointed by Bao Dai —to prevent him from needlessly obstructing any honorable truce which the French might reach with the Vietminh.

From Paris, Bedell came back to Washington where, on the 23rd of June, he gave a full report on Geneva to a group of Legislative leaders of both parties. Bedell's entire performance at the Geneva Conference, his last mission in government service,[11] was a magnificent one indeed. In the middle of the negotiations I had felt impelled to send him the following message:

> I have been keeping track of your Geneva activities as well as I can. As always when you are engaged in a difficult job I am lost in admiration of your patience, ability and skill. I do hope that your physical health is standing up also.
>
> *With warm regard,*
>
> DE

[11] Bedell Smith resigned as Under Secretary of State on October 1, 1954. He was replaced by Mr. Herbert Hoover, Jr.

Though suffering from ill health, he retained the respect and admiration of his colleagues and a steel-trap grasp of the talks at all times. His tact and understanding were remarkable to those who had known him only through his reputation in the Army as a tough and rigid taskmaster.

I have often thought, when uninformed or unthinking people refer to the "narrowness of the military mind," of the accomplishments of a man like General Walter Bedell Smith, who after having served as my wartime Chief of Staff, went on to turn in outstanding performances as ambassador to Moscow, chief of the Central Intelligence Agency, and Under Secretary of State, representing the United States in some of the most difficult negotiations imaginable. The fact that he was Foster Dulles' personal selection to be his Under Secretary has always been a source of my increased pride in his accomplishments.

This was one of the few instances in which I tried to influence a Cabinet officer in the choice of a subordinate. When the Secretary of State had first proposed him, I said:

"Look, Foster, you and I have said we are going to dedicate ourselves to the idea of peace with justice. Now we're going to bring into the effort another military man. With military men immediately above and below you, the world will think we are setting about to establish a *pax romana.*"

Foster smiled and said that he would worry about that later. "Bedell's a man with a wonderful sense of organization, a bear for work, and a driver. I want him."

"Then if you want him," I said, secretly pleased, "you have him."

By mid-June our major foreign preoccupation was preparing for a meeting in Washington with Prime Minister Churchill. We had put the meeting off on a couple of occasions, the last time to allow Anthony Eden to stay a while longer at the Geneva Conference. Now, with Winston and Eden coming to Washington, we could talk out any Anglo-American differences face-to-face. I had written to Winston earlier asking his opinion of the elevation of Mendès-France and the pledges the new Premier had made. I also asked for his ideas regarding the solution of the resulting problems.

The answer was a remarkable statement of his thoughts on the whole sweep of foreign affairs of the moment. He said that if the French had intended to fight for their empire in Indochina, they should have insisted on two years' military service, which would have made it possible for them to have used their military power as a nation. Instead, they had fought on for eight years with untrustworthy local troops, with French elements needed in the structure of their home army, and with the Foreign Legion which, he wrote darkly, was full of Germans. He said he felt that as a result Mendès-France had decided to get out on the best terms he could secure, and Churchill was inclined to agree that Mendès-France was right.

Churchill said that under the circumstances he thought there was all the more reason for discussing ways of keeping Communism from establishing a firm base in the Pacific area. He recommended a SEATO (Southeast Asia Treaty Organization), corresponding to NATO, and felt that the Asian countries' support was paramount. I was delighted with this particular reaction to our earlier suggestion.

For Indochina, he was definite in his recommendation against the use of either British or United States troops, except as a "rescue" operation.

He further said that a SEATO front should be considered in its entirety, in relation to the world front against Communist aggression. Since sectors of the SEATO front were so varied in place and conditions, he felt it best to operate nationally, where possible. The British main sector would have to be Malaya, where they had twenty-three battalions.

Winston was encouraging on the related matters of reinforcements and Suez. By now he had concluded that thermonuclear warfare had made the Suez Base less necessary and that forty thousand fighting troops (of the eighty thousand total garrison still stationed there) could be made available for defense of the Far East. He mentioned other matters on his mind, such as the possibility of our sharing information and possibly resources of thermonuclear devices, the prospects of a possible failure of EDC in Europe, and above all his hope of convincing Russia that there was a better way to a better life than living in an armed camp.

It was a long, useful communication.

We met in Washington on the 25th of June in an atmosphere of furor brought about by exaggeration in the press of Anglo-American differences. Churchill himself, however, put the matter in perspective in his arrival statement when he said: "I have come . . . to talk over a few family matters and to make sure there are no misunderstandings."

Over the course of the weekend we were afforded many opportunities for both informal and official conversation. While it is impossible in the course of a few days' discussions entirely to reconcile differing national viewpoints, the talks were productive. Most significant was the formation of a seven-point joint position between our two nations as to what we would find acceptable in any settlement the French might make with the Indochinese. In essence we agreed that Laos and Cambodia would have to be left as free and independent states, able to maintain their integrity. If partition of Vietnam were to become a fact, approximately half of that country must remain non-Communist, south of the 18th Parallel. On one aspect only did our viewpoints differ. Churchill and Eden merely wished to state a "hope" that the French would settle for nothing less than our "seven points"; we wanted these as minimal. Our agreements were transmitted forthwith to our delegations at Geneva and to the French government.

Meanwhile, Premier Mendès-France had been moving in high gear. After his meeting with Bedell Smith he began negotiations with Chou En-lai, in Bern, Switzerland on the 23rd of June. The attitude of Chou En-lai, as reported to me later, was relatively conciliatory. For example, he recognized the existence of the state of Vietnam, which he had not done before, and accepted for the first time the French thesis that the settlement of the fighting in Indochina should be made in two phases; first a military cease fire, and second a political settlement. He professed a desire to see the two states become unified by direct negotiations at a later time and gave no objection to Mendès-France's assertion that general elections could not be held in the near future. Finally, he promised to speak to the Vietminh and ask them to speed up negotiations at Geneva.

Mendès-France said publicly that his conversation gave reason for hope that the Geneva Conference might produce happy results. The problems of Laos and Cambodia, he suggested, had been surmounted; the present governments would be recognized and all foreign troops would pull out. That day the National Assembly gave him a new and larger vote of confidence—433 to 23.

The military situation in the Red River Delta, however, worsened, and the French outlook seemed to become increasingly desolate. By the first week of July their high command announced the completion of the evacuation of fifteen thousand troops and fifty thousand civilians from the southern part of the Red River Delta, and evacuated a key communications center thirty-five miles south of Hanoi. On the 4th of July representatives of the French Union and the Vietminh high command began technical talks at Trunggia, Vietnam, relating to an Indochina armistice.

Mendès-France now asked that either Secretary Dulles or Under Secretary Smith return to Geneva to head the American delegation, previously downgraded to an "observer" mission.

On July 10 I asked Foster to draft a message to Mendès-France, explaining our reasons for preferring to avoid full diplomatic participation in a conference the results of which we could not approve. He was to send a copy to Eden, and await the results. If the British and French replied in a clear and firm manner so that we could go along with their positions, then I said either Foster or Bedell should go back. Foster drafted the memo, read it to me about 6:30 P.M., and it was dispatched that night.

Working at long distance was to no avail. On Monday morning, July 12, Foster was in my office first thing with a request from Mendès-France that he fly to Paris for a conference. I immediately called Defense Secretary Wilson and asked him to have a Constellation available at a moment's notice to take Foster to Europe, probably the same evening.

Actually, Mendès-France preferred that the two meet in Geneva, but Foster and I informed him that this would not be acceptable. In spite of this slight difference, word from Mendès-France was that he was very pleased and would dine with the Secretary the next evening in Paris.

I called Bedell and warned him that, dependent on the outcome of the talk between Foster and Mendès-France, he might have to go back to Geneva, perhaps Thursday or Friday night. I realized that Bedell was again in ill health, but our friends attached so much importance to "ministerial rank" that it was almost essential that he go. Bedell said in typical fashion that the only thing wrong was a touch of lumbago, which seemed to be clearing up nicely, and he thought he could leave as early as Tuesday night. He declined my offer to send a doctor with him for the duration of his trip.

In the course of the meetings in Paris between the 13th and 15th, in which Anthony Eden participated, Foster reported Mendès-France's statement that the Vietminh had apparently agreed to withdraw their forces from Laos and Cambodia and to recognize the control of the legal governments there. Furthermore, the discussion over the partition line between Vietminh territory and that of South Vietnam, while not settled, seemed to be proceeding favorably. Foster succeeded in obtaining agreement to a position paper which was essentially the same as that agreed between the United Kingdom and the United States at the time of the Churchill visit.

After the conference Foster called from Paris and said that French and British attitudes seemed to be firm enough. I agreed that Bedell should go back to Geneva at the end of the week.

When the Secretary of State returned home, on Thursday, July 15, Mendès-France had only until the next Tuesday to obtain his promised truce or resign as Premier.

On the morning of the deadline, July 20, Secretary Dulles, now in Washington, called to report on cables received from Geneva. The Russians were pressing for a conference resolution and for us to join in adopting all the provisos. We, of course, were refusing to participate in the resolution but were authorizing Bedell to make a declaration which would note the conference decisions and state that we would not use force to disturb them. Foster reported that complete autonomy would be given to Laos and Cambodia and there was a provision for future elections which would give the French nearly two years to get ready for them. Membership of the supervisory committee for a truce would consist of Poland, India, and Canada. Their findings would have to be unanimous. The demarkation line also allowed the French the last remaining road between South Vietnam and Laos.

The next day the declaration was signed, ending the seven-and-a-half-year war in Indochina.

It provided for international controls. Cambodia and Laos were to adopt measures permitting all citizens (including the Communist Pathet Lao forces in Laos) to take their place in the community, with local elections to take place in 1955. The settlement in Vietnam was recognized as a military—not a political or territorial—one. General elections in Vietnam, Laos, and Cambodia were to be held in July 1956, supervised by an international commission. There were to be no reprisals against people who had collaborated with any one of the parties during the war. French troops were to be withdrawn when the three governments of the Associated States requested it.

In my news conference that day, July 21, I tried to put our conclusions in focus. I expressed my satisfaction, of course, that the bloodshed was over. The United States had not been a belligerent in the war and the primary responsibility for the settlement in Indochina had rested with the nations participating in the fighting. Though we had tried to be helpful, we were not a party to or bound by the decisions taken at the conference, but hoped they would lead to establishment of peace. The agreement did contain features, I admitted, that we did not like, but a great deal would depend on how these features worked out in practice. "The United States is issuing at Geneva a statement to the effect that it is not prepared to join in the conference declaration," I said, "but . . . in compliance with the obligations and principles contained in Article II of the United Nations Charter, the United States will not use force to disturb the settlement. We also say that any renewal of Communist aggression would be viewed by us as a matter of grave concern." The United States would actively pursue discussions with other free nations to establish an organization of collective defense of Southeast Asia to prevent further Communist aggression.

On July 23 the French National Assembly, anxious to seal the end of the fighting, approved the conclusion of the armistice in Indochina by the overwhelming vote of 462 to 13.

Nonetheless, there was an element of tragedy in an agreement that put great numbers of people under Communist domination.

The United States Navy was able, during August and September, 1954, to assist in evacuating 250,000 refugees from the northern, Communist-held sections. The flight of the unfortunate is always a striking fact when the Communists take over.

On August 17 I directed that aid to Indochina henceforth be given directly to the Associated States rather than through France.

Reviewing the entire episode in retrospect, I find that four questions merit consideration:

(1) Why, with the superiority in manpower and resources available, were the French unable to win?

(2) Why was the very considerable amount of material American aid not more effective in helping the French?

(3) Why, when the French were in difficulty and the interests of the Free World affected, at least indirectly, were the successive French governments unwilling to take logical and reasonable steps to bring United States' and other support to their assistance?

(4) What lessons or benefits, if any, accrued to the Free World as a result?

I am convinced that the French could not win the war because the internal political situation in Vietnam, weak and confused, badly weakened their military position. I have never talked or corresponded with a person knowledgeable in Indochinese affairs who did not agree that had elections been held as of the time of the fighting, possibly 80 per cent of the population would have voted for the Communist Ho Chi Minh as their leader rather than Chief of State Bao Dai. Indeed, the lack of leadership and drive on the part of Bao Dai was a factor in the feeling prevalent among Vietnamese that they had nothing to fight for. As one Frenchman said to me, "What Vietnam needs is another Syngman Rhee, regardless of all the difficulties the presence of such a personality would entail."

In the earlier stages of the conflict, the fighting was mostly conducted where rough terrain made it impossible to seek out the enemy and bring him to a pitched battle. Later, even when the battle lines became so located that the *groupes mobiles* could be effective, there still existed within the Red River Delta a condition in which the French could control even the main roads for only about two or three hours a day. The rest of the time all lines of communication were in the hands of the Vietminh. This meant that the mass of the population supported the enemy. With such a feeling prevalent, it was inevitable that the French should find it impossible to retain the loyalty of their Vietnamese troops.

In addition to the miserable political situation, the French military activities were puzzling. Most perplexing was taking up the position at Dien Bien Phu. True, the position was strong enough to inflict heavy Vietminh casualties; but in the long run, giving up mobility in favor of occupying an inaccessible static position, dominated by high ground surrounding, was certainly not normal practice.

Had the French been able to establish political and military cooperation with the Vietnamese, the Navarre Plan probably would have worked. Unfortunately, this did not occur. In a press conference held by General

Navarre shortly after the fall of Dien Bien Phu, he reportedly stated that one of the difficulties in the defense of that bastion had been inability of Asiatics to withstand artillery fire. A Vietnamese reporter asked General Navarre how it was that the Vietminh themselves, who were Asiatics, had been so successful in learning how to stand up under French artillery fire. At that point the Asiatic reporters in the meeting got up and left.

With this unsound relationship between the Asiatics and the French, it is not difficult to answer the second question: American aid could not cure the defect in the French-Vietnamese relationship and therefore was of only limited value. The decision to give this aid was almost compulsory. The United States had no real alternative unless we were to abandon Southeast Asia.

We will never know, of course, how much United States aid did to forestall a military disaster worse than the one which actually did occur. The French might have been pushed from the Red River Delta into the sea, with the loss of additional thousands of lives, and the rapid spread of Communism in the region. Willingness to fight for freedom, no matter where the battle may be, has always been a characteristic of our people, but the conditions then prevailing in Indochina were such as to make unilateral American intervention nothing less than sheer folly.

Had the circumstances lent themselves to a logical use of military force, the task of explaining to the American public the necessity for sacrifice would have been an acceptable one. But the losses would have been heavy, and because there never arose a situation justifying intervention, speculation as to "might have beens" is—as always—scarcely more than an exercise in futility.

Air strikes in support of Dien Bien Phu would not have been effective. But American air intervention in case of Communist employment of MIGs in the Red River Delta would certainly have been so. Had the Chinese adopted a policy of regular air support for the Vietminh, we would have assuredly moved in to eliminate this blatant aggression from without. This would have necessitated striking Chinese airfields and would have created some risk of general war with China. As it was, I feel confident that our capability to operate in this fashion had a decisively deterrent effect on the Chinese.

The strongest reason of all for United States refusal to respond by itself to French pleas was our tradition of anticolonialism. This tradition, violated—almost accidentally—for a time in the nineteenth and early twentieth centuries, was born in the circumstance of our own national birth in 1776. Our deep conviction about colonialism has often brought us embarrassment in dealings with our friends in Western Europe, whose histories as colonialists are largely alien to our history. But the standing of the United States as the most powerful of the anticolonial powers is an asset of incalculable value to the Free World. It means that our counsel is sometimes trusted where that of others may not be. It is essential to our position of leadership in a world wherein the majority of the nations have at some time or another felt the yoke of colonialism. Never, throughout the long and sometimes frustrating search for an effective means of defeating the Communist struggle for power in Indochina, did we lose sight of the importance of America's moral position.

Much good, along with much sadness, came out of the Indochinese struggle. It accelerated the independence of Laos and Cambodia and South Vietnam by measures which the French implemented in their desperation during the last days of the conflict; this complete independence, with the removal of French troops, paved the way to an understanding among the free nations of Southeast Asia. It alerted those nations to the dangers of international Communism and finally convinced our European allies, the British and French, of the need for cooperative action in that region. This new realization culminated in the formation of one of our most important regional alliances, the Southeast Asia Treaty Organization.

On September 8, 1954, Secretary Dulles, Senator H. Alexander Smith, and Senator Mike Mansfield signed for the United States the Southeast Asia Collective Defense Treaty, commonly known as the Manila Pact. Signatories to the treaty were France, Britain, Australia, New Zealand, Thailand, the Philippines, Pakistan, and the United States.

This pact proclaims that each party recognizes that armed attack against any one of them in the treaty area[12] endangers its own peace and safety and that each will act to meet common danger. The agreement was directed specifically to the repelling of Communist aggression; in the event of other attack we would "consult."

To combat indirect aggression, we agreed to work together to strengthen free institutions and to cooperate economically and technically.

At the suggestion of President Magsaysay of the Philippines, the United States also entered into a Pacific Charter,[13] affirming the desire of the Western nations to help the Asiatic nations to retain full independence.

The dilemma of finding a moral, legal, and practical basis for helping our friends of the region need not face us again.

By and large, the settlement obtained by the French Union at Geneva in 1954 was the best it could get under the circumstances. It ended a

[12] The treaty area includes, besides the signatory nations, the territories of the states of South Vietnam, Laos, and Cambodia [see Appendix J].
[13] This was inspired by the Atlantic Charter between the United States and Britain in 1941.

bloody war and a serious drain on France's resources. More important, it saw the beginning of development of better understanding between the Western powers and the nations of Southeast Asia. It paved the way for a system of true cooperation between both in the never-ending struggle to stem the tide of Communist expansionism.

CHAPTER XV

Power—Electrical and Political

The legitimate object of government is to do for a community of people whatever they need to have done, but can not do *at all,* or can not *so well do,* for themselves—in their separate and individual capacities. In all that the people can individually do as well for themselves, government ought not to interfere.

—Abraham Lincoln

POWER, especially hydroelectric power, has long been something of a political football in our country. The federal-power zealots have advocated the development of hydroelectrical energy exclusively by the federal government, and some have extended their theories also into the fields of steam and atomic-power production. Some have gone so far as to claim the federal government even has a "public-utility" responsibility (to provide all the power needed in its service areas), which, of course, it does not. The private-power group believe that electrical energy should be developed privately whenever possible. In our country there is almost universal approval of power development by cities, counties, or other subordinate political units. This kind of development is, of course, public rather than private, but because it is likewise local, it does not come within the normal connotation of the expression "public power development." This phrase is usually used to describe federal power development.

The supporters of federal power development rarely label their opponents as anything more complimentary than robbers or exploiters of the public; the retort from those in the opposing camp is equally unflattering, usually referring to the other side as arrogant bureaucrats or promoters of socialism. While I believed the problem, from whichever side viewed, was neither wholly white or black, specific projects that came up for consideration and debate early in my administration brought the whole argument into sharp focus.

One such project involved the Tennessee Valley Authority, the city of Memphis, the Atomic Energy Commission, and privately owned companies engaged in the production of electrical energy. In October of 1953 I met a delegation from Tennessee, headed by Governor Frank Clement, which urged me to approve the building of a steam plant at Fulton, Tennessee, by the Tennessee Valley Authority—a wholly owned and supported federal agency—to supply electrical energy to the city of Memphis. That city, the delegation told me, would otherwise have a serious power shortage within four years.

The delegation asserted that the only power that could be made available to Memphis would necessarily come from the TVA; the organization, they said, had established a power monopoly in the area, and the anticipated shortage, they said, was due to the consumption by Atomic Energy Commission installations at Paducah of great quantities of TVA power. (The AEC installations used about 30 per cent of TVA's total output.) The group therefore took the attitude that the federal government should provide steam-generated electric power to forestall the shortage expected in and around Memphis.

I replied that it had always been my impression that since the federal government had paid the costs of developing the TVA power plants, it was ethical and proper for the federal government to use a reasonable portion of the output. All agreed that the hydroelectric potential of the area had already been fully developed, and that TVA was becoming increasingly dependent upon steam power.[1] But when I suggested that the city build its own plant, the delegation heatedly argued that it could not, under the law, without breaking its exclusive contract with TVA, which ran to 1958.

I told the group that I could see no justification in building a steam plant for Memphis, to be paid for by the nation's taxpayers, any more than for any other city in the United States.

"TVA isn't just a power-producing agency," Governor Clement said in protest. "It's a way of life." He and the others insisted that since with the TVA's monopoly, it was obligated to produce all the power that could be used in the region. I could not accept this contention.

After long and futile discussions I ordered Joseph Dodge, the Director of the Bureau of the Budget, and Lewis L. Strauss, Chairman of the AEC, to begin to find a solution under which the necessary power could

[1] Although the government established the TVA in 1933 principally to control floods, preserve farmland, and improve navigation—with power production as a side-effect —by 1957 the operating expense of its power program totaled nearly $178 million, against expenses for all other functions of about $9 million. Although in 1939 TVA produced nearly all its power in hydroelectric plants, by 1956 its steam plants were producing 70 per cent of the total.

be supplied, without further burdening the federal government with the costs of producing electrical energy in that area. With my approval they began conversations with private industry, exploring the possibility of constructing a plant of sufficient capacity to supply the electrical needs of the Memphis region without affecting the continuity of the power supply of TVA to the Atomic Energy Commission plants at Paducah and other points. (TVA had already refused to buy power directly from a private power company which had offered to sell it at a rate set by the Federal Power Commission.) Because of the size of the project and the possibility that a drop in government demand might someday result in a large oversupply of capacity in the area, it was difficult to find a private corporation in the region that was willing and able to consider such a task; eventually, however, two companies, Middle South Utilities, Inc., and the Southern Company, agreed to explore it seriously. Mr. Edgar H. Dixon was the president of the first of these two companies, and Mr. Eugene Yates was board chairman of the second.

The plan which was eventually worked out became known as "Dixon-Yates," and was the object of loud attack by those who alleged it was a federal "giveaway" or "sellout" to special interests, although these critics did not explain what would be given away by the construction of a commercial steam plant. The attackers did not hesitate to say that the administration favored forces of evil against forces of righteousness, greedy special interests against the common good of all the people of the United States, and "private power" against "public power." If they really believed these allegations, they were sadly and badly confused.

In the first place they erred on the issue. "The issue is not . . . public power versus unregulated private power," I said later that year (1954) at the dedication of the great McNary Dam in Walla Walla, Washington. "The issue posed to us is federal monopoly of power, as against public or regulated power, freely chosen in each instance by the citizens of each area, with the federal government coming in as a cooperating partner where this seems necessary or desirable."[2]

These partners comprised more than the United States' approximately 480 private power companies; they also included some 55 federal organizations, 978 cooperatives, and, the largest group of all, the nonfederal, nonprivate *public power agencies*—agencies of cities, counties, and states—numbering more than 2000.

The administration's power policy had one main purpose; to get every

[2] The idea of partnership came from my statements during the political campaign of 1952 and my 1953 State of the Union message, in which I called for "a partnership of the states and local communities, private citizens, and the federal government, all working together"—working together, among other things, to "advance the development of the great river valleys of our nation and the power they can generate."

one of these organizations pulling in harness to keep up with the expanding electrical needs of the American people, and doing it in such fashion, in each case, as to achieve the maximum efficiency and economy, fullest local control, and fairness to consumers. The administration sided neither with private power nor with politicians who, in their zeal for pet projects, seemed to prefer federal kilowatts in the mind to nonfederal kilowatts on the line.

We wanted power, developed where needed, and under methods and by agencies found most appropriate in the special circumstances of each area. We knew that the country's need for power was growing at a Gargantuan rate—a rate which the federal government would not, and indeed should not, try to satisfy by itself. For example, an estimate made in 1956 by the Federal Power Commission indicated that in the succeeding twenty years we would need to triple our generating capacity, swelling it by approximately 200 million kilowatts—an accomplishment requiring an aggregate investment of more than $96 billion. If the federal government were to set out to supply all these generating facilities, it would have to do two things:

The first would be to reverse its traditional policy against building steam plants outside the TVA area (where federal steam plants level off the gaps or irregularities in the firm energy output of the hydroelectric plants). For the federal government to begin the wholesale construction of steam plants would be a radical step, since the Federal Power Commission estimated that, of our future expansion in the next twenty years, less than 12 per cent could come through additional harnessing of rivers.

Second, the federal government would have to allot to power development an unprecedented slice of the federal tax dollar. To provide the money for this huge effort, the government would have had to invest nearly $5 billion every year for the next twenty years—an annual amount ten times the entire fiscal year 1956 budget for all river-basin development projects of the Bureau of Reclamation and the Corps of Engineers.

Far worse, however, federal monopoly could mean the ignoring of local situations, as well as a radical reversal of our present power investment pattern. In a single year of my administration, for example, federal agencies invested in the construction of power facilities approximately $288 million; nonfederal public organizations about $468 million; investor-owned utilities nearly $3 billion. To put the total investment under one set of managers in Washington—some of whom, at least, could be more interested in partisan advantage than in fair treatment of citizens —would be to lodge with them a dangerous influence over every business, farm, and home in every section of the country. From every state Americans would have to journey to the nation's capital, hat in hand, to plead for power, without which their economies would grind to a stop. Frankly, I thought that those who sought a virtual federal monopoly over the development of electric energy were, in fact, far more interested in the extension of their political power than in the most efficient way of developing electric power.

Historically, the Congress has been reluctant, and I believe rightly so, to finance all the power projects, however worthy, urged by the multitude of pressure groups that come to Washington from north, south, east, and west. The roots of the Dixon and Yates case go back to that reluctance.

In my first year in office both the Senate and the House turned down a $30 million appropriation to the Tennessee Valley Authority for fiscal year 1954 for a new steam-generating plant of about 450,000 kilowatts capacity at Fulton, Tennessee (about thirty miles above Memphis), which would meet the growing needs of its customers in the Memphis area. (They were to turn it down the next year also.[3])

Echoing the predictions of the delegation of Tennessee citizens who had come to the White House in 1953, the chairman of the TVA, Mr. Gordon Clapp, said that the city of Memphis would face a "catastrophe" in power supply by 1957 unless we could find some way to provide additional power facilities in the area. But while I agreed that Memphis would in all likelihood need much more power a few years hence, no good or persuasive reason was ever presented to me for the taxpayers of the entire United States to foot the bill.

Even if we should be persuaded to go the one-way federal-power route—as we were not—it was my conviction that no more federal tax money should be spent in the TVA area for developing steam plants, unless all other power-hungry areas were to receive similar federal favors. By 1951 the TVA's investment in steam-plant facilities amounted to about $18 million. But between 1951 and 1954, under the plans of the preceding administration, that $18 million would increase twenty times to $367 million. By 1956, under the same proposals, it was to increase again, to about $800 million—the 1951 figure multiplied by forty-four.

This plan went far beyond the development of water and land resources, and clearly the time had arrived for a hard look at that cost line soaring rapidly upward on the chart.

I had no desire and certainly no intention to destroy TVA. I said so

[3] Against the request of TVA, President Truman had not included the Fulton plant in either his fiscal year 1952 budget, submitted in January of 1951, or his 1953 budget, submitted in 1952. In 1953, however, just before leaving office, he did include this item in his proposed budget for 1954.

In our downward revision of this budget, we eliminated the Fulton steam plant, as the Truman administration had done in the budget for 1952 and 1953.

Chaos in Indochina

"Indochina at this time was what Bedell Smith aptly called a 'real-estate war.' Both sides pursued each other, occupied territory, and indulged in minor combat only. Dien Bien Phu represented the principal exception."

Above: "Operation Castor" at Dien Bien Phu

Centre: French paratroopers alert for Vietminh forces

Below: Evacuation through the Tonkin marshes

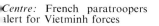

Diplomats W. Bedell Smith, Georges Bidault, and Anthony Eden meet in Geneva, May 22, 1954

A New Look at America's Defenses

"Our military structure and equipment were changing so rapidly that the comforting old slogan 'Tried and true' was gone. In its place had sprung up a disquieting new one: 'If it works, it's obsolete.'"

Above: Hydrogen-bomb explosion photographed at twelve thousand feet

Below: Northrop B–62 Snark guided missile on launcher

Above: Nike missile roars upward

Right: Launching the U.S.S. *Nautilus* after christening by Mrs. Dwight D. Eisenhower

Soviet delegation leaving the Palais des Nations

"It was relatively easy and an interesting silent exercise to categorize them: Bulganin [hand out-stretched], a genial public-relations type, slightly buoyant; Khrushchev [left front], head of the Communist party and new to international conferences, rotund and amiable, but with a will of iron only slightly concealed; Zhukov [smiling, behind Bulganin], on hand as a friendly catalyst, but frightened; Molotov [right], studiously maintaining his reputation as 'the Hammer,' and Gromyko [shielding face, left], stern, unapproachable, unhappy, with little taste for the whole performance." *Also shown:* Yakov A. Malik [at Khrushchev's left].

Representatives of the Big Four: Marshal Bulganin; the author; Premier Faure; Foreign Minister Eden

"Some two years went by with no positive results in developing a promising basis for high-level negotiation in spite of some new and, we thought, reasonable proposals concerning disarmaments and atoms-for-peace. Then, in early spring, 1955, there seemed to arise a new wave of interest."

in public and private, again and again. But I had a clear concern, at times mounting to outrage, which I expressed to the Legislative leaders as early as July 20, 1953, over reliable information from other states that TVA, growing huge on federal taxes and producing cheap, government-subsidized power, was drawing industry away from these other states and creating unemployment in their industrial towns. If the federal government was to supply power—including steam-generated power—in the Tennessee Valley, why, I asked in a news conference on November 10, 1954, should it not supply power also "in the Smoky Hill Valley and in the Penobscot Valley and in the Hudson Valley"?

It was my conviction that if the federal government had a responsibility to supply all the power that any one American region could use, the government had an equal responsibility to supply all the power all American regions needed. I could not countenance an expansion inspired by the illogical contention that the federal government had a public-utility responsibility on the banks of the Tennessee and its tributaries—and nowhere else.

With these convictions and with a determination to prevent a power shortage in the Memphis area, I said in my January 1954 Budget message that arrangements were being made to reduce, by the fall of 1957, existing commitments of the TVA to the AEC for 500,000 to 600,000 kilowatts; this reduction would release an equivalent amount of TVA generating capacity to serve the increasing demands of other customers, specifically those in and around Memphis. If these arrangements did not work out, I added, we should reconsider starting additional TVA steam plants.

The Dixon and Yates plan, which evolved in the succeeding months of 1954, was designed to supply power to the TVA at Memphis in replacement for power which TVA would then continue to furnish at Paducah to plants of the Atomic Energy Commission, with whom Dixon and Yates would contract. For this action there were precedents: in 1951 the AEC contracted with Electrical Energy, Inc., to construct a plant to supply power to the AEC at Paducah, Kentucky. The next year the commission contracted with the Ohio Valley Electrical Corporation to build a plant to supply power to the AEC at Portsmouth, Ohio. Both plants were larger than the one proposed in 1954 for the TVA.

On April 10, 1954, the two private companies submitted a proposal (their second one) to the AEC which the Bureau of the Budget, the AEC, and the TVA considered satisfactory as a basis for negotiations. On June 14, 1954, Rowland Hughes, who had succeeded Joseph Dodge as Budget Director, made a presentation before Executive and Legislative leaders comparing this proposal with a competitive proposal from a group headed by Walter Von Tresckow, and with the original Fulton plant project. Hughes recommended going ahead with Dixon and Yates. When he had finished, I heard no dissent, and I gave approval. But no one in the room doubted that a political storm was sure to come, accompanied by a spate of demagoguery. We were not disappointed. Criticism began immediately.

Two days later Rowland Hughes sent the letters directing that negotiations begin—as they did on July 7. By October 5 the AEC approved the contract, submitting it on November 11, as the law required, for the approval of the congressional committee on atomic energy. It had been cleared by the AEC, the Department of Justice, the Federal Power Commission, the TVA, the Bureau of the Budget, the Securities and Exchange Commission, the General Accounting Office, and the Public Utility Commission of Arkansas. (The plant was to be built across the river from Memphis, at West Memphis, Arkansas.) By a straight party vote (ten Republicans versus eight Democrats) of the Joint Committee on November 13, the contract took effect.

On August 17 I was asked to comment at a press conference on the charge of Stephen A. Mitchell, the Democratic National Chairman, that I had personally ordered the Dixon and Yates contract awarded to a firm in which one of my friends had an interest. Regarding the involvement of my friend, Robert T. Jones, I said that, as I had told the press time and time again, I would not defend myself against this kind of charge. (I had never and would never permit personal relationships to influence a public decision, but I had no intention of saying so every time a political opponent made a baseless accusation. In the negotiations on this case I had never heard that my friend Bob Jones had any interest whatsoever in either of the companies that formed Dixon and Yates, and in all the many contacts I have had with him over all the years before and since the incident, the subject has never been mentioned between us. But I said nothing publicly.)

In the August 17 press conference I did point out that I had approved the recommendations for the Dixon and Yates contract and added that every official action I took involving the contractual relationships of the United States with anybody, except when questions of national security were directly involved, was open to the public. I suggested that any one of the reporters could go to the Bureau of the Budget, or to the Atomic Energy Commission, and get a record of the case.

In the hope of clarifying the issue, the Bureau of the Budget and the AEC prepared for distribution chronologies of the principal events and actions which led up to the signing of the Dixon and Yates contract.

Then, as a result of the 1954 election, the Democrats took control of the Congress. Senator Clinton Anderson became chairman of the Joint Committee on Atomic Energy. On January 28, 1955, the ten Democrats on the Joint Committee outvoted the eight Republicans and recommended—though they could not require—that the AEC cancel the contract. The administration refused.

Soon, the opposition alleged conflict of interest. On February 11, 1955, Senator Lister Hill telephoned Rowland Hughes to ask whether the Bureau of the Budget had ever had in its employ a man named Adolphe Wenzell. Mr. Hughes told the senator that Wenzell had been a consultant for the bureau. One week later Senator Hill attacked the administration on the grounds that Mr. Wenzell had simultaneously been a consultant for the bureau on Dixon and Yates and an official of the First Boston Corporation, which was to handle part of the financing of the Dixon and Yates project. He added, without justification, that Hughes had deliberately tried to conceal the fact.

Mr. Wenzell had twice served as a temporary consultant to the bureau; once from May to September, 1953, when he made a financial analysis of the TVA, trying to estimate the amount and the sources of the federal government's subsidy to it; and again in 1954, between January 18 and April 10, when he took part in a number of conferences, with representatives of the AEC, the Budget Bureau, and Dixon and Yates. His principal task in this period was to analyze power and financing costs—to examine the probable costs of the private-power proposals in comparison with other utility standards and the Fulton plant, as factors bearing on the power rate to be paid by the AEC.

When, at my request, Mr. Hughes handed me in mid-August the Budget Bureau's chronology of the case, Wenzell's name, among others, had not been included because he was not considered one of the principals in the negotiations. He was not involved in or consulted on any major policy decision. The administration's policy on the Fulton steam plant, clearly set forth in the 1955 budget, had been decided upon in the months between his two periods of service. Neither Mr. Hughes nor Mr. Dodge, moreover, knew that Wenzell at times was simultaneously consulting with the Budget Bureau and advising Dixon and Yates on its financing as a representative of First Boston. In fact, as late as June 27, 1955, Mr. Dodge and Mr. Hughes did not know that Wenzell's company, the First Boston Corporation, was one of Dixon and Yates financial agents. Wenzell's working in a dual capacity was a regrettable error. But it was a diversion from the main issue.[4]

[4] On January 16, 1956, I wrote in my diary:
"The Director of the Bureau of the Budget, Mr. Hughes, visited me this afternoon to say that the time had come when he feels he must resign his post. His Deputy in the Budget, Mr. Brundage, is an extremely able man, and I think that this will prevent any major break in policy or method. Nevertheless, I will miss Hughes, who has been a very hardworking and efficient public servant. Strangely enough, he does not give the normal reason for wanting to leave. He merely states that ever since

The stormy history of the contract ended with an action which, I believe, squared with the partnership policy.

Back in February 1954, before Dixon and Yates had submitted their first, and unacceptable, proposal, I had said publicly, "I know of no reason why the city of Memphis, if it wanted to, couldn't do something about this matter itself." Frankly, I was puzzled to realize that a community was sitting around hoping for a federal-government handout to meet its purely local needs, acting like an overindulged child.

But a year and a half later, on June 23, 1955, Memphis, recognizing the firmness of my decision and the impossibility of getting a congressional appropriation for the Fulton steam plant, reversed its original assertion that to build its own plant was impracticable. It now decided, rather than use Dixon and Yates power, to build its own municipal steam-generating plant financed in the usual manner by issuing and selling bonds on the public investment market.

Inasmuch as that decision would make Dixon and Yates power superfluous, the AEC, at my direction, promptly notified Mr. Dixon of our decision to cancel the contract and to proceed with settlement to cover the costs they had incurred, as provided in the contract.

On November 23 the AEC, on advice of counsel, had to tell Dixon and Yates that the United States could not recognize the contract, and therefore could not be liable for any losses until the possible Wenzell conflict-of-interest could be adjudicated. Dixon and Yates thereupon sued the United States in the Court of Claims, and won a judgment of $1,867,545.

I felt that the Court of Claims decision was right. Nonetheless, the Justice Department appealed, for it believed that until the Supreme Court had acted on the matter it would never be finally settled. The case dragged on. It was not until January 9, 1961, that the Supreme Court struck down the Court of Claims award on the ground that the contract was unenforceable because Wenzell's dual status made the negotiations technically illegal.

So Dixon and Yates became the losers in the whole affair—on a technicality.

Some protested that the building of a local plant by the city of Memphis meant the wrecking of TVA. This was nonsense. In a news conference in June 1953, elaborating on a speech reference I once made to "creeping socialism," I had pointed out the danger of federal monopoly

coming down here in 1953 he has not missed a day of duty, and he is tired to the bone. Since in the Budget post it is almost impossible to take an extended leave, he sees no alternative but to resign. Moreover, he has a very bad eye, which demands continuous treatment, and he says he has had to neglect it."

in the TVA area—a monopoly which could not fail to tie the area's economic development to the growth of federal appropriations. No one could be so blind as to fail to see the danger in the spread to other areas of such a practice—a danger which the partnership policy aimed to avoid—but I said time and time again, beginning with a speech in Memphis itself on October 19, 1952, that there is "no disposition on my part to impair the effective working out of the TVA."

The fact is—towering like a mountain above the Dixon and Yates and Wenzell molehill—that during my eight years in office the TVA prospered. Between 1953 and June of 1960 it took on more than nearly 100,000 new customers. It boosted its kilowatt-hour output nearly two and a half times, adding 38 million kilowatts compared to the 25 million added in a similar period prior to my inauguration.[5]

On my recommendation the TVA went on a more businesslike basis than before. On August 6, 1959, I signed Public Law 86-137 authorizing the TVA, under budgetary review, to issue revenue bonds to help finance construction of additional power facilities. Fifty million dollars' worth, the first issue, went on the market on November 15, 1960. This bond authorization was to help TVA get the needed capital to assure its 85,000-square-mile area and its regional population of more than 5 million an abundant and growing supply of the power they will need in the years to come.

Far from the Tennessee Valley, another major power controversy arose over proposed dams on the Snake River in Idaho, specifically at Hells Canyon.

In 1950 the Idaho Power Company had filed an application with the Federal Power Commission for authority to construct a dam on the Oxbow site on the Snake. From that time until January 1953 top officials of the Department of the Interior and other federal-power zealots, by entering objections, blocked initiation of any action by the Federal Power Commission.

These people contended that the power needs of that area would best be served, not by a series of three privately financed dams, which the Idaho Power Company eventually sought permission to build (Hells Canyon, Oxbow, and Brownlee, all on the Snake River), but rather by one huge dam financed by the federal government at the Hells Canyon site.

They had blocked private and local construction not only in Idaho but all over the Pacific Northwest in spite of the fact that the federal govern-

[5] It expanded its net power assets by three quarters of a billion dollars, topping the $636 million added in 1946–53. And it brought its 1960 operating revenues to an all-time high of $242 million—more than double the figure for fiscal year 1953.

ment, because of other problems—including a war—could not keep up construction to meet growing needs. Indeed, even before the Korean War, for fiscal years 1949, 1950, and 1951, for example, the Truman administration had recommended, for the Bureau of Reclamation of the Department of the Interior, only one new start[6] each year. For 1952 it recommended three and for 1953 not one.

Bureaucrats blocked action on privately financed projects even in the face of their own realization that the region was starving for power. On January 25, 1952, the then Secretary of the Interior told a subcommittee of the House of Representatives:

> The power supply outlook in the Pacific Northwest for the next several years will remain critical. Power requirements continue to exceed supply, and the addition of defense-industry loads with associated increases in civilian power requirements will further tax the existing generating transmission facilities. Even with strict adherence to present recommended schedules for installation of new generating plants, it is expected that the Pacific Northwest will be in a power-shortage situation until 1957.

A year later, as I was about to take office, his prediction was coming true. The Pacific Northwest, in late 1952 and early 1953, was suffering curtailments in power consumption, slowdowns in production, slashes in company payrolls, and threats of "brownouts." Possible investors turned their backs on the Northwest and looked elsewhere.

A bill to authorize construction of the federal Hells Canyon Dam had already died twice in Democratic Congresses, the Eighty-first and Eighty-second. (It was to die twice more under the Democrat-controlled Eighty-fourth and Eighty-fifth Congresses.[7]) Yet its political supporters continued to insist on the federal government's exclusive right to the sites on the Snake River.

But in 1953 three events began to crack the ice.

First: on March 16 the United States Supreme Court issued a decision that set a precedent. It upheld the right of the Federal Power Commission[8] to issue a license to the Virginia Electric and Power Company—a privately owned company—to construct a hydroelectric dam on the Roanoke River at Roanoke Rapids, North Carolina. The Flood Control Act of 1944 had provided a comprehensive plan for the development of the Roanoke River Basin. The Department of the Interior in the Truman administration contended that this plan presupposed the federal

---

[6] A "start" is the beginning of construction on an authorized project.

[7] The last time it died, in 1957, its proponents wanted to flood out the work already done by the Idaho Power Company and pay the company for its losses.

[8] An independent commission with five members appointed by the President for five-year terms which may therefore run beyond his.

development of all power sites—however long the wait—and ruled out a Federal Power Commission license for any nonfederal organization, however great the need. In its new decision the Supreme Court rejected the theory of federal pre-emption in this field. That rejection cleared the way for nonfederal power agencies, public and private, to start putting electricity on the line.

The second ice-breaker was a change in attitude in the Department of the Interior. At a Cabinet meeting on April 24, 1953, Secretary Douglas McKay announced that his department was withdrawing the Truman administration's objection to the Federal Power Commission's licensing the Idaho Power Company to build the Oxbow Dam—a project which, with two related dams, Brownlee and Hells Canyon, would ring down the curtain on the long-standing proposal for a giant Hells Canyon federal dam. The department, he said, would simply present facts and leave the final decision to the commission. This withdrawal cleared the way for hearings, which lasted two years, to make certain that the three dams would best assure the comprehensive development of the Snake River. On August 4, 1955, the commission issued the license.

The third change: on August 18, 1953, the administration announced its power policy—a policy which included the assurance that the Department of the Interior would "not oppose the construction of facilities which local interests, either public or private, are able to provide in accordance with licenses or other controls of the Federal Power Commission or other appropriate regulatory bodies and which are consonant with the best development of the natural resources of the area."

These three events sealed the fate of the proposed Hells Canyon Dam, which could have been a massive Snake River monument to political maneuver and federal pre-emption, a monument which, in final estimates, would have cost more than a half billion dollars.

These events assured the presence of power—not ten years hence, but promptly—flowing through transmission lines out of the generators at the three Idaho Power Company dams. This solution, in the view of the Federal Power Commission, was far preferable to the high Hells Canyon Dam project in the comprehensive development of the power potential in the Snake River.

These events, in a very real sense, marked the close of an era. They liberated the Pacific Northwest from a theory which had failed.

When I took office, for example, the record showed that in the preceding twenty years—years of New Deal and Fair Deal pre-emption of power sites—the Federal Power Commission had licensed nonfederal organizations in the states of Washington and Oregon[9] to install only 1,783,200

9 In the West Group of the Pacific Northwest Power Pool.

kilowatts of generating capacity. By January 1961 we could look at the record once again and see licenses for a capacity totaling nearly 5 million kilowatts—more than two and a half times the amount licensed in our predecessors' entire twenty years.

And those licenses were not hunting permits for private predators. In the first place, every investor-owned utility must pay taxes and, under the law, submit to regulation by the Federal Power Commission and often by a state commission. Moreover, of that 5 million kilowatts of licensed capacity, almost 80 per cent went to local *public* organizations, of a sort which, being subject to the control of local people who elect their boards of directors—and often subject to state regulation as well— are far more directly responsive to the will of the people served than are the Bureau of Reclamation, the Corps of Engineers, or the TVA.

Still, the federal government was doing its part, better than ever before.

The United States from 1953 to 1960 was hard at work building power facilities not only in the Columbia Basin but from coast to coast—building them on a scale historically unprecedented.[10]

Between 1953 and 1961 the administration recommended, and the Congress authorized, fifty-three new reclamation projects which would turn desert country into green fields, and produce power as well. These reclamation works included as major projects the Glendo Unit of the Missouri River Basin Project in Wyoming; the Trinity River Division of the Central Valley Project in California; and the giant Glen Canyon Dam,

[10] In January of 1953 we had a total installed capacity of 97.3 million kilowatts. By January of 1960 that figure had soared to 175 million—almost twice as much. Compare our installations with those of the past: between 1944 and 1948 the United States added 7.5 million kilowatts; between 1948 and 1952, 27.6 million; between 1952 and 1956, 40 million; between 1956 and 1960, 50 million—a rate nearly twice that of the best four years of the preceding administration.

Beyond all this work to harness falling water and steam for power, we were driving forward with the newest known source, the atom. By the end of 1960 the United States had three civilian stationary nuclear-power plants in operation: at Shippingport, Pennsylvania (60,000 kilowatts); at Rowe, Massachusetts (180,000 kilowatts); and Morris, Illinois (180,000 kilowatts). And other plants were on their way up, with a total installed capacity of more than half a million kilowatts, at Indian Point, New York; Laguna Beach, Michigan; Hallam, Nebraska; Sioux Falls, South Dakota; and other sites.

By 1965, the AEC estimated, our total civilian stationary nuclear-power capacity would total more than one and a half million kilowatts. We were moving toward the day when we could make economical use of uranium, one pound of which, if completely burned, could equal in heat production nearly 3 million pounds of coal. And in research laboratories—at the University of California, at Princeton, at New York University, at Oak Ridge—American scientists were working, in cooperation with British colleagues, on a fusion process for power production; under this process the total fusion of one kilogram of deuterium, abundant in the ocean, could produce for homes and industries and farms a hundred million kilowatt hours of electricity.

with a capacity of 900,000 kilowatts—part of the giant Upper Colorado storage project, the largest reclamation project ever authorized in a single piece of legislation. Glen Canyon itself, the American dam second in reservoir capacity and third in height, contains, to give a suggestion of its vastness, enough concrete to build a four-foot sidewalk around the world.

In dedicating the gigantic McNary Dam in September 1954, I expressed my hope for the early building of another colossus in the Columbia Basin —one impossible for a nongovernmental organization—the Libby Dam. For years the construction of this dam had been stalled, waiting for an agreement between the United States and Canada. It took time, but on October 19, 1960, this obstacle yielded to patient negotiation;[11] I approved a treaty providing for joint United States and Canadian development of the Columbia River, and I asked the Senate to ratify it early in 1961.

The treaty opened the way, as an initial result, to 1.6 million additional kilowatts of low-cost power for the United States' side of the border; it broke the years-old barrier blocking the road to the Libby Dam, which will have a power output greater than the giant Bonneville Dam on the lower Columbia. Moreover, it laid the foundation for a power structure in the Pacific Northwest of nearly five times the capacity we had when the preceding administration left office.

In the 1952 campaign President Truman had alleged that only the Democratic party could produce power progress. In dedicating the Hungry Horse Dam on October 1, 1952, he said, "All of you who are here today had better go and take another look at this dam because if the Republicans win this election it will be a long time before you see another new structure of this kind."

However, after 1953, as the Brownlee Dam began to rise and the Dixon and Yates headlines began to fade, as the TVA continued to boom and grow, and lights burned and motors spun all over the Pacific Northwest, such talk sounded less and less plausible. So, partisans summoned up a new propaganda package to attack the administration's power policy.

"The Russians will overtake us if we don't watch out," they warned, frightened, so they claimed, by reports—which could just as well have been written without the authors ever leaving Washington—about mas-

[11] On the United States side, these negotiations owed their success, after so many years, largely to four men: former Governor Len Jordan of Idaho (now a United States senator); former Secretary of the Interior Douglas McKay; his successor Fred A. Seaton; and Under Secretary of the Interior Elmer F. Bennett, who, working closely with Secretary Herter and Secretary Seaton, did the major share of the work in bringing the agreement to a close.

sive Russian hydroelectric projects rising on rivers from the Volga to the Ob in Siberia.

What is the evidence? Are we about to trail the Soviet Union?

At the end of 1959, with an installed capacity of 59 million kilowatts, the Soviets were where we were in 1942. By 1975, if they continue to grow as they have, they will be where we were in 1955.

But by 1975, if we continue to add at our present rate, which is nearly three times theirs, we shall have an installed capacity of 355 million kilowatts. So when that year arrives, if past trends continue, the Russians will trail us in installed capacity by nearly one quarter of a billion kilowatts. To take the long leap forward and pull up alongside us, they would have to do all they have been doing and on top of that, for every year between 1959 and 1975, add to their total installed capacity the gigantic equivalent of seven Grand Coulee dams, or one every month and a half.

This review of the administration's accomplishments, however, should lead to no conclusion that we built power projects with no check as to their value. The course of a project from concept to reality is a long one; the scrutiny that precedes the ground-breaking for a new dam often takes years.

This scrutiny ordinarily begins with a congressionally-authorized project report, prepared, normally, by one of the two largest federal water-resource agencies, the Bureau of Reclamation of the Department of the Interior (which builds irrigation projects only in the nineteen Western states, including Alaska and Hawaii) and the Corps of Engineers of the Department of the Army (which builds flood-control and navigation projects from coast to coast).[12]

I consistently held that a project should not be authorized if no analytical survey had been made concerning it, or if its cost outweighed its calculated benefits. However, if a project had a benefit-cost ratio greater than one to one, it stood a chance of approval by the Secretary of the Interior or the Secretary of the Army. If successful there, it was referred to Budget Bureau experts, and to my Special Assistant for Public Works Planning, General John S. Bragdon. These men, calling on long years of experience, advised me as to the worth of the project, the priority which should be assigned to it, and whether it fitted into the over-all annual budget of a given year. If it met these tests, I would then recom-

[12] The project report, which goes to both the President and the Congress, includes comments from state and other federal agencies and analyzes in detail the cost of the proposed work. Alongside the estimated cost it lays out the project's probable benefits—water storage, power, flood control, recreation, fish and wild-life preservation. This relationship is called the "cost-benefit ratio."

mend that the Congress authorize the project and, if advisable that year, appropriate money to start construction.

The Congress, of course, could always and often did authorize projects on its own initiative, without awaiting reports from the Executive-branch experts.

By the beginning of 1958 $5 billion worth of public works projects had, through many years past, received congressional authorization but no appropriations. Behind these were others which had received favorable project reports but no authorization. Despite the clamor of pressure groups, however, the government declined to start more of these than it could prudently hope to finish. Bad planning can always cause great waste.

At the end of 1950, for example, the Bureau of Reclamation had swollen its staff to approximately twenty thousand employees. But by that time the Truman administration—beset by the Korean War and other problems—had cut new starts to the bone. By the end of 1952 those twenty thousand employees had become approximately seventeen thousand; by the end of 1953, thirteen thousand. Over the next seven years my administration never exceeded that number; nevertheless we efficiently carried on one of the greatest reclamation programs in our history. For one thing, by minimizing peaks and valleys in starting resource projects —in spite of a congressional habit of authorizing projects not recommended by the Executive branch, or denying some urgently requested— we avoided the more expensive layoffs followed by frenzied recruiting, and avoided the waste that comes from stretching out a project over years when there is not enough money to finance the work more expeditiously.

This determination to build only well-scrutinized projects was my principal reason for vetoing several pork-barrel bills.

In August 1956, in the middle of the presidential political campaign, I vetoed one such bill because it authorized thirty-two projects, involving financial commitments of more than a half-billion dollars, which had not been reviewed by the individual states affected, or by the Corps of Engineers.

In 1958 I vetoed a rivers-and-harbors appropriation bill because, among other things, it authorized four projects, costing more than $27 million, which had no project reports; and another three projects, costing $115 million, which, the Corps of Engineers experts said, had no economic justification.

Then on August 28, 1959, I vetoed another public-works appropriation bill because it dumped on top of the all-time-high spending of the corps and the bureau ($1.1 billion) another sixty-seven projects which would ultimately cost the taxpayers more than $800 million. On September 2, the Congress upheld this veto. But a week later, after the opposition had introduced a new bill—identical with its predecessor but pared 2.5 per cent from construction estimates—the Senate and House overrode a second veto by narrow margins. The lure of the pork barrel had proved irresistible.

"Despite the cheers," a metropolitan daily said in an editorial the next day, recording the elation of those who, after 145 failures during my administration, had at last overridden a veto, "it is the President who comes off with honor from the affair. He took his stand on the large principle of fiscal responsibility, and it is the overriders who have played the role of irresponsibles."

Another controversy, related in principle and polemic to that between federal and local power devotees, involved the Rural Electrification Administration (REA) and the National Rural Electric Cooperative Association.

The REA came into being in 1935, under a presidential Executive Order. The following year Congress passed the Rural Electrification Act, with Republican Senator George W. Norris of Nebraska and Democratic Congressman Sam Rayburn as co-sponsors.

The REA, an agency of the Department of Agriculture, obtains funds by congressional appropriation to make loans to cooperatives and other organizations which bring power and telephone service to rural areas. These loans are repaid directly into the United States Treasury. Since 1944, REA has been charged a flat interest rate of 2 per cent for these loans, with thirty-five years to repay. Yet to procure the money to make the loans, the Department of the Treasury today must pay about 4 per cent interest.

"The Republican party," I said in a campaign speech at Omaha, Nebraska, on September 18, 1952, "favors a sound program of rural electrification and rural telephone service. . . . We regard REA as an investment in agriculture's future."

Throughout the years of my Presidency many opposition leaders professed to doubt the truth of this assertion. They alleged dismay in 1953 when, in Reorganization Plan Number 2, the administration, with the approval of the Congress, vested in the Secretary of Agriculture authority to carry out REA functions, until that time performed independently by the REA administrator. Oddly enough, they seemed to think that the Secretary of Agriculture would be opposed to electricity for farms. In 1954 Governor Stevenson alluded darkly to "what has happened to REA." And year after year the general manager of the National Rural Electric Cooperative Association, the lobbying organization for the REA, unveiled bits and pieces of an alleged top-secret administration "master plan," which he alone had discovered, to wreck the REA.

The record refutes such contentions. In the first six years of my administration, the REA loaned cooperatives $1.2 billion—nearly a third of all funds loaned since the program began; in those same years it made loans which brought telephone service to more than 800,000 farm families— nearly 80 per cent of all the telephone loans made under the program.

The administration pulled more than its full share of weight in fulfilling the purpose for which the REA was set up in the first place—to carry electric power to America's farmsteads. In 1935, when the program started, only 11 per cent of American farms had electricity; by January 1959 the figure was more than 95 per cent. Of the loans being granted by REA in the last years of my administration, those going to non-farmers outnumbered those going to farmers by three to one.

These facts posed a new question: should the federal government borrow money for REA at about 4 per cent and make loans at 2 per cent, not to bring electricity to farms, but to supply electricity to industries and nonfarm residences located in rural areas? Did it have a right to use tax money collected from all to favor this special group?

I gave my opinion in a message submitted to the Congress in January 1959: I proposed that the present statutory interest rate of 2 per cent for loans made by the Rural Electrification Administration be replaced by a rate which would cover the current cost of interest to the Treasury. I suggested that REA should be permitted to budget through revolving funds, and proposed "that legislation be enacted to assist both electric and telephone borrowers to obtain financing from private sources." In line with this conviction the administration from 1957 to 1961 refused to approve a $60-million loan to a group of Indiana cooperatives planning to supply power to a local aluminum company.

Then, on February 11, 1959, I appeared before the annual meeting of the National Rural Electrification Cooperative Association and told them that they should no longer live at the expense of other taxpayers. The REA had grown out of infancy and adolescence; its consumers' equality of opportunity, I held, had been re-established through governmental assistance; now it was up to them, in maturity, to recognize, as independent, sturdy, and useful members of society, that they did not need, did not deserve, and should not accept subventions from the government.

In reaction, the opposition hit the roof. Standing before the members in the same convention on another day, Senator Lyndon B. Johnson counseled the association members to "fight with beer bottles" if necessary to keep their interest rate at 2 per cent.

"This is a battle for your very existence . . . ," he said. "We are not going to raise the interest rate. We are not going to let the administration send you down the chute to the Wall Street bankers." In fact, Senator Johnson added, the Congress would pass Senator Hubert Humphrey's bill to overturn the REA Reorganization Plan of 1953 and give the REA administrator—not Secretary Benson—the final authority to approve or disapprove REA loans. "REA rates must remain low," Senator John F. Kennedy of Massachusetts told the same audience. I felt it a pity that he did not follow the advice of a great Democratic leader of yesteryear and say, "Let's look at the record."

On the interest rate Senator Johnson's prediction was right: the Congress did fail to raise it as I recommended. On the Humphrey bill, however, he was wrong: on April 27 I vetoed it, and three days later the House sustained the veto.

The subject of power really involves energy of several kinds. Electric power is generated by falling water. This source was long ago tapped by man, who also, resourcefully, began to produce power by constructing steam plants fired by one conventional fuel source or another, and who now taps the abounding, astounding power of the atom. But the other power which charges the question is political—power exercised by lobbies and congressional blocs, power contesting with power, for motives sometimes obvious, sometimes obscure, with little of the seething contest revealed fully and accurately to the public for whom the fight is presumably waged.

The government has the power to help human beings in need. It has also the responsibility to stimulate people to exercise initiative on their own behalf. It has always seemed to me that in the field of power production, government should exercise this power and discharge this responsibility. At least, for eight years, we tried.

CHAPTER XVI

Three Hurdles Cleared:
Western Europe, Trieste,
Guatemala

I feel pretty confident that the Soviet Union doesn't like what is going on. . . . There is behind this program a sense of urgency and momentum, so that I don't believe the Soviet Union will be able to break it up.

—*Secretary of State John Foster Dulles,*
Report to the Cabinet, October 25, 1954

ON April 23, 1945, a reconnaissance unit of the 69th U. S. Infantry Division, then holding positions along the Mulde River in Germany, crossed the river, and soon, in the vicinity of Torgau, the site of one of Frederick's battles, made contact with advance elements of the Russian forces moving westward. This historic day marked the first contact between United States' and Soviet troops, and put the final seal of doom on the once proud but now shattered fighting machine of Hitler.

Two weeks later, in the middle of the night, Colonel General Jodl and my chief of staff, General Walter Bedell Smith, signed at my headquarters in a schoolhouse in Reims the documents of German surrender, thus bringing to an end the war in Europe which had cost the Western nations alone nearly 900,000 lives.[1]

[1] As I reported in *Crusade in Europe,* Marshal Zhukov told me after the close of the war that the Russian civilian losses, west of the Volga, had never been and could never be accurately estimated. But he and others suspected that, in executing Hitler's barbaric order to "depopulate" the country, the lives of something like 15 million men, women, and children had been lost.

Germany that night in early spring of 1945 was a scene of devastation and despair. With her armies destroyed, her cities in ruins, 3.5 million of her youth killed during the war, her economy shattered, there seemed little left of the country which five years before had overrun France, threatened England, occupied the Balkans and locked in a death struggle with Russia. Her population was embittered, partly at the Nazis who had led them into this costly and disastrous war, partly at the Allies, who had engineered their defeat. But they were more than embittered; they were bewildered. The dreams of invincibility built up by Hitler were gone amid the smoking ruins. The people were reduced to beggary and forced to depend upon their former enemies for the mere essentials of life—in this case reduced to minimum food and a ration of coal. Furthermore, the sight of the horror camps, of Dachau, Belsen, and Buchenwald, scenes of crimes beyond human comprehension and yet the work of the Nazi government which the citizenry had supported, struck the national conscience. Railroads and factories were destroyed, making even the distribution of the necessaries of life difficult for the occupying powers. A black market throve to the extent that nearly the only usable tender on the streets of Germany was the American cigarette. Even the occupation Deutsche mark (DM) issued by the Allied powers and the Soviets was considered almost worthless. To top it all, the country was now occupied by two power blocs—the Soviets in the east, and the British, French, and Americans in the west. The future of Germany and its people seemed hopeless.

This was Germany, controlled by the four conquering powers, when in November of 1945 I was recalled from my post as United States commander to return to Washington to take the position of Chief of Staff of the United States Army.

It was a changed land that met my eyes when I returned to Europe early in 1951 to assume command of the military forces of the North Atlantic Treaty Organization. Germany was still technically an enemy nation, under occupation. But in the interim, in 1949, a new West German nation, the Federal Republic of Germany, had come into existence with a constitution and a parliament headed by Chancellor Konrad Adenauer. True, not all of the ruins were gone; in many places devastation still remained. However, the economy was improving and a reawakening sense of pride and self-respect characterized the population. In place of the black market the West Germans now boasted a Deutsche mark that had real value. No longer did the United States have to guarantee artificially a rate of exchange of ten DM to the dollar. The DM now stood on its own at a rate of not ten to one, but 5.3 to one, even on the free market. It was estimated that the budget of Western Germany would be balanced for fiscal year 1951 at a little over 13 billion DM, a figure which included more than four and a half billion DM to be paid to the three occupying powers to defray the costs of occupation. (Between 1945 and 1955 West Germany did receive from the United States approximately $3.5 billion in economic aid.)

Germany was still divided. The cleavage between the two parts was widening. But Western Germany by itself was now a nation to be reckoned with.

Much of the credit for this resurgence of Western Germany must be given to its iron-willed Chancellor, Dr. Adenauer. A strong anti-Nazi, he had refused to bow to Hitler and, as leader of the newborn nation, he remained in spirit the ramrod mayor of Cologne, dealing with former conquerors with dignity, reserve, and wisdom. Adenauer preached to his countrymen the concept that they must turn their backs on the past and replace their former nationalism with an ambition to become "good Europeans." An advocate of closer ties with all of Western Europe, he staked his political fortunes on the concept of a rapprochement with France and an end to the age-old quarrels that had cost both nations so dearly.

A major factor in the restoration of Germany to the family of nations was the West's growing realization of the malevolent designs of the Communist bloc, evidenced by the threat to Greece and Turkey in 1947 and the takeover of Czechoslovakia in 1948. When arrangements were made late in 1950 for integration of the European military forces under a single NATO commander, a common assumption among the participating powers was that eventually Germany must be allowed her own armaments and must participate in European defense. During 1950 Germany had become a participant in the Consultative Assembly of the Council of Europe at Strasbourg beginning in 1950. West Germany was cooperating in the Schuman Plan[2] and in late 1950 had taken part in the thirty-nine nation tariff negotiations, at Torquay in England, under the General Agreement on Tariff and Trade.

Thus when I took command in Europe in early 1951, Germany was in an anomalous position. Still technically in a state of war, occupied by foreign military forces and being forced to pay large sums of money to support this occupation, she was nevertheless cooperating with the occupying powers in peaceful international organizations. The Federal Republic of Germany was ready to become a free and equal member of the North Atlantic Treaty Organization and to make her full contribution to the common defense.

[2] A plan for a West European coal and steel pool, including France, Belgium, the Netherlands, Luxembourg, the Saar, and West Germany.

The first step, the termination of the technical state of war between Germany and the Western powers, began to be taken in the summer of 1951. The United States Congress adopted a resolution officially ending the war, and on the 24th of October a proclamation was duly issued by President Truman.

But plans for rearming Germany created problems. France had to be convinced that if Germany were rearmed she would never again use her power to turn on her Western neighbors. But any means of achieving this legitimate objective which would impose humiliating restrictions on a sovereign—even though lately defeated—nation would be unacceptable to Germany. I became convinced that the best possible solution was the creation of a European Defense Community, conceived by the French and proposed on October 24, 1950, by René Pleven, the French Premier.

The EDC treaty was intended primarily to merge the armed forces of the six signatory nations—France, West Germany, Italy, Belgium, the Netherlands, Luxembourg—but it included additional agreements, such as (1) a treaty of mutual assistance between these six and the United Kingdom against attack from without, (2) a protocol extending to West Germany the guarantees of the fourteen-nation North Atlantic treaty, (3) a declaration by the United States and the United Kingdom that any threat to the integrity of the EDC would be considered a threat to them, and (4) an agreement on the part of the United States and the United Kingdom to station in Europe "such forces as they deem necessary and appropriate to contribute to a joint defense of the North Atlantic area."

EDC, we hoped, was to become a "hard and dependable core" for NATO. The six signatories were to contribute units of no larger than divisional size to a common pool of troops. Eventually there were to be forty-three divisions, all organized under a supreme NATO commander, and with a single budget. The pool was to be controlled by an executive commissariat, a council of ministers, an assembly, and a court of justice. Proponents of an eventual United States of Europe took great hope from the creation of these supranational institutions.

From its inception in 1951 I supported the concept of EDC and, during my tour of duty in NATO, visited every government of the region to urge the signing and subsequent parliamentary approval of the treaty.

A few governments, particularly the French, feared the EDC concept, even though a Frenchman originally had proposed it; the ancient and mutual hostility of the French and Germans persisted and created a strong feeling in France that to include Germany—even a defeated and powerless Germany—in an international defense organization would be to invite the camel into the tent.

But most NATO nations believed that establishment of an effective collective security for Western Europe was not feasible without a strong

West German contribution. Not only did I agree; I also believed that an organization of NATO forces under the EDC plan would minimize or make impossible the resurgence of an independent German military machine that could again threaten her Western neighbors. So, as the NATO commander, I did all I could to induce universal and prompt acceptance of the plan. So important did I consider accomplishment of this purpose that in the spring of 1952 I announced that until the French government signed the EDC treaty I could not, in good conscience, leave my post in NATO to return to the United States.

On May 26, 1952, the United States, the United Kingdom, France, and West Germany signed the Bonn Convention on relations with the Federal Republic of Germany, restoring West Germany's sovereignty. The next day, in an associated action, they signed the Treaty of Paris, which set up the EDC organization itself. The Bonn Convention would go into effect, ending the occupation of Germany, upon ratification of EDC by all signatory powers. Thus EDC became the condition for the restoration of German sovereignty.

But treaties, once signed, must be approved by legislative bodies, and ratification was slow. The lingering reluctance of the French was duplicated in some degree by the Italians. Moreover, elements in these two nations, harassed by the problems of Indochina and Trieste, hoped particularly after the death of Stalin on March 5, 1953, that the West could reach an understanding with the Soviet Union which would make a NATO army unnecessary. On May 11, 1953, Winston Churchill publicly proposed a conference "at the summit," a suggestion which encouraged those who wished to hold out a little longer before agreeing to join in the EDC project. The heart of the problem, however, as Chancellor Adenauer later observed, was France's fear of Germany. "The important points for most Frenchmen," he said, "were that the British should participate on a footing of equality with them, and that France should not be left alone with Germany."

Certainly the French viewpoint was understandable.[3] The men now

[3] General Gruenther in a speech once described this French feeling very aptly:

"Now there are many French who are against it [German rearmament], and I think you should know why they are against it because, whether you agree or not, I feel that it is essential in this alliance that we understand the point of view of the other man. You know well that France and Germany have had three wars in the last eighty years. You know that there was a large resistance movement in France against the Germans during the war and that created a great amount of bitterness. You may not know that there were 700,000 French laborers deported to Germany, and many of them felt that they had a very unhappy existence. In addition to that, there were 240,000 of the so-called upper classes who were shipped to Germany and spent considerable time in prisons like Dachau and Buchenwald, and of that group, heading the French government had themselves suffered under Nazi domination or had lost members of their families in the war. Understandable as the French attitude was, it could not, however, ignore that the principal threat to French peace and tranquillity in 1952 was posed by Soviet imperialism, not by a truncated, partially rearmed Germany. Therefore, upon my inauguration as President, I again set out to use every means at my disposal to indicate what I considered the path of enlightened self-interest to the French. The journey to European capitals of Foster Dulles and Harold Stassen immediately upon my inauguration aimed largely at encouraging European unity. The discussions on the subject at the Bermuda Conference in December 1953 were extensive. In all our diplomatic dealings with the French, the subject was in the forefront; indeed, during the trying and dramatic last days of the Indochina war the dispatches from Paris usually covered two subjects: Indochina and the attitude of the current French government on EDC. At times I suspected that the French, realizing our concern about EDC, could not resist the temptation to use this issue as a bargaining point in seeking our assistance in the Indochina war.

Always we moved in concert with the British. On April 13, 1954, for example, the British signed an association agreement with the six future members of the EDC, strengthening the 1952 British statement of intention to keep their forces in Europe, and three days later I set forth a commitment which the United States would make to the EDC; I indicated that the United States would keep armed forces in Europe, including Germany, as long as the need existed, and would do everything possible to bring about the closest integration between EDC forces on the one hand and United States and other forces (meaning principally British) on the other.

Foster Dulles was able to use this commitment in subsequent discussions, pointing out that my assurance presupposed that EDC would be ratified.

All the signatories had ratified the treaty except France and Italy when the Laniel government fell, over the Indochina issue. We, in Washington,

---

over 100,000 failed to return. So it is not difficult to see that there is a considerable amount of bitterness still existing on this subject.

"And in case you are inclined to be impatient of bitterness, I would recall to you that, after our own Civil War, the last state that came back into the Union returned in 1877—twelve years after the end of that war—and the bitterness did not end then. Those were people that we knew, that spoke the same language and were very good friends."

This address was made before the National Security Industrial Association, in New York, on September 29, 1954.

were understandably concerned that a new Premier might lack the strength and determination to obtain ratification of EDC. Our doubt proved to be well founded. On June 17 the new Premier, Pierre Mendès-France, included in his investiture speech a promise to amend the EDC treaty, presumably before asking for French ratification.[4] This proposal, if accepted by other signatory nations, would have delayed approval for many months, because the whole laborious process of revising, signing, and ratifying the organic document would necessarily be repeated.

When Winston Churchill and Anthony Eden came to Washington late in June 1954, we discussed EDC, as well as Indochina, and began to explore alternative action we might take if EDC should fail to be ratified by the French National Assembly. These discussions were by no means defeatist; we were determined to keep moving ahead, even in the face of temporary setbacks. It appeared that despite France's fear of Germany, the French on the whole were not set against German rearmament as such, but rather were opposed to EDC as a means, largely because of its supranational features.[5]

On July 30, 1954, the Senate made clear that the American people supported the rearmament of Germany; it unanimously adopted a resolution encouraging me in my purpose—to take any steps necessary to "restore sovereignty to Germany and to enable her to contribute to the maintenance of peace and security."

As France approached its crisis of decision, the Soviet Union continued its unremitting efforts to disrupt the movement toward European unity. At this time its tactic, if our estimate of its motives was correct, was to lull Western Europe into a false feeling of security. On August 4 it proposed a preliminary conference of the Big Four Foreign Ministers to consider the convocation of a larger European security conference. A week later it informed Austria that it would take part in a five-power conference on an Austrian peace treaty.

[4] This statement contrasted with what Mendès-France told Bedell Smith on June 20, 1954, when Bedell visited him on the way back from the Geneva Conference. At that time Mendès-France said that he was firmly and solidly in favor of the movement for European unity in every field. He was deferring action on EDC pending the termination of the Indochinese war, he said, at the end of which he correctly assumed that his personal prestige would be enhanced. Then he could obtain ratification by a large majority. France might later consider amendments necessary, but he would attempt to obtain ratification of EDC first, and, after France was committed, he would later propose the amendments to the other signatory nations.

[5] A further reason for France's resistance to EDC was the fact that it would not have a national army; the bulk of its armed forces would be organized in division-sized units only, with all higher levels of command vested in the supranational organization. This was understandably resisted by the proud and influential French officer corps.

Late in August a conference of the six EDC signatories was scheduled to take place in Brussels. Before the meeting convened, however—on August 19—Premier Mendès-France unveiled radical amendments to the treaty which he intended to propose. These included indefinite postponement of plans to standardize the armed forces, veto power for any nation over EDC actions, and deferment for eight years of the time the supranational court might begin to function.

These proposals were shocking. They changed the entire concept of the treaty. The Brussels Conference of the six EDC signatories, meeting on August 19–22, refused to agree on these alterations.

Instantly many cables began to be exchanged among several governments, especially the British, German, and American. Churchill, who had an appointment to see Mendès-France the day after the Brussels meeting, promised me that he would do all he could to change the Frenchman's mind.

When Winston and Anthony Eden met Mendès-France, they warned him of the difficulties of finding and bringing into force any substitute means of rearming Germany, particularly because of the time that would be consumed in getting Germany and other countries to accept. They urged him, they reported, to try to persuade the French National Assembly to accept the EDC as the most feasible answer.

Further, they said that a meeting of the United States, the United Kingdom, Germany, and Benelux had been suggested in the event that France definitely refused to go along with the other nations. Mendès-France argued strongly against such a meeting, but agreed in the event that EDC should fail of ratification to consider Germany's entry into NATO with or without some smaller grouping.

Entreaties were to no avail. On August 30, 1954, after intricate and mysterious maneuverings in a parliament where coalition governments must be made from six approximately equal-sized parties, the French National Assembly rejected EDC by a vote of 319 to 264, with 43 abstentions.

In all capitals, particularly in Bonn, the effects of the rejection of EDC were strongly felt. Chancellor Adenauer had obtained ratification of the EDC several months earlier, though not without opposition. Now, with the rejection of EDC, the Adenauer idea of rapprochement with France was crushed. The dream of German sovereignty, linked as it was to the adoption of EDC, seemed also gone for the moment. And Dr. Adenauer himself was in trouble. The elections of 1953 had given his Christian Democratic Union, the strongest single party in the Federal Republic, a majority of one seat in the Bundestag. To fortify that majority he required the vote of members of several smaller parties. During September the head of one of these called upon Dr. Adenauer to remove himself from the post of Foreign Minister. And into the bargain, the opposition Social Democratic party gave the Chancellor's party a clean defeat in a state election in Schleswig-Holstein. This election, the Social Democrats claimed, was a decisive repudiation of Dr. Adenauer's idea of a sovereign and rearmed German Federal Republic, a policy which the Social Democratic party had attacked continually, charging that any such status for the Federal Republic without East Germany included would demolish all hopes for a united Germany.

Faced with his most serious political crisis, Adenauer had to find a new course of action. Within a few days after France's rejection he demanded immediate sovereignty for Germany and participation in Western defense without discrimination. He promised that Germany would "voluntarily" limit its armaments, thus hoping to allay the fears of the French while preserving German self-respect.

Premier Mendès-France himself did not come off unscathed in his own country. Supporters of EDC now criticized him sharply for failing to give sufficient leadership to the cause. While he had been successful in many of his initial maneuvers, Mendès-France was still in an uncertain position.

In the United States our problems were complicated by a multiplicity of events. Almost simultaneously with the news of the EDC rejection, Foster Dulles had to proceed to Manila to participate in the signing of the SEATO treaty. Shortly thereafter, the Chinese Communists began to shell Quemoy and Matsu. And we were having difficulty with Italy, whose political scene was turbulent and confused. I was therefore frequently moved to say in private that all of us should be grateful for our great superiority in strategic bombing power, for that superiority sometimes seemed to be the only deterrent to an all-out Soviet attack on Europe. But this superiority could not last forever.

Despite the disappointing vote in the French parliament, this was no time for defeatism.[6] The task now was to search for a new device to bring Germany into the NATO family. On the 3rd of September I wrote from Denver to Bedell Smith, Acting Secretary of State in Foster's absence:

[6] The day I got the news of the EDC defeat, I said to an audience in Iowa:

"We have had our setbacks. One of the major setbacks was reported in your papers today: the rejection by the French parliament of the French proposition to establish in Europe the European Defense Community. . . .

"America has never quit in something that was good for herself and the world.

"We will not quit now. . . ."

For some days I have been storing up a few matters regarding which I wanted to write to you.

The first point is the state of our thinking toward the development of a substitute for EDC. I take it, that all of us agree we cannot sit down in black despair and admit defeat.

It seems to me there are two possible approaches—or maybe even three—

(a) Through the revision of the EDC idea by the nations concerned.

(b) Through a meeting of the entire NATO group, with a view of including Germany as an equal partner therein.

(c) Through unilateral agreements with Germany—to which agreements we would, of course, have to get the concurrence of a sizeable number of Western and Atlantic nations. . . .

A week later Foster Dulles advised me that the State Department was considering two alternative approaches: (1) to bring Germany directly into NATO, entrusting the control of the size, composition, and disposition of German defense forces to a NATO agreement with the German government voluntarily agreeing to limit its arms, and (2) if the French should object to this scheme, to take steps along with Britain, Germany, and possibly others, to go ahead with German rearmament under a defense agreement without the cooperation of the French. The second measure, though a last resort, might convince the French of the seriousness of our resolve.

Many leaders seemed to have proposals for solving the problem; none apparently jelled. On Saturday, September 11, Anthony Eden visited the Continent to confer with the Foreign Ministers of some of the EDC signatory nations. Winston reported to me that the visit with the Benelux Foreign Ministers had been successful, but they were disturbed by the rather bitter German reaction the previous week over the failure of EDC. The Benelux Foreign Ministers were apparently favorably disposed, however, to a plan the British government had devised for extending the force, provisions, and membership of the "Western Union" treaty which had been signed in Brussels in 1948 by Britain, France, Belgium, the Netherlands and Luxembourg—that treaty, ironically enough, having been directed ostensibly toward the prevention of a resurgence of German militarism. In his message Winston mentioned to me the possibility of convening in London a nine-power meeting to include those five nations named, plus Italy, Germany, Canada, and the United States.

On the 14th of the month Eden wrote to Foster Dulles (who had returned from Manila) that Chancellor Adenauer, as well as the Benelux ministers, had warmly welcomed the British proposal. On that same day Foster departed for a hurried trip to Bonn and London.

Foster found Adenauer gravely worried and anxious to find a solution quickly to impress his own people with the fact that they were not to remain indefinitely under subjugation. While Adenauer was still dedicated to the principle of European integration, he would be willing to go ahead, if necessary, with a German national army.

After Bonn, Foster's next stop was London, where he conferred with Winston, who wrote to me about the meeting. I was glad to see that despite all our frustrations, the Prime Minister's sense of humor was still intact. Referring to a message of mine thanking him for a full account of Anthony's trip, he said he was glad I thought him a good reporter. He had once made his living as a journalist. Referring—without saying so—to flurries in the press here, he added that he understood we had them in our country, too.

Winston's message explained his attitude on the European defense plan: From the start, he wrote, he had disliked "the sludgy amalgam" of EDC, which he described as mixing races in companies if not platoons. But because the plan had seemed to offer the only way of getting French and German forces to cooperate in a single defense mechanism, he had swallowed his prejudices when he had come to power in 1951. Now his reaction was that he did not blame the French for rejecting EDC but only for inventing it.

On the broad issue, however, that of the necessity for limited German rearmament, Winston's views were basically the same as ours. He recognized the tragedy which had befallen Adenauer in wasting three years pressing for acceptance of a plan which was now defunct. He commended for our consideration the British plan for expansion of the Brussels treaty and expressed hope that as time passed it could lead to a United Europe with German "comradeship."

In the meetings with Winston, Foster emphasized the difficulties which faced our government as a result of the collapse of EDC. The concept of a United States of Europe had great appeal in America. This had been reflected in congressional resolutions and legislation, and the American Chiefs of Staff were engaged in making a strategic reappraisal, seeking an acceptable alternative to earlier plans. There was a danger that if Europe showed little concern for American views, discouragement at home regarding the concept of a collective European defense would arise. This in turn might well jeopardize cooperative efforts with others, because the assurances given to Europe in my declaration of April 1954 had won congressional approval only in the context of EDC.

The nine-power Foreign Ministers' conference,[7] which Winston had suggested, opened in London on September 28. The atmosphere was strained, the main cause being the defensive attitude of Mendès-France.

[7] The United States, Canada, Britain, Belgium, Luxembourg, the Netherlands, Germany, France, and Italy.

When Foster met with him, he seemed to be offended at the criticism which he had received because of his role in the EDC rejection. However, he did agree that a way should be found to bring Germany into NATO.

In the meantime significant developments had been taking place. One was a definitely "on-the-record" statement by General Gruenther to a group of French industrialists visiting his headquarters at Rocquencourt, on September 22. Confidently he expressed the conviction that, with reasonable precautions on the part of the military commander of NATO, the composition and structure of the NATO force itself would prevent the possibility of any member nation's taking military action against the others. To deal with the French desire to bind and hamstring the West Germans with a super-elaborate apparatus of controls, he warned against setting up a "super police state in which inspectors could constantly check up on baby carriage factories to make certain they were not manufacturing guided missiles in secret."

Another development involved Britain. Since Foster's visit to London two weeks previously, the British had been restudying their defense planning. Previously the British had always been reluctant to pledge themselves to keep forces of any specified size on the Continent. (Indeed, it was the fear of a British withdrawal which had prompted so much of the French concern over a rearmed Germany.) Now, at the opening of the conference, Anthony Eden indicated that the British government would be willing to make unprecedented commitments, even in the absence of EDC, and would agree not to withdraw its current forces on the Continent against the wishes of the majority of the enlarged Brussels-treaty powers. Though this policy would not give France a veto, it would commit Britain not to withdraw forces at her sole discretion.

At the conference Foster and Anthony determined to deal in specifics, in the hope of encouraging any who might feel fainthearted. The United States pledged continued support if progress were made toward European unity. Eden, in a dramatic and historic speech, promised that Britain would maintain on the mainland of Europe four United Kingdom divisions and a tactical air force for so long as the majority of the Brussels-treaty powers desired.

The effect of Eden's statement was electric, even though, strangely, this act of British statesmanship was interpreted by some as a victory for Mendès-France. No matter how it was interpreted, the fact was that the French could now, with such assurances from Britain, be confident that they would never be left alone with a rearmed Germany. In his daily report to me Foster Dulles described the reaction:

> This was regarded, and I think rightly, by other countries as an historical decision tying England to the continent in a way which has never been

done before. The seven other countries made responses which were expressive of profound appreciation except that the response of Mendès-France, while formally correct, was somewhat grudging and lacking in the spirit which animated the others. I think he feels that our two statements, and notably the British statement, create a situation which makes it almost impossible for France to reject a reasonable settlement of the conditions which would make possible the admission of Germany to NATO and the creation of European unity with some supranational features on basis of Brussels treaty.

Early in October, I wrote to Winston to express my appreciation:

Foster has kept me informed on the progress of the talks now going forward in the Nine Power Conference. Both officially and personally I am most deeply appreciative of the contribution that Britain has offered to make to advance European unity.

Of course I understand fully your reluctance to move without parallel commitment by us. However, our constitutional processes do not permit this, but I am certain that so long as Europe is moving toward unified action, you can always be sure of our effective cooperation on the continent. In this statement I know I speak for the tremendous majority of the citizens of our country.

In this often confused world, it is encouraging to witness the enlightened and courageous statesmanship exhibited by you and Anthony. In this instance, as in so many others, I have the greatest admiration for your judgment and actions.

Please give my warm regard to Anthony, and, as always, the best to yourself.

As a result of ensuing diplomatic maneuverings, the meeting produced positive and constructive results. While further meetings in Paris would be required to work out the details of plans for integration of the German armed forces, and Mendès-France would still insist that the long-standing Saar question between France and Germany had to be settled before he could proceed affirmatively with the National Assembly, there was no doubt that a tremendous step forward had been taken.

Foster summarized the results:

Have just signed with the eight other foreign ministers the agreements reached here. They still have to be perfected in some detail, but immense amount of work has been accomplished, and I believe that if what was done here is finally realized, we will have saved most of the values inherent in EDC. The Brussels Council will have many supranational responsibilities, and while the present arrangements do not go as far as EDC in creating parliamentary controls, this disadvantage is to an extent offset by the British committal to continental Europe. . . .

In concrete terms the outcome of the meeting was this:

(1) A committee of the Big Three and West German experts was to arrange for an end to German occupation;

(2) West Germany was to be invited to enter NATO and to contribute (as in the EDC agreement) twelve divisions and an air force of one thousand planes; the power of the Supreme Allied Commander in Europe was to be expanded to prevent the independent deployment of German forces;

(3) West Germany and Italy were to join the Brussels-treaty organization, which would fix the maximum size of the Continental members' contributions to NATO and control all arms manufacture;

(4) West Germany was not to manufacture missiles or atomic, biological, or chemical weapons.

Later in the month in Paris the Foreign Ministers of all the NATO countries and West Germany met to declare the virtual sovereignty of the German Federal Republic; to set terms for West German rearmament within a Western European Union (WEU) under the expanded Brussels treaty; to invite Germany to join NATO; and to secure an agreement between France and Germany on the Saar.

Strangely, in this second meeting, even after so much had been accomplished in the first, the fate of the Western European Union seemed to remain in doubt up to the last moment. On October 23 Foster reported:

> We are waiting here Saturday morning not knowing whether or not documents in relation to German sovereignty, Brussels treaty and NATO will or will not be signed this afternoon. Everything hinges on Saar matter, which Adenauer and Mendès-France discussed last night until nearly three. They are apparently in agreement on political issues, but certain economic issues remain unsolved. They meet again at 11:30 Paris time. It seems to me incredible that the margin of difference now remaining should wreck this whole affair, but it is possible because Adenauer has gone close to the tolerable political limit and Mendès-France can be very stubborn.
>
> Everything else has gone extremely well, and the NATO atmosphere is one of strengthened fellowship.

And then later on in the morning, the final message:

> I am happy to inform you that everything including Saar [see Appendix K] has now been signed sealed and delivered. I know you will rejoice with me that the unity and freedom of Europe to which you contributed so indispensably seems likely now to be preserved.

The nine-power meetings were over. Foster Dulles flew home, where, on the evening of October 25, he reported the results in a Cabinet meeting, the first one in history televised for the American people.

I was highly gratified by developments, as was Foster and the entire administration—and there was much reason for satisfaction. On August 30 the European Defense Community had run upon the rocks, and the possibilities of finding a device to bring Germany into the family of independent nations seemed remote. A mere thirty-three days later an accord had been signed, under a different name, Western European Union, encompassing the essentials we had striven so long to realize.

The occupation of Germany was over. Our High Commissioner James Conant became Ambassador Conant.

Soviet efforts to scuttle European unity through biting propaganda during this whole proceeding had failed.

The land that Allied forces under my command had helped to conquer nearly a decade before was no longer the scene of desolation and despair. It was now a rehabilitated and equal member of the Western Alliance. I fervently agreed with Foster that the accomplishment of this transformation was a "near miracle—a shining chapter in history."

*   *   *

For the want of Trieste, an Issue was lost.
For the want of an Issue, the Election was lost.
For the want of an Election, De Gasperi was lost.
For the want of De Gasperi, his NATO policies were lost.
For the want of his NATO policies, Italy was lost.
For the want of Italy, Europe was lost.
For the want of Europe, America . . . ?

This version by Ambassador Clare Boothe Luce of the old "For want of a nail" may have been a little overdrawn, but it held considerable truth. Anyone who becomes immersed in international affairs soon realizes that no important issue exists in isolation; rarely is it only bilateral. A problem which may seem to be of interest to only two countries almost invariably affects a third and, as often as not, a fourth or more. And, save in exceptional circumstances, there is a tendency within any country for one set of problems in its foreign affairs to become linked with others.

A remarkable illustration of this interrelationship was the situation which existed in Italy in 1953 when Mrs. Luce wrote these lines. Three foreign problems of deep concern were foremost in the thinking of the leaders of that country. One was obtaining the ratification of the European Defense Community in the Italian parliament; a second involved negotiations with the United States for NATO bases, to be located on Italian soil; the third and most emotional was the controversy between Italy and Yugoslavia over the Free Territory of Trieste. Given the precarious nature of Italian politics at the time, the fate of Italy's action on the first two—indeed, the entire orientation of the Italian government—depended to a large extent on the outcome of the Trieste negotiations.

Before World War I the city of Trieste was the property and principal port of the Austro-Hungarian Empire. With the defeat and dismemberment of that empire, and as a reward for Italy's participation on the side of the Allies in that conflict, the city of Trieste (which became the capital of the province of Trieste) and a three-thousand-square-mile region around it, Venezia Giulia, were ceded to Italy. This status prevailed between the wars.

In the final days of World War II, Allied armies, dashing across the Po Valley, continued northward to the Alps, and eastward to the head of the Adriatic. They reached and occupied the city of Trieste and its immediate environs, finally coming to a halt face to face with Yugoslav armies which occupied the outlying eastern and northern regions of the former Trieste province. The line on which American and British forces halted was known, after its local British commander, as the Morgan Line. It split Venezia Giulia in half.

Tito, for his own reasons, insisted that the entire area, with its important city and port, should belong to Yugoslavia. He based this claim on the participation of the Yugoslavs against Nazi Germany in World War II and on the initially hostile status of Italy in the war—Italy came in on the side of the Allies only after the fall of Mussolini. Moreover, the city of Trieste was on the Yugoslav side of the Gulf of Trieste, and the population of the hinterlands was primarily Slovenian.

Tito's plans for occupying Venezia Giulia were foiled by the fact that American and British troops along the Morgan Line held half of it, including the city of Trieste. Thus by an agreement of June 9, 1945, each side simply occupied the territory behind its line, in zones which came to be known as Zone A (under the British and Americans) and Zone B (under the Yugoslavs).

The Italian peace treaty, signed in Paris on February 10, 1947, gave most of Venezia Giulia to Yugoslavia. It let Italy keep part of its former province of Gorizia and, out of the former Italian provinces of Trieste and Istria, it carved a new political creation, the Free Territory of Trieste, an area 285 square miles in extent, with its independence guaranteed by the United Nations Security Council.

The Morgan Line, which had split all of Venezia Giulia into two zones, also split this new Free Territory into Zones A and B, Allied and Yugoslav respectively, with the city of Trieste on the Allied side. On implementation of the treaty, British and American forces in the north

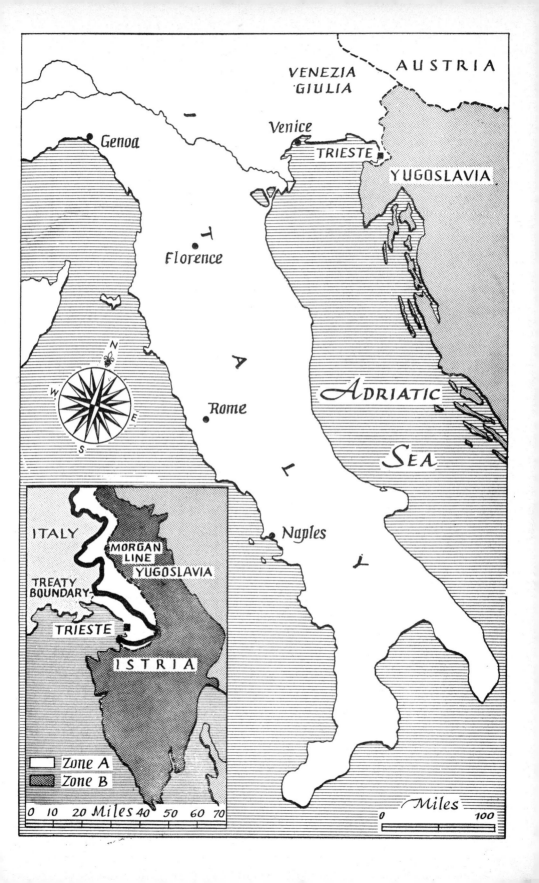

AUSTRIA

VENEZIA GIULIA

Venice

TRIESTE

YUGOSLAVIA

Genoa

Florence

ADRIATIC

Rome

SEA

Naples

ITALY

MORGAN LINE

YUGOSLAVIA

TREATY BOUNDARY

TRIESTE

ISTRIA

Zone A
Zone B

0 10 20 Miles 40 50 60 70

Miles

0   100

withdrew from their positions on the Morgan Line to the line established as Italy's new political boundary. Within the newly established Free Territory, however, they remained in place, against the day when the UN Security Council would set up a territorial government.

The Italians objected to the permanent internationalization of Trieste; it meant, they said, the loss of an Italian city and brought on the danger of increased Yugoslav influence at the head of the Adriatic. The Yugoslavs objected also; they insisted on their right to Trieste as a reward for their wartime sufferings, and moreover, they claimed, the Italians had been mistreating Yugoslav minorities living in Zone A.

Under the peace treaty the UN Security Council was to appoint the governor of Trieste, who in turn was to set up a legislative and police organization. East-West disagreements within the Security Council, however, prevented even the initial appointment. Recognizing this impasse, the United States, Britain, and France sent a note to the Soviet Union (as one of the signatories to the 1947 Italian peace treaty) on March 20, 1948, proposing the return of all of Trieste to Italy. The Soviet Union turned down this proposition.

The whole territory therefore continued under military government, with Communist minorities within the Italian Zone A instigating political strikes, with the Yugoslavs in Zone B threatening to substitute a judicial system of their own for the system in effect, which was still, of course, the Italian system, and with both sides claiming the whole territory. These tensions remained despite the Cominform's expulsion of Tito in the middle of 1948 and Russia's abrogation of its treaty with Yugoslavia in September of 1949.

In February 1952 Tito made a new proposal: the integration of Zones A and B with the provision that Yugoslavia and Italy, not the UN Security Council, should name governors for alternating three-year terms. The Italian Premier, Alcide de Gasperi, seeing the trap, refused to be a collaborator with Communism and wisely turned the suggestion down.

Three months later the Americans, British, and Italians agreed on a share of administrative functions for the Italians in Zone A. The Soviet Union protested, and in retaliation Yugoslavia announced it would extend its own laws into Zone B.

When I took office in 1953, the quarrel was still raging. Tito remained intransigent, and so did the Italian government, which was under constant scrutiny by its domestic opposition for any "concession" or "weakness." Wanting to keep Tito split from the Soviet Union, the United States could no longer, as in 1948, back Italy to the hilt in its claim to everything. But something had to be done. With the aid of our capable ambassador to Italy, Mrs. Luce, we began in the early months of my administration to explore ways of resolving the issue.

By mid-1953 the Italians had unwarrantedly developed a fear, possibly generated by Communist agitators, that the United States was backing Yugoslavia. The miscalculations of the Allies, De Gasperi warned during his last week in office, could endanger NATO. His successor, Giuseppe Pella, refused to push for ratification of the EDC treaty until the Western Allies assured him clear protection for Italian rights in Trieste—rights which, in a speech in August, he based on the 1948 proposal of the three Western Allies, which had suggested the return of all Trieste to Italy.

This speech infuriated the Yugoslavs, to whom it indicated Italy's intention to annex Trieste. Yugoslavia, Tito said, would have to re-examine the whole Trieste question. Pella interpreted Tito's attitude as a threat of armed conflict; accordingly, he sent Italian troops to the northeast frontier and warships up the Adriatic. He warned the West that Italy would have to withdraw from NATO unless it obtained the backing of the United States, Britain, and France. Through General Gruenther he privately sent me a request to consider letting Italian troops occupy Zone A.

In September 1953 I had a lengthy discussion on the Trieste problem with Foster Dulles. Neither the Italians nor the Yugoslavs could back down sufficiently to agree to a settlement which would give the entire territory to the other. Hence, the only answer lay in some form of partition. Each side, naturally, would protest strongly against partition. But both would undoubtedly realize that such a solution was inevitable. As to the mechanism, I felt it would be impossible to amend the peace treaty of 1947 to achieve partition, for the Soviet Union, as a signatory, would have to be a party to an amendment, and could therefore essentially veto such an approach. Hence, it seemed that the solution lay in some informal device to recognize and make permanent the boundaries then existing between Zones A and B within the Free Territory. I asked Foster to pursue the matter in detail and report back to me.

About three weeks later, on September 30, I sent Foster a note asking him what progress we were making. In my note I said that ever since my experience as NATO commander, I had been expecting some kind of solution to this problem "within the month." Foster replied to me the next day that we were pushing the settlement vigorously; he would not, he said, give up hope that the matter could be settled within the month. "I say this with more hope," he wrote, "since this is the first day of the month."

The next week we announced through the State Department (the British Foreign Office did the same) that, because it had proved impossible to set up a permanent regime for Trieste, the Allies were planning to turn over Zone A to Italian administration and to withdraw Allied troops "at the earliest possible date." This would mean, among other things, that Italian troops would enter Zone A for the first time.

On the day of the announcement I wrote in my diary:

> Today, October 8th, the British and American governments made public a previously agreed upon position with respect to Trieste. Trieste has, of course, been for years a source of irritation and mutual recrimination between Italy and Yugoslavia. We need both nations as friends, and we had therefore to try for some solution.
>
> Tito, dictator of the Yugoslav government, has actually made good on his occupation of the so-called Zone B in the Trieste area, and our solution is merely to give similar de facto title to Italy with respect to Zone A. This zone is now occupied by British and American troops, and our announcement means that as soon as practicable, we will physically turn over that area to the Italians.
>
> This is another step in a long series of things we have been attempting to do in order to strengthen America's political and security position vis-à-vis the Soviets. If this works—and I certainly can't think of any better solution of the problem because it is one of those that has no perfect answer—then we will vastly strengthen our position in the Adriatic and generate much greater confidence in all of Western Europe. As of now, the mutual hostility between these two countries has largely neutralized any help that NATO could expect from them in time of emergency. Obviously, if both accept this solution (although both are to have the right to denounce it publicly) we will have the chance to plan confidently for the defense of the whole Alps region.

The announcement, however, created a more enthusiastic reaction on the part of the Italians than was predicted or, as it turned out, desirable. In fact, the reaction, both official and public, was such that Tito apparently felt that he must take a face-saving measure to counter it. He announced that if Italy moved into Zone A, he would consider the movement an act of aggression against Yugoslavia and might well send troops into Zone A himself.

When Foster Dulles informed me on October 14 of the Yugoslav threat, I was surprised but determined to be prepared to deal with any foolhardy movement on Tito's part. A check with the Joint Chiefs of Staff indicated that it would take thirty-six to forty-eight hours to move important elements of the Sixth Fleet into the upper Adriatic. Warships were sent without delay.

At the same time, however, Tito had been proposing a conference (including the United States, Great Britain, Yugoslavia, and Italy) before any transfer of Zone A to Italy. Italy agreed to attend, but only if

Yugoslavia should leave Zone B or if Italy should be given control over the Zone A administration. Yugoslavia remained obdurate on this issue, and the talks never took place.

In early November violence broke out in the city of Trieste itself, instigated by Italian extreme nationalists. The police shot sixty, killing six. Allied troops helped quell the mobs. A United States destroyer anchored in the harbor, and gradually tempers began to cool. In the following weeks both Italy and Yugoslavia, while reiterating their earlier demands, agreed to enter into negotiations with the United States, Britain, and France. Both disputants pulled back their troops from the borders of Zone A.

The political situation in Italy remained tense. On November 1 Ambassador Luce sent me a complete and analytical statement of the situation faced by Italy. She emphasized that the Cominform Left (which included not only the Communists but the Left-wing Nenni Socialists) had polled 37 per cent of the vote in the June elections, and that its strength was growing steadily. If it gained only 4 per cent more at the expense of the Center and Right parties, the Italian President would be required by the Constitution to call upon a Cominform leader (either Nenni or Togliatti) to form the next government. Of all the measures which the United States could take to help halt the political appeal of Communism and strengthen the Center parties, she placed the implementation (partial or complete) of our October 8 decision to withdraw from Trieste as first priority. She expressed urgent hope for rapidity, saying that to delay now threatened to destroy any progress we had made toward checking the growth of the Cominform. The Trieste issue, she said, had now begun to backfire on Pella.

I answered her immediately:

I assure you first that, so far as I know, we have no intention of weaseling on our October 8th decision on Trieste. Because there were some unexpected reactions, there has been a corresponding amount of delay, coupled with some confusion, in trying to get things on the rails again. Specifically, we did not expect the enthusiastic official and public reaction from the Italian side. This unquestionably made Tito feel that he had to react adversely and much more vehemently than he otherwise would have. But whether or not the Italian attitude affected him, a situation has been created where we must observe sufficient caution that we do not almost force Italy and Yugoslavia into even deeper trouble in order to save face on one or both sides. However, I think the State Department is moving as rapidly as it can to correct the current situation.

By now, however, it was becoming apparent that both sides really desired to negotiate in a reasonable manner on the Trieste matter, even though a conference with both Italy and Yugoslavia participating appeared impossible. Accordingly, we determined to begin negotiations secretly with one country at a time.

The first phase of the secret negotiations began in London in February 1954, with the United States, the United Kingdom, and Yugoslavia represented. One of our capable career diplomats, Mr. Llewellyn Thompson, then ambassador to Austria, represented the United States. Meanwhile, internal affairs in Italy appeared somewhat improved. In early March, Acting Secretary of State Bedell Smith reported hopeful developments:

1. A center coalition government including the Social Democrats has been formed by the Christian Democrats and is expected to win parliamentary confirmation. . . .

2. The government has presented an energetic constructive program (housing, social security reform, further tax reform, public works) which may reduce unemployment somewhat and help stem the loss of voter support to the left.

3. The government seems resolved to press for ratification of EDC and for final approval of the United States–Italian agreement on NATO facilities for United States use in Italy.[8] It no longer links these questions to a satisfactory solution of Trieste.

4. The principal anti-Communist trade union has reasserted its opposition to unity of action with the Communist union and is supporting the present government. This also is a blow to the popular front policy.

5. The government and press show a new awareness of the Communist internal threat, and the Berlin conference disillusioned many of the Soviet "peace" campaign.

6. Secret U.S.–U.K. negotiations with the Yugoslavs on Trieste have made progress and have reached the point where specific territorial solutions

---

8 I have always been against negotiations with our allies for United States bases on their territory if those allies showed the least reluctance. Such negotiations, when our friends thought we were overeager, tended to put them in a horse-trading frame of mind. In July of 1954 I wrote the following note to Foster Dulles:

"Mrs. Luce tells me that in her negotiations for bases in Italy, her understanding is that *at all cost* she must secure permission from the Italian Government. . . . Personally, I do not feel that bases in Italy are vital at all, and I think the importance of having them there diminishes every day. If she were able to give the Italians the intimations and information that we were losing interest in the thing, the situation might change.

"Anyway, that applies to all our foreign relations. In selling the United States the idea that 'we cannot live alone' we have also sold the Europeans the idea that we are completely dependent upon their cooperative attitude.

"In a sense this is, of course, true, but if there is not full recognition of a common need and because of this the cooperative effort breaks down, it is equally true that they will feel the pinch long before we will."

are being discussed. If we stand firm there is hope that we may achieve either a compromise settlement the Italians could accept, or the equivalent of implementation of our October 8 decision to transfer Zone A to Italy. Either development would strengthen the Italian Center government. . . .

Of course Italy's basic problems such as over-population and poverty of resources will remain to plague present and future Italian governments. Nevertheless the situation looks better at the moment than it has for some months.

On May 31 the first phase of the Trieste negotiations—those between the United States, the United Kingdom, and Yugoslavia—came to a surprisingly satisfactory end. The Yugoslavs agreed to a territorial settlement which amounted to general acceptance of our announcement of October 8. They agreed that Italy should have Zone A (including the city of Trieste); Yugoslavia was to keep Zone B. The only difference between the terms of this agreement and those of our announcement was that the Yugoslavs would keep a small strip of Zone A at the western end of the interzonal boundary, for which they were willing to give up a smaller segment of Zone B at the eastern end.

The Yugoslavs also gave up their insistence that the territorial settlement be contingent upon a settlement of their financial claims, mostly World War II reparations, against Italy.

Other features of the contemplated settlement were a reciprocal statute for the protection of minorities, and arrangements for maintenance of a free port in Trieste and for some measure of local autonomy.

In June 1954 the second part of the negotiations, those with Italy, began. Progress was tedious and conducted against the background of uncertainties still looming on the Italian political horizon. The matter of NATO bases in Italy remained linked with the Trieste issue, although Foster assured me in this regard that Mario Scelba, who had succeeded Pella as Premier in February, had promised his signature on our base negotiations within twenty-four hours after a Trieste agreement.

On the 31st of August, I received from Ambassador Luce a letter that in its clear perception and forceful expression seemed to me a model of fine ambassadorial reporting and suggestion.

> . . . The day of the funeral [De Gasperi's] was a day of double mourning in Italy. The somber news of Mendès-France's act of mayhem at Brussels foretold the demise of EDC. Italy knew that the noble idea that De Gasperi had labored for so long—the integration of Europe—was being buried with him.
>
> The outcome of the Brussels Conference forced Prime Minister Scelba and his cabinet to make their own "agonizing reappraisal."
>
> Here it is, in the Prime Minister's own words to me:

Except for our fruitless efforts to secure the return of the whole Free Territory of Trieste, since the end of the war Italy's entire foreign policy has been European integration, and solidarity through NATO, with the Western defense system. Today an "integrated Europe" is dead and the strength of NATO may be consequently greatly damaged.

I will not speak of the months of labor we have lost in bringing EDC to where we would have ratified it by a safe margin of 80 votes. I will not speak of the impossibility now of carrying on the Anti-Communist program we had planned to follow upon ratification. I must speak only of one thing: Today the Government's entire foreign policy is seriously discredited: Read this morning's headlines in UNITA [the CP paper]: "Pro-West Policies of Government Total Failure." If we do not shortly have a substitute for EDC, or if we cannot soon say that a rearmed Germany will become a welcome and an effective NATO partner, the Government will have *no* foreign policy to put before the people. Our internal political situation will then deteriorate rapidly, for the Communists will be proven entirely right in their judgment of the European situation. We can then be certain of only one thing: Russian divisions will not invade Italian soil. They will not need to, because our own Communists will ring down the Iron Curtain on Italy in the next election.

If no substitute for EDC and the now acute "German question" can be found shortly, the Scelba Government will not last the winter. That is, *unless* we can produce a settlement of the Trieste question—and immediately.

We must then be prepared to see the collapse of the Scelba Government. And then with no Government and no foreign policy around which a new one can be formed in the interests of the West, if Italy does not revert to strong-arm methods against the Communists the leadership of Italy may soon after fall to Nenni and Togliatti.

The return of Zone A has now become a matter of greatest urgency to the present Italian Government. I, therefore, Mr. President, recommend that you insist on a firm reply from the Yugoslavs at once, which will permit the Italians to dispose of the Trieste question one way or another, before October 8.

By this time the conferences between the United States, the United Kingdom, and Italy were complete. The effort now was to try resolving the results with Yugoslavians and Italians in the same room at the same time. Tito was once again being difficult about putting his final approval on the agreement.

With the Secretary of State spending a large portion of September out of the country in constant negotiations on several outstanding problems, I kept in close touch with Under Secretary Bedell Smith, and on September 3 wrote him:

. . . Still another subject in which I am tremendously interested is Trieste. We have been working on it a long time and my impression is that we have been letting Tito block us, perhaps needlessly. Over a period of many weeks I have been told time and again that it looked as though we were just on the point of securing an agreement, after which there has been nothing but silence. I think that whatever we do must be done soon, if for no other reason than to provide some counter-balance for the EDC flop.

Bedell answered with a request for permission to send Robert Murphy to London to try to give added impetus to the final stages of the negotiations. This I approved.

Four days later Bedell wrote again, his cable illustrating the complicated nature of the negotiations:

Bob Murphy will leave Saturday for Europe in an attempt to push through a final settlement. The basic outstanding issue is over a small piece of territory which both sides insist on getting. The second outstanding issue is the reparations one but we estimate that it will be agreed if a territorial settlement can be reached. The Yugoslavs are in great need of wheat, which we can provide under our law. Harold Stassen is arranging this. In addition the Yugoslavs are greatly worried by their financial problem of converting their short-term liabilities into long-term obligations. They would like our moral and political support in accomplishing this and have proposed sending their Finance Minister here to discuss the problem with us. We have encouraged his coming. Both the wheat and the financial problem give us a certain leverage on the Yugoslavs, which we intend to employ in reaching a Trieste settlement.

On September 24 Foster reported: "Trieste again seems on the verge of settlement, but in view of past experience I must emphasize the word 'verge' rather than the word 'settlement.'" But this time our efforts bore fruit. On October 5, 1954, the long months of wrangling, riots, uncertainty, and tangled diplomacy came to an end. A nine-year quarrel was over. Italy and Yugoslavia signed an agreement on Trieste which was acceptable to both.[9]

Now the way was open for Italian participation in the Western European Union and for success in negotiations for defense bases. The Communist threat to Italy had been averted, and that nation now trod on firmer ground. And the threat of an explosion passed.

[9] The agreement was close to that to which Tito had agreed in London on May 31. It left the city of Trieste in Italian hands. A slight boundary change gave Yugoslavia slightly more square miles and four thousand more people. American and British forces were to withdraw. Italy was to administer Zone A, Yugoslavia, Zone B, in accordance with the Italian peace treaty; Italy was to maintain the free port of Trieste; each government was to protect minority rights on its side of the boundary line.

*   *   *

A region of the world of vital importance to the United States is Latin America, a vast area of undeveloped resources, whose weight in the scales of the balance of power has become steadily more important.

We like to think of Latin America as nearby, in our own back yard, so to speak. In fact, most of it, particularly the large nations of Argentina, Brazil, and Chile, is actually a great distance from the United States. Indeed, Argentina and those portions of Brazil south of the Cape of São Roque are farther by water from the United States than they are from Europe. But distance is only one factor in our relations with these nations. Far more significant is the fact that we both have a tradition of independence and that we both, though separate from Europe, have an inheritance of Western religion and culture.

Nevertheless, from time to time, in fact to an extent all the time, our sister republics to the south feel that the United States pays too little attention to them and their problems. Perhaps, in part, this feeling is justified. Certainly after World War II, United States diplomacy was constantly preoccupied with European and Asian crises, any one of which could have resulted in serious conflict, whereas under normal circumstances it would not be expected that global war would break out as the result of problems in Latin America. Further, our shared ideals of freedom have sometimes led our diplomats to expect our sister republics to stand by us automatically on critical world issues, thus giving them a feeling of being taken for granted.

I was aware of this danger early in my administration and moved to prevent such a feeling from growing. The first state visit to Washington after I entered the White House was, as I have recorded, that of President Remón of Panama, and I had made a special point of attending the dedication of the Falcon Dam with President Ruiz Cortines of Mexico, when for the first time as President I set foot on the soil of another nation, our nearest Latin American neighbor.

But the most important effort to improve Latin-American relations was to recruit the services of my brother Milton, a dedicated diplomat with such exceptional capabilities that were it not for the accident of his being my brother, he would most certainly have been asked to occupy a high Cabinet position in my administration. From 1953 on, Milton served in a highly important capacity as my personal representative with the rank of special ambassador, in making numerous studies in Latin America, and reporting to me the feelings of the people south of the border. He persistently recommended measure after measure to improve our friendships, to establish, as I once wrote to him, "a healthy relationship" which will endure.

We all realized that the fundamental problems of Latin America—which stem from lack of capital; overdependence on the sale of primary commodities; severe maldistribution of wealth; illiteracy, and poverty—would take a long time for the nations themselves to correct even with all the outside help they deserved. No matter how much help we extended—and United States aid to Latin America increased markedly during the 1950s—we realized that we were going to run into difficulties in our relations with individual states before the day came when the major causes of those difficulties could be erased.

The first of these problems was waiting for me when I entered the White House. It involved Guatemala, a beautiful land of Central America whose mountains and moderate climate make it one of the garden spots of the hemisphere. The troubles had been long-standing, reaching back nine years to the Guatemalan revolution of 1944, which had resulted in the overthrow of the dictator General Jorge Ubico. Thereafter, the Communists busied themselves with agitating and with infiltrating labor unions, peasant organizations, and the press and radio. In 1950 a military officer, Jacobo Arbenz Guzmán, came to power and by his actions soon created the strong suspicion that he was merely a puppet manipulated by Communists.

The American republics wanted no Communist regime within their midst. They recognized that subversion by Communism was only another form of aggression, even more evil than that achieved by naked military force. However, in unstable regions where revolutions and rioting were not uncommon, where some governments were being maintained by dictatorial means, where resentments against the United States were sometimes nurtured by groups other than Communist cells, it was difficult to differentiate positively between Communist influence and uncontrolled and politically rebellious groups. For example, on February 24, 1953, the Arbenz government announced its intention, under an agrarian reform law, to seize about 225,000 acres of unused United Fruit Company land. The company lost its appeal to the Guatemalan Supreme Court to prevent this discriminatory and unfair seizure. (Of all lands expropriated, two thirds belonged to United Fruit. In return the company was to receive the woefully inadequate compensation of $600,000 in long-term non-negotiable agrarian bonds.)

Expropriation in itself does not, of course, prove Communism; expropriation of oil and agricultural properties years before in Mexico had not been fostered by Communists.

Approximately six weeks after the announcement of the United Fruit Company land seizure, however, Guatemala withdrew from the five-nation Organization of Central American States, alleging aggression by Guatemala's neighbors. In this instance, the real reason was apparent: Guatemala could not risk participation in a debate on an anti-Communist resolution scheduled for presentation by El Salvador at a forthcoming meeting of the organization.

Arbenz denied that his government was Communist, a denial that was issued in a speech at a May Day celebration featuring seventy thousand marchers. But by the middle of October 1953, the Assistant Secretary of State for Inter-American Affairs, John Moors Cabot, said publicly that Guatemala was "openly playing the Communist game"; for example, it accepted the ridiculous Communist contention that the United States had conducted bacteriological warfare in Korea.

About that time a new ambassador, John E. Peurifoy, was appointed to Guatemala. He was familiar with the tactics of the Communists in Greece, where he had served. Peurifoy soon reached definite conclusions on the nature of the Arbenz government. Later he reported that he had discussed the Arbenz orientation with the Presidente himself within a month after his arrival at his new post. He described his discussion aptly:

> In a six hour conversation he listened while I counted off the leading Communists in his regime, but he gave no ground; many notorious Reds he denied to be Communists; if they were, they were not dangerous; if dangerous, he could control them; if not controllable, he would round them up. He said, in any case, all our difficulties were due to the mal-practices of American business. The trips of Communists to Russia were not to get training and instructions, he said, but merely to study Marxism, just in the same way as other Guatemalans may come to the United States to study economics. Meanwhile, they would continue to enjoy the full advantages accorded all Guatemalans, as they were valuable allies to him in the fight for social reform. . . . It seemed to me that the man thought like a Communist and talked like a Communist, and if not actually one, would do until one came along. I so reported to Secretary Dulles, who informed the President; and I expressed to them the view that unless the Communist influences in Guatemala were counteracted, Guatemala would within six months fall completely under Communist control.[10]

[10] On October 8, 1954, Mr. Peurifoy testified before the Subcommittee on Latin America of the House Select Committee on Communist Aggression as follows:

"It is my understanding, Mr. Chairman, that the purpose of your hearings is to determine:

"1. Whether or not the government of President Arbenz was controlled and dominated by Communists.

Something had to be done quickly. The first task was to marshal and crystallize Latin American public opinion on the issue. The opportunity presented itself at the Tenth Inter-American Conference of the Organization of the American States (OAS) which met in Caracas, Venezuela, in March of 1954. At that meeting the United States urged the adoption of a joint condemnation of Communism, contending vigorously that it should not be permitted to control any state in the Western Hemisphere. Foster Dulles, representing the United States, argued that if Communism should succeed to this extent, it should be treated as a threat to the peace. On March 6 he introduced a draft resolution of a "Declaration of Solidarity for the Preservation of the Political Integrity of the American States against International Communist Intervention."

The draft resolution was harsh. It was meant to be. It condemned international Communism in the Western Hemisphere as a type of foreign intervention; pledged the American states "to take the necessary measures to protect their political independence against" such intervention; declared that the "domination . . . of the political institutions of any American State by the International Communist movement" constituted a "threat to the sovereignty and political independence of the American States, endangered the peace of America, and would call for appropriate action in accordance with existing treaties." It also called for an exchange of data on Communist activity in each country and upheld the right of each state to defend its own independence and to choose its own form of government and its own manner of social and cultural life.

On March 26, in plenary session, the organization approved the resolution by a vote of seventeen to one, with Guatemala opposing, and Argentina and Mexico abstaining—Costa Rica was absent. As passed, it differed in only one respect from the draft; it called not for immediate action to meet the Communist threat but rather for a "meeting to consider the adoption of measures in accordance with existing treaties."

"2. Whether or not the Communists who dominated Guatemala were in turn directed from the Kremlin.

"3. Whether or not the Communists from Guatemala actively intervened in the internal affairs of neighboring Latin American republics.

"4. Whether or not this Communist conspiracy which centered in Guatemala represented a menace to the security of the United States.

"My answer to all four of those questions is an unequivocal 'yes.'

"The Arbenz government, beyond any question, was controlled and dominated by Communists. Those Communists were directed from Moscow. The Guatemalan government and the Communist leaders of that country did continuously and actively intervene in the internal affairs of neighboring countries in an effort to create disorder and overthrow established governments. And the Communist conspiracy in Guatemala did represent a very real and very serious menace to the security of the United States."

This resolution formed a charter for the anti-Communist counterattack that followed. But before these resolutions could become effective, things got worse.

In the two months from March to May, 1954, the agents of international Communism in Guatemala continued their efforts to penetrate and subvert their neighboring Central American states, using consular agents for their political purposes and fomenting political assassinations and strikes. In Guatemala itself the government answered protests by suspending constitutional rights, conducting mass arrests, and killing leaders in the political opposition.

In May things came to a head. On the 17th of that month Foster Dulles reported to the press that the United States had reliable information on a shipment of arms from behind the Iron Curtain. The arms had been loaded on the *Alfhem,* a Swedish ship chartered by a British company, at the East German Baltic port of Stettin. The ship was at that moment being unloaded at Puerto Barrios in Guatemala. The ship had mysteriously changed its announced destination and its course three times en route, apparently in an effort to confuse observers. We learned that the cargo contained two thousand tons of small arms, ammunition, and light artillery pieces manufactured in the Skoda arms factory in Czechoslovakia. This quantity far exceeded any legitimate, normal requirements for the Guatemalan armed forces.

On May 19 Nicaragua broke diplomatic ties with Guatemala. Five days later we announced that the United States was airlifting arms to Honduras and Nicaragua to help counter the danger created by the Czech shipment to Guatemala. Our initial shipment comprised only fifty tons of rifles, pistols, machine guns, and ammunition, hardly enough to create apprehension in neighboring states.

On May 24, 1954, I informed the Legislative leaders of measures we were planning to take. Honduras and Nicaragua had asked for help. Among other things, we would (1) prevent any further Communist arms build-up in Central America by stopping suspicious foreign-flag vessels on the high seas off Guatemala to examine cargo (an action conforming to the United Nations Charter and Caracas resolution) and (2) convene another meeting of the Organization of American States to consider next steps. We would, of course, advise Mexico and other friendly countries of our plans.

Our quarantine measures soon ran into trouble. We were able to hold up at Hamburg some six tons of 20-mm. antiaircraft shells in transit to Guatemala from Switzerland. Action on the high seas, however, was a different matter. While well within the capabilities of the Navy, such measures would require at least the tacit cooperation of our allies, principally Britain, to avoid placing an almost fatal strain on our relations. At first such cooperation was difficult to obtain, at least completely, from the British. Foster communicated with Anthony Eden on the matter, and the latter finally, with misgivings, issued a statement which we considered adequate.[11]

Meanwhile, in Guatemala, Arbenz had declared a state of siege and launched a reign of terror. Then on June 18 armed forces under Carlos Castillo Armas, an exiled former colonel in the Guatemalan Army, crossed the border from Honduras into Guatemala, initially with a mere handful of men—reportedly about two hundred. As he progressed he picked up recruits. Simultaneously three obsolete bombers, presumably under his direction, buzzed Guatemala City and bombed the ordnance depot. Things seemed to be going well for Castillo's small band until June 22. On that date Allen Dulles reported to me that Castillo had lost two of the three old bombers with which he was supporting his "invasion."

A meeting was arranged that afternoon with Foster Dulles, Allen Dulles, and Henry F. Holland, who had succeeded John Cabot as Assistant Secretary of State for Inter-American Affairs. The point at issue was whether the United States should cooperate in replacing the bombers. The country which had originally supplied this equipment to Castillo was willing now to supply him two P-51 fighter-bombers if the United States would agree to replace them. The sense of our meeting was far from unanimous. Henry, a sincere and dedicated public servant and a real expert in Latin American affairs, made no secret of his conviction that the United States should keep hands off, insisting that other Latin American republics would, if our action became known, interpret our shipment of planes as intervention in Guatemala's internal affairs. Others, however, felt that our agreeing to replace the bombers was the only hope for Castillo Armas, who was obviously the only hope of restoring freedom to Guatemala.

"What do you think Castillo's chances would be," I asked Allen Dulles, "without the aircraft?"

His answer was unequivocal: "About zero."

"Suppose we supply the aircraft. What would the chances be then?"

Again the CIA chief did not hesitate: "About 20 per cent."

I considered the matter carefully. I realized full well that United States

[11] The statement by Anthony Eden, dated June 18, 1954, said in part:

"There is no general power of search on the high seas in peace time. The British Government, however, has certain powers under Defense Regulations and otherwise to detain or requisition under certain circumstances. The Commander-in-Chief of West Indies is being instructed to take appropriate action where practicable if the carriage of arms by British ships should be suspected."

intervention in Central America and Caribbean affairs earlier in the century had greatly injured our standing in all of Latin America. On the other hand, it seemed to me that to refuse to cooperate in providing indirect support to a strictly anti-Communist faction in this struggle would be contrary to the letter and spirit of the Caracas resolution. I had faith in the strength of the inter-American resolve therein set forth. On the actual value of a shipment of planes, I knew from experience the important psychological impact of even a small amount of air support. In any event, our proper course of action—indeed my duty—was clear to me. We would replace the airplanes.

As my visitors prepared to leave the office, I walked to the door with Allen Dulles and, smiling to break the tension, said, "Allen, that figure of 20 per cent was persuasive. It showed me that you had thought this matter through realistically. If you had told me that the chances would be 90 per cent, I would have had a much more difficult decision."

Allen was equal to the situation. "Mr. President," he said, a grin on his face, "when I saw Henry walking into your office with three large law books under his arm, I knew he had lost his case already."

Delivery of the planes was prompt and Castillo successfully resumed his progress. After five days, during which the Guatemalan Army announced its refusal to support Arbenz, he announced that he was relinquishing power to a Colonel Díaz as the head of a new provisional government. Two days later a second change deposed Díaz and brought the anti-Communist Colonel Elfego Monzón to power. Thereafter, further negotiations, with Ambassador Peurifoy and President Oscar Osorio of El Salvador as mediators, brought Colonel Castillo Armas into Monzón's new ruling junta, eventually as its head.

Meanwhile the United Nations Security Council had deferred action on the Guatemala matter during an investigation by the Inter-American Peace Committee of the Organization of American States, but the change of government had made furthur action unnecessary.

The major factor in the successful outcome was the disaffection of the Guatemalan armed forces and the population as a whole with the tyrannical regime of Arbenz. The air support enjoyed by Castillo Armas, though meager, was important in relative terms; it gave the regular armed forces an excuse to take action in their own hands to throw out Arbenz. The rest of Latin America was not in the least displeased.

Arbenz fled via Mexico to Czechoslovakia, and Castillo Armas was later confirmed first as head of the military junta and then, by a thundering majority, as President. He proved to be far more than a mere rebel; he was a farseeing and able statesman. For the three years of life remaining to him, he enjoyed the devotion of his people.

By the middle of 1954 Latin America was free, for the time being at least, of any fixed outposts of Communism.

"Now the future of Guatemala," Foster Dulles said in a nationwide broadcast on June 30, "lies at the disposal of the Guatemalan people themselves."

*   *   *

One more event deserves mention to complete the chronicle of 1954: the settlement at Suez.

Probably because of their recognition that in the atomic era large masses of troops at Suez would have doubtful value, the British modified their demands to the government of Egypt, headed after April of 1954 by a new President, Gamal Abdel Nasser. By July 27 the two governments had arrived at an agreement in principle, which they sealed in a final agreement on October 19. Progressively, over the next twenty months, they concluded, the British would withdraw all of their troops. British and Egyptian technicians would, in various zones, keep the Suez Canal Base in working order. The Royal Air Force would have rights of over-flight and landing. In the event of an attack on any of the eight Arab states or Turkey by any non-Arab state, the British could move back into the base and put it on a wartime footing. Freedom of navigation through the canal would remain unimpaired.

On November 7, 1954, having encouraged Egypt to conclude an agreement on Suez, the United States announced a grant of $40 million to further Egypt's economic progress.

*   *   *

By the end of the year a historical pattern was emerging: American political, military, and economic influence was being used to help solve old quarrels, preserve freedom, eliminate traditional antagonisms, and give confidence to weak and exposed nations. We had inherited many problems out of the past. In company with good friends and allies around the globe—from Seoul to Guatemala City to Teheran to London—these problems we had solved, at least for the moment, even though others remained and new ones were certain to arise. But we and our good companions could well feel, as 1954 came to a close, that more than once in the past two years we had made a good end of the beginning.

CHAPTER XVII

Off-Year Election, 1954

History shows that when the Executive and Legislative Branches are politically in conflict, politics in Washington runs riot. . . . The public good goes begging while politics is played for politics' sake.

—Address, Denver, Colorado, October 8, 1954

I N the midst of the manifold foreign and domestic problems which for nearly two years had absorbed our attention, I could not forget the importance of a Republican political success in 1954 to the administration's still-unfolding legislative program and, as I saw it, to the progress of the nation. One significant fact in the 1952 landslide victory of the national ticket had ominous overtones for Republicans who looked beneath the over-all result. While the national ticket had carried thirty-nine of the forty-eight states, and had lost another by a margin of only six hundred votes, the record of Republican victories in the same year at other political levels was not encouraging. True, we had turned a minority into a majority position in both houses of Congress, but in the House the majority was a scant handful of votes; in the Senate only one.

From the beginning, one political fact concerned me deeply. It was obvious that in 1952 a great many persons had voted Republican through the efforts of the "Citizens for Eisenhower and Nixon" national organization and the "Ike and Dick" clubs operating throughout the nation. Their value was immense. Many of these were in the Deep South, for example. It would be fatuous to assume that the 1952 victory had suddenly and permanently transformed the minority party, which the Republicans had been for many years, into the majority party. Yet many people were unthinkingly making that faulty assumption.

There were Republicans who resented the Citizens. I was more than a little startled when, within a few weeks after inauguration, a visiting group of leading Republicans voiced to me their conviction that the first thing Republicans should do was to get rid of "these volunteer politicians," classified by one speaker as "hangers-on." Amazed, I replied that all volunteer groups had not only been useful in 1952 but could be so in the future, if we would only induce them to work with us. They were new blood, new brains and enthusiasm, which the entire political system needed. They had, in fact, helped to create a new and unique political force to elect us. A feminine member among my visitors said impatiently, "All they want is to get their fingers in the patronage pie; it is time we let them know that the Republican party is in charge."

My temper reached the boiling point. I turned to her. "It's true," I said, "that I have been besieged by people seeking appointments for themselves or others and asking for every kind of favor a President could possibly grant. But I must tell you, to their everlasting credit, that not a single member of the Citizens groups who has gained entry to my office, has asked me for any kind of official or unofficial favor.

"Moreover, I have not been approached even indirectly by anyone suggesting that the Citizens and volunteers should receive political rewards of any kind for their help in the campaign. Most of the Citizens in the last campaign were intelligent independents and discerning Democrats who adhere to a moderate philosophy. I think we should court them. We should hold them to us. We should try to make them one of our principal recruiting agencies. It would be sheer stupidity to fail to do so if we want to win more elections."

This stilled that particular verbal exchange, but it did not change the attitudes of those who maintained the same old narrow, inflexible view of partisan politics. And that inflexibility gave a hint of the difficulty the party would have in obtaining from the Citizens in 1954 the same enthusiastic and unselfish support we had received in 1952.

In an early Cabinet meeting I called attention to reports that we were already losing some of the first-voter strength we had enjoyed in the last election and I urged all Cabinet members to search for ways to show the administration's appreciation of and interest in these relatively young voters.

During 1953 the prospects for the 1954 congressional elections came up from time to time. On one occasion the Vice President referred to the issues that would loom important in the next election, observing that in his opinion local matters were normally overrated in congressional elections; he believed that even local contests are decided on the basis of one or two national issues. He felt that in 1954 one of the issues would certainly be the strength and reliability of congressional support for the President.

As early as May 8, 1953, Chairman Leonard Hall of the national committee explained to the Cabinet his conviction as to the most useful contributions government officials could make to Republican success in 1954. He thought it would be a mistake for me to make an intensive coast-to-coast campaign, believing that a President's role in off-year elections was to discuss major issues, standards, records, and programs. He believed, however, that all Cabinet members, with the exception of the Secretary of State and possibly the Secretary of Defense, should make themselves available for speaking engagements according to a schedule he would make up in consultation with them. Of course, in off-year contests the burden of election leadership is supposed to be borne by the senatorial and congressional campaign committees and their respective chairmen. But these committees and chairmen do not exert substantial influence on the electorate as a whole. In many instances even their identity is not generally known. Apart from the candidates themselves, most of the campaign speaking falls upon members of the Executive branch.

A few months afterward, in a press conference, I gave my views on the functions of a President in political campaigns when he himself is not a candidate. I expressed great interest in the political complexion of the Senate and of the House of Representatives, to be sure, but added that it was doubtful whether a President should intervene too intensively and directly in off-year congressional elections. Though he has been elected by only a majority, the President has a duty to exercise leadership in behalf of all the people. His responsibility, I said, was to develop an enlightened and progressive program for the benefit of the nation as a whole, and if he were successful in working with the Congress in such a way as to obtain the enactment of needed legislation, then those candidates who supported the administration's effort would have an umbrella of accomplishment under which to operate. I thought the best thing a President could do for his party and his country was to explain issues, programs, and achievements to the people. I would do everything I could to establish a record that would induce a majority of Americans to approve of our party's program and candidates.

Soon after my inauguration, President Hoover had warned me to expect disappointments in following the course I had set myself.

"In certain respects," he said, "you have probably the most difficult political problem ever encountered by a President. Some people will want you to lead them back at full speed to the 'good old days.' At the other extreme, some will want you to initiate welfare programs regardless of their effect on federal fiscal affairs and on the nation's economy." And then he concluded, "To go back is impossible, but many will not believe this, and will demand miracles of you. To allow present trends to go on is unwise: they will lead to disaster. All you can do is to try to turn away gradually from the path leading to paternalism, until it takes a central course, and then stick with it. And both sides will dislike you."

These sentiments paralleled those I had expressed when I was still NATO commander, to visitors who were urging me to enter politics. So I told President Hoover that I was well aware of the difficulties and expressed the hope that occasionally he would have an admonitory word for those who were not so understanding as he.

As months passed, I continued to emphasize the need to produce an excellent legislative record as an effective basis for the conduct of the next election. I told a news conference on October 28 that I was growing more and more concerned for Republican success, especially in retaining or increasing Republican majorities in the next Congress. I repeated what I had said many times: It was my task, and the task of leaders and members of my party in the Congress (plus others who accepted our philosophy) to produce a program that was so dynamic, so forward-looking, and so adapted to the needs of the United States that anyone running as a supporter of the program would have a distinct advantage.

I have never enjoyed the luxury of being head of a majority party. Perhaps the leader of such a party can be uniformly partisan. But the leader of a minority party has a different set of references. To win, he and his associates must merit the support of hundreds of thousands of independents and members of the opposition party. Attitudes, speeches, programs, and techniques cannot be inflexibly partisan.

In the spring of 1954 I told members of the Cabinet that if our appeal was to be merely to the "Republican versus Democratic" sentiments of the public, we were foredoomed to defeat. I earnestly wanted a Republican Congress. I assumed that all those good friends who had worked with me in 1952 felt the same. So I was somewhat astonished to receive a letter from Cabot Lodge, in July 1954, which argued against my feeling that such a result was essential. In part, he said:

> The basic factor is and always will be the country's confidence in you. This confidence in you can be maintained and, with it, your immense influence for good, no matter what the election results may be.

Former President Truman said on September 17, "It seems to me that President Eisenhower should be secretly wishing for a Democratic Congress . . . and hope that we can save him from the misdeeds of his own party."

The Democrats did not fail to jeer at the Republicans' disappointing failure in 1953 to restore the appropriations committees' cuts of more than a half-billion dollars in the administration's request for mutual-security funds and, in 1954, to give the administration greater support on the Bricker amendment.

I knew, of course, of some disquieting historical precedents in off-year elections. President Wilson failed to get a Democratic Congress in 1918 after he had argued that "in ordinary times divided counsels can be endured without permanent hurt to the country, but these are not ordinary times." Franklin D. Roosevelt in 1938 had unsuccessfully tried to purge Democratic members of Congress who refused to support him. And when the Congress went Democratic in the elections of 1930, Herbert Hoover suffered a crippling blow to his ability to attack the depression.

But despite my troubles with a number of the Republicans in Congress in 1953–54, the Republicans had stood by me far more consistently than had the Democrats.

In the crucial Senate vote on the Bricker amendment, for example, 35 per cent of the Republicans present and voting supported me, in contrast to 30 per cent of the Democrats. On the proposal, which I opposed, to link Hawaiian and Alaskan statehood, and thus kill both, 93 per cent of the Republicans voted with me; all but 5 per cent of the Democrats voted against me. On extending the franchise to eighteen-year-olds, I had from the Republicans 100 per cent support, from the Democrats 23 per cent. And on proposals to improve the Taft-Hartley Act, I had 93 per cent of the Republicans in the Senate behind me, but not one Democrat.

While issues are and should be of paramount importance in any campaign, there can be no doubt that personalities and attitudes of individual candidates also influence voting. We wanted to find in the several states candidates who possessed the understanding, record, personality, and capacity for conducting effective campaigns. There was, I thought, still too much deference paid to party seniority in selecting candidates; many old-line Republicans, of course, still looked on me as a political accident and, worse, as one who was too little respectful of their long-term party membership. But I continued to insist that potential for national service and leadership rather than reward for party longevity should be the guide in choosing candidates.

In 1954 I went against historical tradition and conducted a coast-to-coast off-year campaign unprecedented in the Presidency.

Of all the national and local contests that year the most dramatic was the fight for control of the Senate. In the Eighty-third Congress the Republicans had sustained a slight majority. The death of Senator Taft had resulted in the appointment of a Democrat by the governor of Ohio, Frank Lausche. At stake in the 1954 elections were thirty-eight Senate seats, twenty-two Democratic and sixteen Republican. In an early election a Republican, Margaret Chase Smith, already had been re-elected in

Maine. But many of the Democratic Senate seats came from the South. So in actuality, there were only six seats held by Democrats which the Republicans had a chance of winning—in Ohio, Illinois, Delaware, Colorado, Montana, and Iowa.

On the other hand, many of the remaining Republican seats were in danger. In California it appeared that Senator Thomas Kuchel had the advantage. In Kansas, South Dakota, Nebraska, and New Hampshire (each of the latter two having two Republican seats up for election) we seemed to have the edge. But in Idaho, Kentucky, Massachusetts, Michigan, Nevada, New Jersey, Wyoming, and Oregon our situation was difficult. I made plans to help in these areas those Republicans who had supported my programs—all this, of course, within the framework of my concept of what a President's role should be in an off-year election.

Unfortunately, the issues were not always clear. In Illinois, Senator Paul Douglas, whom the Republicans hoped to unseat, seemed to be prepared to run on the administration's record; he claimed to have supported me on foreign policy, the Bricker amendment, housing, social security, and health. He charged his Republican opponent, Joseph Meek, with wanting to scuttle everything I proposed. Meek had indeed opposed what he called the "foreign giveaway program"; he approved of the Bricker amendment, and cautiously praised Senator McCarthy. In April, I had told him I would not back him until he announced that he would support my program. Consequently, I remained silent on his candidacy until he gave public assurance that "you can count on my loyalties and my support as the junior senator from Illinois." On August 12 I was photographed with seventeen candidates, not yet members of the Congress, who because they promised to support my program had won the approval of the Citizens for Eisenhower, who were again readying themselves for action in the campaign. I wanted and needed a Republican Congress; but I could see no sense in working for office-seekers who were ready to object to every proposal I made.

On August 19, at the Illinois State Fair, I attacked economic "prophets of gloom and doom" who had said that 1954 would turn into another 1929. These prophets, I said, "remind me a little bit of the story of Lincoln's crooked fence. . . . A farmer built a fence that was so crooked that every time a pig bored a hole through it, he found himself on the same side from which he started." No matter how bright a record of accomplishment our party and the economy could show, these critics cried that the nation was going to wrack and ruin.

Not all the speeches I made at this time were strictly political, though during a campaign it is almost impossible for a President to make a strictly nonpartisan talk. [For a typically varied campaign day, see Appendix L.] On August 30, for example, when I addressed a crowd at the Iowa State Fair in Des Moines, it no doubt was expected that my talk would be confined to agriculture, the farm program we were trying to have enacted, and the farmer's stake in electing a Republican Congress. However, on that day I received word that the French National Assembly had rejected the European Defense Community. Consequently, I spoke not of agriculture but of the setback to our hopes which America had sustained in this rejection, and went on to express my determination to continue trying to find a satisfactory arrangement in Europe. It was a mark of the time that a President could speak of foreign relations and of the necessity for mutual security to a group of Iowa farmers and hold their interest in doing so.

During the campaign the Vice President carried on a vigorous effort to explain and give visibility to Republican accomplishments during the administration's first two years. He was assisted by Cabinet officers and other officials, as called upon by the chairman of the Republican National Committee.

Public-opinion polls confirmed that we faced an uphill fight. This was reinforced by the results of the Maine election, held on September 12; Maine voters elected the first Democratic governor in twenty years and Senator Margaret Chase Smith, and three Republican congressmen came closer to defeat than ever before.

In late September I flew to the Pacific Northwest, stopping in the morning to dedicate the McNary Dam at the Washington-Oregon border, near Walla Walla, and to give my views on the federal-state-local partnership principle for the development of America's resources. Then I motored to Pendleton, Oregon, where, before boarding the plane for California, I spoke briefly in support of Senator Cordon, whom we hoped to re-elect in that state. That evening in Hollywood I talked at length to an enthusiastic audience.

Because I had decided to confine myself to broad issues and to Republican accomplishments, there was, I confess, a similarity of content in the speeches I delivered in the campaign. The address that evening in the Hollywood Bowl outlined, as well as any, my convictions:

> Two years ago [I said] the people of our country voted to have clean government. . . .
> Not one appointee of this administration has been involved in scandal or corruption. . . .
> Integrity and decency and dignity have been restored to the federal government. Our government again stands high in the eyes of the people.

I reminded the audience that we had promised reductions in expenses and taxes and that we had fulfilled this pledge by deleting more than $11 billion of projected expenditures from the budget of the previous administration. This had made it possible to approve a general tax cut which saved taxpayers $7.4 billion—or nearly fifty dollars for every person in America. This was, I pointed out, the biggest tax cut in the history of the United States, and the tax laws had been executed without political favoritism and without corruption.

Our people had been longing for a prosperous economy, without war, I went on. The useless Korean fighting had been stopped. Its tremendous costs had ceased, and the nation's economy had adjusted to peacetime conditions with minimum economic disruption. The year 1954 was the best peacetime one in our history. It showed that at last our nation's economic strength could be of an enduring kind. "It is not a prosperity based on the froth of inflation," I said. "We flatly reject the idea that, for America to stay prosperous, we must constantly run an economic fever. We flatly reject the idea that, for America to stay prosperous, the government must always spend more than it has. . . . We do have a prosperous economy—and we have it without war."

I referred to all we had been doing in the world to bring realism where there had been wishful thinking in our foreign dealings; to bring frankness, candor, and force to foreign policy and to distinguish between words and deeds in the conduct of international affairs.

I mentioned the saving of Iran and Guatemala from Communism. Despite the inescapable misfortune of Indochina, I went on, a new concert of nations was building strength in a region where there had been weakness. In national defense we no longer were working on a feast-or-famine program, with skyrocketing expansion due to fear, followed by reckless contraction out of complacency.

To be sure, I called attention to our success in taking the long chance of removing controls from the economy—to the fact that prices had not soared, that inflation had been checked, and that the cost of living had stabilized. At the same time, we followed our conviction that the federal government should not do what enterprising Americans could do better for themselves.[1]

Then I came to the point of the review: "But [our] program is not completed. . . . We must keep on working. We shall keep on, despite those misguided and irresponsible people who, hoping for individual advantage, spread . . . fear of war, fear of atomic disaster, fear of international catastrophe, fear of depression—false fears . . . of tomorrow and of ourselves. . . . Our program is for just one thing: the practical

[1] The government had discontinued many activities and was no longer involved in the manufacture of ice and cement, the retreading of tires, the repairing of shoes, the roasting of coffee, or making clothes and rope, operating rubber plants, and running a commercial bank. It had stopped operating a large fleet of tugs and barges on our inland waterways.

good of 160 million Americans. In two years we have done much toward that goal. But we have much more to do."

Then I turned to subjects more political in character:

"Let us look at a few political facts. Under our system, many millions of our citizens have partisan affiliations. This is as it should be. In no other way can party responsibility be fixed. . . . But for a political party in our nation to be held clearly accountable to the people for its political philosophy and programs to guide the course of our government, it is essential that that party control both the Executive and the Legislative branches of the government. This is what all of you worked for in 1952."

I argued that when the Congress was controlled by one political party and the Executive branch by the other, politics in Washington were rampant. The conduct of government habitually tended, under these conditions, to deteriorate into an endless round of contests for sheer political advantage—an endless round of maneuvering, or of stagnation and inaction—of half measures or no measures at all. These were the compelling reasons why the completion of the administration's program required the election of a Republican-led Congress.

As the campaign progressed I was inevitably drawn more and more into the contest by the importunities of candidates. By the time the campaign was over I had traveled more than ten thousand miles and had given nearly forty speeches,[2] including some which were nonpolitical. October 29 was my most intensive campaigning day. I departed from Washington early in the morning to arrive at Cleveland, Ohio, at 9 A.M., where I talked at the airport in support of Congressman George Bender, who was nominated to succeed the late Senator Taft. Two hours later, I arrived at Cadillac Square in Detroit, Michigan, where I spoke in support of the incumbent Republican Senator Homer Ferguson. By one forty-five I was at Standiford Airport in Louisville, Kentucky, to greet an enthu-

[2] On October 15 I flew to Indiana, where I addressed the Columbia Republican Club and proceeded to the National Institute of Animal Agriculture at Butler University.

On October 20 I began an intensive three days in New York and New England beginning at Trinity College at Hartford, Connecticut, stopped at the West Point Society of New York, and in the evening addressed the Jewish Tercentenary Committee at the Waldorf in New York. The next morning I joined Governor Dewey and Senator Ives to make a tour of hospitals in New York, and dropped in at the Republican state committee rally. I conferred with Mr. Clifford Case, a candidate in a hard race for a Senate seat in New Jersey. That evening I attended the Al Smith dinner.

Two days later, on October 23, I entertained at lunch a group of Republican candidates at Gettysburg, Pennsylvania, soon to be my new home. There Lieutenant Governor Lloyd Wood was facing a difficult contest for the governorship. On October 28 in Washington, I attended a dinner given by the Citizens for Eisenhower Congressional Committee for the District of Columbia.

siastic crowd out to cheer their candidate, John Sherman Cooper. And finally, at 6 P.M. that evening I spoke at New Castle County Airport in Wilmington, Delaware, on behalf of Congressman Herbert Warburton, running for the Senate—and then back to Washington. In brief talks I stressed Republican accomplishments of the previous twenty months, the legislative record of the Eighty-third Congress, and the need for the Executive and Legislative branches of the government not to be controlled by opposing philosophies.

Needless to say, while Republicans were emphasizing numerous achievements, Democrats viewed with alarm. They attacked the Dixon and Yates contract anew.

Pointing to knots of unemployment in Ohio, Pennsylvania, and Michigan, Democrats attacked the Republicans' failure to put everybody back to work at once and expressed shock at the alleged Republican heartlessness of Secretary Wilson's October 11 Detroit press-conference remark: "I've always liked bird dogs better than kennel-fed dogs myself—you know, one who'll get out and hunt for food rather than sit on his fanny and yell." Though he later denied comparing all jobless people to shiftless dogs, Charlie Wilson's remark did not help Senator Ferguson. But Arthur Burns said that Wilson's politically questionable remark was "not only courageous but wise."

By the conclusion of the campaign the Democrats were haphazardly attacking everything. On October 31 Adlai Stevenson declared that the administration had cut the Army, scuttled foreign trade, and intimidated America's allies. It had let production decline, he went on, permitted unemployment to rise, enacted a farm program "on a foundation of broken promises," jammed through the sinister Dixon and Yates scheme, and conducted giveaways from "public power development to grazing lands, from atomic patents to water power sites."

I have always doubted that such obvious misrepresentations actually sway votes as much as the speaker intends. A loss of votes to the other party or candidate seems to me to be more likely.

When I returned to the White House from the campaign circuit, I felt an urge to express my thanks to a tough campaigner. Richard Nixon had always been feared but respected, as an adversary, by the Democrats. This year they had adopted the elevated tactic of accusing him of "McCarthyism in a white collar." Late in October I sent him a letter:

Dear Dick:

Whenever my burdens tend to feel unduly heavy, I admire all the more the tremendous job you have done since the opening of the present campaign. You have personally carried a back-breaking load of hard, tedious, day by day and state by state campaigning. And in doing so you have been undismayed by problems of time, distance, and physical effort.

I know we share the urgent hope that there may be returned to the Congress a Republican majority that will work with the Executive Branch in completing the program that we believe is in the best interests of all America. No man could have done more effective work than you to further that hope. Whatever the outcome next Tuesday, I can find no words to express my deep appreciation of the contribution you have made toward that goal.

Please tell Pat, too, that she has aroused my admiration as an able campaigner; there is no question but that she is the most charming of the lot.

With warm regard,

As ever,
D.E.

At last the results came in.

In the House of Representatives the Democrats gained twenty-one seats from Republicans and one from an independent. Republicans gained five seats formerly held by Democrats. The result was a net gain of seventeen for the Democrats and put control of the House in their hands.

In the Senate the Democrats gained two seats; former Vice President Alben Barkley defeated John Sherman Cooper in Kentucky; Pat Mc-Namara defeated Homer Ferguson in Michigan; Alan Bible, the protégé of Pat McCarran, defeated the incumbent appointee Ernest S. Brown in Nevada; former Senator Joseph C. O'Mahoney defeated Congressman William Henry Harrison in Wyoming; and, most disappointing, in Oregon, a traditional Republican stronghold, Richard L. Neuberger defeated our incumbent Senator Guy Cordon by a handful of votes. Republicans picked up three seats formerly held by Democrats. In Ohio, Congressman George Bender defeated Thomas A. Burke, Governor Lausche's interim appointee; in Iowa, Congressman Thomas E. Martin defeated Senator Guy Gillette, a victory for a supporter of flexible price supports. Finally, a surprise which delighted us all: in Colorado, Lieutenant Governor Gordon Allott defeated John A. Carroll for the seat vacated by Senator Edwin C. Johnson.

Thus, with three gains and five losses, the Republicans also lost control of the Senate (forty-eight Democrats, forty-seven Republicans, and one Independent, Wayne Morse, committed to vote with the Democrats on organizing the Senate).

In the gubernatorial races, though they had no direct bearing on our legislative programs, the effects were also disappointing. In Colorado, for example, former Senator Ed Johnson defeated Donald Brotzman for the seat formerly held by one of my strong advocates, Dan Thornton. In Connecticut, John Lodge was defeated by Abraham Ribicoff. In New York, Senator Irving M. Ives, whom I had supported to succeed Governor Dewey, lost by a few votes to Averell Harriman. In Pennsylvania, George Leader defeated Lieutenant Governor Lloyd H. Wood. And in Arizona, Ernest W. McFarland defeated Howard Pyle, who soon thereafter became a valued member of my staff at the White House.

On the cheerful side, my friend and supporter Allan Shivers had been re-elected in Texas, Theodore McKeldin had been re-elected in Maryland, and Leo Hoegh had defeated his Democratic opponent in Iowa.

The press viewed the 1954 elections as practically a draw. In its column "The Washington Weathervane" the *New York Herald Tribune* said that "Dramatic personal campaigning by the President is credited with holding down what might have been a devastating Democratic sweep last Tuesday." The column said that Republicans were sorry I had not entered the campaign considerably earlier, and that if I had done so I might at least have saved the Senate—a thesis with which I did not agree. Also in the *Herald Tribune,* another syndicated column, seldom friendly to me, asserted that the election had been a political plus for my administration. Probably the most balanced view of the results was in the *New York Times:*

(1) As a midterm election it was normal—but only barely. In the past half-century the average loss for the party in power has been forty House and four Senate seats. The net Republican loss Tuesday was only sixteen and two. On the other hand they had very little ground to lose. The Republicans under Eisenhower conspicuously lacked the momentum toward national dominance that the Democrats displayed under Roosevelt.

(2) The President's personal standing with the voters seemed largely intact. Although his exceptionally vigorous campaigning did not save Congress for the Republicans, it was credited with averting a heavier Democratic sweep.

(3) The impact of specific issues—farm policy, unemployment, "communism in government"—was spotty. Despite heavy electioneering—and in some cases heavy mudslinging—neither party was able to whip up great antipathy for the other.

(4) Nevertheless the signs of a drift to the Democrats were clear. One was the big Democratic gain in governorships. Another was that the Republicans, apart from their actual losses in Congress, had heavier going in contests all across the country.

(5) But it was only a Democratic drift, no more. The election was the fourth in the past five in which Congress has changed hands. In all five the party line-ups have fluctuated within relatively narrow limits. Thus the mood of the U. S. electorate appears to be set on the middle of the road.

Despite these evaluations of the press, I could not help being sorry that the results had not been better. While our losses in both House and Senate were considerably less than predicted,[3] for at least the next two years the United States would have a divided government, with the Executive branch in the hands of the Republicans and the Legislative branch dominated, though ever so narrowly, by the Democrats.

Could we, I wondered, achieve in the year ahead a record which would compare at all favorably with what had been done in 1954? I thought of the struggles which had resulted in these accomplishments in 1954 on the domestic front alone:

(1) The transition, under sensible government policies, from a wartime to a peacetime economy without a depression;

(2) The establishment of a new electric-power policy which was to lead to the greatest multiplication of generating facilities in American history;

(3) An effective check on profligate spending, an unprecedented reduction in taxes, and the restoration of fiscal responsibility in government;

(4) The enactment of a massive amount of constructive legislation, including much previously believed impossible, such as the St. Lawrence Seaway project;

(5) The virtual ending of the fights which set Republican against Republican and American against American, over the Bricker amendment and McCarthyism.

We could only keep on working. My disappointment over the election results would provide no excuse for inaction or defeatism on the part of the administration. Nor would it provide a reason for abandoning the philosophy of government which had led to these accomplishments.

That philosophy I had summed up again and again in the preceding campaign. I had also argued for it in private talks with friends. In July of 1954, for example, in the midst of the legislative session and the troubles with Senator McCarthy, I carried on an extended dialogue by mail with Brigadier General Bradford G. Chynoweth (Retired), with whom I had served in Panama thirty years earlier. With friendly humor and conviction he had written to me deploring my belief in the "Middle Way" for government, and I replied, in part:

Dear Chyn:
  I answered your note with one equally short, but remembering your statement that you differ sharply with my philosophy of the Middle Way,

[3] Not since 1934, when the Democrats gained nine seats in the House of Representatives, had a party in control of the White House gained seats in Congress. In 1938 the Democrats lost seventy-one House seats; in 1942, forty-five; in 1946, fifty-five. In 1950 the Democrats had fared a little better: they had lost only twenty-nine seats.

I was reminded of the very fine and heated arguments we used to have some thirty years ago in Panama, and I decided to write just a little bit further.

Frankly I think that the critical problem of our time is to find and stay on the path that marks the way of logic between conflicting arguments advanced by extremists on both sides of almost every economic, political and international problem that arises. . . .

[In] our own day, we have those individuals who believe that the Federal government should enter into every phase and facet of our individual lives, controlling agriculture, industry and education, as well as the development of every natural resource in our country. These people, knowingly or unknowingly, are trying to put us on the path toward socialism. At the other extreme we have the people—and I know quite a number of them— who want to eliminate everything that the Federal government has ever done that, in one way or another, represents what is generally classified as social advance. For example, all of the regulatory commissions established in Washington are anathema to these people. They want to abolish them completely. They believe that there should be no trade union laws and the government should do nothing even to encourage pension plans and other forms of social security in our industry.

When I refer to the Middle Way, I merely mean the middle way as it represents a practical working basis between extremists, both of whose doctrines I flatly reject. It seems to me that no great intelligence is required in order to discern the practical necessity of establishing some kind of security for individuals in a specialized and highly industrialized age. At one time such security was provided by the existence of free land and a great mass of untouched and valuable natural resources throughout our country. These are no longer to be had for the asking; we have had experiences of millions of people—devoted, fine Americans, who have walked the streets unable to find work or any kind of sustenance for themselves and their families.

On the other hand, for us to push further and further into the socialistic experiment is to deny the validity of all those convictions we have held as to the cumulative power of free citizens, exercising their own initiative, inventiveness and desires to provide better living for themselves and their children. . . .

I shall conclude with this one general observation or aphorism, even though I well recall the old statement of the Frenchman that all generalities are false, including this one. The generality that I advance is merely this: excluding the field of moral values, anything that affects or is proposed for masses of humans is wrong if the position it seeks is at either end of possible argument.

A few days later he came back in zest and good spirits with counterarguments, and several lively proposals—so lively, in fact, as to be alarming. I enjoyed writing him an answer which said, in part:

I find myself in enthusiastic agreement with your rebellion against the reduction of every value, every incentive to the materialistic. If man is only an educated mule, we should eliminate him and turn the earth back to the birds and the fishes and the monkeys.

But the very fact that man is a spiritual thing makes it impossible for any durable governmental system to ignore hordes of people who through no fault of their own suddenly find themselves poverty stricken, and far from being able to maintain their families at decent levels, cannot even provide sustenance. Mass production has wrought great things in the world, but it has created social problems that cannot be possibly met under ideas that were probably logical and sufficient in 1800.

What I mean by the "Middle of the Road" is that course that preserves the greatest possible initiative, freedom and independence of soul and body to the individual, but that does not hesitate to use government to combat cataclysmic economic disasters which can, in some instances, be even more terrible than convulsions of nature.

Despite the setback of the 1954 election, I was resolved to continue on such a course in the years to come.

When we lost control of the House in the 1954 elections, difficulties arose in the Republican leadership in the House. Having lost the Speakership to Sam Rayburn, a Democrat, Joe Martin now elected to resume the post of party leader, a job that Charlie Halleck wanted to keep. Mr. Halleck is a high-tempered man and he wasted little time in making his dissatisfaction felt. He was a fighting leader and was valuable to me. Following our defeat, Mr. Martin had provided for Halleck no official place in the Republican leadership group, so I personally insisted that Halleck still attend the Legislative-leaders meetings at the White House.

Congressman Halleck grew restive and came to me for my "permission" to start a campaign to unseat Mr. Martin. I refused to endorse the idea, telling Mr. Halleck that such an action would cause a definite cleavage from top to bottom in the Republican delegation, and asking him to work, informally, to help get administration programs enacted into law. At the same time, I asked Mr. Martin to find some kind of official role for Halleck in the leadership group that would ease the growing tension between the two. Martin refused, and the situation grew worse rather than better.

BOOK FOUR

I propose, therefore, that we take a practical step, that we begin an arrangement, very quickly, as between ourselves. . . .

To give each other a complete blueprint of our military establishments, from beginning to end. . . .

The quest for peace is the statesman's most exacting duty. Security of the nation entrusted to his care is his greatest responsibility. Practical progress to lasting peace is his fondest hope. Yet in pursuit of hope he must not betray the trust placed in him as guardian of the people's security. . . .

—Statement on disarmament at the Geneva Conference, July 21, 1955

CHAPTER XVIII

A New Look at America's Defenses

To be prepared for war is one of the most effectual ways of preserving peace.

—*Washington*

Two and two continue to make four, in spite of the whine of the amateur for three or the cry of the critic for five.

—*James McNeïll Whistler*

FROM the moment that the Soviets exploded their first atomic bomb and built airplanes capable of carrying them over great distances, Americans realized that, as never before in history, they must thenceforth live under the specter of wholesale destruction. But multimegaton bombs and long-range missiles do not necessarily mean that we must live forever in disabling fear. For one thing, threats and challenge are not new. An analogy can be made, with some validity, between the life we lead today and that led by the American pioneers who made their homes, raised their families, plowed their fields, and lived a full life even under the never-ending threat of attack by hostile Indians. Today, though we know that there is a constant possibility, however remote, of an unprecedented holocaust, we still must be wise and courageous enough to live fully, confident in the knowledge that we have taken every reasonable step to deter aggression, and that we shall always be ready to defend liberty no matter what the price.

I have often been told that deep-seated concern over the possibilities of nuclear war persuaded many people to vote for me in 1952 who under other circumstances might have opposed the candidacy of a professional military man. Whatever the impact on the political campaign, however, my military background assured at least that as President I would hold certain definite convictions on national security. With some oversimplification, it seemed to me, as I took over the office, that five basic considerations provided logical guidelines for designing and employing a security establishment.

I had long been convinced that the composition and structure of our military establishment should be based on the assumption that the United States on its own initiative would never start a major war. This meant that the nation had to maintain forces of greater strength and effectiveness than would be necessary if our purposes had been aggressive. So long as we were to allow an enemy the initiative, we would have to be capable of defeating him even after having sustained the first blow—a blow that would almost certainly be a surprise attack and one that would make Pearl Harbor, by comparison, look like a skirmish. Nevertheless, the assumption did not, in my view, presuppose that America's response to attack would have to accord with the exact nature of the aggression. For example, an invasion of Europe in overwhelming strength by conventional forces did not mean that our reaction had to be limited to force of the same kind.

The second guideline was that since modern global war would be catastrophic beyond belief, America's military forces must be designed primarily to deter a conflict, even though they might be compelled later to fight.

A third was that national security could not be measured in terms of military strength alone. The relationship, for example, between military and economic strength is intimate and indivisible. What America needed, I felt, was a fully adequate military establishment headed by men of sufficient breadth of view to recognize and sustain appropriate relationships among the moral, intellectual, economic, and military facets of our strength. This meant also that they should have the capacity to dispose our forces intelligently, in such a fashion as best to serve peacetime objectives and yet to be of maximum effectiveness in case of attack. They would, of course, have to realize that the diabolical threat of international Communism—and our problems in meeting it—would be with us for decades to come.

A fourth consideration was that our armed forces must be modern, designed to deter or wage the type of war to be expected in the mid-twentieth century. No longer could we afford the folly, so often indulged in in the past, of beginning each war with the weapons of the last.

The fifth important guideline was that United States security policy should take into account the need for membership in a system of alliances. Since our resources were and are finite, we could not supply all the land, sea, and air forces for the entire Free World. The logical role of our allies along the periphery of the Iron Curtain, therefore, would be to provide (with our help) for their own local security, especially ground forces, while the United States, centrally located and strong in productive power, provided mobile reserve forces of all arms, with emphasis on sea and air contingents.

In the early months of my administration the Korean War still dragged on; it would be difficult to effect major changes immediately. But thorough study could be undertaken without delay. An immediate task was to ensure an effective advisory mechanism concerned with all phases of national defense. The basic organ, the National Security Council, was already in existence. To ensure a breadth of viewpoint in considering security problems, I invited the Secretary of the Treasury, the Director of the Budget, and the Director of the United States Information Agency to participate, in addition to the statutory members,[1] in the advisory work of the council.

The brave statement "America can afford anything it needs for national security" was and is true; in the earliest days of my administration I made this plain. But I also emphasized that America could not afford to waste money in any area, including the military, for anything that it did *not* need. I knew from experience that there was much duplication among the three services in research and development, in procurement, and even in roles and missions—these last always at least partly self-assigned.

To aid in the elimination of waste and duplication in the armed services, I felt that some reorganization of the Pentagon was desirable. The result was a reorganization plan[2] which had three basic objectives: (1) to strengthen civilian control by establishing clearer lines of responsibility; (2) to improve administrative procedure in the Department of Defense by eliminating unwieldy boards and committees and substituting instead responsible executive officials; (3) to provide mechanisms for better strategic planning. The plan was prepared with the benefit of a report from a study committee which Secretary Wilson had established as early as January 30, 1953.

This reorganization emphasized the position of the Secretary of Defense as my channel for communicating decisions to the defense establishment; likewise, it clearly recognized the legal responsibilities of the Joint Chiefs of Staff as advisers to the President and to the Secretary of Defense in purely military matters.

The last part of the reorganization plan involved strengthening the

[1] The "statutory" members comprised only the President, Vice President, Secretaries of State and Defense, and Director of the Office of Defense Mobilization. Others besides those mentioned, such as the director of the Central Intelligence Agency, also attended.
[2] Reorganization Plan Number Six, submitted to Congress on April 30, 1953. This took the form of an amendment to the National Security Act of 1949.

structure of the staff whose mission it was to serve the Joint Chiefs of Staff and, indirectly, the President and the Secretary of Defense. This Joint Staff was composed of officers assigned from the military services. They were, inescapably, too much under the divisive influence of the separate services from which they came. My objective was to take at least one step in divorcing the thinking and the outlook of the members of the Joint Staff from those of their parent services and to center their entire effort on national planning for the over-all common defense of the nation and the West. To accomplish this I directed that the selection of every military officer for service on the Joint Staff should require the approval of the chairman of the Joint Chiefs.

Opposition developed in Congress to this plan because of a fear that we were setting up a "Prussian-style general staff." This notion was scarcely based on any real knowledge of Germany's pre-World War I staff concepts, and after I had succeeded in clarifying the matter for the Legislative leaders, Reorganization Plan Number Six went into effect on June 30, 1953.

As the leading civilian executives, we had what I considered a strong combination in the Pentagon. Secretary Wilson's top deputy was Roger M. Kyes, a bold, sharp-minded businessman with a great store of common sense. The Secretary of the Army was Robert T. Stevens; the Secretary of the Navy, Robert B. Anderson; and the Secretary of the Air Force, Harold Talbott—all men of considerable ability.

In the uniformed services the leadership changed during the first few months of my administration. However, this implied no dissatisfaction, on my part, with any of the officers who had been serving in these important posts. Indeed, I knew three of them intimately—General Omar Bradley, chairman of the Joint Chiefs; General J. Lawton Collins, Army Chief of Staff; and General Hoyt Vandenberg, Air Force Chief of Staff. I knew Admiral William M. Fechteler, Chief of Naval Operations, by reputation —which was excellent. Bradley had been my classmate at West Point and my friend for all the years since. He served under me during World War II from early 1943 until its close in 1945. During the final eleven months of that period he commanded the Twelfth Army Group, which was composed entirely of American troops. In this position he had control of the largest exclusively American force of World War II.

The reason for the change was that during 1953 the terms of service of all of the incumbent Chiefs were to expire. General Vandenberg, unfortunately, had been afflicted with what turned out to be his last illness. He had been Chief of Staff of the Air Force since April of 1948 and was retired for disability on May 7, 1953, on which date the announcement was made of General Nathan F. Twining's appointment to succeed him. The term of General Bradley was to come to an end in August, as was that of General Collins. So, in mid-May, to avoid speculation about the identity of their successors, I announced the appointment of Admiral Arthur W. Radford as chairman of the Joint Chiefs of Staff, and simultaneously, General Matthew B. Ridgway's appointment to replace Collins, both changes to become effective on August 15. Ridgway's appointment insured that the Army would continue to have as its head a man of proven leadership qualities, and at the same time it allowed me to elevate General Gruenther, with the hearty concurrence of the other nations of the NATO Alliance, from the post of Chief of Staff in Paris to that of Supreme Commander. To my mind, General Gruenther was, as I have indicated, the best-qualified officer in the service of the United States for this vital post.

On June 2 Admiral Robert B. Carney, who had served as the commander of the Sixth Fleet, attached to NATO, was named as Chief of Naval Operations to replace Admiral Fechteler, whose two-year term was expiring. The term of General Lemuel C. Shepherd, commandant of the Marine Corps, was not to expire until January 1, 1956.[3]

At about the time of the change-over in the Joint Chiefs of Staff, active fighting in Korea ended. This fact, along with the epochal developments which were transpiring in nuclear armaments, occasioned what Admiral Radford described in a talk late in the year as a "New Look."[4] It happened that this term had a definite place in the parlance of the day; it had been coined to describe noticeable changes in the style of women's dresses (not entirely an improvement, some men felt). Thus the tag "New Look" probably suggested to many minds a picture of a far more radical change in the composition of our armed forces than was truly the case.

Conventionally the armed forces of the United States are thought of in terms of the specific services: the Army, the Navy, the Air Force, the Marine Corps, and sometimes the Coast Guard. But a better approach in analyzing strategic requirements is to make what has been called in military terminology a "horizontal analysis," which simply means to examine our armed might in the light of tasks which must be performed and the forces and weapons available to perform them, regardless of parent service.

Thus modern combat forces (as contrasted with logistical support forces) can be classified as follows:

(1) *Nuclear retaliatory or strike forces,* designed primarily for instant destruction of the enemy by large-scale nuclear attack. In the days of my

---

[3] The commandant of the Marine Corps is a member of the Joint Chiefs of Staff for matters pertaining to the Marine Corps.
[4] At the Press Club, Washington, December 14, 1953.

first administration the bulk of this power was invested in the Air Force's Strategic Air Command, the backbone of which was the heavy intercontinental bomber, with the B-52 in the process of replacing the B-36. In addition, the Navy, with its attack carriers, made a contribution, particularly in the Far East.

(2) *Forces deployed overseas.*[5] These forces, including land and tactical air forces, were stationed principally in Europe and the Far East. Their duty was to bolster our allies' defenses in those areas and to insure that the boundaries between freedom and slavery would not be moved to our disadvantage. In Europe these forces came under the command of the man in a U.S. post called CINCEUR, or Commander-in-Chief, Europe (who was also Supreme Commander for the Allied powers of Europe). The United States contribution was made up of the U. S. Seventh Army, the Ninth Air Force, and the Sixth Fleet, the last normally stationed in the Mediterranean.

In the Far East, at the close of the Korean fighting, was the U. S. Eighth Army in Korea, and the U. S. Fifth Air Force, the Seventh Fleet, and units of all services, stationed on the offshore island chain.

(3) *Forces to keep the sea lanes open in the event of emergency.* These forces, primarily Navy and Marine, were deployed in the Atlantic and Pacific.

(4) *Forces to protect the United States from air attack.* These consisted primarily of air-defense units, both Army and Air Force, assigned to the Continental Air Defense Command, with headquarters in Colorado. This command later became a combined command between the United States and the Canadians, and its title was changed to North American Air Defense Command.

(5) *Reserve Forces.* These forces, located primarily within the con-

[5] Forces deployed overseas were all assigned to unified (more than one service) and specified (one service only) commands, whose commanders reported directly to the Secretary of Defense. The unified commands comprised European Command, headquarters in Paris; the Atlantic Command, headquarters in Norfolk; the Caribbean Command, headquarters in the Panama Canal Zone; the Far East Command, headquarters in Tokyo (later disestablished); the Pacific Command, headquarters in Honolulu; the Continental Air Defense Command, headquarters in Colorado Springs; and the Alaskan Command.

The specified commands included the Strategic Air Command; and the Naval Forces, Eastern Atlantic and Mediterranean (whose commander was to serve primarily as the naval-component commander for the Commander-in-Chief, Europe).

The commands were not, however, all located overseas. The Strategic Air Command, a specified command, was deployed largely in the United States as a nuclear deterrent; Continental Air Defense Command, a unified command, was located almost entirely in the United States as a force to protect the United States from air attack.

tinent of the United States, were normally left under the control of their respective service chiefs for training purposes. They consisted of Army divisions, Air Force and Navy wings and fleets, and supporting units.

Keeping these missions in mind, then, we might define the New Look, as first, a reallocation of resources among the five categories of forces, and second, the placing of greater emphasis than formerly on the deterrent and destructive power of improved nuclear weapons, better means of delivery, and effective air-defense units.

Other active combat units, including those deployed overseas and forces to keep the sea lanes open, were to be modernized and maintained at a maximum mobility and effectiveness, but with decreases in numerical strength. Supporting reserves in the United States, while important, were given a lower priority.

The New Look called for a new outlook by the men concerned. This was not easy to acquire, for, as it turned out, the reallocations resulted in an increase in the Air Force, whereas the bulk of the reductions were primarily in the Army and secondarily in the Navy. This came about partly because during the Korean War the Army had expanded far beyond its necessary peacetime size.

This change in emphasis came at a time when the administration was exerting every effort to cut the costs of government everywhere; therefore the two separate efforts came to be associated in many minds.

Protests against the planned changes came from many quarters. Numbers of people were merely prejudiced in favor of one service as against the other two; others were interested in producing, for example, equipment for the Army and Navy rather than for the Air Force; still others, in political life, disliked any closing down of military installations in their respective geographical constituencies. All were ready to accuse us of endangering military security for the political plaudits we might receive for reducing the budget.

I could not help being amused when I heard such accusations. Had their authors been present to listen to the emotional exposition of Senator Taft in April 1953 (when he charged that the defense expenditures I had recommended were at least 50 per cent too large and represented only the thinking of jingoistic and ambitious men in the services), they would have reconsidered their idea that we anticipated plaudits, to say the least. When some claimed I was planning to "wreck" the Army and Navy, I decided that anyone familiar with my background and sentiments would know that these charges did not deserve the dignity of a refutation.

Resistance, however, continued in varying degrees throughout 1954, even though I was proposing a defense establishment in which all three of the services were to remain far larger, stronger, and more effective than ever previously in peacetime. For example, my proposed defense budget was three times that of 1950.

I directed that this concept of defense should be implemented with minimum delay. However, in order to attain the necessary wholehearted cooperation of the senior military officers, I did, from time to time, meet with the Joint Chiefs and other defense officials to review progress.

One important meeting of this kind was held in my office in early December 1954.[6] I pointed out to the group, once again, that long-term security required a sound economy, that no predicted critical danger date could be taken as a decisive factor in the nation's defense planning, and that the only way the United States could be quickly knocked out was by surprise attack on its mainland. I went over, once more, all of the missions for which the armed forces would be responsible and the priorities that had been established.

I indicated the necessity of making a realistic appraisal of what the maintenance of an adequate but not extravagant defense establishment over an extended period of time (say, half a century) could mean to the nation, and urged that we do our best to create a national climate favorable to dynamic industrial effort. I said that, since there could not possibly be any large-scale deployment of military forces from the continental United States to overseas theaters during the first few months of a nuclear war, our requirements in ground forces, other than those already overseas, should be limited to reserves of sufficient strength to meet a "brush-fire" war in one—or at most, two—localities. If conflicts started in a number of places simultaneously, then we would automatically be in a major war, which was a different problem entirely. In this instance, I repeated, our objectives in the first phase of such a global war would have to be to avert disaster, as we, in turn, released our nuclear stockpile on the aggressor. After that we would have time to go on to win.[7]

[6] Secretary Wilson, Deputy Secretary Anderson, General Ridgway, General Twining, Admiral Carney, General Shepherd, and Colonel Goodpaster were present.

[7] To give an idea of the shift in emphasis involved, the following figures might help:

Manpower	December 1953	October 1954	June 1955
Army	1,500,000	1,400,000	1,000,000
Navy/Marines	1,000,000	920,000	870,000
Air Force	950,000	960,000	970,000

Budget (*in billions of dollars*)

Fiscal Year '54		Fiscal Year '55	
Army	12.9	Army	8.8
Navy/Marines	11.2	Navy/Marines	9.7
Air Force	15.6	Air Force	16.4

These views received varying degrees of concurrence. Admiral Carney, for one, reported that the Navy was tailoring its forces to follow these policies, increasing its early striking power and cutting back amphibious forces, not so necessary as formerly, in the early stages of hostilities. General Ridgway, however, recently returned from Europe, was deeply troubled about the security of United States forces then overseas. In event of war it would not be possible to support them quickly unless reinforcements of large size (perhaps ten divisions he felt) were constantly ready to sail at a moment's notice. In his opinion our deployed strength was inadequate, and our ready reserve units at hand too small.

I could not help being sympathetic. The safety of United States troops and their dependents in Europe was my concern as well. I stressed to General Ridgway that I had no intention of allowing Europe to be overrun, as it had been in 1940. But we knew that the Soviets maintained something in the neighborhood of 175 divisions active in Europe at all times. The United States had twenty divisions, only five of which were in Europe. Therefore, in view of the disparity in the strengths of the opposing ground forces, it seemed clear that only by the interposition of our nuclear weapons could we promptly stop a major Communist aggression in that area. Two more divisions or ten more divisions, on our side, would not make very much difference against this Soviet ground force.

But I was not pessimistic. My intention was firm: to launch the Strategic Air Command immediately upon trustworthy evidence of a general attack against the West. So I repeated that first priority must be given to the task of meeting the atomic threat, the only kind of attack that could, without notice, endanger our very existence.

I pointed out that no commander—no nation—ever had, when conflict threatened, all the forces of all kinds that might be considered desirable. Therefore it was the responsibility of leadership—civil and military—to decide upon priorities. This done, the next task was to assure maximum efficiency in the forces calculated to be permanently necessary.

As time went on this doctrine came to be largely accepted in principle. But then there was raised another argument, based on the assumption that as a nuclear balance between the West and the East became foreseeable, the danger of atomic war would recede and our real problem would be to provide more ground forces and conventional support types to win small, brush-fire conflicts. In a climate of mutual deterrence, several of these "small wars" *could* conceivably occur simultaneously; therefore, it was asserted, we must greatly reinforce our conventional forces. The argument was based upon the premise that we would never, under any kind of circumstance, provocation, or aggression, employ our nuclear strength.

In my opinion this kind of solution was the product of timidity—a solution that began by seeing danger behind every tree or bush. This was also an unrealistic solution, one that required massive defense units of such size and capacity that no matter how universal and threatening the danger or how many the local "disturbances," we could quickly defeat them by conventional means.[8] I refused to turn the United States into an armed camp.

To emphasize my convictions, I stressed that the United States would not employ the same policies and resources to fight another war as were used in the Korean conflict.[9] I saw no sense in wasting manpower in costly small wars that could not achieve decisive results under the political and military circumstances then existing. I felt that this kind of military policy would play into the hands of a potential enemy whose superiority in available military manpower was obvious. We should refuse to permit our adversary to enjoy a sanctuary from which he could operate without danger to himself; we would not allow him to blackmail us into placing limitations upon the types of weapons we would employ. Moreover, in the matter of brush-fire wars I pointed out that we would not try to maintain the conventional power to police the whole world, even though we would cooperate with our allies on the spot. The Communists would have to be made to realize that should they be guilty of major aggression, we would strike with means of our own choosing at the head of the Communist power.

If we were wise enough, and sufficiently self-confident to concentrate on making our defense establishment effective, flexible, and economical, rather than heavy, clumsy, and costly, I believed we could be both secure and prosperous.[10]

When it came time to prepare budgets, it was particularly difficult to get the Joint Chiefs of Staff, collectively, to be guided by these policies. Each believed that although the sums allocated to the others were quite sufficient for national safety, the amounts approved for his own particular

[8] It was this kind of fear that later, in 1957 and 1958, saw disastrous bomber gaps in our defense establishment, and though that illusionary gap never existed, spent useless millions to fill it. Finally convinced of the falsity of their allegations, the prophets of doom changed to missiles—the gap here, they cried, was far worse and more fearsome than the earlier one. Again they were proved wrong; but proof of past error cannot still a present, senseless fear.

[9] On July 28, 1953, the United States had nine divisions (eight Army, one Marine) in Korea; the Republic of Korea had fourteen.

[10] This decision, appropriate as it was at the time of its making, applied, like all military decisions, to the situation of the moment and to the proximate future. It must be remembered, however, that the military, economic, and psychological situations in the world are in a constant state of change. These bring new problems—and new solutions.

service were inadequate. The result was that budgetary decisions had to be made, rather than approved, at the civilian echelon. Thus the internal differences in our highest military mechanism tended to neutralize the advisory influence they should have enjoyed as a body.[11]

Strategic deployment of forces, coordination among services, and man-power and budgetary problems, however, are not the only military mat-ters of concern to a President. Equally important is the matter of how the research and development efforts of the Department of Defense are man-aged, for in the process of establishing sensible priorities for high-cost programs of this kind, the nature of the entire military posture is deter-mined.

The most dramatic action in this field during the early years of my administration was, for all practical purposes, the beginning of research and development on ballistic missiles of intermediate and intercontinental

[11] On August 20, 1956, I wrote to Everett Hazlett at some length on the subject.

"Let us not forget that the Armed Services are to defend a 'way of life,' not merely land, property or lives. So what I need to make the Chiefs realize is that they are men of sufficient stature, training and intelligence to think of this balance— the balance between minimum requirements in the costly implements of war and the health of our economy. . . .

". . . When each Service puts down its minimum requirements for its own military budget for the following year, and I add up the total, I find that they mount at a fantastic rate. There is seemingly no end to all of this. Yet merely 'getting tough' on my part is not an answer. I simply must find men who have the breadth of under-standing and devotion to their country rather than to a single Service that will bring about better solutions than I get now.

"Strangely enough, the one man who sees this clearly is a Navy man who at one time was an uncompromising exponent of Naval power and its superiority over any other kind of strength. That is Radford.

"I do not maintain that putting all of these people in one uniform would cure this difficulty—at least not quickly. But some day there is going to be a man sitting in my present chair who has not been raised in the military services and who will have little understanding of where slashes in their estimates can be made with little or no damage. If that should happen while we still have the state of tension that now exists in the world, I shudder to think of what could happen in this country." [See Appendix M.]

Letters to Hazlett, a friend, appear throughout this volume. He and I were raised in the same town. After leaving high school, we decided to try for a military academy. We studied together for a year while both of us were holding down jobs. We questioned each other, using questions not of our own manufacture, but from the examinations used by the Academies in previous years. As it turned out, we were in the same class, that is, we were graduated in the same year. But Hazlett was in the Navy, and I in the Army. In later decades, as junior officers, we visited each other when we could, and I found myself writing letters to Swede Hazlett on all sorts of subjects. He was always a good person with whom to "let go."

ranges.[12] These vehicles, with their nuclear warheads, were destined to make previous concepts of warfare obsolete and could possibly reduce the duration of a modern war to a matter of hours. Our problem in the development of long-range ballistic weapons was complicated by prior neglect of their potential capabilities. For example, in fiscal year 1953, the United States spent only a million dollars on long-range ballistic missiles, less than it was spending to support the price of peanuts.

This lack of concern with the ballistic missile was undoubtedly partly the result of preoccupation with the aerodynamic missile, or pilotless aircraft. Development of the aerodynamic weapon could be expected to be quicker—and at that time it was thought to be more practical than the ballistic type, which had to leave and re-enter the earth's atmosphere. On two aerodynamic projects, the Snark and the Navajo, a great deal of time and money had already been used.

But then, through the conclusions and recommendations of the scientists, presented to me in 1954 and early 1955, it became clear that the matter of developing ballistic missiles was urgent. Indications were that the Soviets had been working on this type of weapon for a number of years, and our development programs were promptly accorded the highest priorities.

While it was easy to direct the Defense Department to go full speed ahead, it was not so easy to devise the best organization of the missile program itself. It might have been best, had it been feasible, to remove the whole missile program from the hands of the regular military services and to establish another "Manhattan Project," similar to that through which the atomic bomb was developed during World War II. This scheme would have had the advantage of concentrating the best scientific minds on one set of programs and eliminating duplication and rivalry among the various service activities. However, by the time the urgency of the program became apparent, each of the services had already organized and was using experimental teams of scientists and engineers for missile development.[13] To tear up all of these organizations and to transplant the scientists, engineers, and officers already engaged in the business, seemed to me, to Secretary Wilson, and to my military-scientific advisers to promise more delay than would continuation of existing procedures.

[12] Intermediate (IRBM): 1200–1500 miles. Intercontinental (ICBM): 5000 miles.
[13] The Army, in particular, had achieved a considerable head start in short-range (two-hundred-mile) ballistic missiles by importing from Germany a group of scientists and engineers headed by Dr. Wernher von Braun, who had developed the German V-2 rocket of World War II. This group was established at Huntsville, Alabama, where it continued work on these weapons which, being ballistic, of course supplied some knowledge and experience applicable to the longer range IRBMs and ICBMs.

This was a close decision. The problems of achieving coordination among services were severe. However, the urgent need for quick results dictated that this disadvantage be accepted. The decision was, I believe, the right one, although interservice rivalries in this field were by no means eliminated.

Another question was whether the priority to be accorded the IRBM deserved to be as high as the more glamorous ICBM. For the immediate military problem, I thought it was. I realized that the political and psychological impact on the world of the early development of a reliable IRBM would be enormous, while its military value would, for the time being, be practically equal to that of the ICBM, since the former, located on bases on foreign soil, could strike any target in Communist areas as well as could an ICBM fired from the United States. However, since in the long term the ICBM promised great advantages over the IRBM, I directed that both phases of the missile program should have the highest possible priority in the use of talent, money, and materials.

In early 1955 it came to my attention that the Navy, by combining techniques all of which had already been proven, could now begin development of a new weapon system which would enable them eventually to fire a ballistic missile from a submerged nuclear submarine.[14] The missiles would carry nuclear warheads and be of sufficient range to hit critical targets in the Sino-Soviet land mass. Thus it would constitute an almost invulnerable retaliatory capability, separate and apart from the missiles and planes located in the United States and on foreign bases. The project was undertaken at once, and before the end of my years in the White House, some of these highly valuable "Polaris" submarines were on station as a growing part of our nuclear deterrent.

* * *

I have pondered, on occasion, the evolution of the military art during the mid-fifties. The Army in which I was commissioned a second lieutenant in 1915 underwent phenomenal changes in the thirty years from then until the German surrender in 1945. Auto-firing guns, motor transport, fighter and bomber airplanes, tanks, and many types of rockets all came into common use. But those changes, startling as they were, faded into insignificance when compared to those of the postwar period, particularly during my first three years in the Presidency.

[14] The missile would be launched as a vertical torpedo and would become a solid-propellant IRBM on leaving the water.

The first nuclear submarine, the *Nautilus,* was christened by Mrs. Eisenhower on January 21, 1954.

New military developments, therefore, brought about important changes in the duties that absorbed the urgent and continuous attention of the President. The title óf Commander-in-Chief of the armed forces had become something real and critical even in peace. I was incessantly involved in basic decisions, planning, and meeting with Defense and Atomic Energy Commission officials to approve annual increments in the national atomic stockpile and its dispersal in far-flung posts around the globe. My every footstep was followed by a courier carrying a satchel filled with draft war orders to be issued by code number in case of emergency.

Our military structure and equipment were changing so rapidly that even the comforting old slogan "Tried and true" was gone. In its place had sprung up a disquieting new one: "If it works, it's obsolete."

CHAPTER XIX

Formosa Doctrine

> . . . that the President of the United States be and he hereby is authorized to employ the Armed Forces of the United States as he deems necessary for the specific purpose of securing and protecting Formosa and the Pescadores against armed attack, this authority to include the securing and protection of such related positions and territories of that area now in friendly hands and the taking of such other measures as he judges to be required or appropriate in assuring the defense of Formosa and the Pescadores.
>
> —*Formosa Resolution*

AT about seven o'clock on the evening of September 3, 1954, the Army Signal Corps at the Summer White House in Denver brought me a message from Deputy Defense Secretary Robert B. Anderson, in Washington. It reported that at one forty-five that morning (Eastern Daylight Time), the Chinese Communists had begun a heavy artillery shelling of Quemoy Island off the Chinese coast. Though the shelling had diminished at about four-twenty in the morning, it was still, at last reports, continuing. Two Americans in uniform had been killed; fourteen were being evacuated.

At daybreak on September 4 (Quemoy local time), one report predicted, the Communists would launch an assault against Quemoy Island. The Commander-in-Chief of the Pacific Fleet, Admiral Stump, alerted, was moving carriers into position, to give support or to undertake a rescue.

The message from Anderson marked the commencement of a sequence of events which was to extend through nine months, threaten a split between the United States and nearly all its allies, and seemingly carry the country to the edge of war, thus constituting one of the most serious problems of the first eighteen months of my administration.

As a result of the Sino-Japanese War of 1894–95, China lost to Japan the important islands of Taiwan (Formosa) and the Pescadores, lying about a hundred miles off the Chinese coast. The Cairo Declaration of December 1943 announced that after World War II these islands would

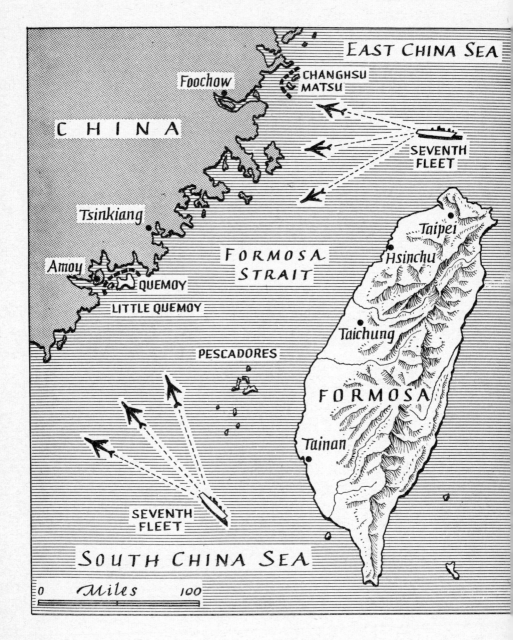

be returned to the "Republic of China." The Japanese peace treaty of 1951 ended Japanese sovereignty over the islands but did not formally cede them to "China," either Communist or Nationalist.

The Quemoy and Matsu groups, much smaller and much nearer the China coast, had always been under the control of the government on the Chinese mainland, until Chiang Kai-shek had fled to Formosa in 1949. Chiang still controlled them and was prepared to defend them with his full strength. An attack on Quemoy and Matsu, in his eyes, would without doubt be the prelude to an attack on Formosa and the Pescadores. If, therefore, the United States were to intervene in the contest over these islands, this country technically would be participating in a Chinese civil war.

The nineteen rocky, treeless Matsus, covering twelve square miles, blocked the port of Foochow on the Chinese mainland, just ten miles away, while the Quemoys, covering sixty square miles of land which supported several thousand farmers and fishermen, blocked the port of Amoy, only two miles away. Thus the two contending forces in China were face to face across a few thousand yards of water. Again and again in the years following the Chinese Communists' takeover in 1949, fearful observers asked whether we and our ally, Chiang, should be so close to Red China. Often they would pose a hypothetical situation which in their view would be similar to the one in Quemoy and Matsu. What would the United States do, they would ask, if Red China or the Soviet Union were encouraging a hostile army stationed on Staten Island? Such critics advised that safety required the abandonment of Quemoy and Matsu— with a Chinese Republic retreat to a relatively safe spot more than a hundred miles away, the islands of Taiwan and the Pescadores.

Chiang's forces held the offshore islands for several reasons. The most important was Chiang's conviction that if he lost Quemoy and Matsu, his main forces would lose their will to fight. Historically, he and his men remembered, Quemoy had been the site of strongholds of men who had defied and fought—sometimes with striking success—the rulers of the mainland. To Chiang and his people, Quemoy and Matsu would one day be stepping stones for the reinvasion of their homeland. Meanwhile, the possession of these islands enabled Chiang to preserve for his forces a jumping-off place for guerrilla raids on the mainland (these had been discontinued, however, in the summer of 1953); to sustain the morale of anti-Communist Asiatics in other areas of the Southwest Pacific, and to compel the Communists to tie down troops to guard against the threat which the island-based forces posed. This threat, angering and irritating the Communists, strengthened their resolve to drive the offshore islands' defenders into the sea.

By the September morning when the shelling started, the Nationalist forces, including guerrillas, numbered approximately 9000 on the Matsus, 15,000 on the Tachens (far to the north), and nearly 50,000 on Quemoy. Facing these units on the Chinese mainland around the port of Amoy were Communist troops numbering more than 150,000—more than enough, once they had landed on the island, for the work of conquest. Incidentally, both sides knew that the months between April and October offered best weather for an attack on Formosa, but that an invasion against Quemoy or Matsu or the Tachens could start any time.

The September 3 shelling did not come as a complete surprise.

In his New Year's message for 1954, Generalissimo Chiang Kai-shek had pledged an attack on the mainland "in the not distant future"; and his Easter message had called for a "holy war" against the Communists. Twice during the month of May, Nationalist and Communist planes had clashed over the waters of the Formosa Strait, and Communist and Nationalist ships had fired on each other.

At a meeting with Republican Legislative leaders on May 24—more than three months before the shelling began—I outlined to them the problems involved in defending Formosa and the outpost islands. Two months later Syngman Rhee, speaking before a joint session of the United States Congress, proposed that the United States join South Korea and Nationalist China in a war against Red China; he called for United States air and naval support for his and Chiang's invasion of the Chinese mainland.[1]

In President Rhee and Chiang Kai-shek the world had to recognize the sturdy qualities of fearless leaders, always ready to incur any risk in support of what they believed right, even though their objectives were based upon local rather than global considerations.

Two weeks after this speech Premier Chou En-lai, as if in reply, called for the "liberation of Formosa"—meaning its capture—and warned that his government would not tolerate interference from the United States or anybody else.

The temperature was rising. And on August 17 I got a news-conference question on it.

"Mr. President," Merriman Smith, White House correspondent for United Press, asked, "there have been reports recently of a build-up of Chinese Communist strength across on the mainland from Formosa. There have been reports from the Far East that the Chinese Communists may

[1] Through the troubled year that followed, he was to continue his call for action, despite the fact that he would rouse little enthusiasm for such a crusade among his friends and allies. On September 20, 1955, for example, he announced his readiness to "fight for unification soon . . . armed even with sticks if necessary. . . . I would like to march north at this minute and save our poor country now."

attack Formosa. What would happen, sir, if the Communists did attack Formosa in force?"

I answered, "In January or February of 1953 instructions went out to the Seventh Fleet. Those instructions regarding the defense of Formosa merely reaffirmed orders that had been in force in that fleet since 1950. Those orders are still in force. Therefore, I should assume what would happen is this: any invasion of Formosa would have to run over the Seventh Fleet."

While Peiping Radio continued to call for Formosa's "liberation," on the 26th of August forty Communist raiders struck on Quemoy Island, killing ten Nationalists. And then on the morning of September 3 the artillery bombardment began.

I now faced the question, "What policy should the United States adopt?" Since the outbreak of the Korean War more than four years earlier, this country had adhered to the conviction that Communists and Nationalists would have to fight out their own differences over the offshore islands, as distinguished from Formosa and the Pescadores. In any purely coastal conflict, the United States would limit its aid to matériel. Should the United States continue this policy or change it?

The message which Deputy Secretary Anderson sent to me in Denver pointed out that the Joint Chiefs of Staff disagreed on the defense of the offshore islands. Some believed the United States should change its policy in order to assure the defense of ten particular islands which they believed were essential in these groups. Though the majority concluded that the offshore islands were not militarily necessary to the defense of Formosa, all but one recognized the overriding fact that the islands' loss would have bad, possibly disastrous, psychological effects. Therefore they believed we should defend them. Only General Ridgway, then Army Chief of Staff, refused to concur; the United States, he said, should not commit any forces to hold the islands. The Joint Chiefs, he went on, should not take upon themselves the nonmilitary job of judging the islands' political and psychological value. What he was setting aside was the effect of their possible loss on the morale of Chiang's main forces and therefore on the defense of Formosa. The Joint Chiefs, however, agreed on two things: (a) the islands were not militarily essential to America's capacity to defend Formosa; and (b) the Chinese Nationalists could not hold them without American assistance.

By Sunday, September 12, the Chinese Communists still had not attacked, they had been confining themselves for the moment to sporadic artillery fire against Quemoy. That Sunday morning, at my temporary White House in Denver, my top foreign-policy and military advisers and I held a special meeting from which came the administration's decision on what Secretary Dulles called "a horrible dilemma."

There were military reasons, Admiral Radford contended, of considerable import for holding the offshore islands (for example, they blocked Communist communications along the coast). He, Admiral Carney, and General Twining therefore urged that the United States commit itself to defend the islands and help the Chinese Nationalists bomb the mainland. With this conclusion I disagreed. Such a course, I said, we could not confine to Quemoy Island. "We're not talking now about a limited, brush-fire war. We're talking about going to the threshold of World War III. If we attack China, we're not going to impose limits on our military actions, as in Korea.

"Moreover," I reminded them, "if we get into a general war, the logical enemy will be Russia, not China, and we'll have to strike there."

Secretary Dulles observed that the problem involved complex and conflicting considerations. The Chinese Communists, he said, were probing; unless we stopped them, we faced disaster in the Far East. But, he added, if we drew a line and committed ourselves to defend Quemoy and Matsu, we might find ourselves, without allies, in a war against Red China. He therefore suggested an alternative: "We should take the offshore-islands question to the United Nations Security Council with the view of getting there an injunction to maintain the status quo and institute a cease fire in the Formosa Strait. Whether Russia vetoes or accepts such a plan," he said, "the United States will gain."

I approved the Secretary's suggestion.

Overseas, however, leading public figures urged on us a variety of different courses. For example, former Prime Minister Clement Attlee, returning early in September from a British Labor-party tour of Red China, confirmed reports that Mao Tse-tung had asked him and his fellow Laborites to pressure the United States into pulling the Seventh Fleet away from the waters around Formosa, which, Attlee added, the Communists have a "strong determination" to capture. In subsequent interviews Attlee suggested neutralizing Formosa and "getting rid of Chiang." Strangely, a "neutralization" agreement seems always to come to the fore when a new crisis impends; but even more strangely, those proposing it seldom suggest an effective plan for enforcement.

Foreign Minister Eden, though less extreme in his counsel, had no enthusiasm for risking a war over Quemoy and Matsu. On September 29, in London, Secretary Dulles met with him and the New Zealand High Commissioner on a proposal to have New Zealand submit the offshore-islands problem to the United Nations Security Council. Foster wanted a Security Council recommendation that military activity both against the islands and in their defense be suspended. Eden enthusiastically agreed, urging the New Zealand government to do anything possible in view of the grim alternatives.

To this plan, however, Chiang Kai-shek objected; going to the Security Council, he contended, was the first step toward letting it decide who owned Formosa and which China had a right to United Nations representation. On October 14 Secretary Dulles wrote the Generalissimo in defense of the plan, predicting that though Chiang's reaction was negative, Mao's would be even more so; and assuring him that the United States would never agree to submit to the United Nations the question of Chiang's right to rule Formosa. I always regarded this suggestion— and my recollection is that Secretary Dulles concurred—as one that could have no harmful results and could give us a much better position in convincing other free nations of our sincerity and honesty in the policies we followed in that area.

On November 1, 1954, Communist planes bombed the Tachen Islands. The next day they shelled other small offshore islands and the build-up of troops opposite Formosa continued. Then on November 23 Peiping Radio reported the verdict of a Communist court on thirteen Americans, eleven of them airmen in uniform. They had been shot down by the Red Chinese (who announced their capture on my first day in office). The court had sentenced them to prison terms ranging from four years to life, for espionage.

In a speech on the Senate floor Senator Knowland demanded that the United States Navy blockade the coast of China, with or without the assent of the United Nations, and thus force Red China to free the American prisoners. Three days earlier at a breakfast meeting I had warned the senator against any such rash step. As President, I of course experienced exactly the same resentments, anger, and frustration as anyone else when such a thing happened to another American, and my impulse, like his, was to lash out. But I knew such a response would be self-defeating.

"The hard way," I said, "is to have the courage to be patient." The United States would work tirelessly for the American prisoners' eventual release. But I rejected the strategy of 'a naval blockade, and in that rejection got backing not only from Republican leaders (not including Knowland, of course) but also from the Democrats George, Johnson, Sparkman, and Fulbright.

Early in December, Secretary Dulles and Dr. George K. C. Yeh, Nationalist China's Foreign Minister, signed a mutual-defense treaty in behalf of the United States and the Republic of China. The two countries pledged separately and jointly to "maintain and develop their individual and collective capacity to resist armed attack and Communist subversive activities"; and they agreed that an armed attack on either of them would endanger the peace and safety of the other. Though the treaty limited these agreements to Taiwan and the Pescadores, it specifically provided that they could be extended to other areas by consent of both sides.

On December 10 Secretary Dulles and Dr. Yeh exchanged letters—kept secret for a month—which included a further key understanding between the two countries:

> In view of the . . . fact that the use of force from either of these areas [under Chinese Nationalist control] by either party affects the other, it is agreed that such use of force will be a matter of joint agreement, subject to action of an emergency character which is clearly an exercise of the inherent right of self-defense.

The Chinese Nationalists, in other words, agreed not to attack the mainland unilaterally.

On December 20 Dr. Yeh came to see me at the White House. Generalissimo Chiang, he assured me, was satisfied with the treaty, but he felt that it would be good psychological warfare for the United States also to assure the Chinese Nationalists it would give them logistic support for the defense of the offshore islands. I felt it would be a mistake, however, to expand the treaty at this time and asked the Foreign Minister to convey this message to the generalissimo. Moreover, I said I was sure that it would be a military mistake to crowd still more Chinese Nationalist soldiers onto these small and exposed islands. Their strength should be in weapons, emplacements, morale, and supply—not in numbers of personnel.

With the beginning of the New Year, events in the Formosa Strait began to take a turn for the worse. Generalissimo Chiang Kai-shek's New Year's message for 1955 forecast war "at any time." The Chinese Communists stepped up construction of jet airfields opposite Formosa—airfields which, by the end of the spring, might permit them to gain air superiority over Quemoy and Matsu.

On January 10 a hundred Communist planes raided the Tachen Islands. These islands, about two hundred miles from Formosa, were much less significant to the Nationalist cause than were Quemoy and Matsu, farther south. But a week later, on January 18, nearly four thousand Chinese Communist troops, with heavy air bombardment and an amphibious attack, overwhelmed one thousand Nationalist guerrillas and seized the island of Ichiang, just seven miles north of the Tachens. The fight had lasted just two hours.

The newspapers headlined the news. At a press conference I pointed out that neither Ichiang, occupied by guerrillas, nor the Tachens, occupied by the regulars, were vital to the defense of Formosa and the Pescadores.

But the time had come to draw the line. The following morning, after discussion with my advisers, I decided on a course of action.

"It is **unlikely**," Secretary Dulles argued at this meeting, "that any of the offshore islands can be defended without large-scale American armed help. But we all agree that we cannot permit the Communists to seize *all* the offshore islands. Therefore," he continued, "I believe we must modify our policy: we should assist in the evacuation of the Tachens, but as we do so we should declare that we will assist in holding Quemoy and possibly the Matsus, as long as the Chinese Communists profess their intention to attack Formosa." I reiterated the serious psychological consequences of abandoning Quemoy and Matsu, and ordered a start in implementing this modified policy—even Chiang saw little value in holding the Tachens.

The next day I approved the wording of a special message to the Congress asking for presidential authority to use American armed force to protect Formosa and the Pescadores and related positions, if necessary, in defense of the principal islands. I believed the Korean War had resulted, partially at least, from the mistaken Communist notion that under no circumstances would the United States move to the assistance of the Korean Republic. I resolved that this time no uncertainty about our commitment to defend Formosa should invite a major Chinese Communist attack.

On the afternoon of January 21 I met with Secretary Dulles, Secretary Wilson, Deputy Secretary of Defense Anderson, Admiral Radford, Admiral Carney, General Twining, General Shepherd, General Bolte, and Mr. Robert Bowie, head of the State Department's Policy Planning Staff. Admiral Carney expressed the view that my proposed message to the Congress advocated an evacuation of the Tachens, which he and the other members of the Joint Chiefs believed both unwise and difficult. Thirty thousand civilians and troops were on those islands, Admiral Carney said. Because a ship had been sunk at the entrance to the harbor, it would be necessary to carry out all American military equipment by lighter. These facts would make evacuation of the islands more difficult than defending them. But, Admiral Carney added, the Chinese Nationalists could not defend the Tachens alone.

I stuck to my proposed message, the purpose of which was to inform the Chinese Communists of the United States' intentions, to dispel doubts in foreign capitals that the United States was acting on constitutional grounds, and to bolster Chinese Nationalist morale.

Three days later the message went to Capitol Hill.

"I do not suggest that the United States enlarge its defensive obligations beyond Formosa and the Pescadores," it said. But the danger of attack against them compelled consideration of "closely related localities and actions which, under current conditions, might determine the failure or the success of such attack." The authority that might be accorded by the Congress, I added, would be used only "in situations which are recognizable as parts of, or definite preliminaries to, an attack" against Formosa and the Pescadores. This explanation was necessary, I thought, for the reason that all the Chinese Communist propaganda constantly proclaimed that their purpose was to capture Formosa; the offshore islands were only incidental in their plans.

In asking for the resolution I did not imply that I lacked constitutional authority to act: "Authority for some of the actions which might be required," I said, "would be inherent in the authority of the Commander-in-Chief." But a "suitable congressional resolution" would "clearly and publicly establish the authority of the President" to act in whatever fashion might be necessary; it would "make clear the unified and serious intentions" of the American Congress, the American government, and the American people and thus reduce the chance of war through Communist miscalculation.

Chou En-lai considered this to be a "war message" and reiterated his intent to liberate not merely the offshore islands but the Pescadores and Formosa as well.

As soon as my message reached the Congress, Senator George and Congressman Richards introduced identical resolutions in the Senate and the House to give the President unlimited authority to act in the Formosa Strait. The next day the House approved the resolution 410 to 3.

In the Senate committee hearing the following day, Senator Kefauver proposed turning over the protection of Formosa and the Pescadores to the United Nations and giving authority to the President only until the United Nations should act. The committee voted the amendment down.

Senator Hubert Humphrey introduced an amendment to limit the President's authority only to Formosa and the Pescadores; the committee members rejected this too.

For three days, senators debated the resolution on the floor. Senator Morse complained that it gave the President "a predatory authorization" to wage war. Senator Herbert Lehman of New York introduced a crucial amendment drawing a line back of Quemoy and Matsu and confining the use of American armed forces to the defense of Formosa and the Pescadores. In the vote on this amendment—the key congressional vote on the entire subject—seventy-four senators rejected Lehman's limitation. Thirteen favored the amendment, including one Republican (Langer) and twelve Democrats (Fulbright, Long, McNamara, Humphrey, Mansfield, Murray, Lehman, Morse, Neuberger, Kefauver, Byrd, and Kilgore).[2]

[2] When this crucial vote was taken, by coincidence Senator Kennedy and Senator Johnson were in the hospital. But they felt so strongly about it as to announce themselves as paired: Senator Kennedy stood with Lehman, Morse, Kefauver, and the rest of the thirteen who wanted to write off Quemoy and Matsu; Lyndon John-

On January 28 the Senate passed the resolution eighty-three to three, and the next day I signed it. The President was now, in the words of the resolution,

> . . . authorized to employ the armed forces of the United States as he deems necessary for the specific purpose of securing and protecting Formosa and the Pescadores against armed attack, this authority to include the securing and protecting of such related positions and territories of that area now in friendly hands and the taking of such other measures as he judges to be required or appropriate in assuring the defense of Formosa and the Pescadores [see Appendix N].

Two weeks later I signed the Formosa mutual-security treaty, also approved by the Senate. Taken together, the two documents left no doubt of the United States' intention regarding Formosa and the Pescadores; in that region we would not be in the situation we had faced in the 1950 Korean crisis.

In the meantime on January 28, Sir Leslie K. Munro, New Zealand's Representative to the United Nations, had proposed a Formosa Strait cease-fire resolution in the United Nations Security Council. Britain and the United States concurred. The Security Council invited Communist China to join in the discussion. Chou refused; the aim of the discussion, he declared, is "obviously to intervene in China's internal affairs," and any decisions the Security Council might take would therefore be "illegal and null and void." He lashed out against "American aggression" against Taiwan.

It was therefore clear that the United Nations was unable to be of any help to us in establishing a cease fire and keeping the peace.

Moreover, it seemed probable that the Soviet Union would do all it could to get the United States bogged down in a debilitating war with Communist China. Indeed, early the following month Bulganin in his inaugural speech to the Supreme Soviet assailed the United States and pledged Russian support to the Chinese Communists in the event of war.

That same day Admiral Radford came to the White House to discuss the orders to go to Admiral Stump, the commander-in-chief of the Pacific Fleet, on the matter of American assistance in evacuating the Tachen Islands. The final instruction gave the American commander the right, in responding to Chiang's request for the evacuation, to attack Red Chinese airfields, if self-defense so required.

---

son joined the ranks of the seventy-four in the majority, following the leadership of Senator Walter George of Georgia who during the debate had declared that turning over Quemoy and Matsu to the Communists would cause a "disintegration that would . . . be swift, quick, speedy, and final," one which would "cut the heart out" of the Nationalist troops.

On February 4 the evacuation began. Within a week the Navy and Air Force, with little difficulty, evacuated approximately twenty thousand civilians and ten thousand troops from the Tachens and from nearby Yushan and Penshan. Two weeks later, and this time without United States aid, the Chinese Nationalists took four thousand troops off Nanki Island, 150 miles north of Formosa and 20 miles from the coast, and moved them to reinforce Matsu.

Throughout, we kept our principal allies informed of the reasons for our actions [see Appendix O]. Early in February, for example, I wrote to Prime Minister Churchill:

I have heard how earnestly you supported throughout the Conference of Prime Ministers the proposition that nothing must create a serious rift in British-American relationships. Not only do I applaud that sentiment, but I am most deeply grateful to you for your successful efforts.

I realize that it has been difficult, at times, for you to back us up in the Formosa question and, for this reason, I want to give you a . . . brief account of our general attitude toward the various factors that have dictated the course we have taken. You understand, of course, that we have certain groups that are violent in their efforts to get us to take a much stronger, even a truculent position. The number that would like to see us clear out of Formosa is negligible. I know that on your side of the water you have the exact opposite of this situation.

Because the Communists know these facts, there is no question in my mind that one of the principal reasons for their constant pressing on the Asian frontier is the hope of dividing our two countries. I am sure that we, on both sides of the water, can make quite clear that, no matter what may be our differences in approach or even sometimes our differences in important convictions, nothing is ever going to separate us or destroy our unity in opposing Communist aggression.

We believe that if international Communism should penetrate the island barrier in the Western Pacific and thus be in a position to threaten the Philippines and Indonesia immediately and directly, all of us, including the free countries of Europe, would soon be in far worse trouble than we are now. Certainly that whole region would soon go.

To defend Formosa the United States has been engaged in a long and costly program of arming and sustaining the Nationalist troops on that island. Those troops, however, and Chiang himself, are not content, *now*, to accept irrevocably and permanently the status of "prisoners" on the island. They are held together by a conviction that some day they will go back to the mainland.

As a consequence, their attitude toward Quemoy and the Matsus, which they deem the stepping stones between the two hostile regions, is that the surrender of those islands would destroy the reason for the existence of the Nationalist forces on Formosa. This, then, would mean the almost immediate conversion of that asset into a deadly danger, because the Communists would immediately take it over.

The Formosa Resolution, as passed by the Congress, is our publicly stated position; the problem now is how to make it work. The morale of the Chinese Nationalists is important to us, so for the moment, and under existing conditions, we feel they must have certain assurances with respect to the offshore islands. But these must be less binding on us than the terms of the Chino-American Treaty, which was overwhelmingly passed yesterday by the Senate. We must remain ready, until some better solution can be found, to move promptly against any Communist force that is manifestly preparing to attack Formosa. And we must make a distinction— (this is a difficult one)—between an attack that has *only* as its objective the capture of an off-shore island and one that is primarily a preliminary movement to an all-out attack on Formosa.

Whatever now is to happen, I know that nothing could be worse than global war.

I do not believe that Russia wants war at this time—in fact, I do not believe that even if we became engaged in a serious fight along the coast of China, Russia would want to intervene with her own forces. She would, of course, pour supplies into China in an effort to exhaust us and certainly would exploit the opportunity to separate us from your country. But I am convinced that Russia does not want, at this moment, to experiment with means of defense against the bombing that we could conduct against her mainland.

In any event, we have got to do what we believe to be right—if we can figure out the right—and we must show no lack of firmness in a world where our political enemies exploit every sign of weakness, and are constantly attempting to disrupt the solidarity of the free world's intentions to oppose their aggressive practices.

Though thus sketchily presented, this has been the background of our thinking leading up to the present day. I devoutly hope that history's inflexible yardstick will show that we have done everything in our power, and everything that is right, to prevent the awful catastrophe of another major war.

I am sending you this note, not merely because of my realization that you, as our great and trusted ally, are entitled to have our thoughts on these vital matters, but because I so value, on the more personal side, the opportunity to learn of your own approach to these critical problems.

Often I had assured the Prime Minister that never would I be a participant in appeasement. Now I wanted to be sure of his understanding that America's determination to defend Formosa and the Pescadores was firm and that our reaction to an attack on the Matsu and Quemoy groups would have to depend on circumstances as they might arise.

On February 15 Winston answered, presenting, in splendid and eloquent words, an argument, some of which I could not accept. As a matter of honor, he wrote, the United States must not permit its loyal ally Chiang Kai-shek to be liquidated and massacred and scuppered by the Chinese Communists. But from this overriding purpose, he urged the United States to disentangle one which he believed secondary: holding the offshore islands as a bridgehead for a Nationalist invasion of Red China. No decisive relationship, he believed, existed between the offshore islands and an invasion of Formosa; in his view, the United States could easily "drown any Chinese would-be invaders of Formosa," no matter where they came from. To Chiang, Winston argued, the United States should give the protection of its shield but not the use of its sword.

On February 19 I again explained to him why we would not abandon the offshore islands.

Dear Winston:

I greatly appreciate the message from you and Anthony. I have studied it long and carefully, as has Foster. . . . We clearly recognize the great importance to the security of the free world of our two governments achieving a step by step progress both in policy and in action.

Diplomatically it would indeed be a great relief to us if the line between the Nationalists and the Communists were actually the broad Strait of Formosa instead of the narrow Straits between Quemoy and Matsu and the mainland. However, there are about 55,000 of the Nationalist troops on these coastal islands and the problem created thereby cannot, I fear, be solved by us merely announcing a desire to transplant them to Formosa. . . .

I pointed out that while the United States could, for itself, assume an attitude of indifference to the fate of the islands, this would not ease, but rather would complicate, our problem, which was to assure the integrity of the island barrier in the Pacific. At all costs, I said:

. . . We must not lose Chiang's army and we must maintain its strength, efficiency and morale. Only a few months back we had both Chiang and a strong, well-equipped French Army to support the free world's position in Southeast Asia. The French are gone—making it clearer than ever that we cannot afford the loss of Chiang unless all of us are to get completely out of that corner of the globe. This is unthinkable to us—I feel it must be to you.

In order to make an express or tacit cease-fire likely, we have, with difficulties perhaps greater than you realize, done, through our diplomacy, many things.

1. We rounded out the far Pacific security chain by a Treaty with the Nationalists which, however, only covered specifically Formosa and the Pescadores, thus making it clear to Chiang and to all the world that we were not prepared to defend the coastal positions as Treaty territory.

2. We obtained from Chiang his agreement that he would not conduct any offensive operations against the mainland either from Formosa *or from his coastal positions,* except in agreement with us. Thus we are in a position to preclude what you refer to as the use of these offshore islands as "bridgeheads for a Nationalist invasion of Communist China," or as a base for "sporadic war against the mainland" or "the invasion of the mainland of China." . . .

3. Furthermore, we obtained an agreement from the Nationalists closely limiting their right to take away from Formosa military elements, material or human, to which we had contributed if this would weaken the defense of Formosa itself.

4. We made possible the voluntary evacuation of the Tachens and the two other islands.

5. Finally, we secured the acquiescence of the Chinese Nationalists to United Nations proceedings for a cease-fire, although the Chinese Nationalists were extremely suspicious of this move and felt that it could permanently blight their hopes.

All of this was done, as I say, in consultation between Anthony and Foster and in the hope that this would provide a basis for a cease-fire.

However, what we have done has apparently been interpreted by the Chinese Communists merely as a sign of weakness. They have intensified their threats against Formosa and their expressions of determination to take it by force. Also, they continue to hold, in durance vile, our airmen who were captured by them in the Korean War and who should have been freed by the Korean Armistice.

There comes a point where constantly giving in only encourages further belligerency. I think we must be careful not to pass that point in our dealings with Communist China. In such a case, further retreat becomes worse than a Munich because at Munich there were at least promises on the part of the aggressor to cease expansion and to keep the peace. In this case the Chinese Communists have promised nothing and have not contributed one iota toward peace in the Formosa area. Indeed, they treat the suggestion of peace there as an insult.

Winston had seemed to think that Communist announcements of their purpose of taking Formosa were just talk; he felt that they would be quite happy with possession of the offshore islands alone. With this view I disagreed:

. . . What they are really interested in is Formosa—and later on Japan —the coastal islands are marginal. They do not want to have another Chinese Government in their neighborhood, particularly one which has military power and which poses a threat to their center if ever they attack on their flanks.

Therefore, I think that if the Chinese Nationalists got out of Quemoy and the Matsus, they would not be solving the real problem, which is far more basic. I repeat that it would more likely mean that this retreat, and

the coercion we would have to exert to bring it about, would so under-
mine the morale and the loyalty of the non-Communist forces on
Formosa that they could not be counted on. Some, at least, might defect
to the Communists or provide such a weak element in the defense of
Formosa that an amphibious operation could give the Communists a
strong foothold on Formosa.

In the meantime we were receiving, almost daily, through diplomatic
and private channels, questions from other Asiatic nations concerning the
firmness of our intentions. So my letter continued:

> All of the non-Communist nations of the Western Pacific—particularly
> Korea, Japan, the Philippines, and, of course, Formosa itself—are watching
> nervously to see what we do next. I fear that, if we appear strong and
> coercive only toward our friends, and should attempt to compel Chiang
> to make further retreats, the conclusion of these Asian peoples will be that
> they had better plan to make the best terms they can with the Com-
> munists. . . .
> We are doing everything possible to work this situation out in a way
> which, on the one hand, will avoid the risk of war, and, on the other
> hand, preserve the non-Communist position in the Western Pacific, a
> position which, by the way, is vital to Australia and New Zealand. How-
> ever, if the Chinese Communists are determined to have a war to gain
> Formosa, then there will be trouble.
> I see I have made this as long, and perhaps as complicated, as a diplo-
> matic note. For that I apologize!
> With warm regard,
>
> *As ever,*
> IKE

On February 21 I cabled Secretary Dulles, who was in Bangkok for
the first meeting of the Manila Pact Council (SEATO), to confirm his
understanding that we would assist Chiang in defending the offshore
areas logistically and, if convinced that any attack was really a military
part of a campaign against Formosa, that we would participate more directly. Any offensive military participation on our part, I said, would be
only by presidential order.

For some time, most of my associates had agreed with me that the
Chinese Nationalists would improve their position if they withdrew the
major part of their forces from the coastal islands, organized the remaining troops and installations as outposts, and held their main forces on
Formosa, poised and ready to move to the attack in response to Chinese
Communist actions. In my cable to Foster Dulles in Bangkok, I agreed
that there was little probability that we could induce Chiang to acknowledge the wisdom of thinning out his forward positions, and of making
those islands tactical outposts for Formosa. I approved Foster's intention

to inform Eden that unless we could soon arrive at a cease fire, we could not much longer insist that the present policy of watchful readiness be observed, which permitted a major Communist build-up or attacks without a reaction from Chiang. I suggested he tell Eden that we did not intend to blackmail Chiang into an evacuation of Quemoy and the Matsus as long as Chiang deemed their possession vital to the spirit and morale of the Formosan garrison and population. On the contrary, I said, we expected to continue our logistic support of Chiang's forces, at all points, as long as there was no mutually agreed-upon or tacit cease fire.

In a long cable on February 25 Secretary Dulles replied that he had talked with Anthony Eden about the Formosa crisis, reminding him that successful pressure on Chiang to surrender Quemoy and Matsu would permit the Chinese Communists to attack from the harbors of Amoy and Foochow, and invite the Chinese Communists to put to the test American resolution to defend Formosa. Dulles said also that the Communists had repeatedly announced their determination to take Formosa by force, and would use each surrendered island as a route toward that objective. Continuing, Foster said that the United States had taken step after step to reduce the chance of war. In addition, we had limited the congressional resolution to Formosa and the Pescadores; we had accepted the idea of a United Nations cease-fire resolution; and we had opposed retaliation against the Chinese Communists for the imprisonment of our airmen.

Eden remained unpersuaded. On returning to England he urged in a speech in the House of Commons on March 8, that the Nationalists withdraw from Quemoy and Matsu and that the Communists agree to abstain from attacking them or Formosa and the Pescadores. This arrangement, he argued, could be followed by discussion of the political issues, which would produce a peaceful settlement. Such a suggestion, more wishful than realistic, in the light of our past experiences, I simply could not accept.

Even in the United States, however, responsible and intelligent citizens questioned the United States policy. For example, Lewis W. Douglas, a former United States ambassador to Great Britain, wrote to me on March 3 saying that Quemoy and Matsu belonged to China. If the United States helped Chiang, he went on, the United States automatically would intervene in a Chinese civil war. Such intervention, he argued, rested completely on strategy; he urged me to reject that policy for one based instead on law.

Again, I could not accept such a strictly legalistic conclusion, and in my answer I explained why:

It is true that our strategic situation would be seriously—possibly even fatally—damaged in the western Pacific if we should lose Formosa to the Communists. However, not only does the legal history of that island give

us a recognized right to assist in [its] defense; it is occupied by a government that the U.S. has recognized as an ally over a number of years. . . .
In spite of what you say about strategic considerations, let us remember
that the Soviets have not hesitated to apply the theory that the strategic
considerations are all important. Seizing on the opportunity given them—
I believe at Yalta—to occupy the Kuriles, they have also occupied Hobomai,
immediately off the shores of Hokkaido, in fact only two or three miles
away. There they sit, and if Japan or ourselves would try to kick them out,
we would probably be accused of provocative action that might lead to
a world war.

Our planes have been shot down as much as twenty miles offshore in
areas that are certainly of the "high seas" variety. The Baltic is a closed
Communist lake.

I do not, by any means, intend to argue against the logic of your opening paragraphs in which you point out the danger of following a doctrine
of strategic convenience. I merely point out that we are living in a time
when our enemies don't even bother to explain—they just act, and
often without any semblance of justification in international law, in
ethics or in custom.

On March 8 Secretary Dulles returned from two weeks in Southeast
Asia and the Western Pacific. Following the initial eight-nation meeting
of the Manila Pact Council in Bangkok, he had gone on to Burma, Laos,
Cambodia, South Vietnam, the Philippines, and Formosa. In conferences
with heads of government, he had done his utmost to make clear the
United States' resolve to defend Formosa and the Pescadores, in the hope
that this message would get through to Mao Tse-tung and Chou En-lai.

When he reported on his trip at a White House meeting on March 10,
however, he took a somewhat gloomy view of the future.

"The situation out there in the Formosa Strait," he said, "is far more
serious than I thought before my trip. The Chinese Communists are determined to capture Formosa. Surrendering Quemoy and Matsu won't end
that determination. If we defend Quemoy and Matsu," he said, "we'll
have to use atomic weapons. They alone will be effective against the
mainland airfields." To this I agreed, but then Foster brought into the
open a nagging doubt he had acquired during his trip. He said he could
not answer one crucial question: how loyal would Chiang's troops be if
attacked?

This disturbed me: "The United States," I pointed out to the meeting,
"cannot possibly save the Nationalists if they don't want to be saved. The
Secretary's report of military morale on Formosa puts the problem in a
different light."

Admiral Radford asserted once more that the Nationalists' morale depended on their hope of returning to the mainland—a hope encouraged
by their possession of Quemoy and Matsu. Foster agreed that the United

States could not sit idly by and watch the Chinese on Quemoy and Matsu suffer a crushing defeat—a defeat which would lead to the loss of Formosa itself.

"Before this problem is solved," he said, "I believe there is at least an even chance that the United States will have to go to war."

I merely observed that if this proved to be true it would certainly be recognized that the war would not be of our seeking.

The next afternoon Foster and Allen Dulles, most of the Chiefs of Staff, General Cutler, and Colonel Goodpaster came to my office to discuss the Chinese Nationalists' capacity to defend Formosa during the coming weeks without active American help or without the American use of the atomic bomb.

To get further information and a sensing of the problem as it appeared to an observer at firsthand, I should ordinarily have called in at such a moment the commander-in-chief of the Pacific Fleet. But in a time of such tension, with the enemy scrutinizing our every move, I could not possibly call Admiral Stump back to Washington. I therefore sent Colonel Goodpaster, the brilliant and trusted White House Staff Secretary, to Pearl Harbor to confer with Admiral Stump. On March 15 Colonel Goodpaster's report was in my hands. After March 25, he said, the Chinese Communists could overcome Nationalist opposition only by an all-out coordinated amphibious attack against Quemoy and Matsu, with artillery and air support: such an attack probably would not come sooner than in four weeks against Matsu and in eight weeks against the Quemoys. But the next ten days (March 15–25), he warned, were the time of greatest danger. The Nationalists were still building up their defenses on Matsu. If a sudden Chinese Communist amphibious attack was launched before they finished, it might succeed.

Through all these tense days Foster and I continued to meet with the press and face public inquiry.

"Would the United States," a reporter asked me on March 16, "use tactical atomic weapons in a general war in Asia?" Against a strictly military target, I replied, the answer would be "yes." I hoped this answer would have some effect in persuading the Chinese Communists of the strength of our determination.

As I was about to cross West Executive Avenue to the Executive Office Building for my press conference the next week, on March 23, Jim Hagerty reported a frantic plea he had just received.

"Mr. President," he said, "some of the people in the State Department say that the Formosa Strait situation is so delicate that no matter what question you get on it, you shouldn't say anything at all."

I could see the point of this advice. But I didn't take it.

"Don't worry, Jim," I told him as we went out the door of my office, "if that question comes up, I'll just confuse them."

One question on this subject came that morning from Joseph C. Harsch, of the *Christian Science Monitor:* "If we got into an issue with the Chinese, say, over Matsu and Quemoy, that we wanted to keep limited, do you conceive of using [atomic weapons] in that situation or not?"

I said that I could not answer that question in advance. The only thing I knew about war was two things: the most unpredictable factor in war was human nature, but the only unchanging factor in war was human nature.

"And the next thing," I said in answer to Mr. Harsch, "is that every war is going to astonish you in the way it occurred, and in the way it is carried out.

"So that for a man to predict, particularly if he has the responsibility for making the decision, to predict what he is going to use, how he is going to do it, would I think exhibit his ignorance of war; that is what I believe.

"So I think you just have to wait; and that is the kind of prayerful decision that may some day face a President."

During that same week Secretary Dulles, addressing the Advertising Club of New York, pointed out that the Chinese Communists' tactics were even more provocative of war than those of the Soviet Union. The Chinese, "dizzy with success," he said, pursue a course of "aggressive fanaticism." Three days later, however, External Affairs Secretary Lester Pearson announced that Canada would not fight over the offshore islands, a remark which led to a pontifical summary by one columnist on the morning of March 25 that "all our Allies, except Generalissimo Chiang Kai-shek, regard this as the wrong war, at the wrong time, and at the wrong place." Evidently there are citizens of the Free World who can never be made to see that any retreat in the face of Communist aggression merely assures another attack.

The next morning the newspapers reported that a high administration official had leaked the news that the President and his advisers feared an imminent Chinese Communist attack against Quemoy and Matsu. The source was Admiral Carney, speaking, he thought, off the record. Insofar as I personally was concerned, his statement was incorrect.

That day I wrote one of my occasional notes to myself:

> Lately there has been a very definite feeling among the members of the Cabinet, often openly expressed, that within a month we will actually be fighting in the Formosa Straits. It is, of course, entirely possible that this is true, because the Red Chinese appear to be completely reckless, arrogant, possibly over-confident, and completely **indifferent** as to human losses.
> Nevertheless, I believe hostilities are not so **imminent** as is indicated by

the forebodings of a number of my associates. It is clear that this gloomy outlook has been communicated to others because a number of articles in the papers state that the Administration is rather expecting hostilities within a month.

I have so often been through these periods of strain that I have become accustomed to the fact that most of the calamities that we anticipate really never occur. No period was more illustrative of this truth than the six months following the outbreak of our war in 1941. Every prophet in those days was one of gloom. Only two or three of the eventualities that sprung up in the mind or in the imagination came to pass.

The Carney leak about the imminence of war brought about a clash in the Senate between Lyndon Johnson, who feared an "irresponsible adventure," and Senator Knowland, who condemned any form of "appeasement."

The newspapers the next morning carried another "leak"—this time one made intentionally by Jim Hagerty—to the effect that "the President did not believe war was upon us."

That same day I wrote another letter to Winston Churchill, still seeking a common understanding between us on our problems in the Far East. In it I compared the aggressiveness of the Red Chinese in the Formosa Strait with that of the Japanese in Manchuria and the Nazis in Europe in the 1930s. Concessions were no answer.

At my news conference the next day, in responding to a question about Admiral Carney's off-the-record prophecy, I said that it was, of course, impossible to predict when war would break out, and I added that the hope for peace was not strengthened by such speculation.

At noon that day and the next, Secretary Dulles and I held bipartisan luncheon meetings with Legislative leaders. At the March 30 meeting with members of the House of Representatives, Secretary Dulles outlined the Formosa Strait problem as it then existed. He listed a number of reasons for the Chinese Communists' obvious arrogance: their successes in Korea three years earlier, where they had driven the United Nations forces from the Yalu back to the 38th Parallel; their 1954 success at Dien Bien Phu, and the recent evacuation of the Tachens. To the Chinese Communist leaders, the Secretary said, these victories might well indicate that the Free World was not only taking reverses but "almost asking for more." Chou En-lai, it was reported, estimated that in a war with the United States, Red China might lose 100 million men and still have 450 million left—apparently believing that this would constitute victory for his side.

The Secretary told the congressmen that the United States had no means of knowing how much the Russians supported the aggressive tactics of the Chinese. A war between the United States and China would require the Russians to increase immensely their deliveries of military equipment to their Chinese allies. On the other hand we should remember, the Secretary went on, that last winter Khrushchev, in a visit with Bulganin to Peiping, ringingly denounced the United States for interference in the Formosa dispute, insisting that Formosa be made part of Red China.

I said that such bluffing was not impressive.

With the highly publicized first conference of Asian-African nations at Bandung in Indonesia coming up in the week of April 17–24, however, the Secretary thought that the Red Chinese might be trying to "clean up" their dubious reputation so as to be accepted as a peace-loving nation; fortifying such an assumption was the fact that Peiping's propaganda on the "liberation" of Formosa had recently dropped from 25 per cent to 5 per cent of the Red's propaganda total.

One congressman asked the Secretary, "Is there any way in which the Chinese Nationalists could withdraw from Quemoy and Matsu without disaster?" Only, the Secretary answered, as a result of a decision made by Chiang Kai-shek *on his own initiative* that such a withdrawal would be good for Chinese Nationalist interests.

At the end of the Secretary's presentation, Speaker Sam Rayburn said he understood from it that if the Communists should attack Quemoy and Matsu, the United States would intervene. I quickly corrected this conclusion.

"To the contrary," I pointed out, "we have not made that decision and will not make it until we know the circumstances surrounding any given attack. Foster and I have been living with this problem twenty-four hours a day. My decision is not to have the United States intervene if the Chinese Nationalists can defend Quemoy and Matsu alone. But a critical consideration is this: before attacking Formosa the Chinese Communists will almost necessarily have to capture or neutralize Quemoy and Matsu, for they block the two most important mainland ports from which an attack on Formosa would be launched. And," I repeated, "the Red Chinese have proclaimed again and again their purpose to capture Formosa; at no time have they shown interest in just the offshore islands. In any event," I assured the Speaker, "the tricky business is to determine whether or not an attack on Quemoy and Matsu, if made, is truly a local operation or a preliminary to a major effort against Formosa."

Through these anxious days, the two unpleasant alternatives remained: assisting Chiang in the defense of the coastal islands, thus risking entry without allies into a global war; or pressing Chiang to change the offshore islands, by partial evacuation and intensive fortification, from population centers into fortress outposts. This solution, unless Chiang concurred, would risk impairment of morale in one of our defensive links, and serious damage to our security position in the Western Pacific.[3] I therefore decided to try to find out whether Chiang, armed with a promise from us to deploy and maintain United States forces on Formosa, including Marines and an air wing, would voluntarily withdraw the bulk of the civil population and unnecessary elements of his forces from Quemoy and Matsu and change those islands from precarious symbols of Chinese Nationalist prestige into strongly defended, workable outposts. If we could find a man who had Chiang's confidence, he might be able to bring the Generalissimo to this view. The fact that the plan came to Chiang from me—from one soldier to another—might possibly convince him to accept it.

As emissaries on this mission to the Generalissimo I named Admiral Radford and Walter Robertson, a former Richmond investment banker and a diplomat with a firsthand knowledge of the Far East, who, as Assistant Secretary of State for Far Eastern Affairs, had since 1953 been a tower of strength to Foster Dulles in the framing of policy.

Admiral Radford and Assistant Secretary Robertson left for Formosa on April 20. They were to seek "to induce the Generalissimo to propose some solution to the Formosa-Quemoy-Matsu problem that will be acceptable both to him and to us"—a solution "that will neither commit the United States to go to war in defense of the offshore islands nor will constitute an implied repudiation of the Generalissimo" by the United States government. Despite their persuasiveness, however, they failed to obtain any encouragement from him; he would not agree to redistribute his forces in the areas under his control.[4]

[3] In any delicate international situation there is rarely shortage of outside advisers who are willing to contribute, at times out of experience, out of naïveté, or out of politics, answers that seem to them to be simple, clear, and decisive.

On April 12 Governor Adlai Stevenson said that he had "the gravest misgivings about risking a third world war in defense of these little islands." He asked whether the offshore islands were essential to the security of the United States and called for the United States and its allies to make a declaration against the use of force in the Formosa Strait. How did the prestige and honor of the great United States, he wanted to know, come to be "staked on some little islands within the shadow of the China coast?"

[4] In the 1960 presidential campaign, Senator Kennedy charged that the administration had tried to persuade Chiang to *withdraw* from Quemoy and Matsu. Vice President Nixon denied this assertion. No one, he said, including Radford and Robertson, had tried to persuade Chiang "to withdraw from and thus to abandon" the offshore islands; the Robertson-Radford discussions sought only a better deployment of Nationalist ground forces among Taiwan, the Pescadores, and Quemoy and Matsu.

Mr. Nixon was correct, as is shown by the instructions under which our representatives acted [see Appendix P].

Despite my disappointment, I could not help reflecting that if I had been in his position, I might well have made the same decision.

The future of the Formosa situation remained obscure. But then the immediate crisis began to dissolve.

The Asian-African conference at Bandung had opened, representing twenty-nine countries and about one and one-half billion people—more than half the world's population. By April 23 reports from there quoted Premier Chou En-lai as saying that Red China had no intention of going to war with the United States, and that it was ready to negotiate with us over Formosa and the Far East.

On April 26 Secretary Dulles, in a news conference, indicated that the United States would be willing to talk with the Chinese Communists about a cease fire, insisting, however, that the United States would not discuss the interests of Nationalist China "behind its back." In addition, he insisted, any talk about the Formosa Strait would imply no official diplomatic recognition of the Red Chinese regime.

More than two weeks later Secretary Dulles reported to me on a talk he had held in Vienna:

> I talked alone with Molotov about the China situation. He said it was very complicated. I referred to the menacing buildup of airpower and said he must know about it because it was being done with Soviet equipment. Molotov said this was purely a Chinese internal affair. I said we were exerting influence on the Chinese Nationalists and they should exert a comparable influence on the Chinese Communists. I said that we needed a situation where as in Germany, Korea and Viet Nam, it was agreed that unification would not be sought by force. Molotov said they wanted peace. He suggested a five-power conference. I said a six-power conference would be better. He said the Chinese Communists would not meet with the Nationalists. I said we would not meet with the Communists without the Nationalists. I urged him to think about a way of solution, and he said he would do so. I said to communicate with us either through our ambassador at Moscow or their ambassador at Washington.
>
> I do not feel that much concrete progress was made, but I think that the Soviet may as a result of our talk put increasing pressure upon the Chinese Communists to avoid war.

Almost simultaneously Chou, in a report on the Bandung Conference, announced, "The Chinese people are willing to strive for the liberation of Formosa by peaceful means as far as this is possible." By May 22 the newspapers reported an informal cease fire on the Formosa Strait: Communist vessels were declining to attack Nationalist ships; Communist MIGs were holding their fire against Nationalist patrol planes. At the end of the month India's Krishna Menon, sent to Peiping by Nehru to intercede on the Formosa crisis, reported China had agreed to release four American fliers. And although on the eve of the Geneva Summit Conference of July 1955 Anthony Eden still looked upon Quemoy and Matsu with alarm, on August 1 the eleven American airmen were released as the United States and Communist Chinese ambassadors began talks on the release of the remaining American civilians and "other practical matters."

During the months of crisis the administration had to contend with not only the threats of the Communists but also with varieties of advice from leaders in the Free World.

Looking at the spectrum from one extreme to the other, the administration heard the counsel of Attlee (liquidate Chiang), Eden (neutralize Quemoy and Matsu), Lehman and Morse and Kennedy (abandon Quemoy and Matsu), Lewis Douglas (avoid entry into a civil war, on legal principle), Radford (fight for the Tachens, bomb the mainland), Knowland (blockade the Chinese coast), and Rhee (join him and Chiang in a holy war of liberation).

The administration rejected all of these suggestions, threading its way, with watchfulness and determination, through narrow and dangerous waters between appeasement and global war. For nine months the administration moved through treacherous cross-currents with one channel leading to peace with honor and a hundred channels leading to war or dishonor.

Mao Tse-tung once expressed his strategy of war in just sixteen words:

Enemy advances, we retreat; enemy halts, we harass; enemy tires, we attack; enemy retreats, we pursue.

In the Formosa Strait in 1955 we refused to retreat, and the enemy, true to his formula, for a while tried harassment but refused to attack. The crisis had cooled; it would not heat up again for three years.

The hard way is to have the courage to be patient.

CHAPTER XX

Laws for a Changing America

The old order changeth, yielding place to new;
And God fulfills himself in many ways,
Lest one good custom should corrupt the world.

—Tennyson

IN 1953 we had seen the end of the Korean War. In 1954 we had won out over the economic hazard of a recession. With these problems behind us, we in the United States entered a new era of unprecedented peace and unprecedented prosperity. The slogan "Peace, Progress, and Prosperity," which was applied to the first-term years and was used in the campaign of 1956, perhaps seemed platitudinous. But compared with any years of the two preceding decades, these surely must have seemed miraculous to most Americans. Not in the lifetime of millions of our citizens—children, adolescents, and men and women entering adult life—had we previously had peace, progress, and prosperity all at one time.

This was not the only change; the nation was humming with change. Between the day I entered office and the end of 1955, the United States had added about 9 million to its population—more than another New York City. We had increased our labor force by 3 million. The birth rate, which in the depression year of 1935 had amounted to seventeen births for every thousand in the population, and which at the end of the war had totaled twenty per thousand, had in the postwar years climbed to about twenty-five and stayed there.

This high plateau of the birth rate meant, among other phenomena, more and more children in school. Between 1930 and 1940 a line representing the total school enrollment in the United States ran across the chart horizontally; at the end of the decade there were approximately as many children in school, and no more, as at the beginning. In the decade of the forties that figure (slightly under 30 million), went up by about 1 million. But in the interval between 1950 and 1956 the line angled upward sharply, as nearly 8 million more students took their places in American classrooms.

Another circumstance helped swell our population: the average American's life expectancy was also climbing; in 1940 it was sixty-three years, in 1950 sixty-eight years, and in 1955 nearly seventy.

Elsewhere in the world, to be sure, birth rates were soaring, going up even faster than ours, while death rates were falling off. But in many countries—particularly in Latin America and Asia—more people meant only more mouths to feed and therefore more grinding poverty. In the United States, on the contrary, it did not, for peacetime prosperity was rising as never before.

From the second quarter of 1954 our gross national product went into a strong and steady ascent, quarter by quarter, from an annual rate of $359 billion to $409 billion by the end of 1955. And it kept on climbing. Between 1952 and 1956 the increase alone—nearly $70 billion—was an amount greater than the 1961 gross national product of France.

In the same period personal incomes of our people went up $55 billion, or 20 per cent. The average weekly earnings of production workers in manufacturing went up by nearly the same rate. Contrary to the political charges of some of our opponents, the fact was that in the middle years of the 1950s the bottom income groups were becoming richer, the rich were paying record taxes, and many from both groups were joining the "middle class." We still had our impoverished and our wealthy, but the new prosperity was reducing the relative size of both groups. The middle class, as sociologists were pointing out, was becoming the widening band around the country. Between 1947 and 1957 the number of American families with incomes of $4000 or more had increased by more than 100 per cent.

One dramatic feature of the expanding middle class was the increase in the number of white-collar workers and professional people. Widespread schooling, increasing domestic and international travel (not a little of it by servicemen), and reasonable prosperity had helped turn people away from becoming laborers, while technology was making many unskilled and semiskilled jobs obsolete. More and more people were working in the catch-all, important category called "services," because more and more people could afford to pay others to do work for them—from shining shoes to surgery.

With higher incomes, Americans in 1955 were filing a record number of federal income-tax returns. In 1940 they had filed less than 15 million returns; in 1950, 53 million; in 1955, 58 million. They also bought securities. Between 1952 and 1956 the number of individual share-holders increased by nearly a third. They bought insurance. Between 1952 and 1956 the amount of life insurance in force went up nearly $140 billion.

Between 1952 and 1956 nearly 5 million families moved into new homes.

And they bought cars, appliances, and similar consumer goods. In 1955 a record number of automobiles was produced—nearly 8 million—to supply a record number of American families, many of whom already owned one car or more. To keep pace with the mounting consumer demand, businesses, between 1950 and 1955, increased their expenditures for new plant and equipment more than 40 per cent.

In all these figures, two trends were noticeably favorable—in unemployment and in prices. In July 1955, as unemployment was then estimated, the United States had 2.5 million unemployed, 3.7 per cent of the civilian labor force. Save for scattered years in the 1920s and immediately after World War II, never in peacetime since 1907 had the rate been so low. There were, of course, pockets of desperate, chronic unemployment in Massachusetts, Pennsylvania, West Virginia, and elsewhere, and we were determined to reduce them. New England, once the industrial bulwark of the United States, had been losing its dominance in manufacturing for years. Many manufacturers had moved to the South, where labor and power costs- were less. Many New England manufacturing towns experienced hard days. Parts of West Virginia and Pennsylvania, dependent on a coal economy, were suffering from coal's competitors—natural gas and oil. But we had come a long way from the time when unemployment had shrouded the entire country and put millions on the dole.

We had come a long way also from the postwar days of skyrocketing prices. For the first time since World War II, all the gains of our people —the value of their production, their wages, their investments, their savings—could be counted in dollars with a stable buying power— dollars not gutted by inflation. Between 1945 and 1952 consumer prices soared 50 per cent. Between 1952 and January of 1955 they increased less than 1 per cent. Unquestionably, the fact that the value of our currency was not eroding away encouraged people to invest in life-insurance policies, with confidence that when the time came to collect, they would not be paid off in dollars greatly depreciated.

One fact about the extraordinary economic expansion of the middle fifties needs to be emphasized: the federal government did not create it. But another fact is equally certain: by unwise policies the federal government might well have wrecked it.

Private efforts had wrought the recovery from the recession of 1954 and wrought the new prosperity of 1955. Between the second quarter of 1954 and the third quarter of 1955 the annual rate of federal spending dropped by $2 billion; at the same time state and community spending rose $3 billion, private investment $18 billion, and consumer spending $24 billion. From the second quarter of 1953 to the third quarter of 1955 the annual rate of federal spending dropped by over $14 billion, the spending of the rest of the economy went up more than three times as much—by $49 billion. More and more, as Dr. Arthur Burns, chairman of the Council of Economic Advisers, said, Americans were "making jobs for one another instead of relying on the federal government to do it for them."[1]

The administration's central economic aim was to encourage this process. Week by week Dr. Burns and Dr. Gabriel Hauge, my Special Assistant for Economic Affairs, came to my office to report on the economy and recommended action to spur its growth.[2] These men were two of the most astute and objective economists I have known. As we conferred, we recalled the lessons of the past—the failures as well as the successes. For example, emerging from the 1954 recession, the country had profited by the existence of the federal-state unemployment-compensation system introduced during the Roosevelt administration—a system which automatically injects money into the economy when unemployment is rising. The country profited also from the action of a Republican President and a Republican Congress in 1954 in broadening this system to include 4 million workers not previously covered and to increase benefits for the 30 million already protected—the greatest single improvement in the unemployment-compensation system since its inception.

But the country profited also from our refusal to repeat the mistakes of the past. In 1932, 1934, 1935, and 1936 the federal government drastically increased taxes. The revenue acts of those years reduced tax exemptions, increased the maximum rate of personal income taxes, boosted the maximum estate-tax rate, and piled on new gift taxes, new excise taxes, and bigger capital-gains and corporate-profit taxes. In a country trying to recover from a depression, these tax increases hobbled the spending power of individuals and businesses; they induced a fear that the national administration was using its power to tax as a power

[1] In contrast to 1954, in these days when Arthur Burns reported to the Cabinet, he had a relaxed, though receptive, audience. The amount or absence of tension in a Cabinet meeting often mirrors the condition of the nation's economy.

[2] Reorganization Plan Number Nine, which became effective August 1, 1953, reorganized the Council of Economic Advisers, giving more authority to the chairman.

to level, to punish, or to destroy; this could not fail to frighten people away from investment and innovation. In 1933 our unemployment rate was 25 per cent. In 1939, after six years of such policies, the rate was still 17 per cent: one man in six in the civilian labor force was still out of work. It was World War II, not the New Deal, which finally provided him a job.

In the middle years of the 1950s we took the opposite way. On October 14, 1955, at the Commonwealth Club in San Francisco—the same forum in which Governor Franklin D. Roosevelt of New York in 1932 had outlined his conviction that our "overbuilt" American economy had already crossed its last frontier—Dr. Gabriel Hauge gave a resounding summary of the economic philosophy of my administration. First, Dr. Hauge said, the Eisenhower conservative "wants to conserve the system of free markets and private initiative as the best means yet devised to plan and organize the production that people want. He is not much taken with the idea that government price fixing, wage control, rationing, production planning and materials allocation can do the job better than the free market system—except, of course, in time of war when people are willing to make special sacrifices and to endure otherwise intolerable regimentation. The energetic enterprise and imagination of the nearly 10 million centers of planning represented by our private businesses and farms have provided the unrivaled creative force for our economic growth.

Second, Dr. Hauge went on, "the Eisenhower conservative intends to preserve our tradition of incentive and reward. His is a deep conviction that in the economic race every man should have an equal place at the starting line, but he knows too, that it has never been part of the American tradition to assure every man the right of breasting the tape at the same instant."

Third, Dr. Hauge noted that the Eisenhower conservative rejects the doctrine that our economy must always run a temperature to stay healthy, rejects inflation as an instrument of national policy—an instrument which cuts down first the millions of Americans who hold savings bonds, savings deposits, life-insurance policies, and pension rights.

Fourth, Dr. Hauge said that the Eisenhower conservative seeks to conserve the market mechanism when the government must act to avert a depression or inflation. Implicit in this principle is the belief that government must not follow a laissez-faire, eyes-upward policy in the midst of human poverty. But it affirms that whenever the government intervenes in the economy, its goal must always be maximum economic freedom for the individual.

Fifth, Dr. Hauge concluded, "the Eisenhower conservative seeks to conserve and strengthen economic ties among free nations." In addition, of course, he emphasized that such things as unemployment insurance and social security reduce the human costs of freedom; while a sound federal budget policy helps to keep our economy growing and stable.

With the recession of 1954 behind us and with the economy moving upward, the administration, in accordance with these principles, began to concern itself with the danger of inflation. Week by week we scrutinized stock prices, figures on credit expansion and debt, and other economic indicators for any sign of danger. In particular we continued to work to cut back on federal spending and produce a surplus for partial payment on the staggering national debt. "If we cannot produce a surplus under conditions of such unprecedented prosperity," Dr. Burns observed on August 12, "a question can be raised as to whether the fiscal affairs of this country can ever be managed satisfactorily over the long term."

Arthur Burns said that reducing federal expenditures would not only redeem our earlier pledges to live, except in emergencies, within our means, but that this was essential to future prosperity. As he spoke, the thought came to me that probably no other single tenet of economic philosophy so emphasized the difference between the majority of the Republicans and the dominant faction of the Democrats. We were dedicated to responsibility, for we recognized, in Arthur's words, that "in an economy like ours, poised on a high plateau, neither the threat of inflation nor of recession can ever be very distant."

One specific feature of the administration's policy was its attitude toward organized labor. The percentage of all estimated working time lost because of strikes between 1949 and 1952 was drastically higher[3] than that lost between January 1953 and August 1956. I believe much of this success was due to our reversal of my predecessor's policy of intervening unwisely in disputes between labor and management, of calling the leaders to conference tables in the East Wing of the White House and trying to get them to agree.

We believed in the principle of collective bargaining, but we did not assume that those collected together for every negotiation ought to include the government. The administration consistently followed a policy of staying out of labor disputes except where grave, nationwide emergencies threatened. I was asked at a news conference in June 1955 about this standard. "In Detroit," a reporter said, "there is apparently increasing danger of an automobile strike in one or two of the big companies. Does the administration feel that the economic results of such a strike would require immediate government intervention, if it comes?"

"This government has gone on the theory that the Executive department, as such," I replied, "will not project itself into the details of private

[3] Sixty per cent.

negotiations between employer and employee." We had a federal media-
tion service. When trouble arose, I said, that service could be called
upon to help settle it; only in the case of a strike creating a real
national crisis, would the Executive branch of the government be justified
in intervening.

The reporter was referring to the negotiation between the United Automobile Workers and the Ford Motor Company for a guaranteed annual
wage, a new demand. I told the news conference that I would express no
opinion at the moment, because this was precisely the subject of the
negotiation between the automobile company and the union; I would not
try to use the great powers of the President to influence the answer.

Soon afterward the negotiators agreed upon a contract that provided
cash benefits for workers who had been laid off, to supplement unemployment insurance. A Ford vice president—John Bugas—called this a "sup-
plemental unemployment benefit." UAW chief Walter Reuther hailed it
as the long-sought guaranteed annual wage.

Apart from the label, the fact remained that the UAW and Ford could
have concluded an agreement like this only in a period of great prosperity.

When I appointed James P. Mitchell to the post of Secretary of Labor,
a reporter asked the union official George Meany how good a Secretary he
would make. "He's a very fine gentleman, a very fine fellow, and I think
he'll be as good a Secretary of Labor," the press story quoted him as
saying, "as Brother Weeks allows him to be." Obviously he did not know
what a rugged character Jim Mitchell was.

Because Secretary Mitchell shared my basic views concerning the need
for economic statesmanship on both sides of the bargaining table, I never
felt any need of limiting him in his efforts to promote industrial peace
and progress. With his keen intelligence, his forthrightness and honesty,
Secretary Mitchell won the confidence of union members and management alike. Even when some disagreed with him, they respected him and
recognized that he was working for the things he believed were in the national interest.

He and I agreed that it would be wise to establish personal and frank
relationships with important men in the labor movement. I met and talked
with many of them. One evening, for example, Mr. David McDonald,
president of the United Steel Workers of America, came to the White
House at my invitation, together with Secretary Humphrey and Secretary
Mitchell. For about an hour and a half we talked about statesmanship in
business, the need for a sound dollar to protect pension and old-age-
insurance moneys, the racial problem, the responsibility of all economic
groups to aid in stopping the wage-price spiral and inflation. Mr. McDonald gave his views freely. His position seemed to be definitely that of
avoiding extremes and of seeking the path that promised the most con-

structive results for the nation as a whole. He said that the efforts of the steelworkers, in their bargaining that year, would be directed more toward the things yielding future security than toward immediate pay increases. He agreed that a sound dollar was essential to our whole future prosperity.

I suggested that labor unions ought to help educate the public on this subject, because whenever a political leader mentioned the "sound dollar" the charge was made that he was interested only in the rich. Mr. McDonald believed that a stable currency was of special significance to the salaried man, and to any of those who had to depend upon pension money, savings accounts, bonds, and insurance policies stored up for their later years.

Speaking of racial problems, McDonald said that the Steel Workers Union in the South had by then been completely integrated. He thought this success would mark the chance for similar progress in other fields.

Our discussion produced nothing that could be called a meeting of the minds with respect to any particular program, nor was it so intended. McDonald was, of course, a man who on occasion—whenever slight signs of a recession appeared—could advocate a stupendous federal public-works program involving billions of dollars, a practice that I felt worse than useless except in most unusual circumstances. Nonetheless, our talk was friendly. I had invited Mr. McDonald to the White House that evening to get his views and to give him a chance to understand what the administration was trying to accomplish in providing an atmosphere of confidence in which the nation's economy could prosper. In this respect it was, like many similar meetings with union officials, a success.

With wages rising, prices staying steady, and the number of "man-days" lost because of strikes going down, it was understandable that George Meany, head of the AFL-CIO, would tell his associates in the middle of 1955, "American labor has never had it so good."

Behind all these other changes in the middle years of the 1950s loomed the changes of science, remaking the world and bringing new problems. More and more, the jet aircraft, the nuclear power plant, the hydrogen bomb, the ballistic missile were coming into the consciousness of all of us. When I entered the White House I traveled in a piston-driven plane, the *Columbine*. But before I left, my Air Force aide, Colonel Draper, had had to go to school to learn how to fly a new presidential airplane, a 707 jet. Medical research was reducing the death rate, conquering diseases. Between the year I entered office and the year I left, for example, the federal appropriations for medical research at the National Institutes of Health multiplied nearly ten times, going from $59 million to $560 million. Actually, I knew that an increase on this scale could not produce a corresponding automatic increase in valuable research. For one thing, you cannot find graduate scientists as you can buy laboratory equipment. But the Congress consistently raised the amounts we recommended for the purpose.

One hot July noon in 1955 Jim Hagerty announced to the White House reporters that he would have an exceptional story for them that day at about one-thirty. That story, as dramatically as any, illustrated the way science was changing our lives. For on that day at the White House, Dr. Detlev Bronk, the head of the National Academy of Sciences, and Dr. Alan Waterman, head of the National Science Foundation, announced the plans for the United States' first launching of an earth satellite.

In October of 1954 scientists from forty countries had met in Rome to draw up plans for the International Geophysical Year, in 1957–58—the first coordinated world-wide study ever made of the physical phenomena of the earth and its atmosphere. This study would include work in meteorology, physics, geology, and a host of other disciplines. But two areas to be explored stood out above the rest. One was the Antarctic—a largely unexplored sixth of the globe. In March 1955 the United States accordingly announced that, along with other countries, we planned to send an expedition down there at the end of 1955 to begin work on three observation sites. Recognizing the strategic as well as the scientific value of such an exploration, the Soviet Union several months later announced that it too planned to establish observation bases on that frozen continent as part of the International Geophysical Year.

The second area was outer space. The scientists at the Rome meeting had urged participating countries to undertake for the first time a program to launch an earth satellite. The plan was approved by the United States government in 1955. Such a program, the scientists recognized, would permit hitherto impossible studies of radiation, of the density of the earth's upper atmosphere, of the composition of the earth's crust, and of the earth's shape. The July news conference announced the United States' response to that scientific challenge. We invited other countries to participate with us in the undertaking and promised to make information on the space vehicle available to the public. The satellite, as originally conceived, would be about the size of a basketball. At that time no one yet knew whether it would or could contain any instruments. Under the label Project Vanguard, the Department of Defense would, with its experience in rocketry, provide the means of shooting it into orbit. For the first time in history men could look with hope, grounded in knowledge, to the possibility of flight toward the stars.

The battle for legislative action in 1955 was fought out against the background of the quiet but immensely significant changes in our country, as well as the change that had occurred in November the year before —the transfer of the control of Congress from Republicans to Democrats.

In my January 1955 State of the Union message I referred to the divided control under which the government would have to operate and offered to meet the new Congress halfway. "We shall have much to do together," I said. "I am sure that we shall get it done."

This may have seemed naïve or overly optimistic. I knew, of course, that, in the words of Bryce Harlow, my experienced assistant for congressional liaison, *"divided* government—with the Congress in one Party's hands and the Executive branch in the other's—is ordinarily the most costly and least efficient arrangement our citizens can have. It produces bills passed only for political advantage, no matter what their fiscal impact; it blocks bills needed by America, only because their passage might credit the administration; it harasses through investigations, through excessive demands on administrators, through misrepresentations, and ends up leaving the people utterly confused as to who did what to whom. In short, it exalts the petty, demeans the noble, rewards irresponsibility, makes a virtue of stagnation, and bamboozles the public."

But although as a Republican President I could not expect the controlling congressional Democrats to welcome my proposals with open arms, there were some reasons for hope. I knew many of the key legislators personally; bipartisan cooperation would be neither impossible nor distasteful. House Speaker Sam Rayburn was a Texan and I had been born, in 1890, within the district he was later to represent in Congress. We had long maintained friendly contact, and for many years prior to my inauguration he had called me "Captain Ike." I had also enjoyed a friendly relationship with Senate Majority Leader Lyndon Johnson, another Texan. When, later that year, he suffered a serious heart attack, I want to see him in the hospital and kept in touch with him through friends and correspondence during his illness.

One good quality of life in Washington is that in most cases government people can differ sharply during the day on specific political issues and yet, after hours, be on cordial terms personally. But there was much daytime trouble in 1955. With the assumption of control of Congress by the Democrats, a great increase in investigations began, some of them obviously partisan. The Eighty-third Congress, under Republican leadership, had a total appropriation for investigations of about $8.1 million; the Eighty-fourth, a Democratic Congress, had $11.3 million. Within two months of the opening of the 1955 session more than thirty investigations were under way. The right of Congress to investigate governmental activities and performance is unchallengeable; we welcomed legitimate inquiry. But appropriations to support investigations should never be used for the harassment of hard-working officials, or to give the man holding elective office a platform to be used primarily to guarantee his re-election.

By January of 1955 the Congress had already spent many hours on the Dixon and Yates contract; it would spend many more. Later, Congress looked into a case involving Air Force Secretary Harold Talbott. He had written a business letter on official Air Force stationery, giving rise to the allegation that this was a clear case of conflict of interest. In the outcome, Secretary Talbott himself said that he had been indiscreet and thought it best to resign. I accepted the offer, even though as an administrator he had not only demonstrated unusual competence but had saved the government significant sums in streamlining procurement and storage practices in the Air Force. In campaign promises I had spoken of the need to go behind the legality of action by members of the government as a standard of satisfactory performance, saying that it was necessary to consider the ethics of the matter and the degree of judgment exercised. From this standpoint the investigation of any irregularity was eminently justified.

At the same time, the Talbott incident illustrates one of the continuing hazards of public service. Successful men from education, business, the professions, agriculture, and labor are needed if the government is to function intelligently and efficiently. Such men have usually developed their own methods of work and are accustomed to different types of staff assistance or to expressing themselves bluntly, quickly, using the tools at hand. Occasional failures on their part to observe every nicety and taboo of bureaucratic procedure do not necessarily imply evil intent; they can be, and often are, the result of personal or staff carelessness. For example, *Harper's* magazine prepared an article late in 1955 suggesting that the American farmer, a "pampered tyrant," was a thief picking the pockets of other Americans. A copy was sent to Secretary of Agriculture Benson. He never saw the article, and an assistant responded for him, writing a short note to the editor of *Harper's,* expressing approval of the article. The magazine editor, delighted to have the letter from the Secretary of Agriculture, printed it. If it were not for the fact that Secretary Benson himself had come from a farm background and an extensive career in agriculture and obviously could never believe this of the American farmer in general, the damage could have been more explosive than amusing.

Another controversy came out of a piece of good news. On April 12, 1955, the nation was electrified by the announcement of the results of an exhaustive test of a vaccine discovered by Dr. Jonas Salk to prevent poliomyelitis, the dread disease that in 1954 alone had killed over thirteen hundred Americans, most of them young, and crippled more than eighteen thousand more. The vaccine, the scientific investigators announced, was "safe, effective, and potent." The world joyously acclaimed Dr. Salk's accomplishment, and a rush began to inoculate as many children as possible before the summer polio season set in.[4]

The same day, the federal government licensed six manufacturers to produce the vaccine under standards set by the United States Public Health Service of the Department of Health, Education and Welfare. Two weeks later the government announced that the manufacturers would produce enough vaccine to immunize every child under the age of nine by the 1st of August. Even before the test results appeared, the National Foundation for Infantile Paralysis (a private organization) had purchased vaccine for 9 million immunizations; when the test proved successful, it announced it would turn this over to state health officials; all children of the first and second grades, the National Foundation announced, would be offered the shots at no charge.

Two days after the announcement I directed Mrs. Hobby to set up a voluntary system of fair allocation for the vaccine (not including that distributed by the National Foundation) to make certain no child in the United States would be denied this emergency protection for want of ability to pay. Accordingly, she established a National Advisory Committee on Poliomyelitis Vaccine, to recommend allocations. At a meeting at the Health, Education and Welfare Department on April 22, the drug manufacturers pledged to ship the vaccine only in accordance with these allocations, once they had produced the vaccine. (In these weeks their entire output was going to meet their contract with the National Foundation.)

Problems arose. On April 27 the Surgeon General ordered a temporary ban on the distribution of vaccine produced by one of the laboratories, because a number of persons inoculated with this vaccine had contracted polio.

On May 6, 1955, the Public Health Service temporarily held up the release of all the new vaccine but recommended a continuation of injections of the vaccine already approved and distributed. The following day the service recommended that all vaccination be halted during a recheck of manufacturing and testing procedures.

Between May 11 and May 15, Public Health Service scientists, working around the clock, rechecked and approved the vaccine manufactured by Eli Lilly and Parke, Davis and Company. But then the service suddenly reported that no vaccine at all would be released for about a week. And on May 20 an advisory committee of scientists, including Dr. Salk, recommended against giving the vaccine at the height of epidemics, ap-

---

[4] I announced that the United States would give "full details" of the manufacture of the vaccine "and the technique of injecting it, to every country that welcomed the knowledge, including the Soviet Union."

parently on the assumption that the vaccine might possibly induce polio by triggering latent viruses.

These events raised both uncertainty and dismay in the minds of parents. They reflected the fact that the problem was not just the simple one of distributing an effective vaccine; it was that, plus the much more complex problem of continuing tests for safety—tests which, to be absolutely final, would take time, slow vaccine production, and delay prevention of the disease for thousands who would be struck down. Understandably, parents were both clamoring for immediate action and fearing the dangers of a possibly unreliable vaccine. The scientists insisted on distributing only a proven product. Tempers rose.

In spite of these disheartening delays and their attendant confusion, Mrs. Hobby proceeded with the preparation of a comprehensive plan for national distribution of the vaccine, to go into effect as soon as the National Foundation's free inoculation program for first and second graders ended and vaccine for others became available. By May 16, Mrs. Hobby was able to send this plan to the White House. The plan recommended that manufacturers allocate amounts of the vaccine for each state, commensurate with the number of each state's children. The states would then set up their own distribution machinery. The federal government would appropriate $28 million to buy vaccine for the needy.

The Democrats roared: Why had not Mrs. Hobby turned up the distribution plan six weeks earlier, when the vaccine was first released? Heartened by their hindsight, and conveniently overlooking all scientific obstacles and difficulties, and the fact that the first vaccine had been bought up by the National Foundation and was therefore not available for distribution under the new plan, they demanded that I fire her for "gross incompetence." I backed her instead. It was plain, I said, that Mrs. Hobby had been, in effect, only the agent of scientists, doctors, and producers, working out for them the plans through which their entire production—dependent on the findings of the scientists—could be brought to the people at the earliest possible time and be so supervised that the people who needed it most—the children—would get it first. In the hue and cry, one shining fact was being shouted down—that we owed our deep thanks to the devoted scientists, doctors, and Public Health Service people who had worked night and day during the current crisis, to bring to us this great boon for the protection of our children and grandchildren.

Shortly thereafter, the necessary checks made, the final tests completed, and the program for distribution and use of the vaccine in order, the fruits of Dr. Salk's experiments and genius began moving out across the country. Within one year deaths from polio declined nearly 50 per cent, to the lowest number recorded in nine years: by 1960 the disease took just 260 American lives—one fifth the number five years earlier.

Some time before the Salk vaccine appeared, Mrs. Hobby had informed me that, for personal reasons, she would have to resign her office, and she had then publicly announced that intention. Inevitably, there were reports that she was leaving under fire. My sincere regret at her leaving was explained in a letter I wrote. I said that we would miss her voice and counsel in government, and added that twice, in a little more than a decade, she had earned the thanks of her fellow citizens. Few—men or women—had brought to heavy tasks and critical challenges the spirit, integrity, and readiness to sacrifice she had. Under her command in World War II the Women's Army Corps had opened a new field of service for American women. As the first Secretary of the newly created Department of Health, Education and Welfare, she had organized many disparate units and agencies into an effective team and in the process helped to make the heart of government a visible fact. Indeed, her associates in Cabinet posts, without exception, assured me that they regarded her resignation as a loss to the nation—as I did.

The administration had trouble with Congress on the fiscal front. "We have arrived," Dr. Burns said in October of 1955, "at the threshold of a $400 billion economy." We could cross this line and go beyond it, he went on, "if public policies continue to encourage individual initiative and enterprise, if they continue to reckon with the humanitarian impulses of our age, and if private citizens together with their government continue to resist courageously any tendencies that they develop toward either recession or inflation." Some of the members of the Congress seemed to have trouble offering such resistance.

In January 1955 I submitted to the Congress a budget for the 1956 fiscal year with a deficit of $2.4 billion—a figure which I hoped, but could not then responsibly promise, to reduce. Referring to the $4.5 billion deficit which we then estimated for the current fiscal year, 1955, I mentioned our continuing "progress toward a balanced budget." On Capitol Hill, however, several legislators thought of a way to arrest this progress, with an extraordinary amount of political appeal; they introduced a proposal to give every American taxpayer a twenty-dollar annual tax cut for each of his dependents.

This was not a measure to benefit the American economy. It was a private political relief bill for the congressmen and senators who attached their names to it.

"Frankly," I wrote to a friend, "I don't care how much the demagogues are gunning for me, but I do get riled when I find them playing fast and loose with the soundness of our economy and the future of 163 million Americans." We could not ignore our enormous national debt and the obligations we had to future Americans to reduce the debt whenever we could appropriately do so. Under conditions of high peacetime prosperity, such as existed then, we could never justify going further into debt to give ourselves a tax cut. (The twenty-dollar tax-cut proposal passed the House by 242 [221 Democrats, 21 Republicans] to 175 [2 Democrats, 173 Republicans]. It failed to pass the Senate by 32 [31 Democrats, 1 Republican] to 61 [16 Democrats, 45 Republicans].) On the contrary—and in fact we did exactly this—we should bend every effort to reduce the projected deficit and produce a budget surplus by 1956.

The inflationists on Capitol Hill pushed through another bill, raising the salaries of postal workers without increasing postal rates to offset the greater costs. I vetoed the bill, and the Congress failed to override my veto. In a Legislative leaders' meeting the following month, Charlie Halleck described as "the most cynical thing yet" the way in which some city congressmen were trying to trade votes for high rigid farm price supports in return for rural votes on a boost in the minimum wage to $1.25 an hour. In my State of the Union message I had recommended that the Congress raise the minimum wage to ninety cents and extend the coverage of the minimum-wage law.[5] But I opposed the prospective adverse effects on costs and prices and employment—however attractive the politics—of raising the rate to $1.25. It finally went through at one dollar, but coverage was not extended to those whom I considered most in need.

In addition to trying to keep the Congress from fiscal frivolity, the administration worked long and hard in 1955 to get legislation to meet new needs of a nation in change.

In some respects we succeeded. In addition to defeating, for example, the dangerous twenty-dollar tax-cut, vote-purchase plan, we persuaded the Congress to extend for one year the excise and corporate-income tax rates then on the books.

We induced the Congress to pass a bill authorizing federal help to the states for assistance in agricultural areas with a heavy concentration of families on small and unproductive farms—a measure which attacked the problem brought on by the ability of fewer farmers with better tools to produce greater quantities of food and fiber—food and fiber which we could not eat or wear or sell or give away successfully.

Most important, the Eighty-fourth Congress in its first session passed an extension of the Trade Agreements Act for three years—not just one, as in 1953 and 1954—and gave the President the authority to cut certain tariffs 5 per cent a year for the following three years. In signing this bill into law on June 21, I called it "an important milestone in the development of our country's foreign economic policy."

[5] I placed a great deal of emphasis on the desirability of extending coverage to the lowest-paid employees, most of whom were unorganized.

The Congress failed, however, to authorize United States membership in the proposed international Organization for Trade Cooperation (OTC). In 1947 the United States and other countries had negotiated a General Agreement on Tariffs and Trade (GATT). In March 1955 the nations which had taken part in that agreement drew up a proposed constitution for the OTC. The OTC would administer the trade rules of the GATT, sponsor international trade negotiations, facilitate consultation on trade, and make recommendations on trade policy. It would come into existence when approved by the nations conducting 85 per cent of the total GATT trade. As the United States conducted more than 20 per cent, its approval was indispensable.

I believed that United States membership in the OTC would be good for the country and for the Free World. Failure to assume membership in the OTC, I argued, could be interpreted throughout the Free World as proof that we were insincere in speaking favorably of the need to trade. It could lead to the imposition of new trade restrictions in other countries and a sharp setback in United States exports.

Nonetheless, using the "constitutional" argument that the Congress had never approved GATT itself (the United States had made the agreement through the authority of the Trade Agreements Act), and that it was "un-American," the opponents of the OTC, including lobbyists for tuna, milk, bicycles, and grapes, successfully pressured the Congress into action.[6]

In other respects too, the Eighty-fourth Congress in 1955 was unresponsive to the needs of the country. Thus, it failed that year to enact into law the Upper Colorado storage project, a giant reclamation project which, by damming the waters of the Colorado River and its tributaries, would bring light and power and irrigation water and flood-control benefits to five mountain states in the growing West. It failed to write into law the administration's proposal for a health-reinsurance program, one which would benefit in particular our growing number of older people without turning the medical profession into a form-filing bureaucracy. It failed to bring Hawaii into the Union, because of the repeated fear that its citizens would probably vote Republican.

Most significantly, the Congress failed to meet the country's urgent need for schools and roads.

Early in February I sent the Congress a long letter urging federal assistance for school construction. As a result of the burgeoning population, there existed an estimated deficit of more than 300,000 classrooms in our country. The current building rate, then 60,000 classrooms a year,

[6] The problem of trade was constantly on my mind. In July of 1954, for example, I wrote Everett Hazlett on the danger of Mexico's possibly turning antagonistic if the United States raised its tariffs; and I criticized those businessmen who, while talking "rugged individualism," clung to tariffs for help.

was doing little more than keeping up with increasing student numbers. Millions of children were receiving substandard education because of unsanitary, overcrowded, and unsafe classrooms. In many places it was possible to provide for only part-time instruction.

It was evident to many of us, but not all, that in view of the financial positions of many states and school districts, the federal government would have to help. The main responsibility for education was still to rest with the states and localities within them. But federal assistance would be available, under the administration's plan, for any district showing a need. The plan was designed to give aid in the most feasible and effective ways. I asked the Congress to authorize, over the next three years, the investment of more than a billion dollars in federal loans and grants, which would stimulate a total investment in that time of more than $7 billion in new school buildings. I opposed involving the federal government in the operation of the schools, such as in paying teachers' salaries. To give Washington the responsibility for the perpetual support of the educational function would, I was convinced, ultimately bring on federal control of education. With every teacher and school administrator looking to the national government for any future pay increases, it would almost inevitably follow that partisanship and the education of our young people would be inextricably mixed. Even a nationalized curriculum might eventually ensue if the trend line of federal aid to education permanently went up. The final result would be the loss of true academic freedom and variety in education.

Despite the need for classrooms, the Congress did nothing.

In November, however, I welcomed to Washington the delegates to an unprecedented White House Conference on Education which I had called —two thousand parents and teachers from forty-eight states, four territories, and the District of Columbia, who had come to Washington to discuss the results of their survey of this country's school needs and how to meet them. In preparation for this conference these men and women had attended fifty-three state and territorial conferences, which in turn were the culmination of thousands of local and regional meetings, bringing together more than a half-million concerned Americans, in the greatest citizen study of our country's public schools—the most comprehensive analysis of their needs—in the history of the United States. At the end of a four-day series of meetings, the conference adopted a report calling for federal funds for public schools, opposing funds for nonpublic schools, and proposing means to increase the number of good teachers and to stimulate public interest in education. Using the findings of this conference, we hoped to get a sound school-construction bill through the Congress the following year.

As it failed on schools that year, the Congress failed also on highways.

The reasons for urgency were incontrovertible. Ours was a nation on the move. Much of our merchandise moved by truck. We took to the roads for recreation. And we needed roads for defense. The weight of the nation was shifting. More people were moving westward. From coast to coast people were leaving the farms and flocking to the cities (those who stayed behind, it was obvious, could produce more food and fiber than we knew what to do with). And the rush carried people not only into the cities but out into the areas just beyond them, creating great suburbs. With these movements and the burgeoning automobile population, the requirements for an efficient arterial network of roads, a true concrete and macadam lifeline, had become acute.

Between 1952 and 1955 the total number of motor vehicles in use increased by 10 million—more than the aggregate owned in 1955 by the British and French together.

We had enough trucks, cars, and buses to cover every traffic lane from coast to coast with vehicles at intervals of seven hundred feet. Every year we were scrapping more vehicles than the total owned by West Germans. Accidents were taking the lives of more than thirty-six thousand persons a year and injuring more than a million. The bad physical condition of our roads was boosting the costs of operating motor vehicles by an annual rate of more than $5 billion. Our roads ought to be avenues of escape for persons living in big cities threatened by aerial attack or natural disaster; but I knew that if such a crisis ever occurred, our obsolescent highways, too small for the flood of traffic of an entire city's people going one way, would turn into traps of death and destruction. And though we were not planning highways for wartime exigencies, if peacetime prosperity kept on rising, the growing number of cars, used by the growing number of people, would slowly clog our road system and make the pace of today's traffic seem a rushing river by comparison.

Accordingly, on February 22, 1955, I sent Congress a special message urging "comprehensive and quick and forward-looking" action to improve the United States highway system. I also sent the text of a report by a special presidential commission headed by General Lucius Clay, which set the ten-year cost of this modernization job at $101 billion, with the federal government putting up more than $31 billion.

A highway bill passed the Senate in 1955 but died in the House, losing by 123 to 292, largely because of differences over financing methods.

The failure of the Congress to enact the road program, Dr. Burns told the Cabinet in a report later that year, not only put the United States behind in its race against time to get the country's streets and roads and highways into shape for the torrents of traffic which would surely be bearing down upon them; it also denied the government an important economic tool.

He recommended that we urge the Congress again to pass the road program. It was so important, he went on, that he would recommend that I even consider calling a special session if necessary.

"Well," I said, somewhat ruefully, "the special session might be necessary—but calling it could be at the cost of the sanity of one man named Eisenhower." There was no sense in spending money to call them back when I knew in advance that the result would be zero.

My lack of enthusiasm for a special session originated in part because of my awareness of the disappointing record that the Congress had turned in during its regular session. When that session ended, it had approved 96 out of 207 of my requests, for an average of 46 per cent, far below that of the Eighty-third Congress (65 per cent), under Republican leadership, the preceding year. At the final Legislative-leaders meeting on August 2, 1955, I said that I was determined to continue fighting on into the election year of 1956 for the measures the country needed. I was set on getting the road program.

The next day I wrote to Charles Halleck on the performance of the Republicans in Congress. Halleck was a hard worker, a driver, and he had done his best.

"I want to say that the events of the past seven months have confirmed once again my high estimate of your loyalty to the cause in which we believe and of your uncommon ability to translate that loyalty into legislative results," I wrote him. "As I mentioned at breakfast, in some ways I have been prouder of our Republican colleagues in the Democratic 84th Congress than I was of their actions in the 83rd, because time and again in this Congress we have had clear-cut evidence, from a unified group, of adherence to the principles and to the sound governmental policies to which we pledged ourselves three years ago. . . .

"In spite of the fact that your talents and devotion played such a large part during the Session in enacting badly needed laws, I feel that the departing Congress laid aside, without action, some extraordinarily important measures. . . . [This] failure . . . gives me the impression that we have a great deal to discuss with the American people in the next five months. . . ."

CHAPTER XXI

Meeting at Geneva

The proof of the pudding is in the eating.

—Traditional aphorism

SINCE the days when President Wilson made his European trips to participate in the formulation of the Treaty of Versailles, many conflicting opinions have been expressed, most often in generalities, as to the wisdom of a President of the United States meeting personally with other heads of government. It seems to me that conclusions of this kind rarely have value if they are meant to apply universally and eternally; each set of circumstances has to provide the answer.

Woodrow Wilson, for example, was criticized by those who held that he should have known better than to have played "international poker" with such shrewd characters as Lloyd George, Clemenceau, and Orlando. Many argued that if Mr. Wilson had remained at home, devoting his talents to molding public opinion in the United States while keeping in touch with the Versailles group through normal diplomatic means, he probably would have been successful in obtaining Senate approval of a satisfactory peace treaty, with provision for the establishment of the League of Nations.

But others saw the Wilsonian pilgrimages as examples of personal sacrifice and extraordinary service to the United States and to humanity— a sacrifice and service that were rejected by arrogant and bigoted men, with resulting disaster to hopes for world peace.

In World War II, President Roosevelt participated in a number of international meetings. One of his objectives, in his role of Commander-in-Chief, was to achieve coordination among the nations fighting against Hitler and the Japanese war lords; another was to reach agreements on many vital problems that were certain to plague the postwar world. Two of these meetings included the Soviet leaders; the others involved primarily the British and ourselves, although a French delegation was consulted at Casablanca and the Chinese at Cairo. Mr. Roosevelt was largely successful in achieving Allied coordination against the Axis. I doubt that this result could have been reached by any other method. But in the settling of postwar problems, the effort was largely a failure. This one stark fact stands out: Every agreement the Soviets entered into at Teheran in 1943 and Yalta in 1945, was ruthlessly broken, save for those palpably to their advantage. The same holds true for the Potsdam Conference of 1945.

But even this dreary record does not furnish proof of the unwisdom of a President's interjecting himself into international exchanges. Certainly his right to do so cannot be questioned, since by the Constitution he is charged with carrying on our foreign relations. Moreover, postwar criticisms of Presidents' meetings with other heads of government have not been confined solely to those that have included Communist representatives. Some writers—either woefully ignorant of facts or attempting to use powers of objective analysis, without noticeable success—have flatly proclaimed that nothing can ever be gained by a President's meeting even with the heads of the most friendly governments or visiting peoples of other lands. I believe the record shows gains for the United States from such meetings. In some I have been a participant.

There are, of course, risks to be encountered in any meeting between the highest officials of two or more nations, no matter how friendly these may be.

Many times after entering politics I asserted my constant readiness and desire to meet formally or informally with the heads of friendly states— meetings that might promote greater solidarity between nations that shared a dedication to the concept of freedom and of self-government. But I was still not willing to meet with Communist leaders unless there was some likelihood that the confrontation could produce results acceptable to the peoples of the West.

From the beginning of my administration the possibility of a conference involving the United States and the U.S.S.R. was suggested frequently in the press or occasionally by foreign officials, apparently under the impression that through face-to-face negotiation the Communists could be led to abandon their most dangerous doctrines, especially that of promoting class conflict throughout the world and trying to achieve global domination in the ensuing turmoil. Few of my associates urged me to seek a "Summit"; indeed, almost without exception they were opposed to the idea. Their skepticism was based on the dim prospects of useful results in view of Communist intransigence. Secretary Dulles, in particular, was emphatically of this view. Nevertheless, the possibility was kept alive by editorials and commentaries, all of which had the effect of creating segments of public conviction that such meetings could "do no harm and might help."

I continued to say that I was ready to meet with anyone, anywhere in the world, provided that there was any logical reason to hope that the world situation could be thereby improved. But I was determined, in the absence of tangible evidence of Soviet sincerity, to avoid a premature meeting because of the probability that failure to achieve worthwhile results would dash the hopes of truly peaceful nations and deepen the atmosphere of world pessimism that had come in the wake of the Soviet's postwar behavior.

The death of Stalin early in 1953 and the rise to power of Malenkov—a man who seemed to bear a less fearful and suspicious attitude than his predecessor toward the West—led Prime Minister Churchill, on May 11, 1953, to call for a meeting at the Summit, saying, "In spite of all the uncertainties and confusion in which world affairs are plunged, I believe that a conference at the highest level should take place between the leading powers without long delay. . . . If there is not at the Summit of the nations the will to win the greatest prize . . . doom-laden responsibility will fall upon those who now possess the power to decide." Yet, at that time, his own Foreign Minister, Anthony Eden, it was reported, did not agree with him.

At home and abroad the subject continued a live one. The constant debate—pro and con—assured the persistent interest of the press; so I developed a stock answer to any question about a possible Summit. "I would not go to a Summit merely because of friendly words and plausible promises by the men in the Kremlin; actual deeds giving some indication of a Communist readiness to negotiate constructively will have to be produced before I would agree to such a meeting."

Some two years went by with no positive results in developing a promising basis for high-level negotiation in spite of some new and, we thought, reasonable proposals concerning disarmaments and atoms-for-peace. Then, in early spring, 1955, there seemed to arise a new wave of interest. The Western European Union was now a fact. More and more in Europe and the United States influential voices joined in the chorus. The distinguished Senator Walter George, chairman of the Senate Foreign Relations Committee; Edgar Faure, Premier of France; and once more, Winston Churchill, all expressed the hope that a Summit might soon be arranged. On April 5, 1955, Anthony Eden replaced Mr. Churchill as Prime Minister. For some reason, whether because of the political exigencies of his new position or the turn of events in the world, Anthony had now reversed his former opposition to a meeting at the Summit. In the campaign for the general election in May, he announced that he was now in favor.

Almost simultaneously the Soviets took a step that gave at least a glimmer of hope that they, under their new leadership, might be genuinely seeking mutually acceptable answers. This act involved Austria.

Since 1946, a joint committee representing the wartime Allies had spent years attempting to negotiate a peace treaty for that nation. It held 379 meetings. Up to this time all the nations, except Russia, had concurred in a draft treaty, but for an inexplicable reason, possibly the Communist desire to continue exploitation of the resources of Austria, the Kremlin had shown no interest in giving final approval to the treaty. Now, without prior notice, while speculation about a possible Summit was rife, the Soviets announced their intention to sign the Austrian State Treaty. This news brought considerable relief to the Western powers—and certainly to Austria.

And to most of the world it was interpreted as a deed auguring well for melting the Soviet ice that had frozen fruitful negotiation between East and West. Coincidentally, Western affairs were better aligned and stronger than before; West Germany was now recognized by the West as a sovereign republic and a member of the Western European Union and NATO.

Because of the Soviet's action, and not wishing to appear senselessly stubborn in my attitude toward a Summit meeting—so hopefully desired by so many—I instructed Secretary Dulles to let it be known through diplomatic channels, that if other powers were genuinely interested in such a meeting we were ready to listen to their reasoning.

On June 13, after an exchange of notes, the Soviet Union agreed that such a meeting would be held in Geneva, Switzerland, beginning on July 18, 1955.

I held no illusions, however. As I wrote to Swede Hazlett on June 4, 1955:

> Personally I do not expect any spectacular results from the forthcoming "Big Four" Conference. Nevertheless, I should think that Foster and I should be able to detect whether the Soviets really intend to introduce a tactical change that could mean, for the next few years at least, some real easing of tensions. If we do not obtain some concrete evidence of such a tactical change, then, of course, the effort must be to determine the exact purpose of recent Soviet suggestions for conferences and easing of tensions and so on.

A full-scale international conference involves difficult and intricate preparation by each participating government. "Position papers"—documents on all conceivable issues, setting forth the position the government intends to present at the meeting—have to be carefully written and approved. Responsible United States officials have to reach agreements with their opposite numbers in other governments about the schedules of meetings, agenda, details of timing, and personnel to be present in the conference room, while advance parties from each country must go to the selected spot to make arrangements for offices and living accommodations, communications, handling of the press, and security. Social activities must be coordinated; even the matter of the exchange of gifts, when this appears appropriate—in this case it did not apply—involves sensitive advance planning.

Position papers can be written only after a chief executive has decided precisely what his position is to be. Priority subjects in my mind were general disarmament, reunification of Germany, cultural exchanges between East and West, the plight of enslaved peoples behind the Iron Curtain, and the aims of international Communism.

The monumental question of what steps the world's major powers might take toward divesting themselves of the massive weaponry built up at such pain, expense, and danger was the topic of highest priority. Disarmament had been much talked about and little acted on. Was there a chance that we might take a step forward? We hoped so.

The division of Germany into two segments was and is both inhuman and dangerous. Countrymen and some families have been cut off from one another; a divided Germany, with Berlin isolated within the Soviet sector, stands constantly as a threat to world peace and as a monument to an unsettled planet.

These were the two critical "action" items. But we wanted to talk, as well, about opening up new paths of contact between East and West. We had little to fear from exchanges of officials, scientists, students, teachers, engineers, and others. Though the Communists would miss no opportunity to gather intelligence when visiting in the West, the chance to show the life of the Free World to visitors from the East promised real results. And we could surely learn more about Communist ideas and culture by sending citizen "ambassadors" eastward.

Not all the talk would be gentle, if the agenda could be arranged to include the two other subjects on which we wanted to speak: of the sad conditions of those living in slavery under Communism, and of the basic purposes of the international Communist conspiracy.

We had no intention of talking about the Far East, if we could help it. This would mean introducing the subject of bringing Mao Tse-tung and the Chinese Communists to the meeting. To this I would not agree.

These decisions made, State Department and other staffs carefully prepared twenty basic documents, with more than 150 secondary papers ready for alternate topics which might come up. Still more reference data and statistical analyses were made ready.

To arrange the format of the conference and to provide an opportunity for preliminary exploration of the positions of both sides, it was decided that the Foreign Ministers of the four nations concerned in the Geneva Conference might meet for a time in San Francisco, where they had gone to celebrate the tenth anniversary of the signing of the United Nations Charter. I had flown to San Francisco to address the anniversary meeting on Monday, June 20; while there, I conferred with Foster Dulles, agreed on the ideas he would offer to the other Foreign Ministers, and then returned to Washington.

When the Foreign Ministers met, Foster at once presented our plan. He proposed a five-day meeting in Geneva, during which the heads of government would attempt only to define the crucial world problems and then issue a directive to the Foreign Ministers to work out the details and conduct negotiations. In general, the routine provided that the Foreign Ministers would meet in the mornings to prepare for the sessions of the heads of government in the afternoon. Molotov initially opposed these arrangements; he later acceded tentatively to most of them.

The exchanges between our Secretary of State and Molotov were later described to me by Foster as the opening guns of the Geneva Conference itself. Molotov emphasized the various moves the Soviets had taken ostensibly to reduce tensions—moves which, aside from the Austrian treaty, were of relatively minor consequence, such as an invitation to Chancellor Adenauer to visit Russia, talks between the Soviets and the Japanese, and a rapprochement between the Soviets and Yugoslavia. Foster, on his part, concentrated on our desire for discussion of the problems of disarmament, German unification, captive nations, and the international Communist conspiracy.

These informed exchanges offered little hope of a truly changed attitude on the part of the Soviets. However, they did not reveal a persuasive reason for canceling plans to go to the conference.

One incident, paradoxically, marred the conference but gave a glimmer of hope. On June 22 the Russians shot down an American Navy patrol plane over the Bering Strait. When Foster protested to Molotov, the latter expressed surprise at this act, and indeed, the Soviet government later issued a statement of regret and paid half the damages—something it had never previously done following an incident of this type.

In Washington prior to our departure, I conferred with Foster to assess once more our own objectives and to anticipate as best we could the Soviet goals and tactics. Foster thought the Soviets would appeal to neutralism, attack power blocs, propose a specious effort to relax armament burdens, such as by "banning the bomb," urge a relaxation of controls on strategic goods sent to the Soviet Union, suggest agreement on a vague statement of principles, propose a "paper" European security system, and seek agreement on a Far East conference to advance the status of Communist China.

The President and Secretary Dulles at the Geneva Conference

" 'We cannot expect here, in the few hours of a few days, to solve all the problems of all the world that need to be solved.' "

Visitors for the President
"When the oxygen tent was removed, I began to ask about my staff. . . . Foster [Dulles] suggested that Governor Adams stay at Fitzsimons General Hospital to act as the avenue through which truly important matters could be brought to my hospital room for decision."

On the sun deck of Fitzsimons General Hospital, Denver, Colorado

"Tuesday, October 25, was a big day in my journey back to health. . . . For the first time in weeks I met my old friends, the members of the press who traveled with us regularly."

The Cabinet in Special Session, October 25, 1954

"Gathered around me were men who were dependable, strong, and reasonable; and in them I knew that the nation had immense resources. With such thoughts in mind, on the appointed day, February 29, I was ready to announce my decision."

Clockwise around the table are: Presidential Aide Persons, Under Secretary of State Hoover, Interior Secretary McKay, Treasury Secretary Humphrey, Attorney General Brownell, Commerce Secretary Weeks, Welfare Secretary Hobby, Civil Service Commissioner Young, Budget Director Hughes, Defense Mobilizer Flemming, Labor Secretary Mitchell, Postmaster General Summerfield, Secretary of State Dulles, the President, Defense Secretary Wilson, Agriculture Secretary Benson, UN Ambassador Lodge, Presidential Aide Rabb, Presidential Assistant Adams.

The detailed conference arrangements I left to others, for I was concerned about the content of a fifteen-minute broadcast I planned to make on the evening of my departure. I wished to dramatize America's spirit and deep yearning for peace. To do this, I intended to deal with the cardinal religious concepts which form the very core of our democratic society. This brought a protest from Foster Dulles, who feared that I would raise the hopes of our people, who might subsequently suffer widespread disillusionment when they realized that no tangible results could come for a year or more, if there were any tangible results at all. It seemed to me, as I planned the talk, that I could do both—I could warn the American people against expecting too much too soon but at the same time emphasize America's quest for peace and make plain that our main objective was to learn whether other nations also truly wanted, in a conciliatory attitude, to follow that quest. All this I felt would have significance beyond our own borders, particularly in counteracting persistent Communist propaganda that pictured the United States as wholly materialistic in its outlook.

Forty-five minutes before our departure for Geneva, I spoke to the nation from the broadcast room on the ground floor of the White House. I pointed out that Presidents of the United States had left the continental limits of our country before to fulfill duties as Commander-in-Chief of our armed forces in time of war or to participate in conferences at the end of a war to work toward peace treaties. "But now, for the first time," I said, "a President goes to engage in a conference with the heads of other governments in order to prevent wars, in order to see whether in this time of stress and strain we cannot devise measures that will keep from us this terrible scourge that afflicts mankind."

There were difficulties inherent in such an undertaking. The President has constitutional responsibilities that cannot be delegated. To perform some effectively he must be at or near to the seat of government. In my talk I acknowledged the cooperation of Congress in holding legislation for my consideration during the time I would be away, and told of my promise to return in a week—that is, by July 24. Obviously, in the time allotted we could not settle major international problems, for they were formidable indeed.

I expressed the conviction that earlier international conferences had paid too much attention to details, or to exploiting nationalistic goals, without enough attention to the spirit in which differences of ambition and ideology might be resolved. The suspicions thus created had meant an increase in armament—and armament created new and greater suspicion. But recognizing the gloomy complexion of the record, I asked, "Do we want to do nothing; do we want to sit and drift along to the inevitable end of such a contest—new tensions and then to war or at least to continuing tensions?" The answer was plain. We want peace, I said, and pessimism never won a battle. Peoples everywhere wanted peace, I said— a peace in which they could live happily and in confidence. To show the world America's earnest desire for peace, I asked that all Americans, on the next Sabbath, crowd their places of worship—all 165 million of us— to ask for help in this undertaking. This would demonstrate to all mankind that we maintained great armaments only because we must. Our armaments did not reflect the way we wanted to live; they merely reflected the way we had to live. I emphasized that Secretary Dulles and I were going in the hope we could represent the convictions, beliefs, and aspirations of all Americans: "We shall be conciliatory because our country seeks no conquest, no property of others. We shall be tolerant because this nation does not seek to impose our way of life upon others. We shall be firm in the consciousness of your material and spiritual strength and your defense of your rights. But we shall extend the hand of friendship to all who will grasp it honestly and concede to us the same rights, the same understanding, the same freedom that we accord to them."

Upstairs on the second floor of the White House my talk was seen on television by my family and several close friends—Bill Robinson, Bob Woodruff, Secretary and Mrs. George Humphrey, and Mr. and Mrs. Gordon Moore. When I joined the group a few moments after completing the talk, the meaning of the occasion was written in all their faces. To my delight I received a call from the statesman who had put so much of himself behind the idea of this Summit meeting, Senator Walter George of Georgia. He was full of emotion and his congratulations and good wishes were heartwarming.

But there was no time for delay. Almost immediately Mamie and I began the trip by auto to the MATS[1] terminal at National Airport, bound for Iceland, the first stop of our journey. Mamie, although she had never completely convinced herself that an airplane flies, was bearing up like a good soldier on what was only her second trip by air across the Atlantic, a trip on which she was to make such a great, though unofficial, contribution. For her the week was a busy one. Without question she gained in Geneva, and brought back with her, the respect and affection of everyone she met, including those Russians with whom she came in contact.

When the plane reached Geneva on July 16, I was astonished at the size and enthusiasm of the crowds that gathered at the airfield and in the streets along the route to our villa. With four delegations scheduled to arrive during the day and the city presumably flooded with visitors,

[1] Military Air Transport Service.

I had told Mamie and my staff that while I anticipated a correct and routine reception, I thought there would be little public interest in the occasion. I was wrong. The Swiss government and people put on an exceptional ceremony of welcome—as I assume they did for other delegations as well—and quickly succeeded in captivating us with the fervor and generosity of their hospitality.

At the conference the principals who were to represent the United Kingdom were Prime Minister Sir Anthony Eden and Foreign Minister Harold Macmillan.[2] The delegation from France was headed by Premier Edgar Faure. He was accompanied by Antoine Pinay, the Foreign Minister.[3] Occupying the forefront for the Soviet Union, as the first among equals, was N. A. Bulganin, chairman of the Council of Ministers of the U.S.S.R. He was accompanied by Marshal G. K. Zhukov, Defense Minister of the U.S.S.R., Foreign Minister V. M. Molotov, N. S. Khrushchev, a member of the Presidium of the Supreme Soviet of the U.S.S.R., and Andrei Gromyko, Deputy Foreign Minister. How many total members there were in each of the three other contingents was not disclosed, but the Soviet Union took over an entire hotel in the center of Geneva and excluded all other guests.

For the United States, I had with me, as my leading official consultants, the Secretary of State; the Special Assistant for National Security Affairs, Dillon Anderson; the United States ambassador to the Soviet Union, Charles E. Bohlen; the director of Policy Planning Staff of the Department of State, Robert R. Bowie; the White House Press Secretary, James C. Hagerty; the counsel of the Department of State, Douglas MacArthur II; the Assistant Secretary of State for European Affairs, Livingston T. Merchant; the legal adviser of the Department of State, Herman Phleger; and the United States ambassador to Austria, Llewellyn E. Thompson. In addition, although not official members of the United States delegation, I had as personal assistants Colonel Andrew J. Goodpaster, Staff Secretary at the White House, and my son, Major John S. D. Eisenhower, who was then between military assignments, having just completed the course at the Command and General Staff College at Fort Leavenworth, Kansas, and scheduled to report to Fort Belvoir at the end of the conference.

Nearly a week before, I had directed that a group of United States advisers be available in Paris on call, including Harold Stassen, who was now my Special Assistant on Disarmament; Nelson A. Rockefeller, my Special Assistant for Cold War Strategy; Admiral Arthur W. Radford, the

---

[2] As well as advisers Sir Ivone Kirkpatrick and Sir Norman Brook.
[3] With Armand Bernard, diplomatic counselor, and R. de Margerie, Director General of Political and Economic Affairs of France.

chairman of the Joint Chiefs of Staff; General Alfred M. Gruenther, then commanding the military forces of NATO; and Robert B. Anderson, the Deputy Secretary of Defense. I felt that I might need these officials for consultation but thought it would be best not to take them to Geneva at the outset.

My tentative plan was to stay in Geneva about one week. This was based on the assumption that nothing much could be accomplished by a shorter stay; on the other hand, damage could be caused by undue prolongation of a conference if it was to be characterized mainly by futile argument and by our combatting Russian propaganda. Always in the background was our caution, based on sad experience, that the Soviets would probably be more interested in using the conference as a convenient platform for confusing the uncommitted nations rather than as an opportunity for the exchange of honest views.

Foster and I each had a country villa loaned to us by generous residents of Switzerland. The one provided for my wife and me, the Villa Creux de Genthod, was owned by André Firmenich, a Swiss businessman. It was a lovely place on Lake Geneva, about five miles from the Palais des Nations.

Secretary Dulles had come to the conference by another plane. On the first evening in Geneva, after we had settled down at the villa and had a quiet dinner, we undertook a final discussion on our planned talks and proposals. We had come to this meeting without having resolved all agenda questions with the Soviets. On the problems of a reunited Germany, general disarmament proposals, and a broadening of East-West contacts we expected the Soviets would be willing to talk, though how constructive and concrete the results would be remained to be seen. We knew the Soviets would refuse to discuss the enslavement of the captive nations of Eastern Europe and the effects on world tensions caused by Communist subversion. Nevertheless I was determined to include these matters in my opening talk so as to leave no doubt of our awareness of their importance.

On Sunday morning Mamie, John, and I left the villa to attend services at the small American church in the center of the city. The congregation comprised, principally, Americans who lived in Geneva; pastors of three different nationalities officiated. One of the high points was the offertory by Miss Fanni Jones, an American, who sang a Negro spiritual, "Sweet Little Jesus Boy," with unusual sincerity and warmth. I later learned from the pastor that she was studying music in Geneva.

That afternoon I spent largely in preparatory conferences. Prime Minister Eden, Foreign Minister Harold Macmillan, Premier Edgar Faure, and Foreign Minister Antoine Pinay, with assistants, came to lunch and we conferred until midafternoon, when I had a chance to relax a while and visit with Jimmy Gault, the Scots Guardsman, who had been my dedicated military assistant in World War II. At four-thirty Anthony Eden and Foster Dulles came again, and at five I had a final conference with Edgar Faure. We were now as well prepared as we could expect to be for any developments.

The next morning we started for the Palais des Nations, where the conference was to be held. The city of Geneva is normally a rather quiet place. Largely French in character, it nestles in a valley between the French and Swiss Alps on a long, peaceful lake which bears its name and through which the Rhone River flows. The town is noteworthy for cleanliness, a cosmopolitan atmosphere, its sidewalk cafés, and the magnificent fountain in the middle of the lake which spouts a geyser more than four hundred feet toward the sky. The population is so accustomed to international conferences that they are reportedly quite blasé about the host of diplomats and world figures who come to their streets from time to time.

In the demeanor of the crowds along our way, however, we quickly saw convincing evidence of peoples' deep longing for peace. These were not holiday crowds, assembled to shout or wave greetings at figures whose names were known around the world; they were hospitable but serious, friendly but devoutly hopeful. Clearly they were praying that from this conference reliable East-West agreements might open the door to a better era.

The edifice which makes an otherwise pleasant resort city a household word throughout the world is the Palais des Nations; once it housed the League of Nations. Now it provides, under auspices of the United Nations, facilities for high-level international conferences. As I entered the building, I was struck by its enormous size. It has several floors of offices, committee rooms, a library of half a million volumes, a restaurant, and meeting rooms. It contained sufficient space to provide office facilities for our sizable delegations—one estimate put the total for the four nations at this conference at twelve hundred. The Council Chamber, where our conference was to be held, was in reality a square amphitheater. Around the gigantic hollow-squared table where forty delegates would sit in two rows were spectator stands arranged in tiers on three sides of the room. On the fourth wall, facing the United States delegation, there were large glassed-in offices of the secretariat, where minutes were kept and translations were broadcast into the earphones of the delegates.

The decoration of the room was remarkable. On the lofty ceilings were murals done in deep bluish-gray and gold. Directly over the table itself the mural depicted figures representing five of the continents of the world in a circle, with arms clasped. The mural is so designed that the viewer sees the five figures peering down at him, as if he were at the bottom of a large well. Around the five continent-figures are scenes depicting man's successful struggle against scourges such as slavery and famine. The scenes are arranged to guide the viewer's eye from one to the next, finally reaching the one unconquered scourge, war, where subhuman beasts drop babies down the muzzles of monstrous cannons, tilted at crazy angles. The mural is effective. The brutish characters remind the participant in this drama of the grim seriousness of his task. It is not a pleasant piece of art, but it is powerful and thought-provoking.

At the table with me were Foster Dulles, Douglas MacArthur II, Herman Phleger, and Livingston Merchant. Simultaneous interpretation was handled by professionals. This was smoothly done in English and French, more laboriously in Russian.[4] As usual I had with me Lieutenant Colonel Vernon A. Walters, one of the most brilliant interpreters I have ever known. Although at the time he was not proficient in Russian, he was completely at home in six or seven other languages, and when he was using any one of them he seemed unconsciously to adopt the mannerisms of the people of that particular country. At this conference he was especially valuable when I was talking with members of the French delegation.

I am certain I could have been more effective in the many conferences I attended during my Presidency if I had previously mastered at least one foreign language. That I had not was unfortunate, but the deficiency was not wholly my fault. A basic difficulty was my lack of talent for learning other languages, due largely to the fact that I was not exposed to them when I was young. Further, I am of the opinion that those people who cannot carry a tune or readily remember one have difficulty in languages; it is rare that I can distinguish or identify even the simplest words spoken in another language even though I have had a fair familiarity with written texts in the same language. A second difficulty for me came about not because of too little academic instruction in other languages, but because of a too varied instruction. In school I had studied Latin, German, French, and Spanish, but I had never wholly mastered them, and the resulting confusion in my mind had made me incapable of using *any* one foreign language satisfactorily. In later years, when I was stationed in foreign areas, I had studied French and Spanish under professional teachers—with no appreciable results. I well remember how in 1929, after being under the tutelage of a Monsieur "Freddy" for months in Paris, he expressed his conviction that I would never become much

---

[4] Russian, which takes longer to translate, was first done unofficially, with the speaker pausing periodically to give the translator time. This was followed by an "official translation" into English by Troyanovsky, the accomplished linguist who had once attended the Friends School in Washington, D.C. Hearing each Russian speech twice was a mixed blessing; at least it gave us more time to study what they said.

good in French. He said, "Major, you are one of the best readers of French and translators of the written language that I have among my American students, but you are the worst candidate as a French linguist I have ever tried to teach. You should stop wasting your money on me." To this, out of native stubbornness, I replied: "I'm inclined to agree, but I engaged you for one year of daily lessons and I'm going through with it. I still hope for miraculous progress." It is no wonder that I have such a deep admiration for a man with the abilities of Colonel Walters.

The initial speeches, delivered formally by the several heads of delegations in order to set out their basic objectives, were later given to the press; of course they were written partly with that in view.

As the only one present who was both head of state and head of government, I was accorded the chairmanship of the first meeting. My talk had been prepared in close collaboration with Foster and his staff, but I had labored long in the effort to make it express my deepest convictions:

> We meet here for a simple purpose. We have come to find a basis for accommodation which will make life safer and happier not only for the nations we represent but for people everywhere.
>
> We are here in response to a universal urge, recognized by Premier Bulganin in his speech of July 15, that the political leaders of our great countries find a path to peace.
>
> We cannot expect here, in the few hours of a few days, to solve all the problems of all the world that need to be solved. Indeed, the four of us meeting here have no authority from others that could justify us even in attempting that. The roots of many of these problems are buried deep in wars, conflicts and history. They are made even more difficult by the differences in governmental ideologies and ambitions. . . .
>
> Nevertheless, we can, perhaps, create a new spirit that will make possible future solutions of problems which are within our responsibilities. . . .
>
> As a preface, may I indicate some of the issues I think we should discuss.
>
> First is the problem of unifying Germany and forming an all-German government based on free elections. Ten years have passed since the German armistice—and Germany is still divided. That division does a grievous wrong to a people which is entitled, like any other, to pursue together a common destiny. While that division continues, it creates a basic source of instability in Europe. . . .

Americans felt strongly, I said, that certain peoples of Eastern Europe had not been given the benefit of wartime pledges of their right to self-government and self-defense.

There was, too, the problem of communication, of human contact. We feared, I said, the consequences of a situation where whole peoples were isolated from the world outside. I went on:

There is the problem of international Communism. For thirty-eight years now, its activities have disturbed relations between other nations and the Soviet Union. Its activities are not confined to efforts to persuade. It seeks throughout the world to subvert lawful governments and to subject nations to an alien domination. We cannot ignore the distrust created by the support of such activities. . . .

Finally, there is the overriding problem of armament. This is at once a result and a cause of existing tension and distrust. Contrary to a basic purpose of the United Nations Charter, armaments now divert much of men's effort from creative to non-productive uses. We would all like to end that. But apparently no one dares to do so because of fear of attack.

Surprise attack has a capacity for destruction far beyond anything which man has yet known. So each of us deems it vital that there should be means to deter such attack. Perhaps, therefore, we should consider whether the problem of limitation of armament may not best be approached by seeking—as a first step—dependable ways to supervise and inspect military establishments, so that there can be no frightful surprises, whether by sudden attack or by secret violation of agreed restrictions. In this field nothing is more important than that we explore together the challenging and central problem of effective mutual inspection. Such a system is the foundation for real disarmament. . . .

. . . I trust that we are not here merely to catalogue our differences. We are not here to repeat the same dreary exercises that have characterized most of our negotiations of the past ten years. We are here in response to the peaceful aspirations of mankind to start the kind of discussions which will inject a new spirit into our diplomacy; and to launch fresh negotiations under conditions of good augury.

In that way, and perhaps only in that way, can our meeting, necessarily brief, serve to generate and put in motion the new forces needed to set us truly on the path to peace. . . .

The British and French opening statements followed. They were harmonious in theme and spirit, though different, naturally, in content. Faure mentioned a proposal for disarmament, which he had discussed with us on Sunday. Eden and I had discouraged him because his plan was based solely on economic controls. We had tried to persuade him that budget limitations would never provide a sufficient measure of protection. But he outlined his plan in his remarks, nevertheless. Far more constructive was Faure's statement on Germany; he described the continuance of a divided and unarmed Germany as "brutal." He dismissed the thought that its problems could ever be solved by reducing Germany further as a power. This was a humane statement for a leading world figure to make and a generous one to come from a political emissary of the emotionally complicated French.

Anthony spoke on the German question. He made our offer for a security pact which would include Germany and the nations present. He announced our readiness to try to reach "agreement as to the total of forces and armaments on each side in Germany and the countries neighboring Germany, with a system of reciprocal control to supervise the arrangement effectively."

"Is there some further reassurance we can give each other?" he asked. One might be considered: "We should be ready to examine the possibility of a demilitarized area between East and West."

Bulganin spoke softly, but his tone could not conceal hard realities. He assumed as a credit for the Soviet Union "the termination of bloodshed in Korea and the cessation of hostilities in Indochina." He said that his country would contribute fissionable materials to the Atoms-for-Peace pool when the international agency was operating, and that he agreed with the need to break down barriers between peoples. Then he moved to their immovable position: "It must be admitted," he said, "that the remilitarization of Western Germany and its integration into military groupings of the Western powers now represent the main obstacles to its unification."

Mr. Bulganin's main proposal was for "a system of collective security" with all of Europe, Russia, and the United States involved—an interesting if impractical notion. In one phase of his program, the Warsaw Pact and NATO would be dissolved. "The Soviet government is of the opinion that our eventual objective should be to have no foreign troops remaining on the territories of European states," Bulganin added, his meaning plain that "foreign troops" were ours. He praised the idea of neutrality, added that my notion of discussing the plight of those caught in Soviet satellite countries was "interference in [their] internal affairs," and that depriving Communist China of its seat in the United Nations was "abnormal."

In other words, the Russian stand, especially on Germany, was as before—adamant and inflexible.

Naturally, I was disappointed. But Bulganin's speech was only an opening gambit. Rarely, in the usual tactics of diplomacy, will a diplomat expose his hand in the early moments of negotiations. It was clear that we had to be patient, watchful, and alert if we were to solve the Soviet enigma. What, we asked ourselves, do the Soviets really want? Who is really in charge among the five who face us across the table—Bulganin, Khrushchev, Molotov, Zhukov, Gromyko?

At my villa that Monday evening I gave a small dinner for the Soviet delegation. Foster Dulles, Charles Bohlen, Livingston Merchant, Douglas MacArthur II, Llewellyn Thompson, James Hagerty, and my son John arrived a few minutes early, and Mamie joined us when the Russian delegation came in; then, according to plan, she withdrew before dinner.

Promptly at 8 P.M. the Soviets arrived in a group: Khrushchev, Bulganin, Molotov, Zhukov, Gromyko, and their interpreter, Troyanovsky. It was relatively easy and an interesting silent exercise to categorize them: Bulganin, a genial public-relations type, slightly buoyant; Khrushchev, head of the Communist party and new to international conferences, rotund and amiable, but with a will of iron only slightly concealed; Zhukov, on hand as a friendly catalyst, but frightened; Molotov, studiously maintaining his reputation as "the Hammer," and Gromyko, stern, unapproachable, unhappy, with little taste for the whole performance.

For reasons of their own, they were seeking good will, but they obviously also had a goal. They drank little and smiled much, with the exception of Gromyko who, when he spared us a rare smile, did so with the greatest effort. Obviously planned and rehearsed, their efforts to ingratiate were carried out with precision and mechanical perfection.

Their first tactical move involved Zhukov. Within a few moments after their arrival, I found myself talking to Zhukov alone; the others had faded into the background. My son, John, joined us. We reminisced about days in Germany and our visit ten years before in Moscow. Then Zhukov said: "There are things in Russia which are not as they seem." Without explaining the meaning of this strange remark, he spoke of personal matters; he announced that his daughter had been married the day before in Russia, and that he had missed the wedding. To my protest over this sacrifice on his part, he said that he would much rather be with me, his old friend and military comrade. Such a statement seemed to me a bit unrealistic; I took it with a grain of salt. Upon learning of this event in his family I sent for and presented to him a pen set and a portable radio to take back to his daughter, a gesture which genuinely seemed to touch him.

After a little more strained but friendly and innocuous talk, we went in to dinner. Here the conversation became serious. In an effort to feel my guests out and to stimulate them to speak candidly, I tried bluntness: I pointed out that with the super weapons of today we could easily and unwittingly destroy the entire Northern Hemisphere. "War has failed," I said. "The only way to save the world is through diplomacy." All nodded vigorous assent, but nothing much of consequence was said.

One thing was sure: the Soviet leaders presented a solid front; it was fruitless to think of one of them at this time without thinking of all five together. Whoever was boss concealed his identity, and each seemed to exercise surveillance over the others. Despite my failure to induce them to reveal their true purposes and ideas, it was a useful evening in that I saw that the implacability of this quintet in a social situation would certainly be encountered in ensuing conferences and we would have to shape our own tactics accordingly. We broke up early because the next day was to be filled to overflowing with formal sessions.

Our plan was to keep the Soviets on the defensive by proposing a series of measures which we hoped would seem logical to the peoples of the world and which we were prepared to support vigorously. We would meet Soviet generalities about their peaceful purposes with specific proposals. If adopted, they would be recognized universally as consonant with any honest effort to promote mutual understanding and peaceful intercourse.

As we proceeded with discussions on disarmament, the Soviets suggested the establishment of certain fixed inspection points as a means of assuring all nations that none could make significant military moves without detection. Their argument—obviously specious, for no practical number of fixed positions could provide adequate inspection—was that by putting a reasonable number of such posts in prominent cities, at railway junctions, and on main highways and large airfields, detection of any mobilization moves would be easy. In this way, the Soviets argued, other nations would be warned of hostile moves and surprise would therefore be impossible—and without surprise any aggressive move would be absurd.

I wasted little time in tearing down this house of cards. I reminded Mr. Bulganin and his delegation that we had seen this scheme tried under the Korean armistice terms. The United Nations inspection teams in Korea, tied down to fixed locations, were freely by-passed by the Communist air and ground forces; the Communists thus were able to dispose their units with impunity and strengthen their forces at will.

This Soviet suggestion, however, offered us an opening for the most effective proposal of the conference, a proposal for mutual aerial inspection. We knew the air forces could provide mobility and that airborne cameras could produce irrefutable information on troops and ground installations—and this without any opportunity to inspect personnel, or to indoctrinate, subvert, or interfere with the populations of the inspected country. It therefore seemed to me that we could present a proposition which, both patently practical and fair, would quickly put Soviet sincerity to the test.

Air inspection had been mentioned casually in many discussions in which I had participated over the years, but never prior to this meeting had I thought of it as a specific proposal to present to the Russians. In the weeks before our departure for Geneva, Nelson Rockefeller enthusiastically advocated mutual inspection, and I had directed that every phase of it receive the most careful study. In Paris on July 18–19 Rockefeller had held intensive discussions on it with Stassen, Anderson, Gordon Gray, and Radford. On July 20, at my direction, Rockefeller and Stassen came to Geneva, where I had that morning talked over the proposal with Anthony Eden, who was most enthusiastic.

After further meetings in which with painstaking care we searched the plan for any possible defects and improvements, I was ready to unveil it to the Russians and the world.

The moment came at the afternoon session on Thursday, July 21. Surprise in presentation I knew might be important. I therefore decided to put forward the plan without delay, even without waiting for a final editing of the text.

As soon as it was my turn to speak, I summarized prior proposals for disarmament which involved inspectional features and showed why none had been mutually acceptable.

Then, quickly and partially extemporaneously, I turned to our new proposal.

"Gentlemen," I said, "since I have been working on this memorandum to present to this conference, I have been searching my heart and mind for something that I could say here that could convince everyone of the great sincerity of the United States in approaching this problem of disarmament.

"I should address myself for a moment principally to ʼhe delegates from the Soviet Union, because our two great countries admittedly possess new and terrible weapons in quantities which do give rise in other parts of the world, or reciprocally, to the fears and dangers of surprise attack.

"I propose, therefore, that we take a practical step, that we begin an arrangement, very quickly, as between ourselves—immediately."

Succinctly, the plan, which came to be called "Open Skies," envisioned:

(1) The exchange of military blueprints and charts, each prepared by one of the conferring nations, on which would be fully described and accurately located the features of every military installation of whatever kind in the territory of that nation or in its bases abroad. The same would, so far as practicable, apply to navies.

(2) Each nation would be furnished with these blueprints and would, under a coordinated plan, station a fixed number of isolated airfields and detachments in the territory of the area to be inspected. The number of planes, cameras, maintenance units, and personnel and the amount of equipment would be agreed on for each unit. The location and specific inspection missions of each detachment would be determined by cooperative action of the nations involved.

(3) Instructions and regulations to govern operating heights of airplanes, speeds, landing procedures, frequency and route of flights would be determined by the staffs. Each plane would be authorized to include in its crew one or more representatives of the nation under inspection.

To avoid captious rejection for technical reasons, I emphasized that if the Soviets would accept the plan in principle, we would be ready to meet them halfway in accommodating details to any reasonable suggestion.

As I finished, a most extraordinary natural phenomenon took place. Without warning, and simultaneous with my closing words, the loudest clap of thunder I have ever heard roared into the room, and the conference was plunged into Stygian darkness. Our astonishment was all the greater because in our air-conditioned and well-lighted room there had been no inkling of an approaching storm.

For a moment there was stunned silence. Then I remarked that I had not dreamed I was so eloquent as to put the lights out. This was rewarded with laughter, only because it was an obvious break in the tension, and in a few moments the lights came back on.

At once, the Prime Minister of Britain and the Premier of France spoke in highly approving terms of the proposal. They declared themselves ready to cooperate and to open their territories to aerial inspection, provided only that all present were in agreement.

Chairman Bulganin spoke last. For a time it appeared that the intransigent Soviet refusal to permit any useful inspection system in the U.S.S.R. might be effectively shaken. The proposal, Bulganin declared, seemed to have real merit, and the Soviets would give it complete and sympathetic study at once. The tone of his talk seemed as encouraging as his words and my first reaction was that the assurance of isolation of inspection teams from the populations, eliminating any possible political indoctrination by such detachments, might prove to be a lead to progress between us.

The hope born of this development was fleeting. Shortly after Premier Bulganin spoke, the session adjourned for the day, all members apparently in high good humor. As was my custom, I mingled with the Soviet delegation. We walked together to the cocktail lounge. Daily, at adjournment time, we participated in what was apparently an international substitute for the British hour of tea. On this occasion, as it happened, I walked with Mr. Khrushchev. "I don't agree with the chairman," he said, smiling—but there was no smile in his voice. I saw clearly then, for the first time, the identity of the real boss of the Soviet delegation.

From that moment until the final adjournment of the conference, I wasted no more time probing Mr. Bulganin; I devoted myself exclusively to an attempt to persuade Mr. Khrushchev of the merits of the Open Skies plan, but to no avail. He said the idea was nothing more than a bald espionage plot against the U.S.S.R., and to this line of argument he stubbornly adhered. He made his points laughingly—but his argument was definite and intractable.

Despite the apparent futility of doing so, I continued the discussion. I urged upon him the value of an effective plan in which both sides could trust. In view of his assertions that the U.S.S.R. had nothing but peaceful intentions while the NATO powers were planning aggressive war, it was greatly to his advantage, I said, to use every legitimate opportunity to keep his government informed of all NATO moves in return for giving NATO powers the same important privileges in the U.S.S.R. I told him also that we in the United States would accept the Soviet plan of fixed posts if they would accept ours of aerial inspection. His protests were, of course, spurious. Khrushchev's own purpose was evident—*at all costs to keep the U.S.S.R. a closed society.* He would permit no effective penetration of Soviet national territory or discovery of its military secrets, no matter what reciprocal opportunities were offered to him. Of course, he was aware that without agreement of any kind there was already available to the Soviet government a vast volume of information about us which was constantly being accumulated at little or no cost from United States newspapers, road maps, aerial photographs, magazines, journals, and government reports—some of it of types that could not be obtained even from aerial reconnaissance.

There was this to say for Mr. Khrushchev. As a member of a dictatorial government, protecting his country's own military and economic fabric from foreign eyes, while having available a fairly well filled-in picture of the military strength, dispositions, and capacity of others, he was, in a selfish nationalistic sense, partly right in the course he pursued. But in the same sense he was also partly wrong, for uncontrolled armaments might well lead in the long run to the destruction of his own country. Certainly for a world statesman, ostensibly concerned with the future peace and well-being of mankind, such a course would be egregiously wrong. Khrushchev, however, does not want peace, save on his own terms and in ways that will aggrandize his own power. He is blinded by his dedication to the Marxist theory of world revolution and Communist domination. He cares nothing for the future happiness of the peoples of the world—only for their regimented employment to fulfill the Communist concept of world destiny. In our use of the word, he is not, therefore, a statesman, but rather a powerful, skillful, ruthless, and highly ambitious politician.

There were, of course, subjects other than the Open Skies plan discussed at the conference. However, once the true intentions of the Communists were made manifest, the conversations, except on this one subject, seemed to become more and more pro forma—an exercise to be completed. Most of it revolved around the problems of a divided Germany.

Here again, the Soviets, though insistently protesting their desire for a peaceful and just resolution of an unnatural situation in Germany, indicated that they would never permit reunification of that country on the basis of free elections by all of its people. I asked Mr. Khrushchev several times: "In view of your repeated declaration that the Soviet concern is for the welfare of the masses and that the people will always prefer a Communist society, why do you fear the result of a free election?" "The German people," he answered at once, "have not yet had time to be educated in the great advantage of Communism! Within a few years this will all be changed."

I took great satisfaction in telling him that the entire Western world would cheerfully abide by the decision of the German electorate, regardless of the outcome. He seemed uncomfortable but reiterated that within a few years the West would not dare propose such a plan.

It was impossible to determine whether the Soviet attitude reflected primarily a fear of a reunited Germany or a desire to extend Communist influence and domination in the West. Possibly it reflected a combination of reasons.

The Soviets talked much of a disarmed and neutral Germany, a concept that, in our conviction, could be nothing but a prelude to final Communist domination of the area; indeed, the history of the prior decade had furnished ample justification for such a conviction.

Moreover, we had obligations to Chancellor Konrad Adenauer and the Federal Republic of Germany. No matter how harmless a Soviet proposal might appear, we were determined to do nothing that might injure the Chancellor or weaken Western resolution to sustain freedom in the German Republic. Though the Soviets continued to reject our proposal that Germany be reunited through free and properly supervised elections, we were quite ready, in order to quiet their fears of such an election, to provide guarantees against any resurgence of Hitlerism or any possibility that Germany might one day become a threat to the safety of the Soviet Union. Arguments on this point were long and seemingly got nowhere. Furthermore, the Soviets insisted that NATO was an organization with aggressive purposes and that its existence made impossible any thought of unifying Germany.

At one point in the seemingly fruitless talk, I reminded the conferees that I had been reluctant to agree to defer talking about the satellite countries and the threatening activities of international Communism. In contrast to this prohibition, I was glad we could talk candidly about the question of Germany and NATO. I wanted, I said, to dispel a fear. I looked pointedly at Marshal Zhukov. Speaking without notes I said to him that he knew that as soldier to soldier I had never knowingly uttered an untrue word to him. He knew, I emphasized, that he could believe me now. There were moral and practical reasons, I pointed out, why NATO could not be an aggressive force. These were self-evident. But if further assurance was needed I would give it. Rather than impede the future of the German people by a concern over that republic's presence in NATO, I said, then insofar as it was possible for the United States to enforce its pledged word, I would say emphatically that there was no need for the Soviets to fear that situation.

Finally, Foster and I, and our delegation, seriously discussed the wisdom of leaving the meeting abruptly as a protest against obvious Soviet resistance to any logical solution to the problem. But by this time it had become evident to us that the Soviet delegation wanted in the final communiqué some kind of "paper agreement" that would be acceptable to world opinion. So we decided to sit out the session patiently to determine exactly what they wanted. In our private consultations we pondered this seemingly paradoxical situation; there was obviously no way of composing the diametrically opposed viewpoints expressed by the West and the East respecting Germany's future.

As all this went on, there were other social gatherings. One formal occasion on the evening of July 22 was a dinner for all delegations—given by the President of the Swiss Republic, Max Petitpierre. The following noon the United States returned the courtesy by entertaining Swiss officials at a luncheon.

I had an interesting and revealing meeting with Marshal Zhukov at my villa. Zhukov, a great personal friend of Stalin's immediately following World War II, and acclaimed as a Soviet hero, had been recalled in 1946 from Berlin for service in Moscow. Then, inexplicably, something cost him his standing with the Soviet hierarchy. Whatever his offense, he was sent into virtual exile and was almost unheard of until long after Stalin's death. For a time I suspected that he was dead. However, a number of years later his name began again to appear in the Soviet news, and before the conference in Geneva he had been appointed Defense Minister of the Soviet Union. Whether this was the result of another reversal of Soviet opinion or whether he was being groomed for Geneva because of his anticipated influence in presenting the Soviet case to me, we did not know. In any event, several members of my staff, early in the conference, began to receive veiled but far from subtle suggestions, usually couched in the form of speculation and seemingly prompted by sheer curiosity, about whether "The President might want to see his old friend Zhukov." I decided to follow up on these heavy-handed hints in the hope that the marshal might be able to give me some explanation of the inconsistencies that seemed always to characterize Russian attitudes and pronouncements.

So I invited him to luncheon, and he promptly accepted. My interpreter was Ambassador Bohlen; Marshal Zhukov's was Troyanovsky. The first part of our meeting was given over to pleasant reminiscences about the war and immediate postwar events.

Once we began to talk about the serious subjects engaging the attention of the conference, however, it became crystal clear that Zhukov was no longer the same man he had been in 1945. In our wartime association he had been an independent, self-confident man who, while obviously embracing Communist doctrine, was always ready to meet cheerfully with me on any operational problem and to cooperate in finding a reasonable solution. This he did on his own; on one occasion he had even abruptly dismissed his political adviser, Andrei Vishinsky, telling him to leave the room so that the two of us might talk confidentially. In many ways it was evident then that Zhukov was just what he appeared to be—a highly important man in the Soviet government, perhaps second only to Stalin himself. During my visit to Moscow in 1945 this evaluation of his position and influence was many times reaffirmed. Now in Geneva, ten years later, he was a subdued and worried man. In a low monotone he repeated to me the same arguments that had been presented to the conference by the chairman of the Soviet delegation. This was not ordinary talk; he spoke as if he was repeating a lesson that had been drilled into him until he was letter perfect. He was devoid of animation, and he never smiled or joked, as he used to do. My old friend was carrying out orders of his superiors. I obtained nothing from this private chat other than a feeling of sadness.[5]

As the conference days passed, the Soviets evinced increasing interest in the final communiqué. The custom of inflicting these documents on the public had become and still remains rather fixed: on the opening day each delegation details its own representative to a combined committee charged with drafting the final joint report. This work goes on steadily throughout the conference. Each representative reports daily to his own delegation concerning emerging areas of agreement and of difference. Hence, we knew that the Soviets wanted a series of meaningless generalities dealing with peace, coexistence, and good intentions. We would not agree to this. We wanted to establish a basis for later negotiation of specific

[5] On July 27 I wrote him:

"During one of our conversations at Geneva, you mentioned that you liked to fish with spinning equipment. I promised to send you one of the types that we use in this country in the hope that you might like it.

"I trust that you will catch a lot of big ones with it, and have a lot of enjoyment during the process.

"It was fine to see you again—possibly some day I shall have the pleasure of once more meeting with you personally. . . ."

agreements—pledges made to the world, so worded that every citizen could, by the later actions of the governments involved, know whether promises were being kept or broken, and who could be held responsible.

In the matter of broadening contacts between East and West, the Soviets talked about quotas and limits. We argued for the principle of free exchange of ideas, documents, addresses, visitors, governmental and business groups, and scholars. In this area we preferred to negotiate on the principle involved, leaving details to our respective Foreign Offices.

We wanted, also, an unequivocal pledge to authorize free elections in Germany, by all its people, preceding the establishment of a unified government for the entire country, which could decide to be pro-Western, pro-Communist, or neutral. We indicated that unless this pledge should be made by all four powers, the United States would not sign the communiqué. Eventually the Russians agreed.

The final meetings were exceedingly tedious as arguments on minutiae went on interminably. But at last it was done. The communiqué took the form of a joint directive to our Foreign Ministers outlining the tasks they were to undertake in furthering the general agreements reached at the Summit Conference. The most important paragraphs, with explanatory material omitted, were:

European Security in Germany:
For the purpose of establishing European security with due regard to the legitimate interests of all nations and their inherent right to individual and collective self-defense, the Ministers are entrusted to consider various proposals, including the following:

A security pact for Europe or for part of Europe including provisions for inclusion of member nations of an obligation not to resort to force and to deny assistance to an aggressor; limitation, control and inspection in regard to armed forces and armaments; establishment between East and West of a zone in which the disposition of armed forces would be subject to mutual agreement; and also to consider other possible proposals pertaining to the solution of this problem.

The heads of government have agreed the settlement of the German question and the reunification of Germany by free elections shall be carried out in conformity with the national interests of the German people and the interests of European security.

Disarmament
The four heads of government
Desirous of removing the threat of war and lessening the burden of armaments
Convinced of the necessity, for secure peace and the welfare of mankind, of achieving a system for the control and reduction of all armaments and armed forces under effective safeguards

Recognizing that achievements in this field would release mass material resources to be devoted to the peaceful economic development of nations, for raising their well-being, as well as for assistance to under-developed countries

Agree: for these purposes to work together to develop an acceptable system of disarmament through the Subcommittee of the United Nations Disarmament Committee.

Development of contacts between East and West

The Foreign Ministers should, by means of experts, study measures, including those possible in organs and agencies of the United Nations which could (a) bring about a progressive elimination of barriers which interfere with free communication and peaceful trade between people; and (b) bring about freer contacts and exchanges as are of the mutual advantage of the countries and people concerned.

The Foreign Ministers of the Four Powers will meet at Geneva during October to initiate their consideration of these questions.

Before leaving Geneva I said, "Only history will tell the true worth and real value of our session together. The follow-through from this beginning by our respective governments will be decisive in the measure of this conference." We watched and waited to detect the results of the meeting.

On July 25 I wrote to my brother Milton:

At the moment, I can't possibly make an objective appraisal of the final results of Geneva. There is no doubt in my mind that in the few days we were there I personally gained insight and understanding that I could never have achieved otherwise. I think, too, that the personal contacts—in some cases, the friendships—that were developed there alone made the trip worthwhile.

The follow-through was to be tested at the Foreign Ministers' meeting scheduled to convene in October.

*   *   *

In the period between the Summit Conference and the Foreign Ministers' meeting, I became ill. Before Foster left to attend the meeting he came to Denver so that we could confer in my hospital room. He had prepared a draft of a reply to Mr. Bulganin, who had asked us for a further explanation of my July proposal for exchanging "blueprints" of military establishments. Inadvertently, Foster had omitted my statement to the Soviet delegation at Geneva that if they would accept an aerial inspection system, I was quite ready to accept their proposition for ground teams. With this correction made, I signed the letter to Bulganin.

Foster felt that preparations for the Foreign Ministers' meeting were going well. We went over in detail the proposals we were preparing to make to implement the directives of the Summit Conference, especially those on German reunification and the broadening of East-West contacts.

Our problem was to find policies which would not rebuff the Soviets' apparently conciliatory attitude in the Geneva communiqué (if it was genuine) but at the same time would not expose us to any individual danger if the Soviets were intent only on using the forthcoming meeting as a tactical maneuver.

Foster reported on the problems involved in completing our proposals for initial disarmament. There were among our top advisers conflicting views. Thus, some felt that nuclear controls could constitute a good first step. Others felt that nuclear disarmament must be part of an agreement for complete disarmament.

Foster returned to Washington, but eight days later came back to see me again. He had little more to report on preparations for the conference which was soon to convene, but with his usual care he was making sure that we had, between us, an up-to-the-minute understanding of what our proposals would be and what we wanted to do.

During the course of the Foreign Ministers' conference, Foster frequently reported by cable from Geneva. When it seemed desirable, I would send him suggestions. For several days the conference seemed to go forward fairly well. While no large areas of mutual agreement had been blocked out, the talks were friendly and on important points it seemed that progress was possible.

Then a short recess of several days was taken. When the conference reconvened, Molotov returned from Moscow to deliver a speech that Foster described in this cable to me:

Dear Mr. President:

Molotov returned from Moscow this morning and this afternoon delivered one of the most cynical and uncompromising speeches which I have ever heard. It involved a sweeping rejection of all Western proposals for European security and German reunification. It repudiated the provision of directive that reunification and European security were closely linked. It stated we could not now speak of "all German elections" as agreed in directive, and in effect said Soviet Union would never permit eastern Germany to be reunified with western Germany except under conditions which clearly implied the communization of all of Germany.

I should welcome any guidance you can get to me by tomorrow. I am deeply disappointed as I know you are at this apparent frustration of the hopes which were born at Geneva and to which you contributed so greatly. However, this development here coupled with developments in Near East seem to me to indicate deliberate Soviet decision to take measures which they must have seen would inevitably involve a sharp increase of tension and resumption of cold-war struggle.

In my reply, I said that I would approve of Foster's taking the position stated by him in the following portion of his cable:

> . . . The clear breach of Summit directive creates a condition where no confidence can be placed on agreements with Soviet Government and that we shall have to conduct our relations accordingly. We feel Soviet position was taken with full recognition of consequences and without any apparent desire to avoid them. It means that further debate on disarmament and contacts will have little substance and we shall probably quickly reach end of our agenda.

In the light of the failure in October, we felt it necessary to re-evaluate the results of the July 1955 Summit meeting.

The Summit Conference had been hailed by the world as a great success, even a diplomatic triumph for the West. It had been held in a cordial atmosphere, which represented a sharp departure from the vitriolic recriminations which had characterized so many meetings in the past. Agreements had been reached to study ways of increasing friendship between the peoples of the West and of the Soviet Union, and these contacts could, we thought, presage the beginning of a more open society in the U.S.S.R. More surprising had been the Soviet agreement that "the settlement of the German question and the reunification of Germany by free elections shall be carried out in conformity with the national interests of the German people and the interests of European security," an agreement which, if acted on, would have done much to re-establish stability and progress among the peoples of the European continent. Most spectacular, in the eyes of the press and public, had been our opportunity to demonstrate to the world, in the Open Skies proposal, the dedication of the United States to world peace and disarmament and our sincerity in offering a concrete way in which we would participate.

Then disillusionment had followed. At the October Foreign Ministers' conference, held in the same room as the Summit Conference, the Soviets had repudiated every measure to which they had agreed in July. Unfortunately, this received less attention in the press than had the earlier agreements; attention had been diverted by other things, such as a crisis in the royal family of Britain, the sale of arms by Czechoslovakia to Egypt, and my own illness. But to those of us responsible for the conduct of foreign relations, the Soviet duplicity was a grievous disappointment indeed.

In the final analysis, however, I believe the Geneva Conference represented a limited success. The record was established: All could now see the nature of Soviet diplomatic tactics as contrasted with those of the Free World. Peoples had been given a glowing picture of hope and, though it was badly blurred by the Soviets, at least the outlines of the picture remained. Moreover, and in spite of what happened thereafter, the cordial atmosphere of the talks, dubbed the "Spirit of Geneva," never faded entirely. Indeed, the way was opened for some increase in intercourse between East and West—there began, between the United States and Russia, exchanges of trade exhibitions, scientists, musicians, and other performers; visits were made by Mikoyan and Kozlov to the United States, and returned, by Vice President Nixon and my brother Milton, to the Soviet Union and Poland. These were small beginnings, but they could not have transpired in the atmosphere prevailing before Geneva.

In the autumn of 1955, lying in a hospital bed in Denver, I could not help thinking: What a disappointment it must have been to Winston Churchill not to have been able to represent Her Majesty's government in this critical period. Three months before the Summit meeting, on April 5, 1955, he had resigned his office, thus bringing to a close, save for the retention of his seat in Parliament, an active public career of more than half of a century, a career which ranged from his serving as a subaltern in the British cavalry to his twice being named head of the British government. During at least one of the most interesting periods of his life I was privileged to be intimately associated with him.

In war he was aggressive, creatively combative, and inspirational in his leadership. Under the organizational arrangement by which the United States and Great Britain fought the war in Europe, he and President Roosevelt together were my joint superiors, exercising their direction over my command through the combined British-American Chiefs of Staff. In most questions arising out of the conduct of the war, he and I found ourselves almost always in full agreement. On those few occasions when we did not see eye to eye, another splendid trait of this many-sided man was unmistakably discernible. On official matters he would argue long, earnestly, and intensively, but no matter what the depth of his convictions, and his fervor in upholding them, never once did he make of the incident anything personal; the quality of our friendship was never diluted in any way. With the war won and the sunlight of public acclaim focused upon him, he was generous in his apportionment of credit to all who had served with or under him. Sometimes he was impatient (what strong-minded man is not?), but I know of no individual who was closely associated with him who did not come out of the war with increased admiration and affection for this man who had so gallantly, so devotedly served the cause of his own nation and of the entire Free World.

I knew him also in the days when, with the war in the Pacific not yet decided, he and his party were rejected by the British electorate and he perforce went back, on the world stage, to relative obscurity. But it was relative only. As interested in world affairs as ever before, and leader of the opposition, he was still Winston Churchill, orator, statesman, historian —almost the personification of Britain.

He came back to power as Prime Minister in the fall of 1951. A year later I was elected President of the United States. In these positions our relationship officially had to rest on a different plane; on the personal side it remained just as close and satisfying as it had ever been. For more than two years, as the heads of our respective governments, we communicated regularly with each other and took every possible opportunity to meet for the type of talk we had always enjoyed.

When finally he laid down the mantle of his high office, I could not help feeling that, for me, a treasured partnership had been broken; but never will I lose any of the affection and admiration I hold for him personally or the great sense of obligation I feel toward one who did so much to preserve freedom, honor, and opportunity in vast portions of the earth.

BOOK FIVE

My answer will be positive, that is, affirmative.

—*Press conference, February 29, 1956*

CHAPTER XXII

Heart Attack

If there be regal solitude, it is a sick bed.
— *Harold Lamb*, The Convalescent

O N the night of September 23, 1955, I was struck with a coronary occlusion. Subconsciously, every healthy man thinks of serious illness as \something that happens occasionally—but always to other people. But when, after spending a most uncomfortable night under sedation, I awakened to the realization that I was in an oxygen tent, with doctors and nurses in attendance, I had thrust upon me the unpleasant fact that I was, indeed, a sick man.

Following my return to Washington from the Geneva Conference in late July, I spent busy weeks in the capital on business growing out of the closing activities of the 1955 congressional session. As I worked, I planned a vacation in Denver, where conveniently located office space for a Summer White House was available at Lowry Field. Denver itself was a favorite spot; I had been married there in 1916, and ever since, my wife and I had periodically spent short vacation periods at her old home. And outside Denver, on the western slope of the Rockies and situated on the Fraser River a short distance west of Berthoud Pass, is the town of Fraser. Near there, as I have said, is the ranch owned by Aksel Nielsen and Carl Norgren. A fishing stream, St. Louis Creek, flows through the property. It was to this fishing spot that Aksel and I immediately retreated upon my arrival from Washington late in the summer.

That year the weather was delightful and the fishing good. I remember it as one of the finest trips I ever made to the mountains. After four days of this idyllic existence we moved back to Denver, where I could more conveniently take care of the volume of work and mail that follows a President wherever he goes.

On Friday morning, September 23, accompanied by Aksel, George Allen, Robert Biggers, General Snyder, and Assistant Press Secretary Murray Snyder, I returned to Denver and went at once to my office at the Lowry Air Force Base. There I was brought up to date on the world situation by Intelligence officers from the Air Defense Command at Colorado Springs. I spent the next couple of hours on work and correspondence and departed shortly after eleven o'clock for the golf course at Cherry Hills. We had hardly started playing when word came that Washington was calling on the telephone.

At the clubhouse I learned that Secretary Dulles wanted to talk to me, but by the time I could answer I was informed that the Secretary was en route to an engagement, and that he would call again in an hour.

At the appointed time I was back at the clubhouse only to be told there was difficulty on the lines. I would be notified as soon as the circuits were ready for us. When word again came that my call was waiting, I went back to the clubhouse once more and this time talked with the Secretary.

Because the morning's golf had been so badly broken up, we decided to remain at the club for lunch and play a few more holes in the afternoon. This was not a particularly ambitious program of physical activity. We were using golf carts, and the exercise, even at Denver's relatively high altitude, was by no means strenuous.

My choice for luncheon was probably not too wise. It consisted of a huge hamburger sandwich generously garnished with slices of Bermuda onion and accompanied by a pot of coffee.

Once again on the golf course I was called back to the telephone after the first hole with a message that the Secretary of State would like to speak to me. After a period of waiting I learned that he had not requested another conversation. Someone along the way had not realized that our business had been concluded. The latest call was in error.

My disposition deteriorated rapidly. I was made the more unhappy by an uneasiness that was developing in my stomach, due no doubt to my injudicious luncheon menu.

One or two doctors have later hazarded a guess that even at that moment I was having heart difficulty, mistaking it for indigestion. We finished the nine holes and later in the afternoon I went to the home of Mrs. Doud (Mamie's mother), accompanied by George Allen.

As the dinner hour approached, George and I were in the basement billiard room knocking the balls about. We declined a drink on the grounds that we were tired and expected to go to bed early. And here again, another after-the-event medical opinion is worth mentioning. At least one doctor of repute later told me that if I had then taken the proffered drink, I might not have experienced the heart attack. He believes that older persons—sixty and above—should take one drink, no more, each evening before dinner, because of the tendency of that amount of alcohol to dilate the arteries and aid circulation.

In any event, after dinner George complained of feeling ill. I offered him milk of magnesia, and then we took a walk in the evening air. Finally he said he felt better; so he and his wife, Mary, went off to their quarters at the Brown Palace Hotel.

I went to bed at about 10 P.M. and slept. Some time later—roughly 1:30 A.M., I think—I awakened with a severe chest pain and thought immediately of my after-luncheon distress the previous noon. My wife heard me stirring about and asked whether I wanted anything. I replied that I was looking for the milk of magnesia again. Apparently she decided from the tone of my voice that something was seriously wrong; she got up at once to turn on the light to have a look at me. Then she urged me to lie down and promptly called the White House physician, General Snyder. She thought I was quite sick.

General Snyder arrived shortly thereafter, and gave me some injections, one of which, I learned later, was morphine. This probably accounts for the hazy memory I had—and still have—of later events in the night. I do remember that one or two doctors came into my room and that later I was helped into a car and taken to a hospital. Then, I think, I slept; but never after that night did I feel any pain or any other symptom connected with the attack.

I followed the doctors' orders exactly, not because I was feeling any differently than the day before but because they said I had a coronary difficulty and should follow a specified routine.

Other doctors arrived on the scene. One was Dr. Paul Dudley White, a noted heart specialist of whom I had heard but had never met. Another was Colonel Tom Mattingly of the Army Medical Corps. I had known him for some time and had the utmost confidence in his skill.[1]

For two or three days I was kept in an oxygen tent, visited only by Mamie and my son, John, who had flown out to Denver on receiving the news. On John's arrival my first thought was to send for my wallet. One of the last things on my mind before the attack was to buy a present for my lovely daughter-in-law, Barbara. Now, as if nothing had happened, I asked John to use the money to take a gift back to her.

[1] Colonel Byron Pollock was in charge of the heart clinic at the Fitzsimons General Hospital, where I was taken. These three men, together with General Martin E. Griffin, Colonel George Powell, of the Fitzsimons staff, and General Snyder made up the group responsible for my care and convalescence. The nurses, under the supervision of Colonel Edythe Turner, were Captain Margaret Williams, Captain Carlene Koger, and Lieutenant Lorraine Knox, all of the Army Medical Corps, all dedicated and more than competent.

During my illness John made two or three trips between Washington and Denver; on one of them he brought me messages from my three grandchildren on a wire recorder. The children were too young, of course, to grasp fully what had happened.

When the oxygen tent was removed, I began to ask about my staff— and whether there was anything important that should come to my attention. There was nothing extraordinary in such a request; I felt fine. I was ready to work. For one thing, I asked Mrs. Whitman to call Acting Attorney General Rogers to ask him about some legal questions I had been examining.

One thing I had already decided. Shortly after my doctors told me that I had suffered a heart attack, they and Jim Hagerty wanted to know my wishes about the kind and amount of information that should be given to the public. I had been one of those who during President Wilson's long illness wondered why the public was kept so much in the dark about his real condition, and thought that the nation had a right to know exactly the status of the President's health. So now I had a quick reply: "Tell the truth, the whole truth; don't try to conceal anything." How well they obeyed this instruction came to my attention some weeks later when I was shown, to my acute embarrassment, an early bulletin describing my health and physiological functions in quite specific terms. When I wryly remarked to Dr. White that I thought he and Jim were carrying "realism" a bit too far, he replied, "That may not mean much to the general public, but to doctors everywhere it will tell a revealing story." I recall thinking, "Well, in any event it's too late to object now; forget it."

Another order I promptly gave was likewise inspired by what I had read of President Wilson's illness. There had come out of Washington in those days a story that Mr. Wilson had become incensed upon learning that Cabinet meetings, without his knowledge or consent, had been called by his Secretary of State. In my case, determined to make sure that during my enforced absence the heads of departments should be kept fully cognizant of world developments, I sent a message to the effect that all regularly scheduled meetings of the Cabinet and National Security Council should be held under the chairmanship of the Vice President.

The most annoying part of my new routine was the taking of blood samples; I quickly tired of having a needle thrust into my arm every few hours or so. The periodic cardiogram was not a bother. It gave me something to do, and I rather liked it. One development was a surprise; I had always heard that a heart patient was condemned to confinement in bed for weeks, virtually without moving. Now I learned that there were different schools of thought among heart specialists. One group believed in a considerable period of immobility; others thought that slight exercise— sitting in a chair by the bedside, as a beginning—should be undertaken within a few days of the accident to the heart and thereafter gradually increased until a normal level of physical activity was achieved. I suspect that among my own doctors there were differences of opinion (these doctors are a secretive lot and a patient at times has to form some of his own conclusions as to their beliefs), but it was decided to put me on a regimen of exercise almost as soon as I was taken out of the oxygen tent.

So one morning two husky orderlies came to the bed, picked me up, and placed me in a chair. This was for only a short period. After a day or so, a sudden change in the procedure occurred: I was sitting in my chair when a doctor came in and, finding me looking a bit white about the nose and mouth, ordered me back to bed without delay—instantly! He said that the exercise routine was abandoned momentarily because my cardiogram showed that the heart wound, which initially was very small, indicated some enlargement and I needed more complete rest.

Apparently this condition soon stabilized, for a little later I started the exercise program again and from then on progressed steadily until I was sitting at my easel, painting, then at the dining table, and then climbing a few steps each day, increasing the number, until I was making trips, every few hours, to the floor above. My convalescence proceeded smoothly. The doctors advised me from time to time on the nature of the routines I should thereafter pursue in order to minimize the chances of a recurrence of any difficulty with my heart. One morning, for instance, four of them brought up the matter of smoking. They earnestly counseled me to avoid tobacco in all its forms. I listened to them politely and attentively. Then noting that all four of them were smoking, I remarked pointedly that I had used no tobacco for more than six years, and wondered why I should be in bed with a heart attack while they were up and working, apparently hale and hearty.

From the beginning the doctors kept the daily newspapers from me. To this practice I readily agreed because I knew that the papers would probably be filled with stories of my illness, speculation about the outcome, comments about possibilities concerning the government's activities during the coming weeks. I had little interest in reading about myself and most certainly I did not want to worry over speculation about me, my work, and my future.

Of course, I was kept informed of important world events, except during the first few days of my illness. I was taken to the hospital on a Saturday, and just a week later Governor Adams, at my request, came out to devise with me a method for carrying on necessary work without undue strain.

When Sherman Adams arrived on Saturday, the 1st of October, he had much to report. I learned from him that on the Monday following my heart attack, Secretary Dulles and Secretary Humphrey had left for Ottawa as previously planned to attend a joint economic conference of the United States and Canada. On that same day Jim Hagerty had told a news conference in Denver that the Attorney General would be asked for an opinion on the possibility of delegating my constitutional powers and duties during my illness. But the medical reports were so favorable that it had become obvious that I could discharge my constitutional duties and the opinion was never developed. The next day a study of the possible delegation by Executive Order of some *non*-constitutional powers had also been considered, but that was soon dropped, too. Governor Adams went on to tell me that on Thursday, September 29, the previously scheduled meeting of the National Security Council had been held with the Vice President presiding.

Later I learned that Secretary Dulles told the group that when President Wilson had been stricken, Mrs. Wilson had kept nearly everyone away from the President; the country came to fear that she and a small White House "palace guard" were running the government. It was during that period that Secretary of State Lansing (Foster Dulles' uncle) had, in effect, tried to change the Cabinet into a decision-making organization. This had been considered unconstitutional and for this act he was dismissed. To guard against any misapprehension of this kind, Foster suggested that Governor Adams stay at Fitzsimons General Hospital to act as the avenue through which truly important matters could be brought to my hospital room for decision.

In my October 1 talk with Sherman Adams, I learned that the Cabinet had met the day before, with Vice President Nixon presiding, and had recommended the following procedure:

(1) On actions which Cabinet members would normally take without consulting either the Cabinet or the President, there would be no change in procedure from the normal.

(2) Questions which would normally be brought before the Cabinet for discussion before decision should continue to be discussed there.

(3) *Decisions* which would require consultation with me should go first to the Cabinet or the National Security Council for thorough discussion and possible recommendation and then go to Denver for my consideration.

(4) The proper channel for submission to me of matters requiring presidential decisions should be to General Persons in the White House and then through Governor Adams to me in Denver.

The Vice President had emphasized that any important new administration policies should be set only by me. A few days after seeing Sherman Adams, I received a full record of this Cabinet meeting, the minutes of which I approved.

In the meantime it occurred to me that because the Vice President, not being technically in the Executive branch of government, was not subject to presidential orders, it would be only courteous to express, in the form of a request, my desire that he preside over all appropriate meetings. The next Monday, nine days after my heart attack, I sent him a note:

> I hope you will continue to have meetings of the National Security Council and of the Cabinet over which you will preside in accordance with procedures which you have followed at my request in the past during my absence from Washington.

When Governor Adams returned to Washington, I sent with him a request that Dick Nixon come out the next Saturday, October 8, to give me the opportunity to tell both the National Security Council and the Cabinet, through him, how much I appreciated their helpful attitude. Governor Adams also took the message back—with full permission of the doctors—that appointments with governmental officials would begin the following week in accordance with their urgency.

When Dick Nixon arrived, we discussed the plan by which Governor Adams would bring to me all matters for action, and Cabinet officers and White House Staff members could come at appointed intervals to discuss their special problems. In the succeeding weeks I conferred with numerous officials who were seeing to it that the government continued to function smoothly. Thus it never became necessary or desirable to surrender temporarily any of the President's powers.

In all conferences in the hospital I had to exercise conscious self-restraint, for I was feeling fine and ready for a full work load. I was cautious only because my doctors insisted that I must be, in order to achieve a full recovery. I had no inclination to quarrel with them.

But I did insist to Governor Adams that I be kept informed on important developments and activities. I was especially eager to see Secretary Dulles, who was in the throes of preparatory work for the Foreign Ministers' meeting scheduled for late October in Geneva. He came to see me on Tuesday, October 11, a little more than two weeks after I entered the hospital. We spent most of our time talking about plans for the conference and the Secretary's activities while he was to be in Europe. I studied one of the drafts he was working on and suggested changes. We also discussed a diplomatic appointment for John Hay Whitney and the possibility of one for Bernard Shanley. The conversation was interesting and I was sorry when we came to the end of the half-hour allotted by the doctors for the visit.

Governor Adams was careful to avoid mentioning any petty or merely annoying news, as distinguished from consequential items of information. In particular, he had nothing to say about newspaper speculation on my chances of recovery, the probable scope of my future activity, and the possible effect of my illness on the next election. Strangely, I had little curiosity about these matters, and so Adams had no difficulty in following the doctors' instructions to the letter.

During the entire period of my hospitalization Mamie occupied adjoining quarters; we conversed daily on a wide range of subjects, but on none that might encourage emotional outbursts.

Mamie took on a task which amazed me at the time and has amazed me ever since: Thousands of letters of sympathy and encouragement flowed in—letters and cables and gifts from all over the world; she answered every one individually. With the help of Mrs. Mary Jane McCaffree, who worked at this exhausting task cheerfully and devotedly, Mamie signed every reply with her own rather lengthy signature, a feat which I have seldom seen duplicated. Mamie, above all others, never accepted the assumption that I had incurred a disabling illness. She told John, and I'm sure she told others, too, that she could not reconcile herself to the idea that efforts in behalf of what I believed in had come to an end. While solicitous above all for my health and welfare, she perhaps more than any other retained the conviction that my job as President was not yet finished.

As soon as I was allowed regular periods out of bed, I asked for my easel and paints and began to derive from them a great deal of enjoyment even if every canvas I attempted, except for one, was, by my orders, destroyed.

But each day I became more eager to meet and talk with friends and members of the administration, and as long as, in the judgment of the doctors, such meetings were not too numerous or too tiring, I was gradually allowed greater freedom.

Aside from doctors and members of the family, my most frequent visitor was Sherman Adams, who came in almost daily, often more than once. Every member of the Cabinet visited me, as did the chairman of the Joint Chiefs of Staff, Admiral Radford, my brother Milton, a number of presidential special consultants, President Castillo Armas of Guatemala, and numerous personal friends. In addition to Secretary Dulles, I saw Secretary Wilson and Admiral Radford about the new defense budget; Attorney General Brownell about the backlog of decisions piling up in federal courts; Arthur Burns and Gabriel Hauge about special help for depressed areas; and Ezra Benson about the farm problem. During those same weeks I was able to take on an increased work load and to give fuller attention to the detailed problems of government. In all, I saw sixty-six official visitors between October 1 and my departure from the hospital in early November. I am sure the doctors were concerned greatly with my avoiding any unusual fatigue or excitement—but they did not allow me to become bored.

Tuesday, October 25, was a big day in my journey back to health. It was the first day I was allowed to take a few steps. Even more enjoyably, I was placed in a wheel chair and transported to the roof of the hospital, where for the first time in weeks I met my old friends, the members of the press who traveled with us regularly. As my uniform of the day—a gift from friends of the press—I wore a pair of flashy red pajamas with five stars inscribed above the left pocket and with lettering, for all to read, saying "MUCH BETTER, THANKS."

Finally, I was told that on November 11 I could return to the East, with the admonition that insofar as work was concerned I should move into full speed only gradually. It was recommended that I convalesce a while longer in Gettysburg, where I would be available to official visitors but not too easily available to people who just "wanted to see the President." Actually, in early October, Dr. Paul Dudley White had told the press that his aim was to have me return to Gettysburg between November 5 and November 12. To avoid having to be wheeled a portion of the distance from an automobile to an airplane, I decided to delay returning until such time as I had recovered sufficiently to walk every place I went and to climb up and down the ramp of the airplane. Thus we set the later date of November 11, which with a stopover at the White House would put me in Gettysburg about November 14. I was glad to go to Gettysburg to recover, not only because of the restful atmosphere there but because I felt that I could do my necessary work as readily at the farm as I could at the White House, including that of preparing for the next session of the Congress.

Our departure on November 11 from Lowry Air Force Base was touching. Experiences such as I had gone through cause a man to develop an unusual gratitude and affection for all those who do so much to help him back to health. In addition to political leaders, present at the airport were Major General John F. Sprague, the commander of Lowry Air Force Base, and Major General Martin E. Griffin, commanding general of Fitzsimons Army Hospital, where I had been for the last six weeks. I was able to express my thanks to the people of both installations and to thank their commanding generals in person. I did not mention, nor did many people realize, that both these officers had suffered coronary occlusions of the same type as mine several years before and both had been restored to full active duty.

Landing in Washington after a calm flight, Mamie and I discovered that some five thousand persons had gathered at the National Airport to meet us. The Vice President, the Cabinet, members of the diplomatic corps, a number of congressmen and senators, and my old friend former President Hoover were there. I said only a few words. The doctors had at least given me a parole, if not a pardon, and I assured them that I expected to be back on duty soon—even though I would be required to ease into it. We climbed into our car for the trip back to the White House.

Then a small detail went wrong that illustrates how good intentions on the part of a staff can sometimes work to a disadvantage. I had specifically requested, before the trip back, that I be provided with an open car so that I would be able to stand up and wave, in the event there were people greeting us on the street. The day was a little brisk, and evidently someone else's better judgment prevailed. I was driven through Washington in a black, closed limousine. The streets were lined with people, who stood and waved in welcome; as a result, instead of standing comfortably in the back, which was my wont, I was forced to "squeegee" around from window to window with considerable physical strain in order to acknowledge their heartwarming salutes. Upon arrival at the White House, I was tired and annoyed by this inconvenience. General Snyder examined me as soon as I reached my bedroom on the second floor and found that no discernible additional damage had been done.

The remainder of the weekend I spent at the White House, seeing Sherman Adams and Jim Hagerty on Saturday and making several trips to the office on Sunday. On Monday, November 14, which happened also to be Mamie's birthday, she and I left the White House after several appointments in the morning and motored to our home at Gettysburg. As we approached Emmitsburg, ten miles south of Gettysburg, we were greeted by the entire student body of a girls' Catholic school, St. Joseph's. The Sisters and the students lined the road on both sides, called out greetings, and displayed signs of welcome. This gesture will always live in our memories.

Once at the farm, I settled down to a routine of exercise—primarily walking—and of work. The doctor said that I should resume my favorite exercise before too long. This was good news. Golf had kept my muscles in good shape and this was partly responsible for the good chances of a full recovery. I had a prescribed medical program, but it was far from rigorous. Only one medicine was required, an anticoagulant called Cumadin, taken in pill form. Beyond this a low-cholesterol diet was ordered; I had to give up eggs, fatty and glandular meats, and certain types of seafood. The principal caution was to avoid excessive fatigue, especially if accompanied by overheating. I was also required to keep my weight at 172 pounds instead of my customary 178, no small item for a man with my love of food. One habit that I had to acquire was that of taking a midday rest, before lunch, of thirty to forty-five minutes. This was difficult; to this day I rather resent the inconvenience it causes in planning a day's schedule.

My first post-illness Cabinet meeting took place on November 22, at Camp David. It was a full meeting, largely concerned with the legislative and budgetary program for the next year, although some other subjects were on the agenda. At its conclusion I felt no fatigue or weariness, and concluded that I would soon resume the daily work schedule to which I was accustomed. Now I felt sure my recovery would be complete.

Reviewing the entire period of my first serious illness, I can be grateful for many things, not the least of which was the fact that I could not have selected a better time, so to speak, to have a heart attack, even if I had been able to pick the date. The economy was booming, Congress was not in session. I had been able to handle with Foster the major foreign-policy problems, and at the moment there was no new crisis pending in the world. Thus it was not necessary for me to consult daily with members of the Council of Economic Advisers, or to approve or veto bills passed by the Congress, or to send messages recommending courses of action to that body. Probably most important was the fact that I was not required to make any immediate operational decisions involving the use of the armed forces of the United States. Certainly, had there been an emergency such as the detection of incoming enemy bombers, on which I would have had to make a rapid decision regarding the use of United States retaliatory might, there could have been no question, after the first forty-eight hours of my heart attack, of my capacity to act according to my own judgment. However, had a situation arisen such as occurred in 1958 in which I eventually sent troops ashore in Lebanon, the concentration, the weighing of the pros and cons, and the final determination would have represented a burden, during the first week of my illness, which the doctors would likely have found unacceptable for a new cardiac patient to bear. As it was, with a period of rest, I was able to keep my mind clear, to talk to members of the government on matters of long-range interest, and to experience a satisfactory recovery.

Of course, not all was smooth sailing. My rapid improvement and the favorable medical reports from Denver took the immediacy out of the issue of presidential disability and threw the matter into the realm of politics. There was much interest expressed in the possibility of modifying the 1947 law relating to presidential succession. That legislation had made the Speaker of the House next in line after the Vice President. In the circumstances of 1955 the Speaker was a Democrat, the President and Vice President were Republicans. Consequently, this subject would have been a difficult one to debate quietly and reasonably. Any attempt to change the law would have caused bitter reaction. Happily, this possibility was averted for the moment, as, with my illness beginning to attract less and less headline space, that space became more than filled with speculation about the probable identities of the opposing presidential nominees in 1956.

CHAPTER XXIII

Election-Year Politics

Liberty exists in proportion to wholesome restraint.

—Daniel Webster

AS the Eighty-fourth Congress assembled in January 1956, it seemed evident in Washington that we would be having a six-months-long political Donnybrook. With a presidential election approaching, with my own intentions in that election not yet formed, much less announced, and with numbers of controversial recommendations to be submitted by a Republican President to a Congress dominated by Democrats, partisan temperatures would inevitably run high.

America in change still needed new highways and new schoolrooms—urgently. I once again put programs to build them at the top of my legislative list. Again I urged the Congress to vote Hawaii into statehood and the United States into a new international Organization for Trade Cooperation. I asked the Congress to liberalize the restrictive McCarran-Walter Immigration and Nationality Act of 1952. And I recommended an unprecedented program to aid depressed industrial areas—regions which, despite the country's general prosperity, suffered from chronic and substantial unemployment.

In my 1956 State of the Union message I repeated my recommendation for "a grand plan for a properly articulated system that solves the problems of speedy, safe transcontinental travel; inter-city communications; access highways and farm to market movements; metropolitan area congestion. . . ."

The need, I pointed out to Congress, had grown through 1955. In that year thirty-eight thousand Americans had lost their lives in accidents. The number of cars, trucks, and buses operating on our roads had increased from 58 to 61 million. Already we could foresee that by 1970 Americans would be driving 118 million cars—the 1955 number doubled. During World War II, I had seen the superlative system of German *Autobahnen*—national highways crossing that country and offering the possibility, often lacking in the United States, to drive with speed and safety at the same time. I recognized then that the United States was behind in highway construction. In the middle 1950s I did not want us to fall still further behind.

To finance a sweeping new system of American highways, a presidential advisory committee, headed by General Lucius Clay, had recommended in 1955 that the federal government issue $20 billion worth of bonds at 3 per cent. This proposal had run into a buzz saw on Capitol Hill; many senators and congressmen wanted the whole project paid for by appropriations out of the Treasury. Though I originally preferred a system of self-financing toll highways, and though I endorsed General Clay's recommendation, I grew restless with the quibbling over methods of financing. I wanted the job done.

This difference disposed of,[1] the Federal Aid Highway Act, with strong bipartisan support, moved quickly through the Congress. On June 29 I signed it into law.

It was not only the most gigantic federal undertaking in road-building in the century and a half since the federal government got into this field by improving the National Pike between Cumberland, Maryland, and Wheeling, West Virginia—it was the biggest peacetime construction project of any description ever undertaken by the United States or any other country.

For primary and secondary roads, the highway act authorized the appropriation, over the next three years, of nearly $2 billion, to be matched by the states. But the big feature of the act was the amount it earmarked for the widening and improving of our interstate and defense highway system, a forty-one-thousand-mile network of roads linking nearly all major cities with a population of fifty thousand or more.

Through the late 1950s and the 1960s work on this system would comprise highways of four, six, or eight lanes wide—in one instance, fourteen. The total pavement of the system would make a parking lot big enough to hold two thirds of all the automobiles in the United States. The amount of concrete poured to form these roadways would build eighty Hoover Dams or six sidewalks to the moon. To build them, bulldozers and shovels would move enough dirt and rock to bury all of Connecticut two feet deep. More than any single action by the government

[1] The bill as enacted included a provision, which I approved, for financing the interstate system out of revenues from increased taxes, including taxes on gasoline, diesel oil, tires, trucks, buses, and trailers.

since the end of the war, this one would change the face of America with straightaways, cloverleaf turns, bridges, and elongated parkways. Its impact on the American economy—the jobs it would produce in manufacturing and construction, the rural areas it would open up—was beyond calculation. And motorists by the millions would read a primary purpose in the signs that would sprout up alongside the pavement: "In the event of an enemy attack, this road will be closed. . . ."

This great highway system will stand in part as a monument to the man in my Cabinet who headed the department responsible for it, and who himself spent long hours mapping out the program and battling it through the Congress—Secretary of Commerce Sinclair Weeks.

Another major program of the administration, started in 1956, will stand as a living memorial to another Cabinet member—Secretary of the Interior Douglas McKay, whose department worked out the most comprehensive plan in this country's history for repairing and improving our system of national parks.

This system of twenty-nine national parks, plus more than 150 other national monuments and historic sites, is one of the United States' most valuable and irreplaceable material treasures. The idea of preserving in a national grouping such spots of scenic beauty and historic memory originated here in this country, with the establishment of Yellowstone National Park in 1872 and a nationwide system of parks in 1916. In Europe, Asia, Africa, and Latin America, other countries have followed our pioneering example and set aside their most magnificent scenic areas as national treasures for the enjoyment of present and future generations.

No one needs to belabor the pride which the American people have in such national parks as Grand Canyon, Yosemite, Glacier, Zion, Bryce Canyon, and the original Yellowstone. In 1947, when new automobiles, plentiful gasoline, and longer vacations were again the prerogatives of American families, the parks had 25 million visitors. By 1954 that figure had nearly doubled.

These statistics warned that the parks were in danger of overuse and damage. Men, women, and children in multiplying numbers were driving over their roads, camping on their grounds, enjoying their lodges and cabins, eating around their barbecue pits, visiting their museums, and listening to their underpaid rangers lecture on their history, animals, trees, and mountains. The National Park Service was predicting that by 1964 the total number of visitors might well reach 80 million—a number equal to half of the United States' 1956 population.

Early in 1954 I received a letter from John D. Rockefeller, Jr., whose family long had taken a constructive and enthusiastic interest in the preservation of public monuments and parks. He was so persuasive in expressing concern about the future of our out-of-doors, that I at once dictated a memorandum to Secretary McKay:

> Recently I have been getting communications from people who seem to be genuinely concerned with what they believe to be the deterioration in our national parks. I must admit to a very considerable ignorance in this field—but I am of the opinion that if we are actually neglecting them merely to save a relatively inconsequential amount of money, then we should take a second look.
>
> Sometime when you are over this way, won't you drop in and inform me about the matter?

This memorandum was dispatched on Saturday morning. At two-fifteen on Monday, Secretary McKay was in my office for a wide-ranging discussion of the problem. After the meeting he and his associates in the Department of the Interior began a survey which led to the launching in early 1956 of a ten-year program to improve and preserve the park system against the strains of the years ahead. On February 2 I wrote to the Vice President and the Speaker of the House announcing that Secretary McKay would soon submit this plan to them; with the appropriations he then had for the park system, the Secretary would begin the work at once.

"Mission 66" derived its name from the date of the scheduled completion of the new program; 1966 would also be the National Park Service's fiftieth anniversary. In the first four years of the program the government invested more money in the park system than it had in the thirteen years preceding 1953. It brought into the system more than a half-million additional acres, and it added the twenty-ninth national park, on the island of St. John in the Virgin Islands.

For increasing millions of Americans, this undertaking, launched in 1956, would bring benefits and enjoyment in great measure over the years.

Secretary McKay, a vigorous proponent of the administration's policies on water, power, and parks, had come under criticism from political extremists in the West. They had attacked his ideas, his honesty, and his character. Responding to this challenge like a champion, he decided in the spring of 1956 to return to his home state of Oregon to face his principal critic in the Senate, Wayne Morse, in an attempt to defeat his effort for re-election.

"As a personal matter," I wrote Secretary McKay on his decision, "I have mingled emotions. You have been a tremendous asset to us in the Cabinet, and you will be missed. At the same time, it is easy to understand your desire to be of maximum personal service to your home state. As a member of the United States Senate, you will add a great deal to the working strength we need and must have in order to carry out the objectives of this Administration."

But Douglas McKay lost the election in 1956. Nevertheless, he continued afterward to perform valuable service in Washington as chairman of the International Joint Commission[2] and did much to help frame the agreement between the United States and Canada on the waters of the Columbia in 1960.

Upon McKay's resignation as Secretary, I appointed to succeed him a former Assistant Secretary of Defense and White House Staff member, Fred Seaton of Nebraska, who performed in a splendid manner throughout the remaining years of my administrations, carrying forward Mission 66 and launching a series of measures which won the applause of frequently critical and always articulate American conservationists.

The Congress of 1956 failed again to vote Hawaii into statehood.

And once again it failed to approve United States membership in the Organization for Trade Cooperation. On May 18, 1956, I wrote in my diary:

> I talked to [House Minority Leader] Joe Martin about . . . the chances of enacting the bill on OTC. . . . There is a very great misunderstanding concerning OTC. . . . Joe understands this, as do the other Congressional leaders. However, since the popular concept is that OTC is a device for lowering tariffs, the project is disliked in manufacturing districts such as Joe's. Consequently, he himself is very lukewarm. I insisted that there be a conference called of Republican Congressmen . . . to make certain that each of them understands exactly what OTC is. Moreover, I insisted that each understand how intensely interested I am in having it favorably considered. I pointed out to Joe that many of these people would, this coming fall, be asking for my blessing in races for re-election. I told him that, as always, I would stand for principles and important measures, and of the measures I would insist [were] needed by our country was this OTC. This would create a very difficult situation if we found a majority of House Republicans opposing me on this point; any request of mine under these circumstances for a Republican House would be greeted with a considerable amount of justifiable ridicule.
>
> I think that Mr. Martin got the point; he promised faithfully to get the group together and allow any Congressman to present the case to the Congress whom I might consider capable of doing well. . . .

Though the House Ways and Means Committee that year reported out an amended bill, nothing further happened. In the course of this year I

[2] A commission established in 1909 by treaty between the United States and Canada to discuss boundary water problems—the St. Lawrence Seaway is a prime example —between the two countries.

was to reflect often on this disappointment. As I wrote to Captain Hazlett in the summer, the United States must learn that "the rich owner of a factory cannot forever live on top of a hill in luxury and serenity, while all around him at the bottom of the hill his workmen live in misery, privation, and resentment."

Hopes for a school-construction bill in 1956 died a death that became inevitable when Congressman Adam Clayton Powell of New York added an amendment to a bill sponsored by Congressman Augustine B. Kelley, a Pennsylvania Democrat, denying school-construction funds to any state which refused to comply with the 1954 Supreme Court decision on segregation. In January, I had sent to the Congress a "revised and broadened program for Education." This proposal had been improved as a result of the information obtained in the White House Conference on Education. I proposed more than a billion dollars in federal grants, to be matched by the states, for the neediest school districts over the next five years, and $750 million to purchase school-construction bonds. I opposed any attempt to tie an antisegregation amendment to a school-construction bill, knowing the amendment would doom the bill to defeat. I was therefore gravely disappointed when the House added the Powell amendment to the Kelley bill. The bill itself authorized federal grants not on the basis of need—as I recommended—but rather on the basis of the states' school-age population.

The congressmen who disliked this latter provision joined with those who disliked the antisegregation rider, and the bill was defeated 224 to 194.

At a news conference on August 8 a reporter said: "I understand the Democrats accuse the administration of having sabotaged its own bill. Would you like to comment on that, sir?"

"Well," I answered, "we will have to get one thing straight. I recommended a particular bill, of which two of the primary features were these: (a) that money, school money, be allocated on the basis of need; and (b) that all of the federal school construction be in addition to the current state programs . . . , because our object was to get more schools and not merely to substitute federal money for state money already appropriated or authorized.

"Now, when that bill was placed before the House in the form of a recommittal motion, the Republicans voted for it, three quarters of them. . . ." Moreover, I added, the Democrats "not only killed my bill but . . . . helped to kill their own."

The Congress that year failed to meet another critical need, namely, help for the depressed areas of the country.

In July 1956, for example, the Department of Labor reported that of 149 major labor-market areas in the United States, twenty-three had persistent unemployment records of 6 per cent or more; of these, three were in Puerto Rico, four in Pennsylvania, and four in Michigan. In addition, sixty smaller areas in eighteen states had a rate equally high.

Shortly after my heart attack, while I was recuperating in the hospital, Arthur Burns came to Denver to tell me that the Cabinet had just approved a plan, on which he and the Council of Economic Advisers had been working for more than a year, for helping chronically depressed areas out of their difficulties. I was so pleased with this news and with the details of the plan itself that I insisted that Arthur announce it at once to the press. As soon as he left my hospital room, he did.

The program was to establish an Area Assistance Administration in the Department of Commerce to give technical assistance to industrial communities with substantial persistent unemployment—assistance in studying their resources and making plans for industrial development. This administration would have a $50 million revolving loan fund to initiate its program.

On July 26 the Senate passed a depressed-areas bill, one which went further and included assistance for rural areas as well as for depressed industrial areas, and which raised the dollar figure in the amount of aid. But the House did not bring the measure to a vote. In this year and those which followed, to the end of my term of office, the fundamental difficulty was that the Democrats in the Congress insisted on two things which had nothing to do with the problem of chronic unemployment. First, they insisted on including rural areas where the problem was low incomes rather than unemployment. Second, they insisted on including urban areas of substantial unemployment regardless of whether that unemployment was temporary or chronic. I resisted this congressional effort to distort a proposal designed specifically to help urban areas characterized by unemployment which was both substantial and persistent.

*   *   *

In 1956 the Congress not only failed to pass legislation to meet obvious needs. It also passed legislation which required a veto.

The first was the natural-gas bill. In 1954 the Supreme Court, in the Phillips Petroleum case, had ruled that under existing law the federal government had to regulate the price which an independent gas producer could charge a transmission company for gas to be piped into another state. From the beginning of my administration I had let it be known that I was in favor of corrective legislation because of my belief that the responsibilities and rights of the states were being involved.

In 1955 Congressman Oren Harris and Senator J. William Fulbright of Arkansas introduced bills exempting such independent producers from federal regulation. Proponents argued that federal regulation of prices would discourage exploration for other sources of gas, force producers to confine their sales of gas to their own states, deprive other regions of this fuel, and thus eventually, like the TVA, draw industry out of some regions, mainly in the North and East, where gas was neither produced nor sold. In such circumstances, consumers' costs would, in the end, rise rapidly.

In 1955 the bill passed the House. When it came up for debate in the Senate in early 1956, arguments pro and con reached unusual intensity. Early in February I set down my own reflections in my diary:

> For some years I have felt that Congress should enact legislation dealing with the confusion into which our natural gas production has lately been plunged. I have wanted a bill that would make clear that the Federal government does not attempt to assume authority to rule upon the prices that may be charged for natural gas at the well head. This seems to be a state matter and the producer of any such well should be enabled to charge whatever he can get by competitive bidding in his particular state.
>
> Admittedly, the natural gas business, when distributed to communities in great quantities, must be classed as a 'public utility' and is therefore subject to the regulations of the state in which consumption of the gas takes place.
>
> Connecting the field with the consuming state is a network of long pipe lines, and since these are an interstate commerce, it seems reasonable that in justice to all sections, the Federal government, through the Federal Power Commission, should exercise proper regulations over these pipe lines. If it did not do so, then in certain areas where a good share of the citizenry became committed to the use of the gas, the long pipe lines would have almost a stranglehold on the economy of that region. So everybody admits that both the state and the Federal government have a responsibility in protecting the interests of the consumers.
>
> However, some time ago the Supreme Court made a ruling which to most people was truly astonishing. This ruling was that the authority of the Federal government over the interstate pipe lines gave it also the authority to determine the price in which gas could enter the interstate pipe line in the state of origin. I suppose it is presumptuous for a mere layman to question the legal ruling by the Supreme Court, but at least I can record the fact that this ruling violated many conceptions of what the Constitution has meant. . . .
>
> My own contention is that the consumers ought to be very much on the side of encouraging production, and that they could not do this if prices in the producing areas were too tightly regulated. In the long run I think that the present system will ruin the gas industry. . . .

There was a great deal of accusation on both sides, but as orators wearied, it became obvious that the bill was headed for passage. Then suddenly a spate of rumors began circulating around the Capitol—rumors of flagrant bribery and corruption connected with lobbying for this bill.

On February 3, 1956, these rumors dramatically changed from speculation into incontrovertible fact. On that day Senator Francis Case, Republican of South Dakota, announced on the Senate floor that he had decided to vote against the bill because, he said, a Nebraska lawyer who was interested in the bill's passage had, on learning of Case's inclination to vote yea, left a $2500 contribution with one of the senator's friends, ostensibly for "campaign" expenses. This had all Washington agog—but three days later the Senate passed the bill.

The Case incident continued to occupy columns in the newspapers and the excitement was felt in every office, hall, and room, of the government. "He's in my pocket," one oil lobbyist at a cocktail party reportedly said of one powerful senator. "The President of an oil company," I wrote in my diary,

> had luncheon with two or three Republicans, among them Len Hall and Cliff Folger. At that luncheon, he announced in unequivocal terms that he had supported Senator Bush of Connecticut with funds for his first election; but because Senator Bush was trying to get the bill reasonably amended, the oil man announced that never again would he support such a fellow and referred to him in indecent language. He further stated that he had helped to see that the Senator's son had been deprived of a large volume of business. In what business the Senator's son is, I do not know, but the blackmailing intent of the oil man was clearly evident.
>
> These are merely two instances of the kind of thing that is coming to light. It is clear that there is a great stench around the passing of the bill, even though it is my firm conviction that the great mass of the oil industry is completely innocent and is deserving of some relief consonant with the *basic* principles of the bill.
>
> This is the kind of thing that has been raising my blood pressure lately.

After thorough study of all the pertinent facts and exhaustive discussions with my associates in the Cabinet, who differed widely in their opinion on the matter, I vetoed the bill on February 17, giving my reasons in the following message:

> I am unable to approve H.R. 6645 "To Amend the Natural Gas Act as Amended." This I regret because I am in accord with its basic objectives.
>
> Since the passage of this bill, a body of evidence has accumulated indicating that private persons, apparently representing only a very small segment of a great and vital industry, have been seeking to further their own interests by highly questionable activities. These include efforts that I deem to be so arrogant and so much in defiance of acceptable standards

of propriety as to risk creating doubt among the American people concerning the integrity of governmental processes.

Legally constituted agencies of government are now engaged in investigating this situation. These investigations cannot be concluded before the expiration of the ten-day period within which the President must act upon the legislation under the Constitution.

I believe I would not be discharging my own duty were I to approve this legislation before the activities in question have been fully investigated by the Congress and the Department of Justice. To do so under such conditions . . . would be a disservice both to the people and to their Congress. Accordingly, I return H.R. 6645 without my approval.

At the same time, I must make quite clear that legislation conforming to the basic objectives of H.R. 6645 is needed. It is needed because the type of regulation of producers of natural gas which is required under present law will discourage individual initiative and incentive to explore for and develop new sources of supply.

In the long run this will limit supplies of gas which is contrary not only to the national interest but especially to the interest of consumers.

I feel that any new legislation, in addition to furthering the long-term interest of consumers in plentiful supplies of gas, should include specific language protecting consumers in their right to fair prices.

The newspapers interpreted my act as a sign that I intended to run again. In a news conference two weeks later, this question was asked: "Would you tell us if you . . . have . . . heard whether your veto of the gas bill has helped or hurt your chances in some sections?"

I explained that I did not have the slightest idea of the effect of my action on the election, but made clear my conviction that only a minor section of a great industry had been guilty of arrogant and indefensible action. Among my many good friends in the oil industry, not one had tried to use that friendship to persuade me to sign the gas bill.

On April 7 a Senate Select Committee, headed by Senator Walter George, reported its conclusion that though "there was neither a bribe nor an intent to bribe, . . . this is a case of irresponsibility run riot," and that the purpose of the gift to Case was to influence his vote. On July 24 Attorney General Brownell announced that a federal grand jury had indicted John M. Neff and Elmer Patman, two lawyers for the Superior Oil Company, and the company itself on charges of conspiracy. On December 14 Patman and Neff were fined $2500 each and given suspended one-year jail sentences after they pleaded guilty to the charge of failing to register as lobbyists. The Superior Oil Company was fined $5000 for "aiding and abetting" this failure.

Despite my call for corrective legislation, the Congress did not pass another gas bill; the issue was too "hot."

That year I also had to veto another major bill—a jumbled-up, election-year monstrosity.

Early in 1956, as in the years before, American agriculture suffered from food, fiber, and grain surpluses, stored in federal warehouses—put there as a result of legislation which set a floor under farm prices, a floor as high as most ceilings.

Since January 1953, vast quantities of surpluses had been moved, and much given away. During all those years we had found outlets for commodities with a value of more than $4 billion—far more than in any comparable period in recent history—but even so the stockpiles grew larger. For each bushel or its equivalent sold, one and a half replaced it in the stockpile. But locking them up was no solution. We could not keep food or fiber there forever. If we tried to move surplus stocks overseas, they might shatter trade and prices abroad, disrupting the economies of friendly nations. If we tried to move them within the United States, they would compete with the products American farms were selling and thus drive prices down. Without the surplus, the Department of Agriculture estimated, farmers might have received 20 per cent—$2 billion—more for their 1955 crop.

In all our work on this tough problem, we constantly had available the assistance of an eighteen-man Agricultural Advisory Commission, a body including, by law, members of both political parties, practical farmers, experts from our agriculture colleges, farm organization officials, and others. Its members served voluntarily and, by and large, their majority opinions and recommendations differed little from the essentials of the program we consistently recommended to the Congress. In addition, Secretary Ezra Benson and I rarely found ourselves in major disagreement with the American Farm Bureau Federation, one of the strongest of the agricultural associations, with 1.6 million members. We also had good support from the 800,000-member National Grange. One organization, however, consistently opposed us—the National Farmers' Union with its 750,000 members, which clings to federal subsidy and prices "made in Washington" as the only hope for the twentieth-century American farmer.

The administration's Agricultural Act of 1954—developed and passed with bipartisan support, as all our agricultural legislation should be— had aimed at gradually lowering governmental price supports so that prices would be more responsive to supply and demand. The principle was sound, but by early 1956 it had not yet been able to make its potential contribution to solving our troubles. First, the law began to take hold only with the harvests of 1955. Second, the new law had to operate under the smothering surpluses amassed under the old program.

In January 1956, therefore, we proposed a new attack on the surplus, one which would give the 1954 program a chance to start gearing production to markets at fair prices.

The principal feature of this new attack was called the "soil bank." It had two parts.

The first part—the "acreage reserve"—was a recommendation for a reduction in the acreage of certain crops then in serious surplus—wheat, cotton, corn, and rice.

In return for voluntarily not planting a certain number of acres, farmers would receive certificates whose value would reflect the normal yields of the acres thus withheld in this reserve. A farmer could redeem his certificates either in cash or in kind at specified rates. If he took the cash, the Commodity Credit Corporation would increase its opportunity to sell off its surplus stocks in the market place. If he took the commodity, he would himself be helping to unload some of the government's holding. The acreage reserve thus used the lever of the surplus to reduce the surplus.

The second part of the soil bank—the conservation-reserve program—would affect both the surpluses and the future needs of our growing population.

Under the pressures of war and the encouragements of price supports, farmers had been cultivating large tracts which wise land use and sound conservation would have reserved to forage and trees.

I proposed that farmers be asked to contract voluntarily with the government to shift into forage, trees, and water storage those lands now under cultivation that most needed conservation measures. Any farmer would be eligible to participate in this program regardless of the crop he produced or the area where his farm was located. We thought that possibly some 25 million acres—an area nearly the size of the entire state of Virginia—would be brought into the conservation reserve.

In any event, with Secretary Benson, I persisted in the stand that high price supports and forced acreage reduction would never solve the mounting difficulties. A gradual decrease in price supports and a voluntary reduction in plantings, along with a temporary subsidy from the government and widening markets for the farmer's crops, would provide the only formula under which our agricultural difficulties could be surmounted.

Feeling on this issue ran high. I learned how intense it was even in my own family when my brother Milton, formerly an official in the Department of Agriculture, sent along a letter from my brother Edgar, written late in 1955:

I am about to make a public blast against the government subsidies to the farmers, but before doing so, I thought that you might give me some moral or economic reason why we should subsidize the farmer.

I am sick of paying the farmer money for his product, wasting that product, and then paying him a higher price for what he puts into the market! I know there are a lot of other people in this country who feel the same way that I do, but it looks to me as though the politicians don't have any backbone, and for that reason, are afraid to do anything about it although in my opinion, legally the action of the government cannot be supported—in spite of the decision of the Supreme Court.

This was originally a war measure, but as far as I am able to learn, we are not now at war, and therefore, the war powers are not enough excuse for this kind of action.

Milton, in a long and thoughtful reply, talked him out of the blast, though I am certain not out of his convictions. When I saw this exchange of letters, the thought crossed my mind that if he had not been my brother, I might have appointed Edgar Secretary of Agriculture to find out what he would propose to do in the circumstances then existing.[8]

The debate on agricultural legislation in the Congress in 1956 was sharp—a contest between the administration's backers and the advocates of a return to the high rigid supports rejected in 1954. In my own party many of the so-called "conservative" or "right-wing" members coming from farm states voted for the rigid, high price supports, usually considered a "liberal" solution.

On February 11, after a crucial vote in the Senate Agriculture and Forestry Committee, I wrote in my diary:

Recognizing that it would take a long time for the 1954 Agricultural Bill (providing for flexible farm supports) to bring about the desired results, the Administration this year brought forward a very comprehensive program to take land out of production to preserve it and enrich it for future generations, and in general, to get the land used better to meet the current needs of the population while keeping it in the best shape for the future.

The bill also had a number of features that would increase farmers' incomes immediately. Their relative income has fallen badly over the past six or seven years, and the past year has seen a continuation of the drop. There seemed to be almost universal approval for the program the Administration submitted. But the Senate Agricultural Committee promptly tacked on it a provision for the return to 90 per cent rigid price supports. They are completely indifferent to the fact that this feature, designed to provide an incentive for increased immediate production, is in direct conflict with the rest of the bill. They seemingly want to bribe the farmers in the hope of getting this year's votes. In the Committee three Republican Senators voted with the Democrats to put over this feature. . . .

[8] It is a standing joke in the Army that any lieutenant caught complaining of the food in the mess hall is automatically given the job—in addition to his other duties—of mess officer.

. . . The Democrats are trying, of course, to put the Republicans in a hole because of the plight of the farmers, the cause of which plight is the 90 per cent rigid price supports of the war that were too long continued. Today we have surpluses that cost us some eight billion dollars and are costing us something like a million dollars a day to store. . . .

Nonetheless, the Congress that year passed a monstrosity of a farm bill, which while incorporating the recommended soil-bank plan, made the great error of going back to the 90 per cent of parity price supports for the six basic crops.[4] It established 80 to 90 per cent supports for whole milk and butter fat, and set up a system of dual parity for certain crops, by which the government would use either the old or the modern formula, whichever was higher. In effect it was less a piece of farm legislation than a private relief bill for politicians in that election year.

Nevertheless, many people in the agricultural areas urged me to sign, saying that the bill was "better than nothing." Many were friends and political supporters; their feeling was that I would be "letting them down" if I failed to approve. A favorite uncle of mine living in the heart of the nation's "breadbasket" forwarded a letter containing the recommendations of an agricultural expert in that area and a loyal Republican. This letter, addressed to me personally, ran:

In view of the fact that the nation's farmers are looking to you for help in their present hour of difficulties, it is the hope of your Republican friends in this part of the country that you will see fit to sign the farm bill that will probably be placed before you for signature in the very near future.

Planting time is here and the bill will probably be completed in just a few days. A veto at this time would just about rule out the possibility of giving agriculture substantial help for this year.

The soil bank combines the effect of conserving our greatest natural resource along with cutting down of production of total agricultural production over the nation as a whole. The full effect of its efficacy will probably not be felt for two or three years but it is the real remedy. On this point alone I and other Republicans interested in agriculture's welfare here think that the bill presented to you should be passed.

On April 16 I vetoed the bill. That night, in a nationwide television address, I said why:

I know you are depending on me to tell you the truth as I see it—and the truth is: I had no choice. I could not sign this bill into law because it was a bad bill. . . .

It was a bad bill for the country. It was confusing—in some aspects

---

[4] Wheat, corn, cotton, rice, tobacco, and peanuts.

self-defeating, and so awkward and clumsy as to make its administration difficult or impractical.

I was happy that the administration's soil bank was still in it.

But the disappointing thing was that other provisions of the bill would have rendered the soil bank almost useless. The fact is that we got a hodge-podge in which the bad provisions more than canceled out the good. . . .

I said, further, that by going back to the wartime rigid price system, we would set in motion forces designed to produce more of certain crops at a time when we needed less of them. It would also tend to shrink both foreign and domestic markets for some of these crops.

I admitted that the bill would temporarily help some farmers, but eventually it would hurt many more than it would help, and in the long run, it would hurt them all.

Of course, it was difficult for me to veto a bill authorizing the soil bank, but I pointed out that the long delay in getting this bill made it too late for most farmers to participate in the soil bank on that year's crops. In the South people were already planting cotton and corn. Spring wheat was already being seeded in the Dakotas. Even the congressional backers of this bill admitted in debate that it was then too late for the soil bank to do much good during the current year.

I urged Congress promptly to enact an acceptable bill, even though some of my advisers believed that the Democrat-controlled Congress would now do nothing.

By May 28 our efforts won out. The Congress enacted a reasonably satisfactory bill, containing the soil bank, and I signed it into law.[5]

[5] At the same time, though the fact was often forgotten in the furor over the price-support bill, the administration continued its constructive work on its Rural Development Program. I had proposed this in April of 1955. It reflected the fact that a million and a half American farm families, one fourth the total, had a cash income every year of less than a thousand dollars. Half the adults in these families had less than eight years' schooling; only one in nine had finished high school. These families lived in concentrations in the Southeast, the Appalachians, the Northern lake states, and the West. The price-support program benefited them little, though some of them in the South came under the program for cotton and tobacco. Under my Rural Development Program the Departments of Agriculture, Labor, Commerce, and of Health, Education and Welfare, together with the states and localities, would work together to increase the earning power of these rural families. This fifteen-measure program included vocational training for agriculture, research, an increase in agricultural credit, retraining for work off the farm, an increase in information about off-farm work, and inducements to bring industries into rural areas. In 1955 the Congress cooperated by enacting part of this program; I called upon them to enact the rest in 1956.

A third agricultural measure successfully proposed by the administration in 1956 was a conservation program specifically for the Great Plains area, which is subject to recurrent droughts and extreme climatic variations.

Neither this law nor any other bill that we were able to get enacted into law during all the years of my Presidency could really get at the roots of the farm problem. This was impossible because the agricultural industry had been legislated into an almost complete separation from the necessary influence of free markets. With this separation, brought about by the federal government, had come constricting federal controls.

The governmental policies which created this situation were, for the most part, war measures, set up to give extraordinary incentives for agricultural production. Though intended as emergency measures, they were found by politicians to have a great appeal for the populations of the farm states. Thereafter, no matter what arguments, what facts or statistics or logical influence could be brought to bear upon the Congress, members from the farm states, regardless of party, consistently refused to overthrow the false doctrine that farm prosperity could be and should be achieved only through governmental price supports.

The pitiful result of this state of affairs is that by and large it enriched those who needed no help and was almost useless to the "small farmers" —those who live and operate on the thin, ragged edge of poverty. The family that lives on a small farm, unable to afford advanced types of labor-saving machinery, sells very little of its product, consuming much of it at home. Two million commercial farms sell 85 per cent of our annual product; 3.5 million families living on small farms sell only 15 per cent. These families, of course, provide a fertile field for political conniving, but they themselves seldom find enough fertility in their inadequate land-holdings to make a decent living.

In the long run the agricultural industry must look to the open market, the still operative laws of supply and demand, for its salvation. Those who, for one reason or another, cannot meet the requirements of these laws must inevitably go wholly or partly into other types of work. Commercial and mechanized farms can earn good rewards without supports because the demand for their products will still be there; under a free system, however, they would no longer get rich on the taxpayers. The huge surpluses, which overhang the market and cost the taxpayer more than a million dollars a day just for storage and maintenance, would start to disappear.

The efforts that I made, for eight years, with Ezra Benson and the whole Department of Agriculture, the Farm Bureau, and the bipartisan Agricultural Advisory Committee, were aimed at gradual reform. Realizing that a sudden withdrawal of artificial supports might spell disaster to millions—both farmers and many others—we tried by a progressive series of actions to reach a goal that forever eluded us. A forward step in one year would almost surely be negated in the next. Majorities in both houses of the Congress refused to respond in the way that logic, common sense, and the nation's welfare clearly indicated. I took some small solace in vetoing bills that were worse than those enacted into laws.

Recognizing the plight of the small farmer and our failure to bring about an effective legislative cure for the real problem, we did develop the Rural Development Program. It was designed to help develop small industry in rural areas so that part-time employment could be secured by people who would otherwise be living on a marginal basis. It had beneficial effects—but it was a palliative not a cure.

The situation, as I write these lines in 1963, is worse rather than better. The only hopeful sign in the bleak farm picture was provided in 1963 by a majority of the nation's wheat farmers, who decisively defeated the Freeman Plan, a proposal that would have fastened governmental controls more rigidly than ever over sectors of the farming community. Despite this one break in the dark clouds surrounding us, the whole farm situation remains a national disgrace.

*   *   *

The record of the 1956 session, though far from brilliant, included good measures, notably the enactment of the highway bill and the fragmentarily helpful farm legislation. But the Congress did nothing on schoolroom construction, civil rights, Hawaiian statehood, postal-rate increases, extension of minimum-wage coverage, the Organization for Trade Cooperation, and a revision of the immigration law. During the session the administration won sixty-nine out of ninety-nine test votes: forty-three times a majority of both Republicans and Democrats (present and voting) supported us; twenty-one times a majority of Republicans supported and a majority of Democrats opposed us. And five times—and this I thought almost tragic—a majority of Republicans opposed administration recommendations, while a Democratic majority supported us. Party loyalty is normally a weak influence indeed when compared to a congressman's desire to cast his vote for whatever he believes may help re-elect him. There were, however, legislators who voted their convictions, not their politics. For 1955–56 as a whole, the Eighty-fourth Congress supported me on roll-call test votes 72 per cent of the time; the Republican-led Eighty-third Congress of 1953–54 had supported me 83 per cent of the time.

The administration's record with both Democratic and Republican Congresses outranked the records of the postwar Democratic administrations, which only once had to work with a Congress controlled by the opposition party.

By the end of four years I had arrived at one strong conclusion regarding the legislative process. I had become convinced that the term of members of the House of Representatives is too short. In the early days of our government it was expected that a congressman would go to the capital of the country, serve there for the months necessary for accomplishing the annual business of the Congress, and then go back to live in his own district the major part of each year. With communications slow and tortuous, it was difficult for him to keep well acquainted with the people of his own region. Undoubtedly the constitutional provision fixing the term in the House of Representatives at two years was adopted with the thought that in this way the representatives would, because of the necessity of campaigning at such short intervals, be kept closer to the people of their localities.

Today all this is changed. Mass media, the telephone, telegraph, and fast postal service have made it possible for information to flow from congressional districts to Washington and vice versa with the greatest of ease. Also, through the years, government has grown in size and has proliferated into many activities that were undreamed of when the nation was young. Sessions of Congress grow longer. If a congressman is to do his job well these days, he simply cannot be forever running for re-election. Yet this is what the two-year terms compel him to do.

*   *   *

So we arrived at the end of the Eighty-fourth Congress. The actual adjournment of a session of Congress follows a prescribed ritual. After the leaders of both houses have agreed among themselves that the main objectives of the session have been achieved or have been definitely abandoned, or when, with the minimum necessary legislation enacted and the members weary of the daily routine and anxious to go home, or sometimes only because there is a general feeling in Congress that there is more profitable political work to be done away from Washington, the leaders of both houses fix the time of adjournment. Just before the critical hour, they approach the President and ask him whether he has any further business to place before them. This approach is sometimes made in person by a committee of each house. In recent years it became the fashion —a far preferable and more convenient one—to make the contact by telephone, since the notification often takes place during the early morning hours. The leader of the majority party in each house is responsible for calling the President; the leader of the minority party is always with him at the Capitol Hill end of the telephone.

Conversations at such hours reflected none of the animosity that occasionally characterizes contacts between the Legislature and Executive. With the senators and congressmen anxious to get home, relations among the principals are quite cordial. The sense of relief expressed at 2 or 3 A.M. is so great that the exchanges during my time were usually carried on in a spirit of camaraderie and good fellowship. This was especially true because the Legislative leaders of both political parties were my friends.

As I went through this midnight ritual in 1956, I was, as usual, seated in a big chair at the end of the darkened West Hall of the White House, clad in bathrobe and slippers. Though the conversations were somewhat enlivened by jocular exchanges, a more serious thought was in my mind. Would I be present in Washington to carry it out again?

CHAPTER XXIV

Second Beginning

The wheel has come full circle.
—*Shakespeare,* King Lear

AFTER a campaign which has just settled one question, any newly-elected President must soon face another: What about a second term? For me the matter came up even before my nomination at Chicago in 1952.

One of the reasons I had given during my sustained refusal to consider myself a candidate was the matter of age. I would be sixty-two years old if elected, I said, and this almost precluded any thought of my occupying the Presidency for eight years. And in my opinion, anyone trying to lead the country into new trends in economic and political thought would need at least two terms to make a significant impression upon the nation. Since a second term would be virtually out of the question for me, I argued, my friends should look for a younger man.

The enthusiastic, determined, biased visitors of 1952 brushed these arguments aside. They were looking to me as the man to break the continuity of New Deal and Fair Deal control of government: they would later take care of the problem of succession.

After my nomination in 1952, I repeatedly told Herb Brownell, General Persons, and Gabriel Hauge that, assuming the Republican party won, we should begin at once to discover intelligent, personable, vital people who could help in the work of changing the direction of government, and to look for one of them who could provide party leadership after 1956.

This determination to limit my political life to the four years ahead became so conscious an intent that, after election, I planned to include such an announcement in my Inaugural Address. Then I found that, the election having settled the immediate problem, my colleagues no longer accepted with tolerant smiles my ideas about re-election. Their attitude was not that I should commit myself to be a candidate again; rather, they expressed concern that I would weaken if not destroy my political influence in the Presidency by announcing in advance my intention to stay in the White House no more than one term. They said it would be bad politics. They produced historical precedents to prove the point, the most recent being Calvin Coolidge's famous "I do not choose to run."

I produced a historical precedent of my own—Rutherford B. Hayes, in his letter accepting the nomination, had declared himself inflexibly determined to serve only one term. I also suggested that the recent Twenty-second Amendment to the Constitution, which limits any President to no more than two terms, meant that any second-term President would be in exactly the same position as a President who, at his first inauguration, announced his determination to decline renomination.

They fell back on the "bad-politics" argument. We were talking about a problem that would not become urgent for another four years; would I please be so discreet as to remain silent on the subject?

Though I said nothing publicly, I had by no means been dissuaded from pursuing the course I had laid out for myself. Letters to my brother Milton and to Captain Hazlett, written in 1953 and 1954, suggest the depth of my disinclination.

I wrote to Milton in December 1953 about a statement I saw in the paper one morning. One of my good political friends had said that of course the President would run for re-election in 1956—who ever heard of a President who didn't want a second term? Admitting that I could not talk publicly yet, I asked Milton's help: "If ever for a second time I should show any signs of yielding to persuasion, please call in the psychiatrist—or even better the sheriff. . . . I feel there can be no showing made that my 'duty' extends beyond a one time performance."

After the 1954 elections, however, on November 18, 1954, General Lucius Clay came to see me at the White House. We had a long conversation that I summarized in my diary:

A drive to force from me a commitment that I be a candidate for the Presidency in 1956 has suddenly developed into a full-blown campaign. For some time, even extending back for some months before the 1954 elections, I have had numerous hints, inquiries and suggestions, all designed to get me to express myself definitely and favorably on this point.

Clay approached the matter circumspectly and even in round-about fashion, but when he once got on to the real purpose of his visit, he pursued his usual tactics, aimed at overpowering all opposition and at settling the matter without further question. . . .

Clay says that he belongs to a group, many of whom were involved in the successful effort to get me nominated in July '52, whose present purpose is to do several things:

(a). Bring about rejuvenation of the Republican Party, beginning both at top and at the grass roots level.

(b). Find and provide the money to keep this kind of effort on the rails.

(c). To watch closely the reform in the Republican Party so as to make certain that in every area we have fine, young, precinct, county and state chairmen, and the same kind of candidates for public office. In doing this particular work, they would try to work effectively in stirring up interest at the grass roots level so that the entire organization would be highly effective and in each case would be in the hands of these forward-looking, dynamic people of whom I speak.

(d). Undertake to provide a better publicity program in support of the "Eisenhower" program.

(e). Elect me as President in 1956. . . .

I tried to make Clay see that what we must all do is work for this kind of idea, principle or doctrine. I admitted that it was probably easier to personalize such an effort and therefore to use my name as an adjective in describing it. But I pointed out that if we focused the whole effort on me as an individual, then it would follow that in the event of my disability or death, the whole effort would collapse. This, I pointed out, was absurd. The idea is far bigger than any one individual.

Here is where we parted company.

Clay said, "I am ready to work for you at whatever sacrifice to myself because I believe in you. I am not ready to work for anybody else that you can name." He also insisted that he and his friends needed now the assurance that I would not "pull the rug out from under them." This is exactly the phrase they used on me in 1951, and I well know how such a foot in the door can be expanded until someone has taken possession of your whole house. . . .

I . . . insisted that while I hoped that I would always make every decision based on what I believed to be for the good of the country, yet I carefully warned him that his idea of what is good for the country and my idea—at least so far as it involved my personal participation—could differ widely indeed. . . .

Six months later, on the eve of the Geneva Summit Conference, I wrote Hazlett:

Some time ago, probably in 1953, I gave you an outline of my intentions with respect to my future in politics. Those intentions have undergone no significant change whatsoever. But as the tension mounts and the bombardment continues, the question that I will have to face next spring will be: "Are the conditions actually prevailing in the world and at home sufficiently serious as to be classed an emergency which should properly override any personal decision or desire?"

As of this moment I feel no qualms as to my ability to hold out. . . .

In spite of all this, the fact that I had consistently refused ever since 1953 to commit myself publicly began to be misinterpreted. On September 12, 1955, I referred to this fact in a letter to my brother, saying that I was concerned by the increasing number of commentators and editors who were beginning to say that my comments, attitude, and actions over the past several months had given to my friends—my very best friends—a clear indication that I was available as a candidate and would undertake to run once more. This bothered me considerably. Whenever I attended political meetings, the question would invariably come up in some form. At a meeting in Denver one of the state chairmen was asked what he thought should be done in case I decided not to run again. "When I get to that bridge," he answered, "I will jump off it."

Then came my heart attack.

Speculation intensified. At first the reaction was, "Of course he will never run again." The question became one of: Who would the next candidate be? Included among those frequently mentioned as a possibility was my youngest brother. Milton wrote to me to say that he was ignoring all queries on the subject because he could not answer such a silly question; it would smack of effrontery on his part to assume it was made seriously. I received his letter just a month after the beginning of my illness. I answered saying: "Don't you know that long before I became President, you were my favorite candidate for that office?"

As the doctors continued to report progress in my convalescence, speculation seemed to grow. The Democratic National Committee chairman, Paul Butler, predicted that I would decline to run, and 88 per cent of the Washington correspondents polled by the Newspaper Enterprise Association agreed with him. In addition to Milton, a number of people were suggested as possibilities for the nomination. About the time I left Denver for Washington, November 11, 1955, the results of a California poll appeared in the press. According to that poll, the strongest Republican candidate, if I should refuse to run, would be Chief Justice Warren, followed in order by Nixon, Dulles, Knowland, Dewey, and Stassen.

Dr. Paul Dudley White, the distinguished heart specialist, who from the first had served as a consultant to the military doctors responsible for my case, told reporters that he and other specialists would require two or three months before they would be able to advise as to my physical ability to withstand the rigors of another campaign and further years of carrying out the duties of the Presidency. This, of course, prolonged and intensified further speculation.

After I arrived at Gettysburg for convalescence, Leonard Hall, chairman of the Republican National Committee, came to see me on November 28 at my temporary office in the town post office. Later I wrote to

Clifford Roberts and said, "This morning Len Hall was here and of course had to talk politics, but I am going to keep pretty still about the whole business [of running again] until at least late winter or early spring." Chairman Hall, however, felt no particular inhibitions about discussing the prospects. As soon as he went out the door, he proceeded three blocks down the street to the Gettysburg Hotel for a press conference. At that conference he held the same line that he had expressed two months earlier—two days after my heart attack—saying that the 1956 Republican ticket would read "Ike and Dick." He acknowledged that I had not said yes or no, but he came away from the meeting very much encouraged, convinced that I would run if I thought myself able to do so.[1]

By now it had been more than two months since my heart attack, and some of those who regarded themselves as likely presidential candidates in the event I should withdraw could be expected to make known their personal ambitions. On November 1 the press had reported that Senator Knowland had made up his mind to announce his own candidacy by early March if I should decide not to run. Now, on December 8, he moved up the date for the announcement, saying that if I did not reveal my plans by January 31, he would "throw his hat into the ring." Since my doctor, General Snyder, announced two days later that I should not make any decision until the middle of February at the earliest, this announcement clearly opened the way for Senator Knowland to do whatever he pleased.[2]

The newspapers of December 30 reported on a poll taken of 134 Republican governors, state chairmen, and national committeemen. More than half of them believed that I, if physically able, would head their ticket.

By this time I was carrying on a regular routine of work and correspondence, at almost the same pace as before my illness. The doctors thought I was doing too much too soon and insisted that I go south for ten days of relaxation and sunshine. I benefited greatly from a stay at Key West, Florida. My Navy hosts spared no pains to make me comfortable and to protect my privacy. On leaving Key West I met with the

[1] In a book written a number of years later, the Vice President reported that the chairman said he had found me that day in a depressed mood. Although it is quite impossible to remember all of one's moods in years past, this seems unlikely. I am reminded of the stories that White House Staff members learned to gauge my morning mood by the color of the suits I wore. A brown suit, it was said, was supposed to mean that I was in a "brown" or foul mood. Perhaps; but inasmuch as Sergeant Moaney was the one who chose and laid out a suit for me each morning, it is quite possible that the conduct of the government was somewhat conditioned by the sergeant's moods.

[2] On November 15 Adlai Stevenson had announced his candidacy.

press but had no more to say in reply to their questions than, "My mind at this moment is not fixed." Mr. Hagerty told me afterward that of fourteen reporters at that conference, twelve thought that I would refuse to run.

At about this time I became aware of the convictions of several men who on the personal side were close to me. My brother Milton, my son, John, and my old friend George Allen all urged me to refuse to run. While each had slightly different reasons for his recommendations, they were unanimous in their belief that a release from governmental responsibilities would increase my longevity prospects. On the other hand, my wife insisted that this was a mistaken notion. She felt, and said, that it would be best for me to do exactly whatever seemed to engage my deepest interest. She thought idleness would be fatal for one of my temperament; consequently, she argued that I should listen to all my most trusted advisers, and then make my own decision. She said she was ready to accept and support me in that decision, no matter what its nature.

Finally in mid-January, ignoring the bugaboo about Friday the 13th, I gave a dinner in the White House. The guests were Herbert Brownell, Leonard Hall, Foster Dulles, Cabot Lodge, Sherman Adams, Jerry Persons, George Humphrey, Arthur Summerfield, James Hagerty, Howard Pyle, and Tom Stephens. My brother Milton was present, too; I had a special job for him, as usual.

After dinner I asked each guest—except my brother—to discuss the pertinent reasons, as he saw them, pro and con affecting my decision to run or not to run. Milton, to whom I gave the task of summarizing the views expressed, did not himself make any recommendation of any kind. All the others argued that it was my duty to run.

Milton, faithfully restating the substance of all the recommendations made by my guests, went on to state the negative case. He said that I should be thinking more of my own health and of removing myself completely from the political caldron. At this conference he took notes and later prepared a two-page memorandum which placed the whole matter in perspective. Several of the points made were flattering, and there is no need to repeat them here in detail. I appreciated the counsel but withheld any decision. A number of thoughts expressed at the meeting had, for me, however, sufficient weight to be quoted here from Milton's summation:

> All felt that you are in a better position than anyone else to prevent global war and to work steadily toward permanent peace. . . .
> The Republican party is being rebuilt (thirty-nine new State Chairmen have been elected during your administration) and this reform will be

more meaningful and dependable four years hence. Since it is believed that only you of all Republicans can be elected in 1956, the continuation of present policies and programs for peace, rising levels of well-being, fiscal stability, and promotion of the general welfare is dependent on your being a candidate for re-election.

However, all present fully understood that only you can decide whether you would feel able to complete your present term, and also serve another four years, and all would respect your decision whether it be negative or affirmative.

A few days after that meeting a primary contest in New Hampshire figured once more in my future. A telegram arrived from the deputy secretary of state of New Hampshire asking whether I had any objection to the entry of my name in their primaries. At my January 19 news conference, I said that my failure to object must not be construed as any final decision on my part relative to a candidacy for a second term:

> It would be idle to pretend that my health can be wholly restored to the excellent state in which the doctors believed it to be in mid-September. At the same time, my doctors report to me that the progress I am making toward a reasonable level of strength is normal and satisfactory. My future life must be carefully regulated to avoid excessive fatigue. My reasons for obedience to the medical authorities are not solely personal; I must obey them out of respect for the responsibilities I carry.

The decision would be given as soon as it was firmly fixed in my own mind, I wrote. It would be based on what, in my judgment, was best for our country.

At a news conference on February 8 I promised to announce my decision by no later than the end of the month. Several days later I went into Walter Reed Hospital for a series of tests, and on February 14 the doctors delivered their verdict: "Medically the chances are that the President should be able to carry on an active life satisfactorily for another five to ten years." In releasing that statement Dr. Paul Dudley White repeated what he had said months earlier—if I ran again, he would vote for me.

Shortly after leaving the hospital I flew to Secretary Humphrey's Thomasville plantation for some quail hunting. On February 25 I returned to Washington.

In the preceding weeks several considerations had come to dominate the rest. Almost unanimously, the men at the dinner were convinced that no other Republican could be elected in 1956; that conviction presented a challenge that I could not ignore. Whether or not their prediction was accurate, it did underscore a political fact of life. "I have just about decided," I later wrote a friend, "that a first-term President—

unless he has been publicly repudiated from the beginning of his term—
can scarcely get his own party to think in terms of a candidate other
than himself."

There were other considerations, among them my certainty that we had

> . . . put together in the Executive branch, the ablest group of civilians
> that has worked in government during the long years I have been around
> Washington. If I had quit, no matter who might be elected in my place,
> there would be a tendency for this band to scatter. After all, two or three
> of them are even older than I, and most of them have business affairs and
> interests that attract them to a freer existence than they can lead here. . . .

The question of becoming a "lame-duck" President? By the Constitution I would be, if elected, the first President unable to be considered as
a potential candidate after his second term. Reflecting, it seemed to me
that this might have advantages. If what the doctors predicted turned out
to be accurate, of one thing I could be sure. I might be a duck, but I
would not be sitting and I would not be lame. A man who is not running
for office can be a formidable political leader. Gathered around me were
men who were dependable, strong, and reasonable; and in them I knew
that the nation had immense resources.

With such thoughts in mind, on the appointed day, February 29, I
was ready to announce my decision.

It was natural, through those many winter months, that I should have
looked back at the years of the term which had passed, to ask the
question: What had those years seen accomplished?

What we had done since January of 1953, we had done in a time of
danger.

Twice in this century the United States, at the end of a war, had celebrated the victory, brought the troops back home, and with relief and
hope tried to return to "normalcy."

In 1953, as the Korean War came to an end, this country, under a
new administration, and with the same unanimity as that with which it
had made those earlier decisions, now made a new and historic reversal.
It recognized that it could not lay down its sword and shield and return
to a peaceful world in which wars would be no more. It faced the fact
that it could no longer throw off the burden of budgets for armaments
on a wartime scale. It realized now that it must learn to live, possibly
for a lifetime or longer, with great arms close at hand, with millions of
men in uniform, and with an implacable enemy always just beyond the
horizon.

With the 1954 truce in Indochina, the march of Communism had been halted and in some parts of the world, as in Iran and Guatemala, certain of its tentacles had been cut off.

It was a clear responsibility of the administration to keep America strong, militarily by maintaining a defense establishment of unequaled power and flexibility; economically by cutting waste, drastically reducing federal expenditures, and removing controls over the economy. In line with this purpose we insisted upon integrity in government and devoted our efforts toward putting an end to much of the bitterness which, when I took office, had so torn segments of our population.

Overseas we had strengthened our alliances, through helping promote the Western European Union, through creating bilateral defense pacts and arrangements with Korea and Free China, and through promoting the Southeast Asia Treaty in 1954 and the Baghdad Pact in 1955.

We had improved the situation of our allies, not only with grants and loans but, more importantly, by the encouragement of freer trade throughout the Free World.

Domestically we had worked toward more responsible fiscal policies, determined to live, except in emergency, within the nation's means. We had inherited in 1953 a budget in the red by nearly $10 billion. This we could not fully redress at once. The government cost curve cannot be abruptly turned down; it has to be gradually bent. By June 30, 1956, we could report that the campaign pledge of balancing the budget, made in Peoria, Illinois, in 1952, had been met. Fiscal year 1956 showed a surplus of more than $2.5 billion.

Our goal was a progressive America. While in some areas we had not been successful—in the attempt to provide federal aid to certain states for needed classroom construction, for example, or in the efforts to eliminate our gigantic farm storage surpluses—other successes more than offset these disappointments. The St. Lawrence Seaway project had been passed after thirty years of effort; a gigantic highway system was approved and under way; research and development had been vastly widened and intensified and a space program had been initiated. Approaching the close of my first administration, America was enjoying unprecedented prosperity.

But these efforts and programs, massive as they were, did not command the whole of our attention during those years of the first term.

Rather, as I thought back over almost four years in the White House, I could recall the hours and days and months on end in which my associates, principally Foster Dulles, and I, had focused our concern not on these giant projects but rather on such things as a tiny patch of land at the head of the Adriatic, a small Central American republic with a population equal to that of the borough of Brooklyn, a strip of sand sixty-five miles long bordering a narrow waterway between the Red Sea and the Mediterranean, a scattering of rocky islands in the China Sea—

areas which taken all together would fit comfortably inside the state of Mississippi.

But on these bits of geography and the handfuls of people within them in those years, war and peace at times could have hung in the balance. And through lonely hours—hours spent in an oval office away from the public view—we wrestled with decisions on these places and people, decisions on which the fate of the world might well have hinged, decisions sometimes incredibly minute: to give airplanes to a Central American revolutionary leader, to encourage an ally to put his Suez Base technicians into civilian dress rather than military uniform, to draw a line on a map of the Free Territory of Trieste which would give Yugoslavia an additional four thousand people—a little over half the population of Gettysburg, Pennsylvania.

And through these decisions, and many others better known, we had kept the peace with honor and preserved the domain of liberty.

We had converted the United States of America from a nation at war to a nation at peace, productive and happy. We had wrought the giant military structures which, coiled for war, would safeguard that peace. We had ringed the globe by signed agreements with our allies. And hour by hour we had made clear to friend and foe our determination to safeguard freedom in those areas where freedom was prized, and we had given hope for a better life to many millions who, unless backed by our strength, would almost certainly lose the freedom and economic opportunities that they now could devote their full energies to achieve.

"I have reached a decision," I told the reporters at my news conference on February 29. Subject to the decision of the Republican National Convention, I said, "my answer will be positive, that is, affirmative." I went on to say, however, that there were so many factors and considerations involved that a simple and bare announcement could not give everyone the information to which they were entitled. After the conference I would ask for time on radio and television that evening to tell the American people the full facts as I saw them.

In that report I described my physical condition as accurately as I possibly could, explained what the doctors believed to be the prospects for my future activities, and then called attention to the record of the programs that had occupied our interest and attention for all the years of my Presidency.

With this, my personal political Rubicon was crossed.

ACKNOWLEDGMENTS

Three men who assisted me in specific and important fields of work on this book were:

My son, Colonel John S. D. Eisenhower, to whom I entrusted the organizing of a mountainous collection of records in such fashion as to make them useful for historic as well as my own purposes, was unique in his qualifications for the task. John was cleared by the government for access to secret documents, for almost three years he had served on the White House Staff, and because of our intimate personal association he was able to communicate with me instantly on any matter that involved a personal decision or opinion.

In addition, as a liaison agent for the publishers, the basic researcher, and myself, he became a virtually indispensable assistant.

My brother, Milton S. Eisenhower, president of the Johns Hopkins University, undertook the onerous work of reading the entire text in one draft and offering notes on its content. He is the one individual who could have done this to my satisfaction, not only because of the close relationship between us for a matter of sixty years, but because he, during the entire period of my two administrations, was a constant adviser, a confidant and, at times, a personal representative.

I am deeply indebted to him for his cheerful acceptance of the duty, and the skill and thoroughness with which he performed it.

Dr. William B. Ewald, Jr., another of my staff in the White House years, was responsible for basic research. While my initial drafts of text contained little more than those things that left rather vivid impressions in my memory, his work brought to light much in the way of facts and statistics, as well as excerpts from my diary, letters, and statements that stimulated recall of my attitudes and thoughts in those years. Without him the book would undoubtedly have reflected only my convictions and concepts of today rather than those of the years that are herein recorded.

To do this work he secured a two years' leave of absence from his position in the International Business Machines organization; I am indebted not only to him but to that company.

I am indebted to members of my administration and other associates for having reviewed certain portions of the manuscript which fell within their areas of interest: Sherman Adams, Robert R. Bowie, Herbert Brownell, Arthur F. Burns, Lucius Clay, Robert Cutler, Thomas E. Dewey, Joseph M. Dodge, Allen W. Dulles, Andrew J. Goodpaster, James C. Hagerty, Bryce N. Harlow, Gabriel Hauge, Henry Cabot Lodge, Kevin McCann, James P. Mitchell, Malcolm Moos, Gerald D. Morgan, True D. Morse, Don Paarlberg, Wilton B. Persons, Maxwell M. Rabb, Clarence B. Randall, Nelson A. Rockefeller, Fred A. Seaton, Thomas Stephens, and Mrs. Ann C. Whitman. Responsibility for accuracy of the text remains, of course, my own.

I would like to express my appreciation to the following ladies for their role in the physical preparation of the manuscript: my personal secretaries, Mrs. Whitman and Miss Lillian H. Brown, and also to Mrs. Weldon (Marian M.) Smith, Mrs. Ray (Joyce E.) McGough, and Miss Elizabeth W. Beverly. I am indebted to the following: Mrs. Eugene Abul, Mrs. Conrad Hoffman, Miss Joyce Schwartz, Mrs. Jeanette Constantino, and Miss Linda Richter for their work in typing the final manuscript.

APPENDIXES

APPENDIX A

SECRETARIES AND UNDER SECRETARIES OF DEPARTMENTS OF THE GOVERNMENT BETWEEN 1953 AND 1961

Secretaries of State
John Foster Dulles — January 21, 1953, to April 21, 1959
Christian A. Herter — April 22, 1959, to January 20, 1961

Under Secretaries of State
Walter Bedell Smith — February 9, 1953, to October 1, 1954
Herbert Hoover, Jr. — October 4, 1954, to February 21, 1957
Christian A. Herter — February 21, 1957, to April 22, 1959
C. Douglas Dillon — June 12, 1959, to January 4, 1961

Under Secretaries of State for Administration
Donold B. Lourie — February 16, 1953, to March 5, 1954
Charles E. Saltzman — June 28, 1954, to December 31, 1954

Under Secretary of State for Economic Affairs
C. Douglas Dillon — July 1, 1958, to June 12, 1959

Under Secretary of State for Political Affairs
Livingston T. Merchant — December 4, 1959, to February 20, 1961

Secretaries of the Treasury
George M. Humphrey — January 21, 1953, to July 28, 1957
Robert B. Anderson — July 29, 1957, to January 20, 1961

Under Secretaries of the Treasury
Marion B. Folsom — January 27, 1953, to August 1, 1955
H. Chapman Rose — August 3, 1955, to January 31, 1956
Fred C. Scribner, Jr. — August 9, 1957, to January 20, 1961

Under Secretaries of the Treasury for Monetary Affairs
W. Randolph Burgess — August 3, 1954, to September 26, 1957
Julian B. Baird — September 26, 1957, to January 20, 1961

Secretaries of Defense
Charles E. Wilson — January 28, 1953, to October 8, 1957
Neil H. McElroy — October 9, 1957, to December 1, 1959
Thomas S. Gates, Jr. — December 2, 1959, to January 20, 1961

Deputy Secretaries of Defense
Roger M. Kyes — February 2, 1953, to May 1, 1954
Robert B. Anderson — May 3, 1954, to August 4, 1955
Reuben B. Robertson, Jr. — August 5, 1955, to April 25, 1957
Donald A. Quarles — May 1, 1957 to May 8, 1959
Thomas S. Gates, Jr. — June 8, 1959, to December 1, 1959
James H. Douglas, Jr. — December 11, 1959, to January 20, 1961

Secretaries of the Army
Robert T. Stevens — February 4, 1953, to July 20, 1955
Wilber M. Brucker — July 21, 1955, to January 20, 1961

Secretaries of the Navy
Robert B. Anderson — February 4, 1953, to May 2, 1954
Charles S. Thomas — May 3, 1954, to April 1, 1957
Thomas S. Gates, Jr. — April 1, 1957, to June 8, 1959
William B. Franke — June 8, 1959, to January 20, 1961

Secretaries of the Air Force
Harold E. Talbott — February 4, 1953, to August 13, 1955
Donald A. Quarles — August 15, 1955, to April 30, 1957
James H. Douglas, Jr. — May 1, 1957, to December 11, 1959
Dudley C. Sharpe — December 11, 1959, to January 20, 1961

Chairmen of the Joint Chiefs of Staff
General Omar N. Bradley — August 16, 1949, to August 14, 1953
Admiral Arthur W. Radford — August 15, 1953, to August 14, 1957
General Nathan F. Twining — August 15, 1957, to September 30, 1960
General Lyman L. Lemnitzer — October 1, 1960, to September 30, 1962

Chiefs of Staff of the U. S. Army
General J. Lawton Collins — August 16, 1949, to August 14, 1953
General Matthew B. Ridgway — August 15, 1953, to June 30, 1955
General Maxwell D. Taylor — June 30, 1955, to June 30, 1959
General Lyman L. Lemnitzer — July 1, 1959, to September 30, 1960
General George H. Decker — September 30, 1960, to September 30, 1962

Chiefs of Naval Operations
Admiral William M. Fechteler — August 16, 1951, to August 17, 1953
Admiral Robert B. Carney — August 17, 1953, to August 17, 1955
Admiral Arleigh A. Burke — August 17, 1955, to August 1, 1961

Chiefs of Staff of the U. S. Air Force
General Hoyt S. Vandenberg — April 30, 1948, to June 29, 1953
General Nathan F. Twining — June 30, 1953, to June 30, 1957
General Thomas D. White — July 1, 1957, to June 30, 1961

Commandants of the Marine Corps

General Lemuel C. Shepherd, Jr. — January 1, 1952, to December 31, 1955

General Randolph McC. Pate — January 1, 1956, to December 31, 1959

General David M. Shoup — January 1, 1960 ——

Attorneys General

Herbert Brownell, Jr. — January 21, 1953, to November 8, 1957

William P. Rogers — November 8, 1957 to January 20, 1961

Deputy Attorneys General

William P. Rogers — January 28, 1953, to November 8, 1957

Lawrence E. Walsh — December 27, 1957, to December 31, 1960

Postmaster General

Arthur E. Summerfield — January 21, 1953, to January 20, 1961

Deputy Postmasters General

Charles R. Hook, Jr. — January 29, 1953, to October 1, 1955

Maurice H. Stans — October 1, 1955, to September 15, 1957

Edson O. Sessions — September 20, 1957, to October 20, 1959

John M. McKibbin — November 2, 1959, to January 20, 1961

Secretaries of the Interior

Douglas McKay — January 21, 1953, to April 15, 1956

Fred A. Seaton — June 18, 1956, to January 20, 1961

Under Secretaries of the Interior

Ralph A. Tudor — March 31, 1953, to September 1, 1954

Clarence A. Davis — September 1, 1954, to January 4, 1957

O. Hatfield Chilson — March 18, 1957, to September 20, 1958

Elmer F. Bennett — October 3, 1958, to January 20, 1961

Secretary of Agriculture

Ezra Taft Benson — January 21, 1953, to January 20, 1961

Under Secretary of Agriculture

True D. Morse — January 29, 1953, to January 20, 1961

Secretaries of Commerce

Sinclair Weeks — January 21, 1953, to November 10, 1958

Lewis L. Strauss — November 13, 1958, to June 30, 1959

Frederick H. Mueller — August 10, 1959, to January 20, 1961

Under Secretaries of Commerce

Walter Williams — January 28, 1953, to November 1, 1958

Frederick H. Mueller — November 3, 1958, to August 10, 1959

Philip A. Ray — August 31, 1959, to January 20, 1961

Under Secretaries of Commerce for Transportation
   Robert B. Murray, Jr. — January 28, 1953, to January 20, 1955
   Louis S. Rothschild — March 2, 1955, to October 24, 1958
   John J. Allen, Jr. — December 20, 1958, to January 20, 1961

Secretaries of Labor
   Martin P. Durkin — January 21, 1953, to September 10, 1953
   James P. Mitchell — October 8, 1953, to January 20, 1961

Under Secretaries of Labor
   Lloyd A. Mashburn — February 24, 1953, to October 9, 1953
   Arthur Larson — April 12, 1954, to November 14, 1956
   James T. O'Connell — February 3, 1957, to January 20, 1961

Secretaries of Health, Education and Welfare
   Oveta Culp Hobby — April 11, 1953, to August 1, 1955
   Marion B. Folsom — August 1, 1955, to July 31, 1958
   Arthur S. Flemming — August 1, 1958, to January 20, 1961

Under Secretaries of Health, Education and Welfare
   Nelson A. Rockefeller — June 11, 1953, to December 16, 1954
   Herold C. Hunt — September 12, 1955, to February 4, 1957
   John A. Perkins — March 26, 1957, to March 1, 1958
   Bertha S. Adkins — August 18, 1958, to January 20, 1961

Chairmen of the Atomic Energy Commission
   Gordon Dean — July 11, 1950, to June 30, 1953
   Lewis L. Strauss — July 2, 1953, to June 30, 1958
   John A. McCone — July 14, 1958, to January 20, 1961

Directors of the Bureau of the Budget
   Joseph M. Dodge — January 21, 1953, to April 15, 1954
   Rowland R. Hughes — April 15, 1954, to April 1, 1956
   Percival F. Brundage — April 2, 1956, to March 17, 1958
   Maurice H. Stans — March 18, 1958, to January 20, 1961

Chairmen of the Council of Economic Advisers
   Arthur F. Burns — August 8, 1953, to December 1, 1956
   Raymond J. Saulnier — December 1, 1956, to January 20, 1961

APPENDIX B

PRESIDENTS AND FIRST LADIES

GEORGE WASHINGTON, 1789–1797
Martha Dandridge Custis Washington

JOHN ADAMS, 1797–1801
Abigail Smith Adams

THOMAS JEFFERSON, 1801–1809
Martha Wayles Skelton Jefferson, died 1782; she therefore did not live to become First Lady.

JAMES MADISON, 1809–1817
Dolley Payne Todd Madison

JAMES MONROE, 1817–1825
Elizabeth Kortwright Monroe

JOHN QUINCY ADAMS, 1825–1829
Louisa Catherine Johnson Adams

ANDREW JACKSON, 1829–1837
Rachel Donelson Robards Jackson, died 1828, before President Jackson entered the White House.

MARTIN VAN BUREN, 1837–1841
Hannah Hoes Van Buren died eighteen years before her husband entered the White House.

WILLIAM HENRY HARRISON, 1841–1841 (died April 4)
Anna Tuthill Symmes Harrison, because of her husband's illness and death, never entered the White House.

JOHN TYLER, 1841–1845
Letitia Christian Tyler (died September 10, 1842)
Julia Gardiner Tyler

JAMES K. POLK, 1845–1849
Sarah Childress Polk

586 APPENDIXES

ZACHARY TAYLOR, 1849–1850 (July 9)
Margaret Mackall Smith Taylor

MILLARD FILLMORE, 1850–1853
Abigail Powers Fillmore

FRANKLIN PIERCE, 1853–1857
Jane Means Appleton Pierce

JAMES BUCHANAN, 1857–1861
He lived and died a bachelor.

ABRAHAM LINCOLN, 1861–1865 (April 15)
Mary Todd Lincoln

ANDREW JOHNSON, 1865–1869
Eliza McCardle Johnson

ULYSSES S. GRANT, 1869–1877
Julia Boggs Dent Grant

RUTHERFORD B. HAYES, 1877–1881
Lucy Ware Webb Hayes

JAMES A. GARFIELD, 1881–1881 (September 19)
Lucretia Rudolph Garfield

CHESTER A. ARTHUR, 1881–1885
Ellen Lewis Herndon Arthur (died 1880)

GROVER CLEVELAND, 1885–1889
Frances Folsom Cleveland

BENJAMIN HARRISON, 1889–1893
Caroline Lavinia Scott Harrison

GROVER CLEVELAND, 1893–1897
Frances Folsom Cleveland

WILLIAM McKINLEY, 1897–1901 (September 14)
Ida Saxton McKinley

THEODORE ROOSEVELT, 1901–1909
Edith Kermit Carow Roosevelt

WILLIAM HOWARD TAFT, 1909–1913
Helen Herron Taft

WOODROW WILSON, 1913–1921
Ellen Louise Axson Wilson (died August 6, 1914)
Edith Bolling Galt Wilson

WARREN G. HARDING, 1921–1923 (August 2)
Florence Kling De Wolfe Harding

CALVIN COOLIDGE, 1923–1929
    Grace Anna Goodhue Coolidge

HERBERT HOOVER, 1929–1933
    Lou Henry Hoover

FRANKLIN DELANO ROOSEVELT, 1933–1945 (April 12)
    Anna Eleanor Roosevelt

HARRY S TRUMAN, 1945–1953
    Bess Wallace Truman

APPENDIX C

EXCERPTS FROM THE CONSTITUTION OF THE UNITED STATES

PREAMBLE

We the People of the United States, in order to form a more perfect union, establish justice, insure domestic tranquility, provide for the common defence, promote the general welfare, and secure the blessings of liberty to ourselves and our posterity, do ordain and establish this Constitution for the United States of America.

ARTICLE I

Section 1 All legislative powers herein granted shall be vested in a Congress of the United States, which shall consist of a Senate and House of Representatives.

Section 2 The House of Representatives shall be composed of members chosen every second year by the people of the several States, and the electors in each State shall have the qualifications requisite for electors of the most numerous branch of the State legislature.

No person shall be a Representative who shall not have attained to the age of twenty-five years, and been seven years a citizen of the United States, and who shall not, when elected, be an inhabitant of that State in which he shall be chosen. . . .

Section 7 All bills for raising revenue shall originate in the House of Representatives; but the Senate may propose or concur with amendments as on other bills.

Every bill which shall have passed the House of Representatives and the Senate, shall, before it become a law, be presented to the President of the United States; if he approve he shall sign it, but if not he shall return it, with his objections, to that house in which it shall have originated, who shall enter the objections at large on their journal, and proceed to reconsider it. If after such reconsideration two thirds of that house shall agree to pass the bill, it shall be sent, together with the objections, to the other house, by which it shall likewise be reconsidered, and if approved by two thirds of that house, it shall become a law. But in all such cases the votes of both houses shall be determined by yeas and nays, and the names of the persons voting for and against the bill shall be entered on the journal of each house respectively. If any bill shall not be returned by the President within ten days (Sundays excepted) after it shall have been presented to him, the same shall be a law, in like manner as if he had signed it, unless the Congress by their adjournment prevent its return, in which case it shall not be a law.

Every order, resolution, or vote to which the concurrence of the Senate and House of Representatives may be necessary (except on a question of adjournment) shall be presented to the President of the United States; and before the same shall take effect, shall be approved by him, or being disapproved by him, shall be repassed by two thirds of the Senate and House of Representatives, according to the rules and limitations prescribed in the case of a bill.

Section 8 The Congress shall have power to lay and collect taxes, duties, imposts and excises, to pay the debts and provide for the common defense and general welfare of the United States; but all duties, imposts and excises shall be uniform throughout the United States;

To borrow money on the credit of the United States;

To regulate commerce with foreign nations, and among the several States, and with the Indian tribes;

To establish a uniform rule of naturalization, and uniform laws on the subject of bankruptcies throughout the United States;

To coin money, regulate the value thereof, and of foreign coin, and fix the standard of weights and measures;

To provide for the punishment of counterfeiting the securities and current coin of the United States;

To establish post offices and post roads;

To promote the progress of science and useful arts, by securing for limited times to authors and inventors the exclusive right to their respective writings and discoveries;

To constitute tribunals inferior to the Supreme Court;

To define and punish piracies and felonies committed on the high seas, and offences against the law of nations;

To declare war, grant letters of marque and reprisal, and make rules concerning captures on land and water;

To raise and support armies, but no appropriation of money to that use shall be for a longer term than two years;

To provide and maintain a navy;

To make rules for the government and regulation of the land and naval forces;

To provide for calling forth the militia to execute the laws of the Union, suppress insurrections and repel invasions;

To provide for organizing, arming, and disciplining the militia, and for governing such part of them as may be employed in the service of the United States, reserving to the States respectively the appointment of the officers, and the authority of training the militia according to the discipline prescribed by Congress;

To exercise exclusive legislation in all cases whatsoever, over such district (not exceeding ten miles square) as may, by cession of particular States, and the acceptance of Congress, become the seat of the Government of the United States, and to exercise like authority over all places purchased by the consent of the legislature of the State in which the same shall be, for the erection of forts, magazines, arsenals, dockyards, and other needful buildings; and

To make all laws which shall be necessary and proper for carrying into execution the foregoing powers, and all other powers vested by this Constitution in the Government of the United States, or in any department or officer thereof.

ARTICLE II

Section 1 The executive power shall be vested in a President of the United States of America. He shall hold his office during the term of four years, and, together with the Vice President, chosen for the same term, be elected. . . .

Section 2 The President shall be Commander-in-Chief of the Army and Navy of the United States, and of the militia of the several States, when called into the actual service of the United States; he may require the opinion, in writing, of the principal officer in each of the executive departments, upon any subject relating to the duties of their respective offices, and he shall have power to grant reprieves and pardons for offences against the United States, except in cases of impeachment.

He shall have power, by and with the advice and consent of the Senate, to make treaties, provided two thirds of the senators present concur; and he shall nominate, and by and with the advice and consent of the Senate, shall appoint ambassadors, other public ministers and consuls, judges of the Supreme Court, and all other officers of the United States, whose appointments are not herein otherwise provided for, and which shall be established by law: but the Congress may by law vest the appointment of such inferior officers, as they think proper, in the President alone, in the courts of law, or in the heads of departments.

The President shall have power to fill up all vacancies that may happen during the recess of the Senate, by granting commissions which shall expire at the end of their next session.

He shall from time to time give to the Congress information of the state of the Union, and recommend to their consideration such measures as he shall judge necessary and expedient; he may, on extraordinary occasions, convene both houses, or either of them, and in case of disagreement between them, with respect to the time of adjournment, he may adjourn them to such time as he shall think proper; he shall receive ambassadors and other public ministers; he shall take care that the laws be faithfully executed, and shall commission all the officers of the United States.

ARTICLE III

Section 1 The judicial power of the United States, shall be vested in one Supreme Court, and in such inferior courts as the Congress may from time to time ordain and establish. The judges, both of the supreme and inferior courts, shall hold their offices during good behaviour, and shall, at stated times, receive for their services, a compensation, which shall not be diminished during their continuance in office.

Section 2 The judicial power shall extend to all cases, in law and equity, arising under this Constitution, the laws of the United States, and treaties made, or which shall be made, under their authority; to all cases affecting ambassadors, other public ministers and consuls; to all cases of admiralty and maritime jurisdiction; to controversies to which the United States shall be a party; to controversies between two or more States; between a State and citizens of another State; between citizens of different States; between citizens of the same State claiming lands under grants of different States, and between a State, or the citizens thereof, and foreign States, citizens or subjects.

In all cases affecting ambassadors, other public ministers and consuls, and those in which a State shall be party, the Supreme Court shall have original jurisdiction. In all the other cases before mentioned, the Supreme Court shall have appellate jurisdiction both as to law and fact, with such exceptions, and under such regulations as the Congress shall make.

The trial of all crimes, except in cases of impeachment, shall be by jury; and such trial shall be held in the State where the said crimes shall have been committed; but when not committed within any State, the trial shall be at such place or places as the Congress may by law have directed.

Section 3 Treason against the United States shall consist only in levying war against them, or in adhering to their enemies, giving them aid and comfort. No person shall be convicted of treason unless on the testimony of two witnesses to the same overt act, or on confession in open court.

The Congress shall have power to declare the punishment of treason, but no attainder of treason shall work corruption of blood, or forfeiture except during the life of the person attainted.

ARTICLE V

The Congress, whenever two thirds of both houses shall deem it necessary, shall propose amendments to this Constitution, or, on the application of the legislatures of two thirds of the several States, shall call a convention for proposing amendments, which, in either case, shall be valid to all intents and purposes, as part of this Constitution, when ratified by the legislatures of three fourths of the several States, or by conventions in three fourths thereof, as the one or the other mode of ratification may be proposed by the Congress; provided that no amendment which may be made prior to the year one thousand eight hundred and eight shall in any manner affect the first and fourth clauses in the ninth section of the first article; and that no State, without its consent, shall be deprived of its equal suffrage in the Senate.

APPENDIX D

In eleven appearances to testify before congressional committees, between November 15, 1945, and March 29, 1950, I urged the strengthening of our defenses. On June 5, 1946, for example, I told the House Committee on Military Affairs: "I cannot overemphasize the necessity for the maintenance of a well-rounded and vigorous research and development program. Our efforts in this field suffered during the prewar years from lack of financial support. During the war we developed a superb organization of scientists and research men. Their scientific knowledge, skill, and ingenuity provided the American soldier with the best equipment and most effective weapons in the world. We must hold together the framework of this superb organization if we are to maintain the superiority of our weapons and equipment and be assured of the availability of proven types superior to those of other nations. In the fields of guided missiles, electronic devices, and high-speed high-performance aircraft the possibilities are unlimited. It would be fatal to permit ourselves to be outdistanced."

"We have cut our requirements to the irreducible minimum, beyond which lies real danger," I told a House subcommittee on February 19, 1947. "As a result of this weakness and sparseness of our forces," I testified on June 28, 1947, "the United States Army has a lessened influence toward deterring aggression. . . . Those who count the existing military power of the United States can scarcely find it negligible; but they can hardly find it impressive. Therefore the United States Army exerts today far less pressure for peace than it did when it was the world's most formidable fighting force."

These warnings reflected the fact that expenditures for the military functions of the military departments had fallen from the wartime peak of $80.3 billion in fiscal year 1945 to $41.6 billion in 1946 and to $11.8 billion in 1947. They remained on approximately that level in 1948 ($10.5 billion), 1949 ($11.3 billion), and 1950 ($11.8 billion), which ended just as the Korean War began. On March 24, 1950, I had observed in an address at Columbia University: "America has already disarmed to the extent—in some directions even beyond the extent—that I, with deep concern for her present safety, could possibly advise, until we have certain knowledge that all nations, in concerted action, are doing likewise." Testifying before a subcommittee of the Senate several days later, because of my service as informal chairman of the Joint Chiefs of Staff during the preparation of the defense budget for fiscal year 1951, I urged additions to that budget, in which the administration had set military expenditures at an estimated $12.5 billion—a figure at once made obsolete by the Korean War.

The administration's persistent tendency to set too low a ceiling on defense spending was one major cause of my decision to resign as informal chairman of the Joint Chiefs.

APPENDIX E

BRICKER AMENDMENT

Senate Joint Resolution 1, Eighty-third Congress
Reported out June 15, 1953

JOINT RESOLUTION PROPOSING AN AMENDMENT TO THE CONSTITUTION OF THE UNITED STATES, RELATING TO THE LEGAL EFFECT OF CERTAIN TREATIES AND EXECUTIVE AGREEMENTS

Resolved by the Senate and House of Representatives of the United States of America in Congress assembled (two-thirds of each House concurring therein), That the following Article is proposed as an amendment to the Constitution of the United States, which shall be valid to all intents and purposes as part of the Constitution when ratified by the legislatures of three-fourths of the several States:

Article —

Section 1. A provision of a treaty which conflicts with this Constitution shall not be of any force or effect.

Section 2. A treaty shall become effective as internal law in the United States only through legislation which would be valid in the absence of treaty.

Section 3. Congress shall have power to regulate all Executive and other agreements with any foreign power or international organization. All such agreements shall be subject to the limitations imposed on treaties by this article.

Section 4. The Congress shall have power to enforce this article by appropriate legislation.

Section 5. This article shall be inoperative unless it shall have been ratified as an amendment to the Constitution by the legislatures of three-fourths of the several States within seven years of the date of its submission.

APPENDIX F

KNOWLAND AMENDMENT

Substitute for Senate Joint Resolution 1
Introduced July 22, 1953

AMENDMENT
(In the Nature of a Substitute)

Intended to be proposed by Mr. Knowland to the joint resolution (S. J. Res. 1) proposing an amendment to the Constitution of the United States relative to the making of treaties and executive agreements, viz: Strike out all after the resolving clause and in lieu thereof, insert the following:

Section 1. A provision of a treaty or other international agreement which conflicts with the Constitution shall not be of any force or effect. The judicial power of the United States shall extend to all phases in law or equity, in which it is claimed that the conflict described in this amendment is present.

Section 2. When the Senate consents to the ratification of a treaty, the vote shall be determined by yeas and nays, and the names of the persons voting for and against shall be entered on the Journal of the Senate.

Section 3. When the Senate so provides in its consent to ratification, a treaty shall become effective as internal law in the United States only through the enactment of appropriate legislation by the Congress.

Section 4. This article shall be inoperative unless it shall have been ratified as an amendment to the Constitution by the legislatures of three-fourths of the several States within seven years from the date of its submission.

APPENDIX G

On June 15, 1953, the Department of the Army awarded the English Electric Company a $1.7 million contract for ten transformers for the Chief Joseph Dam—a Corps of Engineers project on the Columbia River at Brewster, Washington. (An American firm received a $4.2 million contract for four generators, having underbid the British firm, originally the low bidder for transformers and generators together, in a second round of bids based on more exact specifications.) And on December 15 the department awarded the British firm a $3.6 million contract for the last two generators for the McNary Dam on the Columbia River between Washington and Oregon.

Under the Buy-American Act of 1933, which permits a government procurement agency to award a contract to an American bidder if his bid does not exceed that of a foreign competitor by an amount which is "unreasonable," the department might have awarded both British contracts to American firms; the American bid in each instance exceeded the British bid by less than 25 per cent, an amount which, under the usual interpretation of the law, was not "unreasonable." In December of 1954, in accordance with a recommendation of the Randall Commission, I issued Executive Order 10582, which specified that, under the Buy-American Act, an American bid was "unreasonable" if it exceeded a foreign bid by (in two different formulas) 6 or 10 per cent. Friends of free trade here and abroad welcomed these decisions.

APPENDIX H

LETTER TO SECRETARY OF DEFENSE WILSON

Public Papers of the Presidents, May 17, 1954

Dear Mr. Secretary:

It has long been recognized that to assist the Congress in achieving its legislative purposes every Executive Department or Agency must, upon the request of a Congressional Committee, expeditiously furnish information relating to any matter within the jurisdiction of the Committee, with certain historical exceptions—some of which are pointed out in the attached memorandum from the Attorney General. This Administration has been and will continue to be diligent in following this principle. However, it is essential to the successful working of our system that the persons entrusted with power in any one of the three great branches of Government shall not encroach upon the authority confided to the others. The ultimate responsibility for the conduct of the Executive Branch rests with the President.

Within this Constitutional framework each branch should cooperate fully with each other for the common good. However, throughout our history the President has withheld information whenever he found that what was sought was confidential or its disclosure would be incompatible with the public interest or jeopardize the safety of the Nation.

Because it is essential to efficient and effective administration that employees of the Executive Branch be in a position to be completely candid in advising with each other on official matters, and because it is not in the public interest that any of their conversations or communications, or any documents or reproductions, concerning such advice be disclosed, you will instruct employees of your Department that in all of their appearances before the Subcommittee of the Senate Committee on Government Operations regarding the inquiry now before it they are not to testify to any such conversations or communications or to produce any such documents or reproductions. This principle must be maintained regardless of who would be benefited by such disclosures.

I direct this action so as to maintain the proper separation of powers between the Executive and Legislative Branches of the Government in accordance with my responsibilities and duties under the Constitution. This separation is vital to preclude the exercise of arbitrary power by any branch of the Government.

By this action I am not in any way restricting the testimony of such witnesses as to what occurred regarding any matters where the communication was directly between any of the principals in the controversy within the Executive Branch on the one hand and a member of the Subcommittee or its staff on the other.

Sincerely,
                    DWIGHT D. EISENHOWER

APPENDIX I

McCARTHY CONDEMNATION RESOLUTION

Senate Resolution 301, Eighty-third Congress, as finally amended and agreed to on December 2, 1954

Resolved, That the Senator from Wisconsin, Mr. McCarthy, failed to cooperate with the Subcommittee on Privileges and Elections of the Senate Committee on Rules and Administration in clearing up matters referred to that subcommittee which concerned his conduct as a Senator and affected the honor of the Senate and, instead, repeatedly abused the subcommittee and its members who were trying to carry out assigned duties, thereby obstructing the constitutional processes of the Senate, and that this conduct of the Senator from Wisconsin, Mr. McCarthy, is contrary to senatorial traditions and is hereby condemned.

Section 2. The Senator from Wisconsin, Mr. McCarthy, in writing to the chairman of the Select Committee to Study Censure Charges, (Mr. Watkins) after the Select Committee had issued its report and before the report was presented to the Senate charging three members of the Select Committee with "deliberate deception" and "fraud" for failure to disqualify themselves; in stating to the press on November 4, 1954, that the special Senate session that was to begin November 8, 1954, was a "lynch party"; in repeatedly describing this special Senate session as a "lynch bee" in a nationwide television and radio show on November 7, 1954; in stating to the public press on November 13, 1954, that the chairman of the Select Committee (Mr. Watkins) was guilty of "the most unusual, most cowardly thing I've heard of" and stating further: "I expected he would be afraid to answer the questions, but didn't think he'd be stupid enough to make a public statement"; and in characterizing the said committee as the "unwitting handmaiden," "involuntary agent" and "attorneys-in-fact" of the Communist Party and in charging that the said committee in writing its report "imitated Communist methods—that it distorted, misrepresented, and omitted in its effort to manufacture a plausible rationalization" in support of its recommendations to the Senate, which characterizations and charges were contained in a statement released to the press and inserted in the *Congressional Record* of November 10, 1954, acted contrary to senatorial ethics and tended to bring the Senate into dishonor and disrepute, to obstruct the constitutional processes of the Senate, and to impair its dignity; and such conduct is hereby condemned.

APPENDIX J

SEATO TREATY

Department of State Bulletin, September 20, 1954

The Parties to this Treaty,

Recognizing the sovereign equality of all the Parties,

Reiterating their faith in the purposes and principles set forth in the Charter of the United Nations and their desire to live in peace with all peoples and all governments,

Reaffirming that, in accordance with the Charter of the United Nations, they uphold the principle of equal rights and self-determination of peoples, and declaring that they will earnestly strive by every peaceful means to promote self-government and to secure the independence of all countries whose peoples desire it and are able to undertake its responsibilities,

Desiring to strengthen the fabric of peace and freedom and to uphold the principles of democracy, individual liberty and the rule of law, and to promote the economic well-being and development of all peoples in the treaty area,

Intending to declare publicly and formally their sense of unity, so that any potential aggressor will appreciate that the Parties stand together in the area, and

Desiring further to coordinate their efforts for collective defense for the preservation of peace and security,

Therefore agree as follows:

ARTICLE I

The Parties undertake, as set forth in the Charter of the United Nations, to settle any international disputes in which they may be involved by peaceful means in such a manner that international peace and security and justice are not endangered, and to refrain in their international relations from the threat or use of force in any manner inconsistent with the purposes of the United Nations.

ARTICLE II

In order more effectively to achieve the objectives of this Treaty, the Parties, separately and jointly, by means of continuous and effective self-help and mutual aid will maintain and develop their individual and collective capacity to resist armed attack and to prevent and counter subversive activities directed from without against their territorial integrity and political stability.

ARTICLE III

The Parties undertake to strengthen their free institutions and to cooperate with one another in the further development of economic measures, including technical assistance, designed both to promote economic progress and social well-being and to further the individual and collective efforts of governments toward these ends.

ARTICLE IV

1. Each Party recognizes that aggression by means of armed attack in the treaty area against any of the Parties or against any State or territory which the Parties by unanimous agreement may hereafter designate, would endanger its own peace and safety, and agrees that it will in that event act to meet the common danger in accordance with its constitutional processes. Measures taken under this paragraph shall be immediately reported to the Security Council of the United Nations.

2. If, in the opinion of any of the Parties, the inviolability or the integrity of the territory or the sovereignty or political independence of any Party in the treaty area or of any other State or territory to which the provisions of paragraph 1 of this Article from time to time apply is threatened in any way other than by armed attack or is affected or threatened by any fact or situation which might endanger the peace of the area, the Parties shall consult immediately in order to agree on the measures which should be taken for the common defense.

3. It is understood that no action on the territory of any State designated by unanimous agreement under paragraph 1 of this Article or on any territory so designated shall be taken except at the invitation or with the consent of the government concerned.

ARTICLE V

The Parties hereby establish a Council, on which each of them shall be represented, to consider matters concerning the implementation of this Treaty. The Council shall provide for consultation with regard to military and any other planning as the situation obtaining in the treaty area may from time to time require. The Council shall be so organized as to be able to meet at any time.

ARTICLE VI

This Treaty does not affect and shall not be interpreted as affecting in any way the rights and obligations of any of the Parties under the Charter of the United Nations or the responsibility of the United Nations for the maintenance of international peace and security. Each Party declares that none of the international engagements now in force between it and any other of the Parties or any third party is in conflict with the provisions of this Treaty, and undertakes not to enter into any international engagement in conflict with this Treaty.

ARTICLE VII

Any other State in a position to further the objectives of this Treaty and to contribute to the security of the area may, by unanimous agreement of the Parties, be invited to accede to this Treaty. Any State so invited may become a Party to the Treaty by depositing its instrument of accession with the Government of the Republic of the Philippines. The Government of the Republic of the Philippines shall inform each of the Parties of the deposit of each such instrument of accession.

ARTICLE VIII

As used in this Treaty, the "treaty area" is the general area of Southeast Asia, including also the entire territories of the Asian Parties, and the general area of the Southwest Pacific not including the Pacific area north of 21 degrees 30 minutes north latitude. The Parties may, by unanimous agreement, amend this Article to include within the treaty area the territory of any State acceding to this Treaty in accordance with Article VII or otherwise to change the treaty area.

ARTICLE IX

1. This Treaty shall be deposited in the archives of the Government of the Republic of the Philippines. Duly certified copies thereof shall be transmitted by that government to the other signatories.

2. The Treaty shall be ratified and its provisions carried out by the Parties in accordance with their respective constitutional processes. The instruments of ratification shall be deposited as soon as possible with the Government of the Republic of the Philippines, which shall notify all of the other signatories of such deposit.

3. The Treaty shall enter into force between the States which have ratified it as soon as the instruments of ratification of a majority of the signatories shall have been deposited, and shall come into effect with respect to each other State on the date of the deposit of its instrument of ratification.

ARTICLE X

This Treaty shall remain in force indefinitely, but any Party may cease to be a Party one year after its notice of denunciation has been given to the Government of the Republic of the Philippines, which shall inform the governments of the other Parties of the deposit of each notice of denunciation.

Article XI

The English text of this Treaty is binding on the Parties, but when the Parties have agreed to the French text thereof and have so notified the Government of the Republic of the Philippines, the French text shall be equally authentic and binding on the Parties.

Understanding of the United States of America

The United States of America in executing the present Treaty does so with the understanding that its recognition of the effect of aggression and armed attack and its agreement with reference thereto in Article IV, paragraph 1, apply only to communist aggression but affirms that in the event of other aggression or armed attack it will consult under the provisions of Article IV, paragraph 2.

In witness whereof, the undersigned Plenipotentiaries have signed this Treaty.

Done at Manila, this eighth day of September, 1954.

Protocol to the Southeast Asia Collective Defense Treaty

Designation of states and territory as to which provisions of Article IV and Article III are to be applicable:

The Parties to the Southeast Asia Collective Defense Treaty unanimously designate for the purposes of Article IV of the Treaty the States of Cambodia and Laos and the free territory under the jurisdiction of the State of Vietnam.

The Parties further agree that the above-mentioned states and territory shall be eligible in respect of the economic measures contemplated by Article III.

This Protocol shall enter into force simultaneously with the coming into force of the Treaty.

In witness whereof, the undersigned Plenipotentiaries have signed this Protocol to the Southeast Asia Collective Defense Treaty.

Done at Manila, this eighth day of September, 1954.

APPENDIX K

On the Saar, until the signing of a peace treaty, France and Germany agreed that it should remain autonomous and acquire a European status under WEU; that a "European Commissioner"—neither French nor German—should, under appointment by the WEU Council of Ministers, represent the Saar on defense and foreign policy in the WEU; that the Saar should have representation also in the Council of Europe and the coal and steel community; that existing French economic ties with the Saar would be continued; and that agreements would be made on similar economic ties between the Saar and Germany.

France and Germany agreed also that the people of the Saar should vote on the proposed "Europeanizing" statute. In a plebiscite held October 23, 1955, they rejected it overwhelmingly and the following year France and Germany announced agreement on the region's return to Germany.

APPENDIX L

My schedule for the day, August 30, shows the many types of activity a President participates in, even at the beginning of an "off-year" campaign. After a flight from Denver aboard the *Columbine,* I arrived at 6:45 A.M. on August 30 at the MATS Terminal, Washington National Airport, and arrived at the White House at ten minutes of seven. An hour later I had breakfast with Walter Kohler, governor of Wisconsin, General Lucius Clay, Sherman Adams, and Gabriel Hauge, to discuss the highway program that we were so anxious to get under way. At eight forty-five I saw John Lodge, governor of Connecticut, who was up for re-election. Forty-five minutes later I signed H. R. 9757, the Atomic Energy Act of 1954, in the presence of sixteen senators, congressmen, and officials of the AEC and the Executive Office. At nine forty-five I signed an act to authorize and direct the construction of bridges over the Potomac River. At eleven forty-five I left for the National Guard Armory where, accompanied by Douglas McKay, the Secretary of the Interior, and Sherman Adams, I addressed the annual convention of the American Legion at 12 noon. At 2 P.M. I saw a member of the AEC, the Honorable Henry D. Smyth. After a haircut in my office at two-fifteen I conferred with Foster Dulles, then left the White House, accompanied by former President Herbert Hoover, Secretary of Agriculture Ezra Taft Benson, my brother Milton, his daughter Ruth, Congressman Thomas E. Martin and one of my physicians, Major Tkach, and his family. We arrived at the Washington National Airport at three-ten, where we departed for the Des Moines Municipal Airport, Iowa. We arrived in Des Moines at five-twenty and proceeded to the Fair Grounds, where at the grandstand I gave my short talk at six-thirty. By seven-fifteen we were airborne for Denver, Colorado, once more, where I arrived at Mrs. Doud's residence, 570 Lafayette Street, at nine-fifteen.

APPENDIX M

LETTER TO EVERETT HAZLETT
August 20, 1956

Dear Swede:

The probable explanation for the simultaneous arrival in New York of your two letters, one bearing three cents and the other six cents postage, is the institution of a new policy on the part of the Postmaster General. Where a subsidized air line is not involved, and a three cent letter can be carried on a plane without extra cost—and space is available—the policy is to pick up the letter and carry it exactly as if it were bearing a six cent stamp.

Not long ago you expressed some of your irritation that anyone should even dream of putting the Services into the same uniform. I won't quarrel with the idea, but I will attempt to give you a slightly different viewpoint toward the Services than you probably have. . . .

What I have tried to tell the Chiefs of Staff is that their most important function is their corporate work as a body of advisers to the Secretary of Defense and to me. We now have four-star men acting as their deputies, and those men are either capable of running the day-to-day work in the Services or they should not be wearing that kind of insignia. Yet I have made little or no progress in developing real corporate thinking.

I patiently explain over and over again that American strength is a combination of its economic, moral and military force. If we demand too much in taxes in order to build planes and ships, we will tend to dry up the accumulations of capital that are necessary to provide jobs for the million or more new workers that we must absorb each year. Behind each worker there is an average of about $15,000 in invested capital. His job depends upon this investment at a yearly rate of not less than fifteen to twenty billions. If taxes become so burdensome that investment loses its attractiveness for capital, there will finally be nobody but government to build the facilities. This is one form of Socialism.

Let us not forget that the Armed Services are to defend a "way of life," not merely land, property or lives. So what I try to make the Chiefs realize is that they are men of sufficient stature, training and intelligence to think of this balance—the balance between minimum requirements in the costly implements of war and the health of our economy.

Based on this kind of thinking, they habitually, when with me, give the impression that they are going to work out arrangements that will keep the military appropriations within manageable proportions and do it in a spirit of good will and of give and take.

Yet when each Service puts down its minimum requirements for its own military budget for the following year, and I add up the total, I find that they mount at a fantastic rate. There is seemingly no end to all of this. Yet merely "getting tough" on my part is not an answer. I simply must find men who have the breadth of understanding and devotion to their country rather than to a single Service that will bring about better solutions than I get now.

Strangely enough, the one man who sees this clearly is a Navy man who at one time was an uncompromising exponent of Naval power and its superiority over any other kind of strength. That is Radford.

I do not maintain that putting all of these people in one uniform would cure this difficulty—at least not quickly. But some day there is going to be a man sitting in my present chair who has not been raised in the military services and who will have little understanding of where slashes in their estimates can be made with little or no damage. If that should happen while we still have the state of tension that now exists in the world, I shudder to think of what could happen in this country. . . .

Tomorrow Mamie and I leave for San Francisco and what promises to be, for us at least, a hectic and tumultuous two days there. Then Cypress Point—and *I hope* some rest.

Give my love to Ibby.

As ever,

APPENDIX N

TEXT OF JOINT RESOLUTION ON DEFENSE OF FORMOSA

Whereas the primary purpose of the United States, in its relations with all other nations, is to develop and sustain a just and enduring peace for all; and

Whereas certain territories in the West Pacific under the jurisdiction of the Republic of China are now under armed attack, and threats and declarations have been and are being made by the Chinese Communists that such armed attack is in aid of and in preparation for armed attack on Formosa and the Pescadores,

Whereas such armed attack if continued would gravely endanger the peace and security of the West Pacific Area and particularly of Formosa and the Pescadores; and

Whereas the secure possession by friendly governments of the Western Pacific Island chain, of which Formosa is a part, is essential to the vital interests of the United States and all friendly nations in or bordering upon the Pacific Ocean; and

Whereas the President of the United States on January 6, 1955, submitted to the Senate for its advice and consent to ratification a Mutual Defense Treaty between the United States of America and the Republic of China, which recognizes that an armed attack in the West Pacific area directed against territories, therein described, in the region of Formosa and the Pescadores, would be dangerous to the peace and safety of the parties to the treaty: Therefore be it

Resolved by the Senate and House of Representatives of the United States of America in Congress assembled, That the President of the United States be and he hereby is authorized to employ the Armed Forces of the United States as he deems necessary for the specific purpose of securing and protecting Formosa and the Pescadores against armed attack, this authority to include the securing and protection of such related positions and territories of that area now in friendly hands and the taking of such other measures as he judges to be required or appropriate in assuring the defense of Formosa and the Pescadores.

This resolution shall expire when the President shall determine that the peace and security of the area is reasonably assured by international conditions created by action of the United Nations or otherwise, and shall so report to the Congress.

APPENDIX O

EXCERPTS FROM A LETTER TO WINSTON CHURCHILL[1]

January 25, 1955

Dear Winston:

. . . Your paper seems to me to under-emphasize a point of such moment that it constitutes almost a new element in warfare. I refer to the extraordinary increase in the value of tactical or strategic surprise, brought about by the enormous destructive power of the new weapons and the probability that they could be delivered over targets with little or no warning. Surprise has always been one of the most important factors in achieving victory. And now, even as we contemplate the grim picture depicted in your memorandum, we gain only a glimmering of the paralysis that could be inflicted on an unready fighting force, or indeed upon a whole nation, by some sudden foray that would place a dozen or more of these terrible weapons accurately on target.

I personally believe that many of our old conceptions of the time that would be available to governments for making of decisions in the event of attack are no longer tenable. I think it possible that the very life of a nation, perhaps even of Western civilization, could, for example, come to depend on in-stantaneous reaction to news of an approaching air fleet; victory or defeat could hang upon minutes and seconds used decisively at top speed or tragically wasted in indecision. . . .

Respecting the Far East—yesterday I sent a message to the Congress to clarify the intention of this nation in the region of the Formosa straits. It would be a pity if the Communists misinterpreted our forebearance to mean indecision and precipitated a crisis that could bring on a nasty situation.

I note that in the memorandum accompanying your letter, your Govern-ment fears that during the next two or three years the United States may, through impulsiveness or lack of perspective, be drawn into a Chinese war.

I trust that my message to the Congress reassured you as to our basic attitudes and sober approach to critical problems.

It is probably difficult for you, in your geographical position, to under-stand how concerned this country is with the solidarity of the Island Barrier in the Western Pacific. Moreover, we are convinced that the psychological

[1] This letter was written before our scientists had reported to me on the full potential efficiency of long-range ballistic missiles.

effect in the Far East of deserting our friends on Formosa would risk a collapse of Asiatic resistance to the Communists. Such possibilities cannot be lightly dismissed; in our view they are almost as important, in the long term, to you as they are to us.

I am certain there is nothing to be gained in that situation by meekness and weakness. God knows I have been working hard in the exploration of every avenue that seems to lead toward the preservation and strengthening of the peace. But I am positive that the free world is surely building trouble for itself unless it is united in basic purpose, is clear and emphatic in its declared determination to resist all forceful Communist advance, and keeps itself ready to act on a moment's notice, if necessary. . . .

With my continuing warm regard, and with my sincere wishes for your health, strength and happiness,

APPENDIX P

EXTRACTS FROM A MEMORANDUM TO SECRETARY OF STATE DULLES

April 5, 1955

I believe that the situation and actions best calculated to sustain the interest of ourselves and the free world, and to damage the Communists can be roughly described as follows:

(a). Without abandoning the offshore islands, make clear that neither Chiang nor ourselves is committed to *full-out* defense of Quemoy and Matsu, so that no matter what the outcome of an attack upon them, there would be no danger of a collapse of the free world position in the region. . . .

(b). Initiate, immediately, the process of bringing to Chiang's attention the great advantages, political and military, that would result from certain alterations in his present military plans, as follows

(1). To regard the offshore islands as outposts and consequently to be garrisoned in accordance with the requirements of outpost positions. This involves vigilant reconnaissance and a maximum of protective works and with properly sited automatic weapons and light artillery, together with effective obstacles, defensive mine systems, and so on. All this should be reinforced by adequate stores of ammunition, of food and medical supplies, all thoroughly protected and available to the garrison as needed. Excess personnel (except such civilians as might decline to leave) should be removed from the islands.

(2). The Nationalist forces on Formosa should assist these garrisons by aerial and sea reconnaissance and fighting support. Plans for defense should be fully coordinated between the forward units and the mobile elements in Formosa.

(3). Adequate plans should be made for determined and persistent defense, and evacuation should take place (if this finally becomes necessary) only after defensive forces had inflicted upon the attackers heavy and bloody losses.

(4). The process of concentrating, equipping and training of troops on Formosa itself should be expedited. The United States could and would help in this process so as to give to Chiang the greatest possible strength in support of his outpost troops on Quemoy and the Matsus, and in preparing and sustaining the bulk of his forces as a weapon of opportunity, ready to take advantage of any political, military or economic circumstance on the mainland that would give to an invasion a reasonable chance of success.

(5). To protect the prestige of Chiang and the morale of his forces, any alteration in military and political planning should obviously be developed under his leadership; above all, there must be no basis for public belief that the alterations came about through 'American intervention or coercion.

Index

Index

624INDEX

Dondero, George, 302
Donovan, Robert, 233
Doud, Mrs., 536
Douglas, James H., Jr., 582
Douglas, Lewis W., 483
  writes to Eisenhower on Quemoy-
    Matsu, 475
Douglas, Paul, 193, 225
  in 1954 election, 433
Douglas, William, 225
Draper, William, 251, 262, 263, 491
  learns to fly jet plane, 491
Drummond, Roscoe, 233
Dry, Leonard, 265, 266
Duff, James H., 26, 218
  on Eisenhower campaign trip, 60 n
Dulles, Allen, 149
  and Formosa, 477
  and Guatemala, 425, 426
  and Indochina, 339, 341, 344, 358
  at Stalin's death, 143
Dulles, John Foster:
  appointed Secretary of State, 85, 86,
    581
  arms shipments to Guatemala and, 424,
    425
  Berlin Conference and, 342, 343–44
  Bermuda Conference and, 242, 255
  Bohlen appointment and, 212, 213
  Bricker amendment and, 279–81, 283,
    284
  British and, relations between, 150,
    157, 158, 251, 347, 348, 349, 352,
    355, 404–5, 475
  Cabinet contributions, 125, 130
  delegation to Queen Elizabeth's corona-
    tion, 226
  Eisenhower and, relations between, 23,
    139, 142, 167, 191, 212, 217, 227,
    280–81, 343–44, 347–48, 349–50,

364, 367, 413, 416 n, 512, 536, 540,
  542, 545, 571, 574, 611–12
European capitals visited by, 140–43
European Defense Community and,
  404–5, 406–7, 408
foreign-policy plank by, 41
Geneva Conference and, 348, 355, 504,
  506, 508, 509, 510, 511, 512, 513,
  515, 517, 524, 527–28, 541
Guatemala and, 424, 425, 427
Indochina and, 167, 169, 345, 347, 351,
  352, 358, 359, 361, 362, 369–70, 374,
  400
Korea and, 172, 181, 184, 186–87, 191,
  248
Manila Pact Council meeting in Bangkok, 474, 476
Middle East visited by, 155, 156, 157,
  158
mutual-defense treaty signed with Nationalist China, 465–66
nominates Lodge for UN post, 89
Ottawa economic conference, 539–40
quoted, 395
Red China, Formosa and, 463, 464,
  465–66, 467, 475, 476–77, 478, 479–
  80, 481, 482
SEATO treaty signed by, 403
Smith chosen as assistant, 367
speeches by, 169, 172, 279–80, 478
Stalin's death and, 144
Suez problem and, 150
Supreme Court appointment considered, 227
trade agreements and, 210
Trieste and, 413, 414, 416 n, 418, 419
Wake Island conference, 96
Durkin, Martin P., 96–99, 584
  appointed Secretary of Labor, 90–91
Dworshak, Henry, 193
  and Bohlen nomination, 213